Beginning ASP.NET 2.0 Databases

From Novice to Professional

Damien Foggon

Beginning ASP.NET 2.0 Databases: From Novice to Professional

Copyright © 2006 by Damien Foggon

ISBN-13 (pbk): 978-1-59059-577-0

ISBN-10 (pbk): 1-59059-577-7

Printed and bound in the United States of America 9 8 7 6 5 4 3 2 1

Lead Editor: Jonathan Hassell

Technical Reviewers: Ronald Landers, Sahil Malik

Editorial Board: Steve Anglin, Dan Appleman, Ewan Buckingham, Gary Cornell, Jason Gilmore, Jonathan Hassell, James Huddleston, Chris Mills, Matthew Moodie, Dominic Shakeshaft, Jim Sumser, Matt Wade

Project Manager: Richard Dal Porto

Copy Edit Manager: Nicole LeClerc

Copy Editors: Marilyn Smith, Kim Wimpsett

Assistant Production Director: Kari Brooks-Copony

Production Editor: Kelly Gunther

Compositor: Susan Glinert

Proofreader: Linda Seifert

Indexer: Julie Grady

Artist: Kinetic Publishing Services, LLC

Cover Designer: Kurt Krames

Manufacturing Director: Tom Debolski

Distributed to the book trade worldwide by Springer-Verlag New York, Inc., 233 Spring Street, 6th Floor, New York, NY 10013. Phone 1-800-SPRINGER, fax 201-348-4505, e-mail orders-ny@springer-sbm.com, or visit http://www.springeronline.com.

For information on translations, please contact Apress directly at 2560 Ninth Street, Suite 219, Berkeley, CA 94710. Phone 510-549-5930, fax 510-549-5939, e-mail info@apress.com, or visit http://www.apress.com.

The source code for this book is available to readers at http://www.apress.com in the Source Code section.

Contents at a Glance

Contents

About the Author

DAMIEN FOGGON is a freelance programmer and technical author based in Newcastle, England. He is technical director of Thing-E Ltd., a company specializing in the development of dynamic Web solutions for the education sector, and founder of Littlepond Ltd. He started out working for BT in the UK before moving on to progressively smaller companies, finally founding his own company. Now he can work on all the cool new technologies, rather than the massive monolithic developments that still exist out there.

Although this is his first solo outing, Damien has coauthored books for Microsoft Press and Apress and acted as technical reviewer for both Wrox and Apress. He can be reached at http://www.littlepond.co.uk.

About the Technical Reviewers

RONALD LANDERS is the President and Senior Technical Consultant of IT Professionals, Inc. (http://www.itpconsultants.com), a staffing, recruiting, development, and IT project services company located in Calabasas, California. He has more than 20 years of experience in the IT field and specializes in database design and implementation, application design and architecture, and Web-based technologies such as Web services, electronic commerce, and Web portals. In addition to IT Professionals, Inc., Ronald has been teaching IT courses at UCLA Extension for the past 13 years. Currently, his courses include beginning and advanced classes in ASP.NET, SQL Server, Web services, and object-oriented programming.

SAHIL MALIK is a consultant, trainer, and mentor in various Microsoft technologies. He is also the author of the best-selling *Pro ADO.NET 2.0.* He has worked for many large clients across the globe, including a number of Fortune 100 companies and U.S. government organizations. Currently, he leads the study of emerging technologies at a prominent government office, where he is in charge of reviewing, assessing, and recommending various technologies to support the organization. Sahil frequently speaks on a variety of .NET-related topics at local user group meetings and industry events. For his community involvement and contribution, he has been awarded the Microsoft MVP award. He can be reached at http://www.winsmarts.com.

Acknowledgments

The second was definitely easier than the first, but the third was the killer. Thanks to Beckie, Richard, Marilyn, Kelly, and Kim for putting up with me and getting something out there that makes sense.

Introduction

Welcome to the introduction. From this point on, you'll discover the amazing world of ADO.NET, inanimate computer desks, late-night coding sessions, evil bugs, functions, methods, properties, and data. Seriously though, welcome to the world of databases in ASP.NET.

The idea for this kind of book isn't new, but if you're trying to learn something for the first time, having it constantly spelled out to you in a stodgy, primary-school-history-teacher-learn-these-dates-by-rote style probably won't help. Therefore, you'll find one joke per 50 pages to this book to break up the monotony.

Actually, a confession here: I studiously spent several years avoiding anything to do with databases because, despite my love of things techie, I always perceived them to be even more techie than other server products and operating systems. Come on, system administrators defer to database administrators, who have to wear white lab coats, have foreheads the size of Mount Rushmore to hold their huge brains, and speak in some additional language only they understand to commune directly with their charges, don't they? Of course not. Thanks to a little nudging and handholding, I can now build *data-driven Web sites*. These Web sites use databases and other sources of information to define what they present to a user and how they present it, and to learn how the user would like it to work.

With any luck, by the time you've worked through this book, you'll be able to do the same (without the need to stand stubbornly in the corner for several years muttering something about databases being scary and too techie).

How to Use This Book

This book is designed as your all-in-one introduction to the world of building data-driven Web sites using ASP.NET and ADO.NET. It's intended to be read from beginning to end, rather than by dipping in at random points, as you may do with other, more reference-type books.

You may have come across databases already in other books, but this one assumes you really have been sitting at the bottom of a well for the past five years and know nothing at all about databases. It does, however, assume that while you were in your well, you had a book teaching you some ASP.NET and a computer on which to write your first ASP.NET pages.

You can download all the code and sample databases for this book from the Source Code section of the Apress Web site at http://www.apress.com. However, many of the examples are short enough that they can be typed in, and I hope you decide to do this, because it will help you to learn and remember the material.

The only other things you'll need are a computer that runs Windows 2000, Windows XP, or Windows 2003 and has a fast enough connection to the Internet. You may need to download several items to work through this book, as follows:

- .NET 2.0 (22.4MB)

- Visual Web Developer Express Edition (43MB)

- SQL Server 2005 Express Edition (53.5MB), along with SQL Server Management Studio Express (30MB)

- MySQL 5.0 (16.8MB), along with MySQL Query Browser (5.1MB), Connector/ODBC (2.3MB), and Connector/NET (545KB).

This book also covers using Microsoft Access as a database. But unless you have an MSDN subscription, you'll need to buy this as part of Microsoft Office.

Of course, working through the book with just one database—SQL Server 2005, for instance—is fine. I'm just covering all the bases by presenting three of the most commonly used databases.

What This Book Contains

The chapters in the book are broadly divided into three sections: introductory material (Chapters 1 and 2), database-access techniques (Chapters 3–12), and a final chapter looking at some real-world issues (Chapter 13). Here's a quick rundown:

- Chapter 1 takes a high-level overview of how data-driven Web sites work, how ASP.NET and ADO.NET let them work, and what you can use as a source of data for your Web sites.

- Chapter 2 takes a similarly high-level overview of databases, which are the typical data sources for Web sites. It covers the components that make up a database, how a database stores and gives meaning to data, and a few basic rules for storing data in a database.

- Chapter 3 describes how to connect your ASP.NET page to a database by writing a minimum amount of code using the SqlDataSource.

- Chapter 4 covers how to connect your ASP.NET page to a database using code to perform the job of the SqlDataSource from the previous chapter. It presents some of the common database queries that will return data for display on a page. It also looks at how you actually send those queries to the database.

- Chapter 5 discusses how you handle the results of your queries in the page using a DataReader object, which is fast and direct but has drawbacks. It compares the DataReader with a DataSet, which gives you a lot more flexibility with the results of your data, but is somewhat slower and bulkier than a DataReader.

- Chapter 6 starts your look at how to *bind* data ("plug in" data to a page) from a DataReader object, a DataSet, or a SqlDataSource to Web controls on the page. This chapter looks at binding to individual Web controls, as well as binding a list of results to list-aware Web controls.

- Chapter 7 builds on Chapter 6 and shows how you can bind a full table of values to table-aware Web controls, again using a DataReader object, a `DataSet`, or a `SqlDataSource`.

- Chapter 8 shows how you can use form controls and the Command object or a `DataSet` to create, update, and delete data.

- Chapter 9 looks at updating the database using the `GridView`, `DetailsView`, and `FormView` controls in conjunction with a `SqlDataSource` to create, update, and delete data.

- Chapter 10 describes stored procedures and how to use them. Stored procedures are queries stored in a database that, depending on your choice of database, may run faster than queries sent over a connection to a database from the ASP.NET page.

- Chapter 11 looks at the Data Definition Language (DDL), which allows you to create, modify, and delete databases.

- Chapter 12 explores four issues that you'll come across when building your data-aware pages: concurrency, caching, transactions, and multiple result sets.

- Chapter 13 presents an overview of designing a database-driven Web site from scratch. In particular, it covers picking the right data source for your Web site and the right design for your database. It also discusses code style, performance, error handling, debugging, and maintenance.

Finally, the book has four appendices for your reference. In order, they cover the installation of the software used; the data types used by SQL Server 2005, MySQL 5.0, and Microsoft Access; the syntax for all the SQL queries used in this book; and the contents of the sample databases used in the examples.

I hope you enjoy the book and get as much out of reading it as I did out of writing it. If you do get truly stuck or find errors in the book, please let me know via support@apress.com, quoting this book's ISBN (577-7).

Data Sources and the Web

Look around you. No really, look around you. In the past 30 years, computers have taken over from the filing cabinets of the world to become the (almost) universal way people store and look up information. Would you rather spend five minutes rifling through some badly organized stack of paper for the name of a client or the price of a book, or spend ten seconds typing in a search query on a computer and getting the desired information back immediately? I thought so—the computer wins every time.

It's not just in the office that data-driven Web sites have proven popular. Server-side technologies now allow people to hook electronic data sources—databases, spreadsheets, Extensible Markup Language (XML) files, Windows services, and more—to Web sites. This means that today's World Wide Web is a place of dynamic, data-driven Web sites, rather than the collections of static Hypertext Markup Language (HTML) pages it once was. Regardless of whether you develop your Web sites with Active Server Pages (ASP), ASP.NET, PHP, JavaServer Pages (JSP), or one of numerous other technologies, you can use a data source to interact with your users, giving them the information they want to see and safely storing how they want to see it next time.

E-commerce Web sites, such as Amazon and eBay, use databases to provide customers with product information, recommendations, and wish lists, and to store feedback and orders. Portal Web sites use databases to store articles and user settings, so users don't need to reset them each time they visit the Web site.

How you choose to use data in your Web site is up to you. Whatever your goals are for your data-driven Web site, this book will give you the tools you'll need to accomplish them.

In this chapter, you'll look at the world of data-driven Web sites from 50,000 feet, so that by the time you finish it, you'll at least have a rough knowledge of how things hook together. You'll spend the rest of the book parachuting down to the ground, espying the exact details as you get closer.

Up here in the blue sky of Chapter 1, you'll learn the following:

- Why data-driven Web sites are such a good idea

- How a data-driven page actually works

- The different sources of data you can use with ASP.NET Web sites

- How ADO.NET is the glue that joins data sources and ASP.NET Web sites

- How to build your first data-driven page

If you've already read a beginner's book on ASP.NET, such as *Beginning ASP.NET 2.0 in C#2005: From Novice to Professional* by Matthew MacDonald (Apress, 2006), you're probably familiar with some of the material in this chapter already, so you could skip to the next chapter. Still, I encourage you at least to browse through this chapter. You never know what nuggets of information you may find.

Are Data-Driven Web Sites a Good Idea?

Should you even bother with hooking a data source to your Web site? That's the $64,000 question, isn't it really? If you're reading this book, I'll assume you've already come to the conclusion that using databases and other sources of data to turn static Web sites into dynamic data-driven Web sites is a good thing. However, I would be lying if I said there weren't any disadvantages to using data sources—there are. This section, then, covers the pros and cons of creating data-driven Web sites.

On the plus side, data-driven Web sites offer the following:

Maintenance: Using a database makes it a lot easier to maintain your data and keep it up-to-date. Take the example of a bank application that contains lists of customers by name and by branch, and contains profiles for each customer. Each time the customer is mentioned in a list, the customer's account number is also present. If that account number changed, the application would need to change it accordingly on all the lists, which could lead to errors; after all, account numbers aren't the easiest things to remember. A well-designed database usually ensures that easily mistyped data—such as Social Security numbers (SSNs), credit card numbers, International Standard Book Numbers (ISBNs), and so on—is entered or modified in only one place, rather than several. The data-driven Web site would then generate the lists by querying the database. Another reason that data-driven Web sites are easier to maintain is that they typically have fewer actual pages than static Web sites. The pages they do have act as templates that are filled on-the-fly from a database, as opposed to the complete, individual pages that static Web sites contain.

Reusability: Information in databases can easily be backed up and reused elsewhere as required. Compare this to static Web sites, where the information can't be retrieved easily from the surrounding HTML and layout instructions.

Data context: Databases allow you to define relationships and rules for the data in your database. For example, you can create a rule in your database that says if you store some information about a book, you must include an author and an ISBN, which must, in turn, be valid. This means that rather than querying the database for information by a simple index, such as the one in the back of this book, you can specify what to search for, as well as the order in which the information should be returned. A great example of this is the search engine. Can you imagine Google as a table of contents for the Web?

Quality and timeliness of content: Databases are optimized for the storage and retrieval of data and nothing else. They allow you to use and update information on a live Web site almost in real time—something that isn't possible with a Web site consisting of just static pages containing forms. For example, consider what happens when an e-commerce Web site receives an order for some goods. The code running behind the page knows to store the new order in a database and to reduce the inventory count for each item in the order once payment has been received. If the customer wants to change the order, it's still available in the database to be changed. The inventory also can be changed, depending on what the customer does. For instance, if the customer cancels the order, the system can simply reinstate inventory levels and mark the order as canceled. Now consider what happens if the e-commerce Web site has a human on the other side instead of a database, and the customer wants to change the order. The human needs to find the order, check the stock, and so on. This process wouldn't be immediate, and it would be prone to errors. What if the order were lost or incorrectly recorded?

On the downside, data-driven Web sites have some additional requirements:

Development time: It takes a little more time to write code to access the database containing information and to populate the database with the information you require. Likewise, it may take a little more planning initially to accommodate a database in the architecture of a Web site. Sometimes, the data may not lend itself to being used as a data source, which means more development is required to change it into an appropriate form. And actually designing the database is a valuable skill in its own right, which can take a considerable amount of time to develop.

Database round-trip: When a user requests a static page from a Web server, that Web server immediately sends the page back to the client. When a user requests a dynamic page that requires data from a database, the Web server must first make a request to (or *query*) the database for the necessary data, and then wait for it to arrive before it can assemble and send the page the user requested. This extra round-trip means a slight reduction in performance levels from the Web server. This delay might be unnoticeable on small Web sites, but may become more obvious on enterprise Web sites where thousands of pages might be requested per minute.

Tip Although you can't ever completely compensate for the additional round-trips that are made between the Web server and database, you can try to minimize the number of trips made by caching pages when they're created. After all, if the data in a page hasn't changed, why does it need to be retrieved from the database again? You'll look at improving the performance of a data-driven Web site with caching and other techniques in Chapter 12.

Dependence on the database: Using a database in a Web site means that should the database fail for some reason, the whole Web site will fail. The solution may be to run failover servers with synchronized databases, but as you can see from the next point, that could put quite a large dent in your pocketbook.

Cost: Full enterprise-level database solutions don't come cheap. At the top end of the market, Oracle Enterprise Edition starts at $40,000 and SQL Server Enterprise Edition at $25,000 for installation on *one* computer. Obviously, not everything costs that much, and indeed the databases used in this book are free, but things can get quite pricey quickly.

■**Note** Even at a grassroots level, Internet service providers (ISPs) will offer some sort of database use in their hosting packages—typically MySQL or SQL Server—but charge an additional fee per month. Don't forget to check exactly how much, even if you aren't planning to deploy a data-driven Web site immediately. Having the facility in place is always a plus, even if it costs a little more. Of course, hosting your own Web site would solve that problem, but then that costs money to set up as well.

All in all, the decision comes down to how big your Web site is likely to be and whether you would be happy tweaking HTML all day for the rest of your life, rather than putting the effort in initially, letting the database do most of the tweaking for you, and generally enjoying the social scene. You're still a database fan, aren't you? I thought so.

How Do Web Sites Use Data Sources?

So then, you have a database or some other data source, and you have an ASP.NET page. What does the page do to use the data source?

As you know, a static page doesn't do a great deal. It's static. It has a pretty simple structure: a <head>, a <body>, and probably some headings and paragraphs. When you add ASP.NET, that page becomes dynamic and can be generated in many ways, depending on the code you add. However, it still ends up with the same basic HTML structure displayed by the Web browser. The difference is generally the content.

Database Uses in a Web Environment

At its simplest, using a data source in a Web site means getting it to store and then provide the content for a page. You define a page whose structure and layout don't change but whose content does. It becomes a template for you to fill in the gaps with information from the database. For example, Amazon.co.uk (http://www.amazon.co.uk) uses databases to store all the information and feedback for every product it sells, and yet, as Figure 1-1 demonstrates, the basic product page has the same layout, regardless of the item you're viewing.

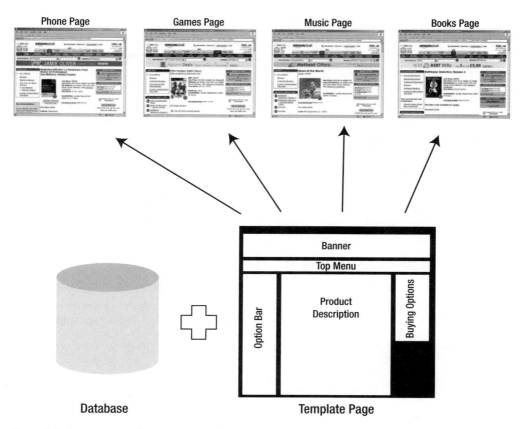

Figure 1-1. *Amazon.co.uk uses one template page and many product pages.*

Amazon.co.uk is also a good example of using a database to store layout and preferences information that changes depending on the page being requested. For example, the basic banner changes color according to the type of product you're browsing, and a combination of cookies and database data stores information about the items you've browsed and bought in the past, so Amazon.co.uk can suggest other content you may like in its recommendation pages.

In portal Web sites such as Slashdot (http://www.slashdot.org), a cookie on your machine identifies who you are to the Web site, and user preferences stored in the Web site's database allow for more radical changes to the Web site's user interface (UI), keeping track of which article groups you're interested in and whether the UI should be text only or full graphics, as Figure 1-2 demonstrates.

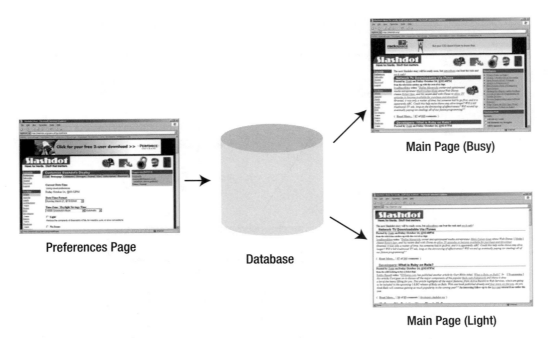

Figure 1-2. *Slashdot uses a database to display its pages according to your preferences.*

Delivering content and keeping track of user preferences aren't the only uses for a database in the Web environment, but they give you the idea. What about login systems, shopping carts, search engines, and bug-tracking systems? They're all variations on a theme, implemented as a database with a Web front end.

How Does the Web Site Get the Data?

It's time to get a little more technical. What actually happens when a data-driven page is requested by a browser? Does the code need to pray to the database gods for enlightenment and a source of knowledge? Of course not. Aside from anything else that ASP.NET may be doing in a page, the task of communicating with a data source takes just three steps, as shown in Figure 1-3.

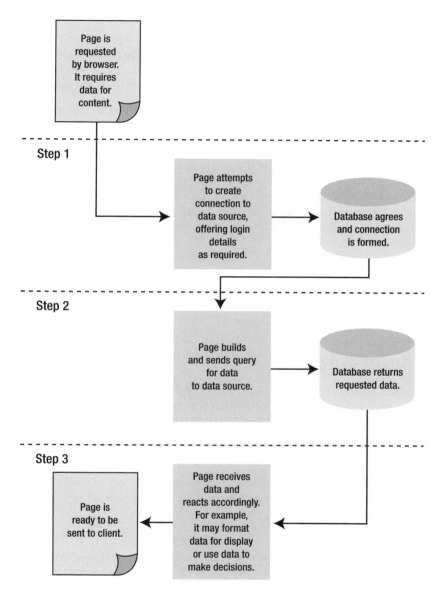

Figure 1-3. *It takes three simple steps to retrieve data and use it in a page.*

The steps are as follows:

1. The page tries to open a connection to a database. The code tells the page which database and where it can be found. In the examples in this book, the databases will be stored on the same machine as the Web server, but this doesn't have to be the case.

2. The page sends a query (also known as a command or statement) to the database. Usually, it's a request for some data, but it could be to update some data, to add some new data, or even to delete some data.

3. The database sends back some information that the page must then handle accordingly. If it's information for display on the page, it's rendered on the page, as with the earlier Amazon.co.uk and Slashdot examples. On the other hand, it may be a confirmation from the database that it updated, inserted, or deleted some data as you requested, or something else that doesn't directly affect the display of the page. It depends on the query sent in step 2.

These three steps are relatively simple, and once you have mastered them, you'll understand the basic requirements for building data-driven Web sites.

Now that you know what a page does when it talks to a data source, it's time to look at what you can actually use as a data source to drive your pages.

Looking for Information

Oranges aren't the only fruit. Databases aren't the only source of data you can use in your Web sites, and it's good to remember this as you start to develop your code. After all, why confine yourself to one central source if it doesn't make sense to do so? For example, you could put your lists of things to do today in a database, but it makes more sense to keep these items as a group of Outlook tasks, as a note in OneNote, or even as a simple text file. With a little tweaking, you can also use these as data sources for your pages.

The following sections cover the five general types of data sources you can use with your Web sites. First, let's look at the data source that you'll be using in this book: database servers.

Database Servers

Hang on, they're just called *databases*, aren't they? Where do the *servers* come into it? Well, strictly speaking, the database software you install—such as SQL Server, Oracle, MySQL, and so on—is a database server, or a database management server, depending on the product you're using. The database itself is just the collection of data you're filling your Web site with, and the server software is what hosts and manages it for you. A server may host many databases at a time, or just one, depending on the server configuration and the size of the database. The database that you'll use in the examples in this book is a few hundred kilobytes (10^5 bytes). One of the largest databases in the world is that of the U.S. Army logistics division, which is almost a couple of hundred terabytes (10^{14} bytes)!

The following are several different types of database servers (and therefore databases), and each works in its own way:

Relational databases: A relational database is the most common type and the one you'll use for the duration of this book. Information about an object or an event is strongly typed (just as .NET variables are) and stored in tables. Each table is given a set of rules as to how it relates to other tables in the database. For example, if you wanted to store some contact information in a database, you could create a table called ContactInfo and include items in it such as your contacts' first names, last names, e-mail addresses, work phone numbers, and Web site URLs. You'll spend Chapter 2 looking at what makes up a relational database, how you store data in it, and how you define relations and rules on that data.

Object-oriented databases: Information about objects and events are stored as objects and manipulated using methods attached to that object's class. This mimics the way you work with objects in .NET.

Object-relational databases: Almost a superset of relational databases, object-relational databases store information in tables, but the tables themselves are given a type and allowed to be operated on in a pseudo-object-oriented fashion.

Native XML databases: These store information about an object or event as an XML document rather than an object or row in a table, reading in and offering information as XML documents only. This kind of database has come into being only recently, following the development of XML as a popular technology.

A lot of commercial database servers are available. More relational and object-oriented databases exist than the others, but XML is gaining a great deal of popularity, so the balance is swiftly being redressed. However, the underlying query technology for XML has yet to be developed fully, so it will be a while before native XML databases are truly as powerful as relational and object-oriented databases.

Flat Files

The information stored in a database is often interrelated. For example, information about cats may be related to information about their owners. You design it that way, and database servers ensure that the relationship is maintained. On the other hand, the information in a flat file doesn't have a "flat file server" to keep track of a relationship between data in two flat files. The information about cats in one flat file may be related to the information about people who own cats in another flat file, but there is nothing to enforce that relationship. If an owner moved, a database server would note that the cat's address also changed. In the flat file, the cat would still be living at the old address.

A flat file lives in its own world and is unaware of any events related to the information it contains. That doesn't mean you can't use it as a source of data, though. Information is usually stored in lists or as comma-separated values (CSVs) such as the following, with each line storing data for one item:

```
Judy, tabby, 12, kitekat
Fred, ginger tom, 2, cat chow
Gene, siamese, 5, live mice
Ann, albino, 8, dog food
```

For example, you can use any of the following types of files in a Web site:

- Text files containing information written in a uniform way—perhaps as a CSV file or as a list of items (such as phone numbers), each on its own line

- Spreadsheet files generated by applications such as Excel and Lotus 1-2-3

- XML files

Web Services

You can also retrieve information from other systems that aren't directly connected to the Web server hosting your Web site. *Web services* allow you to expose functionality on remote servers and call that functionality across the Web. They're also cross-platform, allowing you to call functionality that is running on other operating systems (such as Linux) and other development platforms (such as Java).

You can make use of Web services by returning a data source from the remote server and using it as though it were a local data source. If the remote server is also using .NET, you can return a DataSet and use this as your data source. If the remote server isn't running .NET (perhaps it's a Linux machine), you can return an XML document and use that as the data source.

Objects

The three data sources that we've looked at so far all have one thing in common: they exist outside the code that uses them. The database is a stand-alone application, a flat file exists in the file system, and so on. It is also possible to use *objects* created within code as a data source, provided they're collections and implement the IList interface.

You can use objects for a whole host of different tasks, but a common use is as a wrapper around a set of database entities, where you'll use a collection to store a set of objects. A good example of this is in an e-commerce Web site.

In an e-commerce Web site, each product will be represented as a Product object, and a collection of products will be stored as a ProductCollection object. The ProductCollection implements the IList interface and can be used as a data source. If you want to display a list of products, you can pass the ProductCollection object to a GridView and use it as a data source.

Services

Your computer maintains a lot of information about itself, even if you never use it. It maintains user profiles, hardware profiles, e-mail archives, and more. They can all be used as data sources if you know where to look and how to access them. For example, you can use the following in your Web sites:

- You can tap into an Exchange server and search for messages, contacts, and calendar information.

- You can tap into the Windows registry, search for system settings, and tweak them if you like.

- You can tap into a network's Active Directory and work with users, groups, and other network resources.

Please be careful if you decide to start working with these kinds of data sources. A lot of security measures guard these services, and with good reason. Even with the best intentions, altering and deleting pieces of the registry, for example, can render Windows inert.

Introducing ADO.NET

So, you have a set of pages that need information and a data source to provide it. You know that the Web server will use the information to provide the page's content and influence the way the page displays. You need to tell the page how to retrieve the content from the data source and what to do with it afterward. Does this look like a job for ASP.NET?

Not quite. While it's true that you'll use ASP.NET to react and work with the information once it has been pulled from a data source, you actually use its sibling technology, ADO.NET, to work directly with the database. If you've worked with classic ASP, the relationship between ASP.NET and ADO.NET is the same as the relationship between ASP and ADO; the former deals only with the creation of pages, and the latter deals solely with retrieving information from data sources.

■**Note** While you may be thinking that using ADO.NET will be the same as using ADO, it's not just the "same old thing." Even though ADO.NET shares the same name as ADO, it isn't a simple evolution of ADO. You've already discovered that moving from ASP to ASP.NET was a complete paradigm shift in terms of how you build Web sites, and you'll soon see that moving from ADO to ADO.NET is a similarly large paradigm shift. A lot of the terminology is the same—you still have connections and commands, for instance—but that's about where the similarities end.

Data Access Technology: A Brief History

ADO.NET is the latest in a long line of Microsoft data-access technologies spanning a good ten years with the same aim in mind: to make database access as easy and as painless as possible for anyone who needs that facility.

Back in the late 1980s and beginning of the 1990s, database server vendors all faced the same problem. A lot of third-party vendors wanted to build products backed by a database but didn't want to be limited to using just one database. They wanted to keep the product as generic as possible so customers could use their application backed by their database of choice. The problem was that every database had its own way to access the data inside it, so a third-party vendor had to write new code each time it wanted to support a new database.

The solution the database vendors came up with was called Open Database Connectivity (ODBC). This is a common set of functions and interfaces agreed upon by all the major database vendors at that time to be implemented by all their servers. Third-party vendors needed to write code only against ODBC methods to access a database, and it would then work against any database that supported ODBC, which they all did. The third-party vendors were happy because the size of their products was reduced quite dramatically, and they all worked against every ODBC database. The database vendors were happy because third-party products worked against their database servers, and they could charge the third parties license fees. Everyone's customers were happy because of the increase in competition, product, and, well, wasn't it nice when everyone played nicely with everyone else?

ODBC was extremely successful and is still supported by all the major database servers in use today. However, one thing you can't call it is simple to use. ODBC works at quite a low level. In context, if your program spoke English, you would need to train yourself to write code in the Swahili that ODBC spoke when you wanted to access a database. Microsoft saw this problem and attempted to fix it by creating OLE DB, a set of Component Object Model (COM) components designed for Windows developers. OLE DB makes accessing data a bit simpler—more Spanish than Swahili, so still not English, but easier to learn. It also doesn't presuppose that the data source is a database, as ODBC does. OLE DB was pretty successful and is still supported by several vendors including Microsoft, which decided that OLE DB would be the cornerstone for its Universal Data Access (UDA) strategy.

One of the aims of UDA was to bring an object-oriented interface to ODBC and OLE DB, which were procedural in nature—more C than C++ or Visual Basic (VB). Its first attempts— Data Access Objects (DAO) and Remote Data Objects (RDO)—were designed to work against Access and larger databases such as SQL Server and Oracle, respectively. However, ADO version 2.0 superseded both of these in 1998. ADO is a technology originally designed to give classic ASP pages a way to access databases.

ADO.NET now takes over from ADO. Like its predecessor, ADO.NET gives you the ability to work with a data source through a common set of methods and interfaces, regardless of whether it supports ODBC, OLE DB, or its own proprietary access solution. This is achieved through a set of data providers, which are described in the next section. ADO.NET also provides better support for the following:

- Working with data away from the database itself or, rather, pulling information onto the Web server and working with it there instead of on the database server. This method of using *disconnected data* can improve performance if used wisely.

- The database when it is under attack from a large number of simultaneous queries. Stability and performance have been significantly improved in ADO.NET compared to ADO.

- Binding information to any control on the page, as you'll see in Chapter 6. Strictly speaking, this is more an ASP.NET feature than an ADO.NET feature, but it's an important capability when you're creating data-driven Web sites.

- With the introduction of the data source controls in ASP.NET 2.0 (discussed a little later in this chapter), it has become even easier to write data-aware pages than ever before.

In short, ADO.NET is a lot better than ADO ever was, and it's part of the .NET Framework, which provides a number of development benefits. Developing data-driven Web sites has never been so straightforward. The first release of the ASP.NET made writing data-aware pages almost idiot-proof, and with ASP.NET 2.0, it has become almost child's play. I say "almost" because data access is the one area where you're guaranteed to make mistakes when developing your Web site. Although ASP.NET 2.0 makes developing data-aware Web sites a lot safer, it's still possible to make mistakes.

Data Providers

You know now from your brief history lesson that the hard part of retrieving data from a data source has always been trying to talk to the source. That's why ODBC, OLE DB, ADO.NET, and the rest were created in the first place. Ironically, as you saw earlier, all you really need to do with the data source for a Web site can be reduced into three steps: creating a connection, sending a query, and dealing with the result of the query. ADO.NET provides a common interface for performing those three steps, regardless of whether you're using ODBC, OLE DB, or some other method to access it. It does this with *data providers*.

In this book, you'll see how to use three different data sources, so you have a choice when it comes to working on your own Web sites. MySQL has an ODBC interface. A Microsoft Access database (MDB) file has an OLE DB interface. SQL Server has both ODBC and OLE DB interfaces, as well as its own optimized set of access methods.

Suppose you're going to use MySQL. Writing a bit of pseudo-code for talking to this database, your three steps may look like this:

```
<%@ import Namespace="System.Data" %>
<%@ import Namespace="System.Data.Odbc" %>
<html>
  <script>
    create OdbcConnection object to link to MySQL
    create OdbcCommand object to set up and send a query to MySQL
    get returned an OdbcDataReader object containing the results of the query
    deal with the results....
  </script>
...
</html>
```

If you're using an MDB database file, which has an OLE DB interface, your pseudo-code might look like this:

```
<%@ import Namespace="System.Data" %>
<%@ import Namespace="System.Data.OleDb" %>
<html>
  <script>
    create OleDbConnection object to link to MDB file
    create OleDbCommand object to set up and send a query to MDB file
    get returned an OleDbDataReader object containing the results of the query
    deal with the results....
  </script>
...
</html>
```

The two pieces of pseudo-code are almost identical. The only difference is that the names of the objects are slightly different to correspond to the interface being used. So, for example, it's OdbcConnection for the ODBC database and OleDbConnection for the OLE DB database. As you'll see in Chapter 4, if you look at the real code, the actual calls you make are identical, which means the only things that change between different interfaces are the namespace to use and the names of the objects being used. The same is true if you want to use the native access method for SQL Server. The same method calls and steps are taken, but slightly different namespaces and objects are used, as in this example:

```
<%@ import Namespace="System.Data" %>
<%@ import Namespace="System.Data.SqlClient" %>
<html>
  <script>
    create SqlConnection object to link to SQL Server
    create SqlCommand object to set up and send a query to SQL Server
    get returned an SqlDataReader object containing the results of the query
    deal with the results....
  </script>
...
</html>
```

What you're seeing is the common interface for data-access operations provided by ADO.NET. A common set of base classes and interfaces (one for a Connection object, one for a Command object, and so on) are implemented *and optimized* for each data-access method you may need to use: ODBC, OLE DB, native SQL Server, and so on. Each group of objects is called a *data provider* and is housed in its own namespace. For example, Microsoft ships all of the following data providers:

- System.Data.Odbc is the .NET data provider for ODBC-based databases.

- System.Data.OleDb is the .NET data provider for OLE DB-based databases, such as Microsoft Access. You can also use it to access flat files.

- System.Data.OracleClient is the .NET data provider for Oracle databases.

- System.Data.SqlClient is the .NET data provider for SQL Server.

- System.Data.SqlServerCe is the .NET Compact Framework data provider for SQL Server CE. As you may imagine, its use is limited to applications running on personal digital assistants (PDAs) hosting an instance of SQL Server CE.

And that's one of the beauties of ADO.NET. As long as you know which data provider to use, you need to learn only one set of calls, and every data provider supports that set. Figure 1-4 shows this diagrammatically.

Going one step further, if a vendor would rather have .NET developers use a data provider specifically designed for its database server, instead of the generic OLE DB or ODBC one, all the vendor needs to do is implement the same common set of objects that every other data provider includes. An extra method or property here and there may take advantage of a particular feature unique to the data-access technology being modeled by the data provider, but in general, all the objects have the same methods and properties.

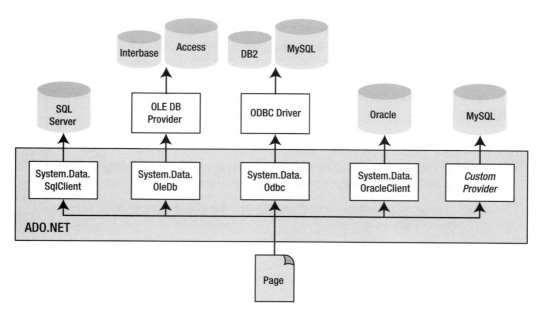

Figure 1-4. *Using data providers means you have easy, optimized access to all databases.*

Every data provider contains implementations of the following:

- **Connection object:** Used to represent the connection between the page and the data source.

- **Command object:** Used to represent the query to be sent to the database. Queries are much like functions and may use parameters filled at runtime rather than hard-coded values filled at compile time. To represent the parameters in a query, a data provider also includes a Parameter object.

- **DataReader object:** Used to represent the data returned by the data source as a forward-only, use-once result of a query. You'll start working with the DataReader object in Chapter 4.

- **DataAdapter object:** Used to populate a DataSet with the results of a query. Unlike with the DataReader, once the results are added to a DataSet, you can access it as many times as you like and however you want. Note that the DataSet isn't part of any data provider, and the same object is used, regardless of which data provider you use. A DataSet uses disconnected data on the Web server; it never works directly with a data source. The DataAdapter provides the bridge between the specific data provider and the DataSet. We'll look at the DataAdapter and DataSet objects in more detail in Chapter 5.

Note Although the objects that interact with the data source are the DataReader and DataAdapter objects, the DataAdapter tends to get short shrift when talking about data access. Although technically incorrect, it's common practice to refer to the DataReader and DataSet as the methods of accessing the database, and that's what I'll use for the rest of the book. Rather than saying DataAdapter/DataSet, I'll stick to just DataSet. Just be aware that wherever you use a DataSet, there's going to be a specific DataAdapter interacting with the data source.

- **Exception object:** Used to allow your page to fail gracefully if something untoward happens and lets you know (in detail) exactly what went wrong.

Figure 1-5 demonstrates how these objects fit into the grand three-step data access scheme you saw in Figure 1-3.

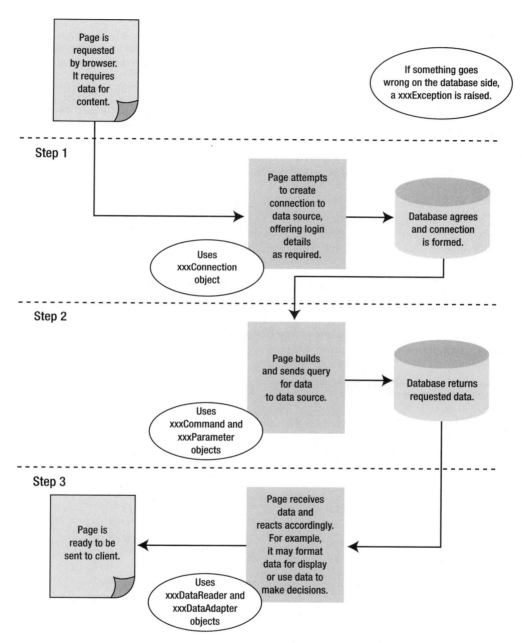

Figure 1-5. *Putting the pieces of a data provider in their place*

Data Source Controls

The paradigm and objects that we've looked at in the previous section were the only way to handle data access in the previous versions of ASP.NET. ASP.NET 2.0 introduces several new controls that simplify the way that you work with data.

The data source controls are a series of controls that allow the interactions with data sources to be handled without writing a single line of code, what I like to call *code-free data access*. Instead of having to create Connection and Command objects in code, you can create an instance of the `SqlDataSource` and point this at the correct data source. Any data source can be accessed, as long as there's a data provider available for it. The `SqlDataSource` handles the interaction with the data source for you automatically. In the next section, you'll see how these controls work.

Although the data source controls do provide an ideal means of building data-aware pages that allow you to view and modify data, you'll soon realize that there are limitations to what you can accomplish using this method. This is where the Connection and Command objects that you'll meet in Chapter 4 come into their element.

Developing Your First Example

Enough theory—it's time for your first example. You're going to discover exactly how easy it is to create a data-driven page by creating one in five seconds flat—well, slightly longer, as you have a little typing to do! The page that we're going to build will look very much like Figure 1-6.

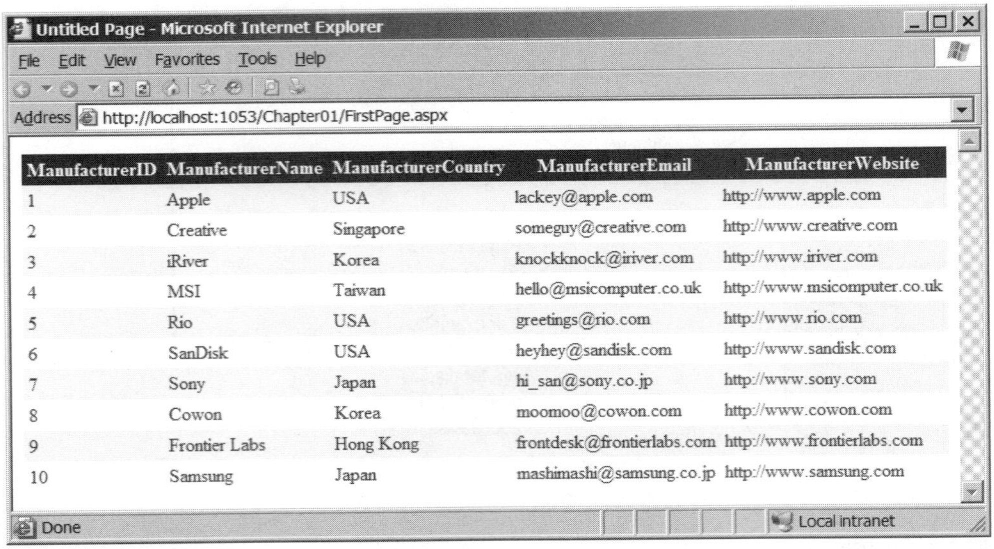

ManufacturerID	ManufacturerName	ManufacturerCountry	ManufacturerEmail	ManufacturerWebsite
1	Apple	USA	lackey@apple.com	http://www.apple.com
2	Creative	Singapore	someguy@creative.com	http://www.creative.com
3	iRiver	Korea	knockknock@iriver.com	http://www.iriver.com
4	MSI	Taiwan	hello@msicomputer.co.uk	http://www.msicomputer.co.uk
5	Rio	USA	greetings@rio.com	http://www.rio.com
6	SanDisk	USA	heyhey@sandisk.com	http://www.sandisk.com
7	Sony	Japan	hi_san@sony.co.jp	http://www.sony.com
8	Cowon	Korea	moomoo@cowon.com	http://www.cowon.com
9	Frontier Labs	Hong Kong	frontdesk@frontierlabs.com	http://www.frontierlabs.com
10	Samsung	Japan	mashimashi@samsung.co.jp	http://www.samsung.com

Figure 1-6. *Your first data-driven page in action*

For the purposes of this book, we're going to use free, or as cheap as possible, tools to build all of the examples. Both of the database servers that we'll use—SQL Server 2005 Express and MySQL 5.0, can be downloaded for free, and we'll use Visual Web Developer 2005 Express as our development environment.

Visual Web Developer 2005 Express is a cut-down version of Visual Studio 2005. Although it doesn't provide any of the high-end features of Visual Studio 2005, it does offer the same environment for building Web sites. Visual Web Developer 2005 Express provides code high-lighting, error checking, and most of the features that you would expect from a full-fledged development environment. It also includes its own mini Web server (the ASP.NET Development Server), so those of you without access to a server running Internet Information Services (IIS) can work through the exercises in this book. At the moment, you can download Visual Web Developer 2005 Express for free from `http://msdn.microsoft.com/vstudio/express/vwd` for the "next year," and after that, you'll have to pay for it.

Although we're using the cut-down versions of SQL Server 2005 and Visual Studio 2005, if you happen to have access to the full-fledged versions, you'll also be able to work through all of the examples in the book. The differences are very minor—for example, some menus may be in slightly different places—so you should find it easy to follow along.

■**Caution** If you're going to run this example (and the rest of the examples in this book), you'll need to install, as a minimum, .NET Framework 2.0 and Visual Web Developer 2005 Express. Refer to Appendix A for full instructions and come back here when you're ready to continue.

Try It Out: Creating a Simple Data-Driven Page

In this example, you'll create a simple data-driven page that pulls some information from a data source and displays it in a table on the page. In this case, the data source is a small MDB database file that you can find in the code download for this book (available from the Downloads area of `http://www.apress.com`). It's called `players.mdb` and should be copied to `C:\BAND`.

For this first example, we're going to use an MDB file as the database. In Chapter 2, we'll look at creating a database in both SQL Server and MySQL. When building real-world Web sites, you're advised to use a full-fledged database server such as SQL Server or MySQL, and avoid using MDB files.

To create the data-driven page, follow these steps:

1. Start Visual Web Developer and create a new Web site by selecting the File ➤ New Web Site menu option. This will launch the New Web Site dialog box, as shown in Figure 1-7.

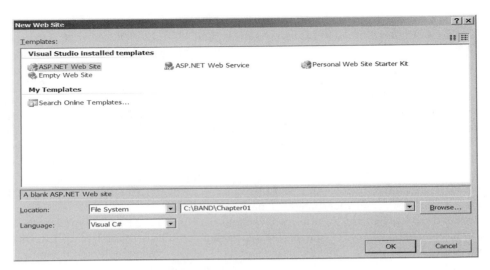

Figure 1-7. *The New Web Site dialog box in Visual Web Developer*

2. We're going to create an empty Web site for each chapter of the book, so select ASP.NET Web Site from the Templates list and enter C:\BAND\Chapter01 for the location of the Web site. Because we're using the ASP.NET Development Server, our access to the Web site is file-based, so ensure that the Location option is set to File System. Make sure that the Language option is set to Visual C#. Then click OK to create the Web site.

3. By default, when creating a new Web site, Visual Web Developer will create a Web Form called Default.aspx in the Web site. We're not going to use this page, so right-click it in the Solution Explorer and select Delete from the context menu. Click OK in the confirmation dialog box to delete the page.

4. Right-click the folder name in the Solution Explorer and select Add New Item from the context menu. This launches the Add New Item dialog box, which allows you to create a whole host of different items, as shown in Figure 1-8.

5. Select Web Form from the Templates list. In the Name text box, enter FirstPage.aspx. Make sure that the Place Code in Separate File check box is *not* checked, and ensure that the language is set as Visual C#. Click Add to add the Web Form to the Web site. This will add the page to the Solution Explorer, as shown in Figure 1-9.

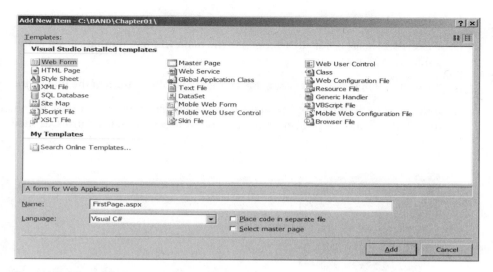

Figure 1-8. *The Add New Item dialog box*

Figure 1-9. *Your new page (Web Form) has been added to the solution.*

6. Right-click `FirstPage.aspx` and select Set As Start Page from the context menu.

7. If `FirstPage.aspx` is not already open in the main window, double-click it in the Solution Explorer to open it.

8. Switch to Design view by clicking the Design tab at the bottom of the main window.

9. If the Toolbox does not appear on the left side of your screen, select View ➤ Toolbox to display it. Expand the Data entry in the Toolbox to see the data controls, as shown in Figure 1-10.

Figure 1-10. *The Visual Web Developer Toolbox contains a plethora of useful controls.*

10. Add a `SqlDataSource` control to the page. This will create an instance of the control called `SqlDataSource1` and open the Tasks menu for the control, as shown in Figure 1-11. If the Tasks menu is not shown, click the control to select it, and then click the little right-pointing arrow in the top right of the control to launch the Tasks menu.

Figure 1-11. *Controls have Tasks menus showing common operations.*

11. Click the Configure Data Source option on the Tasks menu. This will launch the Configure Data Source wizard and allow you to select the data source to use.

12. On the first step of the wizard, click the New Connection button. We're not connecting to a SQL Server database, so select Change in the Add Connection dialog box. Select Microsoft Access Database File as the data source, and then click OK.

13. The database that we want to use is included in the book's code download, and you need to enter this as the database file name, as well as the correct location of the database. Specify the data connection to use as C:\BAND\players.mdb, and then click OK. This will create the correct connection string, as shown in Figure 1-12. Click Next to continue.

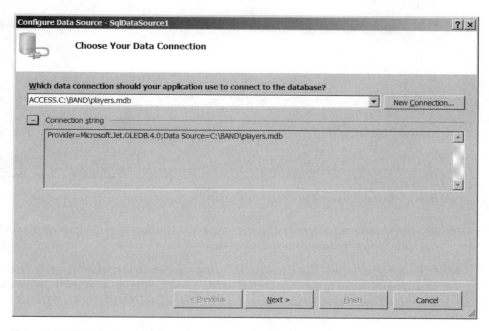

Figure 1-12. *The data source has the correct connection string.*

14. On the Save the Connection String step, make sure the Yes check box isn't checked, and then click Next.

15. On the Configure the Select Statement step, select Manufacturer from the drop-down list and click the * column in the Columns list, as shown in Figure 1-13. Then click Next to move to the next step of the wizard.

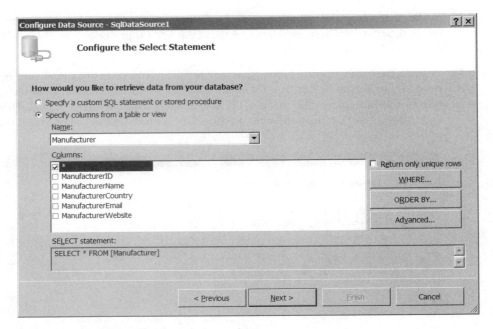

Figure 1-13. *Specifiying the data that we require.*

16. If you wish, you can select Test Query to preview the data that the query will return. Click the Finish button to close the wizard.

17. Add a `GridView` control from the Toolbox to the page below the `SqlDataSource`. From the Tasks menu, select `SqlDataSource1` as the data source for the `GridView` from the Choose Data Source list, as shown in Figure 1-14.

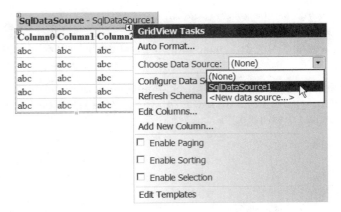

Figure 1-14. *Choosing a data source from the Tasks menu*

18. Reopen the Tasks menu for the GridView and select the Auto Format option. Select Colorful from the Auto Format dialog box, and then click the OK button.

19. Save FirstPage.aspx, and press F5 to debug the Web site. A dialog box will ask if you want to create a Web.config file to enable debugging, as shown in Figure 1-15. Click OK to create a Web.config file.

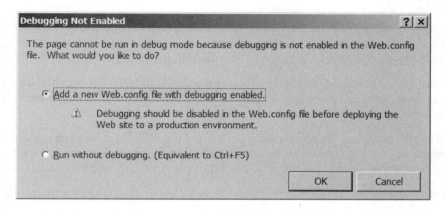

Figure 1-15. *Enabling debugging in Visual Web Developer*

This will start the ASP.NET Development Server, as shown in Figure 1-16. Once the ASP.NET Development Server is running, all being well, you'll see a page in your Web browser looking none too dissimilar from Figure 1-6. Congratulations, you've just made your first data-driven page!

Figure 1-16. *ASP.NET Development Server is used by Visual Web Developer for debugging.*

How It Works

Visual Web Developer allows you to automate a lot of simple tasks when you use it. In this chapter's example, you built a Web Form (Microsoft's terminology for an ASP.NET page) that interacts with a database and displays the results in a graphical format. And you've done this without writing a single line of code!

You saw how to use Visual Web Developer to build a data-driven page using two of the new controls available with ASP.NET 2.0: the SqlDataSource and the GridView. You'll look at these and the various other data controls in more detail in the chapters to come.

It's time to finish this chapter before a bug crops up.

Summary

In this chapter, you've looked at the world of data-driven Web sites from 50,000 feet. You learned how a page interacts with a data source and the different types of data sources that interact with pages. Specifically, you learned the following:

- Databases generally support at least one of the ODBC and OLE DB common database interfaces, although some also support their own optimized data-access methods for speedier results.

- ADO.NET is a relatively new technology—part of the .NET Framework. It presents the developer with a set of data providers, each of which is optimized to access data through OLE DB, ODBC, and so on, but all of these data providers are used in the same way.

- The following are the three steps for accessing a database and using the information retrieved from it in a page:

  1. Create a connection to a database with a Connection object.

  2. Send a query to the database with a Command object.

  3. Handle the data appropriately depending on what you want it to do. Data is returned from the database using a DataReader or DataAdapter object and may be stored on the Web server in a DataSet object, which is generic and not specific to any data provider.

Finally, you created your first data-driven ASP.NET page using a simple MDB database file and Visual Web Developer. You saw how a Visual Web Developer wizard allows you to create a page in simple stages.

In the next chapter, you'll start coming down from 50,000 feet and investigate what makes a database, and in particular a relational database, tick.

CHAPTER 2

∎∎∎

Introducing Relational Databases

In Chapter 1, you learned that you can use almost any kind of data source to drive your dynamic pages. You also learned that the relational database is the most commonly used type of data source for this purpose. In this chapter, you'll take a closer look at how relational databases actually work. You'll see how data is organized inside a database, and to make sure you understand it, you'll build your own sample database from scratch.

If you're wondering why this whole chapter focuses on the theory and setup of a database, it's because a badly designed and badly built database will nearly always come back to bite you once you start to build an application that uses it. And this isn't an issue specific to ASP.NET. Any application on any platform that connects to a database will run into problems if the database isn't designed correctly in the first place. Applications become harder to expand and slower to run as you spot-fix individual problems that wouldn't have come up if you had built the database correctly.

A data-driven Web site relies totally on its data source for content, so having it drag its heels because you built it wrong wouldn't be a good thing. You'll look further at the actual designing of a database in Chapter 13, but you need to be familiar with the basics before you can go there.

This chapter covers the following topics:

- The different pieces that make up a database: the tables that hold the data, the columns that define what the table holds, and the rows that contain the actual data

- The different types of SQL queries and an introduction to the most commonly used queries, as well as stored procedures

- How indexes can make your databases more efficient

- The different types of relationships between tables and how these can be modeled in the database

- How to create and use SQL Server 2005 database diagrams, which show the layout of your database

- An introduction to database views and triggers

The Databases and Tools

We're going to work with three different databases throughout the course of this book. You've already seen one of these, Microsoft Access at the end of Chapter 1. The other two that we'll look at are Microsoft SQL Server 2005 Express Edition and MySQL 5.0.

Microsoft SQL Server 2005 Express Edition is the free version of Microsoft's full SQL Server 2005 database server. The Express Edition lacks several features available in the full-blown version (none of which will cause any problems during the course of this book), and the numerous administration tools SQL Server 2005 comes with aren't included. In previous releases of SQL Server, the lack of administration tools for the free edition was a problem. However, a quite powerful administration tool, SQL Server Management Studio Express Edition, was released along with the SQL Server 2005 Express Edition. We'll use this tool to manage the SQL Server 2005 Express Edition database that we will build in this chapter.

The second, real, database that we'll use is MySQL 5.0. This is a free database server that, in its latest incarnation, provides a very comprehensive range of functionality that rivals other databases. Several free administration tools work with MySQL. We'll use of one of these: MySQL Query Browser.

As you saw in Chapter 1, Visual Web Developer 2005 Express Edition provides functionality for interacting with databases, although that functionality is limited. Visual Web Developer 2005 Express Edition allows you to connect to any data source that has an ODBC driver or OLE DB provider. If you're using ODBC or OLE DB to connect to the data source, you can only view and query the data that it contains. If you're using the SqlClient data provider—that is, connecting to SQL Server—then Visual Web Developer 2005 Express Edition offers most of the same func-tionality provided by SQL Server Management Studio Express Edition.

You can find the instructions for installing SQL Server 2005 Express Edition, SQL Server Management Studio Express Edition, MySQL 5.0, and MySQL Query Browser in Appendix A. You can find the complete details of the sample database you'll be building in this chapter in Appendix D. It's a simple database, which contains the details of several MP3 Players, their Manufacturers, and supported Formats.

Note As marketing people are prone to do, they make the job of talking about their products quite long-winded. What sort of name for a product is Visual Web Developer 2005 Express Edition? If I had to use that every time I talked about the product, this book would be about three times longer! I'm going to use shorter versions of the names: Visual Web Developer, SQL Server 2005, and SQL Server Management Studio. Just keep in mind that I'm referring to the Express Editions.

Tables, Rows, and Columns

The first thing to know and be comfortable with is that a relational database stores all data as *tables*. Each of these tables represents a single, distinct subject: an object or an event. For example, a table may contain details of Manufacturers (as in Figure 2-1), fish, or compact discs. Or it may keep data on appointments, deliveries, or customer service enquiries.

	ManufacturerID	ManufacturerName	ManufacturerCountry	ManufacturerEmail	ManufacturerWebsite
	1	Apple	USA	lackey@apple.com	http://www.apple.com
	2	Creative	Singapore	someguy@creative.com	http://www.creative.com
	3	iRiver	Korea	knockknock@iriver.com	http://www.river.com
	4	MSI	Taiwan	hello@miscomputer.co.uk	http://www.miscomputer.co.uk
	5	Rio	USA	Greetings@rio.com	http://www.rio.com
more rows...					

Figure 2-1. *A simple table*

In general, databases shouldn't store information about several types of objects or events—say, cats and fish—in the same table, unless the application of the database says otherwise. Biologists, for example, will want to keep details on cats and details on fish separate. More than likely, the details they keep for the two species of animal will be quite different. On the other hand, an online pet store may use a single table to keep a record of all the pets it has in stock. Cats and fish would be grouped together as "pets" in one table.

When you create a table in a database, you give it a name to reflect its contents—Book, Compact_Disc, Customer_Service_Enquiry, and so on. The table in Figure 2-1 is named Manufacturer. If you start calling a table Cats_And_Fish, for example, chances are you actually want to be creating two tables: one for cats and one for fish.

Every table contains a number of *rows*, or *records* if you prefer (or even *tuples*, if you're a mathematician). Each row represents exactly one instance of the object or event the table holds details about. In Figure 2-1, each row in the Manufacturer table holds the details for exactly one Manufacturer. These details aren't duplicated or continued elsewhere in the table, so when you locate that particular row, it contains all the information you have on that Manufacturer. In Figure 2-2, for example, the row containing all the information about Creative has been highlighted.

	ManufacturerID	ManufacturerName	ManufacturerCountry	ManufacturerEmail	ManufacturerWebsite
	1	Apple	USA	lackey@apple.com	http://www.apple.com
▶	2	Creative	Singapore	someguy@creative.com	http://www.creative.com
	3	iRiver	Korea	knockknock@iriver.com	http://www.river.com
	4	MSI	Taiwan	hello@miscomputer.co.uk	http://www.miscomputer.co.uk
	5	Rio	USA	Greetings@rio.com	http://www.rio.com
more rows...					

Figure 2-2. *A row in a table contains data about one object instance.*

Every row contains a number of *columns*, also called *attributes* or *fields*. Each column contains a single piece of information indicated by the column's name. Like the name for a table, the name for a column should be as unambiguous as possible. In the example in Figure 2-2, all of the columns are prefixed with *Manufacturer*. If it used a column called Name to represent the Manufacturer's name, for instance, it would not be immediately clear what it's referring to—Name could refer to a person's name, a Web site's name, or any name you like if you take it out of context. With the column name ManufacturerName, it's pretty clear what this column will contain.

■**Note** All table and column names should start with a letter and be followed only by more letters, numbers, or an underscore—never a space. Some, but not all, databases permit using a few punctuation characters in names, but it's easier to stay clear of them altogether.

Retrieving information from a table is reasonably simple, because every table must contain a column or a combination of columns that uniquely identifies any piece of data in the table. This means that it doesn't matter in what order you add rows to the table, because you'll still be able to identify them individually. When you're building a database table, you identify this column or combination of columns as the table's *primary key*. In Figure 2-1, for example, the ManufacturerID column does this job nicely. Because of this primary key, you can access any column in a database with relative ease, as long as you know the column name, the value of the primary key for the row it's in, and the name of the table. For example, say you need a contact e-mail address for iRiver. To get this information, you need to find the Manufacturer table, then the row for iRiver, and then the value in the ManufacturerEmail column in that row, as shown in Figure 2-3.

	ManufacturerID	ManufacturerName	ManufacturerCountry	ManufacturerEmail	ManufacturerWebsite
	1	Apple	USA	lackey@apple.com	http://www.apple.com
	2	Creative	Singapore	someguy@creative.com	http://www.creative.com
▶	3	iRiver	Korea	knockknock@iriver.com	http://www.river.com
	4	MSI	Taiwan	hello@miscomputer.co.uk	http://www.miscomputer.co.uk
	5	Rio	USA	Greetings@rio.com	http://www.rio.com
more rows...					

Figure 2-3. *Pinpointing data in a database*

Every table should have a primary key. It doesn't have to be an ID number (although that's the norm in a simple table) as in this example, but you must be able to guarantee that each value for that primary key column will be unique. A person's last name or an appointment date won't do for a primary key, but a global unique identifier (GUID) or a product's Amazon standard identification number (ASIN) should do fine. Consider the situation where a table doesn't have a primary key. The database server may not be able to identify a specific row in a table, so it might return the wrong one or return many. What if a Web site were trying to retrieve a user's preferences and presented him with the wrong set of options? What if credit card numbers weren't unique but were used as primary keys? You could get sent the wrong bill or be charged with someone else's transactions. You can see why primary keys must be unique.

You can also use a combination of columns, rather than just one column, as a primary key. If a primary key is a single column, it's a *simple primary key*. If it consists of two or more columns, it's a *composite primary key*. For example, you couldn't uniquely identify an album in a table by its name alone (consider 4—the name of albums by Peter Gabriel, Led Zeppelin, and Black Sabbath, no less), so you could set the table's primary key to contain both the band and title. You'll see further examples of composite primary keys in the "Many-to-Many Relationships" section later in this chapter.

You can create a new table in a database in many ways, depending on which database server software and which development environment you're using. In the following sections, you'll investigate how to do this within SQL Server 2005 and MySQL 5.0.

Try It Out: Creating a Table in SQL Server 2005

In this example, you'll create the Manufacturer table shown in Figure 2-1 inside a new SQL Server 2005 database using the tools provided in SQL Server Management Studio. Follow these steps:

1. Start SQL Server Management Studio. You're immediately presented with the Connect to Server dialog box.

2. Enter the server name as `localhost\BAND` and select SQL Server Authentication as the authentication method. Enter a Login of **sa** and a Password of **bandpass**. Check the Remember Password check box. Your dialog box should look like Figure 2-4. Once all the information is entered, click the Connect button to connect to the database server.

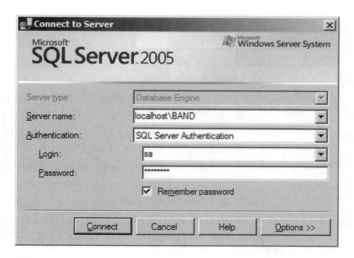

Figure 2-4. *Connecting to the correct SQL Server instance*

3. In the Object Explorer, right-click the Databases node and select New Database from the context menu to open the New Database dialog box.

4. Enter a name of **Players** for the database, as shown in Figure 2-5, and click the OK button to create the database. This will close the dialog box, and you'll see in the Summary window that the database has been created.

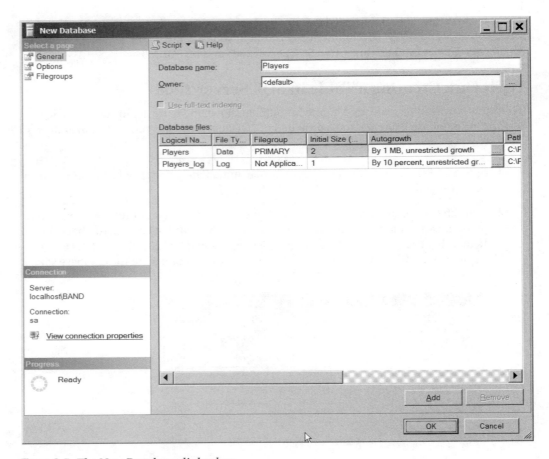

Figure 2-5. *The New Database dialog box*

5. You can also see that the database has been created by expanding the Databases node in the Object Explorer, as shown in Figure 2-6. Expand the new database, right-click the Tables node, and select New Table.

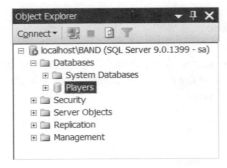

Figure 2-6. *The Players database has been created.*

6. The first task is to create the ManufacturerID column that contains the primary key for this table. Enter **ManufacturerID** in the Column Name field and select int from the drop-down list for the Data Type. Finally, uncheck the Allow Nulls check box. Your column definition should look like Figure 2-7.

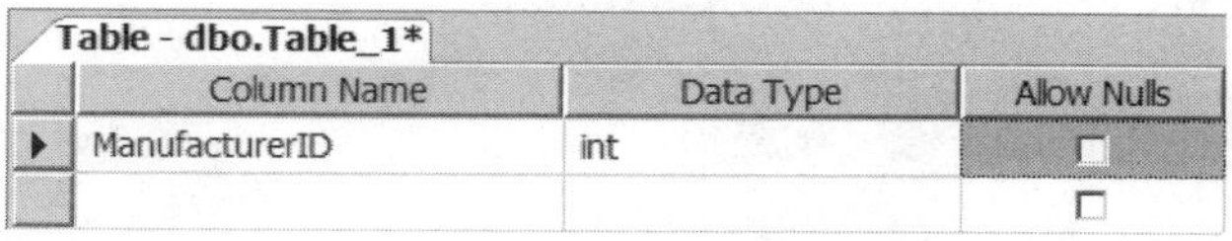

Table - dbo.Table_1*		
Column Name	Data Type	Allow Nulls
▶ ManufacturerID	int	☐
		☐

Figure 2-7. *The basic column details have been entered.*

7. Right-click the column you just created and select Set Primary Key. This marks the column as the primary key for the table. This is indicated by the key icon in the column to the left of the Column Name field, as shown in Figure 2-8.

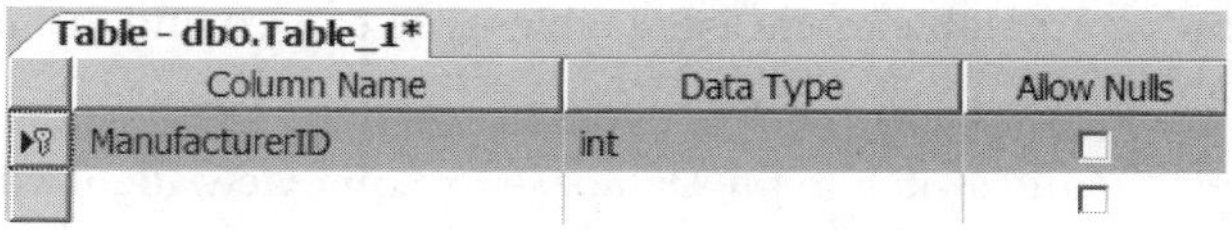

Table - dbo.Table_1*		
Column Name	Data Type	Allow Nulls
▶🔑 ManufacturerID	int	☐
		☐

Figure 2-8. *Primary key columns are indicated graphically.*

8. Now add the four remaining columns to the Manufacturer table, as shown in Figure 2-9. As you enter details for a column in the table, a new blank row is added to the bottom of the list, allowing you to enter the details for the next column. Set up the remaining four columns as follows:

Column Name	Data Type	Allow Nulls
ManufacturerName	Varchar(50)	Not checked
ManufacturerCountry	Varchar(50)	Checked
ManufacturerEmail	Varchar(100)	Checked
ManufacturerWebsite	Varchar(100)	Checked

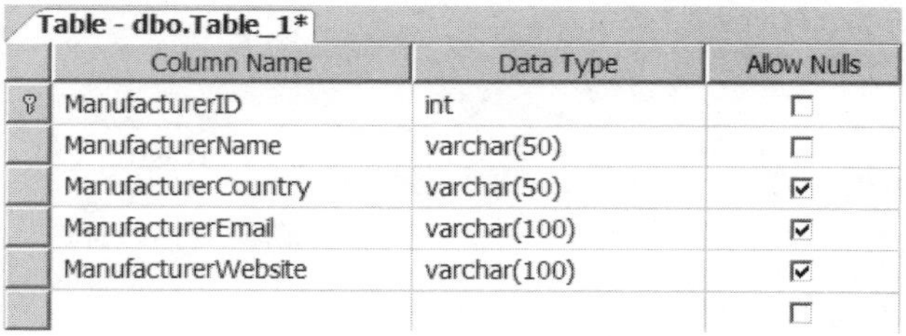

Table - dbo.Table_1*		
Column Name	Data Type	Allow Nulls
🔑 ManufacturerID	int	☐
ManufacturerName	varchar(50)	☐
ManufacturerCountry	varchar(50)	☑
ManufacturerEmail	varchar(100)	☑
ManufacturerWebsite	varchar(100)	☑
		☐

Figure 2-9. *The column definitions for the Manufacturer table in SQL Server 2005*

9. In the Properties window for the table (shown on the right side of the SQL Server Management Studio window), select ManufacturerID as the Identity Column.

10. Save the table by clicking the Save button in the toolbar or by selecting File ➤ Save Table_1 from the menu. In the Choose Name dialog box, enter the name **Manufacturer**, as shown in Figure 2-10, and then click the OK button.

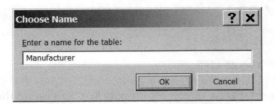

Figure 2-10. *Entering a name for the new table*

11. To confirm that the table has been created, expand the Tables node in the Object Explorer. You'll see the new Manufacturer table in the list of tables (you can expand this to show the full details of the table).

12. Open Visual Web Developer and switch to the Database Explorer view. Right-click the Data Connections node and select Add Connection from the context menu. In the Add Connection dialog box, enter the same information as you used to connect in SQL Server Express Management Studio in step 1. In addition, select Players from the Connect to a Database drop-down list. Once you've entered the information, click OK to add the connection.

13. Expand the connection you just added, and then expand the Tables node in the tree that is presented. You'll see the Manufacturer table that you've just created, as shown in Figure 2-11.

Figure 2-11. *Visual Web Developer can also connect to the SQL Server 2005 database.*

How It Works

As you've just seen, the tools provided by SQL Server Management Studio make creating a new table within a database quite simple. In the example, you actually accomplished three different tasks:

- Creating a new database

- Creating a new table in the database

- Creating new columns in the table

When first launching SQL Server Management Studio, you first connect to a SQL Server 2005 database server. Once you're connected to the database server, you can create a new database quite easily. You specify the name of the database, and SQL Server Management Studio takes care of the details of creating the database and adding it to the list of databases that you can see.

Once you've created the database, you can add new tables to it as required. You can see how easy it is to create a column by simply specifying the column's name and data type, and deciding whether the column can have null values.

You also saw how you can create a primary key on a table very easily by using the context menu for the column. As you learned earlier, primary keys allow you to individually identify a row in a table. You'll see how important primary keys are when we look at relationships between database tables later in the chapter.

The final piece in the puzzle was the setting of the identity column for the table. This allows you to set an auto-incrementing column in the table, which will be incremented by one every time a new row is added to the table. If you look again at the drop-down list that is presented for the table (you can view and edit the design of an existing table by selecting Modify from the table's context menu in the Object Explorer), you'll see that the only column that is available as an identity column is ManufacturerID. ManufacturerID can be an identity column because it contains only integers, and these can be incremented automatically every time a new row is added. As you also have a requirement for ManufacturerID to be your primary key—with unique values—setting it as the identity column makes perfect sense.

SQL Server Management Studio actually interprets your wishes to create databases and tables into queries in the database's own language—Structured Query Language (SQL)—which you'll look at in the "Queries and Stored Procedures" section later in this chapter. Actually, you have several other ways to send these same queries and build the Manufacturer table, including the following:

- Using Visual Web Developer to interact with the SQL Server 2005

- Using the SQL Server 2005 client tools to work with the database

- Using a database's command-line utility, such as `osql.exe`, as you'll see in Chapter 11

- Building your own application to send the query to the database

At the end of the example, you saw how to connect Visual Web Developer to the database you created. From within the development environment, you can see the structure of the databases, view the contents of tables, and run queries against the tables. Since you connected to the database using the SqlClient data provider, the context menu also provides options to modify the database. In later examples, you'll use Visual Web Developer to look at the database, but you will not use its management features. You'll stick to using SQL Server Management Studio for making modifications.

Try It Out: Creating a Table in MySQL 5.0

In this example, you'll create the Manufacturer table shown in Figure 2-1 inside a new MySQL 5.0 database using the tools provided in MySQL Query Browser. Follow these steps:

1. Start MySQL Query Browser. You're immediately presented with the Connect to MySQL Server Instance dialog box.

2. Enter a Server Host of **localhost**, a Username of **root**, and a Password of **bandpass**. Your dialog box should look like Figure 2-12. Once you've entered the information, click OK to connect to the database server.

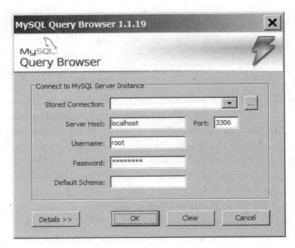

Figure 2-12. *Connecting to the correct MySQL instance*

3. Right-click in the Schemata pane on the right side of the MySQL Query Browser window and select Create New Schema from the context menu to open the Create New Schema dialog box.

4. Enter a name of **Players** for the database, as shown in Figure 2-13, and then click the OK button. This will close the dialog box, and you'll see that the new database has been added to the Schemata pane, as shown in Figure 2-14.

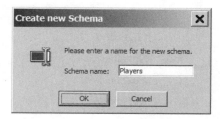

Figure 2-13. *The Create New Schema dialog box*

Figure 2-14. *The Players database has been created.*

5. Right-click the Players database and select Create New Table from the context menu.

6. The first step is to create the ManufacturerID column that contains the primary key for the table. Double-click in the first row of the Columns and Indices grid underneath Column Name and enter **ManufacturerID** as the name. You'll see that the column has already been marked as the primary key and is set to be auto-incrementing.

7. Accept the defaults for the rest of the values. Your column definition should look like Figure 2-15.

Figure 2-15. *The ManufacturerID column has been created.*

8. Now add the remaining four columns to the Manufacturer table, as shown in Figure 2-16. As you enter details for a column in the table, a new blank row is added to the bottom of the list, allowing you to enter the details for the next column. Set up the four columns as follows:

Column Name	Datatype	Not Null
ManufacturerName	Varchar(50)	Checked
ManufacturerCountry	Varchar(50)	Not checked
ManufacturerEmail	Varchar(100)	Not checked
ManufacturerWebsite	Varchar(100)	Not checked

Column Name	Datatype	NOT NULL	AUTO INC	Flags			Default Value	Comment
ManufacturerID	INTEGER	✓	✓	✓ UNSIGNED	☐ ZEROFILL		NULL	
ManufacturerName	VARCHAR(50)	✓		☐ BINARY				
ManufacturerCountry	VARCHAR(50)			☐ BINARY			NULL	
ManufacturerEmail	VARCHAR(100)			☐ BINARY			NULL	
ManufacturerWebsite	VARCHAR(100)			☐ BINARY			NULL	

Figure 2-16. *The column definitions for the Manufacturer table in MySQL 5.0*

9. Enter a table name of **Manufacturer** at the top of the Table Editor dialog box, and then click Apply Changes to save the table. In the Confirm Table Edit dialog box, click Execute to create the table. Once the table has been saved, click Close to close the Table Editor dialog box.

10. To confirm that the table has been created, expand the Players database in the Schemata pane. You'll see the new Manufacturer table in the list of tables (you can expand this to show the columns that make up the table).

11. Open Visual Web Developer and switch to the Database Explorer view. Right-click the Data Connections node and select Add Connection from the context menu.

12. Click the Change button next to the Data Source field, and then select Microsoft ODBC Data Source from the Change Data Source dialog box.

13. Select the Use Connection String option and enter the following connection string:

    ```
    Driver={MySQL ODBC 3.51 Driver};server=localhost;database=players;
    ```

14. Enter a Username of **root** and a Password of **bandpass**.

15. Click OK to add the connection.

16. Expand the connection that you just added, and then expand the Tables node in the tree that is presented. You'll see the Manufacturer table that you just created, as shown in Figure 2-17.

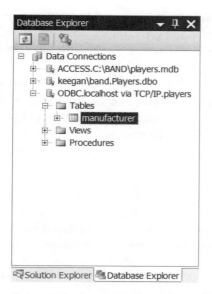

Figure 2-17. *Visual Web Developer can also connect to the MySQL 5.0 database.*

How It Works

As you saw, the tools for MySQL Query Browser are comparable to those available using SQL Server Management Studio, although they work a bit differently.

As with SQL Server Management Studio, the creation of the database and the table are performed in SQL. When you created the table, you had a sneak preview of this SQL in the Confirm Table Edit dialog box. You'll look at the SQL to modify the database structure in Chapter 11.

At the end of the example, you saw how you can use Visual Web Developer to view a MySQL database. Using the SqlClient data provider, the process is quite simple, and Visual Web Developer takes care of a lot of the work for you. However, when you use the ODBC data provider, you must create the connection string yourself. Here, you specified the following connection string:

```
Driver={MySQL ODBC 3.51 Driver};server=localhost;database=players;
```

You need to tell the ODBC data provider which ODBC driver you want to use, and then specify the specific properties for the driver—in this case, the server and database to which you're connecting.

The same is also true when you need to use the OLE DB data provider. You specify the OLE DB provider to use, and then set any properties that are specific for that provider. If you wanted to connect to the Access database, you would use the following connection string:

```
Provider=Microsoft.Jet.OLEDB.4.0;Data Source=c:\BAND\Players.mdb
```

Once the connection has been made, Visual Web Developer treats all non-SqlClient data sources equally. You can view and query the database, but you cannot modify the database in any way. The options to modify the database are simply not displayed in any of the context menus.

Note Each type of ODBC driver and OLE DB provider has a different syntax for its connection string. A good place to look for the connection string that you're after is `http://www.connectionstrings.com`. It has connection string examples for the common ODBC drivers and OLE DB providers.

Column Properties and Constraints

When building even a simple table, you can do a lot more than give the columns in the table a name. You can give each one a series of properties that strongly types and then further restricts the range of values that it can hold. This is akin to the way you give every variable in C# a simple type, or perhaps even a complex type if you want to restrict its values further.

Strictly speaking, you actually give each column a set of *properties* and then apply zero or more *constraints* that restrict the values it can hold.

The following are the column properties and constraints you've seen in the Manufacturer table example:

Column Name: This is the name of the column.

Data Type: This is the data type of the column. In the Manufacturer table, you used only two types—int/integer and varchar—but there are many more. You can find a complete list of data types you can give to a column in Appendix B.

Length: When you specified a data type of varchar, you also specified a number, in brackets, that indicates the maximum number of characters that may be entered in the column. The length property is available only for data types that contain text, such as char and varchar.

Allow Nulls: If you allow null values for a column, you're saying that the column can actually be completely empty, with nothing in it. And by "nothing," I do mean nothing. Spaces, zeros, or any other actual characters are not the same as having a null value in the column.

Primary Key: This sets whether the column is part of the primary key for its table. For the Manufacturer table, you have one column making up the primary key, indicated by the key icon next to the column name. As mentioned earlier, it is possible to have multiple columns making up the primary key, and all the columns in the key would be indicated in the same way.

You also set another property on the ManufacturerID column, making it an identity column and giving it an auto-incrementing value. This is where you'll see the first difference between SQL Server 2005 and MySQL 5.0.

In SQL Server 2005, you specify that the ManufacturerID column is auto-incrementing by setting the Identity Column property for the table. SQL Server Management Studio shields you from some of the details of designing tables, and this is one of those cases. When you set the table's identity column, you're actually modifying the ManufacturerID column directly and setting three properties on that column:

Is Identity: This indicates that the column is an identity column and will have an auto-incrementing value.

Identity Seed: This sets the value given to the first row entered into the table. The default is 1.

Identity Increment: This sets the number added to the most recently created row in the table to produce the next value of the column for a new row yet to come. The default is 1.

By default, an automatically generated integer column will be set to 1 for the first row created in the table, then 2 for the second, 3 for the third, and so on. If you set Identity Seed to 10 and Identity Increment to 2, the first row would get 10, the second 12, the third 14, and so on.

You can actually see these values for the column if you look at the Column Properties tab at the bottom of the main SQL Server Management Studio window and expand the Identity Specification node, as shown in Figure 2-18.

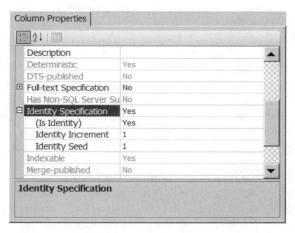

Figure 2-18. *Viewing the Identity Specification details for a column*

MySQL 5.0 specifies that a column is auto-incrementing by setting the AUTO INC property when adding the column. If you look back at Figure 2-16, you'll see that the AUTO INC column is checked for ManufacturerID.

■**Note** You can have only one auto-incrementing column on a table. Although SQL Server Management Studio and MySQL 5.0 specify auto-incrementing columns differently, they both allow you to have only one column set as auto-incrementing at a time. SQL Server Management Studio allows you to select one column from the Identity Column list, and MySQL Query Browser lets you check only one AUTO INC column at a time.

Once you've set the general characteristics for a column, you can narrow them down by applying constraints. We've already looked at two constrains: Allow Null and Primary Key. The Column Properties tab allows you to set a further constraint on the column: its default value.

The default value for a column is specified in the Default Value or Binding property for SQL Server 2005 and as the Default Value for MySQL 5.0. This property allows you to specify a value that is used when the user doesn't enter a value when creating a new row.

You'll learn about one more type of constraint in this chapter. The foreign key constraint is concerned with maintaining the validity of data between two tables that are related. Of course, this doesn't make much sense until you understand how tables can be related, so you'll come back to this topic in the "Relationships Between Tables" section.

Queries and Stored Procedures

Many parallels exist between the way you program in .NET and the way you set up a relational database. You've already come across the idea of strongly typing columns and giving them properties. It shouldn't be a surprise then to learn that relational databases also allow you to perform actions (methods, if you like) on rows, columns, tables, and even the database itself. These actions are written in SQL, and knowing how to write queries in SQL is as fundamental to working with a database as knowing how tables, rows, and columns fit together.

Recall from Chapter 1 that the second step of talking to a database is to send it a query to retrieve, create, modify, or delete some data. This query needs to be defined and called explicitly, much like a method in .NET, and you use SQL to do this.

So, what is SQL, and why do you need to use it? Why can't you just use C# instead? SQL (usually pronounced "sequel") is the de facto standard language for talking to relational databases. Invented by IBM along with the original idea of relational databases, SQL was designed to fit the mathematical concepts that relational databases were built upon, while being straightforward to use. (Interestingly, the man who first published the rules for relational databases, Dr. E. F. Codd, disliked SQL quite a lot and preferred another query language.)

SQL is now in its second version as an International Organization for Standardization (ISO) and American National Standards Institute (ANSI) standard. It essentially works like ODBC as a common interface to a database that all vendors implement and everyone uses. One key difference between SQL and ODBC is that although all vendors implement the majority of the basic elements of the SQL standard, they then add their own proprietary queries to it and badge the whole as their version of SQL. Microsoft SQL Server uses Transact-SQL (T-SQL), Oracle uses PL\SQL, and MySQL aims to implement straight ANSI-standard SQL, although it hasn't managed all of it just yet.

SQL Queries

SQL queries are at the heart of what you'll be doing in the rest of this book. They're the commands the page gives the database, and they can be sent individually or in batches. You need to learn how to write those queries correctly, what kind of results they will return, and how to handle those results.

SQL can be divided into three main parts: a Data Manipulation Language (DML), a Data Definition Language (DDL), and a Data Control Language (DCL). Over the next few pages, you'll take a whirlwind tour through the key queries that you'll use throughout this book. I'll expand on the syntax for each instruction as you use them, and Appendix C provides a summary syntax reference for these queries.

■**Note** Keywords in SQL aren't case-sensitive. However, I write them in all uppercase letters to make them easily distinguishable from the values you add to queries.

DML Queries

SQL's DML contains queries that let you create, retrieve, update, and delete data from a database. It has the following four basic queries:

INSERT: The INSERT query creates a new row in a table, and then adds some new data to it. For example, here is the query to add a new row to the Manufacturer table:

```
INSERT INTO Manufacturer (ManufacturerName, ManufacturerCountry,
  ManufacturerEmail, ManufacturerWebsite)
VALUES ('Apple', 'USA', 'lackey@apple.com'', 'http://www.apple.com')
```

Each column in the row you want to give a value to is named in the first list, and the values they will be given are in the second list, respectively. If the table has an identity column (as the Manufacturer table does), you don't need to specify it, as it is added automatically with the new row.

UPDATE: The UPDATE query changes the values of one or more columns in a table row. For example, to change the name of a Manufacturer from Apple to Pear, issue the following query:

```
UPDATE Manufacturer
SET ManufacturerName = 'Pear'
WHERE ManufacturerName = 'Apple'
```

As mentioned earlier, every column can be identified uniquely using the table name, primary key value, and column name. UPDATE queries can use all three to pinpoint exactly which piece of data to change, but they can also effect more sweeping changes, modifying several rows at a time by being less specific.

DELETE: The DELETE query removes a row or rows from a table. For example, to remove the entry in the Manufacturer table for the Manufacturer Pear, issue the following query:

```
DELETE FROM Manufacturer
WHERE ManufacturerName = 'Pear'
```

Like UPDATE, DELETE can target many rows in a table at a time. You need to be careful using DELETE. One false step, and you might delete all the data in a table by accident.

SELECT: The SELECT query fetches data from the database and returns it to the waiting page. For example, to retrieve a list of all Manufacturers and their e-mail addresses, issue the following query:

```
SELECT ManufacturerName, ManufacturerEmail
FROM Manufacturer
```

The SELECT query is incredibly powerful. You can use it to preprocess data, retrieve data across several tables at once, and then work on that data again before the page gets it. You can return tables of data or single values. You can present data using aliases or using a column's name as it is in the table. You can filter the results that you're returning using the WHERE clause.

Note There are books dedicated to just the SELECT query, so don't be disheartened if you don't get your SELECT queries working first time round. One of the best books about SELECT queries is *SQL Queries for Mere Mortals* by Michael J. Hernandez and John L. Viescas (0201433362: Addison-Wesley, 2000).

The basic syntax for all four queries is pretty straightforward. To begin with, you'll just plug in values to those simple queries and go. Then you'll start to vary and tweak. You can already see that the WHERE keyword is used in UPDATE, DELETE, and SELECT queries. It can match more than one row if you want to affect more than one row and can concatenate conditions together with Boolean operators (AND, NOT, and OR) to create specific clauses that may not match any rows at all.

DDL Queries

A DDL query lets you build, alter, and remove databases, tables, relationships, constraints, indexes, and more. For example, the sample database that you'll build in this chapter can also be built using a mixture of DDL and DML: DDL to create the Players database, construct the tables within it, and the columns within the tables, and some DML to add the values to the tables.

DDL has three basic queries:

CREATE: The CREATE query allows you to create a new database or object within the database. For example, to add a new table called Player with PlayerID and PlayerName columns, issue the following query:

```
CREATE TABLE Player (PlayerID INT, PlayerName VARCHAR(50))
```

The CREATE TABLE query is quite powerful. You can create as many strongly typed columns for the table as you like, specify a primary key, and set some of the column properties and constraints you saw earlier.

ALTER: The ALTER query allows you to modify a database object that already exists. For example, to add a new column called PlayerStorage to the Player table, issue the following query:

```
ALTER TABLE Player ADD PlayerStorage VARCHAR(50)
```

It's possible for a database to refuse to execute an ALTER query and return an error. This is usually because in changing the table, constraint, and so on, the altered version of the database will break the rules that still apply to the database and violate its integrity. Or rather, it will render the data invalid. For example, changing the type of the ManufacturerName column in the Manufacturer table to integer isn't allowed.

DROP: The DROP query allows you to delete any object in a database. For example, to delete the Player table from the database, issue the following query:

```
DROP TABLE Player
```

As with ALTER, a database may not execute a DROP query if the altered version of the database breaks its integrity rules.

■**Caution** As long as your page has the appropriate privileges to delete a database, the server will go ahead and delete anything you tell it to if it doesn't violate a constraint, regardless of whether you've backed up anything or the database still contains data. Database servers have no concept of a recycle bin either, so once you say delete, it's gone. Be very careful using DROP. It can kill anything—database, table, constraint, and so on—just as CREATE and ALTER can create and modify anything.

DCL Queries

All database servers can also restrict which of the previous SQL queries a user may execute. The DCL queries are used to control access to the database. The following are the three most common DCL queries:

GRANT: The GRANT query allows you to give a user account the permission to run a certain kind of SQL query. For example, to let the user account Damien INSERT and SELECT data from the Manufacturer table, issue the following query:

```
GRANT INSERT, SELECT ON Manufacturer TO Damien
```

DENY: The DENY query allows you to prevent a user account from running a certain SQL query that it already has permission to run indirectly, say, because the permission was given to a group or role to which the user was assigned. For example, to prevent the user account Jill from running DELETE and DROP queries against the Manufacturer table, issue the following query:

```
DENY DELETE, DROP ON Manufacturer TO Jill
```

REVOKE: The REVOKE query completely removes the permission to run a certain SQL query from a user account. For example, to remove all permissions from an exEmployee user, issue the following query:

```
REVOKE ALL FROM exEmployee
```

ALTERNATIVES TO SQL

SQL won't be going anywhere for quite some time to come, because it's too well established and because it's the de facto standard language that all database servers use. Indeed, millions of lines of SQL run every day. But that doesn't mean you'll always need to use it.

With the release of SQL Server 2005, Microsoft has moved the goal posts quite a bit by allowing queries to be written in any of the .NET languages (C#, VB.NET, and so on), as well as in traditional SQL. For more information about using a .NET language this way, visit the SQL Server 2005 Web site at `http://www.microsoft.com/sql/2005/default.mspx`. You can also refer to *Pro SQL Server 2005* by Louis Davidson (1-59059-477-0; Apress, 2005).

If you think XML may be your calling, then you also have a third option. The World Wide Web Commission (W3C) has been working on an XML-based database querying language for some time. XQuery is still a working draft—the biggest the commission has ever created—but will be pretty solid when it's finished. The big companies such as Microsoft, IBM, and Oracle are all working on this with the W3C, so it will be well supported. For more details, go to `http://www.w3.org/XML/Query`.

Stored Procedures

Most relational database servers allow you to store SQL queries along with the databases they query. These are known as *stored procedures*, and they allow you to insulate the application developer from the intricacies of your database. After all, if all the developer is after is a list of Manufacturers from the database, does she really need to know that the table is called Manufacturer and then issue the SELECT query against that table to return the required columns?

Stored procedures allow you to create something like a GetManufacturers stored procedure and let the developer use that. Rather than the SELECT query itself, the page now sends a call to a stored procedure on the database, along with any parameter values it may require, just as you call a method on an object.

You'll look at using stored procedures in much greater detail in Chapter 10.

Indexes

While constraints help ensure that any modifications to the database don't disturb the validity of the data it contains, and so potentially slow down the rate at which you interact with a database, the aim of indexes is to increase the rate at which you can retrieve information. Consider a situation where you want to find all the references to SQL Server in this book. You could read this book from cover to cover and write them all down, or (if the publisher has done a particularly good job) you could turn to the back of the book, look in the index under SQL Server, and turn to the pages listed under that entry. The second method—using an index—is obviously a lot faster, and a database index works in the same way for the same reason.

Consider a situation where you want to retrieve information about all the Manufacturers who are based in Japan. Even with just ten Manufacturers, the database must work through all of the rows to make sure it has found all the entries that fit the criteria before returning the results to the page. As you can see in Figure 2-19, this search returns only two Manufacturers.

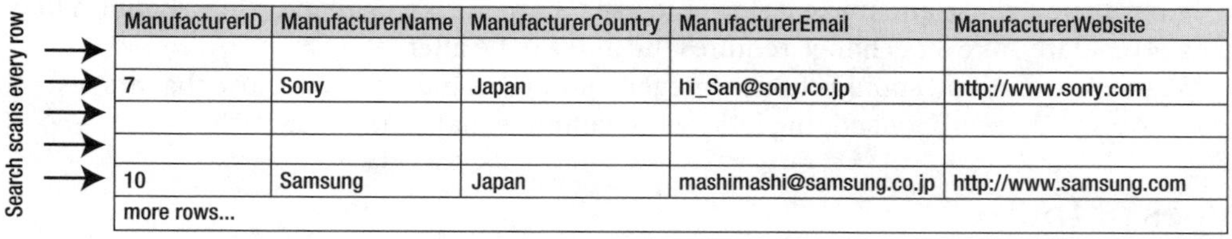

Figure 2-19. *Scanning through a table without an index*

By asking it to create an index on the ManufacturerCountry column of the Manufacturer table (the ManufacturerCountry column is to referred to as the *index key* in this context), the database server makes available to any searches an ordered list of the values in the ManufacturerCountry column. Essentially, this works in the same way the index in the back of a book works. When it needs to look up a Manufacturer, the search knows that titles are ordered alphabetically in the index you've created, so it just looks under *J*, finds the Manufacturers that have Japan as the location, and follows the index links to the correct rows. Rather than search through all of the rows in the Manufacturer table, it looks through two, as shown in Figure 2-20.

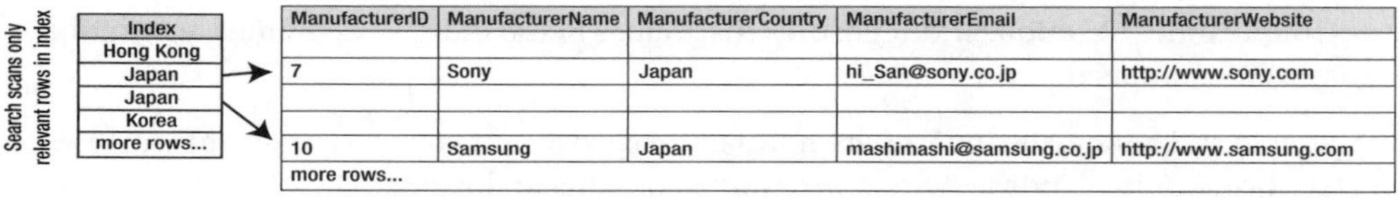

Figure 2-20. *Scanning through a table with an index*

Database indexes work exclusively behind the scenes, and aside from adding and removing indexes, you never need to reference them in your code. If an index exists it will be used automatically.

Adding the right indexes to the right tables can significantly improve performance. If you frequently issue a query that requests information to be ordered on or grouped by a certain column, it makes sense to add an index to the database based on that column.

Of course, there are always downsides. The database server must maintain every index added to the database, which means a performance hit if items are frequently added, deleted, or changed. With each modification, the server must first make that change, see if it affects any index, and then update the index if it does. That's three operations per modification. An index also consumes a fair amount of additional disk space. Therefore, overusing indexes has downsides, especially when they contain large amounts of data.

The power of indexes is in creating them wisely. For example, the effectiveness of an index whose index key column contains values that are usually the same will be much less than one where the values are unique. Consider also that a database server silently copies all the values in a nonclustered index (the default type, as described in the next section) key column in order to sort them and maintain the index. Therefore, choosing a column for the index key that contains sizable values (in other words, values that require a lot of storage) will increase the resources needed by the database and make it slower to use. The same is true of indexing a column that changes regularly, as every change requires the index to be altered.

Where possible, you should choose integer columns as indexes over those that are text-based. You should also avoid adding indexes on columns that change regularly.

Types of Index

You can add several kinds of indexes to a database:

Simple index: A simple index uses only one column as the index key.

Composite index: A composite index uses two or more columns in its index key.

Nonclustered index: A nonclustered index contains a list of index key columns in the correct order with links to the actual rows in the table (see Figure 2-20).

Clustered index: This is the most important kind of index in a database. It determines the order in which rows in a table are stored in the database. Because the clustered index changes the ordering of the rows in the table, you can have only one clustered index per table. Creating a primary key column in a table automatically creates a simple clustered index using the primary key column as the index key.

Unique index: A unique index ensures that values in the index key columns are unique, as well as orders them.

Simple and composite indexes are mutually exclusive, but you can create nonclustered, clustered, and unique indexes with one or more columns in the index key.

In the sample database, you'll add a simple index to the Manufacturer table using the ManufacturerCountry column as the index key. With only a few records in the table itself, this will have a small effect on performance, but it's important to know how to add indexes to your databases.

Try It Out: Adding Indexes in SQL Server 2005

In this example, you'll add a simple index to the ManufacturerCountry column in the Manufacturer table of the database using SQL Server Management Studio. Follow these steps:

1. Start SQL Server Management Studio. Connect to the `localhost\BAND` server using the login details that you used in the first example.

2. Expand the Databases node in Object Explorer. Expand the Players database, and then expand the Tables node.

3. Right-click the Manufacturer table and select Modify from the context menu.

4. Right-click in the table definition window and select Indexes/Keys from the context menu to open the Indexes/Keys dialog box.

5. Click Add to create a new index. Under the Identity grouping, enter **IX_ManufacturerCountry** as the index's Name, as shown in Figure 2-21.

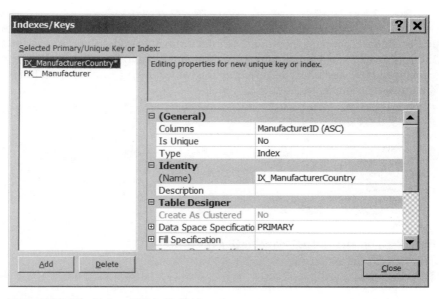

Figure 2-21. *The Indexes/Keys dialog box*

6. Click the Columns property under the (General) grouping, and then click the ellipsis in the right column.

7. In the Index Columns dialog box, select ManufacturerCountry from the Column Name drop-down list, as shown in Figure 2-22.

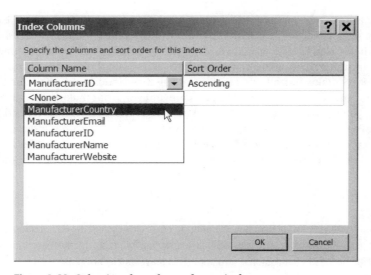

Figure 2-22. *Selecting the column for an index*

8. Click OK to close the Index Columns dialog box.

9. Click Close to close the Indexes/Keys dialog box.

10. Click Save on the toolbar to save the changes to the database.

11. In the Object Explorer, expand the Manufacturer table node, and then expand the Indexes node, as shown in Figure 2-23. (You may need to refresh the node, by right-clicking Indexes and select Refresh from the context menu, to see the two indexes that are present on the table.)

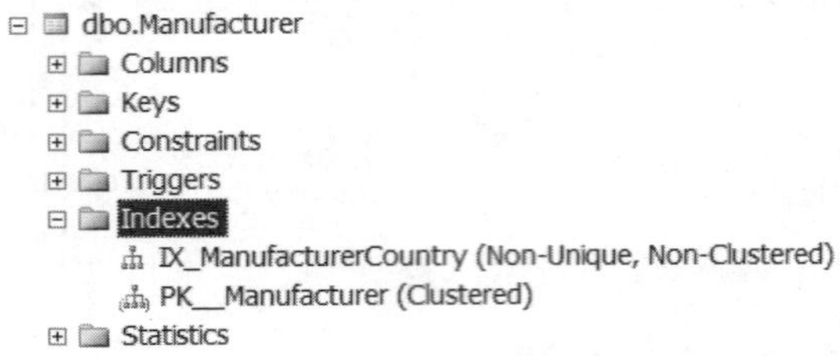

```
⊟ ▭ dbo.Manufacturer
    ⊞ ▭ Columns
    ⊞ ▭ Keys
    ⊞ ▭ Constraints
    ⊞ ▭ Triggers
    ⊟ ▭ Indexes
        ▭ IX_ManufacturerCountry (Non-Unique, Non-Clustered)
        ▭ PK__Manufacturer (Clustered)
    ⊞ ▭ Statistics
```

Figure 2-23. *Indexes can be viewed in Object Explorer.*

How It Works

As you can see, creating an index using SQL Server Management Studio is very simple. You give it a name, and then specify the columns that you want to include in the index. SQL Server Management Studio deals with sending the correct queries to the database to create the index. We'll look at the SQL queries for creating database indexes in Chapter 11, but for the curious, what is actually sent is as follows:

```
CREATE INDEX IX_ManufacturerCountry
ON Manufacturer (ManufacturerCountry)
```

If you need to create a clustered or unique index, you use the query CREATE CLUSTERED INDEX or CREATE UNIQUE INDEX, respectively. A nonclustered index is the default for the CREATE INDEX query, but you could have used CREATE NONCLUSTERED INDEX to accomplish the same thing.

In the same way, the indexes you create from the Indexes/Keys dialog box are nonclustered by default. The Indexes/Keys dialog box allows you to create all three index types (nonclustered, clustered, and unique), and it provides a bit of logic to prevent you from making any simple errors. In Figure 2-21, you see two options that allow you to alter the index that you're adding: Is Unique and Create As Clustered. However, since you already have a clustered index on the table (for the ManufacturerID primary key), the Create As Clustered option is disabled.

You can also delete indexes by selecting the index in the Indexes/Keys dialog box and selecting Delete.

■**Note** You'll notice that in the very last step of this example, you explicitly clicked the Save button to save the changes to the database. SQL Server Management Studio allows you to modify the database tables and doesn't automatically save changes to the database structure. This prevents any errors that you may make from affecting data that you don't really want to change. To keep the changes that you've made, you must explicitly save the changes. If you try to close the table without doing so, SQL Server Management Studio will prompt for you to save the changes.

Try It Out: Adding Indexes in MySQL 5.0

In this example, you'll add a simple index to the ManufacturerCountry column in the Manufacturer table of the database using MySQL Query Browser. Follow these steps:

1. Open MySQL Query Browser, if it isn't already running. Connect to the `localhost` server using the login details that you used earlier.

2. Expand the Players database in the Schemata pane.

3. Right-click the Manufacturer table and select Edit Table to open the Table Editor dialog box. The Indices tab in the lower half of the dialog box allows you to create, edit, and delete any indexes on this table. Initially, it displays the primary key index created automatically when you first built the table, as shown in Figure 2-24.

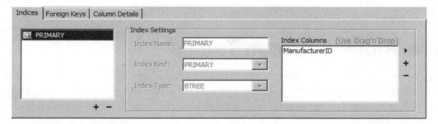

Figure 2-24. *The Indices tab in MySQL Query Browser*

4. To add the index, click the plus sign under the list of indexes. A dialog box pops up and asks for the name of the new index. Type **IX_ManufacturerCountry**, and then click OK.

5. The new index now appears in the list of indexes. This index contains only the ManufacturerCountry column. Select the column from the column list at the top of the dialog box and drag it to the Index Columns box at the bottom of the dialog box. The new index should now look like Figure 2-25.

Figure 2-25. *Building an index for MySQL 5.0*

6. Click Apply Changes to save the changes to the database, and then click Execute in the Confirm Table Edit dialog box.

7. Click Close to close the Table Editor dialog box.

How It Works

The two distinctly different methods with which you created this simple index in the two databases demonstrates nicely that, although you use a graphical tool to work with the database, all the tool actually does is generate some SQL in the background to send to the database. SQL Server Management Studio hides this from you completely, whereas MySQL Query Browser shows you the SQL that is going to be executed (in the Confirm Table Edit dialog box).

Although SQL Server Management Studio executes a `CREATE INDEX` query to create the index, MySQL Query Browser uses an `ALTER TABLE` query:

```
ALTER TABLE players.manufacturer
  ADD INDEX IX_ManufacturerCountry(ManufacturerCountry)
```

This `ALTER TABLE` query is functionally equivalent to the `CREATE INDEX` query that you saw earlier. In fact, the `CREATE INDEX` query works equally well in MySQL 5.0, as you'll see in Chapter 11 when we look at the SQL queries for creating database indexes.

Relationships Between Tables

Ironically, the term *relational databases* was coined because this kind of database was developed using mathematical set theory—a relation is a part of set theory—rather than because you can create relationships between tables. Regardless, this ability is one of the core concepts in relational databases.

Tables are said to have a *relationship* between them if the records they contain are somehow associated with each other. For example, a Player is "built by" a Manufacturer and "supports" different Formats. Thus, in a database, a Player table would have a relationship with a Manufacturer table and a Format table.

When you design databases to drive an application, you should strive to build relationships between the objects and events modeled by the various tables you've established. This allows you to bind the data closer together, make it easier to update, and allow the database to help you establish whether new changes are valid.

Suppose that your database includes a second table called Player, which contains details of various Players built by the Manufacturers listed in the Manufacturer table. The initial design of the table, with various flaws that we'll look at shortly, is shown in Figure 2-26.

PlayerID	PlayerName	PlayerManufacturer	PlayerCost	PlayerStorage	PlayerFormats
1	iPod Shuffle	Apple	99.00	Solid State	wav, mp3, aac
2	MuVo V200	Creative	96.00	Solid State	mp3, wma
3	iFP-700 Series	iRiver	149.00	Solid State	mp3, wma, asf, ogg
4	iFP-900 Series	iRiver	199.00	Solid State	mp3, wma, asf, ogg
5	MegaPlayer 521	MSI	93.00	Solid State	wav, mp3, wma
more rows...					

Figure 2-26. *The Player table*

The Players detailed in this table have a relationship to several other tables in the database. Every Player needs a Manufacturer to build it, and each Player supports one or more Formats.

The PlayerManufacturer column details which Manufacturer builds the Player. This looks okay, but hang on a minute; it's not terribly efficient. The following two problems spring to mind:

What happens if a Manufacturer changes its name? Suppose that a Manufacturer changes its name, say from iRiver to iStream. Potentially, you would need to look through every row in the Player table and any other tables in the database that are related to the Manufacturer table and change any reference to iRiver. If you miss an entry, and then a page looks up details for iRiver, it won't exist according to the database because it has changed its name. Things could easily start to go wrong.

What happens if a Manufacturer ceases to exist? A Manufacturer may go out of business or get bought by someone else. In this case, you might delete the row in the Manufacturer table while Players in the Player table still have references to the Manufacturer. This doesn't make sense.

Fortunately, it's easy to fix this so that, if a Manufacturer changes its name, all you need to do is change the name in the Manufacturer table. Likewise, it's easy to make sure that the computer checks whether it's valid to delete data still used by other tables. It's just a matter of creating the right relationship between the two tables and creating the right foreign key constraint over the relationship.

Establishing a relationship between tables usually means copying one table's primary key column into the second table. At this point, it becomes a *foreign key*—foreign because it isn't directly relevant to the object or event the second table models. Values of a foreign key must be drawn from the table where it's the primary key. It makes no sense for a foreign key to contain a value that doesn't identify a row in the other table.

Types of Relationship

Three types of relationships exist: one-to-one, one-to-many, and many-to-many. It's quite important that you understand how each of them works.

One-to-One Relationships

When a row in one table can be associated with just one row in another table, and a row in that table can be associated with only one row in the first table, those two tables are said to have a *one-to-one* (1:1) relationship. For example, a Player can have only one design budget, and a design budget is specific to a particular Player. Thus, a table containing Players has a one-to-one relationship to a table containing design budgets.

To establish this relationship in a relational database, the primary key in one table is copied across to become the primary key of the second table, as shown in Figure 2-27. To determine which design budget belongs to which Player, you just use the value of the primary key as a reference.

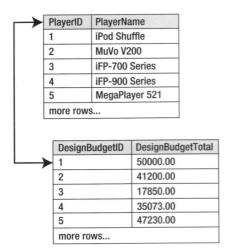

PlayerID	PlayerName
1	iPod Shuffle
2	MuVo V200
3	iFP-700 Series
4	iFP-900 Series
5	MegaPlayer 521
more rows...	

DesignBudgetID	DesignBudgetTotal
1	50000.00
2	41200.00
3	17850.00
4	35073.00
5	47230.00
more rows...	

Figure 2-27. *Player and DesignBudget tables in a one-to-one relationship*

One-to-Many Relationships

When a single row in one table can be associated with many rows in another table, but a single row in that table can be associated with only a single row in the first table, you have a *one-to-many* (1:n) relationship. This fits in with the Player and Manufacturer example from earlier. A Manufacturer can build many Players, but a Player can be built by only one Manufacturer at a time.

To establish this relationship, you need to copy the primary key from the table on the "one" side—in this example, the Manufacturer table—and use it as a foreign key in the "many" table—the Player table, as shown in Figure 2-28. To determine who built the Player, you use the PlayerManufacturerID in the Player table to look up the name in the Manufacturer table.

ManufacturerID	ManufacturerName	ManufacturerCountry	ManufacturerEmail	ManufacturerWebsite
1	Apple	USA	lackey@apple.com	http://www.apple.com
2	Creative	Singapore	someguy@creative.com	http://www.creative.com
3	iRiver	Korea	knockknock@iriver.com	http://www.river.com
4	MSI	Taiwan	hello@miscomputer.co.uk	http://www.miscomputer.co.uk
5	Rio	USA	Greetings@rio.com	http://www.rio.com
more rows...				

PlayerID	PlayerName	PlayerManufacturerID	PlayerCost	PlayerStorage	PlayerFormats
1	iPod Shuffle	1	99.00	Solid State	wav, mp3, aac
2	MuVo V200	2	96.00	Solid State	mp3, wma
3	iFP-700 Series	2	149.00	Solid State	mp3, wma, asf, ogg
4	iFP-900 Series	3	199.00	Solid State	mp3, wma, asf, ogg
5	MegaPlayer 521	4	93.00	Solid State	wav, mp3, wma
more rows...					

Figure 2-28. *Establishing a one-to-many relationship*

Every Player now points to one place where Manufacturer details are stored. If you change the details in the Manufacturer table, they're changed for every Player as well.

Many-to-Many Relationships

The third type of relationship between tables occurs when rows in one table can be associated with many rows in another, and when rows in that other table can be associated with many rows in the first table. In this case, the two tables are said to have a *many-to-many* (m:n) relationship. In our example, this is certainly the case of the relationship between Players and the Formats that they support. A Player can support multiple Formats, and a Format may be supported by multiple Players.

In Figure 2-28, the Player table contains a column called PlayerFormats. An alarm should already be ringing, because the column name is plural. Columns should contain single pieces of information, rather than several. So then, say that every Player has only one supported Format. If that were the case, you would create a new table called Format, which is in a one-to-many relationship with the Player table, much as in Figure 2-29.

FormatID	FormatName
1	wav
2	mp3
3	aac
4	wma
5	asf
6	ogg
7	atrac
8	aiff
more rows...	

PlayerID	PlayerName	PlayerManufacturerID	PlayerCost	PlayerStorage	PlayerFormatID
1	iPod Shuffle	1	99.00	Solid State	1
2	MuVo V200	2	96.00	Solid State	2
3	iFP-700 Series	2	149.00	Solid State	2
4	iFP-900 Series	3	199.00	Solid State	2
5	MegaPlayer 521	4	93.00	Solid State	1
more rows...					

Figure 2-29. *If Players supported only one Format, this would be correct.*

Of course, most Players support more than one Format. But how many? You could add a couple more columns to the Player table to account for a Player supporting two or three Formats, but what happens when you have a fourth? This relationship is still unresolved. Logic dictates there has to be a better solution than this, and there is.

Databases cannot express a many-to-many relationship directly. A many-to-many relationship is modeled as two one-to-many relationships. To express this many-to-many relationship properly, you remove PlayerFormat columns from the Player table, and you create a *link table* (with its own name—for example, WhatPlaysWhatFormat) that contains at least two columns: one for each of the two table's primary keys, as shown in Figure 2-30.

To discover which Formats a Player supports, you now look up the PlayerID in the link table and follow all the FormatIDs associated to the Player for the details. You just need to be aware that the PlayerID will occur in several rows in the link table—one for each supported Format. The combination of the two foreign keys, WPWFPlayerID and WPWFFormatID, is then used as the primary key for the table.

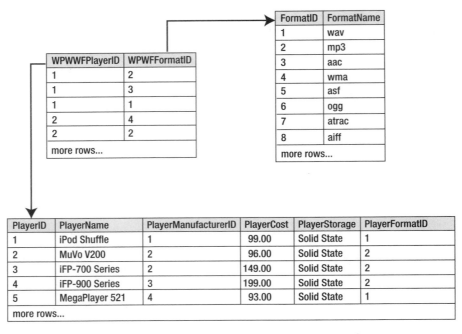

Figure 2-30. *Using a link table to model a many-to-many relationship*

Foreign Keys and Foreign Key Constraints

To model any of the three kinds of relationship between two tables, you create a column in one table that contains only the values from the primary key in another. For example, in Figure 2-30, you reference the primary key column PlayerID from the Player table in the WhatPlaysWhatFormat table as the WPWFPlayerID column. WPWFPlayerID is known as a *foreign key* column.

■**Note** A foreign key is a column that references values of a primary key in another table. If the primary key is a composite one, the foreign key may also consist of more than one column.

This all makes sense, but what keeps track of these relationships as you build them? After all, the foreign key column is just another column. When you start adding, changing, and deleting data to and from those related tables, do you need to keep making sure that the data makes sense according to those relationships, or can you get the database to do it for you? Say, for example, you delete a Player from the Player table. What happens to the entries relating to that Player in the WhatPlaysWhatFormat table? They don't reference a Player anymore, so do you delete those entries, too? Do you set them to null?

If the data in a database remains valid and obeys the rules and relationships set out over the tables containing it, then the integrity of the database is intact. If you delete a Player, that integrity isn't intact, because the WhatPlaysWhatFormat table now references a Player that has been deleted. How do you manage this and restore the (referential) integrity of the database?

The answer lies in the fifth type of constraint I mentioned earlier in the section about properties and constraints: a *foreign key constraint*. By applying this kind of constraint to the two columns concerned, you can lay out exactly how the database will react when you delete an entry from the table containing the primary key in a relationship. A foreign key constraint lets you define three particular things:

- Which columns are the primary key and the foreign key

- If the database should check newly entered data against this constraint

- If the database should enforce this constraint when data in either column is modified or deleted, and if so, what the database should do about it

By default, the database won't allow you to violate the integrity of the database by modifying or deleting information, but you can reverse this so that either the action is just allowed (and the database's integrity is violated) or the database updates/deletes the appropriate rows in the corresponding tables. This is known as *cascading changes* between the tables in the relationship, and any changes to the table containing the primary key will cause the data in the other tables to be modified. If you delete a row that is the primary key in the relationship, then any rows that reference that primary key are also deleted. If you update a primary key, then all rows that reference that foreign key are updated with the new key value. In the majority of cases, you won't use cascading changes in your database.

Now you'll look at relationships in practice by adding some tables to your sample database, and then creating some constraints to enforce the relationships between the tables. In the previous set of examples, you saw how to build a single table—the Manufacturer table—and add some data to it. The next step is to build the remaining three tables—Player, Format, and WhatPlaysWhatFormat—and then add the appropriate foreign key constraints that ensure their relationships are maintained and the integrity of the data within them stays intact.

You'll add three foreign key constraints to your database. The first is between the Manufacturer and Player table and will strengthen the one-to-many relationship between Players and their Manufacturers. The second and third will strengthen the many-to-many relationship between Players and their supported Formats using the WhatPlaysWhatFormat table as the middleman.

Figure 2-31 illustrates the relationships between the different tables. This relationship diagram was drawn using the built-in tools in SQL Server Management Studio, which we'll look at shortly.

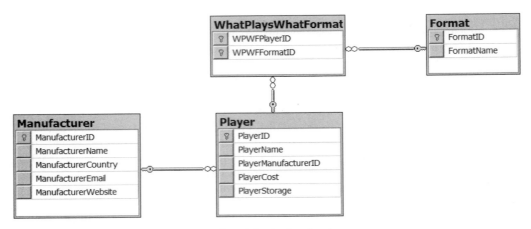

Figure 2-31. *The relationships between the tables in the database*

Try It Out: Adding Relationships in SQL Server 2005

In this example, you'll add two relationships to the SQL Server 2005 database. Of course, first you need to add the other tables. To create the remaining three tables, follow the steps again in the "Try It Out: Creating a Table in SQL Server 2005" section, but use the table information for the other tables as listed in Appendix D.

Follow these steps to add the relationships:

1. Start SQL Server Management Studio. Connect to the localhost\BAND server using the login details that you used earlier.

2. In the Object Explorer, expand the Databases node, then the Players database, and then the Tables node.

3. Right-click the Player table and select Modify from the context menu.

4. Right-click in the table definition window and select Relationships from the context menu to open the Foreign Key Relationships dialog box. Click the Add button to create a new relationship. This adds a new relationship to the dialog box, as shown in Figure 2-32.

5. Click the ellipsis button in the right column of the Tables and Columns Specification node under the (General) option to open the Tables and Columns dialog box.

6. Select Manufacturer as the primary key table and ManufacturerID as the primary key. For the foreign key, select PlayerManufacturerID. Your dialog box should look like Figure 2-33.

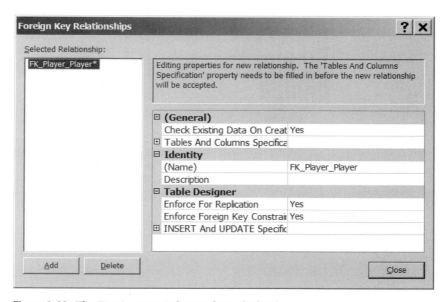

Figure 2-32. *The Foreign Key Relationships dialog box*

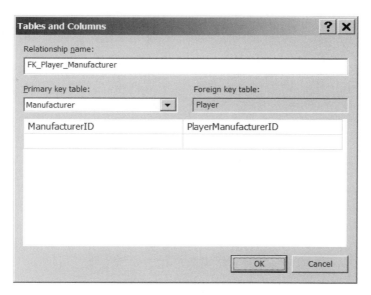

Figure 2-33. *The Tables and Columns dialog box*

7. Click OK to close the Tables and Columns dialog box.

8. In the Foreign Key Relationships dialog box, expand the Tables and Columns Specification node under the (General) option. You'll see the details for the relationship, as shown in Figure 2-34.

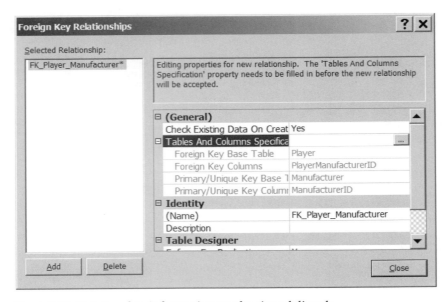

Figure 2-34. *Relationship information can be viewed directly.*

9. Click Close to close the Foreign Key Relationships dialog box, and then click Save on the toolbar to save the changes to the database. In the Save dialog box, click Yes to confirm the changes.

10. In the Object Explorer, expand the Player table node, and then expand the Keys node, as shown in Figure 2-35. (You may need to refresh the node, by selecting Refresh from the Keys context menu, to see that the relationship has been added to the table.)

Figure 2-35. *Relationships can be viewed in Object Explorer.*

11. From the Object Explorer, open the table definition for the WhatPlaysWhatFormat table, and then open the Foreign Key Relationships dialog box.

12. Click Add to create a new relationship, and open the Tables and Columns dialog box for the new relationship.

13. Select Player as the primary key table and PlayerID as the primary key column.

14. Select WPWFPlayerID as the foreign key.

15. In the second row, select <NONE> for the foreign key instead of WPWFFormatID.

16. Click OK to complete the relationship, and then click Close to close the Foreign Key Relationships dialog box.

17. Click Save on the toolbar to save the changes to the database, confirming the changes as required. If you now expand the Keys node under the WhatPlaysWhatFormat table, you'll see that the new relationship has been created.

How It Works

This example demonstrated how easy it is to create relationships using the graphical tools provided by SQL Server Management Studio. You created two relationships with very little work. The only thing that you need to remember is that the relationship is added to the foreign key side of the relationship; the relationship between the Manufacturer table and the Player table is added to the Player table, as this table contains the foreign key.

The eagle-eyed among you will notice that you created only two relationships, when I said there would be three relationships. You'll see how to add a relationship between the Format and WhatPlaysWhatFormat tables when we look at another way of creating relationships with database diagrams.

When we look at DDL queries in detail in Chapter 11, you'll appreciate how much work SQL Server Management Studio is doing on your behalf. For each relationship, SQL Server Management Studio is creating an ALTER TABLE query and executing this against the database. For example, the Manufacture to Player relationship is created using the following SQL query:

```
ALTER TABLE dbo.Player
ADD CONSTRAINT FK_Player_Manufacturer
FOREIGN KEY (PlayerManufacturerID)
REFERENCES dbo.Manufacturer (ManufacturerID)
```

I'm sure you'll agree that the graphical tools make this process a lot less painful than having to create a SQL query like this. As you'll see shortly, database diagrams make it even simpler to create a relationship.

Although we've not explicitly looked at editing and deleting existing relationships, it is a painless task and can be accomplished from the Foreign Key Relationships dialog box. Selecting an existing relationship will allow you to edit the details for the relationship. You can choose to delete the relationship by clicking the Delete button.

Try It Out: Adding Relationships in MySQL 5.0

In this example, you'll add all three relationships to the MySQL 5.0 database. Unlike SQL Server Management Studio, MySQL Query Browser doesn't provide a diagramming tool, so you need to design all the relationships using the Table Editor dialog box.

Again, you first need to create the other tables. To create the remaining three tables, follow the steps again in the "Try It Out: Creating a Table in MySQL 5.0" sections, but use the table information for the other tables as listed in Appendix D.

Follow these steps to add the relationships:

1. Open MySQL Query Browser if it isn't already running and connect to the localhost server using the login details that you used earlier.

2. Expand the Players database in the Schemata pane.

3. Right-click the Player table and select Edit Table to open the Table Editor dialog box. The Foreign Keys tab in the lower half of the dialog box allows you to create, edit, and delete any foreign keys on this table. Initially, it will not contain any relationships, as shown in Figure 2-36.

Figure 2-36. *The Foreign Keys tab in MySQL Query Browser*

4. To add the relationship, click the plus sign under the list of foreign keys. A dialog box pops up and asks for the name of the new foreign key. Type **FK_Player_Manufacturer**, and then click OK.

5. Select Manufacturer from the Ref. Table drop-down list. The reference column will be populated with ManufacturerID automatically. You need to select PlayerManufacturerID as the column in the list on the right of the tab. You can do this by clicking underneath the Column heading in the list and selecting the column from the drop-down list or by dragging the PlayerManufacturerID column from the column list. The new relationship should now look like Figure 2-37.

Figure 2-37. *Building a relationship for MySQL*

6. Click Apply Changes to save the changes to the database, and then click Execute in the Confirm Table Edit dialog box.

7. Click Close to close the Table Editor dialog box.

8. Select the WhatPlaysWhatFormat table in the Schemata pane and select Edit Table from the context menu.

9. Switch to the Foreign Keys tab and click the plus icon to create a new relationship.

10. In the Add Foreign Key dialog box, give the relationship the name **FK_WhatPlaysWhatFormat_Player**, and then click OK.

11. Select Player as the Ref. Table and the WPWFPlayerID column as the foreign key column.

12. Add another relationship, and give this one the name **FK_WhatPlaysWhatFormat_Format**.

13. Select Format as the Ref. Table and the WPWFFormatID column as the foreign key column.

14. Click Apply Changes to save the changes to the database, and then click Execute in the Confirm Table Edit dialog box.

15. Click Close to close the Table Editor dialog box.

How It Works

MySQL Query Browser makes it quite easy to create relationships between tables without needing to remember the syntax of the ALTER TABLE query. You can see the exact queries that are being executed. If you compare the queries that it executes against the basic ALTER TABLE query, shown in the description of how adding relationships to SQL Server 2005 works, you'll begin to appreciate more fully how well the graphical tools shield you from the SQL. We'll come back to the ALTER TABLE query in Chapter 11.

Although both tools are creating the same relationships, MySQL 5.0 works in a slightly different way and requires an index on every column that participates in a relationship. And not just any index—the column that is referenced must be the first column in the index. Thankfully, MySQL 5.0 will automatically create any necessary indexes when it creates the relationships.

If you look at the indexes in the Table Editor dialog box for the Players table, you'll see that an index, FK_Player_Manufacturer, containing the PlayerManufacturerID column, has been added. If you look at the Manufacturer table, you won't see a new index, because the ManufacturerID column is already indexed, as it's the primary key for the table.

The WhatPlaysWhatFormat table is slightly different. Even though both columns are in the primary key, and so are already indexed, an extra index has been created. MySQL 5.0 requires that the column must be the first column in the index, and as the existing index contains two columns, it can't be fully used for the relationship. If you look at the PRIMARY index, you'll see that the WPWFFormatID column is the first column in the index, so it can be used for the relationship. MySQL 5.0 has added a new index, FK_WhatPlaysWhatFormat_Player, containing the WPWFPlayerID column, as shown in Figure 2-38.

Earlier versions of MySQL required you to manually add the indexes before you could add relationships, and an error was thrown if the correct indexes were not in place. Thankfully, you don't need to remember to add the indexes now, as MySQL 5.0 will do it for you. It will throw an error if you try to delete an index that is required for a relationship.

Figure 2-38. *Composite primary keys require a separate index when they are in a relationship.*

Database Diagrams

It's time for a quick aside before leaving the topic of relationships. Consider a situation where you want to share with others how you've designed the structure of the tables in your database and how they relate. You could write a document containing descriptions of each table, the columns they contain, and the relationships you've established between them, but that's a bit long-winded. Alternatively, you can prepare a relationship diagram for the database.

It's said that a picture is worth a thousand words, and in this case, that's true. A relationship diagram allows you to capture all this information in one fell swoop, and it can be handy to know how to use them. SQL Server Management Studio allows you to build tables in a database, and then create relationship diagrams for those tables. As you do so, the relationships you draw are then enforced by the databases as they generate the appropriate constraints to match your diagram.

Unfortunately, MySQL Query Browser doesn't support database diagrams. When you use that tool, you'll need to stick to creating a document that details each table, the columns they contain, and the relationships between the tables.

In the following examples, you'll use the diagramming facilities of SQL Server Management Studio to create a database diagram showing the relationships that you've already added. You'll then add the final relationship graphically.

Try It Out: Creating a Database Diagram in SQL Server 2005

Follow these steps to create a database diagram:

1. Start SQL Server Management Studio and connect to the `localhost\BAND` server using the login details that you used in earlier examples.

2. Expand the Databases node in Object Explorer, and then expand the Players database. Right-click the Database Diagram node and select New Database Diagram from the context menu.

3. If this is the first time that you've tried to view the Database Diagrams node, you'll receive a message informing you that some necessary database objects are missing, as shown in Figure 2-39. Click Yes to create the necessary objects.

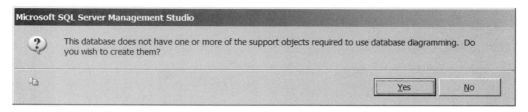

Figure 2-39. *New objects are required to allow database diagramming.*

4. In the Add Table dialog box, select the four tables: Manufacturer, Player, Format, and WhatPlaysWhatFormat. Then click the Add button. This adds all four tables to a new diagram, along with indicators of their relationships, as shown in Figure 2-40 (you may need to drag things around a little to get your diagram to look like this one).

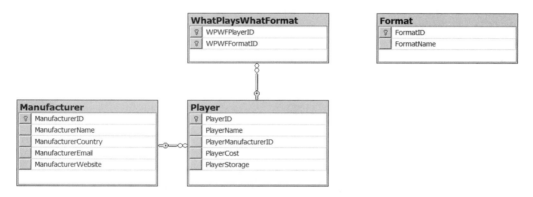

Figure 2-40. *The relationship diagram for the sample database*

5. Click the Save button on the toolbar and give the diagram a name of **Relationships**. You'll see that the diagram is added under the Database Diagrams node.

How It Works

SQL Server Management Studio provides quite a powerful tool for displaying database architectures. The basic diagram that you added shows the database structure at a glance. A database diagram contains the tables that you specify. The default view shows the name of the table, as well as the names of the columns within the table.

The diagram allows you to do a lot more than simply lay out the tables. If you right-click a table in the diagram—for instance, the WhatPlaysWhatFormat table—you'll get an idea of what you can do, as shown in Figure 2-41.

The first thing that you'll notice is that you have access to the Relationships and Indexes/Keys options, which allow you to modify the relationships and indexes that are present on a table.

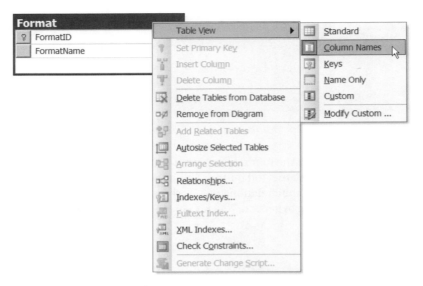

Figure 2-41. *Database diagrams allow you to do a lot more than view the database structure.*

In Figure 2-41, the Table View menu is expanded to show a submenu containing six options. These allow you to see a lot more data about a table than just the names of the columns. For instance, if you select Standard, you'll also see the data type of the column and whether it can allow null values. If you select Modify Custom, you can choose what you see from a list of 15 different properties and constraints.

A database diagram also shows the relationships between the tables on the diagram (if a table has a relationship to another table that isn't on the diagram, you will not see that relationship on the diagram). These are shown as lines between tables. At the ends of each line are a key and an infinity symbol. The table on the key side contains the primary key being used as a foreign key in the table on the infinity symbol side.

It's not immediately obvious, however, to which columns the relationship refers. In order to see this, you must click one of the tables in the relationship and select the Relationships option from the context menu.

Try It Out: Using a Database Diagram to Create a New Relationship in SQL Server 2005

In this example, you'll use the graphical tools provided by SQL Server Management Studio to create the missing relationship in your database. Follow these steps:

1. If you've closed the diagram you created in the last example, open it by double-clicking it in the Object Explorer.

2. Select the key icon next to the FormatID column in the Format table, and then drag your cursor over the WPWFFormatID column of the WhatPlaysWhatFormat table. This adds a plus symbol to the mouse cursor. Once you're sure you've selected the correct

column, release the mouse button. The Tables and Columns dialog box opens, already populated with the correct primary and foreign keys, as shown in Figure 2-42.

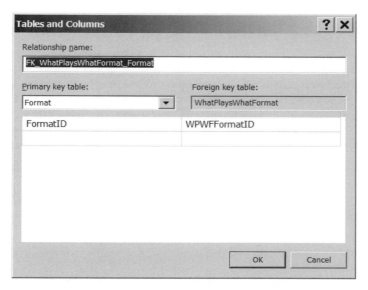

Figure 2-42. *Creating relationships graphically prepopulates the dialog box.*

3. Click OK to close this dialog box, and then click OK to close the Foreign Key Relationship dialog box. As shown in Figure 2-43, the new relationship is created, and the diagram is updated.

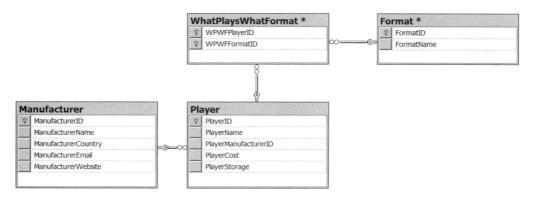

Figure 2-43. *The database with all the relationships completed*

4. Click Save on the toolbar to save the changes to the database.

How It Works

As you saw, creating a relationship by dragging and dropping the primary key over the foreign key is a breeze. By using the graphical tools, you can create relationships between tables in seconds.

Deleting a relationship is also simple. Just right-click the relationship and select Delete Relationship from Database from the context menu.

Users, Roles, and Permissions

Just like any other modern server product or operating system, a database server has a security layer that restricts access to its contents based on the credentials a user or program supplies when logging in. A database server maintains a list of all user accounts that can log in to a specific database, as well as exactly what those users can do to the contents of that database.

All databases are installed with one user already set up: the system administrator. This account, called sa in SQL Server 2005 and root in MySQL 5.0, has the complete run of the system. When logged in as the system administrator, a user or program can back up the system, add data, delete everything, and do whatever, so it's vital that this account is secured properly.

■**Note** If you've followed the instructions in Appendix A, the system administrator account will have a password of bandpass.

Now it won't come as a surprise to learn that connecting to the database from a page using the system administrator account isn't a good idea. Any malcontents might find a way to hijack the connection to the database through a page, and if you used the system administrator account to make that connection, they would have the run of the system. Instead, you must create your own user accounts for use by your applications. This process has the following three steps:

Add a user account to the database server's user table. You need to give the account a user ID and a password.

Give the account the correct permissions on the application's database. You need to tell the server whether the account is restricted to just retrieving data from the database and whether it can modify data, add data, delete data, or even modify the structure of the database itself.

Give the account any server permissions, if appropriate. An account can also be given varying levels of permissions to work with all the databases being hosted by the server. For example, an account can be given permissions for backing up, securing, and optimizing the databases on the server. Unless you're writing a Web-based data administration application, though, there's no reason to give a user account any of these permissions.

The best rule of thumb when it comes to adding users is to give them the fewest permissions possible to do the job they need to do. You need to use your common sense, evaluate exactly what may need to be done to the database, and connect to a database with a user account with permissions for those specific actions. Any more is wasteful.

You'll now follow this advice and add a new user account called band to access the sample database during the course of the book. In the next few chapters, you'll see how to add, modify, retrieve, and delete information from the database, so those are the permissions you will give it, along with the password letmein.

Try It Out: Creating User Accounts in SQL Server 2005

In this example, you'll create a user account, which you'll use to access your SQL Server 2005 database. Follow these steps:

1. Start SQL Server Management Studio and connect to the `localhost\BAND` server using the login details you used in the earlier examples.

2. Expand the Security node, right-click Logins, and select New Login.

3. Enter a login name of **band** and select the SQL Server Authentication radio button. Enter **letmein** as the password, and then confirm it.

4. Uncheck the Enforce Password Expiration option. Your dialog box should look like Figure 2-44. Click OK to create the login.

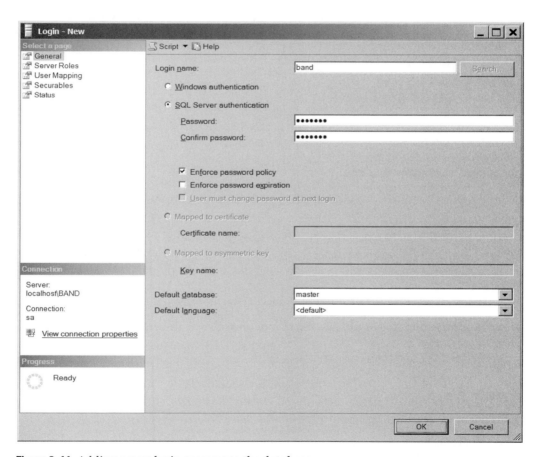

Figure 2-44. *Adding a new login account to the database server*

5. Expand the Logins node to see the new login (you may need to refresh the list from the context menu for the Logins node), as shown in Figure 2-45.

6. Expand the Databases node in Object Explorer, and then expand the Players database.

7. Right-click the Security node, and select New, then User from the context menu.

8. Enter **band** as both the username and login name. Click OK to create the user.

Figure 2-45. *Server access is shown under the Logins node for the server.*

9. Expand the Security node, and then expand the Users node to see that the user has been added to the database (you may need to refresh the list from the context menu for the Logins node) as shown in Figure 2-46.

```
□ 📁 Security
    □ 📁 Users
        🔒 band
        🔒 dbo
        🔒 guest
        🔒 INFORMATION_SCHEMA
        🔒 sys
    ⊞ 📁 Roles
    ⊞ 📁 Schemas
    ⊞ 📁 Asymmetric Keys
    ⊞ 📁 Certificates
    ⊞ 📁 Symmetric Keys
```

Figure 2-46. *Database access is shown in the Users node for the database.*

10. Right-click the Players database and select New Query from the context menu.

11. Run the following query to give the user permissions to query the database:

```
GRANT SELECT, INSERT, UPDATE, DELETE TO band
```

How It Works

In this relatively short example, you've performed three different security tasks:

- Created a login called band on the localhost\BAND server so that the user can connect to the server. If you stopped at this point, the user would be able to connect to the server but would not be able to access any databases.

- Created a user, also called band, with access rights to the Players database. Although this user can now access the Players database, the account still does not have permissions to do anything in the database.

- Gave the user of the database permission to perform SELECT, INSERT, UPDATE, and DELETE queries on the Players database.

Setting up security correctly in SQL Server 2005 is not a trivial task. The graphical tools make it very easy to create logins and users, but also make it dangerously very easy to delete logins and roles. The main thrust of setting your security settings should be to give users the minimum permission that you can.

You've given the band account the minimum privileges possible. The account can query and modify the contents of the tables within the database, but it has no permissions to alter the structure of the database. That's a permission that you should not give to anyone.

Now that you have a reduced-permission account, you'll use it from now on within the database, as you're finished making changes to the structure of the database.

Try It Out: Creating User Accounts in MySQL 5.0

In this example, you'll create a user account in MySQL 5.0, which you'll then use to access your MySQL 5.0 database. Follow these steps:

1. Open MySQL Query Browser if it isn't already running and connect to the localhost server.

2. In the query box at the top of the MySQL Query Browser window, enter the following query:

```
GRANT SELECT, UPDATE, INSERT, DELETE ON players.* TO band
  IDENTIFIED BY 'letmein';
```

3. Click Execute.

How It Works

Unlike SQL Server Management Studio, the MySQL Query Browser doesn't provide a graphical interface for adding users. Therefore, you need to execute a SQL query to create the user:

```
GRANT SELECT, UPDATE, INSERT, DELETE ON players.* TO band
  IDENTIFIED BY 'letmein';
```

This one query performs all three steps that are required to access the Players database in one query. It creates the login, gives the login access rights to the Players database, and then grants the correct permission within the database.

You can break the query down to four parts:

- GRANT: You grant SELECT, INSERT, UPDATE, and DELETE permissions.

- ON: Using the players.* syntax, you specify that you want to give the permissions to everything within the Players database.

- TO: You specify the login that you want to use. If the login doesn't exist, it will be created.

- IDENTIFIED BY: You assign a password for the login.

You've given the band account the minimum privileges possible. It can SELECT, INSERT, UPDATE, and DELETE data within the tables of the Players database, but nothing else.

Now that you have a reduced-permission account, you'll use it within the database, since you're finished making changes to the structure of the database.

Data for the Sample Database

Now that you've done all the hard work building the sample database, all you have left to do is put some data in it. You'll spend a lot of Chapter 8 and Chapter 9 learning how to add, alter, and delete data through a page. Right now, you'll fill the database using the same tools you used to build it.

Try It Out: Adding Data to a SQL Server 2005 Database

Follow these steps to add data to a database table using SQL Server Management Studio:

1. Start SQL Server Management Studio and connect to the localhost\BAND server using the account you just created: a login of band and a password of letmein.

2. Expand the Databases node, and then expand the Players database.

3. Expand the Tables node, right-click the Manufacturer table, and select Open Table from the context menu.

4. In the main window, enter the data for the table as specified in Appendix D. You'll be able to enter all the data, except for the entries in the ManufacturerID column. Since ManufacturerID is a primary key, its values will be generated automatically.

5. Once you've entered all the data for the Manufacturer table, close the window.

6. Repeat steps 3 to 5 for the remaining three tables in the database: Player, Format, and WhatPlaysWhatFormat. The data for each is in Appendix D.

How It Works

Using SQL Server Management Studio, you can enter data into the database very quickly. You enter a row of data. As soon as you move to the next row of data, the entry is sent to the database, and a new primary key value is generated automatically.

As with the other tasks you've accomplished with SQL Server Management Studio, the work is actually handled by a SQL query. In this case, a new INSERT query is sent to the database whenever you move to enter a new row in the table.

Try It Out: Adding Data to a MySQL 5.0 Database

In this exercise, you'll add data to a database table using MySQL Query Browser. Follow these steps:

1. Start MySQL Query Browser and connect to the localhost server using the login that you just created: username of band and a password of letmein.

2. Expand the Players database.

3. Double-click the Manufacturer table to build the SELECT query for the table. Click Execute to return the existing data in the table (which should be empty).

4. Click the Edit button at the bottom of the results window, as shown in Figure 2-47. Now, you can enter the data for the table in the main window, as specified in Appendix D.

Figure 2-47. *Switching MySQL Query Browser into Edit mode*

5. To start editing data, double-click in the blank row underneath the ManufacturerName column heading. You can then enter a single row of data. Use Tab to jump to the next column or double-click in the column. Don't enter a value for the ManufacturerID column, as this is auto-generated. All new data that you enter will be shown with a green background. Figure 2-48 shows some of the data entered in the table.

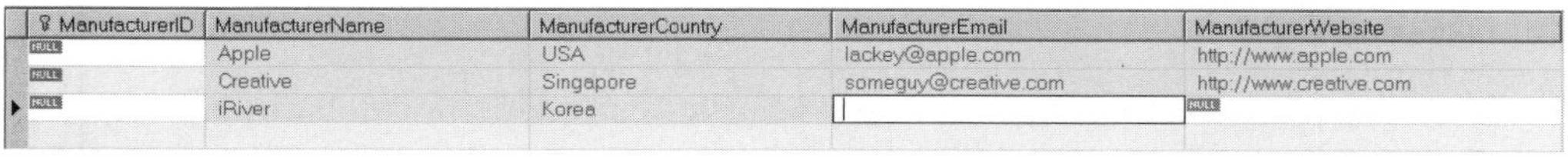

ManufacturerID	ManufacturerName	ManufacturerCountry	ManufacturerEmail	ManufacturerWebsite
NULL	Apple	USA	lackey@apple.com	http://www.apple.com
NULL	Creative	Singapore	someguy@creative.com	http://www.creative.com
NULL	iRiver	Korea		NULL

Figure 2-48. *Editing data in MySQL Query Browser*

6. After you've entered all the data for the Manufacturer table, click the Apply Changes button, as shown in Figure 2-49. (This button became active as soon as you started entering the data.)

Figure 2-49. *Changes must be explicitly accepted.*

7. Repeat steps 3 to 6 for the remaining three tables in the database: Player, Format, and WhatPlaysWhatFormat. The data for each is in Appendix D.

How It Works

The MySQL Query Browser isn't quite as easy to use as SQL Server Management Studio. However, once you get used to the way that it expects you to do things, it's an adequate interface for adding data.

Database Views and Triggers

You may find that two other facets to a relational database server are handy in future projects. (You won't use them in the examples in this book.)

One drawback of the "one object or event per table" rule is that quite often the information you actually need for a page is spread across several tables. For example, it wouldn't be a stretch to imagine a page displaying a Player's name and the name of its Manufacturer. This means pulling information from two different tables, using a complex SELECT query. Like indexes, *views* are designed to save you some time. They're virtual tables containing related columns from many tables in one place. You could, for example, create a view on your sample database containing PlayerName and ManufacturerName. All you do then is write a SELECT query on this view, and the database server does the complex part of pulling all the information together without you knowing.

You can also set up *triggers*—the database equivalent of an event in ASP.NET. These triggers monitor the state of a database table or group of tables. They are fired when a certain kind of query—for example, a CREATE query—is run on that table, or when a certain condition in your database occurs.

If you would like to learn more about SQL views, check out this MSDN tutorial about them at http://msdn.microsoft.com/library/en-us/architec/8_ar_da_2d9v.asp. For more on SQL triggers, check out a two-part article from MSDN Magazine at http://msdn.microsoft.com/msdnmag/issues/03/12/DataPoints/default.aspx and http://msdn.microsoft.com/msdnmag/issues/04/01/DataPoints/default.aspx.

Summary

In this chapter, you've taken a crash course in what makes a relational database (and its server) tick. You've also used some of that theory to build your own database for use in the following chapters. This chapter has covered a lot of ground. Here's a recap of what you've learned:

- All relational database management systems use tables to store information about a single type of object or event. Each row in a table represents one instance of that object or event, and every column in the row contains a single piece of information about that instance.

- Every column has a number of properties and constraints that determine the range of values the column may contain.

- Every table must contain a column or a combination of columns that uniquely identifies that row in the table. This (combination of) column(s) is designated as the primary key for the table. Together, the table name, primary key value for the row, and column name allow you to pinpoint any single piece of information in the database.

- You can model three kinds of relationships between a pair of tables in a database: one-to-one, many-to-one, and many-to-many. Each type of relationship is realized by using one table's primary key as a foreign key in another. Each relationship should be enforced with a foreign key constraint on the tables.

- You use queries written in SQL to convey your wishes to the database.

- You can use stored procedures, indexes, views, and triggers to improve the performance of the database.

In Chapter 3, you'll start building data-driven pages and discover how easy ASP.NET 2.0 makes it to create quite complex data-driven Web pages.

One final note: Congratulations for building the sample database for this book. It would be a bit unfair to expect you to rebuild it each time something went wrong, so you'll find SQL scripts that will rebuild the database included with the code downloads for this book (available from the Downloads section of the Apress Web site, `http://www.apress.com`). You can find instructions on how to run the script in Appendix D.

CHAPTER 3

■ ■ ■

Displaying Data on a Page

The previous two chapters covered the fundamentals required to start using databases. Chapter 1 showed the various types of data sources available. Chapter 2 then moved on to talk about relational databases, and by the end of the chapter, you had fundamentally the same database in three different flavors: SQL Server 2005, MySQL 5.0, and Microsoft Access.

We've covered an awful lot of theory so far. Now, you'll see how to put some of this into practice. In this chapter, you'll look at how to display read-only data on a page using the new (to ASP.NET 2.0) SqlDataSource and GridView.

Now, the phrase *read-only* may sound limiting to you, but Web sites send you a lot more read-only data than data you can alter. Consider search engine results, product details on an e-commerce Web site, news reports from the innumerable feeds on the Web, auction pages, and so on. They're all read-only, unless you have the administrative privileges to change them. Regardless, you may be itching to get straight onto editable data, and you'll look at how to handle that in Chapters 8 and 9.

For the less impetuous, you'll see that working with read-only data isn't a yoke to bear, but on the other hand, it isn't a bag of feathers. You have less to do when you don't have to accommodate creating, updating, and deleting data, but you still have plenty of ways to make mistakes.

We'll spend most of the chapter looking at how to interact with SQL Server 2005. However, there are a few wrinkles when you want to use MySQL 5.0 or Microsoft Access. At the end of the chapter, we'll look at those differences and how they affect the pages you build.

This chapter covers the following topics:

- The data source Web controls that have been added in ASP.NET 2.0, focusing on how the SqlDataSource simplifies the process of connecting to a data source

- How to use SELECT queries to return the results you require, starting with basic SELECT queries and then expanding to those that order results and work across multiple tables in the database

- How to combine a SqlDataSource with a DropDownList to filter the results using a WHERE clause and display them in a GridView

- How to modify the WHERE clause to support both filtered and nonfiltered results returned from the same query

Introducing the Data Source Web Controls

When dealing with databases prior to ASP.NET 2.0, you had to write quite a lot of code, even for the simplest of pages. You needed to create a connection to the database using a Connection object, create a query to execute against the connection using a Command object, and then decide whether you wanted to retrieve the data using a DataAdapter object (into a DataSet object) or via a DataReader object.

Compare this to how you retrieved the data in the very brief example in Chapter 1 using a SqlDataSource object. You didn't write any code, but instead used a wizard to create the correct object. The SqlDataSource is perfect when data-binding the results to a GridView or similar Web control.

This drag-and-drop approach is a far simpler way of retrieving data than writing code to access the database. However, it isn't suitable for every situation, and you probably won't be able to build an entire Web site that doesn't contain code to access the database. We'll look at writing code to access the database in Chapter 4.

ASP.NET 2.0 introduces five Web controls that retrieve data from a particular data source. These Web controls can be broadly categorized into two categories, depending on the type of data that they're retrieving:

- **Set-based:** *Set-based data* is the type of data that you've seen in the two previous chapters—data that is organized into columns and rows. ASP.NET 2.0 provides three set-based data source Web controls:

  - AccessDataSource: This control works exclusively with Access databases. It's limited to retrieving data from the database and won't allow data to be written back to the database. If you need to do more than retrieve data from the database, you need to use the SqlDataSource.

  - ObjectDataSource: This control provides an abstraction layer between an object and a data-bound Web control such as the GridView. Commonly used with a multitiered architecture, the control enables you to use data-bound Web controls while still retaining that architecture.

  - SqlDataSource: This control acts as the bridge between the data-bound Web controls and a database. Although the name SqlDataSource sounds as though it will work with only SQL Server databases, it actually works with any data provider (and therefore with any ODBC- or OLE DB-compliant data source).

- **Hierarchical:** Hierarchical data sources are used to retrieve data that is, well, hierarchical—data that isn't in column-and-row form. ASP.NET 2.0 provides two Web controls that work with hierarchical data:

  - SiteMapDataSource: ASP.NET 2.0 introduces a complete new set of features that make building navigational functions into a Web site extraordinarily easy. For more information about site maps, see http://msdn.microsoft.com/en-us/library/k36h0dfh.aspx.

  - XmlDataSource: This control is designed to work with XML data. For more information about the XmlDataSource, see http://msdn.microsoft.com/en-us/library/51ew3eby.aspx.

As you can see, ASP.NET 2.0 provides five different data source Web controls that you can use in different circumstances, depending on the data that you need to view. By far, the one that you'll use most often is the SqlDataSource, as this allows you to connect to any data source that can be accessed using a data provider, including databases with an ODBC driver or OLE DB provider. As you'll see when you look at using the GridView to modify data in Chapter 9, the SqlDataSource can also modify the data within the database.

Introducing SELECT Queries

To return data from a database, you use a SELECT query. The basic format of the SELECT query is as follows:

```
SELECT <select column list>
FROM <table list>
[ WHERE <constraints> ]
[ ORDER BY <order column list> ]
```

A SELECT query has four parts; two of them are required, and two are optional. A SELECT query must always have a *select column list* and a *table list*, but the WHERE and ORDER BY clauses are optional (indicated by the square brackets in the definition). These optional clauses allow you to filter and sort the data you're retrieving.

Note I'm not trying to teach you every little nuance of SQL here; I'm showing only a small subset of what's possible. Appendix C contains more details of the various SQL commands. For a complete reference, refer to *The Programmer's Guide to SQL* by Christian Darie and Karli Watson (1-59059-218-2; Apress, 2003).

The SELECT query can get confusing quickly, so we'll start with a simple example of querying a single table. Then we'll expand on the example, demonstrating how to sort the results, select data from more than one table, and filter the results returned from the database.

Note In the examples in this chapter, you'll use the SQL Server 2005 database. Using MySQL 5.0 or Microsoft Access is very similar. For details about the differences, see the "Connecting to MySQL 5.0 and Microsoft Access" section later in this chapter.

Try It Out: Querying a Single Table

The easiest form of SELECT query you can make against the database is to query for values from a single table. In this case, you'll list all the Players in the database. This example is the basis for the rest of the examples in this chapter.

Follow these steps:

1. Start Visual Web Developer and create a new Web site called Chapter03 in the C:\BAND\ folder.

2. Delete the Default.aspx file and create a new Web Form by selecting Add New Item from the Web site's context menu in the Solution Explorer.

3. Enter Select.aspx as the name for the Web Form. Make sure that the language is Visual C# and that the Place Code in a Separate File option is unchecked. Click Add to create the Web Form.

4. Right-click Select.aspx in the Solution Explorer and select Set As Start Page.

5. In the Source view, change the name of the page to SELECT by changing the <title> tag as follows:

    <title>SELECT</title>

6. Switch to the Design view by clicking the Design tab at the bottom of the window.

7. Expand the Data entry in the Toolbox on the left side of the screen (if the Toolbox is not visible, select View ➤ Toolbox) and add a SqlDataSource onto the page.

8. From the SqlDataSource Tasks menu, shown in Figure 3-1, select the Configure Data Source option. (If the Tasks menu isn't shown, click the right-facing arrow at the top right of the SqlDataSource to open the menu.)

Figure 3-1. *The SqlDataSource Tasks menu*

9. You'll see that the connections to the databases you created in Chapter 2 are available in the Data Connections drop-down list. However, you want to use the reduced privilege account, rather than the administrator account, so you need to create a new connection. Click the New Connection button.

10. In the Add Connection dialog box, enter the server name as localhost\BAND and select SQL Server Authentication as the authentication method. Enter a username of **band** and a password of **letmein**. Check the Save My Password option. Also select the Players database from the Select or Enter a Database Name drop-down list. Your dialog box should look like Figure 3-2. Click OK to create the new connection.

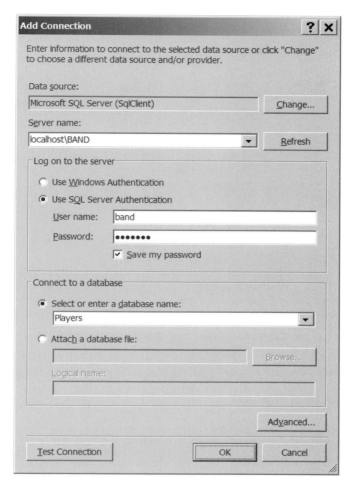

Figure 3-2. *Creating a new connection in Visual Web Developer*

11. In the Configure Data Source wizard, the drop-down list will have been prepopulated with a new entry for the reduced privilege account. The entry will have a name that ends with band.BAND.dbo1; in this case, keegan\band.BAND.dbo1. As shown in Figure 3-3, you can expand the Connection String entry to show the actual connection string being used. Click Next to continue.

12. On the Save the Connection String step, make sure the Yes, Save This Connection option is selected, and enter a name for the connection of SqlConnnectionString. Then click Next.

13. The next step of the wizard allows you to create the SELECT query that the SqlDataSource will use. Select the Player table in the Name drop-down list, and check the PlayerName and PlayerManufacturerID columns, as shown in Figure 3-4. Click Next.

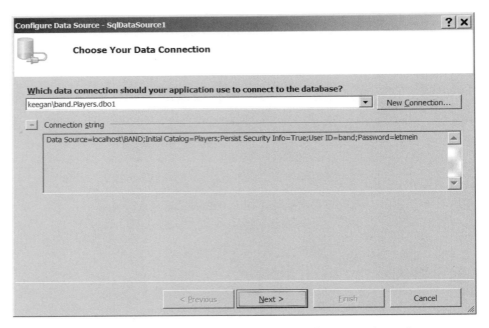

Figure 3-3. *Selecting the correct connection and verifying the connection string*

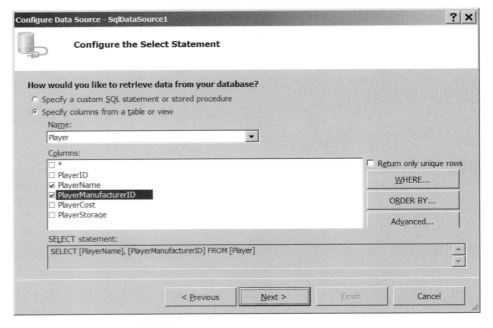

Figure 3-4. *Creating the SELECT query*

14. On the Test Query step, you can click the Test Query button to test that the query is correct. Once you're happy that it is (if it isn't, click Previous to go back to the previous step and modify the query), click Finish to close the wizard.

15. Switch back to the Design view of the page. Add a GridView from the Data section of the Toolbox to the page, below the SqlDataSource.

16. From the GridView Tasks menu, select Auto Format, and then select Colorful from the list. (If you don't like Colorful, you can pick another format, although the pages you build won't look exactly like the illustrations in this chapter.) Click OK.

17. From the Choose Data Source drop-down list, select SqlDataSource1, as shown in Figure 3-5.

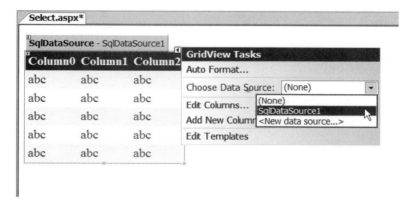

Figure 3-5. *Selecting the correct DataSource from the GridView Tasks menu*

18. As shown in Figure 3-6, the GridView will change to show the columns from the SELECT query that you defined for the SqlDataSource earlier.

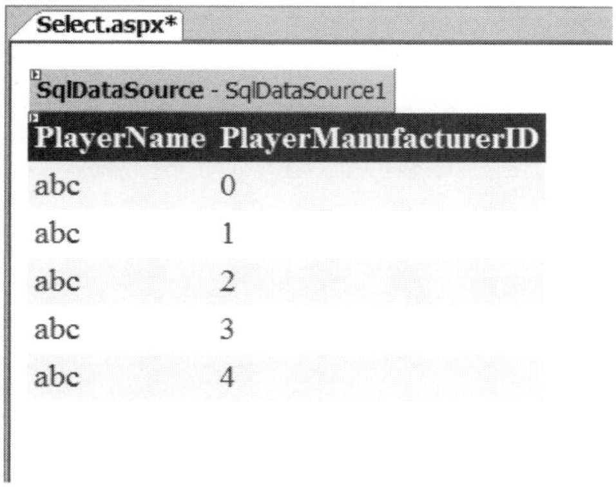

Figure 3-6. *At design time, the GridView shows correct column information.*

19. Run the page in debug mode by clicking the Start Debugging button in the toolbar, selecting Debug ➤ Start Debugging, or pressing F5. All three methods will start the debugging process. Debugging isn't enabled by default for Web sites, so the Debugging Not Enabled dialog box will appear, as shown in Figure 3-7. Accept the Modify option by clicking OK.

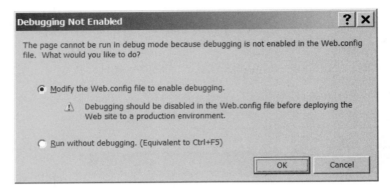

Figure 3-7. *Enabling debugging for the Web site*

20. Visual Web Developer's built-in Web server will start (which you'll see in the system tray), and the page will be displayed in your browser, as shown in Figure 3-8.

Figure 3-8. *Results of running a SELECT query against the Player table*

How It Works

In this example, you built a relatively simple page, showing the name of all of the Players in the database alongside details of their Manufacturer. (Granted, the PlayerManufacturerID data isn't particularly helpful, and you'll see how to improve this in the "Try It Out: Querying Multiple Tables" section later in this chapter.)

As you saw in step 19, Visual Web Developer needs to modify the Web.config file to enable debugging. By clicking OK in the Debugging Not Enabled dialog box (Figure 3-7), you've told Visual Web Developer to add the code shown in bold to the Web.config file:

```
<configuration>
  <system.web>
    <compilation debug="true"/>
  </system.web>
</configuration>
```

This tells ASP.NET that the Web site is running in debug mode and to allow a debugger to attach to the Web site.

Visual Web Developer has also made a further change to Web.config. In step 12, you told it to save the connection string, and it has done just that, placing the connection string in the <connectionStrings> element. In previous versions of ASP.NET, all user settings—database connection strings, file paths, and so on—were usually stored in Web.config in the <appSettings> element. ASP.NET 2.0 introduces the new <connectionStrings> element, which is used exclusively to store database connection strings:

```
<configuration>
  <connectionStrings>
    <add name="SqlConnectionString"
      connectionString="Data Source=localhost\BAND;Initial Catalog=Players;
        Persist Security Info=True;User ID=band;Password=letmein"
      providerName="System.Data.SqlClient"/>
  </connectionStrings>
</configuration>
```

Entries are added to <connectionStrings> in much the same way as they were added to <appSettings> by using an <add> element. But unlike <appSettings>, where you could supply only a key and a value, you add connection-specific information, as follows:

- connectionString: The string that is used to make the connection to the database. The actual value depends on the provider that you're going to use (as determined by the providerName attribute).

- name: Define is the name that is used to refer to this particular connection string.

- providerName: Tells ASP.NET which data provider this connection uses. It can be one of the following values: System.Data.Odbc, System.Data.OleDb, System.Data.OracleClient, or System.Data.SqlClient.

In this example, you specified SqlConnectionString as the name of the connection string, and this is used as the value of the name attribute. The remaining two attributes were completed by Visual Web Developer using the information that you supplied.

You're connecting to a SQL Server database, so `System.Data.SqlClient` is used, and the `connectionString` attribute, which is the connection string itself, is built from the details that you entered in the Add Connection dialog box, as follows:

```
connectionString="Data Source=localhost\BAND;Initial Catalog=Players;
    Persist Security Info=True;User ID=band;Password=letmein"
```

The properties are as follows:

- `Data Source`: This is the server to which you're connecting. This can either be a server name or an IP address, as well as the specific instance that you require. For example, `localhost\BAND` is the BAND instance of SQL Server on the local machine.

- `Initial Catalog`: The database on the server to which you want to connect; `Players` in this example.

- `Persist Security Info`: When set to `True`, this property allows the username and password that are used to connect to the database to be viewed when programmatically looking at the connection string. Ideally, it should always be set to its default value of `False` but it is set to `True` by Visual Web Developer when you're using an existing connection that has its password stored. You can remove this property from the `connectionString` without causing any problems.

- `User ID`: The username to use when connecting to the database; `band` in this example.

- `Password`: The password to use when connecting to the database; `letmein` in this example.

Note You have a multitude of options for connecting to data sources. For a comprehensive list, see `http://www.connectionstrings.com`.

Now that we've covered the various "background" parts of the sample page, it's time to look at the two Web controls that you used to do all the work: the `SqlDataSource` for connecting to the database and retrieving the results and the `GridView` for displaying those results.

The SqlDataSource Web Control

The `SqlDataSource` is the brains of the operation. It handles connecting to the database and executing the query against the database to return the results you requested. Here is the markup produced for it:

```
<asp:SqlDataSource ID="SqlDataSource1" runat="server"
  ConnectionString="<%$ ConnectionStrings:SqlConnectionString %>"
  SelectCommand="SELECT [PlayerName], [PlayerManufacturerID] FROM [Player]">
</asp:SqlDataSource>
```

In its simplest form, there isn't a lot to it. As well as the obligatory ID and runat properties, it has only two other properties: ConnectionString and SelectCommand.

The ConnectionString property is used to specify the data source that you want to use. In this instance, the value indicates that you want to use a connection string, SqlConnectionString, which is stored in the Web.config file:

```
<%$ ConnectionStrings:SqlConnectionString %>
```

As you saw earlier, Visual Web Developer created an entry in the <connectionStrings> section of Web.config that provided the full details of the connection to the database. By specifying the ConnectionString in this way, you're telling the SqlDataSource that you want to use it.

STORING CONNECTION STRINGS

You've stored all of your connection strings within Web.config, as this allows the most flexibility when building Web sites. You have one connection string that you need to change should the database details change.

You should always store your connection strings in Web.config, as this makes for far easier maintenance of the Web site. If the database details change, you can easily modify the connection string in Web.config. However, you can also store the connection string directly within the page, as follows:

```
<asp:SqlDataSource ID="SqlDataSource1" runat="server"
  ConnectionString="Data Source=localhost\BAND;Initial Catalog=BAND;
    Persist Security Info=True;User ID=band;Password=letmein"
  ProviderName="System.Data.SqlClient"
  SelectCommand="SELECT [PlayerName], [PlayerManufacturerID] FROM [Player]">
</asp:SqlDataSource>
```

You need to provide enough information to fully configure the connection, so you must also specify a ProviderName to tell the SqlDataSource which provider to use.

The property of most interest here is SelectCommand. This contains the SELECT query that will be run against the database when data is requested.

The SELECT query you use to select all of the Players is about as simple as it can get. You specify the columns you want to retrieve and the table you want to retrieve them from, like so:

```
SELECT [PlayerName], [PlayerManufacturerID]
FROM [Player]
```

Okay, it could have been simpler—you could have returned only one column, but returning two is just a little more complex. The columns to retrieve are specified as a comma-separated list (in this case, PlayerName and PlayerManufacturerID) after the SELECT query, and the table from which you want the data to be returned is specified after the FROM statement.

■**Note** Instead of listing the columns you want to retrieve with the query, you can use SELECT * to return all the columns from the query. However, it's better to explicitly list the columns to return, rather than relying on returning all the columns. Not only is it quicker (the database doesn't have to retrieve a list of columns to return before it executes the query) and produces less network traffic (you're not returning columns you don't need), but it also makes the code more readable, because anyone can see what the query is returning without having to look at the database structure.

Notice that the column names have square brackets around them, so the PlayerName column is retrieved as [PlayerName]. Although not required in this instance, the square brackets are used by SQL Server to delimit the name of the column. Column names can contain spaces, so the square brackets set off the entire name. For example, a column called Player Name not surrounded by brackets would cause an error, as the database would look for a column called Player. You should avoid using spaces in names within the database—whether for tables, columns, or any other database object—at all costs. It's quite easy to forget that you need to have square brackets around the names, which can lead to all kinds of problems with the queries that you're trying to execute. As you've been good and designed your database without any table or column names without any spaces, we will not need to use square brackets at all. From now on, we will not show any SQL queries with square brackets. Just be aware that Visual Web Developer may add them to the queries that it creates.

■**Note** Although you can refer to the columns using only the name of the column, such as PlayerID, the correct name of the column—its *full name syntax*—is Player.PlayerID. The database allows you to use this shorthand version because there's no confusion as to which table the column belongs. There's no restriction on the names of columns, and when you join tables, it's likely that columns with the same name will appear in multiple tables. The only way you can distinguish which column you're after is to use the full name syntax for specifying the column name.

The GridView Web Control

The GridView is a new control introduced in ASP.NET 2.0 that replaces the DataGrid from previous versions of ASP.NET. As you've seen, it's used to display data from a data source in a tabular format. But it can do a whole lot more than that, including automatic sorting and paging of results. We'll take a much more detailed look at this control starting in Chapter 7. For now, we'll focus on the way that you're using the GridView in this example.

Looking at the markup generated for the GridView, you can start to appreciate how it works (this snippet has formatting instructions removed for simplicity):

```
<asp:GridView ID="GridView1" runat="server"
  AutoGenerateColumns="False" DataSourceID="SqlDataSource1">
  <Columns>
    <asp:BoundField DataField="PlayerName"
      HeaderText="PlayerName"
      SortExpression="PlayerName" />
    <asp:BoundField DataField="PlayerManufacturerID"
      HeaderText="PlayerManufacturerID"
```

```
        SortExpression="PlayerManufacturerID" />
   </Columns>
</asp:GridView>
```

The `DataSourceID` property of the `GridView` tag specifies the name of the data source being used; in this case, you're using `SqlDataSource1`, which is the `SqlDataSource` described in the previous section.

If the `AutoGenerateColumns` property is set to `True`, then the `DataSourceID` is the only property that you need to set on a `GridView` for it to display the data from the data source Web control. The columns that it displays will be generated automatically from the results returned from the data source, and every column in the results will be displayed. However, you may not want this automatic generation—you may want to display just a subset of that data. In this case, you would set the `AutoGenerateColumns` property to `False`, and then manually define the columns you want to display using the `<Columns>` collection. In the example, Visual Web Developer has created a `Columns` collection for you, because you selected the PlayerName and PlayerManufacturerID columns (in step 13).

The `<Columns>` collection contains the columns, or *fields* in `GridView` terminology, that will be displayed. Although you defined only one column type in this example, `BoundField`, a total of seven types are available. Table 3-1 gives you an idea of what is possible using the `GridView`. We'll come back to this list starting in Chapter 7. For now, we're interested only in the `BoundField`.

Table 3-1. *GridView Column Types*

Name	Description
BoundField	Displays data directly from the data source. The `DataField` property indicates which particular column of the results you want to show, and you can use the optional `DataFormatString` property to format the results as required.
ButtonField	Shows a button that causes a postback to the server, allowing an action to be performed on the selected row.
CheckBoxField	Shows a check box. This type of column is usually used to display columns from the database with Boolean values.
CommandField	Creates a column in the results that contains Edit, Update, and Cancel buttons (as appropriate) to allow editing of the data within the selected row.
HyperLinkField	Shows a hyperlink.
ImageField	Shows an image.
TemplateField	Allows full control over what is displayed for the column: the header, the item displayed, and the footer. The `TemplateField` contains various templates controlling what is displayed and, within these templates, you can place whatever content you desire. This makes the `TemplateField` the most customizable of the column types.

A `BoundField` has only one property that is always required when displaying data: `DataField`. This property indicates which column in the data source you want to display. In this example, you have two columns in the `GridView`, and the `DataField` properties are set to `PlayerName` and

PlayerManufacturerID. These are the names of the columns that you want to show from the data source, and they correspond to the columns that you're returning from the SELECT query.

Visual Web Developer also adds two further properties for you: HeaderText is the text that is displayed in the header row of the table, and SortExpression is the value used to control the sorting applied to this column if sorting is enabled. The default for both of these is the name of the column that is being displayed, so you'll see that DataField, HeaderText, and SortExpression all have the same value. For this example, what is displayed in the header for the column is not important, and you're free to change it to whatever you like. Similarly, you're not concerned with sorting, so the SortExpression is not relevant at the moment; you're free to remove it. We'll come back to sorting in Chapter 7.

■**Note** You'll notice that the GridView on the page that you built has a lot more properties than we've looked at here. You'll see six *xxx*Style elements defined, as well as some style properties applied directly to the GridView. Feel free to experiment with the elements and properties, as they won't affect how the GridView works. You can change them directly from the Source view of the page or from the Styles section of the Properties window for the Web control. Just remember that if you get to a point where you can't see anything (blue text on a blue background, anyone?), you can always select Auto Format from the GridView Tasks menu to remove any style information that you've applied or to change to one of the predefined styles.

Try It Out: Ordering the Results

One of the problems with the results you've received in the previous example is that they're not ordered. You've returned all of the Players in the database in whatever order they were entered. If you look back at Figure 3-8, you'll see that trying to find a specific Player will require a lot of work on the behalf of the user.

What you need to do is order the results, and SQL provides this ability with the ORDER BY clause of the SELECT query. In this example, you'll build on the simple SELECT query of the last example and sort the Players alphabetically. Follow these steps:

1. If you've closed Select.aspx from the previous example, reopen it.

2. Switch to the Design view of the page. Open the Tasks menu for SqlDataSource1 and click the Configure Data Source option.

3. You've already configured the data source in the previous example, so click Next to skip past the Choose Your Data Connection step. On the Configure the Select Statement step, click the ORDER BY button.

4. In the first drop-down list of the Add ORDER BY Clause dialog box, select the PlayerName column, as shown in Figure 3-9. Then click OK.

5. Click Next, and then click Finish to close the wizard.

6. Open the page. The results will be the same as the previous example, except that the Players will be in alphabetical order, as shown in Figure 3-10.

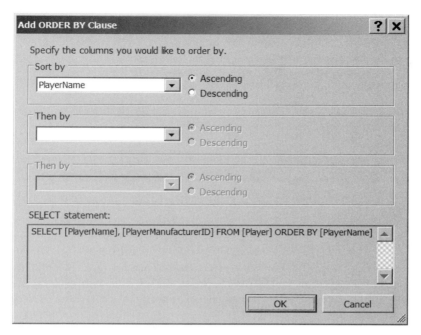

Figure 3-9. *Specifying ORDER BY clauses for a SELECT query*

Figure 3-10. *Ordering the results that are returned*

How It Works

You used the Configure Data Source wizard to modify the query that you're executing against that database. You appended an ORDER BY clause to return the results in alphabetical ascending order. If you look at the Source view of the page, you'll see that the SelectCommand property of SqlDataSource1 has been changed like so:

```
SELECT PlayerName, PlayerManufacturerID
FROM Player
ORDER BY PlayerName
```

■Tip Although you used the wizard to add the ORDER BY clause, you could have quite easily modified the SelectCommand property manually and added the clause.

Adding the ORDER BY clause and specifying a text column sorts the results alphabetically on that column. If you specify a column for the ORDER BY clause, the sort order is, by default, ascending. The query you've used to sort the results is equivalent to specifying a sort order of ASC along with the column, like so:

```
SELECT PlayerName, PlayerManufacturerID
FROM Player
ORDER BY PlayerName ASC
```

You can also sort in descending order using DESC, like so:

```
SELECT PlayerName, PlayerManufacturerID
FROM Player
ORDER BY PlayerName DESC
```

Executing this query has the effect of sorting the results by Player name in descending alphabetical order, as shown in Figure 3-11.

PlayerName	PlayerManufacturerID
Zen Touch	2
Zen Micro	2
Network Walkman NW-HD3	7
Network Walkman NW-E99	7
Napster YH-920	10

Figure 3-11. *Sorting by PlayerName in descending alphabetical order*

Although the examples you've seen sort on a text column, PlayerName, you can sort on any type of column. Dates will be sorted earliest to latest if you specify an ascending order, and latest to earliest if you specify descending. Numbers are sorted smallest to largest or largest to smallest. Each type of column follows its own rules, and the ordering they impose generally makes sense.

You can see how ordering applies to nontext columns if you order the results by PlayerManufacturerID, like so:

```
SELECT PlayerName, PlayerManufacturerID
FROM Player
ORDER BY PlayerManufacturerID
```

Executing this query returns the results in ascending PlayerManufacturerID order, as shown in Figure 3-12.

PlayerName	PlayerManufacturerID
iPod Shuffle	1
iPod	1
iPod Mini	1
iPod Photo	1
MuVo V200	2

Figure 3-12. *Sorting by an integer column, PlayerManufacturerID*

You could also return the results in descending PlayerManufacturerID order, and the entries that have a PlayerManufacturerID of 10 would be at the beginning of the results.

The ORDER BY clause also allows you to sort the results on multiple columns, as you saw offered in the Add ORDER BY Clause dialog box (Figure 3-9). If you look at the results in Figure 3-12, you'll see that, although you've sorted by PlayerManufacturerID, the PlayerName column is unsorted. What you really want is the results sorted by PlayerManufacturerID, and then by PlayerName. You can accomplish this relatively easily by specifying the two columns you want to order, separated by commas after the ORDER BY clause, like so:

```
SELECT PlayerName, PlayerManufacturerID
FROM Player
ORDER BY PlayerManufacturerID, PlayerName
```

This will order the Players by PlayerManufacturerID and PlayerName. Both of the sorts will be in ascending order, as you can see from the results returned in Figure 3-13.

PlayerName	PlayerManufacturerID
iPod	1
iPod Mini	1
iPod Photo	1
iPod Shuffle	1
MuVo V200	2

Figure 3-13. *Sorting on multiple columns*

It's also possible to have different sort orders on different columns by specifying the sort order you want for each column, like so:

```
SELECT PlayerName, PlayerManufacturerID
FROM Player
ORDER BY PlayerManufacturerID DESC, PlayerName
```

You want the results by PlayerManufacturerID in descending order and then by PlayerName in ascending order. As shown in Figure 3-14, this is exactly the order in which the results are returned.

PlayerName	PlayerManufacturerID
Napster YH-920	10
L1	9
iAudio M3	8
Network Walkman NW-E99	7
Network Walkman NW-HD3	7

Figure 3-14. *Sorting on multiple columns with different sort orders*

Try It Out: Querying Multiple Tables

Looking at the results you received from the previous example (Figure 3-10), you'll see that although you return the title of the Player correctly, the Manufacturer is simply an integer. Recall from Chapter 2 that the PlayerManufacturerID column in the Player table corresponds to the ManufacturerID column in the Manufacturer table. Unless you're capable of remembering vast quantities of data, the integer on its own won't be a lot of use. You need some way of joining the Player and Manufacturer tables so that, instead of returning the PlayerManufacturerID, you return the name of the Manufacturer.

SQL allows you to return data from multiple tables by using the JOIN clause when you specify from which tables you want to return data. You'll now see a JOIN in action by building on the previous example and returning the name of the Manufacturer instead of the ID integer. Follow these steps:

1. If you've closed Select.aspx from the previous example, reopen it.

2. Select SqlDataSource1, and from the Properties window, click the ellipsis for the SelectQuery property.

3. In the Command and Parameter Editor dialog box, click the Query Builder button. The Query Builder dialog box isn't easy to use in its default size, so expand the window until it's at a reasonable size, as shown in Figure 3-15.

4. Click the top part of the dialog box next to the Player table and select Add Table from the context menu.

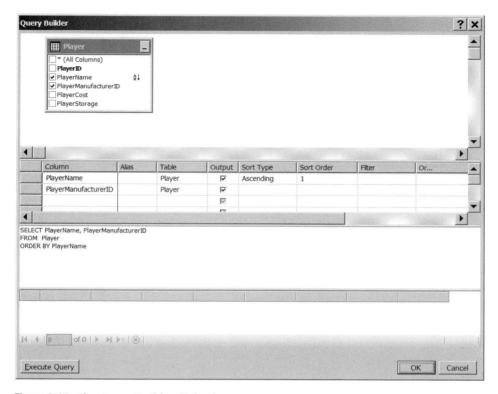

Figure 3-15. *The Query Builder dialog box*

5. From the Add Table dialog box, select the Manufacturer table, and then click OK. This adds the Manufacturer table and shows the relationship it has with the Player table, as shown in Figure 3-16.

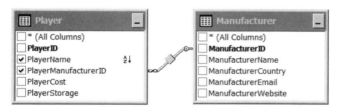

Figure 3-16. *Relationships are shown in the Query Builder dialog box*

6. Uncheck the PlayerManufacturerID check box in the Player table, and check the ManufacturerName check box in the Manufacturer table. This updates both the column list in the second part of the Query Builder dialog box and the SQL view in the third part.

7. Click OK to close the Query Builder dialog box, and then click OK to close the Command and Parameter Editor dialog box.

8. Open the Tasks menu for GridView1 and select the Refresh Schema option. You're presented with a confirmation dialog box, as shown in Figure 3-17.

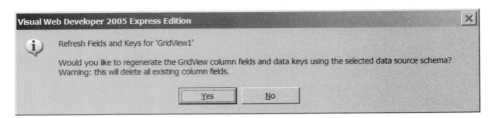

Figure 3-17. *You must confirm that you want to change the schema for a GridView.*

9. Click Yes to confirm that you want to refresh the GridView. You'll see that the GridView has been updated correctly.

10. Open the page. The new query runs against the database, and the results are returned, as shown in Figure 3-18.

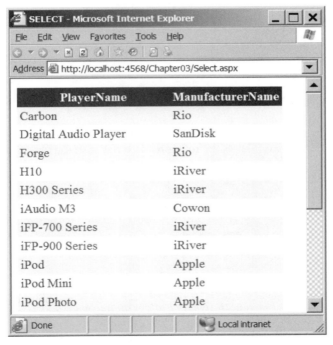

Figure 3-18. *Results of a SELECT query against the Player and Manufacturer table*

How It Works

Before we look at what actually changed in the query, it's worth taking a quick detour into the interaction of the SqlDataSource and GridView.

The first couple of steps of the example were concerned with changing the query that you are executing. When you closed the Command and Parameter Editor dialog box for the SelectQuery property, SqlDataSource1 was updated with the new SELECT query—with PlayerManufacturerID replaced by ManufacturerName—but GridView1 was still looking for the old column. If you had run the page at this point, you would have seen an error message instead of any results, as shown in Figure 3-19.

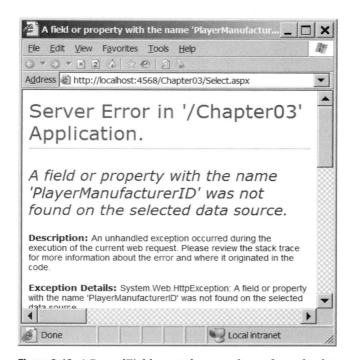

Figure 3-19. *A BoundField must show a column from the data source.*

If you had been using automatically generated columns, this wouldn't have been a problem, as the ManufacturerName would have been returned. However, as you saw in the first example in this chapter, you're explicitly saying which columns you want to show, so you would have gotten an error.

To avoid this error, you refreshed the schema for GridView1 before running the page. When the schema is refreshed, Visual Web Developer looks at the specified data source and replaces the <Columns> collection with a new collection for the data source as it stands at that point in time.

Now, let's look at the changes to the SELECT query that you're running. The query has been changed to the following:

```
SELECT Player.PlayerName, Manufacturer.ManufacturerName
FROM Player INNER JOIN Manufacturer
  ON Player.PlayerManufacturerID = Manufacturer.ManufacturerID
ORDER BY Player.PlayerName
```

First, notice that you're now using the full name syntax to refer to the columns. Although the database doesn't have any column names that could clash, it's good practice when returning data from multiple tables to use the full name, even if you don't have to do so. Not only does it make it easier to see which table a column comes from, it should also make the query a little faster, because the database won't need to work out which table contains the column since you've already specified it.

The following FROM clause, and in particular the INNER JOIN you added, is the important part of the query:

```
FROM Player INNER JOIN Manufacturer
  ON Player.PlayerManufacturerID = Manufacturer.ManufacturerID
```

When joining tables using an INNER JOIN, the database combines both tables into one "supertable" and returns only records that exist on both sides of the join. It does this by using the table specified after the FROM clause as the master table and by appending matching records in the table specified after the INNER JOIN based on the ON criteria.

Note Using INNER JOIN rather than simply JOIN should give you a clue that this isn't the only type of join. SQL also defines RIGHT JOIN, LEFT JOIN, and CROSS JOIN, which allow you to change how the tables are actually joined. The INNER JOIN is by far the most commonly used type of join.

The ON criterion specifies how the two tables you're joining are being joined. In this case, you specify that the PlayerManufacturerID column in the Player table is joined to the ManufacturerID column in the Manufacturer table. This tells the database that the two columns are equal and to combine the tables based on this.

If you could view the constructed supertable for this join of the Player and Manufacturer table, you would initially see all of the columns in both tables, as shown in truncated form in Figure 3-20.

PlayerID	PlayerName	PlayerManufacturerID	PlayerCost	PlayerStorage	ManufacturerID	ManufacturerName	ManufacturerCountry
18	Carbon	5	169.00	Hard Disk	5	Rio	USA
7	Digital Audio Player	6	119.00	Solid State	6	SanDisk	USA
6	Forge	5	93.00	Solid State	5	Rio	USA
16	H10	3	189.00	Hard Disk	3	iRiver	Korea
17	H300 Series	3	319.00	Hard Disk	3	iRiver	Korea

Figure 3-20. *A "supertable" from the join of the Player and Manufacturer tables*

As you can see, you have the PlayerID, PlayerName, PlayerManufacturerID, PlayerCost, and PlayerStorage columns from the Player table, and the ManufacturerID, ManufacturerName, and ManufacturerCountry columns from the Manufacturer table. The supertable contains two more columns that aren't visible in Figure 3-20: ManufacturerEmail and ManufacturerWebsite. In addition, both the PlayerManufacturerID and ManufacturerID columns have the same value, as these are the columns that you specified in the INNER JOIN statement.

The query specifies that only the Player.PlayerName and Manufacturer.ManufacturerName columns should be returned, and the remaining columns are ignored, as shown in Figure 3-21.

PlayerName	ManufacturerName
Carbon	Rio
Digital Audio Player	SanDisk
Forge	Rio
H10	iRiver
H300 Series	iRiver

Figure 3-21. *Returning a subset of the columns from the supertable*

When you looked at sorting columns in the previous example, you learned that you can sort a set of results by more than one column. The same is also true if you have multiple tables, and you can sort across any of the columns that are in the supertable. So to sort by ManufacturerName and then by PlayerName, you would add both of these to the ORDER BY clause in the order you wanted the sorting to take place, like so:

```
SELECT Player.PlayerName, Manufacturer.ManufacturerName
FROM Player INNER JOIN Manufacturer
  ON Player.PlayerManufacturerID = Manufacturer.ManufacturerID
ORDER BY Manufacturer.ManufacturerName, Player.PlayerName
```

So, rather than having a list of Players sorted by name, you would now have a list of Players sorted by the name of the Manufacturer and then the name of the Player, as shown in Figure 3-22.

PlayerName	ManufacturerName
iPod	Apple
iPod Mini	Apple
iPod Photo	Apple
iPod Shuffle	Apple
iAudio M3	Cowon

Figure 3-22. *You can also sort using columns from different tables.*

■**Note** It's possible to have multiple joins in the same SQL query and also to mix different join types within the same SQL query. Joins can quickly become hideously complex. You can find more information about joins and SQL in general in *The Programmer's Guide to SQL* by Christian Darie and Karli Watson (1-59059-218-2; Apress, 2003).

Try It Out: Filtering the Results

In the previous three examples, you've come from writing a simple query that takes data from one table to being able to order the results you get and join two tables to retrieve user-friendly data. Now, let's look at how to filter the results of your queries to return only the results that meet the criteria you specify.

You filter the results of a query by using a WHERE clause to constrain the records that are returned. In this next example, you'll again build on the previous example and allow users to select the Manufacturer in which they're interested. Once a selection has been made, only the Players for that Manufacturer will be returned. Follow these steps:

1. If you've closed Select.aspx from the previous example, reopen it.

2. In the Design view, add a second SqlDataSource to the page. Then add a DropDownList from the Standard section of the Toolbox to the page above the GridView. Your page should look something like Figure 3-23.

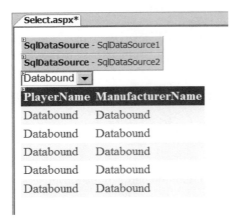

Figure 3-23. *Adding the second SqlDataSource and a DropDownList*

3. Click SqlDataSource2, the second SqlDataSource, and select Configure Data Source from its Tasks menu.

4. On the Choose Your Data Connection step, select SqlConnectionString from the drop-down list, and then click Next.

5. On the Configure the Select Statement step, select Manufacturer from the Name drop-down list, and then select the ManufacturerID and ManufacturerName columns.

6. Click the ORDER BY button. In the Add ORDER BY Clause dialog box, select ManufacturerName in the first Sort By drop-down list and leave the sort order as Ascending. Then click OK. Click Next to continue with the wizard.

7. Test that the Manufacturers are being returned correctly by clicking the Test Query button on the Test Query step. Once you're satisfied that the query works as expected, click Finish to close the wizard.

8. Select the drop-down list, DropDownList1, and open the Tasks menu. Check the Enable AutoPostBack check box. Select the Choose Data Source option.

9. On the Choose a Data Source step, select SqlDataSource2 as the data source and ManufacturerName as the data field to display, as shown in Figure 3-24. Click OK to close the wizard.

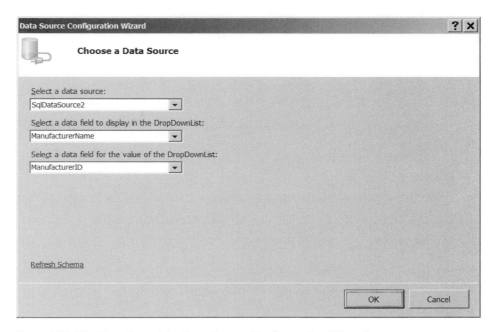

Figure 3-24. *The DropDownList Data Source Configuration Wizard*

10. Select SqlDataSource1 and click the ellipsis in the SelectQuery property to launch the Command and Parameter Editor dialog box.

11. Click the Add Parameter button and give the parameter a name of ManufacturerID. Then select Control as the Parameter source and DropDownList1 as the ControlID.

12. Click the Query Builder button, and then expand the Query Builder dialog box to a usable size.

13. In the top of the Query Builder dialog box, click the check box next to the ManufacturerID column in the Manufacturer table. In the list of columns in the query, uncheck the Output column next to ManufacturerID.

14. In the Filter column, enter @ManufacturerID. Make sure that the filtered column is set correctly. In the table view at the top, you should see that the ManufacturerID column is highlighted with an icon to show that it is filtered. The SQL query also should have changed to show that the ManufacturerID column is being filtered using @ManufacturerID, as shown in Figure 3-25.

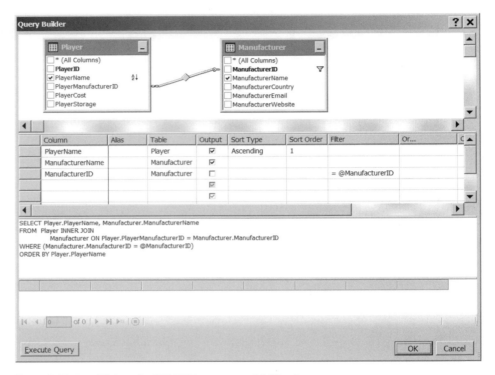

Figure 3-25. *Modifying the SELECT query to add filtering*

15. Click OK to close the Query Builder dialog box, and then click OK again to close the Command and Parameter Editor dialog box.

16. Open the page. You'll see that the drop-down list is populated with the available Manufacturers in the database and the grid shows only the Players manufactured by Apple, as shown in Figure 3-26.

17. Select any of the other Manufacturers from the drop-down list to see that the list of Players is indeed modified to display only the correct list of manufactured Players.

Figure 3-26. *Players can be filtered by Manufacturer*

How It Works

Although you've looked at several examples so far in the book, this is the first page you've seen that starts to give you an idea of what's possible with data-driven pages—you've responded to a user selection to modify the results that are returned as part of the query.

We'll look at this example in two parts: how to populate the drop-down list with the list of Manufacturers in the database, and then the changes necessary to make the GridView's data source handle the filtering.

Populating the DropDownList Web Control

You used a new SqlDataSource, SqlDataSource2, which returns all of the Manufacturers in the database in alphabetical order by executing a simple SELECT query:

```
SELECT ManufacturerID, ManufacturerName
FROM Manufacturer
ORDER BY ManufacturerName
```

Using the Configure Data Source wizard, you specified SqlDataSource2 as the data source for the drop-down list, as well as the text to display and the value to use from the data source. Looking at the markup generated from this wizard, you can start to see what is actually happening:

```
<asp:DropDownList ID="DropDownList1" runat="server"
  DataSourceID="SqlDataSource2"
  DataTextField="ManufacturerName"
  DataValueField="ManufacturerID"
  AutoPostBack="True">
</asp:DropDownList>
```

As you can see, the DataSourceID property is set to the name of the data source that you want to use.

The DataTextField and DataValueField properties are used to control what is shown on the page to the user and what is used as the value of the user's selection. So, by setting ManufacturerName as the DataTextField property value, you're telling ASP.NET to show the Manufacturer names—Apple, Cowon, Creative, and so on. By setting the DataValueField property to ManufacturerID, you're saying that you want the ID of the Manufacturer—1, 2, 3, and so on— to be returned when you request the SelectedValue of the drop-down list.

The AutoPostBack property is set to True to cause any selection changes in the drop-down list to automatically cause a postback to the server to update the grid that is displayed. If you left AutoPostBack set to the default value of False, you would need to add a button (or some other Web control) to the page to force the postback. By having an automatic postback, the page will react immediately to the user's selection.

So you have a drop-down list that contains the different values that you want to filter. Now, let's look at how the results are filtered for the GridView.

Filtering the GridView's Data Source

The GridView simply displays the data that it's told to display from the data source that it's bound to; in this case, SqlDataSource1. To filter the results, you change what the data source is returning from the database by modifying the SELECT query to take into account the value that you've selected in DropDownList1.

First, let's look at the SELECT query that you now use to interrogate the database. This is the same query as you used in the previous example, but with the addition of the WHERE clause (shown in bold):

```
SELECT Player.PlayerName, Manufacturer.ManufacturerName
FROM Player INNER JOIN Manufacturer
  ON Player.PlayerManufacturerID = Manufacturer.ManufacturerID
WHERE (Manufacturer.ManufacturerID = @ManufacturerID)
ORDER BY Player.PlayerName
```

The query still returns the Player and Manufacturer names ordered alphabetically on the Player's name. Here, you use the WHERE clause to constrain the results that are returned. We'll look at the WHERE clause in a lot more detail in the next section, but the simple one that you used here should be quite easy to understand.

The WHERE clause compares the ManufacturerID column in the Manufacturer table to a parameter called @ManufacturerID. If the ManufacturerID matches the value of @ManufacturerID, the row will be returned. So, if you select Apple as the Manufacturer, which has a value of 1, only the Players that have a ManufacturerID of 1 will be returned.

But what's @ManufacturerID? It's a parameter to the query, as indicated by @ at the front of its name. *Parameters* in SQL are the means whereby you can pass information into a query at runtime without making any changes to the query. You could have written (quite a lot of) code to extract the value of the Manufacturer that you want to filter for and changed the query that you're running at runtime, but using parameters allows a lot of the hard work to be done for you. You can use the same query every time and simply vary the value of the parameter that you pass into the query.

■**Note** Only when using the `SqlClient` data provider to connect to SQL Server 2005 can you use named parameters. Neither the `Odbc` data provider when connecting to MySQL 5.0 nor the `OleDb` data provider when connecting to any database (such as Microsoft Access) support named parameters. Therefore, the queries for those databases are written a little differently. See the "Connecting to MySQL 5.0 and Microsoft Access" section later in this chapter for more information.

The @ManufacturerID parameter is defined for SqlDataSource1 using the following markup:

```
<SelectParameters>
  <asp:ControlParameter ControlID="DropDownList1"
    Name="ManufacturerID" PropertyName="SelectedValue" />
</SelectParameters>
```

The `<SelectParameters>` element indicates that all the parameters that you're adding here are to be applied to the `SelectCommand` of the data source. You add one parameter here, a `ControlParameter`, which takes its value from another Web control on the page. Table 3-2 lists the various parameters you can use. We'll come back to these in more detail in later chapters, where you'll see a lot more examples of using parameters, but for now we'll concentrate on the `ControlParameter`, the one you're using here.

Table 3-2. *Query Parameter Types*

Name	Description
ControlParameter	Takes its value from another Web control on the same page. The Web control to use is specified by ControlID, and the property on the Web control to retrieve the value from is indicated by PropertyName.
CookieParameter	Uses a value specified in a cookie, indicated by the CookieName attribute, to set the value of the parameter.
FormParameter	Uses a value specified in a form variable, indicated by the FormName attribute, to set the value of the parameter.
QueryStringParameter	Uses a value in the page's query string, indicated by the QueryStringField attribute, to set the value of the parameter.
SessionParameter	Uses a value in the user's session, indicated by the SessionField attribute, to set the value of the parameter.

All parameters, irrespective of their type, must specify a Name property, which is the name used to refer to the parameter within the query. You set a name of ManufacturerID here, and this will be passed to the query as @ManufacturerID. The leading @ is added automatically by the SqlClient data provider; if you were to add it to the name in the parameter definition, the result would be @@ManufacturerID, which isn't what you want.

■**Note** Several other properties are common across all the parameter types. In most instances, you won't need to use them. However, one that can be quite important is the DefaultValue parameter, which sets the value that is used if the parameter that you've defined cannot be evaluated. Examples of all of these properties are available in the MSDN documentation.

For the rest of the parameter definition, you use the ControlID and PropertyName attributes to specify the Web control to interrogate and the property you want from the Web control. You're filtering the Players based on a Manufacturer selected in the drop-down list, and so you use the name of the Web control, DropDownList1, as the ControlID. You set the PropertyName to SelectedValue, to specify from which of the Web control's properties you want to retrieve the parameter's actual value.

Try It Out: Filtering Results and Showing All Results

In the previous example, you saw how the results could be filtered, but there was no way to show the Players for all of the Manufacturers at the same time. It is possible to show both filtered and nonfiltered results using the same Web controls, as you'll see in this example. Follow these steps:

1. If you've closed Select.aspx from the previous example, reopen it.

2. Switch to Design view. Select the drop-down list, DropDownList1.

3. In the Properties window, switch to the Events view (by clicking the lightning bolt icon). Under the Data section, double-click in the DataBound event to create the DropDownList1_DataBound event handler. Enter the following code within the event:

```
DropDownList1.Items.Insert(0,
    new ListItem("-- All Manufacturers --", "0"));
```

4. Switch back to Design view and select the SqlDataSource1. Click the ellipsis in the SelectQuery property to launch the Command and Parameter Editor dialog box.

5. Click the Query Builder button and expand the Query Builder dialog box to a usable size.

6. In the list of columns in the middle of the screen, add a new column called @ManufacturerID, uncheck the Output column, and in the first Or... column, enter a value of 0. You should have the column list and SQL query shown in Figure 3-27.

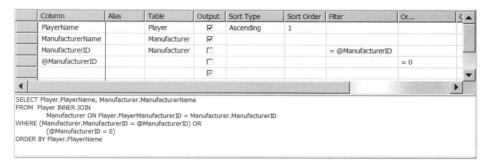

	Column	Alias	Table	Output	Sort Type	Sort Order	Filter		Or...		C
	PlayerName		Player	☑	Ascending	1					
	ManufacturerName		Manufacturer	☑							
	ManufacturerID		Manufacturer	☐			= @ManufacturerID				
	@ManufacturerID			☐					= 0		
				☑							

```
SELECT Player.PlayerName, Manufacturer.ManufacturerName
FROM  Player INNER JOIN
           Manufacturer ON Player.PlayerManufacturerID = Manufacturer.ManufacturerID
WHERE (Manufacturer.ManufacturerID = @ManufacturerID) OR
           (@ManufacturerID = 0)
ORDER BY Player.PlayerName
```

Figure 3-27. *Adding a second column to the WHERE clause*

7. Close OK to close the Query Builder, and then click OK again to close the Command and Parameter Editor dialog box.

8. Open the page. You'll see that the drop-down list has a new first entry of -- All Manufacturers --, and the grid itself is populated with the Players for all the Manufacturers, as shown in Figure 3-28.

Figure 3-28. *The Players for all Manufacturers can now be viewed.*

9. Select any of the Manufacturers from the drop-down list, and you'll see that the list of Players is still modified, depending on your selection.

How It Works

With a little more work (and our first line of code!), you've modified the page so that you can view all of the Players in the database or a list filtered by Manufacturer.

First, you changed the query to return the Players from the database by adding an OR to the WHERE clause:

```
SELECT Player.PlayerName, Manufacturer.ManufacturerName
FROM Player INNER JOIN Manufacturer
  ON Player.PlayerManufacturerID = Manufacturer.ManufacturerID
WHERE (Manufacturer.ManufacturerID = @ManufacturerID)
  OR (@ManufacturerID = 0)
ORDER BY Player.PlayerName
```

There are now two parts to the clause, and these are OR'd together; if either of the parts is true, then the row that you're dealing with will be returned.

The first part of the OR statement works as it did in the previous example: it filters the results based on the value of the @ManufacturerID parameter. The second part of the OR statement will return true if the value of the @ManufacturerID parameter is equal to 0. This isn't a valid Manufacturer in the database, and as you'll soon see, it's the value used to indicate -- All Manufacturers --.

Because this is an OR statement, the parts of the WHERE clause work together to filter the Players. If you have a @ManufacturerID that isn't 0, the Players will be filtered for that Manufacturer. If you have a @ManufacturerID of 0, all of the Players will be returned.

By populating the drop-down list with the Manufacturers from the database, it will be possible to filter the results based on the Manufacturer, but it removes the ability to not filter the results. The SELECT query on the database returns the list of Manufacturers, but it doesn't return a "no manufacturer" entry. In order to allow the user to select to view all of the Players in the database, you need to add an -- All Manufacturers -- entry to the drop-down list.

The DataBound event fires for the drop-down list after any data binding has occurred, and the OnDataBound property of the GridView is used to point to the event handler that you want to execute. In this case, DropDownList1_DataBound is called after the query to populate the list of Manufacturers has completed, and at this point, you can add the -- All Manufacturers -- entry:

```
DropDownList1.Items.Insert(0,
  new ListItem("-- All Manufacturers --", "0"));
```

You're inserting a new ListItem at position 0 to the Items collection of the drop-down list, ensuring that it's the first item in the list and that when the page first loads, all of the Players in the database (the nonfiltered results) are displayed.

In this example, you've seen that you can use the WHERE clause to restrict the records that you've returned based on the criteria you specify. Now, let's take a closer look at what else you can do with the WHERE clause.

Introducing the WHERE Clause

Not only is the WHERE clause used with the SELECT query, it can also be used with the UPDATE and DELETE queries to restrict your actions within the database. You'll look at UPDATE and DELETE queries starting in Chapter 8, but for now, you'll concentrate on what you can do with the WHERE clause. In the previous filtering examples, you've looked at comparing only two values to see if they're equal. Now, let's look at the other operators that are available.

Using Comparison Operators

Table 3-3 describes the standard comparison operators. You should be familiar with most of the comparison operators; they work in the way that you would expect.

Table 3-3. *The SQL Comparison Operators*

Operator	Definition	Example
=	Equality	`PlayerManufacturerID = 1`
<>	Inequality	`PlayerManufacturerID <> 1`
<	Less than	`PlayerManufacturerID < 3`
>	Greater than	`PlayerManufacturerID > 4`
<=	Less than or equal to	`PlayerManufacturerID <= 3`
>=	Greater than or equal to	`PlayerManufacturerID >= 4`
IS NULL	Test for null values	`PlayerManufacturerID IS NULL`

The only comparison operator that you may not be unfamiliar with is the `IS NULL` operator. Null values in the database can't be compared to any other value and won't appear in any comparison. So, if you execute the following query, you would expect to return every Player that had a `PlayerManufacturerID` of any value other than 1:

```
SELECT PlayerName
FROM Player
WHERE PlayerManufacturerID <> 1
```

However, this isn't the case, and if null values are allowed for PlayerManufacturerID, you would need to test for this condition explicitly, like so:

```
SELECT PlayerName
FROM Player
WHERE PlayerManufacturerID <> 1 OR PlayerManufacturerID IS NULL
```

This will return the correct results: Players that have a PlayerManufacturerID that isn't equal to 1 and Players that have a null value for PlayerManufacturerID.

Using Logical Operators

You've already seen the `OR` logical operator in action when you filtered the results in the previous example, and I sneaked it in again at the end of the discussion of comparison operators. Table 3-4 lists all of the SQL logical operators.

Table 3-4. *The SQL Logical Operators*

Operator	Definition	Usage
AND	Returns true if both conditions are true	a AND b
OR	Returns true if either condition is true	a OR b
NOT	Returns true if the condition is false	NOT a

Using the IN and BETWEEN Operators

SQL also defines two other handy operators that you can use within the WHERE clause to make some of the clauses that you need to execute a little simpler.

The IN operator allows you to specify that you're looking within a series of noncontiguous values and is equivalent to using the OR operator to chain together several different equality comparisons. For example, to return all the Players that have a PlayerManufacturerID of 1, 3, or 5, you could execute the following query:

```
SELECT PlayerName, PlayerManufacturerID
FROM Player
WHERE PlayerManufacturerID = 1
  OR PlayerManufacturerID = 3
  OR PlayerManufacturerID = 5
```

The IN operator allows you to do this more simply:

```
SELECT PlayerName, PlayerManufacturerID
FROM Player
WHERE PlayerManufacturerID IN (1,3,5)
```

Both queries will return the same results, as shown in Figure 3-29.

PlayerName	PlayerManufacturerID
iPod Shuffle	1
iFP-700 Series	3
iFP-900 Series	3
Forge	5
iPod	1

Figure 3-29. *Selecting from a series of values using the IN operator*

Similarly, you can use the BETWEEN operator to specify that you're looking within a contiguous range of values. If you wanted to return all the Players that have a PlayerManufacturerID of 3, 4, or 5, you could use the AND, <=, and >= operators in conjunction to retrieve the correct Players:

```
SELECT PlayerName, PlayerManufacturerID
FROM Player
WHERE PlayerManufacturerID >= 3 AND PlayerManufacturerID <= 5
```

The BETWEEN operator allows you to simplify this, like so:

```
SELECT PlayerName, PlayerManufacturerID
FROM Player
WHERE PlayerManufacturerID BETWEEN 3 AND 5
```

Both of these queries will return the results shown in Figure 3-30.

PlayerName	PlayerManufacturerID
iFP-700 Series	3
iFP-900 Series	3
MegaPlayer 521	4
Forge	5
H10	3

Figure 3-30. *Selecting from a range of values using the BETWEEN operator*

One word of warning when using the BETWEEN operator: You'll notice that you use AND to specify the upper and lower values of the range. This isn't the same as using the AND operator as a logical comparison, so don't get the two confused.

Connecting to MySQL 5.0 and Microsoft Access

Now that we've looked at the SQL Server 2005 pages, it's time to see what the differences are when you use MySQL 5.0 and Microsoft Access pages. As I've noted earlier, when you use the SqlDataSource, you're shielded quite a lot from the intricacies of data access, so the pages to connect to the three databases are the same apart from one area: parameters to queries.

■**Note** In the code download for this chapter, and indeed for every chapter (available from the Downloads section of the Apress Web site at http://www.apress.com), you'll find two folders: odbc and oledb. The odbc folder contains a copy of the SQL Server 2005-based pages modified to connect to MySQL 5.0, and the oledb folder contains modified pages to connect to Microsoft Access.

Let's first look at the connection strings for the database types, and then review how MySQL and Access handle query parameters.

Connection Strings

So, what sort of things does a connection string contain? This depends on the data provider you're using, and in the case of OleDb and Odbc data providers, also on the underlying provider/driver you're using.

As you've already seen, the connection strings should be stored in the `<connectionStrings>` section of `Web.config`. In the code download for all of the chapters, you'll see that there are three different connection strings defined in `Web.config`:

```
<connectionStrings>
  <add name="SqlConnectionString"
    connectionString="Data Source=localhost\band;Initial Catalog=Players;
      Persist Security Info=True;User ID=band;Password=letmein"
    providerName="System.Data.SqlClient"/>
  <add name="OdbcConnectionString"
    connectionString="Driver={MySQL ODBC 3.51 Driver};
      server=localhost;database=players;uid=band;pwd=letmein;"
    providerName="System.Data.Odbc" />
  <add name="OleDbConnectionString"
    connectionString="Provider=Microsoft.Jet.OLEDB.4.0;
      Data Source=C:\band\players.mdb"
    providerName="System.Data.OleDb" />
</connectionStrings>
```

We've already looked at `SqlConnectionString` earlier in this chapter.

For the `OdbcConnectionString`, the first thing you specify is the ODBC `Driver` being used. Each driver has its own connection string specification, and if you don't specify the driver, the rest of the connection string cannot be parsed correctly.

For MySQL 5.0, the connection string must specify the `server`, `database`, `uid`, and `pwd` that are to be used to connect to the database.

The `OleDbConnectionString` specifies the OLE DB `Provider` being used, and then the connection string details specific to the provider. When using the `JET` provider to connect to Microsoft Access, you specify the `Data Source` as the filename, including the path, to the `.mdb` file.

■Note You have a multitude of options for connecting to data sources. For a comprehensive list, see `http://www.connectionstrings.com`.

Parameters and Queries

The only difference when using MySQL 5.0 or Access for the examples in this chapter involves the parameters for queries.

With named parameters, the `SqlClient` data provider can determine which parameter is required. In the examples, you used a named parameter called @ManufacturerID, and even though the parameter was used twice in the query, only one parameter was defined.

The `Odbc` data provider when connecting to MySQL and the `OleDb` data provider when connecting to any database rely on the order that the parameters are added to the `SqlDataSource` to determine how they're inserted into the query. This means that they require a slightly different query than the `SqlClient` data provider. Rather than the @ syntax to refer to a parameter, you use a question mark (?) instead, like so:

```
SELECT Player.PlayerName, Manufacturer.ManufacturerName
FROM Player INNER JOIN Manufacturer
  ON Player.PlayerManufacturerID = Manufacturer.ManufacturerID
WHERE Player.PlayerManufacturerID = ?
  OR ? = 0
```

As there are two parameters (indicated by the two question marks), you must specify two parameters, even if, as in this case, the two parameters take the same value. As these aren't named parameters, you don't need to specify a name (if you do, it will simply be ignored):

```
<SelectParameters>
  <asp:ControlParameter ControlID="DropDownList1"
    PropertyName="SelectedValue" />
  <asp:ControlParameter ControlID="DropDownList1"
    PropertyName="SelectedValue" />
</SelectParameters>
```

If you look at the two modified Select.aspx files in the odbc and oledb folders, you'll see that apart from these two changes—the change to the query and the addition of the duplicate parameter—the pages are the same.

Summary

This chapter covered quite a lot of ground. You've learned about the following:

- You were introduced to the GridView and SqlDataSource, and through the course of the examples, saw how easy it is to build data-driven pages with a minimum of code.

- You were introduced to the SELECT query by writing a simple query for one table.

- You expanded your understanding of the SELECT query by looking at ordering results and joining tables to retrieve information from both tables in the same query.

- You looked at filtering the results that you returned by using parameters with values taken from other Web controls on the page.

- You looked at the comparison and logical operators you can use with the WHERE clause and saw the IN and BETWEEN operators you can use to simplify the constraints that you add to queries.

- You looked at the connection strings that are required for the SQL Server 2005, MySQL 5.0, and Microsoft Access databases, and saw how to store all three connection strings in the <connectionStrings> element of Web.config.

- You saw that SQL Server 2005 supports the concept of named parameters where the same parameter can be used several times in the same query. With MySQL 5.0 and Microsoft Access, you need to provide a separate value for each parameter within the query, even if you want to reuse the same parameter.

Now that you've had a taste of how data-driven pages work, we'll move on to look at how you can connect to the database using code, rather than relying on the SqlDataSource to do all of the work for you.

CHAPTER 4

■ ■ ■

Database Access in Code

The previous three chapters covered the fundamentals required to start using databases. Chapter 1 showed the various types of data sources available, and you saw how you can use text files, XML files, spreadsheets, and the Active Directory store, not to mention *real* databases as data sources. Chapter 2 then moved on to talk about relational databases, and by the end of the chapter, you had fundamentally the same database in SQL Server 2005, MySQL 5.0, and Microsoft Access.

In Chapter 3, you took the first look at actually using the database in a page. You used a `GridView` to display the results returned from a `SqlDataSource` using three different databases: SQL Server 2005 using the native SQL Server provider, MySQL 5.0 using an ODBC driver, and Microsoft Access using an OLE DB provider. In all three cases, the returned results were displayed in a tabular format by the `GridView`.

But as you learned in Chapter 1, this isn't the end of the story. You have several objects that you can use to communicate with the database: Command, Connection, Parameter, DataReader, and DataAdapter. The approach you took in Chapter 3 completely hid these, and wrapped all the requests to the database inside the `SqlDataSource`. You created the correct `SqlDataSource` and `GridView` controls, and ASP.NET performed all the necessary data access automatically.

You do, however, need to be able to interact with the database in code, as there are certain things that you can't do using the `SqlDataSource`. In this chapter, we'll look at dealing directly with the database in code, rather than relying on ASP.NET to do all of this for you.

This chapter covers the following topics:

- The connection and command life cycle

- How to connect to databases using the correct Connection object (the `SqlConnection`, `OdbcConnection`, and `OleDbConnection` objects)

- Connection pooling to reuse database connections and improve performance

- How to use the Command object to modify the query that is being executed based on the user's actions

- How to use parameters to change the query being executed

- The SQL scalar functions that you can use to return information from a database

- Error handling in code to access a database

The Connection and Command Life Cycle

We can summarize the life cycle for connecting to a data source and executing queries against it as follows:

- Create the Connection object and specify the data source.

- Create the Command object.

- Tell the Command object which Connection to use.

- Specify the query to execute and pass to the Command object.

- Open the connection to the data source.

- Execute a query against the data source.

- If there are query results, you may need to do something with them.

- Close the connection to the data source.

In practice, the sequence in this list is what would ideally happen, but it isn't always the case. You can perform several of the tasks in the life cycle list in a slightly different order without causing any problems. As with most coding tasks, you can do these in several slightly different ways, and usually none of them is more correct than the others.

We're going to look at this life cycle in three stages. We'll first look at the Connection object and how to configure this to connect to the data source, and how the connection is opened and closed. Next, we'll deal with the Command object and how to configure it to use a specific Connection object and a given query. You'll see that there are several different ways that you can execute the query, depending on what the query does. The queries that we've looked at in Chapter 3 have always returned a set of results (a list of Manufacturers, for instance), and we'll spend some time looking at how to connect to the database and return a DataReader containing the set of results using the `ExecuteReader()` method.

■**Note** As you saw in Chapter 1, you can also return data using a DataAdapter to populate a `DataSet`. The DataReader is the easier method of accessing the database, and we'll concentrate on it in this chapter. In Chapter 5, we'll look at the differences between the DataReader and the `DataSet`, and in Chapter 6, we'll start using the DataAdapter and `DataSet` objects to query the database.

As you'll see, not all queries to a database produce a set of results. You can write queries that only return single values, most commonly when returning the result from a scalar function, and we'll spend some time looking at scalar functions and how you can use the `ExecuteScalar()` method to retrieve these values from the database.

You can also write queries that don't return any results at all. Any INSERT, UPDATE, or DELETE queries that you execute against the database won't return any results. You use a third method, `ExecuteNonQuery()`, to execute those queries. You'll see how to use `ExecuteNonQuery()` in Chapter 8.

Connection Objects

As you saw in Chapter 1, the data provider for a particular data source contains implementations of several objects. Each of these objects handles a specific task, and a Connection object, unsurprisingly, handles a connection to a data source. The Connection object (as was the case with traditional ADO) is the basis for all interactions with the data source you want to use. You must open the connection before you access the data source, and you must close it when you're finished.

■**Note** Unlike with traditional ADO, you must always create a Connection object when talking to a data source. With ADO, you could pass an ADODB.Connection object or a connection string to an ADODB. Command object, but when using ADO.NET, you must create an instance of a Connection object and pass this to the Command object.

Again, as you saw in Chapter 1, the data provider architecture allows a data provider to be specifically designed for a data source. Here, we'll look at three implementations of the Connection object:

- The `SqlConnection` object to connect to a SQL Server database

- The `OdbcConnection` object to connect to a data source using an ODBC driver

- The `OleDbConnection` object to connect to a data source using an OLE DB provider

---

■**Note** If you're trying to connect to SQL Server version 6.5, you can't use the `SqlConnection` object because it works with only SQL Server version 7.0 and newer. With SQL Server 6.5, use the `OleDbConnection` object and the OLE DB provider for SQL Server.

Try It Out: Connecting to SQL Server 2005 Using SqlConnection

To connect to a SQL Server 2005 database, you use the `SqlConnection` object. As this is part of the `SqlClient` data provider, you can assume that it's the quickest way of accessing the database.

In this example, you'll use the `SqlConnection` object to connect to the database and the `SqlCommand` object to return all of the Players that are in the database.

1. Start Visual Web Developer and create a new Web site in the `C:\BAND\Chapter04` folder. Delete the auto-created `Default.aspx` file.

2. Add a new `Web.config` file by selecting Add New Item from the Web site's context menu. Click Web Configuration File, and then click the Add button.

3. Find the `<connectionStrings />` element in `Web.config` and replace it with the following:

```
<connectionStrings>
  <add name="SqlConnectionString"
    connectionString="Data Source=localhost\BAND;Initial Catalog=Players;
    User ID=band;Password=letmein" />
</connectionStrings>
```

4. Add a Web Form by selecting the Add New Item option from the Web site's context menu. Click Web Form and make sure that the Place Code in Separate File option is unselected and Visual C# is selected as the Language. Give the page a name of Select.aspx and click the Add button.

5. In the Source view of the page, change the `<TITLE>` element to **Displaying Data with SqlClient**. Then add the following to the top of the page after the `<% Page %>` tag:

```
<%@ Import Namespace="System.Data" %>
<%@ Import Namespace="System.Data.SqlClient" %>
```

6. Switch to the Design view of the page and add a GridView from the Data tab of the Toolbox onto the page. (If the Toolbox is not visible, select View ➤ Toolbox.)

7. From the GridView Tasks menu, select AutoFormat and choose the Colorful scheme. (If you don't like that scheme, choose a different one.)

8. Double-click somewhere on the page that isn't the GridView to add a Page_Load event to the page. Add the following code to the event handler:

```
protected void Page_Load(object sender, EventArgs e)
{
  if (Page.IsPostBack == false)
  {
    // create the connection
    string strConnectionString = ConfigurationManager.
      ConnectionStrings["SqlConnectionString"].ConnectionString;
    SqlConnection myConnection =
      new SqlConnection(strConnectionString);

    // create the command
    string strCommandText = "SELECT Player.PlayerName, ➡
      Manufacturer.ManufacturerName FROM Player INNER JOIN ➡
      Manufacturer ON Player.PlayerManufacturerID = ➡
      Manufacturer.ManufacturerID ORDER BY Player.PlayerName";
    SqlCommand myCommand =
      new SqlCommand(strCommandText, myConnection);

    // open the database connection
    myConnection.Open();
```

```
      // show the data
      GridView1.DataSource = myCommand.ExecuteReader();
      GridView1.DataBind();

      // close the database connection
      myConnection.Close();
    }
}
```

9. In the Solution Explorer, right-click Select.aspx and select Set As Start Page.

10. Run the Web site. If you're presented with the Debugging Not Enabled dialog box, click OK to modify Web.config and start debugging. This will load your browser and display the page as shown in Figure 4-1.

Figure 4-1. *Results of the query using the SqlConnection object*

How It Works

That wasn't too hard was it? You needed only seven lines of code to connect to the database, retrieve the data, and then bind the results returned to the GridView for display. Let's start by looking at using a SqlConnection.

First, you added a connection string for the SQL Server database that you'll use in the connectionStrings section of Web.config:

```
<add name="SqlConnectionString"
  connectionString="Data Source=localhost\BAND;Initial Catalog=Players;
  User ID=band;Password=letmein"/>
```

This is similar to the connection strings that you used in Chapter 3. The only difference is the absence of the providerName property here. The providerName property is used by the SqlDataSource to decide which Connection and Command objects to use, but as you're manually specifying the Connection and Command objects in this example, you don't need this property. To use the same connection string in both situations, you can simply add the correct providerName to the connection string.

Before you can use any of the database objects, you must reference the namespaces that contain those objects. You could use fully referenced names to refer to them, but this requires a lot of typing and some unwieldy lines of code. As you saw in Chapter 1, a general namespace exists for all the data objects and a namespace exists for the SQL Server-specific objects. You included a reference to both of these namespaces, which allows you to refer to the objects using much shorter names:

```
<%@ Import Namespace="System.Data" %
<%@ Import Namespace="System.Data.SqlClient" %>
```

Because the page needs to populate the GridView when the page is loaded, you need to use the page's Page_Load event. The Page_Load event handler executes every time the page is loaded (whether a first view or a postback responding to a request from the user). In data-driven Web sites, you'll want to perform some actions only once, such as populating the GridView, rather than every time the page is loaded. You can check for the type of page request using the IsPostBack property of the Page object, which returns true if there has been a postback because of a user request.

The GridView remembers the data that it's populated with, so you need to populate it only once. First, you check that the page is not responding to a postback from the client by seeing if the IsPostBack property is false. If it is, you're showing the page for the first time, and you execute the code to populate the GridView.

The first line of code retrieves the connection string, SqlConnectionString, that you're going to use from the Web site configuration and stores this in the strConnectionString local variable:

```
string strConnectionString = ConfigurationManager.
  ConnectionStrings["SqlConnectionString"].ConnectionString;
```

The ConfigurationManager.ConnectionStrings property accepts the name of the connection string that you want and returns a ConnectionStringSettings object that contains the details specified in Web.config for the connection string. There's a Name property for the name element, a ProviderName property for the providerName element, and—the one you're after— a ConnectionString property for the connectionString element.

Once the connection string has been populated, it's time to create the SqlConnection object and point it at the correct database. You do this by passing the connection string into the constructor, like so:

```
SqlConnection myConnection = new SqlConnection(strConnectionString);
```

■**Note** Although you pass the connection string into the constructor to initialize it, you can create a connection without passing in a connection string. In this case, you must set the ConnectionString property of the Connection object to the correct connection string before you attempt to open the connection.

The next two lines of code are concerned with the query that you pass to the database and the SqlCommand object that you use to actually execute the query. We'll come back to this when we discuss the Command object later in the chapter; for now, just be assured that it works. However, you should recognize the query—you saw it in the previous chapter. It returns all of the Players in the database along with the name of the Manufacturer, in Player name order.

Although you've now created a SqlConnection object to connect to the database and the SqlCommand object to query the database, you still haven't made the connection to the database. Only a finite number of database connections are available, and you shouldn't open a connection if you're not actually doing anything with it. While you have the connection open, you're preventing everyone else from using that connection. The connection should be opened at the last possible moment by calling the Open() method on the SqlConnection object, like so:

```
myConnection.Open();
```

Once the connection is opened, you carry out the tasks on the data. In this case, you're doing a little data binding:

```
GridView1.DataSource = myCommand.ExecuteReader();
GridView1.DataBind();
```

Once you're finished with the connection to the database, you should close the connection to the database as soon as it isn't required anymore. Again, keeping it open once you're finished with it prevents anyone else from using that connection. To close the database connection, use the Close() method, like so:

```
myConnection.Close();
```

That's all there is to connecting to the database. You've created a connection, opened the connection, and then closed it. It doesn't get any more complex than that.

Try It Out: Connecting to MySQL 5.0 Using OdbcConnection

For some data sources, such as SQL Server, you'll have a native data provider to use. In a production environment, you should always use the specific data provider if one is available. If one isn't available, then you need to use the OleDb or Odbc data provider with the correct OLE DB provider or ODBC driver for your database.

Indeed, MySQL has its own data provider that you can download from the MySQL Web site at http://dev.mysql.com/downloads/connector/net/1.0.html. However, we're going to forgo the native data provider (until Chapter 10 anyway) and connect through the Odbc data provider using the MySQL ODBC driver.

Using the OdbcConnection object to connect to a MySQL database is no different from using the SqlConnection object to talk to a SQL Server database. The same is also true if you were to use the MySqlClient data provider (MySqlConnection) or OleDb data provider (OleDbConnection) to connect to using an OLE DB provider. Although you use different objects, the methodology remains the same.

In this example, you'll build the same page as in the previous example, but using the OdbcConnection object to talk to a MySQL database. Follow these steps:

1. Start Visual Web Developer and open the Chapter04 Web site from C:\BAND\Chapter04.

2. Open Web.config and add a new connection string to the connection string element:

```
<add name="OdbcConnectionString"
  connectionString="Driver={MySQL ODBC 3.51 Driver};
    server=localhost;database=players;uid=band;pwd=letmein;" />
```

3. Create a new folder called odbc and add a new Web Form called Select.aspx to the folder.

4. In the Source view of the page, change the <TITLE> element to **Displaying Data with Odbc**. Then add the following to the top of the page after the <% Page %> tag:

```
<%@ Import Namespace="System.Data" %>
<%@ Import Namespace="System.Data.Odbc" %>
```

5. Switch to the Design view of the page and add a GridView to the page. Set its AutoFormat property to Colorful (or another scheme that takes your fancy).

6. Double-click somewhere on the page that isn't the GridView to add a Load event to the page. Add the following code to the event:

```
protected void Page_Load(object sender, EventArgs e)
{
  if (Page.IsPostBack == false)
  {
    // create the connection
    string strConnectionString = ConfigurationManager.
      ConnectionStrings["OdbcConnectionString"].ConnectionString;
    OdbcConnection myConnection =
      new OdbcConnection(strConnectionString);

    // create the command
    string strCommandText = "SELECT Player.PlayerName, ➥
      Manufacturer.ManufacturerName FROM Player INNER JOIN ➥
      Manufacturer ON Player.PlayerManufacturerID = ➥
      Manufacturer.ManufacturerID ORDER BY Player.PlayerName";
    OdbcCommand myCommand = new
      OdbcCommand(strCommandText, myConnection);

    // open the database connection
    myConnection.Open();
```

```
      // show the data
      GridView1.DataSource = myCommand.ExecuteReader();
      GridView1.DataBind();

      // close the database connection
      myConnection.Close();
    }
  }
```

7. Right-click Select.aspx in the odbc folder in the Solution Explorer and select View in Browser. This will launch your browser and display the results for the query, as shown in Figure 4-2.

Figure 4-2. *Results of the query using the OdbcConnection object*

How It Works

If you compare the code for the previous example and this one, you'll see they're similar.

In order to connect to the MySQL database, you need to add a new connection string to Web.config. This time, it's simplicity itself:

```
<add name="OdbcConnectionString"
  connectionString="Driver={MySQL ODBC 3.51 Driver};
    server=localhost;database=players;uid=band;pwd=letmein;" />
```

You create a new connection string with the name OdbcConnectionString and tell it that you're using the MySQL ODBC driver. As you'll recall from Chapter 3, you can use this driver by specifying the server, database, uid, and pwd that you want to use to connect to the database.

First, you include the correct namespaces in the page. You again use System.Data to allow access to the base data objects, but instead of the System.Data.SqlClient namespace, you use the System.Data.Odbc namespace, like so:

```
<%@ Import Namespace="System.Data" %>
<%@ Import Namespace="System.Data.Odbc" %>
```

The connection string is retrieved from Web.config in the same way as the previous example, except that you're retrieving the OdbcConnectionString setting rather than the SqlConnectionString. You store this in the strConnectionString local variable so that you can use it in the constructor of the OdbcConnection object:

```
OdbcConnection myConnection = new OdbcConnection(strConnectionString);
```

You pass in the connection string you want to use as the only parameter to the OdbcConnection object constructor, and you have a properly configured Connection object that you can use. This is exactly the same process as with the SqlConnection object.

As with the first example, the next two lines of code don't really concern us at the moment, but you will notice that you're using the OdbcCommand object rather than the SqlCommand object.

You then open the connection to the database using the Open() method, do the necessary data binding using the OdbcCommand object you created and configured, and then close the database connection using the Close() method.

From this brief description, you can see that the process for creating and using the objects to communicate with MySQL using an ODBC driver is the same as that for communicating with SQL Server. Once you had the correct connection string defined, you could have simply copied the page from the previous example and replaced all references to Sql objects in the Page_Load event with their Odbc equivalents, and the code would have worked perfectly.

As the databases in SQL Server 2005 and MySQL 5.0 contain the exact same data, the results of executing this page are identical to those of the previous example, as you'll see if you compare Figure 4-2 with Figure 4-1.

Try It Out: Connecting to Microsoft Access Using OleDbConnection

The easiest way to connect to an Access database is by using the Microsoft Jet database engine, more commonly known as the Jet engine, which is an OLE DB provider. You can access this provider using the OleDbConnection object. The Jet engine allows you to connect to various other data sources, such as dBASE and Paradox databases, Excel spreadsheets, and text files.

Note Since the release of MDAC 2.6, the Jet engine isn't installed as standard. Therefore, if you don't have Microsoft Access installed, you may not have it. You can download the latest version of the Jet engine, Service Pack 8, from `http://support.microsoft.com/?kbid=239114`.

In this example, you'll build the same page as in the previous two examples, but this time use the `OleDbConnection` object to talk to a Microsoft Access database. Follow these steps:

1. Start Visual Web Developer and open the Chapter04 Web site from `C:\BAND\Chapter04`.

2. Open `Web.config` and add a new connection string to the connection string element:

   ```
   <add name="OleDbConnectionString"
     connectionString="Provider=Microsoft.Jet.OLEDB.4.0;
     Data Source=C:\BAND\Players.mdb" />
   ```

3. Create a new folder called `oledb` and copy the `Select.aspx` page from the `odbc` folder to this new folder.

4. Open the `Select.aspx` page in the `oledb` folder and change the `<TITLE>` element to **Displaying Data with OleDb**.

5. Change the `Import` for the `Odbc` namespace to its `OleDb` equivalent:

   ```
   <%@ Import Namespace="System.Data.OleDb" %>
   ```

6. In the `Page_Load` event, you need to change from using the `Odbc` objects to the `OleDb` equivalents. You also need to use the correct connection string. The changed lines are as follows:

   ```
   string strConnectionString = ConfigurationManager.
     ConnectionStrings["OleDbConnectionString"].ConnectionString;
   OleDbConnection myConnection = new OleDbConnection(strConnectionString);

   ...

   OleDbCommand myCommand = new OleDbCommand(strCommandText, myConnection);
   ```

7. Right-click `Select.aspx` in the `oledb` folder in the Solution Explorer and select View in Browser. This will launch your browser and display the results for the query, as shown in Figure 4-3.

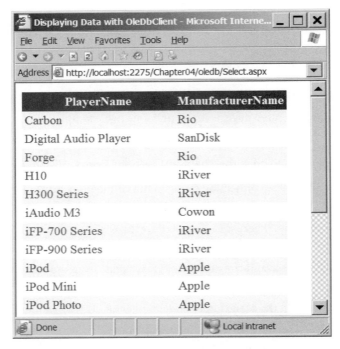

Figure 4-3. *Results of the query using the OleDbConnection object*

How It Works

This time, you really did just replace the Odbc objects with their OleDb equivalents to get the code to work with the different database objects—did you really want to build the same exact page again? All you've needed to do was use the correct connection string, and then change from using the OdbcConnection and OdbcCommand objects to the OleDbConnection and OleDbCommand objects.

As you can see if you compare the results of all three examples, the page returned is exactly the same, regardless of the data source and method of accessing the data source.

Connection Object Methods and Properties

You've already seen two of the methods of the Connection object, Open() and Close(). Now, you'll look at a couple of properties that come in quite handy: ConnectionString and State.

Other properties and methods are available on every implementation of the Connection object, including a common set of properties and methods (inherited from the DbConnection abstract class) that each Connection object implements. Additionally, each object can also implement its own properties and methods. Several are rarely used, and others will never be used except in very advanced situations. If you need further details, you can find more information on MSDN at the following locations:

- SqlConnection:
  http://msdn.microsoft.com/en-us/library/system.data.sqlclient.sqlconnection.aspx

- OdbcConnection:
  http://msdn.microsoft.com/en-us/library/system.data.odbc.odbcconnection.aspx

- OleDbConnection:
  http://msdn.microsoft.com/en-us/library/system.data.oledb.oledbconnection.aspx

The ConnectionString Property

In the examples you've looked at so far, you've always created the Connection object by passing the connection string to the constructor. The Connection object also exposes the ConnectionString property, which you can use instead to specify the connection string after you've created the Connection object. So, for the first example in this chapter, you could have used the alternative method of setting the connection string, like so:

```
SqlConnection myConnection = new SqlConnection();
myConnection.ConnectionString = strConnectionString;
```

The State Property

One of the more useful properties of the Connection object is the State property. This allows you to check the state of the connection to the data source. The State property is read-only and may take, in the current release of the .NET runtime, a value of ConnectionState.Open or ConnectionState.Closed.

Connection Pooling

When connecting to a database, several time-consuming tasks must be performed before the connection can be classed as open. A physical connection to the database is created, the login details parsed and authenticated against the database, and so on. If this occurred every time you connected to the database, the connection preparation time soon mounts up.

In your Web site, you will probably use a limited number of different databases, or maybe only one database. This is where *connection pooling* can help.

Connection pooling works under the covers and creates a pool of connections that are used when you call the Open() method on the Connection object. When you call the Open() method, the data provider will look to see if there are any connections in the pool. If there are, then a pooled connection will be reused. If not, the data provider will create a new connection to the database. On closing the connection with the Close() method, the connection will not actually be closed yet. It will be returned to the pool to be used again on another call to the Open() method.

So how do you enable connection pooling? The answer is you don't. If your data provider supports connection pooling, it will be enabled by default. But it does depend on which data provider you're using:

- The SqlClient data provider uses connection pooling for all connections to the database.

- The OleDb data provider will use connection pooling if the underlying OLE DB provider supports it.

- Connection pooling for ODBC drivers is controlled at the ODBC level and not within the Odbc data provider. If the ODBC driver has connection pooling enabled, it will be enabled.

The key to connection pooling is the connection string that you use for the Connection object. Each different connection string has its own connection pool, and if the connection strings you're using differ, even very slightly, connections will not be reused across the connection pools.

So if you have one SqlConnection object using this:

```
Data Source=localhost\BAND;Initial Catalog=Players;User ID=band;Password=letmein;
```

And you have another SqlConnection object using this:

```
Server=localhost\BAND;database=Players;uid=band;pwd=letmein;
```

The two SqlConnection objects will not be able to use the same connection pool, because the connection strings are different—even though they go to the exact same database on the same server with the same security credentials.

For now, you should just be aware that connection pooling can happen. Be sure to keep connections to the database open for the minimum amount of time, by opening the connection at the last opportunity before you need it and closing the connection at the first opportunity once you're finished with it.

Command Objects

In the examples so far, you've used a Connection object to connect to the database. You then have two lines of code that create the correct Command object. For the SqlConnection version of the code, the SqlCommand object was created as follows:

```
// create the command
string strCommandText = "SELECT Player.PlayerName, ➥
  Manufacturer.ManufacturerName FROM Player INNER JOIN ➥
  Manufacturer ON Player.PlayerManufacturerID = ➥
  Manufacturer.ManufacturerID ORDER BY Player.PlayerName";
SqlCommand myCommand = new SqlCommand(strCommandText, myConnection);
```

In this code, you've simply created a string, strCommandText, to hold the query that you want to execute, and passed both strCommandText and myConnection (the connection to the database that you created) to the constructor of the SqlCommand object.

In this section, the discussion will focus on the SqlClient data provider. However, everything that's discussed in relation to SqlClient is equally applicable to the OleDb and Odbc data providers. Where you prefix objects with Sql, you can, unless noted, replace these with an OleDb or Odbc version of the same object. I'll point out when the code required is slightly different depending on which database you're using.

■**Note** In the code download for each of the chapters (available from the Downloads section of the Apress Web site at http://www.apress.com), you'll find odbc and oledb folders that contain the corresponding code for MySQL 5.0 and Microsoft Access.

Creating a Command Object

Creating a Command object is straightforward. In the code that you've already used in this chapter, you saw one way of doing this: by passing the query and connection to the Command object constructor.

The SqlCommand object has four constructors:

- SqlCommand(): This constructor creates a Command object that has nothing configured, and you must, at a minimum, specify a connection to use and the query you want to execute. You can specify these by using the Connection and CommandText properties.

- SqlCommand(string): This allows you to specify the query you want to execute, although you'll still need to provide a connection, using the Connection property.

- SqlCommand(string, SqlConnection): This specifies both the query you want to execute and the connection you want to use.

- SqlCommand(string, SqlConnection, SqlTransaction): This allows you to specify, along with the connection and query, the transaction in which you want to participate. You'll look at transactions in more detail in Chapter 12.

You can use whichever version of the constructor you prefer, or as Microsoft likes to say, "You have a lifestyle choice."

In the previous examples, you've used the two-parameter version, like so:

```
SqlCommand myCommand = new SqlCommand(strCommandText, myConnection);
```

This is equivalent to the following:

```
SqlCommand myCommand = new SqlCommand(strCommandText);
myCommand.Connection = myConnection;
```

This is also equivalent to the following:

```
SqlCommand myCommand = new SqlCommand();
myCommand.CommandText = strCommandText;
myCommand.Connection = myConnection;
```

There is also a fifth way of creating a SqlCommand object: get the SqlConnection object do it for you. Using the CreateCommand() method of the SqlConnection object creates a SqlCommand object with its Connection property already set to the correct connection, like so:

```
SqlCommand myCommand = myConnection.CreateCommand();
myCommand.CommandText = strCommandText;
```

All the different methods available for creating the SqlCommand object may seem confusing at first. Just pick one that you're comfortable with and stick to it. You won't have any problems as long as you remember to set all the necessary properties before you open the connection and attempt to execute the query against the database.

When you're executing queries directly against the database, the two-parameter version is the one that requires the least number of lines of code, so that's the form you'll continue to use for the rest of the chapter.

Returning the Results

Once the SqlCommand object has been created correctly, you can use the ExecuteReader() method to return the results that you want to display as a SqlDataReader object. You can use this object directly as a data source for the GridView, so you pass it directly into the DataSource property:

```
// show the data
GridView1.DataSource = myCommand.ExecuteReader();
GridView1.DataBind();
```

We'll take a much more detailed look at the SqlDataReader object in Chapter 5. For now, it's enough to know that it returns a read-only, forward-only view of the results of the query.

Once the DataSource for the GridView is set, you call the DataBind() method to actually populate the GridView with the results. Without this call, no results will be shown, as the automatic data binding that you saw when using the SqlDataSource doesn't apply when you set the DataSource manually. We'll look at data binding in great detail in Chapters 6 and 7. For now, you can just rely on the fact that it works.

Filtering the Results

So far in this chapter, you've looked at the basics of connecting to a data source, executing a query, and returning the results to the page. However, you've hard-coded the query that you want to execute, so it's not very dynamic. You can show the Players for all of the Manufacturers, but you don't have any way to filter those results to show only the Players for a single Manufacturer.

You can filter the results of a query by using a WHERE clause to constrain the records that are returned. You can do this in two ways:

- By modifying the query that you're executing at runtime and specifying the variables within the WHERE clause directly

- By placing parameters within the WHERE clause of the query at design time and changing the values of these parameters at runtime

You'll look at each of these methods in turn.

Try It Out: Modifying the Query

In this example, you'll build on the previous example and allow the user to select the Manufacturer of interest. Once a selection has been made, only the Players for that Manufacturer will be returned. Follow these steps:

1. If you've closed Select.aspx from the root of the Chapter04 Web site, reopen it.

2. Switch to the Design view of the page and add a DropDownList to the top of the page, above the GridView that is already there.

3. From the DropDownList Tasks menu, check the Enable AutoPostPack option, as shown in Figure 4-4.

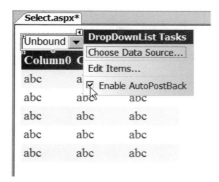

Figure 4-4. *Enabling the DropDownList to post back automatically*

4. Double-click the DropDownList to add the SelectedIndexChanged event. Add the following code (this is pretty much what is in the Page_Load event so you could copy it and modify the bits that are changed to avoid any extra typing):

```
protected void DropDownList1_SelectedIndexChanged(object sender, EventArgs e)
{
  // create the connection
  string strConnectionString = ConfigurationManager.
    ConnectionStrings["SqlConnectionString"].ConnectionString;
  SqlConnection myConnection = new SqlConnection(strConnectionString);

  // build the basic query
  string strCommandText = "SELECT Player.PlayerName, ➥
    Manufacturer.ManufacturerName FROM Player INNER JOIN ➥
    Manufacturer ON Player.PlayerManufacturerID = ➥
    Manufacturer.ManufacturerID";

  // add the filter
  string filterValue = DropDownList1.SelectedValue;
  if (filterValue != "0")
  {
    strCommandText += " WHERE Player.PlayerManufacturerID = " + filterValue;
  }

  // add the ordering
  strCommandText += " ORDER BY Player.PlayerName";

  // create the command
  SqlCommand myCommand = new SqlCommand(strCommandText, myConnection);

  // open the database connection
  myConnection.Open();
```

```
      // show the data
      GridView1.DataSource = myCommand.ExecuteReader();
      GridView1.DataBind();

      // close the database connection
      myConnection.Close();
  }
```

5. Replace the code within the Page_Load event with the following (again, you could just amend what is already there to avoid any unnecessary typing):

```
protected void Page_Load(object sender, EventArgs e)
{
  if (Page.IsPostBack == false)
  {
    // create the connection
    string strConnectionString = ConfigurationManager.
      ConnectionStrings["SqlConnectionString"].ConnectionString;
    SqlConnection myConnection = new SqlConnection(strConnectionString);

    // create the command
    string strCommandText = "SELECT ManufacturerID, ManufacturerName ➥
      FROM Manufacturer ORDER BY ManufacturerName";
    SqlCommand myCommand = new SqlCommand(strCommandText, myConnection);

    // open the database connection
    myConnection.Open();

    // show the data
    DropDownList1.DataSource = myCommand.ExecuteReader();
    DropDownList1.DataTextField = "ManufacturerName";
    DropDownList1.DataValueField = "ManufacturerID";
    DropDownList1.DataBind();

    // close the database connection
    myConnection.Close();

    // force the first data bind
    DropDownList1_SelectedIndexChanged(null,null);
  }
}
```

6. Switch back to the Design view of the page. Select the DropDownList and from the Properties window, add a DataBound event by double-clicking the DataBound entry.

7. Add the following code to the DataBound event:

```
protected void DropDownList1_DataBound(object sender, EventArgs e)
{
   DropDownList1.Items.Insert(0, new ListItem("-- All Manufacturers --", "0"));
}
```

8. Execute the page. On the first load of the page, you'll see that the GridView displays a list of all of the Players for all the Manufacturers, as shown in Figure 4-5.

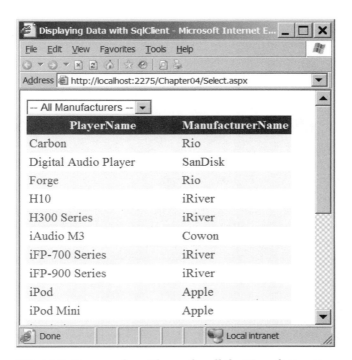

Figure 4-5. *You can show Players for all the Manufacturers.*

9. If you expand the drop-down list, you'll see that it contains all of the Manufacturers in the database. Select Apple from the drop-down list. This will post the page back to the server and execute the DropDownList1_SelectedIndexChanged event handler, populating the GridView with the Players manufactured by Apple, as shown in Figure 4-6.

Figure 4-6. *You can filter the Players by Manufacturer.*

10. Select any of the other Manufacturers to see that the list of Players is indeed modified to display only the correct list. Select -- All Manufacturers -- to see that the page shows all the Players in the database when that option is selected.

How It Works

Here, you've built the same page as you did in the examples in Chapter 3, but using code to query the database instead of the SqlDataSource. The code that you've built is executed in three different event handlers: Page_Load, DataBound, and SelectedIndexChanged. We'll look at each of these in turn.

The Page_Load Event

The Page_Load event handler executes every time the page is loaded, and you want to populate the list of Manufacturers when this occurs. However, you don't want to repopulate the Manufacturers every time the page is loaded; the drop-down list remembers what data it contains automatically, so there is no need to reconnect to the database again to retrieve the list of Manufacturers. You check that the page is not a postback and populate the list of Manufacturers only if this is the first load of the page.

The data-access code is remarkably similar to all of the other code that you've seen so far. You create a connection to the database, specify the query you want to execute, and then set the DataSource for DropDownList1 to the query results by using the ExecuteReader() method.

The query that you're executing to retrieve the results is a simple one that you've already looked at in Chapter 3:

```
SELECT ManufacturerID, ManufacturerName
FROM Manufacturer
ORDER BY ManufacturerName
```

You retrieve the ManufacturerID and ManufacturerName from the Manufacturer table, ordering the results by ManufacturerName. Looking at the query should give you a clue as to what the two new lines of code introduced here are for:

```
DropDownList1.DataTextField = "ManufacturerName";
DropDownList1.DataValueField = "ManufacturerID";
```

We'll look at data binding in a lot more detail in Chapters 6 and 7, but you need to understand what the DataTextField and DataValueField properties do. All list Web controls, of which the DropDownList is one, show a text description for each row returned and have a "hidden" value that is returned whenever you want to know what the selected value is. The DataTextField and DataValueField properties are used to set what is displayed and what is returned.

You've set the DataTextField value to be ManufacturerName, as this is what will make sense to the user; showing a numeral such as 2 as a ManufacturerName is meaningless. Similarly, the numeral that you don't want to show the user makes sense as the value of the Web control. The ManufacturerID is a value you can easily search for within the database, as it's the primary key for the Manufacturer table and is used as a foreign key within the Player table.

Once you've set these values, you can call the DataBind() method on the drop-down list to populate the list.

Once the data binding is complete, you can then close the connection to the database and call the DropDownList1_SelectedIndexChanged event handler to force the GridView to be populated.

The DataBound Event

As you'll recall from the previous chapter, when the data binding has completed, the DataBound event is fired for the Web control. This occurs during the execution of the DataBind() method in Page_Load; execution will move from Page_Load to the DataBound event handler and then back once the event handler is complete.

As you're retrieving the data from the database, you won't get an -- All Manufacturers -- entry automatically. Therefore, you need to manually add one at the start of the list. The Manufacturers in the database have an ID value of 1 and upwards, so you add the -- All Manufacturers -- entry with a value of 0, which won't match a real Manufacturer in the database.

The SelectedIndexChanged Event

Unlike the data binding you saw in Chapter 3, Web controls are not automatically data-bound when using code to query the database. You must manually tell the Web controls to bind to their data source using the DataBind() method. As you'll soon see, all of the code to populate the GridView is contained within the DropDownList1_SelectedIndexChanged event handler, so you call it manually, passing in null as both parameters. Although you're calling the event handler, this doesn't cause the page to postback to execute the handler. An event handler is just a normal method that is called by ASP.NET to respond to a particular event. You're free to call this from your own code if you desire.

The `DropDownList1_SelectedIndexChanged` event handler is used to populate the `GridView` with the list of Players based on the Manufacturer the user selected and is the part of the code that is of most interest now.

Unlike in the previous examples, here the query is built dynamically based on the user's selection. The first part of the query is as follows:

```
SELECT Player.PlayerName, Manufacturer.ManufacturerName
FROM Player INNER JOIN Manufacturer
  ON Player.PlayerManufacturerID = Manufacturer.ManufacturerID
```

This is a perfectly valid query in its own right, and it will return all the Players in the database, regardless of the Manufacturer. In fact, it's the same query as you used in the previous example with the `ORDER BY` clause removed. If you recall the `SELECT` syntax from Chapter 3, you'll remember that the `WHERE` clause to constrain the query must come before the `ORDER BY` clause— you must filter the query before you can order it—and you need to remove the `ORDER BY` clause so that you can add the `WHERE` clause.

To constrain the query, you first retrieve the value of the user's selection from the drop-down list using the `SelectedValue` property. You store this in a local variable, `filterValue`, because you'll use it in several places, like so:

```
string filterValue = DropDownList1.SelectedValue;
```

You've stored this value because you can't simply use it to constrain the query—if you've requested all the Manufacturers, you don't want to add a constraint. You'll recall that you added an -- All Manufacturers -- entry to the drop-down list, and if you've selected this, you want to return all the Players in the database as opposed to a list of Players for a particular Manufacturer. It's when a Manufacturer has been selected that you want to modify the query. You can check whether a specific Manufacturer has been selected by checking for a value that's nonzero. If it's nonzero, you want to add a `WHERE` clause:

```
strCommandText += " WHERE Player.PlayerManufacturerID = " + filterValue;
```

The effect of this `WHERE` clause is to tell the database you want only the records that have a PlayerManufacturerID that's equal to the value you've specified.

■**Note** Although you specify that you want to constrain the query on the Player.PlayerManufacturerID column, nothing is stopping you from using the Manufacturer.ManufacturerID column instead. As they're the columns that make the join, you can use either of them and still return the same results.

Regardless of whether a `WHERE` clause has been added to the query, you add an `ORDER BY` clause so that the Players are ordered alphabetically, like so:

```
ORDER BY Player.PlayerName
```

Now that you know how the query is built, you can look at what's actually executed against the database. If you've selected the -- All Manufacturers -- option, you're not adding a WHERE clause, and the query that's executed is the query you had in the previous example:

```
SELECT Player.PlayerName, Manufacturer.ManufacturerName
FROM Player INNER JOIN Manufacturer
  ON Player.PlayerManufacturerID = Manufacturer.ManufacturerID
ORDER BY Player.PlayerName
```

This query returns all the Players in the database because you're not constraining the query. However, if you select the Apple option, you want to add a WHERE clause, and the query you execute is as follows:

```
SELECT Player.PlayerName, Manufacturer.ManufacturerName
FROM Player INNER JOIN Manufacturer
  ON Player.PlayerManufacturerID = Manufacturer.ManufacturerID
WHERE Player.PlayerManufacturerID = 1
ORDER BY Player.PlayerName
```

You constrain the query to return only the results that have a PlayerManufacturerID equal to 1, which is the ManufacturerID value for Apple.

Open to SQL Injection Attacks

Before we move on, it's worth taking a quick detour into why you shouldn't construct queries at runtime using string concatenation. When constructing queries using string concatenation, it is far too easy to leave the database wide open to attack—SQL injection attacks in particular.

Consider the case where you want to execute the following query to return the user's profile from the database:

```
SELECT * FROM tblUser WHERE UserName = '<<USERNAME>>';
```

Now suppose the user enters her username on a page. The majority of users will enter the correct username, and the query will run as expected. But what if the user entered the following:

```
' OR '1' = '1
```

The string concatenation would merge the entered username with the query that you've defined and actually execute the following against the database:

```
SELECT * FROM tblUser WHERE UserName = '' OR '1' = '1';
```

Oh! Do you really want to show all of the users in tblUser? Even worse, what if the user entered the following:

```
'; DELETE FROM tblUser; --
```

Granted, the user needs a little understanding of your table structure, but you've potentially lost all of the data in tblUser. The database would actually be executing two queries:

```
SELECT * FROM tblUser WHERE UserName = '';
DELETE FROM tblUser;
```

To prevent SQL injection attacks, you might perform checking on the string that the user has entered to make sure that it doesn't do anything it shouldn't. If you go down this route, you'll be fighting a losing battle, but thankfully there is a solution. You can use parameters to fixed queries, rather than constructing the query using string concatenation at runtime.

Try It Out: Using Parameters in Queries

Rather than constructing a SQL query at runtime and passing it to the database to be executed, you can instead use parameters to modify a fixed SQL query. This example will use that methodology to replicate the functionality you saw in the previous example. Follow these steps:

1. Open `Select.aspx` from the root of the Chapter04 Web site and switch to the Source view of the page.

2. In the `DropDownList1_SelectedIndexChanged` event, replace the code that creates the SQL query to be executed with the following:

```
string strCommandText = "SELECT Player.PlayerName, ➥
    Manufacturer.ManufacturerName FROM Player INNER JOIN Manufacturer ➥
    ON Player.PlayerManufacturerID = Manufacturer.ManufacturerID ➥
    WHERE @ManufacturerID = 0 OR Player.PlayerManufacturerID = ➥
    @ManufacturerID ORDER BY Player.PlayerName";
```

3. Remove the existing lines of code that add the filter and the ordering to `strCommandText`.

4. Add the following code before the call to open the database:

```
// add the parameter
SqlParameter myParameter = new SqlParameter();
myParameter.ParameterName = "@ManufacturerID";
myParameter.SqlDbType = SqlDbType.Int;
myParameter.Value = DropDownList1.SelectedValue;
myCommand.Parameters.Add(myParameter);
```

5. Execute the page. You'll see that the page performs exactly as you would expect, with the list of Players filtered correctly according to the Manufacturer that is selected.

How It Works

All that you've changed is the query used to select the Players from the database. Rather than having a query constructed at runtime, you have a complete query that you modify using a parameter.

As you saw in Chapter 3, parameters are the means whereby you can pass information into a query at runtime without making any changes to the query itself.

The query that you're using is the same query that you had for the filtering example in Chapter 3. That query used a parameter called @ManufacturerID to allow the Manufacturer to be specified by the user's selection:

```
SELECT Player.PlayerName, Manufacturer.ManufacturerName
FROM Player INNER JOIN Manufacturer
  ON Player.PlayerManufacturerID = Manufacturer.ManufacturerID
WHERE @ManufacturerID = 0 OR
  Player.PlayerManufacturerID = @ManufacturerID
ORDER BY Player.PlayerName
```

You therefore need to provide a parameter to the query based on the user's selection. When you used a SqlDataSource, you added a ControlParameter to the SelectParameters collection, and passing the selected value was handled automatically; the query executed with the correct value for the selected Manufacturer. However, you need to provide the parameter and its value, and this is what the extra code that you've added to the example shows.

To add the value of @ManufacturerID to the query, you use a SqlParameter object. You must first create the necessary SqlParameter object:

```
SqlParameter myParameter = new SqlParameter();
```

Before you can use this parameter, you must set various properties on it. At a bare minimum, you must set the name, the data type, and the value of the parameter, like so:

```
myParameter.ParameterName = "@ManufacturerID";
myParameter.SqlDbType = SqlDbType.Int;
myParameter.Value = DropDownList1.SelectedValue;
```

The ParameterName value must match the name in the query, and Value is simply the value that you want to assign to the parameter—in this case, the SelectedValue of the drop-down list.

You specify the data type using the SqlDbType property and passing in a member of the SqlDbType enumeration. There are values in the enumeration corresponding to all the data types that are available in SQL, and you can use any of them in parameters. In this case, you want a simple integer, so you specify SqlDbType.Int. You'll find a list of the values available in the SqlDbType enumeration in Appendix B, along with the equivalent .NET and SQL types.

Once you've created the parameter, you must add it to the SqlCommand object before the query executes:

```
myCommand.Parameters.Add(myParameter);
```

Other Methods for Adding Parameters

Although you've created a SqlParameter object and added this to the Parameters collection, this isn't the only way you can add parameters to the SqlCommand object. The Parameters property returns a SqlParametersCollection that has several different methods for adding parameters:

- Add(SqlParameter): Adds a SqlParameter that you've already created to the collection.

- Add(string, SqlDbType): Adds a new SqlParameter to the collection with the specified name and type. The parameter will not have a value.

- Add(string, SqlDbType, int): Adds a new SqlParameter to the collection with the spec-ified name, type, and size. This is useful when you're using a text type, as you can set the length of the string. The parameter will not have a value.

- AddWithValue(string, Object): Adds a new SqlParameter with the specified name and value. The type will be inferred from the object that is passed to the method.

Another way of creating a SqlParameter object is to have the SqlCommand object do it for you. Using the CreateParameter() method of the SqlCommand object creates a new SqlParameter object that has already been added to the Parameters collection, like so:

```
SqlParameter myParameter = myCommand.CreateParameter();
myParameter.Name = "@ManufactuerID";
myParameter.SqlDbType = SqlDbType.Int;
myParameter.Value = DropDownList1.SelectedValue;
```

You can use any of these methods to add parameters. I chose to use the Add() overload that requires a SqlParameter object because it introduces the concept of using names, types, and values for parameters.

Protected from SQL Injection Attacks

As I explained after the example of modifying the query, creating queries using string concate-nation isn't the correct way to do things. One big problem is that it leaves your database wide open for SQL injection attacks. As I said, parameters are the solution.

You're executing this query to return the user's profile from the database:

```
SELECT * FROM tblUser WHERE UserName = '<<USERNAME>>';
```

Even if the user enters one of the strings that would break the previous example, such as:

```
' OR '1'='1
```

this won't actually cause a problem, other than that the user won't be found in the database.

The value entered as the parameter is treated as the whole parameter, so the WHERE clause is actually checking whether the UserName value in the database is equal to the entire string that the user entered: ' OR '1' = '.

I don't think any user will have picked that as a username (although with users, you never know!), so the query will not return any results—exactly what you would hope to happen.

Parameters and Queries

Using parameters is one of the few instances where the query to be executed and the corre-sponding code changes depend on the Command object you're using. Each of the Command objects uses parameters in slightly different ways and requires different queries and changes to the way parameters are added.

Recall from the previous example that the parameters were added with the ParameterName of the SqlParameter matching the name of the parameter in the query passed to the SqlCommand. The query had a parameter called @ManufacturerID, and a SqlParameter with its ParameterName set to @ManufacturerID was added to the SqlCommand. With named parameters, the SqlConnection object can determine which SqlParameter is required, and even though the parameter was used twice in the query, only one SqlParameter is required.

Only when using the `SqlClient` data provider to connect to SQL Server 2005 can you use named parameters. Neither the `Odbc` data provider when connecting to MySQL 5.0 nor the `OleDb` data provider when connecting to any database (such as Microsoft Access) support named parameters. Both the `OdbcCommand` and `OleDbCommand` objects rely on the order that the Parameter objects are added to the Command object to determine how they're inserted into the query.

As named parameters are no longer used, `OdbcCommand` and `OleDbCommand` require a slightly different query than `SqlCommand`. You can no longer use the @ syntax to refer to a parameter; you use a question mark (?) instead, like so:

```
SELECT Player.PlayerName, Manufacturer.ManufacturerName
FROM Player INNER JOIN Manufacturer
  ON Player.PlayerManufacturerID = Manufacturer.ManufacturerID
WHERE ? = O OR Player.PlayerManufacturerID = ?
```

As you have two parameters (indicated by the two question marks), you must have two Parameter objects added to the Command object, even if, as in this case, the two parameters take the same value. As these aren't named parameters, you can add them by specifying only their type and value; you don't need to give the parameter a name.

For the `OdbcCommand` object, you need to create two `OdbcParameter` objects and add them to the `OdbcCommand` object, like so:

```
// add the first parameter
OdbcParameter myParameter1 = new OdbcParameter();
myParameter1.OdbcType = OdbcType.Int;
myParameter1.Value = DropDownList1.SelectedValue;
myCommand.Parameters.Add(myParameter1);

// add the second parameter
OdbcParameter myParameter2 = new OdbcParameter();
myParameter2.OdbcType = OdbcType.Int;
myParameter2.Value = DropDownList1.SelectedValue;
myCommand.Parameters.Add(myParameter2);
```

For the `OleDbCommand` object, the process is the same. You create the following two `OleDbParameter` objects and add these to the `OleDbCommand` object:

```
// add the first parameter
OleDbParameter myParameter1 = new OleDbParameter();
myParameter1.OleDbType = OleDbType.Integer;
myParameter1.Value = DropDownList1.SelectedValue;
myCommand.Parameters.Add(myParameter1);

// add the second parameter
OleDbParameter myParameter2 = new OleDbParameter();
myParameter2.OleDbType = OleDbType.Integer;
myParameter2.Value = DropDownList1.SelectedValue;
myCommand.Parameters.Add(myParameter2);
```

> ■**Note** Although you don't need to give the parameter a name, it's a good idea to do so. Both `OdbcCommand` and `OleDbCommand` will ignore the name, but the name can still be used to access the individual parameters in the `Parameters` collection. If you ever need to change the value of the parameter, it's much easier to access the parameter using a name rather than the parameter's position in the `Parameters` collection.

Command Object Methods and Properties

Although you've looked at querying data sources using three different Command objects, there are a few properties and methods that, while not essential for querying the data sources, allow you greater control over the query. Here, we'll look at some of the most useful properties and methods. If you would like more details about the others that are available, you can find more information on MSDN at the following locations:

- `SqlCommand`:
  http://msdn.microsoft.com/en-us/library/system.data.sqlclient.sqlcommand.aspx

- `OdbcCommand`:
  http://msdn.microsoft.com/en-us/library/system.data.odbc.odbccommand.aspx

- `OleDbCommand`:
  http://msdn.microsoft.com/en-us/library/system.data.oledb.oledbcommand.aspx

The CommandText Property

In the examples you've looked at so far, you've always created the Command object by passing the query to execute directly to the constructor. The Command object also exposes the `CommandText` property, which you can use instead to specify the query after you've created the Command object. So, you can create a `SqlCommand` object and specify the query to execute as follows:

```
SqlCommand myCommand = new SqlCommand();
myCommand.CommandText = "SELECT ManufacturerID, ManufacturerName ➦
  FROM Manufacturer ORDER BY ManufacturerName";
```

The CommandType Property

So far, we've looked at passing SQL queries directly to the database. However, this isn't the only way that you can query the database. For instance, as you'll see in Chapter 10, you can also use stored procedures.

A SQL query is the default query type, and this is represented by a value of Text from the `CommandType` enumeration. Table 4-1 shows all the different values for the `CommandType` enumeration.

You've already implicitly used the `CommandType.Text` value. as you've been executing queries against the database without specifying a value for the `CommandType` property. In this case, the default value was used automatically.

Table 4-1. *Values of the CommandType Enumeration*

Value	Description
StoredProcedure	Indicates that the value passed as the CommandText is the name of a stored procedure to execute (discussed in Chapter 10).
TableDirect	Specifies that the CommandText is the name of a table within the data source and all the data within the table should be returned. This value is not supported by either the SqlClient or Odbc data providers.
Text	Indicates that the CommandText property contains a SQL query to execute. This is the default value.

The Execute Methods

The Execute methods of the Command object, listed in Table 4-2, allow you to execute queries against the database. We've already looked at one of these: the ExecuteReader() method.

Table 4-2. *The Execute Methods*

Value	Description
ExecuteNonQuery()	Executes the specified query against the database and doesn't return any results from the query, even if the query had results to return. Instead, the query returns the number of rows affected by the query. Use this method when executing INSERT, UPDATE, and DELETE queries (see Chapter 8).
ExecuteReader()	Returns a read-only, forward-only view of the query results.
ExecuteScalar()	Returns a single value, rather than one or more rows of data. You can use the ExecuteScalar() method to return information from the database without the overhead of using a DataReader object.

Next, you'll see how to use the ExecuteScalar() method to return data from a database.

Scalar Commands

Although you've looked at the most common method for returning data from a database (the ExecuteReader() method), sometimes you can avoid the overhead that goes with returning the results as a DataReader object. If the query you're executing returns only a single value from the database, you can use the ExecuteScalar() method. Yes, you could perform the same task using the ExecuteReader() method and manipulating the DataReader object that's returned. However, that requires a lot more code and is slower than using the ExecuteScalar() method.

A common reason to return only one value from a query is when you're using scalar functions to query a table within the database.

Scalar Functions

Scalar functions, or *aggregate functions* as Microsoft likes to call them, are mathematical functions defined within SQL that return a single value. Table 4-3 describes some of the more common scalar functions.

Table 4-3. *Common Scalar Functions*

Scalar Function	Description
AVG(column)	Returns the average value of the specified column
COUNT(DISTINCT column)	Counts the number of distinct values in the specified column
COUNT(*)	Gives the number of rows in the specified table
MAX(column)	Returns the maximum value in the specified column
MIN(column)	Returns the minimum value in the specified column
SUM(column)	Returns the total of all the values in the specified column

You can use scalar functions in several places in SQL, but by far, the most common usage is returning them as columns from SELECT queries.

Note You can also use scalar functions as constraints in SELECT queries, but only if you've grouped the columns in the query using the GROUP BY clause. In this case, you would use the HAVING clause in place of the WHERE clause to apply the constraint. For more information about using the GROUP BY and HAVING clauses, see *SQL Queries for Mere Mortals* by Michael J. Hernandez and John L. Viescas (0-20143-336-2; Addison-Wesley, 2000).

Try It Out: Using the ExecuteScalar() Method

In this example, you'll build on one of the previous examples. You'll use the COUNT(*) scalar function and return the number of records that your query has matched. Follow these steps:

1. Open the Chapter04 Web site in Visual Web Developer.

2. Copy Select.aspx, and rename the copied version to Scalar.aspx.

3. On the Design view of the page, on a new line after the DropDownList, enter **Players for this Manufacturer:**. Then add a Label from the Toolbox. Change the ID of the label to lblCount, and remove its default text. You should have a page that looks similar to the one shown in Figure 4-7.

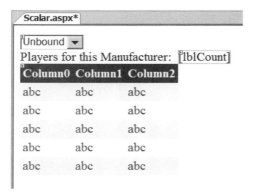

Figure 4-7. *Adding a count of the number of Players*

4. Switch to the Code view of the page. Add the following code immediately before opening the database connection in the DropDownList1_SelectedIndexChanged event handler (the additional code is shown in bold):

```
// create the count query
string strCommandTextCount = "SELECT COUNT(*) FROM Player WHERE ➡
  @ManufacturerID = 0 OR Player.PlayerManufacturerID = @ManufacturerID";
SqlCommand myCommandCount =
  new SqlCommand(strCommandTextCount, myConnection);
SqlParameter myParameterCount = new SqlParameter();
myParameterCount.ParameterName = "@ManufacturerID";
myParameterCount.SqlDbType = SqlDbType.Int;
myParameterCount.Value = DropDownList1.SelectedValue;
myCommandCount.Parameters.Add(myParameterCount);

// open the database connection
myConnection.Open();

// count the players for the manufacturer
lblCount.Text = Convert.ToString(myCommandCount.ExecuteScalar());
```

5. Execute the page. As well as seeing the selected Manufacturer's Players, the number of Players available will be displayed. Initially, the count will be 20, as you're not filtering the results. Selecting a Manufacturer, such as Apple, will filter the results, and the count of the Players will be adjusted accordingly, as shown in Figure 4-8.

Figure 4-8. *The count of the number of Players is returned.*

How It Works

You've used an earlier example as the basis for this example, and you've simply added a label to the page that you populate with the count of the number of Players for the selected Manufacturer. The count is returned by using the following COUNT(*) scalar function and returning this as the result from a SELECT query:

```
SELECT COUNT(*)
FROM Player
WHERE @ManufacturerID = 0 OR Player.PlayerManufacturerID = @ManufacturerID
```

You're filtering the results using a parameter, and by specifying COUNT(*) as the only column, the query will return a single row containing a single column. This is how you use the ExecuteScalar() method.

The ExecuteScalar() method returns an object representing the value that has been returned from the query. In this case, you're returning an integer, and you need to convert this to a string before you can assign it to the Text property of the label, like so:

```
lblCount.Text = Convert.ToString(myCommandCount.ExecuteScalar());
```

Error Handling

As any programmer will tell you, you're never going to write code that doesn't fall over at some point—whether it's caused by an error within the code or something outside the scope of the code (such as someone unplugging the database server).

Unless you have some way of handling any errors that occur, any problems you encounter can have the side effect of leaving connections to the database open. As you've already learned, database connections are a finite resource, so leaving connections open is definitely not a good idea.

If you're using SqlDataSource objects to connect to the database, as in Chapter 3, you don't need to worry about error handling to close the database connections. The SqlDataSource handles all the connections to the database internally, so you can be sure that any open database connections are handled before any error is thrown. However, when you're interacting with the database in code, you do need to catch and handle errors.

Try It Out: Catching and Handling Errors

You should already be familiar with the try..catch..finally syntax for handling errors, so you'll now see how to use this syntax to handle any errors that may occur within a page. If an error occurs, you'll write the error to a log file and close the open database connection.

1. Open Select.aspx from the root of the Chapter04 Web site and switch to the Source view of the page.

2. Add the following Import statement to the top of the page after the existing Import statements:

   ```
   <%@ Import Namespace="System.IO" %>
   ```

3. Change the Page_Load event as follows (the changed lines of code are shown in bold, and note that the name of the table is deliberately incorrect, with an *s* at the end):

   ```
   protected void Page_Load(object sender, EventArgs e)
   {
     if (Page.IsPostBack == false)
     {
       // create the connection
       SqlConnection myConnection = new SqlConnection();

       try
       {
         // configure the connection
         string strConnectionString = ConfigurationManager.
           ConnectionStrings["SqlConnectionString"].ConnectionString;
         myConnection.ConnectionString = strConnectionString;
   ```

```
      // create the command
      string strCommandText = "SELECT ManufacturerID, ManufacturerName ➡
        FROM Manufacturers ORDER BY ManufacturerName";
      SqlCommand myCommand = new SqlCommand(strCommandText, myConnection);

      // open the database connection
      myConnection.Open();

      // show the data
      DropDownList1.DataSource = myCommand.ExecuteReader();
      DropDownList1.DataTextField = "ManufacturerName";
      DropDownList1.DataValueField = "ManufacturerID";
      DropDownList1.DataBind();

      // force the first data bind
      DropDownList1_SelectedIndexChanged(null, null);
    }
    catch (Exception ex)
    {
      // write the error to file
      StreamWriter sw = File.AppendText(Server.MapPath("~/error.log"));
      sw.WriteLine(ex.Message);
      sw.Close();

      // now rethrow the error
      throw (ex);
    }
    finally
    {
      // close the database connection
      myConnection.Close();
    }
  }
}
```

4. Execute the page. You should immediately be presented with the error shown in Figure 4-9.

5. In Windows Explorer, navigate to the C:\BAND\Chapter04 folder, and you'll see that a file called error.log has been created. Open that file. You'll see the error has been logged, as shown in Figure 4-10.

Figure 4-9. *The error presented to the user*

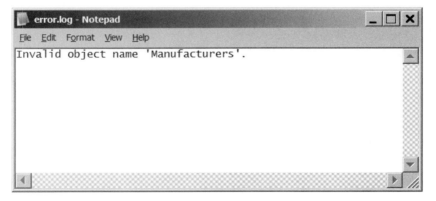

Figure 4-10. *The error has been logged in the error.log file.*

6. Switch back to the Source view of the page and fix the intentional error by changing the query to be executed within Page_Load as follows:

```
// create the command
string strCommandText = "SELECT ManufacturerID, ManufacturerName
  FROM Manufacturer ORDER BY ManufacturerName";
```

How It Works

You should already be familiar with error handling in .NET. Here, you've simply moved some of the code for accessing the database around to fit within the try..catch..finally syntax.

First, within the Page_Load event handler, before you get to any error-handling code, you need to create the Connection object. You must do this here, because the Connection object needs to be global to the entire event handler. If you created it in the try block, it wouldn't be available in the catch or the finally block. You create the Connection object without specifying the connection string, like so:

```
SqlConnection myConnection = new SqlConnection();
```

You then move into the try block. The code here is the same as you've seen in the previous example; the only difference is that instead of creating the Connection object with the correct connection string, you set the ConnectionString property of the existing Connection object, like so:

```
// configure the connection
string strConnectionString = ConfigurationManager.
  ConnectionStrings["SqlConnectionString"].ConnectionString;
myConnection.ConnectionString = strConnectionString;
```

The rest of the code is the same as you had previously (barring the intentional naming of the Manufacturer table incorrectly), except you've removed the code to close the database connection:

```
// create the command
string strCommandText = "SELECT ManufacturerID, ManufacturerName
  FROM Manufacturers ORDER BY ManufacturerName";
SqlCommand myCommand = new SqlCommand(strCommandText, myConnection);

// open the database connection
myConnection.Open();

// show the data
DropDownList1.DataSource = myCommand.ExecuteReader();
DropDownList1.DataTextField = "ManufacturerName";
DropDownList1.DataValueField = "ManufacturerID";
DropDownList1.DataBind();

// force the first data bind
DropDownList1_SelectedIndexChanged(null, null);
```

Whether or not you have an error, you always need to close the database connection. You've moved the call to Close() to the finally block.

If any of the code in the try block generates an error, then execution is automatically passed to the catch block, and it's in here that you log the error to the log file:

```
// write the error to file
StreamWriter sw = File.AppendText(Server.MapPath("~/error.log"));
sw.WriteLine(ex.Message);
sw.Close();
```

To write entries to the file, you create a StreamWriter using the System.IO.File.AppendText() static method. This method accepts a filename and opens the file for writing. If the file doesn't exist, it is created automatically.

You then use the WriteLine() method to write the error message to file, and then Close() the open StreamWriter.

Note When using IIS to host your Web site, you must ensure that the user running the ASP.NET process (ASPNET under IIS5 or NETWORK SERVICE under IIS6) has the required permissions to write to the folder where you want to store the log file. In this example, the page has been running under the account that you're logged on to the machine as, and you'll have write access to the C:\BAND\Chapter04 folder, as you created it in an earlier example.

You then reraise the error that you've handled, like so:

```
// now rethrow the error
throw(ex);
```

If you don't rethrow the error, ASP.NET will, since you've caught the error, assume that it has been handled and that any problems have been rectified. As you're only logging the error and not doing anything to fix it, you rethrow the error so that ASP.NET is aware that a problem occurred. If you don't rethrow the error, the user would be presented with a page that's equally as unhelpful as an ASP.NET error message, as shown in Figure 4-11.

Whether or not an error occurred, the finally block then executes. All you want to do here is close the connection to the database, like so:

```
// close the database connection
myConnection.Close();
```

Although it's possible to check the state of the connection using the State property and close the connection only if it's open, this isn't necessary. If the connection is already closed, then calling the Close() method won't have any unwanted side effects.

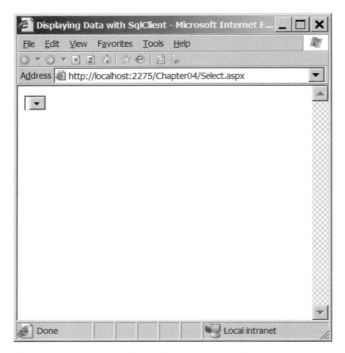

Figure 4-11. *You shouldn't hide errors from ASP.NET.*

Summary

As you saw in Chapter 1, before you can do anything with a data source, you must make a connection to it. You've spent some time in this chapter looking at connecting to several different data sources using the following Connection and Command objects:

- SQL Server 2005 using the SqlConnection and SqlCommand objects

- MySQL 5.0 using the OdbcConnection and OdbcCommand objects

- Microsoft Access using the Jet engine through the OleDbConnection and OleDbCommand objects

Although you've looked at all three different data sources and three different sets of objects, the beauty of the data provider architecture in ASP.NET is that the paradigm for all of the Connection and Command objects is exactly the same.

You also briefly looked at some of the other properties and methods of the Connection and Command objects.

Next, you learned about passing parameters into queries, and got your first look at how the different objects behave slightly differently. The SqlCommand object can handle named parameters, whereas the OdbcCommand and OleDbCommand objects, in our scenario, require parameters presented in the order in which they're to be used.

You then took a brief look at scalar functions and the `ExecuteScalar()` method as an alternative for returning information from the database when you want to return only one value.

At the end of the chapter, you looked at basic error handling and wrote an error handler that ensures you never leave any open connections.

The examples that you've seen so far have been simple pages that performed one task to give you a foundation in using databases and the different queries you can perform. In the next four chapters, you'll build on the techniques you've developed and learn how to build interactive pages. You'll also start to see the real power that's available to data-driven Web sites.

CHAPTER 5

■ ■ ■

DataReader and DataSet

In Chapters 3 and 4, you saw how to build and pass queries to a database, both by using a SqlDataSource and by writing code to connect to the database and retrieve the required results using the ExecuteReader() and ExecuteScalar() methods. Although we've only scratched the surface of what is possible, we've actually looked at the basics of everything you need to do, and you should now be able to build data-access pages that display data to the user.

This isn't the end of the story by any means. You have a large number of options for displaying data, but they all boil down to whether you're going to work with the data directly from the database or store it on the Web server as *disconnected data*. You'll look at both options in this chapter: using the DataReader to work with the results of a query directly from the database or storing query results in a DataSet object on the Web server away from the database. You'll also see how to create a DataSet locally with your own data, independent of an external data source.

Along the way, you'll look in some detail at the DataReader and DataSet objects, their makeup, and their differences. At least one of these two objects will feature in every data-driven page you create, so it's good to be up to speed on how they work. Indeed you've actually looked at both the DataSet and DataReader objects. The examples in Chapter 4 returned data from the database as a DataReader, and the SqlDataSource you used in Chapter 3 actually uses a DataSet by default when retrieving data from its data source.

This chapter is only the first part of five in your journey through data handling. For now, we'll assume that the data you request doesn't need to be displayed on screen. In Chapters 6 and 7, we'll assume that the data will be displayed on screen but is read-only and won't need to be updated. In Chapter 8, you'll continue with building pages that allow you to create, modify, and delete data and reflect those changes back to the data source. In Chapter 9, we'll take an in-depth look at three of the new Web controls introduced in ASP.NET 2.0: GridView, FormView, and DetailView.

Why not just look at the DataReader and DataSet as you go along? Why put this interlude first? These are good questions, but they have a simple answer (borrowed from the world of Perl). For every data-related task you'll be looking at over the coming chapters, you can follow this motto: There's More Than One Way to Do It. But all of these ways stem from how the DataReader and DataSet work. If you don't look at these objects now and see the situations in which they're useful, you'll be less likely to choose the right option when building data-driven pages of your own.

This chapter covers the following topics:

- How to iterate through a DataReader

- Some useful properties and methods of the DataReader

- How the DataSet works with a DataAdapter

- How to iterate through a DataSet

- How to build a DataSet from scratch

- How to set the SqlDataSource to access a database as a DataReader or a DataSet

- Differences between the DataReader and DataSet

- Tips for coding DataReader and DataSet access

The DataReader Object

The key to the whole topic of data handling is the DataReader object, or if you prefer to be data provider-specific, the SqlDataReader, OleDbDataReader, and OdbcDataReader objects. True, they're optimized as appropriate for their associated technology, but their method calls and properties are, for all intents and purposes, identical.

The DataReader is a strange object. You may use it all the time, but it's intangible, representing only a pipeline in memory between the database and the page waiting for the data. In functional terms, it works much like a phone connection. While the phone connection is open, the page can communicate queries to the database, which in turn can communicate its results back to the page, but once the connection is closed, there's no trace of it or record of the data returned from the database, except in the page itself. Only if you use another object, such as the DataSet, can you maintain an in-memory record of the results from the query. If you like, the DataSet is the equivalent of an answering machine or phone-tapping mechanism.

The upshot of a DataReader being only a conduit in memory, rather than a permanent place of storage, is that when you access the data in a DataReader, the data is read-only. It also means you can access the results only one row at a time, and once you finish with a row and move on to the next one, you can't go back to it. You can go only forward. Of course, this means there are pros and cons to using only DataReader in your page. On the plus side, you have the following:

- Using a DataReader is quick and efficient, as it doesn't need to worry about keeping track of every bit of data.

- A DataReader doesn't need to store data in memory, so it uses fewer resources in creating a page.

The disadvantages are as follows:

- You can't do anything with the data, such as sending changes back to the database. This would mean referring to data already passed through the reader, which isn't possible; DataReaders work only from database to client. If you need to send changes back to the database, you'll need to make a separate query to the database, as you'll see in Chapter 8.

- DataReaders require exclusive access to a connection. Once a DataReader is open, nothing else can use a connection until the DataReader is closed.

A DataReader isn't picky about the amount of data passed through it. You could request a single item of information from a column or the entire contents of the database. As long as you understand how to access the DataReader, it won't complain.

As you'll recall, a DataReader is the resulting object from a call to `ExecuteReader()` on a Command object.

```
SqlDataReader myReader = myCommand.ExecuteReader();
```

The general practice at this point is to assign (or *bind*) the values in a DataReader to Web controls on the page, and indeed, that's what you've already done in the examples in Chapter 4. You've created a `GridView` on the page, bound the data to it, and let ASP.NET take care of the display:

```
GridView1.DataSource = myReader;
GridView1.DataBind();
```

So far, all you've seen is the data displayed as a table thanks to the `GridView`, but you can bind information to several more data-aware Web controls. For example, you can use a drop-down list, a set of radio buttons, or a calendar. We'll spend all of Chapters 7 and 8 on data binding, but there's another way to work with DataReader objects that you'll look at here, and that's to iterate through them row by row.

How to Read Through a DataReader

It may seem a waste of time to work through the results of a query row by row and work with each when you can just bind it to a Web control and let the Web control take care of it all, but consider that data isn't always for display. You may be using a database table to store user information and site preferences. Rather than displaying it on the screen, information from these tables may be assigned directly to Web controls' properties or stored in a business object for use across the whole site. For example, you may create a Preferences object to store theme information for the whole site, store values from the database in its properties, and save it as a session-level variable. Rather than accessing the database again, you just access the session variable. If any preferences are changed during the session, they're saved to the session variable, and when the session is over, the changes are sent back to the database. This minimizes both database access for this purpose and also the overhead of using many session variables at a time. You just use one with a lot of information, rather than several containing individual pieces of information.

To iterate through the contents of a DataReader, you use its Read() method. If you haven't worked with reader objects in general before, the idea is simple. A reader has a pointer that you use to keep track of where you are in the information coming through your reader. If you like, it's the same kind of thing that happens when you use your finger to keep your place on a book page. Until you open the book and start to read, you can't see anything. The same thing applies in code. You can't access anything until you call Read() the first time, and each time you call Read() after that, the DataReader lets another row through for you to use. Read() will also return a Boolean value each time you call it: true if there's another row for you to work with and false if you've reached the end of the query results, as shown in Figure 5-1.

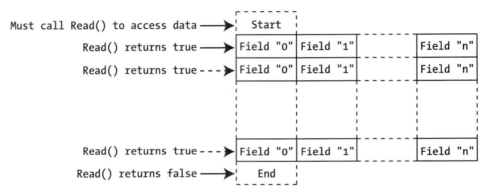

Figure 5-1. *Working through rows in a DataReader using the Read() method*

This means that you can use the call to Read() as the condition in a while loop. If your query returns no results, the first call to Read() ends the loop before you do anything. If not, the code will keep looping until there are no more results. In short, your page needs to have this skeleton code in it:

```
// create the connection
SqlConnection myConnection = new SqlConnection();

try
{
  // configure the connection

  // create the command

  // open the database connection

  // run the query
  SqlDataReader myReader = myCommand.ExecuteReader();

  // parse the results
  while (myReader.Read() == true)
  {
```

```
      // processing instructions for each row in DataReader
   }

   // close the reader
   myReader.Close();
}
finally
{
   // close the database connection
   myConnection.Close();
}
```

Take care not to call Read() in the while statement and then again within the loop—say, in a method call—or the code could skip some of the results. It's easy to do but hard to track down later in the code.

Besides the actual data processing, it's important that you close the DataReader once you've finished with it. Once a DataReader has been opened through a connection, nothing else can use that connection until the DataReader is closed. You can close the DataReader by either closing the SqlConnection (which has the effect of closing the DataReader if it is open) or by explicitly closing the DataReader, as in the previous code fragment:

```
myReader.Close();
```

If an error were to occur on the page before the call to the Close() method of the DataReader, the database connection is still isolated until the .NET garbage collector comes to dispose of the open DataReader. You also have a maximum number of database connections that can be open at any one time, so under heavy loads, not closing your connections could actually generate errors, which is definitely not a good thing.

Therefore, you enclose all of the code that interacts within the database, as you saw in Chapter 4, in a try..catch..finally block, so that you can always close the open database connection within the finally section:

```
finally
{
   // close the database connection
   myConnection.Close();
}
```

Try It Out: Iterating Through a DataReader

In this example, you'll see that you can do more than just fill a GridView with the results of a database query by passing the results into the grid and calling DataBind(). Here, you'll write a custom Manufacturer class, create an instance of it, and use a row of the Manufacturer table to populate it. In real life, you would probably then use it in the business rules tier of your Web site, but as this is a straightforward example, you'll define a simple method on the Manufacturer object that neatly prints the values of its properties to the page.

1. Start Visual Web Developer and create a new Web site in the `C:\BAND\Chapter05` folder. Delete the auto-created `Default.aspx` file.

2. Add a new `Web.config` file and add a new setting to the `<connectionStrings />` element:

   ```
   <add name="SqlConnectionString"
       connectionString="Data Source=localhost\BAND;Initial Catalog=Players;
       User ID=band;Password=letmein" />
   ```

3. Add a new class called `Manufacturer.cs` by selecting Add New Item from the folder's context menu and selecting the Class option. When you click the Add button, you're presented with the dialog box shown in Figure 5-2. Click Yes to create the `App_Code` folder and add the `Manufacturer.cs` file to the new folder.

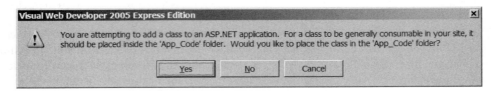

Figure 5-2. *Class files belong in the App_Code folder.*

4. Replace the code in `Manufacturer.cs` with the following:

   ```
   using System.Text;

   public class Manufacturer
   {
     public string Name;
     public string Country;
     public string Email;
     public string Website;

     public Manufacturer()
     {
     }

     public override string ToString()
     {
       StringBuilder sbDescription = new StringBuilder();

       // add the name
       sbDescription.Append("Name: ");
       sbDescription.Append(this.Name);
       sbDescription.Append("<BR/>");
   ```

```
    // add the city
    sbDescription.Append("Country: ");
    sbDescription.Append(this.Country);
    sbDescription.Append("<BR/>");

    // add the email
    sbDescription.Append("Email: ");
    sbDescription.Append("<a href='mailto:");
    sbDescription.Append(this.Email);
    sbDescription.Append("'>");
    sbDescription.Append(this.Email);
    sbDescription.Append("</a>");
    sbDescription.Append("<BR/>");

    // add the website
    sbDescription.Append("Website: ");
    sbDescription.Append("<a href='");
    sbDescription.Append(this.Website);
    sbDescription.Append("'>");
    sbDescription.Append(this.Website);
    sbDescription.Append("</a>");
    sbDescription.Append("<BR/>");

    return (sbDescription.ToString());
  }
}
```

5. Add a new Web Form to the site called DataReader_Iterating.aspx. In the Source view, change the name of the page to **Iterating through a DataReader**.

6. In the Design view, add a Label to the blank page. You'll use this to demonstrate that your objects have been created. Set its Text property to an empty string.

7. In the Source view of the page, make sure the correct data provider is included at the top of the page, like so:

```
<%@ Page Language="C#" %>
<%@ Import Namespace="System.Data.SqlClient" %>
```

8. The second piece of code to add is for the Page_Load handler:

```
protected void Page_Load(object sender, EventArgs e)
{
  // create the connection
  SqlConnection myConnection = new SqlConnection();
```

```csharp
try
{
  // configure the connection
  string strConnectionString = ConfigurationManager.
    ConnectionStrings["SqlConnectionString"].ConnectionString;
  myConnection.ConnectionString = strConnectionString;

  // create the command
  string strCommandText = "SELECT ManufacturerName, ➥
    ManufacturerCountry, ManufacturerEmail, ManufacturerWebsite ➥
    FROM Manufacturer ORDER BY ManufacturerName";
  SqlCommand myCommand = new SqlCommand(strCommandText, myConnection);

  // open the database connection
  myConnection.Open();

  // run the query
  SqlDataReader myReader = myCommand.ExecuteReader();

  // parse the results
  while (myReader.Read())
  {
    // create the manufacturer object
    Manufacturer objManufacturer = new Manufacturer ();
    objManufacturer.Name = Convert.ToString(myReader["ManufacturerName"]);
    objManufacturer.Country =
      Convert.ToString(myReader["ManufacturerCountry"]);
    objManufacturer.Email =
      Convert.ToString(myReader["ManufacturerEmail"]);
    objManufacturer.Website =
      Convert.ToString(myReader["ManufacturerWebsite"]);

    // output the manufacturer object details
    Label1.Text += objManufacturer.ToString() + "<BR/>";
  }

  // close the reader
  myReader.Close();
}
finally
{
  // close the database connection
  myConnection.Close();
}
}
```

9. Save the page, and then run it. When the page loads, you'll see that the Label contains details of all the Manufacturers in the Manufacturer table written out, as in Figure 5-3, but not in tabular form. You have hyperlinks that work and an easier-to-read collection of data instead.

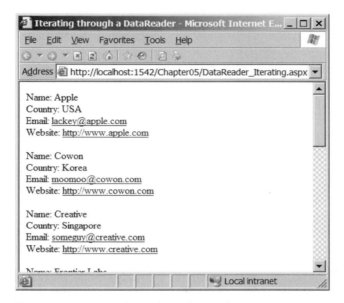

Figure 5-3. *Iterating through a DataReader*

How It Works

The aim of this page is to demonstrate that you can use a DataReader to provide values for any objects you create, so you start by defining a new object, Manufacturer, to use. This is created in the App_Code special folder, as it's not specific to a particular page. If you look at the DataSet code you'll use later in this chapter or the MySQL 5.0 and Microsoft Access versions of this page, you'll see that they use the same Manufacturer object.

The Manufacturer object has properties cunningly mirroring the information stored in the Manufacturer table.

```
public class Manufacturer
{
  public string Name;
  public string Country;
  public string Email;
  public string Website;

  public Manufacturer()
  {
  }
```

To demonstrate that you've achieved this aim, you can add a method that presents the information in a Manufacturer object neatly on the screen:

```
public override string ToString()
{
   StringBuilder sbDescription = new StringBuilder();

   // add the name
   sbDescription.Append("Name: ");
   sbDescription.Append(this.Name);
   sbDescription.Append("<BR/>");

   // country, email, website removed for brevity

   return (sbDescription.ToString());
 }
}
```

All objects within the .NET Framework inherit from System.Object, and they all have a ToString() method that returns a string representing the current object. You override the ToString() method so that the override version is called rather than the version on System.Object—after all, simply outputting the name of the class doesn't really show that you've achieved the aim of mirroring the database in the Manufacturer class.

All that's left is the Page_Load event, and apart from the following section, it's the same as the previous examples. Instead of plugging the results of myCommand.ExecuteReader() into a GridView, you can access the DataReader directly, like so:

```
// run query
SqlDataReader myReader = myCommand.ExecuteReader();
```

The following is the while loop where you work through each row in turn. The Read() method of a DataReader returns false if there isn't a row to retrieve and true if there is. So, if there is a row to be returned from myReader, the while loop will execute.

```
while (myReader.Read())
{
```

Inside the loop, you create a new Manufacturer object and give each of its properties values from the corresponding columns in the DataReader. The properties of the Manufacturer object are named the same as the columns in the database, so the process of constructing the Manufacturer object is relatively easy.

You can access columns in the current row from the DataReader in any order, and you don't need to access all the information in a particular row. Just don't forget that you can't come back to it later. You construct each Manufacturer object as follows:

```
Manufacturer objManufacturer = new Manufacturer();
objManufacturer.Name = Convert.ToString(myReader["ManufacturerName"]);
objManufacturer.Country = Convert.ToString(myReader["ManufacturerCountry"]);
objManufacturer.Email = Convert.ToString(myReader["ManufacturerEmail"]);
objManufacturer.Website = Convert.ToString(myReader["ManufacturerWebsite"]);
```

You use the name of the column you're after and pass this as the required value to the myReader indexer. The indexer allows you to specify the name of the column you want to retrieve, and returns it as a generic System.Object. Therefore, you call Convert.ToString() to convert the object returned to a string to pass to the Manufacturer properties.

When you've finished creating the object, you display its details in the Label by calling the ToString() method of the Manufacturer object. If there's more information in the DataReader, the while loop will start creating another object. If not, the while loop finishes, and you close the DataReader by calling Close(), like so:

```
Label1.Text += objManufacturer.ToString() + "<BR/>";
}

// close the datareader
myReader.Close();
```

■**Note** Remember to close a DataReader object using Close() when you're finished with it. Until you do, you can't use your Connection object for any other queries or purpose. A DataReader has exclusive access to a connection until it's closed. This is true in all data providers. However, DataReaders rely on their connections to work, so make sure that the connection isn't closed before the DataReader is finished, or the results won't be pretty.

DataReader Properties and Methods

The DataReader also provides some handy support properties and methods to help you process its contents with fewer errors and more intelligence. Table 5-1 describes the DataReader properties, and Table 5-2 describes the DataReader methods.

Table 5-1. *DataReader Properties*

Name	Type	Description
FieldCount	int	Returns the number of columns in the current row
HasRows	bool	Returns true if the DataReader contains any rows
IsClosed	bool	Returns true if the DataReader is closed
Item	Object	Returns the contents of a column in a row*

* *Never use Item by name. Instead, this is used in the background to access DataReader columns with, for instance, myReader["columnname"].*

Table 5-2. *DataReader Methods*

Name	Type	Description
Close()	void	Closes the DataReader object
Read()	bool	Moves to the next row in the DataReader; returns true if a row exists, or false if at the end of the DataReader
GetXXX(int)	Varies*	Returns and casts the contents of a column at index int in the row**
GetOrdinal(string)	int	Returns the column index for the specified column name
IsDBNull(int)	bool	Returns true if the column at index int contains a null value pulled from the database, or false otherwise
NextResult()	bool	Moves to the next table in the DataReader; returns true if the next table exists, or false otherwise

* *The GetXXX() methods return a type corresponding to the request. For example, the GetString() method returns a string, and GetInt32() returns an integer.*

** *You must use the appropriate method for the type of object you want to retrieve. There are 37 different GetXXX() methods for the SqlDataReader and 25 for the OleDbDataReader and OdbcDataReader, so check the .NET documentation.*

You've already seen the Read() method in action in the example, and we'll look at NextResult() in Chapter 12. The NextResult() method is used when you send a group of SQL queries to the database in one go, and the resulting DataReader contains more than one result set to scan.

You can use the remainder of these properties and methods to extend the previous example. Let's start with the GetXXX(int) methods. These methods allow the DataReader to be queried and the requested data returned in the correct format, so there are, for example, GetString(int), GetInt32(int), and GetBoolean(int) methods. In the previous example, you could construct the Manufacturer object as follows:

```
Manufacturer objManufacturer = new Manufacturer();
objManufacturer.Name = myReader.GetString(0);
objManufacturer.Country = myReader.GetString(1);
objManufacturer.Email = myReader.GetString(2);
objManufacturer.Website = myReader.GetString(3);
```

This does indeed do what you need it to do, and you don't have to do any casting, as the row you require is returned in the correct format. However, using this method has two drawbacks. One is that the code is a lot less readable. In the example, you can see that the Email property of the Manufacturer class is set to the ManufacturerEmail column from the database. Using a value of 2 for the GetString() method means you have to look at the SQL query you're executing to know which column you're actually returning.

Another problem with using the GetXXX(int) methods is that the code is directly tied to the specific way that the SQL query is constructed, as the ordering of the columns in the SELECT query is fixed. Suppose you were to change the SQL query to change the ordering of the columns returned, like so:

```
SELECT ManufacturerName, ManufacturerCountry,
  ManufacturerWebsite, ManufacturerEmail
FROM Manufacturer
ORDER BY ManufacturerName
```

Then the e-mail and Web site values for the Manufacturer would be incorrect. This is because column 2 is now the Web site instead of the e-mail address, and column 3 is the e-mail address instead of the Web site.

For these two reasons alone, it's worth taking a little extra time to use column names rather than the index, removing the possibility of the order of the SELECT query causing errors that may be extremely tricky to track down. You've already looked at one way of doing this in the previous example—casting the object from the DataReader to the correct type:

```
objManufacturer.Name = Convert.ToString(myReader["ManufacturerName"]);
```

You also have an alternative method that combines the Get*XXX*() methods with the GetOrdinal() method to return the correct type from the DataReader. The GetOrdinal() method returns the column index for a named column. Here's how you can combine these two methods:

```
Manufacturer objManufacturer = new Manufacturer();
objManufacturer.Name =
  myReader.GetString(myReader.GetOrdinal("ManufacturerName"));
objManufacturer.Country =
  myReader.GetString(myReader.GetOrdinal("ManufacturerCountry"));
objManufacturer.Email =
  myReader.GetString(myReader.GetOrdinal("ManufacturerEmail"));
objManufacturer.Website =
  myReader.GetString(myReader.GetOrdinal("ManufacturerWebsite"));
```

The HasRows property returns a Boolean value that's true if a DataReader does contain some information and false if it doesn't. Now, you can already detect this using while(DataReader.Read()), but HasRows allows you to be a bit neater and gives you an alternate check for a positive query if you aren't going to run straight through the while loop. You can add it to the earlier code, like so:

```
if (myReader.HasRows)
{
  while (myReader.Read())
  {
    ...
  }
}
else
{
  Label1.Text = "No rows returned.";
}
```

Once you know there's some information, you can make sure it's safe to retrieve the data by using a combination of `FieldCount` and `IsDBNull()`. Before retrieving data from the row, you can scan it for any columns containing null values, like so:

```
while (myReader.Read())
{
   for (int i=0; i<=(myReader.FieldCount-1); i++)
   {
      if (myReader.IsDBNull(i))
      {
         Label1.Text += "Warning: Column " + i + " is NULL.";
      }
   }

   // create the manufacturer object
}
```

Finally, you can verify that the DataReader is closed when you finish with it by checking its `IsClosed` property. As with the Connection object, telling a closed DataReader to close itself will not cause any problems. But if you need to, you can check before closing the DataReader, like so:

```
if (myReader.IsClosed == false)
{
   myReader.Close();
}
```

That about covers everything for DataReaders by themselves. You know how to iterate through them, and you'll learn how to bind data from them to Web controls in the next chapter. You've even looked at some useful properties such as `HasRows` and `IsClosed`.

One problem is that once you move past a row in a DataReader, you can't go back to it again, because a DataReader is forward-only. An option is to persist the data in a business object, as you've already seen. Another option for accessing the same data more than once is to use a `DataSet`.

The DataSet Object

DataReaders are quick and fast, but they're much like pay-per-view television. The only way to watch a film again once you've finished watching it is to go back to the channel and request it again. A `DataSet`, on the other hand, works like a video recorder; you can record the film off the television and watch it as many times as you like, rewinding and fast-forwarding through it as much as you like.

With a `DataSet`, you can store any data that you may have use for throughout the lifetime of a page. This idea of persisting data away from the database is known as *disconnected data*. In fact, it's even better than a video recorder, because once you have data inside a `DataSet`, you can alter that data, add to it, delete from it, and send all the changes back to the database relatively easily. This is handy (don't you wish you could do that with some movies?).

Of course, there's no reason why you can't use a DataSet just for displaying data in a page as well. In Chapter 6, you'll see how to use both a DataSet and a DataReader to supply read-only information to a page.

■**Caution** A DataSet may not rely on a connection to a database, but it still lasts only for the lifetime of the page. If the page posts back and must be reassembled, so, too, must the DataSet. Either that, or it must be persisted somehow for retrieval by the next page. As a result, take care to query only for the data that will be needed on the page. A DataSet is resident in memory, so the smaller it is, the fewer resources required to keep it there, and the better the page performs and scales.

How to Fill a DataSet

The basic code to use a DataSet as a data source still follows the same three steps you saw back in Chapter 1, but in a slightly different way than creating a DataReader.

First, you set up the Connection and Command objects as usual. You also need to create the DataSet object, like so:

```
// create the connection
SqlConnection myConnection = new SqlConnection();

// create the DataSet object
DataSet myDataSet = new DataSet();

try
{
  // configure the connection
  string strConnectionString = ConfigurationManager.
    ConnectionStrings["SqlConnectionString"].ConnectionString;
  myConnection.ConnectionString = strConnectionString;

  // create the command
  string strCommandText = "SELECT ManufacturerName, ➥
    ManufacturerCountry, ManufacturerEmail, ManufacturerWebsite ➥
    FROM Manufacturer ORDER BY ManufacturerName";
  SqlCommand myCommand = new SqlCommand(strCommandText, myConnection);
```

Now it's time for something new. You use a DataAdapter as the intermediary between the database and the DataSet itself, so you need to set this up before you can populate the DataSet itself, like so:

```
  // create a DataAdapter
  SqlDataAdapter myAdapter = new SqlDataAdapter();
  myAdapter.SelectCommand = myCommand;
```

Next, you open the connection and use the DataAdapter's `Fill()` method to transfer the query results from the database to the DataSet, like so:

```
// open the database connection
myConnection.Open();

// populate the DataSet
myAdapter.Fill(myDataSet);
}
finally
{
// close the database connection
myConnection.Close();
}
```

At this point, the DataSet is ready for work. You can iterate through it as you did with the DataReader earlier, or simply bind the information it contains to a GridView:

```
// bind the data
GridView1.DataSource = myDataSet;
GridView1.DataBind();
```

Note You can find the code for this page in the Chapter05 directory of the code download for this book (available from the Downloads section of the Apress Web site, http:www.apress.com). It's called DataSet_Simple.aspx.

This code is the simplest DataSet example possible, so you'll now add some more detail. There are two new data-aware objects in the code, and you need to learn more about them.

The DataAdapter Object

The eagle-eyed among you may have spotted what looks like an error in the previous code. It appears that it left out the prefix for the DataSet object that identifies which data provider it is a part of:

```
DataSet myDataSet = new DataSet();
```

However, this isn't an error. The DataSet (and the family of objects it contains) are independent of any data provider. You can find their definitions in the System.Data namespace. In the grand scheme of things, this makes a lot of sense. Data providers are there to provide optimized access to a data source and nothing more. The DataSet just stores data in memory and so should be optimized as best for .NET, rather than for the database that it personally never contacts.

The key, as you may have guessed, is the DataAdapter object—or the SqlDataAdapter, OleDbDataAdapter, and OdbcDataAdapter objects, if you prefer. These are the objects that translate the data from the format associated with that particular data provider to the generic .NET format that the DataSet uses. These *are* data-provider-specific. However, their basic mechanisms are the same across the board. Their Fill() method causes data to be pulled from the database into a DataSet, and their Update() method pushes any changes made to the DataSet back to the database, as shown in Figure 5-4.

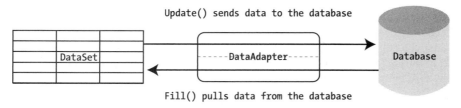

Figure 5-4. *A DataAdapter object plays the middleman between a DataSet and the database.*

Fill() and Update() are, unfortunately, not psychic, so you need to provide a DataAdapter with details of the Connection object it should use to access the database and the various SQL queries it should run when using Fill() and Update(). In the DataSet_Simple.aspx example, this takes place in two easy lines of code. First, create a SqlDataAdapter object; second, assign the SqlCommand object you've already built (which holds a SELECT query to the Manufacturer table) to its SelectCommand property. The Command object is already associated with a Connection object, so the DataAdapter is also by proxy.

```
SqlDataAdapter myAdapter = new SqlDataAdapter();
myAdapter.SelectCommand = myCommand;
```

Using the alternate constructor for the SqlDataAdapter, you could write this in a single line, like so:

```
SqlDataAdapter myAdapter = new SqlDataAdapter(myCommand);
```

Indeed, two other versions of the SqlDataAdapter constructor (and of the OleDbDataAdapter and OdbcDataAdapter, too) lead to providing the same information. The first takes two arguments, like so:

```
public SqlDataAdapter(queryString, SqlConnection);
```

In this case, the string is the SQL SELECT query written out in full, and the Connection object is as you would expect. In the final variant, the SqlConnection object is replaced by another string parameter containing the connection string written out in full, like so:

```
public SqlDataAdapter(queryString, connectionString);
```

The SQL query in these constructors is always the SELECT query that will be sent to the data source when Fill() is called. You can find it in the DataAdapter's SelectCommand property. You'll also need to provide its UpdateCommand, InsertCommand, and DeleteCommand properties with the respective queries for updating, inserting, and deleting data in the database before you can call Update() on the DataAdapter. You'll work with these three properties and Update() in Chapter 8.

Note Each of these four *xxx*Command properties of a DataAdapter object contains a Command object, rather than just a string containing the relevant SQL query.

Both Fill() and Update() can open a database connection if it's closed when they're called and will close it again once they're finished. If a connection is already open, it will remain open. If you want to close the connection, you must call Close() on the Connection object as you have in the code. In the Fill() method's case, you can use one of its many overloaded variations, which allows you to specify that it must close the connection after it has finished.

```
myAdapter.Fill(DataTable, myCommand, CommandBehavior.CloseConnection);
```

This particular variation of Fill() brings up another question. What's the first DataTable parameter? Well, it turns out there's a lot more to a DataSet than meets the eye.

DataSet Components

The DataSet is much more than a simple receptacle for query results. A DataSet is, more technically, a container for one or more DataTable objects that contain the data you retrieve from the database.

- A DataSet contains a DataTableCollection of DataTable objects. Each DataTable is referenced as myDataSet.Tables["TableName"] or myDataSet.Tables[index].

- Each DataTable contains a DataColumnCollection of DataColumn objects to represent the different pieces of information stored in the table. Each column can be referenced as myDataSet.Tables["TableName"].Columns["ColumnName"]. Properties such as AllowDBNull, Unique, and ReadOnly mimic those available in SQL Server 2005, MySQL 5.0, and Microsoft Access.

- Each DataTable also contains a DataRowCollection of DataRow objects to represent individual rows stored in the DataTable. Each row can be referenced as myDataSet. Tables["TableName"].Rows[RowNumber].

- Individual columns in a DataRow object can be referenced as myDataSet.Tables["TableName"].Rows[RowNumber]["ColumnName"].

- A DataSet also contains a DataRelationCollection of DataRelation objects that models the relationships between tables. Each DataRelation object contains the parent and child columns that are related. By default, a UniqueConstraint object is applied to the parent column, and a ForeignKeyConstraint object is applied to the child column. Thus, it mimics the way in which databases handle relationships. DataRelation objects can be referenced as myDataSet.Relations["RelationName"].

So, where was the DataTable in the previous example, DataSet_Simple.aspx? Looking at the code, there was no mention of a DataTable anywhere when you called the following:

```
myAdapter.Fill(myDataSet);
```

True, but by default, the `Fill()` method will create a `DataTable` called `Table` if one isn't specified and add the data to this. Also, when you set the `DataSource` property of the `GridView` to just the `DataSet`, by default, this means it will be bound to the first table in the `Table` collection. This can lead to a lot of problems with binding to the wrong `DataTable`, so it's better to not leave the default values.

You can name the `DataTable` to be filled and bound with the following lines of code:

```
myAdapter.Fill(myDataSet, "Manufacturer");
GridView1.DataSource = myDataSet.Tables["Manufacturer"];
```

The `Tables` property can also be accessed using an integer specifying the position in `Tables` like so:

```
GridView1.DataSource = myDataSet.Tables[0];
```

Unless you're iterating through the collection (as you'll soon see), you should always use the table name version of the indexer. Then changes to what is contained within the `Tables` collection by other parts of the code (such as adding an extra table before the table you're after) won't cause problems.

■**Note** For what seems a simple method, `Fill()` has many variations and rules. The online documentation at `http://msdn2.microsoft.com/system.data.common.dataadapter.fill.aspx` is complete and should be the first place to look for more information about it.

Now, let's see how the components of the `DataSet` fit together by re-creating the first example and iterating through a `DataTable` to create custom objects.

Try It Out: Iterating Through a DataSet

In this example, you'll take what you've learned about the `DataSet`, `DataTable`, and the other objects in the group and replicate the previous example of iterating through a DataReader. Follow these steps:

1. In Visual Web Developer, create a new Web Form in the `Chapter05` Web site called `DataSet_Iterating.aspx`. In Source view, change the name of the page to **Iterating through a DataSet**.

2. Add a `Label` to the view of the page and set its `Text` property to an empty string.

3. In the Source view of the page, make sure the correct data provider is included at the top of the page, like so:

```
<%@ Page Language="C#" %>
<%@ Import Namespace="System.Data " %>
<%@ Import Namespace="System.Data.SqlClient" %>
```

4. Add a Page_Load event handler to the page. First, add the code to populate the DataSet with the contents of the Manufacturer table.

```
protected void Page_Load(object sender, EventArgs e)
{
  // create the connection
  SqlConnection myConnection = new SqlConnection();

  // create the DataSet object
  DataSet myDataSet = new DataSet();

  // configure the connection
  string strConnectionString = ConfigurationManager.
    ConnectionStrings["SqlConnectionString"].ConnectionString;
  myConnection.ConnectionString = strConnectionString;

  // create the command
  string strCommandText = "SELECT ManufacturerName, ➥
    ManufacturerCountry, ManufacturerEmail, ManufacturerWebsite ➥
    FROM Manufacturer ORDER BY ManufacturerName";
  SqlCommand myCommand = new SqlCommand(strCommandText, myConnection);

  // create a DataAdapter
  SqlDataAdapter myAdapter = new SqlDataAdapter();
  myAdapter.SelectCommand = myCommand;

  // populate the DataSet
  myAdapter.Fill(myDataSet, "Manufacturer");
```

5. Add the following code that iterates through the DataTable containing the data and populates the Manufacturer objects:

```
  // now iterate through the rows in the table
  for (int i = 0; i <= myDataSet.Tables["Manufacturer"].Rows.Count - 1; i++)
  {
    Manufacturer objManufacturer = new Manufacturer();
    objManufacturer.Name = Convert.ToString(
      myDataSet.Tables["Manufacturer"].Rows[i]["ManufacturerName"]);
    objManufacturer.Country = Convert.ToString(
      myDataSet.Tables["Manufacturer"].Rows[i]["ManufacturerCountry"]);
    objManufacturer.Email = Convert.ToString(
      myDataSet.Tables["Manufacturer"].Rows[i]["ManufacturerEmail"]);
    objManufacturer.Website = Convert.ToString(
      myDataSet.Tables["Manufacturer"].Rows[i]["ManufacturerWebsite"]);
```

```
        Label1.Text += objManufacturer.ToString() + "<BR/>";
    }
}
```

6. Save this code, and then run it. When the page loads, you'll see the same results as the previous example, as shown earlier in Figure 5-3.

How It Works

You see a few more lines of code in this example than in the DataReader example. We reviewed most of the code in the "How to Fill a DataSet" section, where you discovered how to pull information from a database into a `DataSet`. Indeed, the only thing that has changed in the first half of `Page_Load` is to name the `DataTable` in which the results of the query will be saved.

```
myAdapter.Fill(myDataSet, "Manufacturer");
```

You may be wondering where the error-handling code that you've come to expect has gone. If you look back at the code in the "How to Fill a DataSet" section, you'll see that the reason for the error handling was to always close the database connection. Rather than manually opening and closing the database connection, you've taken advantage of the ability of the DataAdapter to open and close the connection automatically. You've removed the explicit calls to the `Open()` and `Close()` methods of the `SqlConnection` object, so you don't need to worry about the error handling in order to close the database connection.

Beyond that, the only new code in the example is for pulling individual columns into the respective properties of a `Manufacturer` object. For example, you use the following code to retrieve the name of the Manufacturer:

```
objManufacturer.Name = Convert.ToString(
    myDataSet.Tables["Manufacturer"].Rows[i]["ManufacturerName"]);
```

You start with the `DataSet` you created called `myDataSet`. You saved the contents of the Manufacturer table from the sample database into a `DataTable` called `Manufacturer`, which you can reference as `myDataSet.Tables["Manufacturer"]`. A `DataTable` contains a `DataRowCollection`, which you can query using its `Count` property to see how many rows you need to iterate through in code.

```
for (int i=0; i<=myDataSet.Tables["Manufacturer"].Rows.Count-1; i++)
```

You can access the rows inside the collection using their index number rather than their name, so you can reference each row as `myDataSet.Tables["Manufacturer"].Rows[i]`. You can then reference each column in a row either by name, as in the example, or by index. If you aren't sure how many columns are in a row (users of wildcards take heed!), you can use the `Count` property of the row's `DataColumnCollection` and use another `for` loop to iterate through them again, like so:

```
for (int i=0; i<=myDataSet.Tables["Manufacturer"].Rows[i].Columns.Count-1; i++)
```

One awkward thing about using the `DataSet` and `DataTable` is the syntax, which can get quite long. However, you can make it easier to read by accessing the `DataTable`, `DataRow`, and `DataColumn` objects directly rather than through the `DataSet` collections every time:

```
// get the manufacturer table
DataTable ManufacturerTable = myDataSet.Tables["Manufacturer"];

// now iterate through the rows in the table
for (int i = 0; i <= ManufacturerTable.Rows.Count - 1; i++)
{
  DataRow rowManufacturer = ManufacturerTable.Rows[i];

  Manufacturer m = new Manufacturer();
  objManufacturer.Name = Convert.ToString(
    rowManufacturer["ManufacturerName"]);
  objManufacturer.Country = Convert.ToString(
    rowManufacturer["ManufacturerCountry"]);
  objManufacturer.Email = Convert.ToString(
    rowManufacturer["ManufacturerEmail"]);
  objManufacturer.Website = Convert.ToString(
    rowManufacturer["ManufacturerWebsite"]);

  Label1.Text += objManufacturer.ToString() + "<BR/>";
}
```

This is a bit more manageable. You extract the table you're after from the DataSet as ManufacturerTable, and then extract the row you're after from the ManufacturerTable.

In the next section, you'll go one step further and build everything manually, even to the point of adding the data manually. This is a little extreme, but it demonstrates that the life of a DataSet isn't wholly dependent on a call to DataAdapter.Fill().

Creating a DataSet from Scratch

In this section, you'll walk through building a DataSet that mirrors the sample database in terms of tables, strongly typed tables, and relationships. The point is to give you a feeling for the child objects and collections that a DataTable contains. Although you'll repeat the same tasks a few times, you'll try to look at several different ways of achieving them. Also, this will help you to understand a bit more about relationships between tables.

Note You can find the complete example in the Chapter05 directory of the code download for this book. It's called DataSet_Building.aspx.

The actual page generated is nothing fancy. It contains four GridView controls, one for each table in the sample database. They're there purely to demonstrate that the DataSet does indeed mimic the database.

```
<body>
  <form id="form1" runat="server">
  <div>
    <asp:GridView ID="grdManufacturer" runat="server">
    </asp:GridView>
    <asp:GridView ID="grdPlayer" runat="server">
    </asp:GridView>
    <asp:GridView ID="grdFormat" runat="server">
    </asp:GridView>
    <asp:GridView ID="grdWPWF" runat="server">
    </asp:GridView>
  </div>
  </form>
</body>
```

As usual, the action takes place in the Page_Load event handler. However, you'll see a fair amount of code, so rather than have it all in one place, it's split into several methods. Inside Page_Load itself, it's pretty straightforward. You start by creating the SqlConnection object, as follows:

```
void Page_Load(object sender, EventArgs e)
{
  // create the connection
  string strConnectionString = ConfigurationManager.
    ConnectionStrings["SqlConnectionString"].ConnectionString;
  SqlConnection myConnection = new SqlConnection(strConnectionString);
```

Then you create a new DataSet object and build it to match the sample database, like so:

```
  // create a new DataSet
  DataSet myDataSet = new DataSet();

  // create the data
  GenerateDataSet(myDataSet, myConnection);
```

Finally, you bind each table in the DataSet to its own GridView and call DataBind(), like so:

```
  // bind each to table to a grid
  grdManufacturer.DataSource = myDataSet.Tables["Manufacturer"];
  grdPlayer.DataSource = myDataSet.Tables["Player"];
  grdFormat.DataSource = myDataSet.Tables["Format"];
  grdWPWF.DataSource = myDataSet.Tables["WhatPlaysWhatFormat"];

  // data bind the page
  Page.DataBind();
}
```

The key is the GenerateDataSet() method, but again, you're just marshaling your forces in this method. All you do here is call the methods that do the real work, like so:

```
void GenerateDataSet(DataSet dset, SqlConnection conn)
{
  // add four tables
  AddPlayerTable(dset);
  AddManufacturerTable(dset);
  AddFormatTable(dset);
  AddWhatPlaysWhatFormatTable(dset);

  // add the relationships
  AddRelationships(dset);

  // fill the tables
  FillManufacturerTable(dset, conn);
  FillPlayerTable(dset, conn);
  FillFormatTable(dset, conn);
  FillWhatPlaysWhatFormatTable(dset, conn);
}
```

■**Note** Strictly speaking, you should never need to model an entire database in a DataSet for the purposes of data binding, especially considering the resources it consumes. However, for demonstration purposes, you can live with it.

Adding DataTables to a DataSet

Adding a DataTable object to a DataSet object in code may seem new, but the methods you need to call and the properties you need to set mirror almost exactly the actions you took back in Chapter 2 when you built the sample database against an actual database server. Those actions are as follows:

- Create and name the table.

- Create and name the columns within the table.

- Set the column's data type.

- Set any other properties the column should have.

- Establish the table's primary key.

Variations exist in how you do this; indeed, you don't actually need to perform all of these tasks to have a valid and working DataTable. The only mandatory steps are the first two: creating the table and creating the columns. The remaining three steps are optional, but they do give you more control over the type of table that you're creating.

Now, let's look at the AddPlayerTable() method. You start by creating a new DataTable object that you'll name Player. You don't have to give a name to the DataTable constructor right away; you can set it later in the TableName property, but there's less code to work through this way.

```
void AddPlayerTable(DataSet dset)
{
  // create the table
  DataTable PlayerTable = new DataTable("Player");
```

Every DataTable has a Columns collection object containing a DataColumnCollection, so to add a new DataColumn, you simply call the collection's Add() method. This will add a DataColumn object that you've already defined to the table or create a new one, add it to the collection, and return it as its result. As demonstrated, you can either set the new DataColumn to a variable for later reference or ignore the return value and just refer to the new DataColumn through the Columns collection, like so:

```
  // create the columns
  DataColumn PlayerID =
    PlayerTable.Columns.Add("PlayerID", typeof(Int32));
  PlayerTable.Columns.Add("PlayerName", typeof(String));
  PlayerTable.Columns.Add("PlayerManufacturerID", typeof(Int32));
  PlayerTable.Columns.Add("PlayerCost", typeof(Decimal));
  PlayerTable.Columns.Add("PlayerStorage", typeof(String));
```

Notice that the Add() method specifies a .NET data type as the second parameter. This allows you to constrain what is stored within the column. However, it isn't necessary to always specify the type of the column. The default data type of a column in a DataTable is String, so if you don't specify a data type, the column will contain strings. So the following declaration of the PlayerStorage column is functionally identical to the one that you're actually using:

```
  PlayerTable.Columns.Add("PlayerStorage");
```

■**Note** If you're specifying a data type for a DataColumn, you must specify a .NET base type; thus, varchar(255) has no meaning here and would create an error. For a list of supported data types, refer to http://msdn2.microsoft.com/system.data.datacolumn.datatype.aspx.

With the columns in the table established, you can attend to their behavior. Should their contents be unique in each column, can they be null, and so on? Each DataColumn object has a set of properties that match those you saw in Chapter 2. When a column is created, the most common properties have the following default values: AllowDBNull is true, Unique is false, and ReadOnly is false. Also, for String types, MaxLength equals –1 by default, which implies there's no maximum length for the column. For a database column containing an autonumber, you must also set the AutoIncrement property to true, along with the AutoIncrementSeed property for a start value, such as 1. This latter property doesn't have a default value, but the AutoIncrementStep property does: 1.

You need to make the following adjustments:

```
// set the properties
PlayerTable.Columns["PlayerName"].MaxLength = 50;
PlayerTable.Columns["PlayerName"].AllowDBNull = false;
PlayerTable.Columns["PlayerManufacturerID"].AllowDBNull = false;
PlayerTable.Columns["PlayerCost"].AllowDBNull = false;
PlayerTable.Columns["PlayerStorage"].MaxLength = 50;
PlayerTable.Columns["PlayerStorage"].AllowDBNull = false;
```

Finally, you need to set PlayerID to be the table's primary key. This will automatically set its AllowDBNull property to false, and its Unique property will be true. Note that the PrimaryKey property actually requires an array of DataColumn objects in case the table's primary key is a composite one and contains more than one column. You'll see this at work when you build the WhatPlaysWhatFormat table.

```
// set the primary key
PlayerTable.PrimaryKey = new DataColumn[] { PlayerID };
PlayerTable.Columns["PlayerID"].AutoIncrement = true;
PlayerTable.Columns["PlayerID"].AutoIncrementSeed = 1;
```

Last, but not least, you add the whole DataTable to the Tables collection of the DataSet, like so:

```
// add the table
dset.Tables.Add(PlayerTable);
}
```

So, as long as you stick to the same methodical way of adding columns to a table in a database, adding a DataColumn to a DataTable will remain a straightforward process in code. You'll now look at a couple of variations in the other AddxxxTable() methods.

AddManufacturerTable() neatly shows that you don't need to add a DataTable to a DataSet once it has been fully defined. Like the Add() method for a DataTable's Columns collection, the Add() method for a DataSet's Tables collection allows you to create and add a blank DataTable with a given name, as well as add an already established one. Thus, you can make the following call and use the DataTable returned by Add() to define the table:

```
void AddManufacturerTable(DataSet dset)
{
  // create and add the table
  DataTable ManufacturerTable = dset.Tables.Add("Manufacturer");

  ...
}
```

AddWhatPlaysWhatFormatTable() also demonstrates how you deal with composite primary keys. You simply add all the DataColumn objects in the primary key to the DataTable's PrimaryKey array, like so:

```
void AddWhatPlaysWhatFormatTable(DataSet dset)
{
```

```
// create the table
DataTable WhatPlaysWhatFormatTable = new DataTable("WhatPlaysWhatFormatTable");

// add the columns
WhatPlaysWhatFormatTable.Columns.Add("WPWFPlayerID", typeof(Int32));
WhatPlaysWhatFormatTable.Columns.Add("WPWFFormatID", typeof(Int32));

// set the primary key
WhatPlaysWhatFormatTable.PrimaryKey = new DataColumn[] {
  WhatPlaysWhatFormatTable.Columns["WPWFPlayerID"],
  WhatPlaysWhatFormatTable.Columns["WPWFFormatID"] };

// add the table
dset.Tables.Add(WhatPlaysWhatFormatTable);
}
```

Note that if more than one `DataColumn` is added to the `PrimaryKey` array, only their `AllowDBNull` properties will be changed from their default to true. Their `Unique` property remains false, in contrast to the situation where the primary key is only one column when `Unique` is set to true.

Setting Up Relationships in a DataSet

In Chapter 2, you learned how a relationship between two columns was first established and then clarified by a constraint. A unique constraint would ensure that the parent column contained unique values in each column, and a foreign key constraint would cover what happened to all the entries in a child table when the corresponding entry in the parent table was altered somehow. The same is true of relationships between the `DataTable` objects in a `DataSet`, as you'll see in this section.

If you recall, the sample database has three relationships between tables, as shown in Figure 5-5. Each is backed by a foreign key constraint that says that a change in the parent table cannot be made if there are corresponding entries in the child table.

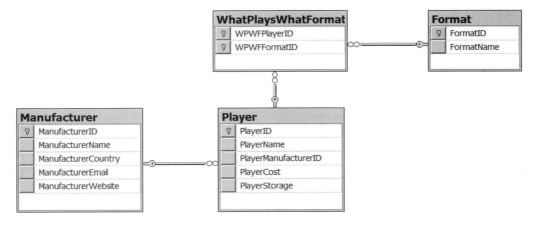

Figure 5-5. *Three relationships to create*

All three relationships are built in the same way in the AddRelationships() method, so you'll look at just one: the relationship between the Player and Manufacturer tables. The relationship between the tables is modeled using a DataRelation object and any constraints on the relationship by accessing either the ParentKeyConstraint or ChildKeyConstraint properties of the DataRelation.

To establish a relationship, you need to create a new DataRelation object, specifying its name (ManufacturerToPlayer) and the parent and child columns that form the relationship:

```
// create the Manufacturer to Player relationship
DataRelation ManufacturerToPlayerRelation = new DataRelation(
  "ManufacturerToPlayer",
  dset.Tables["Manufacturer"].Columns["ManufacturerID"],
  dset.Tables["Player"].Columns["PlayerManufacturerID"]);
```

Once the DataRelation object has been created, it can be added to the Relations collection using the Add() method:

```
dset.Relations.Add(ManufacturerToPlayerRelation);
```

Note that unlike all the Add() functions you've seen in this section, this Add() method won't create a blank DataRelation for you to use. You *must* provide the related columns for the DataRelation to be created.

With the relation established, you can set constraints on the parent or child column by assigning one to the ParentKeyConstraint or ChildKeyConstraint property, respectively. In this case, you need to establish a ForeignKeyConstraint on the child column. You need to block DELETE and UPDATE queries that would cause an orphan row in the Player table, like so:

```
ForeignKeyConstraint ManufacturerToPlayerConstraint =
  ManufacturerToPlayerRelation.ChildKeyConstraint;
ManufacturerToPlayerConstraint.DeleteRule = Rule.None;
ManufacturerToPlayerConstraint.UpdateRule = Rule.None;
```

Setting the DeleteRule and UpdateRule properties to Rule.None stops any deletions or updates to the Manufacturer table that would cause orphan rows in the Player table.

And that's it. The rest of AddRelationships() essentially repeats this code to put the other two relationships in place.

Creating DataRows

With each DataTable and the relationships between them established, all that's left is to add some data to the tables. You've already seen how to use Fill() to fill tables, but that's not the only way to add information to a DataTable. You can also create and populate DataRow objects, adding them individually to the corresponding DataTable. The FillManufacturerTable() method demonstrates this.

■**Note** You may be wondering why you create the Player table first but populate the Manufacturer table first. You need to do this as there is a relationship between the two tables, and you can't have a Player without a Manufacturer (you'll get an `InvalidConstraintException`), so you must add Manufacturers before you can add Players. The order that you add data to the database is important, but the order in which you add unrelated (at least when they're created) tables to the database is irrelevant.

The first option to work with a DataRow (and the recommended one) is to create an empty DataRow object by calling NewRow() on the DataTable object for which you want to create the row.

```
void FillManufacturerTable(DataSet dset, SqlConnection conn)
{
  DataRow NewRow = dset.Tables["Manufacturer"].NewRow();
```

The advantage with this method is that the DataRow object will know what each column is called and the type of value it should contain, having ascertained it from the DataTable object to which the row is being added. It will therefore generate an exception if you try to add values that go against the rules on the table. When you have added values as appropriate, you use Add() to add it to the Rows collection for that DataTable, like so:

```
// create a row on the table
NewRow["ManufacturerID"] = 1;
NewRow["ManufacturerName"] = "Apple";
NewRow["ManufacturerCity"] = "USA";
NewRow["ManufacturerEmail"] = "lackey@apple.com";
NewRow["ManufacturerWebsite"] = "http://www.apple.com";
dset.Tables["Manufacturer"].Rows.Add(NewRow);
```

The second option to add data to a DataTable is to create an array of generic objects that matches the columns in the table, rather than creating a DataRow object. The disadvantage here is that you can create an illegal value for a column that will be picked up only when you try to Add() it to the Rows collection.

```
// create a row from an array
Object[] NewRowColumns = new Object[5];
NewRowColumns[0] = 2;
NewRowColumns[1] = "Cowon";
NewRowColumns[2] = "Korea";
NewRowColumns[3] = "moomoo@cowon.com";
NewRowColumns[4] = "http://www.cowon.com";
dset.Tables["Manufacturer "].Rows.Add(NewRowColumns);
```

Several of the examples in the .NET Software Development Kit (SDK) build up rows of data using loops to generate values, which is handy for examples, but in general, you'll probably end up using a DataAdapter to fill a DataTable once you've created it. You should know the following about using Fill() in this situation:

- If you call Fill() on a DataTable with no columns, as you did in the earlier "Iterating Through a DataSet" section, the DataTable will be filled with the data from the table, and none of the extra details that you added in the last example—none of the DataTable schema definition—will be created. The Fill() method will assign each column in the DataTable a name and data type as best it can from the columns in the query results it's storing. However, properties such as AllowDBNull and ReadOnly will remain at their defaults, and the PrimaryKey for the table won't be set.

- In contrast, if you call Fill() on a DataTable whose details you've defined, as you have in this example, the DataAdapter will try to match DataColumn names with column names in the query results and fill in the values accordingly. If it can't match a column name with a DataColumn, it will create a new DataColumn with the same name as the column and use that instead. Make sure that the column and DataColumn names match up, or use aliases in your SQL query.

That said, one version of Fill() you didn't try earlier allows you to specify a subsection of the results from a query to add to a DataTable. This fits in nicely with the problem you now have with the DataTable copy of the Manufacturer table in FillManufacturerTable (). Using code to create the first two rows manually means that the versions of Fill() you've used so far would try to duplicate those two rows if you called them now. Moreover, this would cause an error because values in the primary key column would be duplicated, which isn't allowed.

You first need to create the Command and DataAdapter objects that return the information:

```
// create the Command and DataAdapter
SqlDataAdapter ManufacturerAdapter = new SqlDataAdapter();
SqlCommand ManufacturerCommand = new SqlCommand(
    "SELECT * FROM Manufacturer ORDER BY ManufacturerID", conn);
ManufacturerAdapter.SelectCommand = ManufacturerCommand;
```

This new version of Fill() allows you to say which row in the results you start filling from and how many rows you want to add to the DataTable. The first parameter identifies the DataSet you're working with, the second is the index number of the row in the results of the SelectCommand to start filling with, and the third is the number of rows (with 0 meaning all), to add to the DataTable, which is identified by the fourth parameter.

```
// fill the DataTable
ManufacturerAdapter.Fill(dset, 2, 0, "Manufacturer");
}
```

Note that the SelectCommand still retrieves all the rows from the Manufacturer table, even though you don't use the first two. If you wanted to retrieve only the seven rows required, you would need to alter the SELECT query rather than use this variant of Fill().

SqlDataSource—DataSet or DataReader?

As you've seen in this chapter, you have two ways to access data in the database:

- As a DataReader, allowing forward-only access to the data

- As a DataSet, allowing full control over the disconnected data

This still doesn't explain how the SqlDataSource accesses the database. Does it do it using a DataReader or a DataSet? Well, actually, it can do both!

By default, the SqlDataSource connects to the database and stores the data internally as a disconnected DataSet. However, you can tell the SqlDataSource to access the database using a DataReader by setting its DataSourceMode property, which has two possible values:

- DataReader: Retrieves data from the database using a DataReader. The type of DataReader (SqlDataReader, OleDbDataReader, or OdbcDataReader) is determined from the connection used for the SqlDataSource.

- DataSet: Retrieves the data from the database into a DataSet. This is the default value.

So why would you want to change the default behavior and use a DataReader to connect to the database? The main reason is speed. As you've learned, the DataReader is the fastest way of talking to a database; a DataSet adds overhead.

If you're simply using a SqlDataSource to get a set of results from the database to display to the user, you should set the DataSourceMode property to SqlDataSourceMode.DataReader. You've already looked at this use of the SqlDataSource in Chapter 3, when you populated the list box containing the list of Manufacturers in the database. In that case, you just show this data to the user, so you should have used a DataReader.

For every other use of the SqlDataSource, you should leave the DataSourceMode as the default value of SqlDataSourceMode.DataSet. Although so far, you've looked at only displaying data in a GridView from the SqlDataSource, it can do a lot more. As you'll see in Chapter 9, a SqlDataSource in association with a GridView can allow paging, sorting, and filtering of the data that you've retrieved. A SqlDataSource can also allow the user to modify the data and have the changes propagated back to the underlying database. In these cases, you need to access the data using a DataSet.

DataSet vs. DataReader

Now that you have a rough idea of how a DataSet works, it's time to take a look at how it compares with a DataReader. The two have some obvious differences. Table 5-3 lists the differences you've seen so far and a few related ones.

You'll also see a comparison of the DataSet and DataReader objects at the end of Chapter 7, with respect to the theory and techniques you learn there. The intention is that by the end of Chapter 7, you'll be able to make a sound judgment as to which object should be used as the source of data for any ASP.NET pages you're writing.

Table 5-3. *Characteristics of DataReaders and DataSets*

DataReader	DataSet
A DataReader is specific to a data provider (for example, SqlDataReader, OdbcDataReader, and OleDbDataReader).	The DataSet class isn't a part of any data provider. It's specific to .NET only. However, the DataAdapter used to fill the DataSet with Fill() is specific to a data provider (for example, SqlDataAdapter, OdbcDataAdapter, and OleDbDataAdapter).
The data retrieved through a DataReader is read-only.	The data retrieved through a DataSet is read-write.
The data retrieved through a DataReader is forward-only. Once the data has been cycled through, the DataReader must be closed and re-created in order to reaccess the data.	You can work with data in a DataSet in any order you choose as many times as you like.
A DataReader presents data through a direct connection to the data source. Only one row of data is stored in memory at any one time.	A DataSet stores all the data from the data source in memory at once.
A DataReader takes up few IIS and memory resources but annexes the database connection until it's closed.	A DataSet takes up a lot more IIS and memory resources to store all the data, but it doesn't hold up a database connection until it's closed. The connection needs to be open only when Fill() is called.
A DataReader lasts as long as the connection to the database is open. It can't be persisted in a cookie or a session variable.	A DataSet lasts only until the page is reloaded (posted back), unless it's somehow persisted (for example, in a session variable).
Columns in a DataReader are referenced by index or name.	You can reference columns in a DataSet by name, but you must also name the DataTable and identify the row (index) that contains the column.
A DataReader has no concept of primary keys, constraints, views, or any other relational database management system concepts, except rows and columns.	A DataSet contains a collection of DataTable objects. A primary key may be set for each DataTable, and relationships and constraints may be established between them.
You can't update a data source through a DataReader.	You can make changes to data in a DataSet, and then send those changes back to the data source.
A DataReader connects to only one data source.	A DataSet can be filled with Fill() from multiple data sources but, once the data is retrieved, is not connected to any of them.

Good Practices

The next chapter looms, but before you start putting data on the screen, let's quickly recap some useful coding tips covered in this chapter.

- Query only for the information you want to use. For example, don't query for three columns per row if you're using only two. Likewise, use a WHERE clause in a SELECT query to retrieve only the rows of information that are required, rather than every row in the database.

- If you're using a DataReader, make sure you close it with Close() as soon as you can. Similarly, make sure you use Close() for your Connection as well.

- Use the DataReader's HasRows and IsDBNull properties to avoid any unwanted error messages when working with data.

- If you're using a DataSet, be aware of how calling Fill() will work with the DataSet you're using. Will it create new columns in a DataTable or use the other ones there? Make sure the columns you're querying for in the database match those in the DataTable you're targeting.

- Don't forget that primary keys and relationships in a DataSet won't be copied over from a database. You must create them in code.

Summary

In this chapter, you looked in detail at the DataReader and DataSet objects. These are the two objects most commonly used as the receptacle for query results by data-driven pages.

You learned that the DataReader is a read-only, forward-only, data-provider-specific window on the results of the query sent by a page, and that you can iterate through those results a row at a time using the DataReader's Read() method. Individual pieces of information can be identified in the current row in a DataReader by name and by index and can be vetted before being used with the DataReader's HasRows and IsDBNull properties.

In contrast, you saw that the DataSet is data-provider-independent. It's a container for a group of objects that can describe with some accuracy the table structure and relationships in a database, and because it's all in memory, the query results stored in a DataSet are read-write and can be accessed in any order. You can either build a complete data structure in code from scratch or Fill() it using a DataAdapter object.

In the next chapter, you'll begin your exploration of data binding, beginning with inline and list binding.

CHAPTER 6

■ ■ ■

Inline and List Binding

In Chapter 5, you looked at two of the most important objects in ADO.NET: the DataReader and the DataSet. You saw how the DataReader is a transient object and provides forward-only, read-only access to the results of any query you send to the data source. In contrast, the DataSet is a read-write, random-access representation of any data source that stays in memory even when the connection to the data source closes. You learned how they both can be populated with data from a data source, and how you can pull that data into something more useful for your Web site, such as a business object.

In this and the next chapter, you'll continue your work with these two objects, as well as the SqlDataSource, and discover the various ways of retrieving and displaying read-only data on a page. You'll also see that the trade-off between the speed of the DataReader and the availability of the DataSet often makes a difference in the way you build even simple pages.

In this chapter, you'll learn the following:

- The three types of data-binding: inline binding, list binding, and table binding

- The differences between binding a DataReader or DataSet in code and binding using the SqlDataSource

- How to perform inline binding to both a DataReader and DataSet

- An alternative to inline binding that returns the same results

- How to perform list binding to a DataReader, DataSet, and SqlDataSource

- How to perform listing binding with Web list controls that allow multiple selections

Data-Binding Techniques

In Chapter 1, I described how a data-aware page is basically a static template into which data is added dynamically from a data source. This "plugging in" of data to a page is more commonly known as *data binding*. You saw data binding in action in Chapter 3 with the SqlDataSource, and then in Chapter 4, when you actually wrote code to return the results that you wanted from the database.

How you implement data binding depends on how you're accessing the database (are you using a SqlDataSource or writing code to access the database?), how much data you want to bind, and to which Web controls you want to bind the data. However, although there are many variations in data-binding techniques, they all fall into one of the following three categories:

- Binding single columns to the properties or value of a Web control. This is often known as *inline binding*.

- Binding a list of values (one column in a table) to a Web control. For convenience, I'll call this *list binding*.

- Binding a table of values to a Web control. For convenience, I'll call this *table binding*.

In this chapter, we'll explore inline binding and list binding. Table binding is covered in the next chapter. But before we look at the specifics for each technique, let's review the general process for data binding with code, how data binding works with the SqlDataSource, and the Web controls that can be data-bound.

Data Binding in Code

When accessing the database in code, the process for adding a data-bound Web control is as follows:

1. Add a data-aware Web control to the page.

2. Associate a source of data with the Web control using the DataSource property.

3. Call DataBind() on the Web control or on the Page.

All the examples in Chapter 4 followed these three steps with the barest minimum of code, binding the query results to a GridView object:

```
GridView1.DataSource = myCommand.ExecuteReader();
GridView1.DataBind();
```

Calling DataBind() seems straightforward, but there's one catch: on what object? Every Web control implements this interface because it must as a derivative of its parent class, System.Web.UI.Control. A call to DataBind() on a Web control will also call DataBind() on any Web controls contained within it. So, you could call it on a Label, and just that particular binding would occur. On the other hand, you could call Page.DataBind(), and the command would also filter down to every Web control on the page.

You need to also consider a second issue here. Should a page rebind to a data source each time a page posts back? Consider a page containing a lot of Web controls populated by binding RadioButtonList controls, CheckBox controls, and other elements to a data source with the eventual aim to update the user's answers back to the database. You don't need to bind the Web controls to the data source more than once, because its purpose is purely to set up the page, not to record the answers given to it. It would be a huge waste of resources to rebind the data every time the page was posted back to the Web server, especially if the page were complex. It would also lose the values the user had entered onto the page if it were posted back, because the rebinding would write over them. This is obviously not ideal. We'll look at how to manage when the data binding occurs in this chapter's examples.

Data Binding and the SqlDataSource

In Chapter 3, you used a `SqlDataSource` to populate both a `DropDownList` with the list of Manufacturers in the database and a `GridView` with a filtered list of Players. The one thing you didn't do was write any code to access the database. You used the following process to add a data-bound Web control using a `SqlDataSource`:

1. Add a `SqlDataSource` to the page.

2. Add a data-aware Web control to the page.

3. Associate the `SqlDataSource` with the data-aware Web control using the `DataSourceID` property.

You'll notice that you do not make an explicit call to `DataBind()`, as you do when you write code to access the database. So how is the data binding done? Automatic data binding occurs, with a call to `DataBind()` on the Web control, after the `OnPreRender` event and before the `OnPreRenderComplete` event in the page life cycle.

Although the `DataBind()` method is called automatically when using a `SqlDataSource`, that doesn't mean that you can't call `DataBind()` on the Web control to force the data binding to occur if necessary.

Data-Aware Web Controls

All three data-binding techniques—inline binding, list binding, and table binding—apply *only* to Web controls because the whole process takes place on the server before the page is sent to the client. Technically speaking, every Web control must understand how to bind data to its properties, because it inherits the `DataBind()` method as something it must implement from its parent `System.Web.UI.Control` class. At the least, this means that every Web control understands inline binding and can set its properties to values from a database. Some Web controls also know how to bind lists and tables of data into their structure.

Table 6-1 shows which groups of Web controls support which type of binding.

■**Note** Table 6-1 doesn't list any Web controls derived from `System.Web.UI.HtmlControl`. You can use `HtmlControl`-derived Web controls for inline binding but, in all cases, there is a `WebControl` equivalent that you should use instead.

Table 6-1. *Web Controls and the Data Binding They Support*

Control Type	Control Names	Binding Supported
Text-based controls	HyperLink, Label, Literal, Localize, Xml	Inline
Form items	Button, CheckBox, FileUpload, HiddenField, ImageButton, LinkButton, RadioButton, TextBox	Inline
Form lists	BulletedList, CheckBoxList, DropDownList, ListBox, RadioButtonList	Inline, list
Images and spaces	AdRotator, Image, ImageMap, Panel, PlaceHolder	Inline
Tabular	Calendar, Table, TableCell, TableFooterRow, TableHeaderCell, TableHeaderRow, TableRow	Inline
Validation	CompareValidator, CustomValidator, RangeValidator, RegularExpressionValidator, RequiredFieldValidator, ValidationSummary	Inline
Data-aware controls	DataGrid, DataList, DetailsView, FormView, GridView, Menu, Repeater, SiteMapPath, TreeView	Inline, list, table
Master page controls	Content, ContentPlaceHolder	Inline
Profile controls	ChangePassword, CreateUserWizard, Login, LoginName, LoginStatus, LoginView, PasswordRecovery	Inline
Wizard controls	CompleteWizardStep, CreateUserWizardStep, MultiView, TemplateWizardStep, View, Wizard, WizardStep	Inline
Web part catalog controls	DeclarativeCatalogPart, ImportCatalogPart, PageCatalogPart	Inline
Web part editor controls	AppearanceEditorPart, BehaviorEditorPart, LayoutEditorPart, PropertyGridEditorPart	Inline
Web part part controls	ErrorWebPart, UnauthorizedWebPart	Inline
Web part zone controls	CatalogZone, ConnectionsZone, EditorZone	Inline

As you can see in Table 6-1, a lot of the Web controls allow only inline binding, which is the same for all Web controls. With more than 70 Web controls, it may seem that only a few support list and table binding. But these Web controls are pretty powerful, and you'll be surprised at what you can actually do with them.

Associating Data to the Web Control

The following sections contain three questions to ponder:

- How much data do you need to pull from your data source?

- Which object do you stream it into?

- How do you associate it to a Web control?

How Much Data Do You Need?

You've already learned that you can use the SELECT query to query for as much or as little data as is required for binding to the Web controls on your page. It makes sense to query only for what you need.

For example, inline binding requires you to identify individual columns to take values from, so why take a whole table's worth? Depending on the object you're sourcing the data from (see the next section), it may not matter if it contains several rows of data, because you can specify which row and column to use. As you know, however, the DataReader presents only a row at a time, so you may want to query only for a specific row of data with a query such as the following:

```
SELECT UserCategory, PreferredColorScheme, ConnectionSpeed
FROM UserPreference
WHERE UserName = 'Damien Foggon'
```

In a similar vein, if you're interested in list binding, you need to present the Web control with a set of rows in the order you want to display them. Each row needs to contain only *two* columns: one that represents the text for items in the list and one that provides the values for items that will be passed on when selected by a user. So, for example, when you displayed the list of Manufacturers in Chapters 3 and 4, you returned only the two columns you needed from the database: the ManufacturerName column to display to the user and the ManufacturerID to make a note of the selections:

```
SELECT ManufacturerID, ManufacturerName
FROM Manufacturer
ORDER BY ManufacturerName
```

In the case of table binding, you can retrieve more data, but try to restrict your query to just what you need. It's possible to hide columns in a GridView, but why bother if you don't need the column in the first place? Don't forget that there's no reason a GridView or similar Web control can't be bound to a query whose results contain only one or two columns.

Which Object Should You Use?

Although we're restricting our discussion to the DataReader, DataSet, and SqlDataSource, it's worth noting that you can use many other objects as the source of the data to which you're binding a Web control. For list and table binding, you can use any class that implements the IEnumerable interface. Some examples of classes that support the IEnumerable interface and can be used for list and table binding are as follows:

- ArrayList objects

- Collections (any class that implements the ICollection interface)

- DataRow objects

- DataTable objects

- DataView objects

If you're inline binding a single value to a Web control property, you can use practically any other single value from any other object available to you, as long as you know the syntax to get the value from the object.

How Do You Create the Association?

The step to create the association comes before the call DataBind() is made (whether in code or automatically in the case of the SqlDataSource), and as such, means that a Web control or property can't be bound to data based on the values bound into some other Web control—not unless you're using a postback in the page to react to choices made by the user.

Inline binding is quite different from list or table binding at this stage, because you must associate the property with the column that will fill it in the HTML markup of the page, rather than the code. For those of you who have worked with classic ASP, inline binding is reminiscent of the way you inserted ASP code into pages.

Let's say you wanted to bind the Text property of a Label. You would use the following in the page:

```
<asp:Label id="Label1" runat="server" text="<%# expression %>">
```

The expression in the text must identify the source for the value you want bound to the Text property and must be surrounded by <%# ... %> tags.

In contrast, list and table binding can be set up in both the code and the HTML markup of the page. For both, you need to set the DataSource or DataSourceID property for the Web control you're binding to the data source. If you're binding to a Web list control, you also need to set its DataValueField and DataTextField properties to the columns in your queried data.

■**Note** Inline binding is one of those things that you'll either love or you'll hate. Personally, it's something that I never do. ASP.NET was supposed to free us from the problems of spaghetti code, but using inline binding makes the code look like a plate of pasta. As you'll see after the Inline Binding section, you can accomplish the same task without relying on data binding.

Inline Binding

Although inline binding data from a DataSet may be more common, the technique is no less valid against a DataReader. In the next two examples, you'll try both approaches.

■**Note** Although a SqlDataSource performs essentially the same function as a DataReader or DataSet, you can't use the SqlDataSource for inline binding. The SqlDataSource can be used only in list and table binding.

Try It Out: Inline Binding to a DataReader

In this example, you'll mimic the results from the "Try it Out: Iterating through a DataReader" section in the previous chapter and print the details of a single Manufacturer in your sample database. Rather than use a single Web control to present the results, you'll use two Label controls and two HyperLink controls to echo the results.

1. In Visual Web Developer, create a new Web site at C:\BAND\Chapter06 and delete the auto-generated Default.aspx file.

2. Add a new Web.config file to the Web site and add a new setting to the <connectionStrings /> element:

```
<add name="SqlConnectionString"
  connectionString="Data Source=localhost\BAND;Initial Catalog=BAND;
    Persist Security Info=True;User ID=band;Password=letmein"
  providerName="System.Data.SqlClient" />
```

3. Add a new Web Form called Inline_DataReader.aspx to the Web site.

4. In the Source view, find the <title> tag within the HTML at the bottom of the page and change the page title to **Inline Binding to a DataReader**.

5. In the Design view, add two Label controls to the page. Name the first lblName and the second lblCountry. Now add two HyperLink controls onto the page. Name them lnkEmail and lnkWebsite. Finally, add one more Label called lblError to house any error messages should something untoward happen (oh, the horror!). Now clear the Text properties for all five Web controls. With a bit of added text (**Country, Email,** and **Website**), your page should look something Figure 6-1.

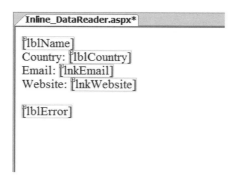

Figure 6-1. *Basic layout for Inline_DataReader.aspx*

6. In the Source view, make sure you've included the correct data provider at the top of the page.

```
<%@ Page Language="C#" %>
<%@ Import Namespace="System.Data.SqlClient" %>
```

7. You need to set up a DataReader to query for Manufacturer details and add your standard code for database access.

```
// must declare the DataReader globally; else the page can't see it.
SqlDataReader myReader;

protected void Page_Load(object sender, EventArgs e)
{
  // set up connection string and SQL query
  string ConnectionString = ConfigurationManager.
    ConnectionStrings["SqlConnectionString"].ConnectionString;
  string CommandText = "SELECT ManufacturerName, ManufacturerCountry, ➥
    ManufacturerEmail, ManufacturerWebsite FROM Manufacturer ➥
    WHERE ManufacturerID = 1";

  // create SqlConnection and SqlCommand objects
  SqlConnection myConnection = new SqlConnection(ConnectionString);
  SqlCommand myCommand = new SqlCommand(CommandText, myConnection);

  // use try finally clauses when the connection is open.
  try
  {
    // open the database connection
    myConnection.Open();

    // run query
    myReader = myCommand.ExecuteReader();

    if (myReader.Read())
    {
      // Process results here.
    }
    else
    {
      // show the error
      lblError.Text = "No results to databind to.";
    }

    // close the reader
    myReader.Close();
  }
  finally
  {
    // always close the database connection
    myConnection.Close();
  }
}
```

8. Now you need to set which data should be bound and to what. Scroll to the bottom of the Source view and find the <body> tag in the HTML. Modify the HTML so that it's as follows (the changed parts are shown in bold):

```
<body>
  <form id="form1" runat="server">
  <div>
    <asp:Label ID="lblName" runat="server">
      Name: <%# DataBinder.Eval (myReader, "[ManufacturerName]") %>
    </asp:Label>
    <br />
    Country:
    <asp:Label ID="lblCountry" runat="server"
      Text='<%# DataBinder.Eval (myReader, "[ManufacturerCountry]") %>'>
    </asp:Label>
    <br />
    Contact:
    <asp:HyperLink ID="lnkEmail" runat="server"
      NavigateUrl='mailto:<%# DataBinder.Eval (myReader, "[2]") %>'
      Text='<%# DataBinder.Eval (myReader, "[ManufacturerEmail]") %>'>
    </asp:HyperLink>
    <br />
    Website:
    <asp:HyperLink ID="lnkWebsite" runat="server"
      NavigateUrl='<%# DataBinder.Eval (myReader, "[3]") %>'>
      <%# DataBinder.Eval (myReader, "[ManufacturerWebsite]") %>
    </asp:HyperLink>
    <br /><br />
    <asp:Label ID="lblError" runat="server"></asp:Label><br />
  </div>
  </form>
</body>
```

9. You've added the data-aware Web controls to the page and associated them with the required data retrieved from the database. All that's left to do is call DataBind(). Scroll back to the <script> block at the start of the page and modify the Page_Load event as follows:

```
if (myReader.Read())
{
  // bind the data
  Page.DataBind();
}
else
{
  // show the error
  lblError.Text="No results to databind to.";
}
```

10. Save the code, and then view the page in a browser. When the page loads, all appears to be well, but is it? Move your cursor over the e-mail link, as shown in Figure 6-2, and you'll see that the link isn't `mailto: lackey@apple.com`. You'll have to change it.

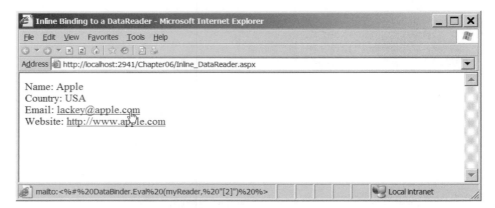

Figure 6-2. *All is not well with this link.*

11. To fix the problem, you need to use a different version of the `DataBinder.Eval()` method. An overloaded version takes a format string as its third parameter, so you can alter the `NavigateUrl` property of `lnkEmail` to be as follows:

```
NavigateUrl='<%# DataBinder.Eval (myReader, "[2]", "mailto:{0}") %>'
```

12. You've solved the problem. Save the file, and then test the code again. You'll see that the link now works, as shown in Figure 6-3.

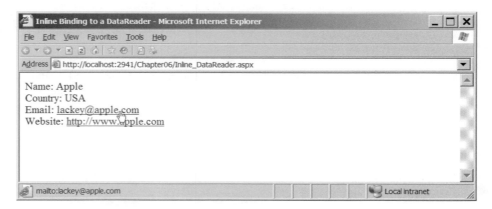

Figure 6-3. *Inline binding to a DataReader*

How It Works

The aim of the page is to display a Manufacturer's details, just as you did in the example in Chapter 5. However, here you limited your results to just a single Manufacturer (displaying a list of Manufacturers would imply list binding, which we'll cover later in this chapter):

```
SELECT ManufacturerName, ManufacturerCountry,
  ManufacturerEmail, ManufacturerWebsite
FROM Manufacturer
WHERE ManufacturerID = 1
```

Let's see how what you've done follows the three-step process for data binding outlined earlier.

Adding Data-Aware Web Controls

The first step is to add some Web controls to the page. Here, you added a Web control for each detail in the database. That way, you can experiment a bit with combinations of text and bound data to see what works and what doesn't.

Associating the Columns of Data to the Web Controls

The second step is to associate the columns of data to the Web controls. For the first Label, lblName, you've mixed the binding expression with the text value of the Web control's tag. In the expression itself, you call DataBinder.Eval(), which is a static method and thus always available.

```
<asp:Label id="lblName" runat="server">
  Name: <%# DataBinder.Eval (myReader, "[ManufacturerName]") %>
</asp:Label>
```

This requires two arguments: the name of the data source object (myReader) and a string stating from which column to take the value. Because you're using a DataReader, you can reference the column using either the name of the column or its index value in the row. You use the column name here, because it makes it a little easier to see what you're actually binding to the Web control.

■**Tip** Using the name of the column, rather than its index, when data binding reduces the chances of errors that can sometimes be difficult to spot. If you're accessing columns by index and the columns in the SELECT query change, the indexes may no longer be valid, and you could swap two columns around that shouldn't be swapped. When you use the name of the column, as long as the column is still returned by the SELECT query, changing the columns that are returned won't cause any problems.

In the second Label, lblCountry, you're binding a value to the Text property. Of course, this amounts to the same thing, but it does show that you can bind to both a property and a value.

```
<asp:Label ID="lblCountry" runat="server"
  Text='<%# DataBinder.Eval (myReader, "[ManufacturerCountry]") %>'>
</asp:Label>
```

▓**Caution** You must use double quotes around the second parameter of `DataBinder.Eval()` and therefore single quotes around the binding expression as a whole. This is because ASP.NET associates single quotes with single-character values, not strings, and it will throw an error when it tries to parse [ManufacturerCountry] as a single character. HTML, on the other hand, isn't as picky about quotes, as long as they're paired correctly.

In the third `Label`, `lnkEmail`, you've attempted to bind to two properties, `NavigateUrl` and `Text`. However, you encountered the problem that hyperlinks require e-mail addresses to be prefixed with `mailto:` for them to be recognized as e-mail addresses rather than Web site addresses by the browser. Thus, you tried to concatenate text and binding expression inside the Web control's attribute, like so:

```
NavigateUrl='mailto: <%# DataBinder.Eval (myReader, "[2]") %>'
```

This doesn't work, because you can't mix the two inside a Web control's property. As soon as you do, ASP.NET regards the binding expression as literal text instead of as a placeholder for data. Also, *you have no way to alter the value of the column in the DataReader*. But it *is* possible to format the value of the column as it's being bound to the Web control using an alternate version of `DataBinder.Eval()`. You just pass it the format string `mailto:{0}` as its third parameter, and `DataBinder.Eval()` will retrieve the column from the DataReader, substitute it for the placeholder `{0}`, and assign the newly formatted string to the property:

```
<asp:HyperLink ID="lnkEmail" runat="server"
  NavigateUrl='mailto: <%# DataBinder.Eval (myReader, "[2]") %>'
  Text='<%# DataBinder.Eval (myReader, "[ManufacturerEmail]") %>'>
</asp:HyperLink>
```

Also notice that you've used both methods of referring to a column here. The column index is used by `NavigateUrl`, and the column name is used by the `Text` property. As noted earlier, these are interchangeable and, at least with the `SELECT` query as it stands at the moment, both refer to the same column within the row.

Finally, the fourth `Label` on the page demonstrates that you can bind to both the properties and the text value of a Web control at the same time:

```
<asp:HyperLink ID="lnkWebsite" runat="server"
  NavigateUrl='<%# DataBinder.Eval (myReader, "[3]") %>'>
  <%# DataBinder.Eval (myReader, "[ManufacturerWebsite]") %>
</asp:HyperLink>
```

Calling DataBind() on the Page

With all the placeholders for the data set up, it's just a matter of creating the DataReader, accessing the first row (you still have to call `Read()` or else there's nothing to bind to), and calling `DataBind()`:

```
// run query
myReader = myCommand.ExecuteReader();

if (myReader.Read())
{
  Page.DataBind();
}
else
{
  lblError.Text="No results to databind to.";
}

// close the reader
myReader.Close();
```

Notice that you've called `DataBind()` on the whole page rather than the individual Web controls. If you comment out this call, nothing at all will get set. As a slight extension of this example, try experimenting with binding individual Web controls just to prove that binding to one label won't affect the others unless they, too, are explicitly bound. Perhaps create a `Panel` that contains some of the Web controls and call `DataBind()` on that to prove that it's not just the `DataBind()` method in the `Page` that filters down to its children.

Try It Out: Inline Binding to a DataSet

Inline binding to values stored in a `DataSet` works in much the same way as the previous example with a DataReader. The main difference is that the binding expression is slightly different to accommodate the syntax used to identify tables, rows, and columns inside a `DataSet`. To see it in action, you'll adapt the previous example to do the same job using a `DataSet` instead of a DataReader.

1. In Visual Web Developer open `Inline_DataReader.aspx` and resave it as `Inline_DataSet.aspx`. Change the `<title>` tag of the page to be **Inline Binding to a DataSet**.

2. Add the `System.Data Import` statement to the top of the page:

   ```
   <%@ Page Language="C#" %>
   <%@ Import Namespace="System.Data" %>
   <%@ Import Namespace="System.Data.SqlClient" %>
   ```

3. Switch to the Source view. Rather than a DataReader, you need to alter `Page_Load` to use a `DataSet`. You'll use the same basic code you saw in Chapter 5, as follows (the changed lines are shown in bold):

```
// must declare the DataSet globally; else the page can't see it.
DataSet myDataSet = new DataSet();

void Page_Load(object sender, EventArgs e)
{
  // set up connection string and SQL query
  string ConnectionString = ConfigurationManager.
    ConnectionStrings["SqlConnectionString"].ConnectionString;
  string CommandText = "SELECT ManufacturerName, ManufacturerCountry, ➥
    ManufacturerEmail, ManufacturerWebsite FROM Manufacturer";

  // create SqlConnection and SqlCommand objects
  SqlConnection myConnection = new SqlConnection(ConnectionString);
  SqlCommand myCommand = new SqlCommand(CommandText, myConnection);

  // create a new DataAdapter
  SqlDataAdapter myAdapter = new SqlDataAdapter();
  myAdapter.SelectCommand = myCommand;

  // use try finally clauses when the connection is open.
  try
  {
    // open the database connection
    myConnection.Open();

    // use the DataAdapter to fill the DataSet
    myAdapter.Fill(myDataSet, "Manufacturer");
  }
  finally
  {
    // always close the database connection
    myConnection.Close();
  }

  // bind the data
  Page.DataBind();
}
```

4. Now you set which property is bound to which column in the DataTable. Scroll to the bottom of the page to the <body> tag, and change the HTML to the following:

```
<body>
  <form id="form1" runat="server">
  <div>
    <asp:Label ID="lblName" runat="server">
    Name: DataBinder.Eval (myDataSet.Tables["Manufacturer"].Rows[0],
      "[ManufacturerName]")
    </asp:Label>
```

```
      <br />
      Country:
      <asp:Label ID="lblCountry" runat="server"
        Text='<%# DataBinder.Eval
          (myDataSet.Tables["Manufacturer"].Rows[0],
          "[ManufacturerCountry]") %>'>
      </asp:Label>
      <br />
      Contact:
      <asp:HyperLink ID="lnkEmail" runat="server"
        NavigateUrl='mailto: <%# DataBinder.Eval(
          myDataSet.Tables["Manufacturer"].Rows[0],"[2]","mailto:{0}") %>'
        Text='<%# DataBinder.Eval(
          myDataSet.Tables["Manufacturer"].Rows[0],
          "[ManufacturerEmail]") %>'>
      </asp:HyperLink>
      <br />
      Homesite:
      <asp:HyperLink ID="lnkWebsite" runat="server"
        NavigateUrl='<%# DataBinder.Eval(
          myDataSet.Tables["Manufacturer"].Rows[0], "[3]") %>'>
        <%# DataBinder.Eval (myDataSet.Tables["Manufacturer"].Rows[0],
          "[ManufacturerWebsite]") %>
      </asp:HyperLink>
      <br /><br />
      <asp:Label ID="lblError" runat="server"></asp:Label><br />
    </div>
    </form>
</body>
```

5. Save the page, and then view it in a browser (see Figure 6-4). The results are the same as for binding to a DataReader, as you saw in Figure 6-3.

Figure 6-4. *Inline binding to a DataSet*

6. Go back to the Source view, and duplicate the Web controls and binding expressions on the page. The ID properties will be changed automatically to default values, but you should change them to lblName2, lblCountry2, lnkEmail2, and lnkWebsite2.

7. Change the binding expressions so that they bind to columns from a different row in the table. This is as simple as changing the Rows index, as this example shows:

```
<asp:Label ID="lblName2" runat="server">
  Name: DataBinder.Eval (myDataSet.Tables["Manufacturer"].Rows[4],
    "[ManufacturerName]")
</asp:Label>
<br />
Country:
  <asp:Label ID="lblCountry2" runat="server"
    Text='<%# DataBinder.Eval
    (myDataSet.Tables["Manufacturer"].Rows[4],
    "[ManufacturerCountry]") %>'>
</asp:Label>
```

8. Save the page, and then view it again (see Figure 6-5). You'll see that the DataTable has no problem. The DataReader would, of course, choke on this. The only way to work at random with a table with a DataReader is to keep rebuilding it.

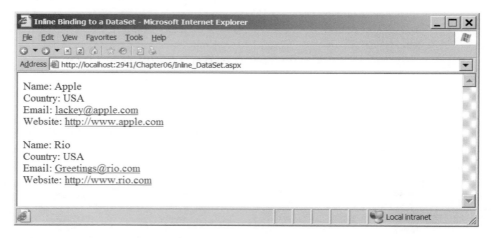

Figure 6-5. *The DataSet gives you random access through a table.*

How It Works

Only two major differences exist between this and the previous example. The first is that you're using a DataSet containing a DataTable to provide the data to bind to, and the second is the syntax you use in the binding expressions. Everything else is the same, demonstrating that there's no limit to inline binding text and properties at the same time.

This example may seem to contradict my earlier advice to query only for what you'll use in a page. You queried only the same four columns, but all of the rows from the Manufacturer table, like so:

```
SELECT ManufacturerName, ManufacturerCountry,
  ManufacturerEmail, ManufacturerWebsite
FROM Manufacturer
```

However, you did this to demonstrate a point: unlike with a DataReader, you can work backward in the DataSet as well as forward.

Inside the binding expressions, you should recognize the slightly unwieldy syntax by now. Each expression identifies a column in a DataSet unambiguously. The second parameter of a call to DataBinder.Eval() names the specific column, and the first identifies the specific row that contains the column. If you recall from the previous example, the call when binding to a column in DataReader looked like this:

```
Name: <%# DataBinder.Eval (myReader, "[ManufacturerName]") %>
```

You can do this because a DataReader contains only one row at a time. It's therefore enough to identify the reader and then the position of the column in that row.

If you're using a DataSet, you need to use a call like this:

```
Name: <%# DataBinder.Eval (myDataSet.Tables["Manufacturer"].Rows[0],
  "[ManufacturerName]") %>
```

This slightly unwieldy syntax is required because you must first identify the DataSet, then the DataTable within it, and the specific row within that in one go, so that the second parameter can name the column in that row. You still have no way to alter the actual value of the column because it's bound to the Web control. However, if you need to format the value of the column, you just add the format string as the third parameter of the call to DataBinder.Eval():

```
NavigateUrl='<%# DataBinder.Eval
  (myDataSet.Tables["Manufacturer"].Rows[4], "[2]", "mailto:{0}") %>'
```

The Inline Binding Alternative

I mentioned earlier that you have other options to inline binding, and that I prefer to avoid inline binding. But why not use data binding?

The main reason that you wouldn't want to use inline binding is performance. Inline binding uses reflection to determine what you're trying to show, and this is slower than using the DataReader and DataSet directly.

Another reason to avoid inline binding is code maintenance. If you use inline binding, you're mixing *real* code with the HTML using <% and %>. Those of you who've written ASP code in the past will remember doing this, with the result being the most horrible spaghetti code imaginable that was an absolute nightmare to debug. ASP.NET was supposed to fix all the problems with ASP, and yet here's one area where we have not moved forward.

Now, let's take a look at how you can show the results from a database query without resorting to data binding.

Try It Out: Showing Data from a DataReader

In this example, you'll display the same data from the DataReader without relying on inline binding. You'll build essentially the same pages as you've already seen, but without a call to DataBind() in sight.

1. Open Inline_DataReader.aspx and save it as Showing_DataReader.aspx.

2. In the Source view, scroll to the bottom of the page and change the <title> of the page to **Showing from a DataReader**.

3. Remove all the data-binding tags from within the <body> element. You should have HTML that looks similar to the following:

```
<body>
  <form id="form1" runat="server">
  <div>
    Name:
    <asp:Label ID="lblName" runat="server"></asp:Label>
    <br />
    Country:
    <asp:Label ID="lblCountry" runat="server"></asp:Label>
    <br />
    Email:
    <asp:HyperLink ID="lnkEmail" runat="server"></asp:HyperLink>
    <br />
    Website:
    <asp:HyperLink ID="lnkWebsite" runat="server"></asp:HyperLink>
    <br /><br />
    <asp:Label ID="lblError" runat="server"></asp:Label><br />
  </div>
  </form>
</body>
```

4. Within the code for the page, remove the global SqlDataReader definition and change the code within the Page_Load event to the following (the changed code is shown in bold):

```
// run query
SqlDataReader myReader = myCommand.ExecuteReader();

if (myReader.Read())
{
  // set the properties on the controls
  lblName.Text = Convert.ToString(myReader["ManufacturerName"]);
  lblCountry.Text = Convert.ToString(myReader["ManufacturerCountry"]);
  lnkEmail.Text = Convert.ToString(myReader["ManufacturerEmail"]);
  lnkEmail.NavigateUrl = "mailto:" +
    Convert.ToString(myReader["ManufacturerEmail"]);
```

```
      lnkWebsite.Text = Convert.ToString(myReader["ManufacturerWebsite"]);
      lnkWebsite.NavigateUrl =
        Convert.ToString(myReader["ManufacturerWebsite"]);
  }
  else
  {
    // show the error
    lblError.Text="No results to databind to.";
  }
```

5. Save the page, and then view it in a browser (see Figure 6-6). The results are the same as for binding to a DataReader (Figure 6-3).

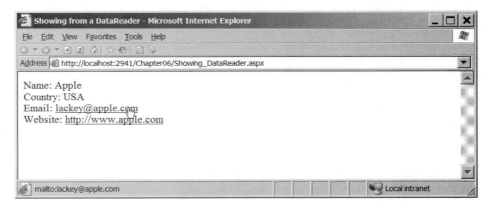

Figure 6-6. *Showing from a DataReader without binding*

How It Works

In this example, you changed quite a lot around compared to the corresponding inline binding exercise. The benefit is that these changes have made the split between what is code and what is presentation a lot easier to see.

The first change is to remove any data-binding code from the HTML. Here's how you created the Label controls in the data-binding example:

```
<asp:Label ID="lblName" runat="server">
  Name: <%# DataBinder.Eval (myReader, "[ManufacturerName]") %>
</asp:Label>
<br />
Country:
<asp:Label ID="lblCountry" runat="server"
  Text='<%# DataBinder.Eval (myReader, "[ManufacturerCountry]") %>'>
</asp:Label>
<br />
```

Compare this to what you have now:

```
Name:
<asp:Label ID="lblName" runat="server"></asp:Label>
<br />
Country:
<asp:Label ID="lblCountry" runat="server"></asp:Label>
<br />
```

It certainly makes the HTML a lot easier to follow, now that no data-binding code is mingled among the HTML.

You also now need to set the properties in code. You need to move the data binding from the DataBinder.Eval() calls within the HTML to the code. And you do this by replacing the Page.DataBind() with code that sets the properties directly on the four Web controls:

```
// set the properties on the controls
lblName.Text = Convert.ToString(myReader["ManufacturerName"]);
lblCountry.Text = Convert.ToString(myReader["ManufacturerCountry"]);
lnkEmail.Text = Convert.ToString(myReader["ManufacturerEmail"]);
lnkEmail.NavigateUrl = "mailto:" +
  Convert.ToString(myReader["ManufacturerEmail"]);
lnkWebsite.Text = Convert.ToString(myReader["ManufacturerWebsite"]);
lnkWebsite.NavigateUrl =
  Convert.ToString(myReader["ManufacturerWebsite"]);
```

You return the column you're after from the current row in the DataReader by passing the column name as the index to the myReader object. This returns the column contents as an Object, and this is cast to the correct type, in this case a String, before the properties on the Web controls are set.

The only change to the way that you set the properties is the NavigateUrl property of the e-mail link. You need to prepend the e-mail address with mailto: to ensure that it appears in the browser correctly. You can do this easily by setting NavigateUrl to the concatenation of the two strings.

Try It Out: Showing Data from a DataSet

As well as querying a DataReader directly, it is also possible to query a DataSet directly. This example will show how you can query the DataSet to return the correct data and use this to set properties on the Web controls on the page.

1. Open Inline_Binding_DataSet.aspx and save it as Showing_DataSet.aspx.

2. Change the <title> of the page to **Showing from a DataSet**.

3. Remove all the data-binding code from the <body> element. You should have HTML similar to the following:

```
<body>
  <form id="form1" runat="server">
  <div>
    Name:
    <asp:Label ID="lblName" runat="server"></asp:Label>
    <br />
    Country:
    <asp:Label ID="lblCountry" runat="server"></asp:Label>
    <br />
    Contact:
    <asp:HyperLink ID="lnkEmail" runat="server"></asp:HyperLink>
    <br />
    Homesite:
    <asp:HyperLink ID="lnkWebsite" runat="server"></asp:HyperLink>
    <br /><br />
    Name:
    <asp:Label ID="lblName2" runat="server"></asp:Label>
    <br />
    Country:
    <asp:Label ID="lblCountry2" runat="server"></asp:Label>
    <br />
    Contact:
    <asp:HyperLink ID="lnkEmail2" runat="server"></asp:HyperLink>
    <br />
    Homesite:
    <asp:HyperLink ID="lnkWebsite2" runat="server"></asp:HyperLink>
    <br /><br />
    <asp:Label ID="lblError" runat="server"></asp:Label><br />
  </div>
  </form>
</body>
```

4. Within the code for the page, remove the global DataSet definition and move it to the Page_Load event, as follows:

```
// create a new DataAdapter
SqlDataAdapter myAdapter = new SqlDataAdapter();
myAdapter.SelectCommand = myCommand;

// create the DataSet
DataSet myDataSet = new DataSet();

// use try finally clauses when the connection is open.
try
```

5. Replace the `Page.DataBind()` call at the end of the `Page_Load` event with the following:

```
// show the first results
DataRow myFirstRow = myDataSet.Tables["Manufacturer"].Rows[0];
lblName.Text = Convert.ToString(myFirstRow["ManufacturerName"]);
lblCountry.Text = Convert.ToString(myFirstRow["ManufacturerCountry"]);
lnkEmail.Text = Convert.ToString(myFirstRow["ManufacturerEmail"]);
lnkEmail.NavigateUrl = "mailto:" +
  Convert.ToString(myFirstRow["ManufacturerEmail"]);
lnkWebsite.Text = Convert.ToString(myFirstRow["ManufacturerWebsite"]);
lnkWebsite.NavigateUrl =
  Convert.ToString(myFirstRow["ManufacturerWebsite"]);

// show the second results
DataRow mySecondRow = myDataSet.Tables["Manufacturer"].Rows[4];
lblName2.Text = Convert.ToString(mySecondRow["ManufacturerName"]);
lblCountry2.Text = Convert.ToString(mySecondRow["ManufacturerCountry"]);
lnkEmail2.Text = Convert.ToString(mySecondRow["ManufacturerEmail"]);
lnkEmail2.NavigateUrl = "mailto:" +
  Convert.ToString(mySecondRow["ManufacturerEmail"]);
lnkWebsite2.Text = Convert.ToString(mySecondRow["ManufacturerWebsite"]);
lnkWebsite2.NavigateUrl =
  Convert.ToString(mySecondRow["ManufacturerWebsite"]);
```

6. Save the page, and then view it in a browser (see Figure 6-7). The results are the same as for binding to a `DataSet` (Figure 6-5).

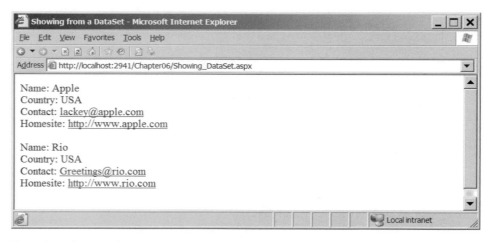

Figure 6-7. *Showing from a DataSet without binding*

How It Works

As with the DataReader example, you've removed the code from the HTML and placed it where it should be: within the code part of the page.

As you've already seen, when dealing with a DataSet, the first thing you need is a reference to the correct row within the correct table of the DataSet. Rather than having to repeat a rather unwieldy syntax every time you need to access the row, you store a reference to the row:

```
DataRow myFirstRow = myDataSet.Tables["Manufacturer"].Rows[0];
```

So, whenever you need to retrieve a column from the row, you can do so relatively easily. One of the indexes for a DataRow is the name of the column that you're after, so the syntax is remarkably similar to that for the DataReader earlier:

```
lblName.Text = Convert.ToString(myFirstRow["ManufacturerName"]);
```

After showing the data for the first row in the DataTable, you then repeat the process, but this time, show the details for the fifth row by getting a reference to a different row in the table:

```
DataRow myFirstRow = myDataSet.Tables["Manufacturer"].Rows[4];
```

List Binding

In comparison to inline binding, list binding is a somewhat less complex way to pass data into a data-bound Web control, but usually it requires more work beyond the call to DataBind() to finesse your Web control into a useful piece of the page for the user. If you consider the four Web controls you can list-bind to—the CheckBoxList, RadioButtonList, DropDownList, and ListBox—you can see that their purpose is to elicit a response from the user for information to be used elsewhere in the page.

■**Note** There is a fifth Web list control, the BulletedList, which is more of a display-only Web control and doesn't allow the user to select options from the list. Even though we're not going to look at it here, the method for populating the Web control is the same as for the other four Web controls.

As you know from using these Web controls and working with HTML option lists, the key to finding out what the user has chosen is to establish a unique value for each option that can be retrieved from the page once the choice has been made. And, of course, you also need some text to display against each choice. In HTML, that means something like this:

```
<select name="ListBox1" size="5" id="ListBox1">
    <option value="1">Apple</option>
    <option value="2">Creative</option>
    <option value="3">iRiver</option>
    <option value="4">MSI</option>
    <option value="5">Rio</option>
</select>
```

On the screen, it looks something like Figure 6-8.

Figure 6-8. *You can build a simple check box by list binding.*

Apple, Creative, iRiver, and so on are displayed in the browser, and the choice registers in the page as 1, 2, 3, and so on. When you're list binding to a Web control, you need to establish a data source containing two columns per row: one for the text to be displayed and the other to identify the choice the user has made. Here's an example:

```
SELECT ManufacturerID, ManufacturerName FROM Manufacturer
```

With the data source established (either by setting the DataSource or DataSourceID property, in code or in the HTML markup of the Web control), you need to tell the Web control which column does what. You do this by setting the DataTextField and DataValueField properties as appropriate. You can do this either in HTML:

```
<asp:RadioButtonList id="RadioButtonList1" runat="server"
  DataTextField="ManufacturerName" DataValueField="ManufacturerID" />
```

or in code:

```
RadioButtonList1.DataTextField = "ManufacturerName";
RadioButtonList1.DataValueField = "ManufacturerID";
```

■**Caution** If you do set the DataTextField and DataValueField properties in code, make sure you specify the data source before the other two properties, or you'll get an error.

The Web list controls have the following two relevant properties:

- DataMember: This property is for use with a DataSet, as you'll see in the example in the upcoming "Try It Out: Using Lookup Lists and Events with a DataSet" section. As a DataSet can contain multiple tables, this property is used to specify which table to use from the DataSet.

- DataTextFormatString: This property lets you set the format for the text displayed in the list and comes in handy when you're dealing with currency, dates, and numbers. See http://msdn.microsoft.com/en-us/library/system.web.ui.webcontrols.listcontrol. datatextformatstring.aspx for examples.

Once the Web list control has been configured correctly, it's time to actually perform the data binding. Using a SqlDataSource, the data binding takes place automatically. If you're using a DataSet or a DataReader as the data source, or you need the data binding to occur at a specific place in code, then all that's left to do is call DataBind() on the Web list control.

So, the core code for the whole three-stage binding process could be as simple as the following:

```
myConnection.Open();
myReader = myCommand.ExecuteReader();
RadioButtonList1.DataSource = myReader;
RadioButtonList1.DataTextField = "ManufacturerName";
RadioButtonList1.DataValueField = "ManufacturerID";
RadioButtonList1.DataBind();
myReader.Close();
myConnection.Close();
```

This is true of all four Web list controls.

Another thing that you'll soon discover is that you can use a DataReader as a Web list control's data source only on a one-to-one basis. Unlike inline binding, where you can bind many properties to the same column in a DataReader, you can't bind many Web list controls to the same columns in a DataReader. Actually, you can't bind more than one Web list control to the same DataReader. Once DataBind() has been called on one of the Web list controls, it works through all the rows in a DataReader, which, of course, is forward-only, so you can't go back to the beginning and bind the same information. The only way to bind all three Web controls from the same source is to use something other than a DataReader—a DataSet, for example—as the data source.

That said, you'll now look at a common application of data-bound lists: using the selection from a list to look up data from another table. First, you'll see how to do this using a DataReader as the source of the list to populate a GridView based on the user's selection from a DropDownList, a RadioButtonList, or a ListBox.

You can accomplish the same task using a DataSet instead of a DataReader, but in order to do that, you need to start dealing with events. So, first we'll look at the two relevant events, DataBound and SelectedIndexChanged, and then we'll extend the DataReader example before moving on to build the corresponding page using a DataSet.

Try It Out: Using Single-Value Lookup Lists with a DataReader

In this example, you'll build a page with two stages. In the first stage, you'll populate a DropDownList with information from the Manufacturer table. Specifically, you'll make the name of all the Manufacturers in the database appear on the screen and use their respective ManufacturerID values to track which Manufacturer has been clicked. The DropDownList allows only one value to be selected in the list, and in the second stage, you'll use the ManufacturerID of the selected Manufacturer to search the Player table for all the Players made by that Manufacturer, and then display that in a GridView.

1. In Visual Web Developer, add a new Web Form called List_DataReader.aspx.

2. In the Source view, change the title of the page to **List Binding to a DataReader**.

3. In the Design view, add a DropDownList and a GridView to the page. Rather than having the Web controls lined up underneath each other, use an HTML table to lay out the Web controls in a more pleasing manner, as shown in Figure 6-9.

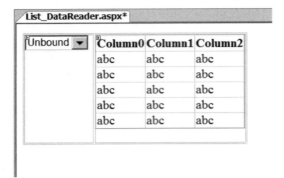

Figure 6-9. *Laying out the DropDownList and GridView*

4. Select the DropDownList and set its ID to lstManufacturers. Also set DataTextField to ManufacturerName, DataValueField to ManufacturerID, and AutoPostBack to True.

5. In the Source view, make sure that you've included the correct data provider at the top of the page, like so:

```
<%@ Page Language="C#" %>
<%@ Import Namespace="System.Data.SqlClient" %>
```

6. All the code for the page is in the Page_Load event handler. It begins by setting up the Connection and Command objects, like so:

```
protected void Page_Load(object sender, EventArgs e)
{
  // create SqlConnection object
  string ConnectionString = ConfigurationManager.
    ConnectionStrings["SqlConnectionString"].ConnectionString;
  SqlConnection myConnection = new SqlConnection(ConnectionString);

  // create SqlCommand object
  SqlCommand myCommand = new SqlCommand();
  myCommand.Connection = myConnection;

  try
  {
    // open the database connection
    myConnection.Open();
```

7. Inside the try loop, you need to run two different queries: one for setting up the DropDownList and the other for the GridView. To set up the DropDownList, add the following code:

```
if (Page.IsPostBack == false)
{
  // If this page isn't posted back
  // you need to set up the list control
  // set up SQL query for the Manufacturer table
  myCommand.CommandText =
    "SELECT ManufacturerID, ManufacturerName FROM Manufacturer";

  // run query
  SqlDataReader myReader = myCommand.ExecuteReader();

  // set up the list
  lstManufacturers.DataSource = myReader;
  lstManufacturers.DataBind();

  // close the reader
  myReader.Close();
}
```

8. To set up the GridView, you need the following code. Again, you're using only the DropDownList, so the calls against the other Web list controls are commented out.

```
else
{
  // If this page is posted back get the selected value and display
  // players made by manufacturer. You don't need to rebind the value
  // for the lists either. They are stored in the viewstate.

  // set up SQL query for the Player table
  myCommand.CommandText =
    "SELECT PlayerID, PlayerName, PlayerManufacturerID, PlayerCost, ➥
    PlayerStorage FROM Player WHERE PlayerManufacturerID = " +
    lstManufacturers.SelectedItem.Value;

  // run query
  SqlDataReader myReader = myCommand.ExecuteReader();

  // setup the GridView
  GridView1.DataSource = myReader;
  GridView1.DataBind();

  // close the reader
  myReader.Close();
}
```

9. And last but not least, you need to tidy things up, like so:

```
    }
    finally
    {
      // always close the connection
      myConnection.Close();
    }
}
```

10. Save the page, and then view it in a browser. Select one of the Manufacturers from the drop-down list. The page will post back to the server and, presto, return with the details for the Players made by that Manufacturer, as shown in Figure 6-10.

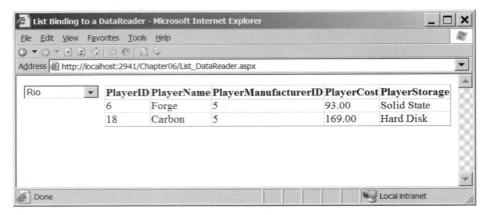

Figure 6-10. *Selecting a single value using a DropDownList*

11. Now that you've seen how this works with a DropDownList, you can experiment with both the RadioButtonList and ListBox to perform the same task. Switch back to Visual Web Developer and change the <asp:DropDownList> and </asp:DropDownList> tags to <asp:RadioButtonList> and </asp:RadioButtonList>. Save the page, and then view it in the browser. Selecting a Manufacturer from the radio button list will post back to the server and populate the Players automatically, as shown in Figure 6-11.

12. Switch back to Visual Web Developer and change the <asp:RadioButtonList> and </asp:RadioButtonList> tags to <asp:ListBox> and </asp:ListBox>. Save the page, and view it in the browser. Selecting a Manufacturer from the list box will post back to the server and populate the Players automatically, as shown in Figure 6-12.

13. Switch back to Visual Web Developer and revert back to using a DropDownList by changing the <asp:ListBox> and </asp:ListBox> tags to <asp:DropDownList> and </asp:DropDownList>.

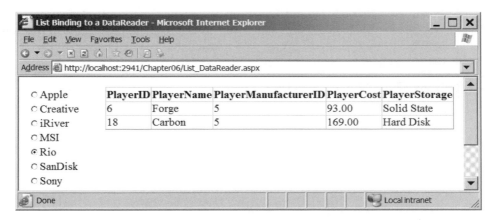

Figure 6-11. *Selecting a single value using a RadioButtonList*

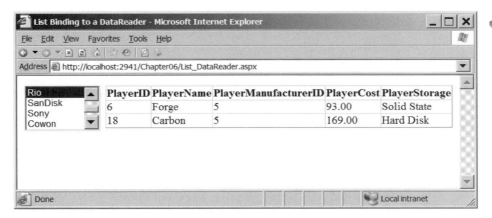

Figure 6-12. *Selecting a single value using a ListBox*

How It Works

We've discussed a great deal of this code already, but it makes a lot of difference to see it in action. Seeing how DataTextField and DataValueField translate inside a data-bound list, for example, is helpful.

When the page is first loaded, you need to populate the list from the database. However, this list will never change as you use the page, so you don't need to repopulate it each time you click the values it contains. Consequently, you set up a simple test to check whether the page has posted back. If it hasn't, you'll populate the list.

```
if (Page.IsPostBack == false)
{
```

Although the `DataTextField` and `DataValueField` properties specify what will populate the list, there's still no need to query the database for any more than those columns. You're using a `DataReader`, so you can't access any extra information from it anyway once you `DataBind()` it to the list.

```
// set up SQL query for Manufacturer table
myCommand.CommandText =
  "SELECT ManufacturerID, ManufacturerName FROM Manufacturer";

// run query
SqlDataReader myReader = myCommand.ExecuteReader();

// set up the list
lstManufacturers.DataSource = myReader;
lstManufacturers.DataBind();

// close the reader
myReader.Close();
}
```

Note You set the `DataSource` property within the code rather than the HTML (as you saw when we looked at inline binding), as this makes the code a little more self-contained. This way, you don't need to have a global reference to the DataReader for the page.

You set the `AutoPostBack` property of the `DropDownList` to true, so any time you select an option from the list, the page posts back, and you can update the `GridView` accordingly.

The `DropDownList`, and indeed all three Web list controls, expose the currently selected item in the list through the `SelectedItem` property. You can use its `Text` and `Value` properties to retrieve the exact details. In this case, you need the ManufacturerID for the Player search, so you use `SelectedItem.Value` because you set ManufacturerID to `DataValueField` in the Web list control.

```
else
{
  // set up SQL query for Player table
  myCommand.CommandText =
    "SELECT PlayerID, PlayerName, PlayerManufacturerID, PlayerCost, ➥
    PlayerStorage FROM Player WHERE PlayerManufacturerID = " +
    lstManufacturers.SelectedItem.Value;

  // run query
  SqlDataReader myReader = myCommand.ExecuteReader();
```

```
  // set up the GridView
  GridView1.DataSource = myReader;
  GridView1.DataBind();

  // close the reader
  myReader.Close();
}
```

An alternate way to go here would be to use the Web list control's SelectedValue and SelectedText properties instead of SelectedItem.Value and SelectedItem.Text. That approach produces the same results in this scenario, where you can select only one item from the list. However, this doesn't work with multiple-selection lists, as you'll see in the "Multiple-Selection Lists" section later in this chapter. Nor can you use the SelectedItem property to find all the list items selected in a group. You must choose another tack.

The last two steps in the example changed the Web list control from a DropDownList to a RadioButtonList and then to a ListBox. You simply changed the HTML tags from <asp:DropDownList> to <asp:RadioButtonList> or <asp:ListBox>. Nothing else on the page changes—all Web list controls have exactly the same interface, and the same methods and properties are available.

List Binding Events

In the previous example, you saw how easy it is to build a list from a DataReader. Before you can see how to do the same thing using the DataSet and SqlDataSource, you need to be aware of the events that are exposed by the Web list controls.

The main problem with the previous example is that there is no way to know which Web list control the user used to cause the postback to the page. As you have only one visible Web list control, this isn't a problem. You can assume that if there has been a postback, the visible Web control caused the postback, and so populate the GridView accordingly. This is exactly what you've done:

```
if (Page.IsPostBack == false)
{
  // populate the list control
}
else
{
  // populate the GridView
}
```

However, when you start adding more Web controls to the page, such as a button or indeed another Web list control that has its AutoPostBack property set to true, you have a problem. How do you know which Web control has caused the postback? A button has a Click event, but what about a Web list control?

Thankfully, a Web list control has its own event that is raised whenever the page is posted back because of a user selection within the list: SelectedIndexChanged. As you'll soon see, you can use this event to modify other Web controls.

As well as the SelectedIndexChanged event, Web list controls have another very helpful event. Introduced in ASP.NET 2.0, the DataBound event is fired immediately after the Web control has been data-bound—whether this is automatic or caused by an explicit call to DataBind() for the Web control or its parent.

Try It Out: Using Lookup Lists and Events with a DataReader

In this example, you'll modify the previous DataReader example to use the SelectedIndexChanged and DataBound events, rather than relying on the fact that the page has been posted back to assume that the user has made a selection.

1. Open List_DataReader.aspx and save it as List_Binding_Events.aspx.

2. Change the <title> of the page to **List Binding with Events to a DataReader**.

3. In the Source view, change the Page_Load event handler to the following:

```
protected void Page_Load(object sender, EventArgs e)
{
  if (Page.IsPostBack == false)
  {
    // create SqlConnection object
    string ConnectionString = ConfigurationManager.
      ConnectionStrings["SqlConnectionString"].ConnectionString;
    SqlConnection myConnection = new SqlConnection(ConnectionString);

    // create SqlCommand object
    SqlCommand myCommand = new SqlCommand();
    myCommand.Connection = myConnection;

    try
    {
      // open the database connection
      myConnection.Open();

      // set up SQL query for Manufacturer table
      myCommand.CommandText =
        "SELECT ManufacturerID, ManufacturerName FROM Manufacturer";

      // run query
      SqlDataReader myReader = myCommand.ExecuteReader();

      // set up the list
      lstManufacturers.DataSource = myReader;
      lstManufacturers.DataBind();
```

```
      // close the reader
      myReader.Close();
    }
    finally
    {
      // always close the connection
      myConnection.Close();
    }
  }
}
```

4. In the Design view, double-click the DropDownList. This will add the SelectedIndexChanged event handler. Change the code within the handler to the following:

```
protected void lstManufacturers_SelectedIndexChanged(object sender,
  EventArgs e)
{
  // create SqlConnection object
  string ConnectionString = ConfigurationManager.
    ConnectionStrings["SqlConnectionString"].ConnectionString;
  SqlConnection myConnection = new SqlConnection(ConnectionString);

  // create SqlCommand object
  string CommandText = "SELECT PlayerID, PlayerName, PlayerManufacturerID, ➥
    PlayerCost, PlayerStorage FROM Player WHERE PlayerManufacturerID = " +
    lstManufacturers.SelectedItem.Value;
  SqlCommand myCommand = new SqlCommand(CommandText, myConnection);

  try
  {
    // open the database connection
    myConnection.Open();

    // run query
    SqlDataReader myReader = myCommand.ExecuteReader();

    // set up the GridView
    GridView1.DataSource = myReader;
    GridView1.DataBind();

    // close the reader
    myReader.Close();
  }
  finally
  {
    // always close the connection
    myConnection.Close();
  }
}
```

5. Save the page, and then view it in the browser. Selecting one of the options will populate the results with the Players for the selected Manufacturer, similar to the results you've already seen in Figure 6-10. However, when the page is first loaded, the DropDownList is showing Apple, but the GridView doesn't appear!

6. Switch back to Visual Web Developer, and in the Design view, show the properties for the DropDownList. Switch to the Events view and double-click the DataBound event to add the event handler, as shown in Figure 6-13.

Figure 6-13. *Setting the DataBound event for a DropDownList*

7. Add the following code to the DataBound event:

```
protected void lstManufacturers_DataBound(object sender, EventArgs e)
{
    ListItem myListItem = new ListItem();
    myListItem.Text = "please select...";
    myListItem.Value = "-1";
    lstManufacturers.Items.Insert(0, myListItem);
}
```

8. Modify the code within the lstManufacturers_SelectedIndexChanged event handler as follows:

```
protected void DropDownList1_SelectedIndexChanged(object sender, EventArgs e)
{
    if (lstManufacturers.SelectedValue != "-1")
    {
        // code as it stands at the moment
    }
```

```
    else
    {
      // clear the GridView
      GridView1.DataSource = null;
      GridView1.DataBind();
    }
  }
```

9. Save the page, and then view it in the browser. This time, notice a new entry, "please select...," added to the DropDownList. Select one of the Manufacturers, and the Player list changes to the selected Manufacturer's Players. Select "please select...," and notice that the list of Players disappears.

10. Experiment with changing the DropDownList to a RadioButtonList and a ListBox. Notice again that all three Web controls will have the "please select..." entry, as well as the list of Manufacturers, and selecting an option displays the same results, regardless of the type of Web list control that you're using.

How It Works

The first thing that you'll notice about this code is that the Page_Load event is no longer populating the GridView, and this is now handled by the SelectedIndexChanged event of the Web list control.

The Page_Load event is now solely responsible for creating the list of Manufacturers for the Web list control. As you saw in the previous example, this must be done only when the page is first loaded, so the first thing that you check is that this is indeed the first load of the page. If it is, you populate the Web list control in the same way as the previous example, by querying the Manufacturer table for the ManufacturerID and ManufacturerName combinations.

Within the SelectedIndexChanged event, you first need to create a connection to the database, and then create the correct SQL query to execute:

```
// create SqlConnection object
string ConnectionString = ConfigurationManager.
  ConnectionStrings["SqlConnectionString"].ConnectionString;
SqlConnection myConnection = new SqlConnection(ConnectionString);

// create SqlCommand object
string CommandText = "SELECT PlayerID, PlayerName, PlayerManufacturerID, ➥
  PlayerCost, PlayerStorage FROM Player WHERE PlayerManufacturerID = " +
  lstManufacturers.SelectedItem.Value;
SqlCommand myCommand = new SqlCommand(CommandText, myConnection);
```

The SQL query is constructed in the same way as in the previous example. You retrieve the value selected from the drop-down list using the SelectedItem.Value property and concatenate this with the rest of the query.

Once you have a Command object, you can run the query and pass the results to the DataSource of the GridView and bind the results:

```
// run query
SqlDataReader myReader = myCommand.ExecuteReader();

// set up the GridView
GridView1.DataSource = myReader;
GridView1.DataBind();

// close the reader
myReader.Close();
```

The only difference from the previous example is that you've changed the page to respond to a specific event, SelectedIndexChanged, to bind the Players to the GridView.

The one new piece of code that you've added here is the DataBound event, which you use to add the "please select..." entry to the list.

A DropDownList always has an item selected, since it must display something, even if the user hasn't made a selection. When you first loaded the page Apple was the selected entry, but the list of Players made by Apple wasn't shown in the list. Contrast this with both the RadioButtonList and the ListBox, which don't have a selected item when they're first loaded. So, you need some way of dealing with this, which is the purpose of the "please select..." entry to the Web list control.

All additions to a Web list control must be made once any data binding has occurred. Before ASP.NET 2.0, any additions to a Web list control had to be made after the Web list control had been data-bound, as follows:

```
// data-bind the list
DropDownList1.DataBind();

// add the "please select..." entry
ListItem myListItem = new ListItem();
myListItem.Text = "please select...";
myListItem.Value = "-1";
lstManufacturers.Items.Add(myListItem);
```

While this works without any problems, you're using an event-driven programming model, and the new DataBound event can be used for this purpose:

```
protected void lstManufacturers_DataBound(object sender, EventArgs e)
{
  ListItem myListItem = new ListItem();
  myListItem.Text = "please select...";
  myListItem.Value = "-1";
  lstManufacturers.Items.Insert(0, myListItem);
}
```

Once the data binding of the Web list control is complete, the DataBound event is fired and the new entry added to the Web list control. Either option works to do the same task, but using the event separates the different parts of the code more cleanly and will make the code easier to maintain later.

Obviously, you can't use the dummy entry "please select ..." as a Manufacturer. Therefore, you check that the selected entry is a real one when handling the SelectedIndexChanged event.

You know that the ManufacturerID values in the database start at 1, so you set the dummy entry to have a value that can't exist, -1. If this is the value that the user has selected, you don't attempt to bind to a set of results from the database. Instead, you remove any data binding already in place by telling the GridView to bind to a null data source:

```
protected void DropDownList1_SelectedIndexChanged(object sender, EventArgs e)
{
  if (DropDownList1.SelectedValue != "-1")
  {
    // code to show the players
  }
  else
  {
    // clear the GridView
    GridView1.DataSource = null;
    GridView1.DataBind();
  }
}
```

You'll notice that you've added the dummy entry to all Web list controls that you may use, including the RadioButtonList and ListBox, even though they can display themselves without having an entry selected. It's only the DropDownList that cannot and needs the dummy entry. Therefore, you may want to remove the DataBound event handler when using a RadioButtonList or a ListBox.

Try It Out: Using Lookup Lists and Events with a DataSet

In this exercise, you'll see how the code for list binding a DataTable in a DataSet to a Web control is almost identical to list binding to a DataReader.

1. Open List_DataReader_Events.aspx and save it as List_DataSet_Events.aspx.

2. Change the <title> of the page to **List Binding with Events to a DataSet**.

3. Add the System.Data Import statement to the top of the page:

```
<%@ Page Language="C#" %>
<%@ Import Namespace="System.Data" %>
<%@ Import Namespace="System.Data.SqlClient" %>
```

4. If the page is using a Web list control other than the DropDownList, change it back to a DropDownList and, if necessary, add the DataBound event that you used in the previous example.

5. Add a RadioButtonList to the page beneath the DropDownList. Set its DataTextField property to ManufacturerName, DataValueField to ManufacturerID, and AutoPostBack to True.

6. You need to populate a DataSet from three different places, so you're going to move the code to do so to a new method called BuildDataSet(). Add the following:

```csharp
private DataSet BuildDataSet(string commandText, string tableName)
{
  // DataSet we're going to return
  DataSet myDataSet = new DataSet();

  // set up connection string
  string ConnectionString = ConfigurationManager.
    ConnectionStrings["SqlConnectionString"].ConnectionString;

  // create SqlConnection and SqlCommand objects
  SqlConnection myConnection = new SqlConnection(ConnectionString);
  SqlCommand myCommand = new SqlCommand(commandText, myConnection);

  // Create the SqlDataAdapter
  SqlDataAdapter myAdapter = new SqlDataAdapter(myCommand);

  try
  {
    // open the database connection
    myConnection.Open();

    // fill the DataSet
    myAdapter.Fill(myDataSet, tableName);
  }
  finally
  {
    // always close the connection
    myConnection.Close();
  }

  // return the DataSet
  return(myDataSet);
}
```

7. Modify the Page_Load event to use the BuildDataSet() method to retrieve the data and populate the Web list control. Since this needs to be done only when the page first loads, the code needs to run only when the page hasn't been posted back.

```csharp
protected void Page_Load(object sender, EventArgs e)
{
  if (Page.IsPostBack == false)
  {
    // set up SQL query for Manufacturer table
    string CommandText =
      "SELECT ManufacturerID, ManufacturerName FROM Manufacturer";
```

```
    // DataSet with list of manufacturers
    DataSet myDataSet = BuildDataSet(CommandText, "Manufacturer");

    // set up the DropDownList
    lstManufacturers.DataSource = myDataSet;
    lstManufacturers.DataMember = "Manufacturer";
    lstManufacturers.DataBind();

    // set up the RadioButtonList
    RadioButtonList1.DataSource = myDataSet;
    RadioButtonList1.DataMember = "Manufacturer";
    RadioButtonList1.DataBind();
  }
}
```

8. You now need to change the SelectedIndexChanged event handler for the DropDownList to use the new BuildDataSet() method to retrieve the results from the database. Change the lstManufacturers_SelectedIndexChanged as follows:

```
protected void lstManufacturers_SelectedIndexChanged(object sender,
  EventArgs e)
{
  if (lstManufacturers.SelectedValue != "-1")
  {
    // set up SQL query for Player table
    string CommandText = "SELECT PlayerID, PlayerName, PlayerManufacturerID, ➡
      PlayerCost, PlayerStorage FROM Player WHERE PlayerManufacturerID = " +
      lstManufacturers.SelectedItem.Value;

    // set up the GridView
    GridView1.DataSource = BuildDataSet(CommandText, "Player");
    GridView1.DataMember = "Player";
    GridView1.DataBind();
  }
  else
  {
    // clear the GridView
    GridView1.DataSource = null;
    GridView1.DataBind();
  }
}
```

9. Switch to the Design view and double-click the RadioButtonList to add its SelectedIndexChanged event. Add the following code to the event handler:

```
protected void RadioButtonList1_SelectedIndexChanged(object sender,
    EventArgs e)
{
  // set up SQL query for Player table
  string CommandText = "SELECT PlayerID, PlayerName, PlayerManufacturerID, ➥
    PlayerCost, PlayerStorage FROM Player WHERE PlayerManufacturerID = " +
    RadioButtonList1.SelectedItem.Value;

  // set up the GridView
  GridView1.DataSource = BuildDataSet(CommandText, "Player");
  GridView1.DataMember = "Player";
  GridView1.DataBind();
}
```

10. Save the page, and then run it in a browser. Select one of the Manufacturers from either the DropDownList or the RadioButtonList. The page will post back to the server, and the list of Players will be presented, based on the Manufacturer selected, as shown in Figure 6-14.

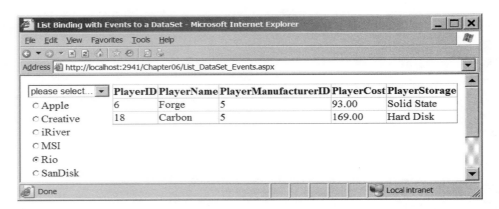

Figure 6-14. *Backing lookup lists with a DataSet*

How It Works

The most immediate difference between this example and its DataReader equivalent is that both the DropDownList and the RadioButtonList are displayed simultaneously. Because of its forward-only nature, you can bind only one Web list control to a DataReader at a time, which is why you had only one Web list control in the DataReader examples. In contrast, you can reuse the contents of a DataTable as many times as you like, so you can use it as a data source to as many Web controls as you like.

Beyond this fairly large functional difference, however, the code is more or less the same. You still identify a DataTextField and a DataValueField for each Web list control, and they work as usual, as does the DataSource property. But there's a slight variation here that applies when using a DataSet as the data source. For either type of binding to work, you must identify the specific `DataTable` for the Web control to bind to. In the example, you've done this by specifying the `DataMember` property in code:

```
GridView1.DataSource = myDataSet;
GridView1.DataMember = "Player";
```

Alternatively, you could just set the `DataSource` to the `DataTable` directly:

```
GridView1.DataSource = myDataSet.Tables["Player"];
```

The event handlers are all straightforward. Because each handler is associated with a specific Web list control, you know which one to check for the newly selected Manufacturer. With that, you can derive the correct SQL query and populate the waiting `GridView` from the `DataTable` storing the results of the query.

Try It Out: Using Lookup Lists and Events with a SqlDataSource

In this example, you'll perform list binding using the `SqlDataSource` to provide the data. You'll see that if we use the `SqlDataSource`, rather than a DataReader or a `DataSet`, you can build quite complex pages with very little code.

1. Open `List_DataReader_Events.aspx` and save it as `List_DataSource_Events.aspx`.

2. Change the `<title>` of the page to **List Binding with Events to a SqlDataSource**.

3. If the page is using a Web list control other than the `DropDownList`, change it back to a `DropDownList` and, if necessary, add the `DataBound` event that you used in the previous example.

4. Remove all of the code from the page other than the `lstManufacturers_DataBound` event handler.

5. Switch to the Design view and add a `SqlDataSource` to the page. Select Configure Data Source from the Tasks menu.

6. Select `SqlConnectionString` from the drop-down list on the Choose Your Data Connection step, and then click the Next button.

7. On the Configure the Select Statement step, select Manufacturer from the Name drop-down list and check the ManufacturerID and ManufacturerName columns, as shown in Figure 6-15. Click the Next button.

8. If you want to test that the results returned are as expected, click the Test Query button. If they're not what you expect, click the Previous button to return to the previous step. Once you're happy that the results are as expected, click the Finish button.

9. Select the `DropDownList` and set its `DataSourceID` property to `SqlDataSource1`. Switch to the events list for the control and remove the `SelectedIndexChanged` event handler.

10. Add another `SqlDataSource` to the page, select to configure the data source, and select `SqlConnectionString` as the connection string to use. Click the Next button.

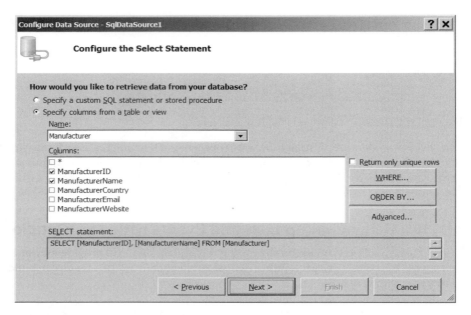

Figure 6-15. *Configuring the SELECT query for a SqlDataSource*

11. On the Configure the Select Statement step, select Player from the Name drop-down list and the * entry in the columns list. Click Next, and then click Finish to complete this part of the configuration.

12. In the Properties window for SqlDataSource2, click the ellipsis next to the SelectQuery property to open the Command and Parameter Editor dialog box.

13. Click the AddParameter button and give the new parameter a name of ManufacturerID. Select Control as the Parameter Source, and from the ControlID drop-down list, select lstManufacturers.

14. Click the Query Builder button to launch the Query Builder dialog box. As shown in Figure 6-16, add @ManufacturerID as the filter for the PlayerManufacturerID column. You can click the Execute Query option to test that the query is correct.

15. Click the OK button to close the Query Builder, and then click OK again to close the Command and Parameter Editor dialog box.

16. Select the GridView and change its DataSourceID property to SqlDataSource2.

17. Save the page, and then run it in a browser. Select one of the Manufacturers from the DropDownList. The page will post back to the server, and the list of Players will be presented based on the Manufacturer selected. Clicking the "please select..." entry will cause the GridView to be cleared.

18. Experiment with changing the DropDownList to a RadioButtonList and a ListBox. Notice again that all three Web controls will have the "please select..." entry, as well as the list of Manufacturers, and selecting an option displays the same results, regardless of the type of Web list control that you're using.

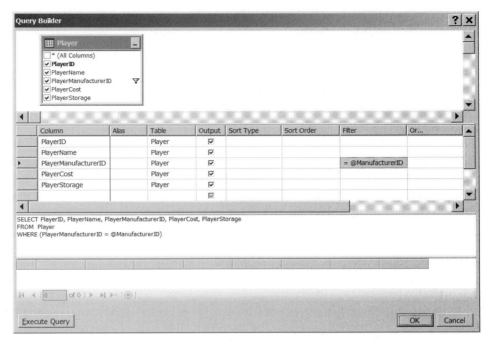

Figure 6-16. *Using the Query Builder to filter the list of Manufacturers*

How It Works

After having to write code to populate the list and grid, you've now come to an example that requires very little code in order to offer the same functionality. Instead, you've used the graphical tools provided with Visual Web Developer to build the page.

First, we'll look at the DropDownList and the first SqlDataSource that you added to the page. Then we'll look at the GridView and its SqlDataSource, as well as the parameters that it requires. Finally, we'll consider some of the limitations of the SqlDataSource.

The DropDownList Control

If you look at the HTML markup for SqlDataSource1, you'll see that apart from the ID and runat properties that all Web controls have, the SqlDataSource has two other properties that enable you to configure the Web control for your purposes: ConnectionString and SelectCommand.

```
<asp:SqlDataSource ID="SqlDataSource1" runat="server"
  ConnectionString="<%$ ConnectionStrings:SqlConnectionString %>"
  SelectCommand="SELECT ManufacturerID, ManufacturerName FROM Manufacturer">
</asp:SqlDataSource>
```

The ConnectionString property sets the connection string that the SqlDataSource will use. This can be any valid connection string. In this case, you're using a new construct added in ASP.NET 2.0 that allows you to automatically retrieve the connection string from the

`<connectionStrings>` section of `Web.config` by specifying the name of the connection string—in this case, SqlConnectionString:

```
<%$ ConnectionStrings:SqlConnectionString %>
```

The SelectCommand property is the query that the SqlDataSource will use to query the database to return the results. In this case, you return a list with the ManufacturerID and ManufacturerName entries for all of the Manufacturers in the database.

■ **Note** SelectCommand hints that the SqlDataSource can be used for a whole lot more than just data binding. As you might guess, it also has corresponding DeleteCommand, InsertCommand, and UpdateCommand properties, which allow you to do much more. Now that I've tempted you with the possibilities, I'm going to make you wait until Chapter 9 before you get to see these in action.

That completes the configuration of SqlDataSource1. All that's left is to tell the drop-down list about its data source. You do this by setting the DataSourceID property of DropDownList1 to SqlDataSource1.

With the drop-down list, you're again making use of the DataBound event to add the dummy entry to the options available. The code is identical to the code you've used in the previous two examples.

Once you've configured the DropDownList and the SqlDataSource that it's binding to, you don't need to worry about the data binding, as it takes place automatically between the OnPreRender and OnPreRenderComplete events in the page life cycle. And it's here that ASP.NET applies some intelligence to the data binding.

In the previous examples, the first decision you had to make within the Page_Load event was whether you needed to bind the DropDownList. You'll recall that you need to do this only once, as the contents of the list are remembered across postbacks. The DropDownList is intelligent enough to know when it needs to bind to the data source and does this only the first time the page is loaded. You can see this by adding a breakpoint to the DataBound event and watch how many times it's reached—only once when the page is first loaded.

The GridView Control

In the previous examples, you've had to respond to the OnSelectedIndexChanged event to pass a SQL query to the GridView and tell it to bind itself. We'll look at the GridView in a lot more detail in the next chapter, when we cover table binding. Here, we'll look at how the SQL query that is executed is constructed.

If you take a look at the data source for the GridView, SqlDataSource2, you'll see that it's remarkably similar to the data source that you've used for the DropDownList:

```
<asp:SqlDataSource ID="SqlDataSource2" runat="server"
  ConnectionString="<%$ ConnectionStrings:SqlConnectionString %>"
  SelectCommand="SELECT PlayerID, PlayerName, PlayerManufacturerID,
    PlayerStorePrice, PlayerStorage FROM dbo.Player
    WHERE (PlayerManufacturerID = @ManufacturerID)">
```

```
    <SelectParameters>
      <asp:ControlParameter ControlID="lstManufacturers"
        Name="ManufacturerID" PropertyName="SelectedValue" />
    </SelectParameters>
</asp:SqlDataSource>
```

There's a ConnectionString that points to the correct database, and again, you have a SelectCommand that details the query that you want to execute. There's also a new child element, SelectParameters, which you haven't seen before.

The SelectParameters collection allows you to specify various parameters to the SelectCommand query, as shown in Table 6-2.

Table 6-2. *SelectCommand Parameter Types*

Name	Description
ControlParameter	Takes its value from another Web control on the same page. The Web control to use is specified by the ControlID attribute. The property on the Web control to retrieve the value from is indicated by the PropertyName attribute.
CookieParameter	Uses a value specified in a cookie, indicated by the CookieName attribute, to set the value of the parameter.
FormParameter	Uses a value specified in a form variable, indicated by the FormName attribute, to set the value of the parameter.
QueryStringParameter	Uses a value in the page's query string, indicated by the QueryStringField attribute, to set the value of the parameter.
SessionParameter	Uses a value in the user's session, indicated by the SessionField attribute, to set the value of the parameter.
System.Data.SqlServerCe	Provides native access to SQL Server CE for the .NET Compact Framework

By setting the parameters in the SelectParameters collection, you can build queries that are automatically modified depending on form values, query string values, values stored in cookies or the session, or, as in this case, the value of another Web control on the page:

```
<asp:ControlParameter ControlID="lstManufacturers"
  Name="ManufacturerID" PropertyName="SelectedValue" />
</SelectParameters>
```

The ControlID and PropertyName properties of the ControlParameter tell you which Web control and which property to use. In this case, you have lstManufacturers.SelectedValue, which returns the ManufacturerID of the selected Manufacturer. The other property that you need is Name, which is the property, common to all the different parameter types, that allows you to tie the parameter to the query.

If you take a look at the SelectCommand property, you'll see that the query actually has a WHERE clause added that takes a parameter:

```
WHERE (PlayerManufacturerID = @ManufacturerID)
```

The parameter you need to provide is @ManufacturerID, and the ControlParameter object has a name of ManufacturerID. The @ is added automatically, and whatever value is selected in the DropDownList is used to modify the query to return the correct list of Players.

■**Note** DeleteCommand, InsertCommand, and UpdateCommand properties also have parameter collections. We'll look at DeleteParameters, InsertParameters, and UpdateParameters in Chapter 9.

The SqlDataSource: Panacea?

You may now be thinking that the SqlDataSource is the perfect data source and gets rid of all of that horrible code that no one really likes writing. Well, to a certain extent it is. However, as you'll see shortly when we look at lists that allow multiple selections, there are times when the SqlDataSource doesn't quite make the grade.

You also have a little problem here that you didn't see when you used code to connect to the database. Although this page appears to have the same functionality, it doesn't. What happens when the user selects the dummy entry? In the DataReader and DataSet examples, you wrote code to clear the GridView when the user selects that entry. You're not manually data binding when you use the SqlDataSource, so you have no way, as it stands, of clearing the list instead of performing the query. When you select the dummy entry, a query is made to the database that returns no results:

```
SELECT PlayerID,PlayerName,PlayerManufacturerID,
  PlayerStorePrice,PlayerStorage
FROM dbo.Player
WHERE (PlayerManufacturerID = -1)
```

In the simple example, this isn't necessarily an issue, as the number of needless hits that you're going to make to the database is quite limited. But what happens when the page is being used by a hundred or a thousand users?

One solution is to stop the data binding from occurring if the user has selected an invalid entry. You can do this by responding to the SelectedIndexChanged event of the DropDownList:

```
protected void lstManufacturers_SelectedIndexChanged(object sender, EventArgs e)
{
  if (lstManufacturers.SelectedValue == "-1")
  {
    GridView1.DataSourceID = null;
  }
  else
  {
    GridView1.DataSourceID = "SqlDataSource2";
  }
}
```

This isn't the most elegant of solutions, but it does prevent needless hits on the database. Selecting the dummy value in the DropDownList sets the DataSourceID of the GridView to a null data source. This has the effect of turning off automatic data binding, as the GridView no longer has a data source to bind to. If the selected entry in the DropDownList isn't the dummy value, then you set the DataSourceID back to the correct SqlDataSource, and the data binding takes place as expected.

You also have the same problem when you first load the page, as the GridView has a valid data source even if the query that is executed will return no results. There are several ways that this can be remedied; I'll leave it up to you to experiment to find out what they are.

Note There's nothing stopping you from using the SqlDataSource and its properties within code. Indeed, any property that you can set within the HTML markup can be modified within code. You'll see this when you start changing the SQL query that is executed by directly modifying the SelectCommand property.

Connecting to Other Data Sources

In this example, you're connecting to a SQL Server database, and the definition of the SqlDataSource is complete, simply specifying the ConnectionString will connect to the database. However, this isn't the whole story. You're actually providing, by omission in this example, one further piece of information that the SqlDataSource needs.

The SqlDataSource can be used to connect to any data source, provided that there is a data provider for it, but as yet, you have not told the SqlDataSource what type of connection string you've provided. You need to do this using the ProviderName property. The ProviderName property can have several different values, depending on which data provider you want to use. The standard data providers are listed Table 6-3.

Table 6-3. *Standard Data Providers*

ProviderName	Description
System.Data.Odbc	Any data source that is accessed through an ODBC driver
System.Data.OleDb	Any data source that is accessed through an OLE DB provider
System.Data.OracleClient	Provides native access to Oracle databases
System.Data.SqlClient	Provides native access to SQL Server databases (default value)
System.Data.SqlServerCe	Provides native access to SQL Server CE for the .NET Compact Framework

As you can see, the default ProviderName is System.Data.SqlClient, so you don't need to specify it when you're connecting to a SQL Server database; the SqlDataSource assumes, unless you specify otherwise, that you're using a SQL Server database.

However, if you're not connecting to a SQL Server database, as in the MySQL and Access examples in the code download, you must specify that you want to use a different provider. You add the ProviderName attribute to the SqlDataSource definition, like this:

```
<asp:SqlDataSource ID="SqlDataSource1" runat="server"
  ConnectionString="<%$ ConnectionStrings:OdbcConnectionString %>"
  SelectCommand="SELECT ManufacturerID, ManufacturerName FROM Manufacturer">
  ProviderName="<%$ ConnectionStrings:OdbcConnectionString.ProviderName %>"
</asp:SqlDataSource>
```

You can either specify the provider you want directly, as in System.Data.Odbc, or set it as part of the connection string in Web.config:

```
<add name="OdbcConnectionString"
  connectionString="Driver={MySQL ODBC 3.51 Driver};
    server=localhost;database=players;uid=band;pwd=letmein;"
  providerName="System.Data.Odbc" />
```

If you set it in Web.config, you can access the providerName property of the required connection string using this syntax:

```
<%$ ConnectionStrings:OdbcConnectionString.ProviderName %>
```

Note As a shortcut, you can specify the connection string, as we've done here, as just OdbcConnectionString. If you don't specify a specific part of the connection string, it's assumed that you mean OdbcConnectionString.ConnectionString.

Multiple Selection Lists

The Web list controls that you've looked at so far have allowed only a single item to be selected from the Web control. But what if you want the user to be able to select multiple entries from the same list?

The ListBox allows you to do this by changing its SelectionMode property from the default value of Single to Multiple. The one remaining Web list control that we haven't looked at yet, the CheckBoxList, also allows the selection of multiple values.

Note Now that you've seen how easy it is to change between a DataReader and a DataSet, you won't use both in the example presented here. List_DataSet_Multiple.aspx in the code download is the corresponding DataSet example.

Try It Out: Using Multiple-Value Lookup Lists with a DataReader

In this example, you'll see what alternative methods you can employ to deal with Web list controls that allow multiple selections. You can't rely on using the SelectedItem property, because that will return only the first item selected in the list. Instead, you must iterate through the list each time and build up a SQL query accordingly.

1. In Visual Web Developer, create a new Web Form called
   List_DataReader_Multiple.aspx.

2. Change the `<title>` of the page to **Multiple Selection Using a DataReader**.

3. Make sure you've included the correct Import statements at the top of the page.

```
<%@ Page Language="C#" %>
<%@ Import Namespace="System.Data.SqlClient" %>
<%@ Import Namespace="System.Text" %>
```

4. In the Design view, add a ListBox, a Button, and a GridView to the page. Change the Text
   for the Button to **Select**. You can use a table to lay out the Web controls in a more user-
   friendly manner, as shown in Figure 6-17.

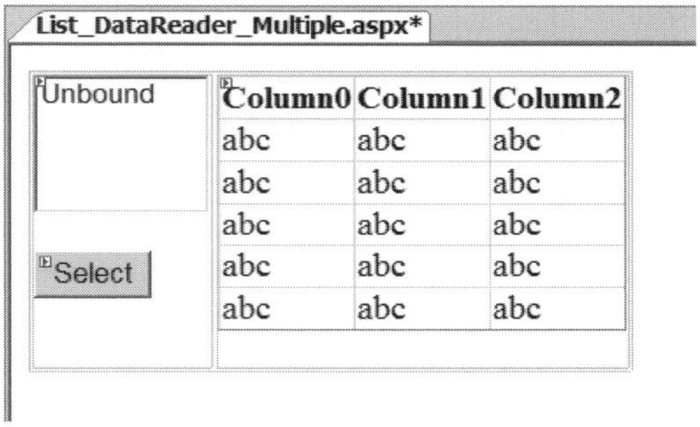

Figure 6-17. *Laying out the Web list controls*

5. For the ListBox, set DataTextField to ManufacturerName, DataValueField to
   ManufacturerID, and SelectionMode to Multiple.

6. The code for the Page_Load event is pretty much the same as in the previous
   DataReader example:

```
protected void Page_Load(object sender, EventArgs e)
{
  if (Page.IsPostBack == false)
  {
    // create SqlConnection object
    string ConnectionString = ConfigurationManager.
      ConnectionStrings["SqlConnectionString"].ConnectionString;
    SqlConnection myConnection = new SqlConnection(ConnectionString);

    // create SqlCommand object
    SqlCommand myCommand = new SqlCommand();
    myCommand.Connection = myConnection;
```

```
    try
    {
      // open the database connection
      myConnection.Open();

      // set up SQL query for Manufacturer table
      myCommand.CommandText =
        "SELECT ManufacturerID, ManufacturerName FROM Manufacturer";

      // run query
      SqlDataReader myReader = myCommand.ExecuteReader();

      // set up the list control
      ListBox1.DataSource = myReader;
      ListBox1.DataBind();

      // close the reader
      myReader.Close();
    }
    finally
    {
      // always close the connection
      myConnection.Close();
    }
  }
}
```

7. Add a Click event handler for the Button. First, add the code to create the Command and Connection objects, and then open the connection:

```
protected void Button1_Click(object sender, EventArgs e)
{
  // create SqlConnection object
  string ConnectionString = ConfigurationManager.
    ConnectionStrings["SqlConnectionString"].ConnectionString;
  SqlConnection myConnection = new SqlConnection(ConnectionString);

  // create SqlCommand object
  SqlCommand myCommand = new SqlCommand();
  myCommand.Connection = myConnection;

  try
  {
    // open the database connection
    myConnection.Open();
```

8. To determine which items were selected in the Web list control, you must iterate through the Web control and build up the query from the results:

```
// set up SQL query for Player table
StringBuilder Query = new StringBuilder("SELECT PlayerID, PlayerName, ➥
  PlayerManufacturerID, PlayerCost, PlayerStorage FROM Player ➥
  WHERE PlayerManufacturerID IN (");

bool gotResult = false;

for (int i=0; i<ListBox1.Items.Count; i++)
{
  if (ListBox1.Items[i].Selected)
  {
    if (gotResult == true) Query.Append(",");
    Query.Append(ListBox1.Items[i].Value);
    gotResult = true;
  }
}

Query.Append(")");
```

9. Now you find out if any items were checked. If so, you run the query you built. If not, you clear the grid.

```
// get results if we have a selection
if (gotResult)
{
  // set the query to execute
  myCommand.CommandText = Query.ToString();

  // run the query
  SqlDataReader myReader = myCommand.ExecuteReader();

  // set up the GridView
  GridView1.DataSource = myReader;
  GridView1.DataBind();

  // close the reader
  myReader.Close();
}
else
{
  // clear the GridView
  GridView1.DataSource = null;
  GridView1.DataBind();
}
}
```

10. And again, matching the last example, you handle any errors and wrap up the code by closing the connection:

```
finally
{
    // always close the connection
    myConnection.Close();
}
}
```

11. Save the page, and then run it in your browser. You'll see the ListBox containing the familiar list of Manufacturers. To select more than one item, hold down the Ctrl key. Clicking the Select button will cause the GridView to be populated with the Manufacturers you've selected, as shown in Figure 6-18.

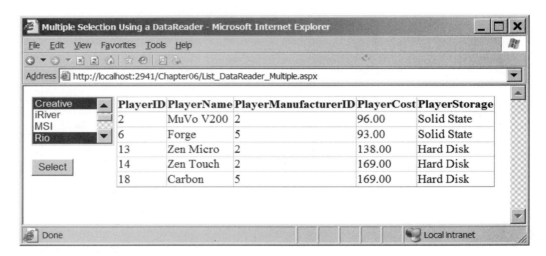

Figure 6-18. *Multiple selections from a ListBox*

How It Works

Much of the code is the same as the previous example, so we won't go over it here. The major change is to the code to generate a query for Player information for the GridView.

Rather than responding to the user's every selection in the list box, you've placed the code to populate the GridView in a button's Click event. This will allow the user to select several different Manufacturers before clicking the button to have the Players for the selected Manufacturers displayed.

The SELECT query uses the IN keyword to let you search for columns with one of a given set of values, so you use that to build your query. Your queries take the following shape:

```
SELECT PlayerID, PlayerName, PlayerManufacturerID, PlayerCost, PlayerStorage
FROM Player WHERE PlayerManufacturerID IN (1,2)
```

You'll need code that inserts the ID number for each selected Manufacturer into the query. You're using a StringBuilder, rather than normal string concatenation, as the StringBuilder is more efficient. You first add the start of the SELECT query you want to execute, like so:

```
// set up SQL query for Player table
StringBuilder Query = new StringBuilder("SELECT PlayerID, PlayerName, ➡
  PlayerManufacturerID, PlayerCost, PlayerStorage ➡
  FROM Player WHERE PlayerManufacturerID IN (";
```

The strategy here is to iterate through each item in the list and see if it has been selected. Fortunately, each ListItem object has a Selected property, which is true if it has been selected and false otherwise. If it has been selected, you pull its Value into the query.

```
bool gotResult = false;

for (int i=0; i<ListBox1.Items.Count; i++)
{
  if (ListBox1.Items[i].Selected)
  {
    if (gotResult == true) Query.Append(",");
    Query.Append(ListBox1.Items[i].Value);
    gotResult = true;
  }
}
```

You've included the Boolean gotResult to keep track of whether anything has been selected. You need to comma separate the selected entries, so you use gotResult to decide if you need to add a comma to the end of the query.

The gotResult variable is also used to decide whether you need to populate the GridView. If the user has selected at least one entry in the ListBox, you set the CommandText property of the Command object and execute the query to populate the GridView. If the user has unselected all the items in the list, you clear the GridView. This will ensure that the list of Players doesn't appear when you don't have a Manufacturer selected:

```
if (gotResult)
{
  myCommand.CommandText = Query.ToString();

  // run the query
  SqlDataReader myReader = myCommand.ExecuteReader();

  // set up the GridView
  GridView1.DataSource = myReader;
  GridView1.DataBind();

  // close the reader
  myReader.Close();
}
```

```
else
{
  // clear the GridView
  GridView1.DataSource = null;
  GridView1.DataBind();
}
```

So nothing much has changed really. You're modifying the query that you want to execute to handle multiple selected values, but the rest of the code remains the same. The same is true if you look at the DataSet version of the page in the code download.

However, all is not the same when you want to use a SqlDataSource.

Try It Out: Using Multiple-Value Lookup Lists with a SqlDataSource

In this example, you'll see how you need to write code when you want to control how the SqlDataSource behaves.

1. In Visual Web Developer, create a new Web Form called List_DataSource_Multiple.aspx.

2. Change the <title> of the page to **Multiple Selection Using a SqlDataSource**.

3. Make sure you've included the correct Import statement at the top of the page.

   ```
   <%@ Page Language="C#" %>
   <%@ Import Namespace="System.Text" %>
   ```

4. In the Design view, add a ListBox, a Button, and a GridView to the page. Change the Text for the Button to **Select**. You can use a table to lay out the Web controls in a more user-friendly manner, as shown earlier in Figure 6-17.

5. For the ListBox, set DataTextField to ManufacturerName, DataValueField to ManufacturerID, and SelectionMode to Multiple.

6. You need two SqlDataSource controls for this example, but rather than using the graphical tools to create them, you can add them directly to the HTML markup. Switch to the Source view and add the definitions for the two SqlDataSource controls at the top of the page:

   ```
   <asp:SqlDataSource ID="SqlDataSource1" runat="server"
     ConnectionString="<%$ ConnectionStrings:SqlConnectionString %>"
     SelectCommand="SELECT ManufacturerID, ManufacturerName FROM Manufacturer">
   </asp:SqlDataSource>
   <asp:SqlDataSource ID="SqlDataSource2" runat="server"
     ConnectionString="<%$ ConnectionStrings:SqlConnectionString %>">
   </asp:SqlDataSource>
   ```

7. Switch to the Design view and set the DataSourceID for the ListBox to SqlDataSource1 and for the GridView to SqlDataSource2.

8. Add a Click event handler for the Button. Then add the following code:

```
protected void Button1_Click(object sender, EventArgs e)
{
  // set up SQL query for Player table
  StringBuilder Query = new StringBuilder("SELECT PlayerID, PlayerName, ➥
    PlayerManufacturerID, PlayerCost, PlayerStorage FROM Player ➥
    WHERE PlayerManufacturerID IN (");

  bool gotResult = false;

  for (int i = 0; i < ListBox1.Items.Count; i++)
  {
    if (ListBox1.Items[i].Selected)
    {
      if (gotResult == true) Query.Append(",");
      Query.Append(ListBox1.Items[i].Value);
      gotResult = true;
    }
  }

  Query.Append(")");

  if (gotResult)
  {
    // set the correct SelectCommand
    SqlDataSource2.SelectCommand = Query.ToString();
  }
  else
  {
    // clear the GridView
    SqlDataSource2.SelectCommand = null;
  }
}
```

9. Save the page, and then run it in your browser. You'll see the ListBox containing the list of Manufacturers. To select more than one item, hold down the Ctrl key. Clicking the Select button will cause the GridView to be populated with the Manufacturers you've selected, as shown earlier in Figure 6-18.

How It Works

Here's one good example of where the SqlDataSource is not the panacea you might have initially thought it was.

The SqlDataSource is ideal when the query that you're executing is simple—or more correctly, any parameters that you want to add to it are simple. It works well when all you need to do is find if x = 1 or y < 3, and so on. But it falls down when you need to use conditional statements such as IN, and the parameter can't just be added to the query that you want to execute. In these cases, you need to massage the query and change the SelectCommand for the SqlDataSource.

The first change that you'll notice is that the second SqlDataSource on the page has a ConnectionString, but it doesn't have a SelectCommand:

```
<asp:SqlDataSource ID="SqlDataSource2" runat="server"
  ConnectionString="<%$ ConnectionStrings:SqlConnectionString %>">
</asp:SqlDataSource>
```

This is perfectly valid, and all it means is that no data binding will take place when a Web control uses this as its data source—no SelectCommand, no automatic data binding. So the page when it first loads won't connect to the database to try to show a list of Players in the GridView.

In order for the automatic data binding to occur, you must add a SelectCommand. And this is exactly what you do in the Click event handler for the button on the page.

The query is constructed in exactly the same way as you saw in the DataReader example. If the user has made a selection from the list, you have a query that you want to run, and you set the SelectCommand property:

```
SqlDataSource2.SelectCommand = Query.ToString();
```

Once you've set the SelectCommand to the query, you can let the automatic data binding occur. As you'll recall, this happens after the OnPreRender event, so as long as you've set the SelectCommand before, you'll be able to rely on the automatic data binding.

If no selection has been made, you don't want to run a query. So, you remove the SelectCommand by setting it to null:

```
SqlDataSource2.SelectCommand = null;
```

As there's no query to execute, the automatic data binding won't occur, thus clearing the GridView.

Summary

You don't have to surf far on the Web to find parallels between the examples you've seen in this chapter and, for example, the pages of an e-commerce or a business Web site where individual pieces of information are placed all around the page, as well as in an orderly list or grid. Dealing with read-only data is a big subject, and you've learned just the basics in this chapter.

In this chapter, we've looked at several ways to handle data binding:

- You learned how to inline-bind a piece of information from the current row in the DataReader or from a DataSet to the property or the text value of a Web control on the page.

- You learned about an alternative to inline binding that involves directly accessing the data source to return the required information directly.

- You learned how to list-bind Web controls such as the DropDownList, RadioButtonList, and ListBox. This requires you to nominate a column for the text of each list item and another column to act as the value for each list item.

- You saw that the DataReader, DataSet, and SqlDataSource can be used as the data source for list binding.

- The SqlDataSource, though a great Web control to have in our toolbox, isn't the panacea that you may have thought it was. You saw various examples of when you need to massage it a little to get it to perform exactly as desired.

In the next chapter, we'll continue our exploration of data binding by looking at table binding. You'll learn how to show the list of results in pretty much any format you require using the Repeater, DataList, and GridView.

You'll also start to see the power that the GridView provides, as well as how you can implement pages that, in the past, would have required a lot of hard work to develop. Because the GridView can perform a lot of complex functions automatically, hard-working developers now have time for the finer things in life.

CHAPTER 7

■■■

Table Binding

In the previous chapter, we focused on two of the three types of data binding. You saw that inline binding allows you to bind individual columns from the database to specific properties of Web controls on the page. I also explained why I prefer to avoid inline binding, and described another solution: using the DataReader or DataSet directly in code, rather than requiring a Page.DataBind() call. We then looked at list binding, which allows you to bind a series of name/value pairs into a Web list control, such as the DropDownList or the RadioButtonList.

This chapter covers the last of the three binding varieties in ASP.NET. For simplicity's sake, I'll call it *table binding*. With table binding, you can bind any number of columns per row from a data source to a Web control that supports it.

You've already looked at table binding, although it wasn't referred to as such. In the examples in Chapters 3 and 4, you used the GridView to display the list of Players from the database. In Chapter 3, you were introduced to data-aware pages by using a SqlDataSource to display the list of Players from the database. In Chapter 4, you saw that you can accomplish the same result in code using a DataReader.

Chapter 5 introduced you to the DataSet, and you saw that it is possible to create a disconnected representation of the results. In Chapter 6, you saw that the DataSet can be used as the data source for inline and list binding, and it will come as no surprise that you can also use the DataSet as the data source for table binding.

This chapter covers the following topics:

- The six table-binding Web controls

- How to use the Repeater, which allows you complete control over the output

- The differences between inline binding and event-based binding

- An introduction to the DataList, which is halfway between the Repeater and the GridView

- How to table-bind to the GridView and add sorting and paging to the displayed results

- A comparison of the DataReader and the DataSet

The Table-Binding Web Controls

Six Web controls support table binding in ASP.NET 2.0: the GridView, DetailsView, FormView, Repeater, DataList, and DataGrid. These are summarized in Table 7-1. If you've built Web sites using ASP.NET 1.1, you'll recognize the DataGrid, DataList, and Repeater, as their ASP.NET 2.0

versions are almost identical. They've been updated to support the use of a SqlDataSource as their data source, but fundamentally nothing has changed.

Table 7-1. *Web Controls That Support Table Binding*

Control	Description
Repeater	This is the simplest of the Web controls that supports table binding. The Repeater supports the "display data and nothing else" model.
DataList	This Web control is a step up from the Repeater. It outputs its content in a table and allows inline editing of the content that it is displaying. By defining different templates, you can control how the output is rendered when viewing data and how this changes when an item is selected or being edited.
DataGrid	This is the predecessor of the GridView. Much like the GridView, the DataGrid displays its output in a tabular format, with one row in the HTML table corresponding to one row of data from the data source. It also allows inline editing of the data that it is displaying, but this tends to involve writing quite a lot of code for all but the simplest tasks.
GridView	This renders as a tabular list of the data that it's bound to, with each row in the HTML table representing a row from the database.
DetailsView	This is used to output a single row of data from a data source in a tabular format. Unlike the GridView, each row in the HTML table represents a column from the selected row. The DetailsView supports inline editing and makes an ideal partner for the GridView, allowing you to build quite powerful master/detail pages with very little code.
FormView	This is similar to the DetailsView in that it displays a single row from the data source. But whereas the DetailsView is output as an HTML table, the FormView has no constraints on its output, and you're free to display the data however you wish. The FormView also supports inline editing, and, like the DetailsView, makes an ideal partner for the GridView when building master/detail pages.

In this chapter, we'll look at three of the table-binding Web controls: the Repeater, the DataList, and the GridView. We'll defer our discussion of the DetailsView and FormView until Chapter 9. We're not going to spend any time looking at the DataGrid. Although the DataGrid is present in ASP.NET 2.0, it doesn't appear in the Toolbox. The idea is to use the GridView instead for all tabulated data.

■Note You can find a very good resource for all of the different table-binding Web controls on MSDN at http://msdn.microsoft.com/en-us/library/a63e36w2.aspx. This includes a discussion of the different Web controls and links to further information.

You've already seen how to associate and bind data to a GridView, and the process for binding to a Repeater or DataList is exactly the same. At its simplest, the whole operation needs only the following four lines of code:

```
myReader = myCommand.ExecuteReader();
GridView1.DataSource = myReader;
GridView1.DataBind();
myReader.Close();
```

If you're using a SqlDataSource, you need to declare the DataSourceID in the markup for the Web control. So, to bind a GridView to a data source called SqlDataSource1, you would need the following as a minimum:

```
<asp:GridView ID="GridView1" runat="server" DataSourceID="SqlDataSource1">
</asp:GridView>
```

The same process is repeated for all of the table-bound Web controls. However, as you can see from TableBinding.aspx (which you'll find in the code download for this book) shown in Figure 7-1, there is more to these three Web controls than simply binding the data source to the Web control.

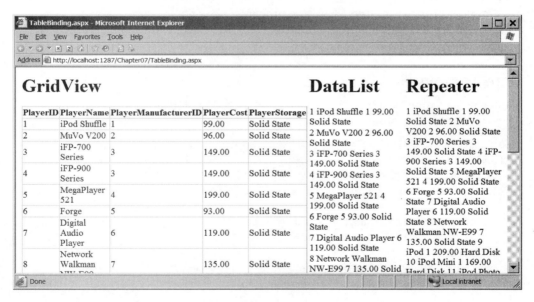

Figure 7-1. *GridView, DataList, and Repeater Web controls*

Repeater, DataList, and GridView Differences

The page shown in Figure 7-1 demonstrates binding and displaying the entire Player table. The GridView takes care of itself; it already understands what rows and columns are and that each column in the row should be placed in its own table cell. In contrast, a DataList only knows what a row is. When you bind a database table to it, a DataList still works row by row, but it doesn't create individual table cells for each column in a row. A Repeater knows even less, and simply spouts out everything bound to it in one paragraph, distinguishing neither column nor row.

Whereas the GridView understands rows and columns, the DataList and Repeater both rely on templates that are used to display each row in the data source. You need to define these templates. This may sound complex, but it isn't really, as you'll see in the next section.

The following summarizes the differences between the three Web controls:

- A Repeater is completely dependent on the template you provide for displaying data. For example, unless you include line breaks in the template, it will display incoming data on one line (as in Figure 7-1). You must do any customization through the templates. The Repeater supports templates for rows, alternate rows, headers, footers, and row separators. However, the data is read-only and can't readily support paging or sorting.

- A DataList displays your data, one item per row, according to a template you must provide. It won't separate individual pieces of information unless told to do so in the template. You can customize the display of the DataList extensively through various properties to match up with the templates you define. The DataList supports the editing, adding, and deleting of data but not sorting or paging. It supports templates to define the header of the list, to define the footer of the list, to highlight alternating rows in the list, and to highlight the row either currently selected or currently being edited.

- A GridView displays your data as a neatly formed grid by default. You can customize the GridView extensively through various properties, as you'll see shortly. You can even switch from the automatic generation of columns in favor of the template approach used by the DataList and Repeater.

Item Templates

Templates are defined using <ItemTemplate>. The DataList in the previous example has the following <ItemTemplate> defined:

```
<asp:DataList ID="DataList1" runat="server" DataSourceID="SqlDataSource1">
  <ItemTemplate>
    <asp:Label ID="PlayerIDLabel" runat="server"
      Text='<%# DataBinder.Eval(Container, "DataItem.PlayerID") %>'>
    </asp:Label>
    <asp:Label ID="PlayerNameLabel" runat="server"
      Text='<%# Eval("PlayerName") %>'>
    </asp:Label>
    <asp:Label ID="PlayerManufacturerIDLabel" runat="server"
      Text='<%# Eval("PlayerManufacturerID") %>'>
    </asp:Label>
    <asp:Label ID="PlayerCostLabel" runat="server"
      Text='<%# Eval("PlayerCost") %>'>
    </asp:Label>
    <asp:Label ID="PlayerStorageLabel" runat="server"
      Text='<%# Eval("PlayerStorage") %>'>
    </asp:Label>
  </ItemTemplate>
</asp:DataList>
```

If you look at the source for the page, you'll see that the Repeater has exactly the same <ItemTemplate> defined, yet it displays the data differently on the page. As the DataList understands rows, it shows each item template on its own row (we'll look at how it does this shortly).

However, the Repeater doesn't really understand anything, so it simply puts each item template one directly after another, and you can't see where one row ends and the next one begins.

You can define several kinds of row templates for the DataList and Repeater, and we'll get to them in a minute. The basic one is the ItemTemplate, as shown here. You can think of each template as a mini-page where you can place any combination of text, HTML, Web controls, and, most important, instructions on how and where to bind the columns in the data source in that row. When the call to DataBind() is made (either directly in code or automatically as part of the page life cycle), the mini-page template is repeated for each row in the data.

The ItemTemplate in the example is simple. It declares that each row will contain five Label controls, one for each column in the Player table. To associate a column in the data with the Label, you inline-bind it with the following binding expression:

```
<%# DataBinder.Eval(Container, "DataItem.PlayerID") %>
```

You saw the static DataBinder.Eval method when we looked at inline binding in the previous chapter. The first parameter locates the data source, and the second locates the column that will be bound. Container in this case means that the data source is the container for this template, or, rather, the DataList or Repeater. You can use this nomenclature in any template. As you may have noticed, a row corresponds to an item here, and you can refer to the column you want by name through the DataItem object.

When using table binding, you also have a slightly different way of inline binding, as shown in the sample ItemTemplate:

```
<%# Eval("PlayerName") %>
```

This is a shorthand way of saying the following:

```
<%# DataBinder.Eval(Container, "DataItem.PlayerName") %>
```

These two inline-binding statements perform exactly the same task, but one of them involves a whole lot less typing! Feel free to use whichever method you prefer. The only word of warning is that you can use the shorthand version only within a Web control that supports table binding. If you're inline binding to Web controls that exist directly on a page, you need to use the longhand version.

Now, we'll take a closer look at using the Repeater. It provides an ideal introduction to using templates without any of the added complications of the other table-binding Web controls.

The Repeater Web Control

As you saw in Figure 7-1, when using the Repeater to display data, you're completely responsible for the layout of that data. The Repeater is the most flexible of the table-binding Web controls, and it allows you to show data in whatever format you desire. However, the flexibility of the Repeater comes at a price—without specifying, as a minimum, an ItemTemplate, the Repeater will not display anything.

We'll first look at the different templates that can be defined for the Repeater, and then you'll see how to use inline binding to extract the data that you want to display. Next, we'll look at the events that the Repeater exposes and when they might be useful.

The Repeater Templates

As explained in the previous section, you must supply at least an ItemTemplate in order for the data that you're trying to show to be visible. As shown in Table 7-2, this isn't the only template that the Repeater supports.

Table 7-2. *Templates Supported by the Repeater*

Name	Description
AlternatingItemTemplate	The AlternatingItemTemplate, if specified, is output alternatively with the ItemTemplate. It can be used to change the formatting that is applied to the row (such as changing the background color of alternating rows) to provide a visible division between the different data items.
FooterTemplate	The HTML content of the FooterTemplate is output once all of the data presented to the Repeater has been displayed.
HeaderTemplate	The HTML content of the HeaderTemplate is output before the Repeater outputs any data via the ItemTemplate and AlternatingItemTemplate.
ItemTemplate	The ItemTemplate is used to display the data returned from the data source in the format that you specify. As a minimum, this template must be specified in order for the Repeater to output the returned data.
SeparatorTemplate	The SeparatorTemplate is output between instances of the ItemTemplate and AlternatingItemTemplate. It allows you to add any HTML that you wish between the data that the Repeater generates. If only the ItemTemplate is specified, the Repeater will output ItemTemplate, SeparatorTemplate, ItemTemplate. If both an ItemTemplate and an AlternatingItemTemplate are specified, the output will be ItemTemplate, SeparatorTemplate, AlternatingItemTemplate.

Each of the templates can contain any combination of HTML and Web controls, but only the ItemTemplate and AlternatingItemTemplate can use data binding to actually output the data that is given to the Repeater. You use the FooterTemplate, HeaderTemplate, and SeparatorTemplate to present the data in the format that you require.

Try It Out: Using the Repeater to Display the Manufacturers

In this first example, you'll use a Repeater to output the list of Manufacturers in the database. You'll use a DataReader to query the database for the Manufacturers and see how to use the different templates to present the data in a usable format.

1. In Visual Web Developer, create a new Web site at C:\BAND\Chapter07 and delete the auto-generated Default.aspx file.

2. Add a new Web.config file to the Web site and add a new setting to the <connectionStrings /> element:

```
<add name="SqlConnectionString"
  connectionString="Data Source=localhost\BAND;Initial Catalog=Players;
    Persist Security Info=True;User ID=band;Password=letmein"
  providerName="System.Data.SqlClient" />
```

3. Add a new Web Form to the Web site called Repeater_DataReader.aspx. Make sure that the Place Code in Separate File check box is unchecked and Language is set to Visual C#.

4. In the Source view, find the `<title>` tag within the HTML and change the page title to **Binding a DataReader to a Repeater**.

5. In the Design view, add a Repeater to the page. Switch back to the Source view and make sure you've included the correct data provider at the top of the page.

```
<%@ Page Language="C#" %>
<%@ Import Namespace="System.Data.SqlClient" %>
```

6. You need to set up the DataReader to query for the Manufacturers and add your standard code for database access.

```
protected void Page_Load(object sender, EventArgs e)
{
  if (Page.IsPostBack == false)
  {
    // set up connection string and SQL query
    string ConnectionString = ConfigurationManager.
      ConnectionStrings["SqlConnectionString"].ConnectionString;
    string CommandText = "SELECT ManufacturerName, ManufacturerCountry, ➡
      ManufacturerEmail, ManufacturerWebsite FROM Manufacturer";

    // create SqlConnection and SqlCommand objects
    SqlConnection myConnection = new SqlConnection(ConnectionString);
    SqlCommand myCommand = new SqlCommand(CommandText, myConnection);

    // use try finally when the connection is open
    try
    {
      // open the database connection
      myConnection.Open();

      // run query
      SqlDataReader myReader = myCommand.ExecuteReader();

      // set the data source and bind
      Repeater1.DataSource = myReader;
      Repeater1.DataBind();

      // close the reader
      myReader.Close();
    }
```

```
      finally
      {
        // always close the database connection
        myConnection.Close();
      }
    }
}
```

7. Save the page, and then view it in a browser. As you didn't define any templates, the Repeater won't output anything to the page.

8. Switch back to Visual Web Developer and, in the Source view, add the HeaderTemplate inside the <asp:Repeater> and </asp:Repeater> tags:

```
<asp:Repeater ID="Repeater1" runat="server">
  ...
  <HeaderTemplate>
    <div style="background-color:Bisque">
      <font size="+2">Manufacturers</font>
    </div>
    <hr style="color:blue"/>
  </HeaderTemplate>
  ...
</asp:Repeater>
```

9. Add the ItemTemplate to the Repeater as follows:

```
<asp:Repeater ID="Repeater1" runat="server">
  ...
  <ItemTemplate>
    <div style="background-color:Ivory">
      <b>
      <asp:Label ID="lblName" runat="server"
        Text='<%# Eval("[ManufacturerName]") %>'>
      </asp:Label>
      </b>
      <br />
      Country:
      <asp:Label ID="lblCountry" runat="server"
        Text='<%# Eval("[ManufacturerCountry]") %>'>
      </asp:Label>
      <br />
      Email:
      <asp:HyperLink ID="lnkEmail" runat="server"
        NavigateUrl='<%# Eval("[ManufacturerEmail]", "mailto:{0}") %>'
        Text='<%# Eval("[ManufacturerEmail]") %>'>
      </asp:HyperLink>
      <br />
```

```
        Website:
        <asp:HyperLink ID="lnkWebsite" runat="server"
          NavigateUrl='<%# Eval("[ManufacturerWebsite]") %>'>
          <%# Eval("[ManufacturerWebsite]") %>
        </asp:HyperLink>
      </div>
    </ItemTemplate>
    ...
</asp:Repeater>
```

10. Add the `SeparatorTemplate` to the Repeater as follows:

```
<asp:Repeater ID="Repeater1" runat="server">
    ...
    <SeparatorTemplate>
      <hr style="color:blue"/>
    </SeparatorTemplate>
    ...
</asp:Repeater>
```

11. Add the `AlternatingItemTemplate` to the Repeater as follows:

```
<asp:Repeater ID="Repeater1" runat="server">
    ...
    <AlternatingItemTemplate>
      <div style="background-color:Azure">
        <b>
        <asp:Label ID="lblName" runat="server"
          Text='<%# Eval("[ManufacturerName]") %>'>
        </asp:Label>
        </b>
        <br />
        Country:
        <asp:Label ID="lblCountry" runat="server"
          Text='<%# Eval("[ManufacturerCountry]") %>'>
        </asp:Label>
        <br />
        Email:
        <asp:HyperLink ID="lnkEmail" runat="server"
          NavigateUrl='<%# Eval("[ManufacturerEmail]", "mailto:{0}") %>'
          Text='<%# Eval("[ManufacturerEmail]") %>'>
        </asp:HyperLink>
        <br />
        Website:
        <asp:HyperLink ID="lnkWebsite" runat="server"
          NavigateUrl='<%# Eval("[ManufacturerWebsite]") %>'>
          <%# Eval("[ManufacturerWebsite]") %>
        </asp:HyperLink>
      </div>
```

```
  </AlternatingItemTemplate>
  ...
</asp:Repeater>
```

12. Finally, add the `FooterTemplate` to the `Repeater`:

```
<asp:Repeater ID="Repeater1" runat="server">
  ...
  <FooterTemplate>
    <hr style="color:blue"/>
    <div style="background-color:Bisque">
      <br />
    </div>
  </FooterTemplate>
  ...
</asp:Repeater>
```

13. Save the page, and then view it in a browser. When the page loads, you'll see that the list of Manufacturers is presented in a rather unattractive color scheme. Figure 7-2 shows the output.

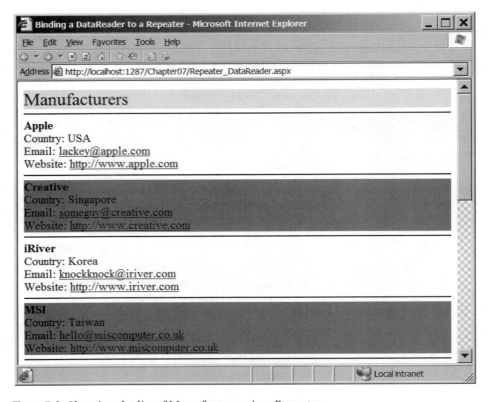

Figure 7-2. *Showing the list of Manufacturers in a Repeater*

How It Works

In this example, you used a DataReader to return the list of Manufacturers from the database and then used this as the data source for the Repeater. You could have used a DataSet to return the list of Manufacturers, and, as you've learned in the previous chapter, very little of the page would change. (Repeater_DataSet.aspx in the code download contains this page using a DataSet rather than a DataReader.)

Whether you're using a DataReader or a DataSet, the code that you use to query the database is the same as you've used in the previous examples. You set up the connection to the database, create the command, open the connection, and close the connection in the same way as you've already seen.

Only three lines of code are a little different:

```
// run query
SqlDataReader myReader = myCommand.ExecuteReader();

// set the data source and bind
Repeater1.DataSource = myReader;
Repeater1.DataBind();
```

You query the database to return the list of Manufacturers using the ExecuteReader() method of the Command object. ExecuteReader() returns a DataReader (in this case, a SqlDataReader), which you store in the myReader variable and then use as the DataSource of the Repeater.

Once the DataSource has been set, you must call the DataBind() method to perform the actual data binding. If you forget to call DataBind(), no data binding will occur. The data binding will not occur automatically as it would if you were using a SqlDataSource and specifying the DataSourceID.

At the point where the DataBind() method is called, the data binding occurs, and the Repeater takes the data that is supplied and outputs the different templates, as necessary, to create the output that you see in Figure 7-2.

Since the Repeater, unlike the DataList and GridView, does not output any layout details of its own, you need to define your own layout. You do this through a combination of <div> and <hr> tags.

The first template that the Repeater will output is the HeaderTemplate:

```
<HeaderTemplate>
  <div style="background-color:Bisque">
    <font size="+2">Manufacturers</font>
  </div>
  <hr style="color:blue"/>
</HeaderTemplate>
```

Anything between the opening and closing tags will be output once to the page (if there is no HeaderTemplate, nothing will be output). In this case, you're outputting a simple title contained within a <div> tag with a slightly odd background color followed by an <hr> tag colored blue. You've used a <div> element to contain the title, so that each part of the template is displayed on a new line; the <div> element is a block element that starts on a new line.

The HeaderTemplate contains an <hr> tag to separate the header from the first ItemTemplate that is output. Although you can use a SeparatorTemplate to specify what you want to appear between the ItemTemplate and AlternatingItemTemplate templates, the separator appears only between the templates, not before or after. The <hr> tag here is used to show the separation between the HeaderTemplate and ItemTemplate more easily.

The ItemTemplate is the first template that is shown that contains data returned from the database. This output is remarkably similar to the output that you saw in Figure 6-3 in the previous chapter. You show the Name of the Manufacturer on the first line, followed by the Country, Email, and Website of the Manufacturer on separate lines, as shown in Figure 7-3.

Apple
Country: USA
Email: lackey@apple.com
Website: http://www.apple.com

Figure 7-3. *The output from the ItemTemplate of the Repeater*

Each ItemTemplate contains four Web controls separated by <br> tags to ensure that each Web control is on a separate line. It has two Label controls and two HyperLink controls. The inline binding is the same for all four Web controls. Looking at the Country and Email markup, you can see that you use the Eval method to show what you want:

```
Country:
<asp:Label ID="lblCountry" runat="server"
  Text='<%# Eval("[ManufacturerCountry]") %>'>
</asp:Label>
<br />
Email:
<asp:HyperLink ID="lnkEmail" runat="server"
  NavigateUrl='<%# Eval("[ManufacturerEmail]", "mailto:{0}") %>'
  Text='<%# Eval("[ManufacturerEmail]") %>'>
</asp:HyperLink>
<br />
```

So for lblCountry, you're setting the Text property of the label to the ManufacturerCountry column from the DataReader. You do the same for the Text property of the lnkEmail hyperlink, except that you use the ManufacturerEmail column from the DataReader.

The NavigateUrl property is slightly different. As you discovered when you looked at inline binding in the previous chapter, you can't mix text with data-binding tags. So the following will not work:

```
NavigateUrl='mailto: <%# Eval("[ManufacturerEmail]") %>'
```

Instead, you need to use a slightly different version of Eval and format the data that you're trying to display:

```
NavigateUrl='<%# Eval("[ManufacturerEmail]", "mailto:{0}") %>'
```

You can also use the column index rather than the column name within the Eval statement. This works fine, unless the query to retrieve the data changes and column 2 is no longer the e-mail address. For that reason, it's always better to use the column name to reference a column.

Once the `ItemTemplate` has been processed, the `Repeater` will then output the `SeparatorTemplate` if one is present. In this case, you output a blue horizontal line:

```
<SeparatorTemplate>
  <hr style="color:blue"/>
</SeparatorTemplate>
```

If a `SeparatorTemplate` isn't specified, nothing will be output, and the `Repeater` will immediately show the `AlternatingItemTemplate`.

As you can see in Figure 7-2, the `AlternatingItemTemplate` is shown, not surprisingly, alternating with the `ItemTemplate`. If an `AlternatingItemTemplate` isn't specified, the `ItemTemplate` is simply repeated.

The usual use of the `AlternatingItemTemplate` is to provide a quick means of showing alternating rows in a slightly different way. In this example, you've simply changed the background color, as shown in Figure 7-4.

Figure 7-4. *The AlternatingItemTemplate shows rows slightly differently.*

In this case, the `AlternatingItemTemplate` and the `ItemTemplate` are the same other than the color specified for the background. The `ItemTemplate` has an ivory background:

```
<ItemTemplate>
  <div style="background-color:Ivory">
```

Whereas the `AlternatingItemTemplate` has an azure background:

```
<AlternatingItemTemplate>
  <div style="background-color:Azure">
```

Once all of the data has been shown using the `ItemTemplate` and `AlternatingItemTemplate` templates, the `Repeater` then shows the `FooterTemplate`:

```
<FooterTemplate>
  <hr style="color:blue"/>
  <div style="background-color:Bisque">
    <br />
  </div>
</FooterTemplate>
```

Again, you start with the horizontal rule, as the `SeparatorTemplate` isn't shown after the final *real* template. You then show an empty `<div>` in the odd background color that you used for the header. In this example, the footer just ties back to the header to round things off. You wouldn't lose anything if you didn't include this `FooterTemplate`.

The Repeater Control Events

You've seen how easy it is to use a Repeater to output data. With the requisite HTML and inline binding, you can create quite complex pages. However, this isn't the end of the story. What if you need to make decisions based on the data returned? Inline binding allows you to only display the data. By using some of the events that the Repeater exposes, you can make complex decisions based on the data that you want to show. For example, you could display an image depending on a value returned from the database.

Like all Web controls, the Repeater acquires some events from its inheritance hierarchy, but we're not particularly interested in the standard events (such as Init and Load). What we're interested in here are the events that are specific to the Repeater, as shown in Table 7-3.

Table 7-3. *The Important Events of the Repeater*

Name	Description
ItemCommand	Fired when a button Web control (a Button, LinkButton, or ImageButton) within the Repeater is clicked.
ItemCreated	Fired for each row that is output by the Repeater, for all five supported templates. If this event is fired in response to an ItemTemplate or an AlternatingItemTemplate, you don't have access to the data that is to be output. You need the ItemDataBound event for that.
ItemDataBound	Fired for each row that is output by the Repeater, for all five supported templates. If the row that is being output is an ItemTemplate or an AlternatingItemTemplate, you have access to the row from the data source that is being output.

In the next example, you'll see how to use the ItemCommand event to respond to the selection of a Manufacturer. The other two events, however, may cause a little confusion.

The ItemDataBound event is fired immediately after the ItemCreated event for every row that the Repeater is going to output. The only difference between the two events is that for the ItemTemplate and AlternatingItemTemplate, the ItemDataBound event has access to the row of data that is to be displayed. The ItemCreated event doesn't have access to this information. Because of this, you'll see the ItemDataBound event used far more often than the ItemCreated event. This is true not only for the Repeater, but the DataList, GridView, DetailsView, and FormView also support both of these events—although the GridView events are called RowDataBound and RowCreated. Again, the ItemDataBound (or RowDataBound) event will be used more frequently.

Try It Out: Using the Repeater to Display the Players

In this example, you'll build on the previous example and add a link button for each Manufacturer, allowing the user to view the Players for that Manufacturer. The list of Players will be shown on its own page, which will use a SqlDataSource to query the database.

1. In the code download for this chapter, you'll find an images folder. Copy this folder to your Chapter07 Web site.

2. If you've closed `Repeater_DataReader.aspx` from the previous example, reopen it and switch to the Source view.

3. Change the query in the `Page_Load` event to also return the ManufacturerID:

```
string CommandText = "SELECT ManufacturerID, ManufacturerName, ➡
  ManufacturerCountry, ManufacturerEmail, ManufacturerWebsite ➡
  FROM Manufacturer";
```

4. Add a `LinkButton` to the end of the `ItemTemplate` for the `Repeater`:

```
      <%# Eval("[ManufacturerWebsite]") %>
      </asp:HyperLink>
      <br />
      <asp:LinkButton ID="btnProducts" runat="server"
        CommandName="Players" Text="View Players"
        CommandArgument='<%# Eval("[ManufacturerID]") %>' />
    </div>
  </ItemTemplate>
```

5. Add the same `LinkButton` to the end of the `AlternatingItemTemplate` for the `Repeater`:

```
      <%# Eval("[ManufacturerWebsite]") %>
      </asp:HyperLink>
      <br />
      <asp:LinkButton ID="btnProducts" runat="server"
        CommandName="Players" Text="View Players"
        CommandArgument='<%# Eval("[ManufacturerID]") %>' />
    </div>
  </ItemTemplate>
```

6. Switch to the Design view and select the `Repeater`. In the Properties window, look at the events and double-click the `ItemCommand` event to add the event handler to the page.

7. Add the following code to the `Repeater1_ItemCommand` event:

```
protected void Repeater1_ItemCommand(object source,
  RepeaterCommandEventArgs e)
{
  if (e.CommandName == "Players")
  {
    Response.Redirect("./Repeater_DataSource.aspx?ManufacturerID=" +
      e.CommandArgument);
  }
}
```

8. Add a new Web Form to the Web site, called `Repeater_DataSource.aspx`.

9. In the Source view, find the `<title>` tag within the HTML and change the page title to **Binding a DataSource to a Repeater**.

10. Switch to the Design view and add a SqlDataSource to the page. Select Configure Data Source from the Tasks menu.

11. Select SqlConnectionString from the drop-down list on the Choose Your Data Connection step, and then click the Next button.

12. On the Configure the Select Statement step, select Player from the Name drop-down list and check the PlayerName, PlayerCost, and PlayerStorage columns. Click the WHERE button.

13. As shown in Figure 7-5, select PlayerManufacturerID from the Column drop-down list. Then select QueryString from the Source drop-down list and enter **ManufacturerID** in the QueryString Field text box.

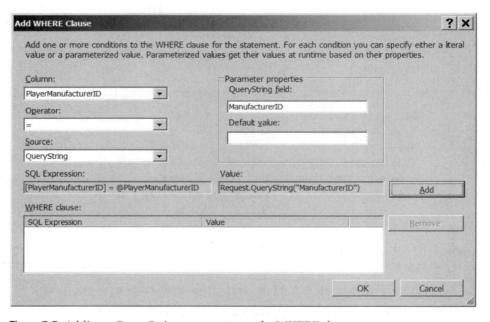

Figure 7-5. *Adding a QueryString parameter as the WHERE clause*

14. Click the Add button to add the parameter to the WHERE clause, and then click the OK button to close the dialog box.

15. Click the Next button. If you want to test the query, you can do so. You'll need to enter a valid ManufacturerID when prompted.

16. Once you're happy that the query returns a filtered list of Players, click the Finish button to close the Configure Data Source dialog box.

17. In the Design view, add a Repeater to the page. Select SqlDataSource1 as the data source from the Tasks menu.

18. Switch to the Source view and make sure you've included the correct data provider at the top of the page:

```
<%@ Page Language="C#" %>
<%@ Import Namespace="System.Data" %>
```

19. Add the following two templates to the Repeater:

```
<asp:Repeater ID="Repeater1" runat="server">
  <HeaderTemplate>
    <div style="background-color:Bisque">
      <font size="+2">Players</font>
    </div>
    <hr style="color:blue"/>
  </HeaderTemplate>
  <ItemTemplate>
    <table>
      <tr>
        <td rowspan="2">
          <asp:Image ID="imgType" runat="server" />
        </td>
        <td>
          <b><asp:Label ID="lblName" runat="server" text="name" /></b>
        </td>
      </tr>
      <tr>
        <td>
          <asp:Label ID="lblCost" runat="server" text="cost" />
        </td>
      </tr>
    </table>
  </ItemTemplate>
</asp:Repeater>
```

20. Switch to the Design view and select the Repeater. Switch to the Events view in the Properties window and double-click the ItemDataBound event. Add the following code to the event handler that is created:

```
protected void Repeater1_ItemDataBound(object sender,
  RepeaterItemEventArgs e)
{
  if (e.Item.ItemType == ListItemType.Item
    || e.Item.ItemType == ListItemType.AlternatingItem)
  {
    // get the item that we're binding to
    DataRowView objData = (DataRowView)e.Item.DataItem;

    // set the two labels
    ((Label)e.Item.FindControl("lblName")).Text =
      objData["PlayerName"].ToString();
    ((Label)e.Item.FindControl("lblCost")).Text =
      String.Format("{0:n}", objData["PlayerCost"]);
```

```
        // set the correct image
        if (objData["PlayerStorage"].ToString() == "Hard Disk")
        {
          ((Image)e.Item.FindControl("imgType")).ImageUrl =
            "./images/disk.gif";
        }
        else
        {
          ((Image)e.Item.FindControl("imgType")).ImageUrl =
            "./images/solid.gif";
        }
      }
    }
}
```

21. Save both pages, and then view `Repeater_DataReader.aspx` in your browser. The list of Manufacturers from the previous example will be displayed, along with a View Players link, as shown in Figure 7-6.

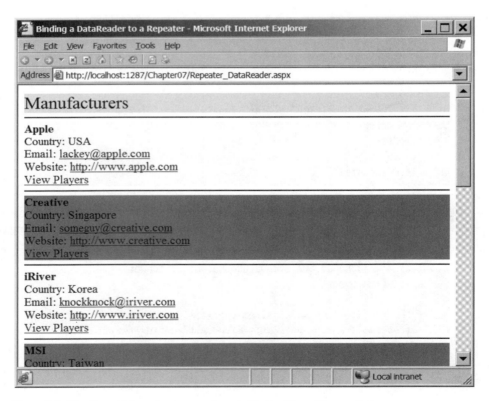

Figure 7-6. *The list of Manufacturers along with the View Players link*

22. Click the View Players link for Apple, and the list of Players for Apple will be displayed, as shown in Figure 7-7.

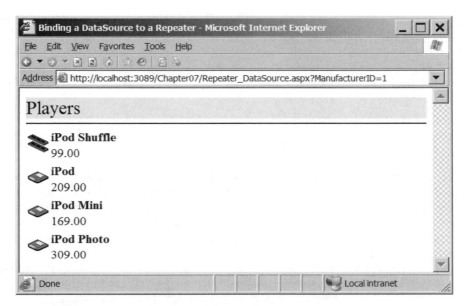

Figure 7-7. *Showing the Players made by Apple*

23. Click the back button in your browser and select any of the other Manufacturers. You'll see that the list of Players changes to show only those for the selected Manufacturer.

How It Works

You've used the ItemCommand and ItemDataBound events to create a little interactive example that starts to show some of the functionality that you can use to build your own pages. This example also uses the SqlDataSource, rather than accessing the database in code, to show that data binding to the Repeater can be done either way. You can also use the ItemDataBound event when using a DataReader or DataSet as the data source. Any time DataBind() is called—either in code or automatically—the ItemCreated and ItemDataBound events will be fired when a row of data needs to be displayed.

The Data Source and the Repeater

First, you modified the query to retrieve the list of Manufacturers from the database. In order to filter the list of Players by Manufacturer, you need to know which Manufacturer you're filtering; the query from the previous example didn't return us the ManufacturerID. You modified the query to add this:

```
string CommandText = "SELECT ManufacturerID, ManufacturerName, ➥
  ManufacturerCountry, ManufacturerEmail, ManufacturerWebsite ➥
  FROM Manufacturer";
```

Since you're modifying the query, you need to be careful that you don't break any data binding that is set up to use column indexes rather than column names. Thankfully we're sensible developers, and we always use column names rather than the index, so this isn't a problem here.

In order to display the list of Players, you need to link to a separate page. You could do this using a HyperLink and set the NavigateUrl property to the correct page, specifying the ManufacturerID that you want to show. While that would be the better solution in a real Web site (after all, you don't want a round trip to the server if you can avoid it), here, you're seeing how the ItemCommand event works. So, you add a LinkButton and set its CommandName and CommandArgument properties:

```
<asp:LinkButton ID="btnProducts" runat="server"
  CommandName="Players" Text="View Players"
  CommandArgument='<%# Eval("[ManufacturerID]") %>' />
```

Once the Repeater has output a row of data, that data is no longer available to the Web control. Thus, if you don't somehow pass the ManufacturerID to the ItemCommand event, there would be no way for you to know which Manufacturer was selected. The CommandArgument allows you to pass any arbitrary data that you want with the button click, and it will be available within the ItemCommand event. You need the ManufacturerID, so you use this as the value of the CommandArgument property.

The CommandName property works in a similar fashion. You're not limited to one button within an ItemTemplate or AlternatingItemTemplate, nor are you limited to using only one type of button; you can also use Button and ImageButton controls. In the case, where you want several different buttons (maybe View, Edit, and Delete buttons), you need some way of determining which button was pressed. You can pass any arbitrary text as the CommandName, and this will be available within the ItemCommand event. Although it's not required, as you have only one button in the row, you use the string Players to indicate that you want to see the list of Players. This will avoid problems in the future if you decide to add a second button.

Although you have a button that, when clicked, will post back to the server, you still haven't hooked up the ItemCommand event. You do this by adding the OnItemCommand property to the <asp:Repeater> tag. Even though you added the event using the Properties window, the event is still added to the markup for the Repeater:

```
<asp:Repeater ID="Repeater1" runat="server"
  OnItemCommand="Repeater1_ItemCommand">
```

You then need to handle the event in code. The first thing that you do is to check the CommandName for the clicked button:

```
if (e.CommandName == "Players")
```

The e argument passed to the event has CommandName and CommandArgument properties that simply pass in the settings from the button that was clicked. You check that the CommandName is the expected value, Players, and if it is, you redirect the user to Repeater_DataSource.aspx to display the correct list of Players using the CommandArgument property:

```
Response.Redirect("./Repeater_DataSource.aspx?ManufacturerID=" +
  e.CommandArgument);
```

The second page in the example, Repeater_DataSource.aspx, uses a SqlDataSource to populate the Repeater. You've seen several SqlDataSource examples already. The one thing that is different here is the parameter that you use to filter the list:

```
<SelectParameters>
  <asp:QueryStringParameter Name="PlayerManufacturerID"
    QueryStringField="ManufacturerID" Type="Int32" />
</SelectParameters>
```

In all the previous examples, you've used parameters based on the values from other Web controls using a ControlParameter. Here, you use another type of parameter: QueryStringParameter. As with all parameters, you have Name and Type properties that tie the parameter to the query that you're executing. For the QueryStringParameter to function, you need to tell it what value to extract from the query string, which you do by using the QueryStringField property.

The value of ManufacturerID in the query string is passed to the SELECT query as the @PlayerManufacturerID parameter, and the results are filtered correctly:

```
SELECT PlayerName, PlayerCost, PlayerStorage
FROM Player
WHERE (PlayerManufacturerID = @PlayerManufacturerID)
```

As you've already seen, the SqlDataSource is associated with a Web control using the DataSourceID property:

```
DataSourceID="SqlDataSource1"
```

Data Binding

Now that the data source and the Repeater have been combined, we can concentrate on the heart of the matter: the data binding that takes place. In the previous example, all of the binding took place inline using the Eval method. In this example, you do all the data binding within the ItemDataBound event. The event handler is attached using the OnItemDataBound attribute of the <asp:Repeater> tag:

```
<asp:Repeater ID="Repeater1" runat="server"
  DataSourceID="SqlDataSource1"
  OnItemDataBound="Repeater1_ItemDataBound">
```

When the ItemDataBound event is called, the first thing that you need to check is that you're actually trying to show a row of data. The ItemDataBound event is called for all five templates, and you need to check which type of template you're showing. You can check for any of the template types using the ListItemType enumerator. As you want to perform the data binding only if the template is an ItemTemplate or AlternatingItemTemplate, you use the Item and AlternatingItem values from the enumeration.

```
if (e.Item.ItemType == ListItemType.Item
  || e.Item.ItemType == ListItemType.AlternatingItem)
{
```

You check for Item and AlternatingItem, even though only an ItemTemplate is specified, because the Repeater is actually outputting Item, followed by AlternatingItem, followed by Item. If the alternating template isn't specified, the Repeater simply uses the item template—it's still classed as alternating row that is being displayed.

The data that you're trying to bind is available to the ItemDataBound event as e.Item.DataItem. This returns an Object that you need to cast to the correct type to use. The SqlDataSource, by default, accesses the database and returns a DataSet. Each row from the DataSet passed to the ItemDataBound event passes as a DataRowView, and e.Item.DataItem is cast to the correct type and stored for later use:

```
// get the item that we're binding to
DataRowView objData = (DataRowView)e.Item.DataItem;
```

This is the case whether you use a SqlDataSource to query the database or use code to construct a DataSet, and use this as the DataSource and call DataBind(). However, if you're using a DataReader (either through code or by setting the DataSourceMode of the SqlDataSource to DataReader), then you don't have a DataRowView. Instead, you have a DbDataRecord that you must cast slightly differently:

```
// get the item that we're binding to
DbDataRecord objData = (DbDataRecord)e.Item.DataItem;
```

Thankfully, both the DataRowView and the DbDataRecord have indexes that you can access using either a column name or a column index. Once you've cast e.Item.DataItem to the correct type, the way that you access the different values is the same.

In order to data-bind, you need to be able to access the Web controls that make up the row. As you're actually dealing with a template, the Web controls don't exist directly on the page, so you can't access them directly. You need to use the e.Item.FindControl() method to return the Web controls that you want to access, as you do for the two labels that make up the ItemTemplate:

```
// set the two labels
((Label)e.Item.FindControl("lblName")).Text =
    objData["PlayerName"].ToString();
((Label)e.Item.FindControl("lblCost")).Text =
    String.Format("{0:n}", objData["PlayerCost"]);
```

The FindControl() method returns a System.Web.UI.Control object that must be cast to the correct type before any of the Web control-specific properties can be accessed. In this case, you're dealing with labels, so you cast the object to a Label before setting the Text property.

Again, you can access the data either using a column name or a column index, but you should, ideally, always use the column name if you can. The index for both the DataRowView and DbDataRecord objects returns an Object, so you need to convert this to a string to set the Text property. You do this slightly differently for each of the labels, as you want to format the cost correctly.

The last piece of data binding that you perform shows why you sometimes need to use the ItemDataBound event. Simply setting Web control properties to a value from the database can be performed quite easily using inline binding. When you want to do something slightly different, then you need to use the ItemDataBound event. In this case, you want to display different images for the Players depending on whether the Player uses a hard disk or a solid-state storage format. You can find out which type the Player is by using the PlayerStorage column. This column is stored in the database as a string, so you can check what the value is by doing a simple string comparison. If the Player is a hard disk-based Player, then you want to show a disk for the

Player, so you set the ImageUrl of the Image (remember that you need to cast to the correct type) to disk.gif:

```
// set the correct image
if (objData["PlayerStorage"].ToString() == "Hard Disk")
{
  ((Image)e.Item.FindControl("imgType")).ImageUrl =
    "./images/disk.gif";
}
```

Otherwise, you want to show that it's a solid-state-based Player, so you set the ImageUrl to solid.gif:

```
else
{
  ((Image)e.Item.FindControl("imgType")).ImageUrl =
    "./images/solid.gif";
}
```

Inline Binding vs. Event-Based Binding

In the preceding couple of examples, we've looked at the two ways that you can perform table binding: with *inline binding* using the Eval() method or *event-based binding* within the ItemDataBound event.

Apart from the instances where you can't use inline binding, such as you saw with the example of changing the image depending on the type of Player, there really is no functional difference between the two types of binding. The main difference is performance. Inline binding uses reflection to evaluate the arguments that are passed in and to return the results. If you use the ItemDataBound event you're not using reflection, so it will be quicker.

Inline Binding Alternative

One of the main problems with inline binding is that fact that the Eval statement uses reflection to query for the requested column. This is perhaps the slowest way of getting at the data and, not surprisingly, there is an alternative.

Rather than using the Eval statement, you can cast the DataItem that you're displaying in much the same way as you do for event-based binding. So where you would use an Eval statement like the following:

```
<%# Eval("ManufacturerName") %>
```

you can instead cast the DataItem, accessed as with normal inline binding using Container.DataItem, to the correct type.

If you're using the DataSet to provide the data source, you need to cast to a DataRowView:

```
<%# ((DataRowView)Container.DataItem)["ManufacturerName"] %>
```

And if you're using a DataReader, you need to cast to a DbDataRecord:

```
<%# ((DbDataRecord)Container.DataItem)["ManufacturerName"] %>
```

Mixing Binding Types

It is also possible to use both inline binding and event-based binding within the DataBind() call. If you choose to use both types of binding at the same time, you need to be aware that the inline binding will occur before the event-based binding.

So, if you were to set the Text property of two Label controls using inline binding as follows:

```
<asp:Label ID="lblName" runat="server"
  Text='<%# Eval("[ManufacturerName]") %>'>
</asp:Label>
<asp:Label ID="lblCountry" runat="server"
  Text='<%# Eval("[ManufacturerCountry]") %>'>
</asp:Label>
```

And then in the ItemDataBound event change the Text property of lblCountry as follows:

```
((Label)e.Item.FindControl("lblCountry")).Text = "COUNTRY";
```

you would not get the results that you're expecting. During the inline binding, both lblName and lblCountry will be bound to the correct values from the database. As soon as the ItemDataBound event is fired, the correct value for lblCountry is replaced by the string COUNTRY.

Granted, this is a very contrived example, as you wouldn't set the Text property to a meaningless value like this, but it does serve to illustrate the point.

The DataList Web Control

The DataList is a Web control that sort of sits in no-man's land. It allows you to display data to the user, and with some coding in the background, it allows you edit data inline and propagate these changes back to the database. However, it's one of those Web controls that you don't see used very often and tends to get overlooked. We're not going to spend too much time looking at the DataList, because it follows the same principles as the Repeater.

■**Note** If you want to use a DataList for editing data, refer to http://msdn.microsoft.com/en-us/library/9cx2f3ks.aspx for full details.

We'll dive straight into an example. You'll see that when displaying data, the DataList and Repeater have a lot in common.

Try It Out: Using the DataList to Display the Players

In this example, you'll use a SqlDataSource to query the database for a complete list of Players from the database. The list of Players will be displayed in a DataList.

1. Add a new Web Form to the Chapter07 Web site called DataList_DataSource.aspx.

2. In the Source view, find the <title> tag within the HTML and change the page title to **Binding a DataSource to a DataList**.

3. Switch to the Design view and add a `SqlDataSource` to the page. Select Configure Data Source from the Tasks menu.

4. Select `SqlConnectionString` from the drop-down list on the Choose Your Data Connection step, and then click the Next button.

5. On the Configure the Select Statement step, select Player from the Name drop-down list and check the PlayerName, PlayerCost, and PlayerStorage columns.

6. Click the ORDER BY button and select PlayerName as the Sort By column. Click OK to close the Add ORDER BY Clause dialog box.

7. Click the Next button. If you want to test the query, you can choose to do so on the next step. Once you're happy that the query returns a complete list of Players, click the Finish button to close the Configure Data Source dialog box.

8. Add a `DataList` onto the page. Select `SqlDataSource1` as the data source from the Tasks menu.

9. Select the `DataList`, and from the Properties window, set `RepeatDirection` to Horizontal and set `RepeatColumns` to 3.

10. Switch to the Source view and make sure you've included the correct namespace declaration at the top of the page:

```
<%@ Page Language="C#" %>
<%@ Import Namespace="System.Data" %>
```

11. Replace the auto-generated `ItemTemplate` with the following `ItemTemplate` and `AlternatingItemTemplate`:

```
<ItemTemplate>
  <table bgcolor="Ivory">
    <tr>
      <td rowspan="2">
        <asp:Image ID="imgType" runat="server" />
      </td>
      <td>
        <b><asp:Label ID="lblName" runat="server" text="name" /></b>
      </td>
    </tr>
    <tr>
      <td>
        <asp:Label ID="lblCost" runat="server" text="cost" />
      </td>
    </tr>
  </table>
</ItemTemplate>
<AlternatingItemTemplate>
  <table bgcolor="Azure">
    <tr>
```

```
        <td rowspan="2">
          <asp:Image ID="imgType" runat="server" />
        </td>
        <td>
          <b><asp:Label ID="lblName" runat="server" text="name" /></b>
        </td>
      </tr>
      <tr>
        <td>
          <asp:Label ID="lblCost" runat="server" text="cost" />
        </td>
      </tr>
  </table>
</AlternatingItemTemplate>
```

12. Switch to the Design view and select the DataList. Switch to the Events view in the Properties window and double-click the ItemDataBound event. Add the following code to the event handler that is created:

```
protected void DataList1_ItemDataBound(object sender,
  DataListItemEventArgs e)
{
  if (e.Item.ItemType == ListItemType.Item
    || e.Item.ItemType == ListItemType.AlternatingItem)
  {
    // get the item that we're binding to
    DataRowView objData = (DataRowView)e.Item.DataItem;

    // set the two labels
    ((Label)e.Item.FindControl("lblName")).Text =
      objData["PlayerName"].ToString();
    ((Label)e.Item.FindControl("lblCost")).Text =
      String.Format("{0:n}", objData["PlayerCost"]);

    // set the correct image
    if (objData["PlayerStorage"].ToString() == "Hard Disk")
    {
      ((Image)e.Item.FindControl("imgType")).ImageUrl =
        "./images/disk.gif";
    }
    else
    {
      ((Image)e.Item.FindControl("imgType")).ImageUrl =
        "./images/solid.gif";
    }
  }
}
```

13. Save the page, and then view it in a browser. When the page loads, you'll see that the list of Players is presented, as shown in Figure 7-8.

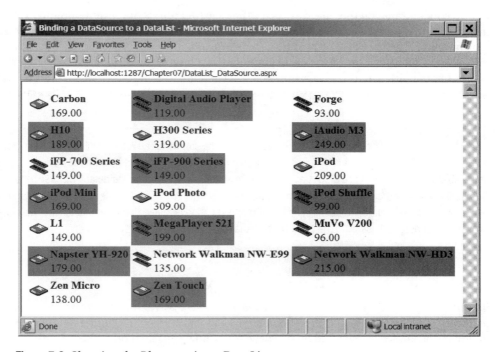

Figure 7-8. *Showing the Players using a DataList*

How It Works

The main difference here is the definition of the DataList. The first thing that you'll notice is that you've set two properties on the DataList: RepeatDirection to Horizontal and RepeatColumns to 3. As the DataList outputs in a table, you're effectively telling it to show three rows from the database on a line before moving to the next line. The list of Players is sorted by the name of the Player, and you can see that they are displayed horizontally before vertically.

Within the DataList, you've used the same ItemTemplate and AlternatingItemTemplate as you did with the Repeater. You've altered the color of the table that is displayed so that you can see the templates alternating, but apart from that, the templates are the same. Each template is output in its own cell within the table, and you've chosen to keep a table structure within the template, as it provides a nice enough display for your purposes.

When the DataList is data-bound, you've used the ItemDataBound event to perform some more complex processing than is available with inline binding. The code within the ItemDataBound event is the same as the Repeater; not a single line has changed.

As you can see in this very brief example, the DataList can provide a little more control over the output than a Repeater, but basically how you control what is displayed is the same.

The GridView Web Control

So far, we've looked at table binding in the context of the Repeater and, very briefly, the DataList. We've concentrated on the Repeater, as it's the "least-featured" of the table-binding Web controls, and it allowed us to cover most of what you need to know without being distracted by any functionality that other Web controls may provide.

Now, we'll look at the GridView, beginning with a brief recap of what we've looked at in previous chapters. Then you'll see how you can customize the layout and the columns for the GridView. Finally, we'll cover the sorting and paging functionality that the GridView supports.

■**Note** As you've already seen, you can construct the data source for a Web control in four ways. You can write code that populates a DataSet or returns a DataReader that you pass to the DataSource property of the Web control, or you can use a SqlDataSource (in either DataReader or the default DataSet mode) and set the DataSourceID property of the Web control. With ASP.NET 2.0, Microsoft has tied the SqlDataSource and GridView quite closely together, and by far the best option is to use them in conjunction. Therefore, all the examples here will use a SqlDataSource as the data source to the GridView.

Try It Out: Showing Data in a GridView

In this example, you'll build a page that displays the list of Players and let the GridView take care of creating all the columns. This is the same page as you've seen in Chapters 3 and 4. In the following examples, you'll build on this page to see how you can modify the GridView to create much more useful pages.

1. In Visual Web Developer, add a new Web Form called GridView_Players.aspx. Make sure that the Place Code in Separate File check box is unchecked.

2. In the Source view, find the <title> tag within the HTML at the bottom of the page and change the page title to **Players in a GridView**.

3. Switch to the Design view and add a SqlDataSource to the page. Select Configure Data Source from the Tasks menu.

4. Select SqlConnectionString as the connection string to use on the first step of the wizard. Click the Next button.

5. Select the Player table. In the Columns list, select all five columns individually. Click the Next button.

6. If you want to test that the query returns the correct results, you can do so. When you're happy that the results are correct, click the Finish button.

7. Switch to the Source view. Within the body of the page, between the <form> and </form> tags, add a GridView to the page:

```
<asp:GridView ID="GridView1" runat="server"
  DataSourceID="SqlDataSource1">
</asp:GridView>
```

8. Save the page, and then view it in a browser. When the page loads, you'll see that the list of Players is presented in a tabular format, as shown in Figure 7-9.

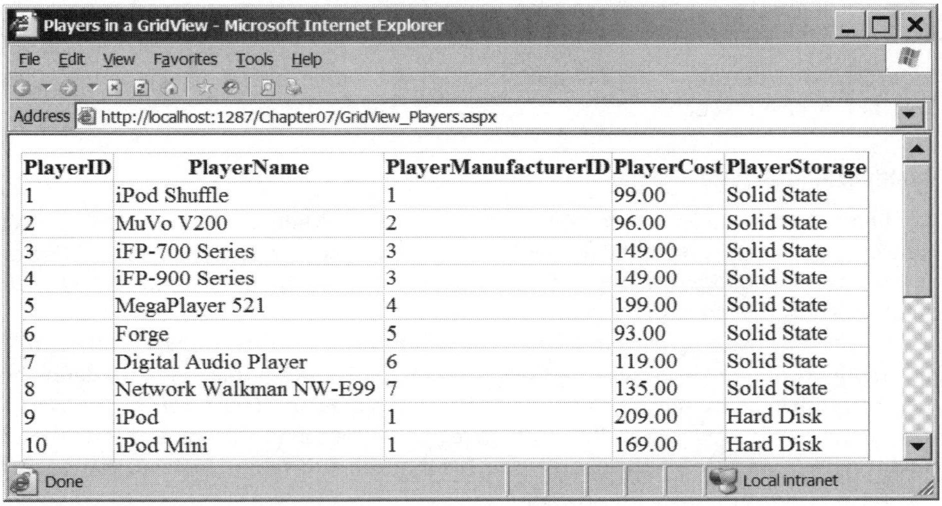

Figure 7-9. *Showing the Players in a GridView*

How It Works

This is perhaps the simplest example that we've looked at so far! Within the markup, you've let the automatic features of the GridView take control. It's the simplest data-bound Web control definition you've seen:

```
<asp:GridView ID="GridView1" runat="server"
  DataSourceID="SqlDataSource1">
</asp:GridView>
```

You have not defined any columns or told the GridView how you want the data presented. It took its complete definition from the SQL query that you ran against the database via the SqlDataSource:

```
SELECT PlayerID, PlayerName, PlayerManufacturerID, PlayerCost, PlayerStorage
FROM Player
```

Every column you specified in the query is output by the GridView, and the name of the column in the table is the name of the column in the database.

Although you've achieved your goal of using the GridView, I think you'll agree that the data isn't presented in the best way. We'll now look at how you can make the output from the GridView more presentable, before moving on to look at how you can allow the user to page through results and to sort the results that they are viewing.

GridView Customization

In this section, you'll look at the following ways to improve the example's dreary black-and-white table:

- Changing the column headings and making the data itself more readable

- Adding some color to the table by defining styles

- Defining the columns that are displayed

You'll stick to using a SqlDataSource as the data source, but these techniques apply to all four data-access mechanisms.

Customizing the Data

The first task is to make the data itself more presentable. When data is bound to a GridView, the column name used in the database table is presented as the column header. That's fine when you're designing databases, but PlayerManufacturerID isn't suitable for user viewing. It's preferable to show the name of the Manufacturer instead.

You could customize the GridView by setting its AutoGenerateColumns property to False and explicitly defining the columns that you want to display. In this case, you define how the GridView renders each particular column with BoundField and TemplateField objects, rather than templates for each row, but the principles are the same. You'll look at this method shortly, but for now, leave AutoGenerateColumns as True (the default value). Instead, you'll see how to use the SQL query to make the change.

You saw in Chapter 3 how to use an INNER JOIN in a SQL query to retrieve data from one table based on values from another. You can use that technique here to return the Manufacturer's name for each Player, rather than the ManufacturerID number. Instead of the following:

```
SELECT PlayerID, PlayerName, PlayerManufacturerID, PlayerCost, PlayerStorage
FROM Player
```

You now have this:

```
SELECT Player.PlayerID, Player.PlayerName, Manufacturer.ManufacturerName,
  Player.PlayerCost, Player.PlayerStorage
FROM Player INNER JOIN Manufacturer
  ON Player.PlayerManufacturerID = Manufacturer.ManufacturerID
```

That sorts the contents of the query, but how do you influence the column names? You alter the SQL query again and use *aliases* as needed for each column. In SELECT queries, you use the AS keyword to tell a database to return an alternate name for a column in its results for a query. If you wanted to show the PlayerName column in the Player table as just Name in the results of a query, SELECT Player.PlayerName AS Name would do the trick. For this example, you can add aliases to the query and complete the first of the tasks:

```
SELECT Player.PlayerID, Player.PlayerName AS Name,
  Manufacturer.ManufacturerName AS Manufacturer,
  Player.PlayerCost AS Cost, Player.PlayerStorage
FROM Player INNER JOIN Manufacturer
  ON Player.PlayerManufacturerID = Manufacturer.ManufacturerID
```

You can see the results in Figure 7-10.

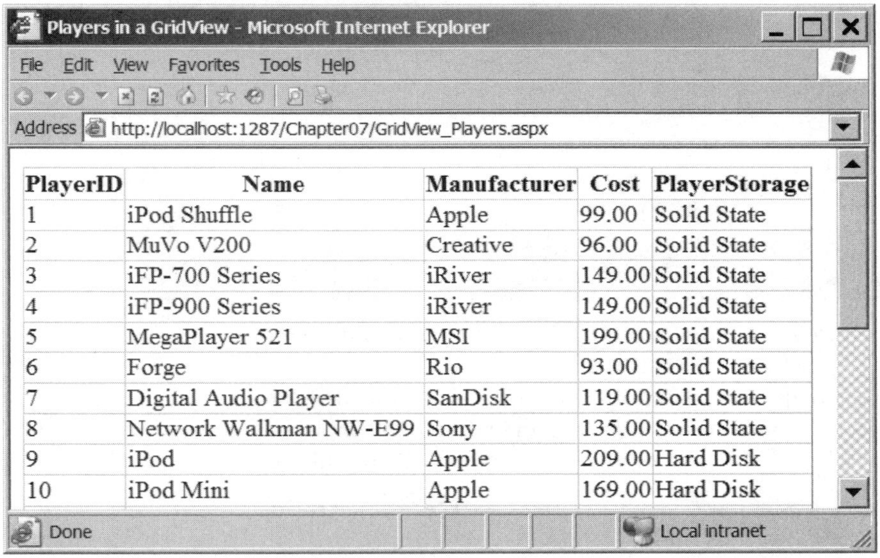

PlayerID	Name	Manufacturer	Cost	PlayerStorage
1	iPod Shuffle	Apple	99.00	Solid State
2	MuVo V200	Creative	96.00	Solid State
3	iFP-700 Series	iRiver	149.00	Solid State
4	iFP-900 Series	iRiver	149.00	Solid State
5	MegaPlayer 521	MSI	199.00	Solid State
6	Forge	Rio	93.00	Solid State
7	Digital Audio Player	SanDisk	119.00	Solid State
8	Network Walkman NW-E99	Sony	135.00	Solid State
9	iPod	Apple	209.00	Hard Disk
10	iPod Mini	Apple	169.00	Hard Disk

Figure 7-10. *Column aliases appear as column headers.*

Although the column headings are now more readable, the data that is displayed may not be quite correct. This is where explicitly defining the columns that you want to display comes into its own.

Adding Styles

The contents of the GridView are now a bit more readable, so you'll now focus on the GridView itself. It's a bit drab in black and white, so you might want to add some color. To do this, you can define style templates for the rows. The whole process is similar to the ItemTemplate in the Repeater, but as the GridView automatically generates a grid for a row, all you need to decide is how each row will be presented: colors, fonts, text alignment, cell padding, cell width, and so on.

The whole process is actually made quite easy by Visual Web Developer as it contains several predefined color schemes to apply directly to the GridView. Simply select your GridView in the Design view, and then click the Auto Format option on the Tasks menu. A dialog box will appear, allowing you to select a color scheme on the left and preview it on the right, as shown in Figure 7-11.

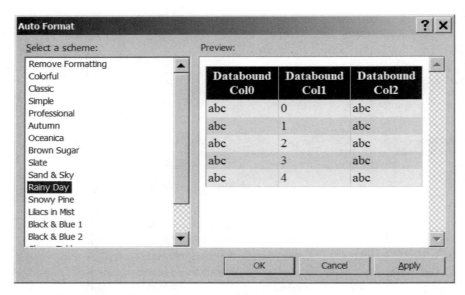

Figure 7-11. *The Auto Format dialog box lets you choose several predefined styles.*

Selecting one of the format options from the Auto Format dialog adds the required definitions for the selected style to the markup for the GridView. For example, you could choose the Rainy Day scheme (which uses most of the available row styles). The resulting code looks like this:

```
<asp:GridView ID="GridView1" runat="server" BackColor="White"
  BorderColor="#999999" BorderStyle="None" BorderWidth="1px"
  CellPadding="3" GridLines="Vertical">
  <FooterStyle BackColor="#CCCCCC" ForeColor="Black" />
  <RowStyle BackColor="#EEEEEE" ForeColor="Black" />
  <SelectedRowStyle BackColor="#008A8C" Font-Bold="True"
    ForeColor="White" />
  <PagerStyle BackColor="#999999" ForeColor="Black"
    HorizontalAlign="Center" />
  <HeaderStyle BackColor="#000084" Font-Bold="True"
    ForeColor="White" />
  <AlternatingRowStyle BackColor="#DCDCDC" />
</asp:GridView>
```

The style information in the <asp:GridView> tag itself sets the defaults for the whole grid, and the various <*xxx*Style> tags define deviations from that default, similar to how CSS works. In fact, there are eight different styles you can work with, as shown in Table 7-4.

Table 7-4. *The GridView Styles*

Name	Description
AlternatingRowStyle	Defines a style for every other row in the GridView, making it easier for the reader to follow a line across the grid
EditRowStyle	Applied to a row when it is being edited
EmptyDataRowStyle	Defines the style to be used when the GridView has no content to display
FooterStyle	Defines the style for the footer of the GridView
HeaderStyle	Defines the style for the header of the GridView
PagerStyle	Applied to the footer when it displays page-navigation links
RowStyle	Sets up the default style for a row in the GridView
SelectedRowStyle	Applied to a row when it's selected

Explicitly Defining the Columns

As you've seen, by default, the GridView automatically defines the columns it displays. However, this isn't always what you want, and with auto-generated columns, you must be very specific in the data that is used to populate the GridView. The column headings are the names of the columns from the database (or aliases, if you define them), and any changes to the query will change the layout of the GridView.

Setting the AutoGenerateColumns property to False prevents the GridView from generating the columns automatically and allows you to explicitly define the columns that you want to show. You do this by specifying a list of columns, or *Field controls* in GridView parlance. Table 7-5 lists the seven Field controls that you can define.

Table 7-5. *The GridView Field Controls*

Name	Description
BoundField	Displays data directly from the data source. The DataField property indicates which particular column of the results you want to show, and you can use the optional DataFormatString property to format the results as required.
ButtonField	Shows a button that causes a postback to the server, allowing an action to be performed on the selected row.
CheckBoxField	Shows a check box. This type of column is usually used to display columns from the database with Boolean values.
CommandField	Creates a column that contains Edit, Update, and Cancel buttons (as appropriate) to allow editing of the data within the selected row.
HyperLinkField	Shows a hyperlink.
ImageField	Shows an image.
TemplateField	Allows full control over what is displayed for the column: the header, the item displayed, and the footer. The TemplateField contains various templates controlling what is displayed and, within these templates, you can place whatever content you desire. This makes the TemplateField the most customizable of the column types.

Although the seven Field controls provide completely different functionality, they are all derived from the same base class, System.Web.UI.WebControls.DataControlField, and so share some very basic functionality. The most important properties are summarized in Table 7-6.

Table 7-6. *Important Properties for Field Controls*

Name	Description
FooterStyle	Sets the style of an individual column's footer. If the FooterStyle is specified for a column and any of the values clash (such as defining a background color in both), the setting here overrides the setting applied to the GridView as a whole.
FooterText	Sets the text to be displayed in the footer. The footer is shown only if the GridView has its ShowFooter property set to True.
HeaderStyle	Sets the style of an individual column's header. If the HeaderStyle is specified for a column and any of the values clash (such as defining a background color in both), the setting here overrides the setting applied to the GridView as a whole.
HeaderText	Sets the text to be displayed in the header. The header is shown only if the GridView has its ShowHeader property set to True.
ItemStyle	Sets the style of an individual column. If the ItemStyle is specified for a column and any of the values clash (such as defining a background color in both), the setting here overrides the setting applied to the GridView as a whole (either in the ItemStyle or the AlternatingItemStyle).

The TemplateField is the most versatile column supported by the GridView. It allows you to display and edit data using whatever Web controls you desire. It does this by allowing you to specify templates that you want to use in the different situations. The four templates that the TemplateField supports for displaying data are summarized in Table 7-7.

Table 7-7. *Templates Supported by the TemplateField in a GridView*

Name	Description
AlternatingItemTemplate	Defines the template for every other row in the GridView, making it easier for the reader to distinguish between the rows in the grid.
FooterTemplate	The HTML content of the FooterTemplate is output as the footer of the column being displayed. If a FooterTemplate is defined, any value set for the FooterText property of the column is ignored.
HeaderTemplate	The HTML content of the HeaderTemplate is output as the header of the column being displayed. If a HeaderTemplate is defined, any value set for the HeaderText property of the column is ignored.
ItemTemplate	The ItemTemplate is used to display the data returned from the data source in the format that you specify. As a minimum, this template must be specified in order for the GridView to output the returned data.

Templates in the GridView serve the same purpose as those in the Repeater. They allow you to control how the data is displayed. However, whereas the templates in the Repeater work on the entire row of data, the templates in the GridView are for a single column.

Note The GridView allows you to edit data inline. To support this functionality, there is also an EditItemTemplate that you can use to specify what is displayed when the GridView is in edit mode. The GridView shares the use of the Field controls with its sibling the DetailsView. When using a TemplateField within the DetailsView, you can specify another template, the InsertItemTemplate. We'll look at these two templates when we cover editing using the GridView, DetailsView, and FormView in Chapter 9.

Try It Out: Customizing the GridView

In this example, you'll customize a GridView by defining the exact columns that you want to show. By combining the three techniques discussed in the preceding sections, you'll extend the previous example and build a page that is much more user-friendly.

1. Open GridView_Players.aspx from the previous example and switch to the Source view.

2. Change the query that is executed by the SqlDataSource to return a more usable set of data as follows:

```
<asp:SqlDataSource ID="SqlDataSource1" runat="server"
  ConnectionString="<%$ ConnectionStrings:SqlConnectionString %>"
  SelectCommand="SELECT Player.PlayerID, Player.PlayerName,
    Manufacturer.ManufacturerName, Player.PlayerCost,
    Player.PlayerStorage FROM Player INNER JOIN Manufacturer
    ON Player.PlayerManufacturerID = Manufacturer.ManufacturerID">
</asp:SqlDataSource>
```

3. Add the correct namespace declaration at the top of the page:

```
<%@ Page Language="C#" %>
<%@ Import Namespace="System.Data" %>
```

4. Switch to the Design view for the page and select Auto Format from the GridView Tasks menu. Choose the Rainy Day style for this example.

5. Select the GridView. From the Properties window, set the AutoGenerateColumns property to False.

6. Switch to the Source view for the page and add the following to the GridView definition, after the style elements that have been added:

```
<Columns>
  <asp:BoundField DataField="PlayerID" HeaderText="PlayerID" />
  <asp:BoundField DataField="PlayerName" HeaderText="Name" />
  <asp:BoundField DataField="ManufacturerName"
    HeaderText="Manufacturer" />
  <asp:BoundField DataField="PlayerCost" DataFormatString="{0:n}"
    HeaderText="Cost" />
  <asp:TemplateField>
    <ItemTemplate>
      <asp:Image ID="imgType" runat="server" />
    </ItemTemplate>
  </asp:TemplateField>
</Columns>
```

7. Switch to the Design view. You'll see that the columns are displayed correctly, as shown in Figure 7-12.

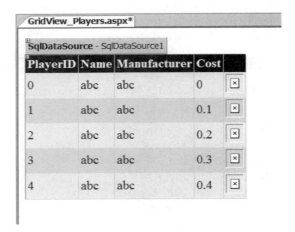

Figure 7-12. *Defined columns are shown correctly in the Design view.*

8. Add a RowDataBound event for the GridView and add the following code to the event handler:

```
protected void GridView1_RowDataBound(object sender,
  GridViewRowEventArgs e)
{
  if (e.Row.RowType == DataControlRowType.DataRow)
  {
    // get the item that we're binding to
    DataRowView objData = (DataRowView)e.Row.DataItem;
```

```
      // set the correct image
      if (objData["PlayerStorage"].ToString() == "Hard Disk")
      {
        ((Image)e.Row.FindControl("imgType")).ImageUrl =
          "./images/disk.gif";
      }
      else
      {
        ((Image)e.Row.FindControl("imgType")).ImageUrl =
          "./images/solid.gif";
      }
    }
  }
}
```

9. Save the page, and then view it in a browser. As shown in Figure 7-13, when the page loads, you'll see that the list of Players is presented in a much more user-friendly format. You'll see different images, depending on the storage format of the Player.

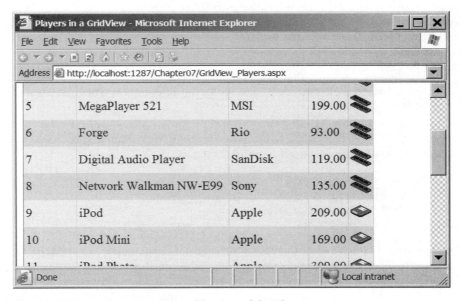

Figure 7-13. *A much more presentable view of the Players*

How It Works

Now you're starting to see how powerful the GridView can be, but also that it's quite similar, when displaying data, to the Repeater and DataList.

The first change that you've made to the example is to return a different set of results from the database. You've added an INNER JOIN to the query, and rather than returning the ManufacturerID, you return the ManufacturerName:

```
SELECT Player.PlayerID, Player.PlayerName, Manufacturer.ManufacturerName,
  Player.PlayerCost, Player.PlayerStorage
FROM Player INNER JOIN Manufacturer
  ON Player.PlayerManufacturerID = Manufacturer.ManufacturerID
```

The main changes that you made in the example are to the GridView definition itself. You selected the Rainy Day style from the Auto Format dialog box, and this has added several different styles to the definition:

```
<asp:GridView ID="GridView1" runat="server" BackColor="White"
  BorderColor="#999999" BorderStyle="None" BorderWidth="1px"
  CellPadding="3" GridLines="Vertical">
  <FooterStyle BackColor="#CCCCCC" ForeColor="Black" />
  <RowStyle BackColor="#EEEEEE" ForeColor="Black" />
  <SelectedRowStyle BackColor="#008A8C" Font-Bold="True"
    ForeColor="White" />
  <PagerStyle BackColor="#999999" ForeColor="Black"
    HorizontalAlign="Center" />
  <HeaderStyle BackColor="#000084" Font-Bold="True"
    ForeColor="White" />
  <AlternatingRowStyle BackColor="#DCDCDC" />
</asp:GridView>
```

The style has added settings that apply to the GridView as a whole (the attributes on the <asp:GridView> element itself) and added settings for the different row types (shown as children of the <asp:GridView> element).

Rather than let the GridView show the columns automatically, you specify the columns that you want to show in the <Columns> element. You have five columns, specified as five Field controls, and three of these are about as simple as it gets:

```
<asp:BoundField DataField="PlayerID" HeaderText="PlayerID" />
<asp:BoundField DataField="PlayerName" HeaderText="Name" />
<asp:BoundField DataField="ManufacturerName"
  HeaderText="Manufacturer" />
```

You use a BoundField to show the data returned from the database as a string on the page. The DataField property specifies the column from the results that you want to bind to, and the HeaderText property sets what is displayed in the header of the column. You used the HeaderText property to make the results a little more user-friendly. Rather than the column names from the database, you use Name and Manufacturer.

■Note The PlayerID column is pretty meaningless to the reader. Here, you've left it in the GridView for a later example. When we look at sorting and paging shortly, you'll see that this column offers a quick and easy way to see that the data being displayed is indeed changing. In a real page, you probably would not display it.

The fourth column is a little more complex. It's again a BoundField, but you specify an additional property, DataFormatString. One of the problems with the auto-generated columns was that it was impossible to show the data in the correct format. The DataFormatString property allows you to apply whatever format you require to the data that you're displaying. In this case, you want to show the price of the Player as a decimal:

```
<asp:BoundField DataField="PlayerStorePrice" DataFormatString="{0:n}"
  HeaderText="Cost" />
```

The last column that you define is a TemplateField. We define an ItemTemplate to display data, and use an Image to show a different image depending on the storage mechanism of the Player:

```
<asp:TemplateField>
  <ItemTemplate>
    <asp:Image ID="imgType" runat="server" />
  </ItemTemplate>
</asp:TemplateField>
```

In order to set the URL of the image that you want to display, you use the RowDataBound event. You could use inline binding, but as you saw with the Repeater earlier in the chapter, the RowDataBound event gives you a little more control over what you're going to display. As with the ItemDataBound event for the Repeater and DataList, the RowDataBound event is fired whenever a row of data is bound to the GridView.

Within the event handler, you add code that's remarkably similar to the ItemDataBound event handler that you saw for the Repeater earlier. You first check whether the row you're displaying is a DataRow (this is equivalent to checking for the ItemType being an Item or an AlternatingItem for the Repeater or DataList). If you are binding a DataRow, you cast the DataItem to the correct type:

```
if (e.Row.RowType == DataControlRowType.DataRow)
{
  // get the item that we're binding to
  DataRowView objData = (DataRowView)e.Row.DataItem;
```

You're using a DataSet to populate the GridView (as you're using the default access mode for the SqlDataSource), so you need to cast to a DataRowView. You then set the ImageUrl of the Image based on the PlayerStorage column returned from the database:

```
  // set the correct image
  if (objData["PlayerStorage"].ToString() == "Hard Disk")
  {
    ((Image)e.Item.FindControl("imgType")).ImageUrl =
      "./images/disk.gif";
  }
  else
  {
    ((Image)e.Item.FindControl("imgType")).ImageUrl =
      "./images/solid.gif";
  }
}
```

Now that we've covered the basics of the GridView, it's time to move forward and look at some of the interactive functionality that is available. We'll look at paging and sorting the results, and then move on to look at the events that are available for the GridView.

Paging and Sorting

Now that you've made the GridView more presentable and the information it contains more readable, you have one other card to play: to have the GridView present the information interactively. At the moment, it just displays all the information that results from a query in one go.

One interactive feature is *sorting*. You can set up the GridView so that clicking a column header sorts the information it contains by the entries in that column. A GridView that sorts can come in handy for users when they're checking data. On eBay, for example, it's a lot more helpful if you can sort which auctions are finishing first than having the information sorted by description. In the examples so far, it would be a lot easier to see which Manufacturer is associated with which Players if you could sort the data in the GridView by the contents of the Manufacturer column.

Another useful feature is *paging*. As you've no doubt experienced, unless you're incredibly specific in searching the Web, chances are that the search engine returns thousands of results. It would be impractical to display all those on one page, so they're divided into pages of 10 (or 25 or whatever you've set the default to) results, so you can move through them more effectively. You can apply this same technique to your GridView, setting it up so that it displays only a small number of rows per page, making it easier to read, with links to move through other pages of data until it has all been shown.

Try It Out: Sorting the GridView

Now you'll build on the previous example and implement sorting on the GridView.

1. Open GridView_Players.aspx from the previous example.

2. In the Source view, modify the column definitions for the GridView and add SortExpression attributes to the PlayerID, Name, and Manufacturer columns:

   ```
   <asp:BoundField DataField="PlayerID" HeaderText="PlayerID"
     SortExpression="PlayerID" />
   <asp:BoundField DataField="PlayerName" HeaderText="Name"
     SortExpression="PlayerName" />
   <asp:BoundField DataField="ManufacturerName"
     HeaderText="Manufacturer" SortExpression="ManufacturerName" />
   ```

3. Switch to the Design view and select the GridView. From the Tasks menu, set the EnableSorting property to True.

4. Execute the page. You'll see that the PlayerID, Name, and Manufacturer column headings are now hyperlinks. Clicking one of the columns, such as the Manufacturer column, sorts the data on the column, as shown in Figure 7-14.

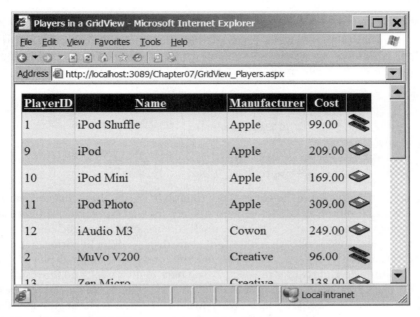

Figure 7-14. *The GridView can be sorted in ascending order.*

5. Click the same column heading again. You'll see that the results are now sorted in reverse order, as shown in Figure 7-15.

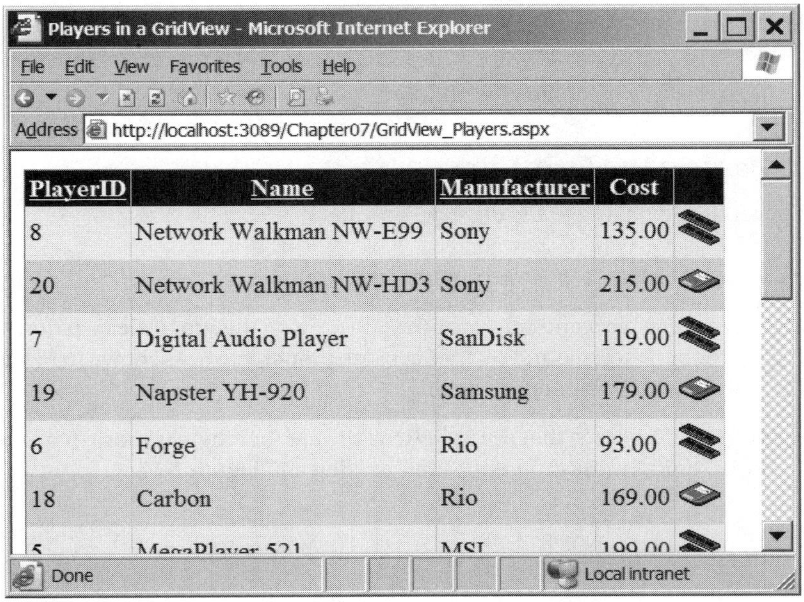

Figure 7-15. *The GridView can also be sorted in descending order.*

How It Works

Before enabling sorting on the GridView, you made some changes to the columns that you're displaying. In the example, you want to sort on only three of the five columns, so you add a SortExpression to only those columns:

```
<asp:BoundColumn DataField="PlayerID" HeaderText="PlayerID"
  SortExpression="PlayerID" />
<asp:BoundColumn DataField="PlayerName" HeaderText="Name"
  SortExpression="PlayerName" />
<asp:BoundColumn DataField="ManufacturerName"
  HeaderText="Manufacturer" SortExpression="ManufacturerName" />
```

You set the SortExpression to the name of the column in the database that you want to sort. If you were using column aliases (as you saw earlier), the SortExpression would be set to the alias rather than the actual name of the column. If you use auto-generated columns and enable sorting for the GridView, all of the columns that are displayed can be sorted. In this case, the SortExpression is added automatically as the column (or its alias) being displayed.

Clicking a column heading causes the page to post back to the server, and the results to be sorted, either in ascending or descending order. But what the code doesn't do is requery the database. As you'll recall, the SqlDataSource, when in DataSet mode, is clever enough to know that it doesn't always have to go back to the database to retrieve the results. Because the DataSet within the SqlDataSource is disconnected from the database, the sort can occur without requiring the database to be requeried.

As well as automatic sorting of the results, the GridView also raises two events when sorting:

- **Sorting**: The Sorting event is fired before the sort operation takes place and allows you to see which column the user wants to sort and gives you the opportunity to cancel the sort operation.

- **Sorted**: The Sorted event is fired after the sort operation has taken place.

Try It Out: Paging the GridView

In this example, you'll add paging to the displayed results.

1. Open GridView_Players.aspx from the previous example.

2. Switch to the Design view and select the GridView. From the Properties window, set the AllowPaging property to True and set the PageSize property to 5. As shown in Figure 7-16, the GridView shows that it's paging-enabled.

3. Execute the page. You'll see that the GridView is aware that there is more than one page and has added links for the different pages, as shown in Figure 7-17.

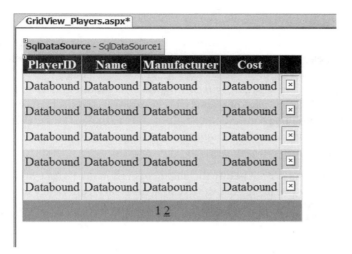

Figure 7-16. *The GridView shows that it's paging-enabled.*

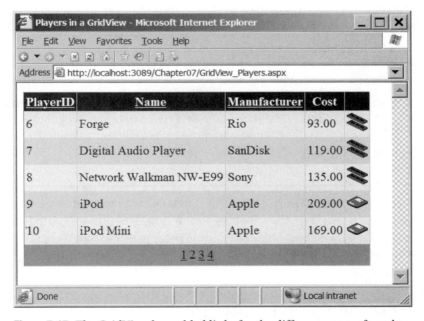

Figure 7-17. *The GridView has added links for the different pages of results.*

4. Click the link for any of the other pages, and you'll see that the correct set of results is displayed. Also try changing the sort ordering and then selecting any of the other pages to view. You'll see that the sorting and paging work in conjunction with each other.

How It Works

This example shows how easy the SqlDataSource and the GridView make it to add paging. All you need to do is set the AllowPaging property to True and the GridView will page the results automatically, showing the number of results set as the PageSize on each page.

The interesting point to note is that paging and sorting work in conjunction. If you have sorted results, then selecting a different page of results will preserve the sort order. In previous versions of ASP.NET, this functionality required quite a bit of code to make it work. Using the SqlDataSource and GridView, you get this functionality for free.

As with sorting, the GridView also raises two events when paging:

- PageIndexChanging: This event is fired before the paging operation takes place and allows you to see which page the user wants to navigate to and, if necessary, cancel the navigation.

- PageIndexChanged: This event is fired after the paging operation has taken place.

GridView Events

When we looked at the Repeater earlier in this chapter, you saw how to add buttons to the output and respond to the user clicking a button. Not surprisingly, the GridView also supports this functionality. You can respond to user events within the GridView through the following:

- ButtonField: This allows you to add a single button within a column, specify a CommandName, and then respond to the user clicking the button. You'll see how to use this type of column in the following example.

- CommandField: This is a column that you'll use only when you're allowing the user to edit the data in the GridView. The state of the GridView determines what buttons the CommandField displays. As this column is only used when editing, we'll discuss it in Chapter 9.

Note Rather than using a ButtonField or CommandField to display buttons that the user can click, you could use a Button, ImageButton, or LinkButton within a TemplateField and respond to the user clicking these buttons. The ButtonField and CommandField simply provide a shortcut way of adding the same functionality.

Try It Out: Responding to Events

In this example, you'll build a new page to show the list of Manufacturers and add a View Players button that allows the user to select a Manufacturer and view the list of Players. To filter the Players list, you'll also make a few changes to the Player list as well.

1. In Visual Web Developer, add a new Web Form called GridView_Manufacturers.aspx. Make sure that the Place Code in Separate File check box is unchecked.

2. In the Source view, find the <title> tag within the HTML at the bottom of the page and change the page title to **Manufacturers in a GridView**.

3. Switch to the Design view and add a `SqlDataSource` to the page. Select Configure Data Source from the Tasks menu.

4. Select `SqlConnectionString` as the connection string to use on the first step of the wizard. Click the Next button.

5. Select the Manufacturer table from the drop-down list. In the Columns list, select the ManufacturerID and ManufacturerName columns. Click the Next button.

6. If you want to test that the query is returning the correct results, you can do so. When you're happy that the results are correct, click the Finish button.

7. Add a `GridView` to the page. From its Tasks menu, set `SqlDataSource1` as the data source. Also open the Auto Format dialog box and select Colorful.

8. Switch to the Source view and add a `ButtonField` to the end of the `<Columns>` collection for the `GridView`:

```
<asp:ButtonField ButtonType="Link" CommandName="Players"
  Text="View Players" />
```

9. In the Design view, make sure that the `DataKeyNames` property of the `GridView` is set to ManufacturerID.

10. Add the `RowCommand` event to the `GridView`. Then add the following code to the event handler:

```
protected void GridView1_RowCommand(object source,
  GridViewCommandEventArgs e)
{
  if (e.CommandName == "Players")
  {
    int intIndex = Convert.ToInt32(e.CommandArgument);
    string strManufacuterID =
      Convert.ToString(GridView1.DataKeys[intIndex].Value);
    Response.Redirect("./GridView_Players.aspx?ManufacturerID=" +
      strManufacuterID);
  }
}
```

11. Open `GridView_Players.aspx` from the previous example.

12. Modify the `SelectCommand` property for the `SqlDataSource` as follows:

```
SELECT Player.PlayerID, Player.PlayerName,
  Manufacturer.ManufacturerName, Player.PlayerCost,
  Player.PlayerStorage FROM Player INNER JOIN Manufacturer
  ON Player.PlayerManufacturerID = Manufacturer.ManufacturerID
  WHERE Player.PlayerManufacturerID = @ManufacturerID
```

13. Add the following parameters to the SqlDataSource:

```
<SelectParameters>
  <asp:QueryStringParameter Name="ManufacturerID"
    QueryStringField="ManufacturerID" Type="Int32"  />
</SelectParameters>
```

14. Save the pages, and then view GridView_Manufacturers.aspx in your web browser. As shown in Figure 7-18, each row in the GridView now has a View Players link at the end.

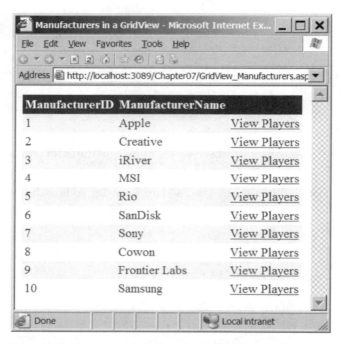

Figure 7-18. *The page now offers the ability to view the Players for a Manufacturer.*

15. Select one of the View Players links, and the filtered list of Players for the Manufacturer will be displayed. As shown in Figure 7-19, the list allows sorting of the filtered results.

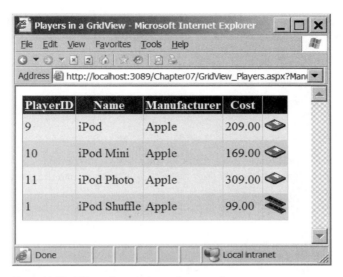

Figure 7-19. *Filtered results can be sorted.*

How It Works

In this example, you've seen further evidence of how data binding the different Web controls is similar, no matter which Web controls you use. Here, you've responded to the RowCommand event (the GridView equivalent of the ItemCommand) to handle the user clicking a button.

To add a button to a GridView, you need to add a ButtonField to the <Columns> collection:

```
<asp:ButtonField ButtonType="Link" CommandName="Players"
  Text="View Players" />
```

You specify the Text that you want to appear on the button and a CommandName that you can use to determine which button was clicked. You can also specify what type of button you want to use. You've specified a Link in this case, but you could have used a normal button by setting the ButtonType property to Button.

The one piece of information that you're missing from this definition is a way to determine which row was clicked. If you recall from the Repeater example earlier, you used the CommandArgument property of the LinkButton to store the ManufacturerID, and you used this to filter the displayed results, but the ButtonField doesn't support setting the CommandArgument property. Instead, the row index of the selected row is automatically passed as the CommandArgument to the RowSelected event handler. You need to use that index in conjunction with the GridView to determine the correct ManufacturerID.

The GridView is capable of storing an ID value for each row by setting the DataKeyNames property:

```
<asp:GridView DataKeyNames="ManufacturerID">
...
</asp:GridView>
```

When the GridView is bound, all the ManufacturerID values for the rows that are displayed are stored in a collection that can be accessed via the DataKeys property of the GridView.

So, when the user clicks a button, the RowCommand event is fired. After checking that you're responding to the correct button, you retrieve the row index from the CommandArgument, and then use this to interrogate the DataKeys collection:

```
int intIndex = Convert.ToInt32(e.CommandArgument);
string strManufacturerID =
  Convert.ToString(GridView1.DataKeys[intIndex].Value);
```

The DataKeys collection is stored in the same order as the rows are displayed. You can therefore use the row's position, from the CommandArgument property, to return the correct ManufacturerID.

You cast this to a string which is then used to construct the correct URL for the Players list:

```
Response.Redirect("./GridView_Players.aspx?ManufacturerID="
  + strManufacturerID);
```

In order to filter the results, you need to make a slight change to the query that is constructed by adding a simple WHERE clause that returns only the Players where the ManufacturerID matches the value passed as part of the query string:

```
SELECT Player.PlayerID, Player.PlayerName,
  Manufacturer.ManufacturerName, Player.PlayerCost,
  Player.PlayerStorage FROM Player INNER JOIN Manufacturer
  ON Player.PlayerManufacturerID = Manufacturer.ManufacturerID
  WHERE Player.PlayerManufacturerID = @ManufacturerID
```

You pass the correct value for ManufacturerID to the SqlDataSource by using a QueryStringParameter object as part of the SelectParameters collection:

```
<asp:QueryStringParameter Name="ManufacturerID"
  QueryStringField="ManufacturerID" Type="Int32"  />
```

Note that the paging and sorting of the Players list still works, even though you have a filtered result set. Because the DataSet inside the SqlDataSource is populated when the page first loads with the filtered results, any sorting or paging applied to the SqlDataSource by the GridView works against the filtered results.

DataSet vs. DataReader

Now, let's quickly look at how the DataSet and DataReader compare across the techniques demonstrated in this and the previous chapters. So, before you learn how to update a data source, you'll take stock and compare DataReader and DataSet. Each has its own advantages and disadvantages, so it's pretty key to make the right choice for each page. This is true whether you're using code to access the database or using a SqlDataSource—you have the choice to use a DataReader or DataSet in both cases. Table 7-8 outlines the main differences.

Table 7-8. *DataSet vs. DataReader for Displaying Data*

DataReader	DataSet
The DataReader is "connected" to the data source at all times.	The DataSet, once populated, is no longer connected to the data source. This allows the DataSet to be persisted between postbacks, reducing the usage of the data source.
The data retrieved through a DataReader is forward-only and must be cycled through by calling Read(). Once the data has been cycled through, the DataReader must be closed and re-created to reaccess the data.	You can work with data in a DataSet in any order you choose as many times as you like.
Binding expressions can use either the index number of the column in the DataReader or the column name itself. Thus, they're quite simple to write and use.	Columns in a DataSet can be referenced by name, but you must also name the DataTable and identify the row that contains the column. This means more complex binding expressions.
Data retrieved through a DataReader must be requeried for after a postback.	A DataSet may be stored during postbacks if it isn't too great a drain on resources.
A DataReader connects to only one data source.	A DataSet can be filled using Fill() from multiple data sources and isn't tied to a particular data source. You can even create a DataSet manually without ever using a data source, as you saw in Chapter 5.
A DataReader is most suitable for quickly binding data to Web controls.	A DataSet is most suitable for working with complex data and data that needs to be updated on a page.
You can bind only one list or table to a DataReader. It must be re-created for other Web controls on the same page.	You can bind as many list or table Web controls to a single DataSet as you want.

Summary

In this chapter, you learned how to bind the query results to a table-based Web control such as a GridView, DataList, or Repeater. Unless you tell it otherwise, the GridView will present the results in a preformatted grid, one column per table cell; the DataList and Repeater, on the other hand, must be given a template for each row of information to be displayed.

You learned that you can customize the GridView quite heavily, even when it auto-generates a grid to display query results. You can use SQL to make the data more readable, use styles to make it more attractive, and implement simple sorting and paging functions to improve the way that users can view the results.

In the next chapter, you'll finish your look at handling the data from a query by exposing it as read-write data. You'll also learn how to send the changes made to that data back to the database.

CHAPTER 8

■■■

Writing to the Database

So far, you've dealt with only read-only data—pulling some data from a database without altering it. In this chapter, you'll discover how to create pages that allow users to add, modify, and delete the contents of a database. At the core of these three operations are three SQL queries: INSERT, UPDATE, and DELETE.

First, we'll look at modifying the data in separate pages that neatly wrap up the three different types of operations using a Command object. Then you'll see how to use a DataSet to make changes to tables.

This chapter covers the following topics:

- How to use single-value and list Web controls to build a query sent directly to the database with a call to ExecuteNonQuery() or ExecuteScalar()

- How to validate data entered through Web controls to make sure no invalid changes are made

- How to use a DataSet to hold several different tables and propagate any changes back to the database in one call to Update() through the DataAdapter

Making Changes to a Database

Those three basic steps you first heard about back in Chapter 1—creating the connection, sending the query, and handling the results—still hold true for making changes to a database. However, you have a lot more things to consider, and the changes must play by the database's rules.

The main difference is in sending the query, where you'll need to use the appropriate query for what you want to do. The results of the query will generally be a scalar value indicating the number of rows in the database that have changed as the result of the query. It's your choice whether you use this result, but it does provide quite a good indication of whether the query that you've executed has worked correctly.

In this chapter, you'll learn how to use the following queries:

- The SQL INSERT query to add new rows to a table in a database

- The SQL UPDATE query to change rows already in a database

- The SQL DELETE query to remove rows from a database

Unlike the SELECT query, which just retrieves data, these three queries must obey the rules you created when you built the database and created relationships between tables. What was the data type for this column? What was its maximum length? Was it a key? Can it be null? The onus is on you to make sure that the data you try to add to a table obeys its rules. As with dealing with data for display, the basics are straightforward, but you need to expend a little more effort to make the page user-friendly (and idiot-proof).

Inserting Data into the Database

You'll always have information to change and new data to collect, so providing a way to add new information to your databases is pretty crucial. Some sites may hide this functionality away in an administration section. How inserting data is handled depends on what the database models and who is logged on. For instance, Amazon hides the functionality to add new product information from you, the public, but it does let you add new feedback, and user information to its database, provided you're logged in. Similarly, eBay allows anyone to add a new auction to its database, but only the auctioneer can change those details. Security, then, is also a very important issue to consider.

The INSERT Query

At the heart of the code to add new information to a database is the SQL INSERT query. Although it may seem otherwise, sending an INSERT query to a database is the only way to do this. Compared to the complexities of the SELECT query, the INSERT query is quite simple.

```
INSERT [INTO] <table name>
[ (column list) ]
VALUES ( column value list )
```

The query doesn't need to be split over three lines, but that format makes it easier to see that it has six pieces:

- The keyword INSERT denotes the action to the database.

- The optional keyword INTO makes the query more readable.

- The *table name* identifies the table to which you're adding information.

- The (comma-separated) *column list* names the columns in the new row to which you're giving values. Although this isn't required, it is a good idea to specify it. It makes the query easier to follow and can reduce the risk of problems when you make changes to the database structure.

- The keyword VALUES separates the *column list* from the *column value list*.

- The (comma-separated) *column value list* contains a value for each of the columns in the *column list* for the new row. The number of the items in the *column list* should equal the number of items in the *column value list* and be ordered in the same way. Thus, the first column named in the *column list* will be filled with the first value in the *column value list*, the second with the second, and so on. Each value can be one of the following:

- A literal

- An expression saying how a value is to be determined from the values of other columns (firstname + surname, for example)

- The keyword DEFAULT, indicating that the column should take its default value as defined in the database

- NULL

With this in mind, it shouldn't be too difficult to construct a simple INSERT query for any of the four tables in the sample database. To insert a new Player, for instance, you could use the following query:

```
INSERT Player (PlayerName, PlayerManufacturerID, PlayerCost, PlayerStorage)
VALUES ('New Player', 1, '199.99', 'Solid State')
```

As you'll recall, the Player table actually has five columns, and you have not specified one of them. This isn't an error!

If a column is an identity column or has a default value, then you don't need to specify it when you're adding a new row; the database takes care of populating the column. So, even though you haven't specified the PlayerID column, the value is entered automatically by the database.

It's also possible to insert data into a database using the INSERT query without specifying the columns you want to insert the data into, as long as you specify the data for all the columns (bar the identity columns) in the order they appear in the database. Even columns that have default values must be specified.

So, you could change the previous INSERT query to the following without any problems:

```
INSERT Player
VALUES ('New Player', 1, '199.99', 'Solid State')
```

Although inserting data without specifying a list of columns is perfectly valid, it makes more sense to name the columns. As with the SELECT query, specifying the columns makes the query slightly quicker and shows which columns you're trying to affect. With the INSERT query, it also avoids putting data in the wrong column if columns have been added to or removed from the table.

■Note One point to remember about INSERT is that it works with only a single table at a time. If you're working with complex data that would be sourced from two or more tables in a database, you'll need to write an INSERT query for each table to be updated. For example, to add details for a new Player to the sample database, you would have to write an INSERT query for both the Player table and the WhatPlaysWhatFormat table at the least. If the new Player were manufactured by a Manufacturer not in the database, you would need to create an INSERT query for the Manufacturer table as well.

The database-generation scripts in the code download for this book illustrate this point. The scripts contain INSERT queries for each row in each table, with each table populated in the correct order so that no data entry breaks any of the database constraints.

Working to the Database's Rules

Unlike playground rules, database rules aren't made to be broken, and you need to keep the following in mind when you're inserting new data into a table using INSERT:

Primary keys: You must provide a unique value for the column(s) in a table's primary key. If you don't, the database will return an error. Thus, you need to ensure that when you insert a new row into a table using INSERT, it contains a valid and unique value for the primary key. Things are a bit simpler if the primary key you use in the table is an identity column, such as the PlayerID column in the Player table, the ManufacturerID column in the Manufacturer table, or the FormatID column in the Format table. By establishing such a primary key, you can omit this column from the INSERT query's *column list*, because the database will automatically generate the value for you as you add the new row.

Foreign keys: If one of the columns in a table is a foreign key, you must ensure that any value you try to add to that column already exists as a value for the primary key in the corresponding table. When adding a Player, for example, the Manufacturer must exist before you can use it for the Player.

Mandatory columns: If a table doesn't allow a column to be null, you must give it a value when you add a new row. Either the user provides a value or you give it a default value when the user doesn't.

Column data types: Each column must be given a value of the appropriate type.

Each of these rules complicates things. Can you ensure that values are unique? What Web controls best suit data entry for each column? How do you enter a default value and make sure a column is given a certain value? You'll learn the answers to these questions as you work through this chapter's examples.

Try It Out: Inserting a New Player with INSERT

In this example, you'll build a page that allows you to add details of a new Player to the sample database. However, you won't include the selection of the supported Formats for the Player, which is handled in a later example.

1. In Visual Web Developer, create a new Web site at C:\BAND\Chapter08 and delete the auto-generated Default.aspx file.

2. Add a new Web.config file to the Web site and add a new setting to the <connectionStrings /> element:

```
<add name="SqlConnectionString"
  connectionString="Data Source=localhost\BAND;Initial Catalog=Players;
    Persist Security Info=True;User ID=band;Password=letmein"
  providerName="System.Data.SqlClient" />
```

3. Add a new Web Form to the Web site called `Players.aspx`. Make sure that the Place Code in Separate File check box is unchecked.

4. In the Source view, find the `<title>` tag within the HTML at the bottom of the page and change the page title to **Players**.

5. Switch to the Design view and add a `SqlDataSource` to the page. Choose to configure the data source and use `SqlConnectionString` to connect to the database. Select the PlayerID, PlayerName, and PlayerCost columns from the Player table to configure the `SELECT` query.

6. Switch back to the Source view and add the following markup after the definition of the `SqlDataSource`:

```
<asp:HyperLink ID="HyperLink1" runat="server"
  NavigateUrl="./Player_Insert.aspx">Add player</asp:HyperLink>
<br /><br />
<asp:GridView ID="GridView1" runat="server" AutoGenerateColumns="False"
  DataSourceID="SqlDataSource1">
  <Columns>
    <asp:BoundField DataField="PlayerID" HeaderText="PlayerID" />
    <asp:BoundField DataField="PlayerName" HeaderText="Name" />
    <asp:BoundField DataField="PlayerCost" DataFormatString="{0:n}"
      HeaderText="Cost" />
  </Columns>
</asp:GridView>
```

7. Add a new Web Form to the Web site called `Player_Insert.aspx`. Make sure that the Place Code in Separate File check box is unchecked.

8. In the Source view, find the `<title>` tag within the HTML at the bottom of the page and change the page title to **INSERT Player**. Add the required `Import` statement to the top of the page:

```
<%@ Page Language="C#" %>
<%@ Import Namespace="System.Data.SqlClient" %>
```

9. Add some Web controls to allow the addition of the Player to the database: a `Button` to insert the Player, a `Button` to return to the list of Players, a `TextBox` for the user to add the Player's name, a `DropDownList` for the Manufacturer, a `TextBox` for the Player's cost, and a final `TextBox` to specify the storage type for the Player. Call these `SubmitButton`, `ReturnButton`, `PlayerName`, `ManufacturerList`, `PlayerCost`, and `PlayerStorage`, respectively. Also add a `Label`, called `QueryResult`, to show the results from the query that was actually executed. You can see how the Web controls are laid out in Figure 8-1.

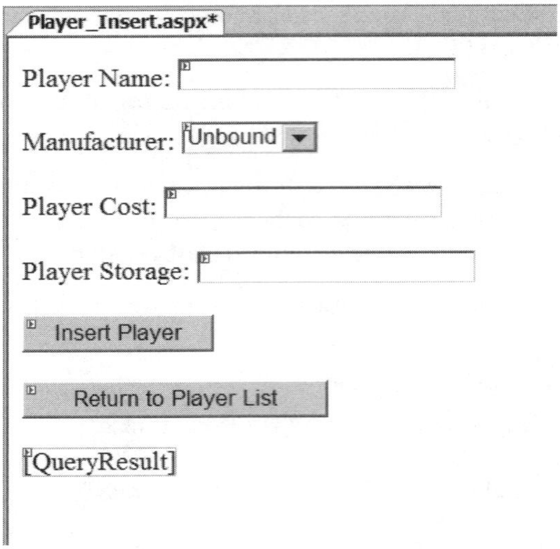

Figure 8-1. *The Web control layout for Player_Insert.aspx*

10. Add a `Page_Load` event handler to the page, as follows:

```
protected void Page_Load(object sender, EventArgs e)
{
  if (Page.IsPostBack == false)
  {
    // populate the list of manufacturers
    PopulateManufacturers();
  }
}
```

11. Add the `PopulateManufacturers()` method:

```
private void PopulateManufacturers()
{
  // create the connection
  string strConnectionString = ConfigurationManager.
    ConnectionStrings["SqlConnectionString"].ConnectionString;
  SqlConnection myConnection = new SqlConnection(strConnectionString);

  try
  {
    // query to execute
    string strQuery = "SELECT ManufacturerID, ManufacturerName ➡
      FROM Manufacturer ORDER BY ManufacturerName";

    // create the command
    SqlCommand myCommand = new SqlCommand(strQuery, myConnection);
```

```
      // open the database connection
      myConnection.Open();

      // run query
      SqlDataReader myReader = myCommand.ExecuteReader();

      // set the data source and bind
      ManufacturerList.DataSource = myReader;
      ManufacturerList.DataTextField = "ManufacturerName";
      ManufacturerList.DataValueField = "ManufacturerID";
      ManufacturerList.DataBind();

      // close the reader
      myReader.Close();
    }
    finally
    {
      // always close the database connection
      myConnection.Close();
    }
}
```

12. Switch to the Design view of the page and add a DataBound event handler for the ManufacturerList control. Add the following code to the event handler:

```
protected void ManufacturerList_DataBound(object sender, EventArgs e)
{
  ListItem myListItem = new ListItem();
  myListItem.Text = "please select...";
  myListItem.Value = "0";
  ManufacturerList.Items.Insert(0, myListItem);
}
```

13. With the Web control layout sorted and populated as required, you need to implement the code to insert the Player into the database. Switch back to the Design view of the page and double-click the SubmitButton control to add a Click event handler. Add the following code to the event handler:

```
protected void SubmitButton_Click(object sender, EventArgs e)
{
  // save the player to the database
  int intPlayerID = SavePlayer();

  // did an error occur?
  if (intPlayerID == -1)
  {
    QueryResult.Text = "An error has occurred!";
  }
```

```
      else
      {
        // show the result
        QueryResult.Text = "Save of player '" + intPlayerID.ToString()
          + "' was successful";

        // disable the submit button
        SubmitButton.Enabled = false;
      }
    }
```

14. To insert the Player into the database, you call a function named SavePlayer(). This function returns the PlayerID for the new entry, or it returns -1 if an error occurs:

```
private int SavePlayer()
{
  int intPlayerID = 0;

  // create the connection
  string strConnectionString = ConfigurationManager.
    ConnectionStrings["SqlConnectionString"].ConnectionString;
  SqlConnection myConnection = new SqlConnection(strConnectionString);

  try
  {
    // query to execute
    string strQuery = "INSERT Player (PlayerName, PlayerManufacturerID, ➥
      PlayerCost, PlayerStorage) VALUES (@Name, @ManufacturerID, ➥
      @Cost, @Storage); SELECT SCOPE_IDENTITY();";

    // create the command
    SqlCommand myCommand = new SqlCommand(strQuery, myConnection);

    // add the parameters
    myCommand.Parameters.AddWithValue("@Name", PlayerName.Text);
    myCommand.Parameters.AddWithValue("@ManufacturerID",
      ManufacturerList.SelectedValue);
    myCommand.Parameters.AddWithValue("@Cost", PlayerCost.Text);
    myCommand.Parameters.AddWithValue("@Storage", PlayerStorage.Text);

    // open the connection
    myConnection.Open();

    // execute the query
    intPlayerID = Convert.ToInt32(myCommand.ExecuteScalar());
  }
  catch
  {
```

```
      // return -1 to indicate error
      intPlayerID = -1;
    }
    finally
    {
      // close the connection
      myConnection.Close();
    }

    // return the ID
    return(intPlayerID);
  }
```

15. Finally, you need to provide a means for the user to return to the list of Players. Switch to the Design view and double-click the ReturnButton. Add the following code to the Click event handler:

```
protected void ReturnButton_Click(object sender, EventArgs e)
{
  Response.Redirect("./Players.aspx");
}
```

16. Save the page, and then open the Web site in your browser. In the list of Players, click the Add Player link. On the following page, add the details for a new Player. Then click the Insert Player button to execute the INSERT query and return the ID of the Player added, as shown in Figure 8-2.

Figure 8-2. *Adding a new Player to the database*

17. Click the Return to Player List button. You'll see that the new Player has been added to the end of the list of Players, as shown in Figure 8-3.

Figure 8-3. *The new Player added to the database*

How It Works

This example has provided you with the means to add a Player to the database. The first 12 steps of the example should be quite familiar to you by now. You built a page that lists basic details for all of the Players in the database using a SqlDataSource and a GridView. We looked at table binding a GridView in Chapter 7.

The second page is the one that lets you insert data into the database.

Web Control Selection

The first stage of this page needs to take the rules of the sample database into consideration. You're adding a new row to the Player table, so the first task is to figure out which Web control is most suitable for adding the value for each column, as follows:

PlayerID: This is the primary key for the Player table, but it's also an identity column, so you don't need to insert a value for this column. It will be added for you automatically.

PlayerName: A Player's name is just text, so a TextBox is appropriate.

PlayerManufacturerID: This is a foreign key from the Manufacturer table, so it can hold only values already in the Manufacturer table. It makes sense to give the user a choice of Manufacturers from a list, so you use a DropDownList and bind the ManufacturerName to DataTextField and the ManufacturerID to DataValueField. You could use any data-aware list Web control, but DropDownList works fine.

PlayerCost: The cost of the Player is a decimal, and the best way for entering this value is using a TextBox.

PlayerStorage: At this point, it becomes obvious that the sample database design is (deliberately) flawed and that the Storage Type entries should really be in their own table. This would mean you could bind the available Storage Types to a list Web control and keep control of the Storage Types for the Players. But since the types are in the Player table, we're allowing users to enter any Storage Type that they want. This is a good example of one of the repercussions of bad database design.

The list of Manufacturers is populated using a simple query to return just the ManufacturerID and ManufacturerName columns from the Manufacturer table. You saw how to do this in Chapter 6. You could also have used a SqlDataSource to populate the DropDownList.

Once the Web controls are set up as required, the user can enter the details of the new Player and click the Insert Player button to save the Player to the database. Here, you see the first problem with the page.

Error Handling

Rerun the Web site and enter a new Player without a name, cost, or storage type. Now save the Player. Instead of the Player being saved, an error has been trapped and an error message displayed, as shown in Figure 8-4.

Entering invalid data and trying to save it causes a SqlException to be raised and handled by the catch clause of your data-access code. If you add a breakpoint to the code within the catch clause, you'll see that the exception is thrown because you're trying to convert an empty string (an nvarchar) to a numeric value, and it's not a valid cast. Figure 8-5 shows this information.

A multitude of different errors can arise if you don't validate entries made by the user when inserting and updating data to the database. We'll look at validating the user's input in the "Validating Data" section later in this chapter, and you'll update this example so that invalid data can't make its way to the database. For now, you must enter values in all of the columns.

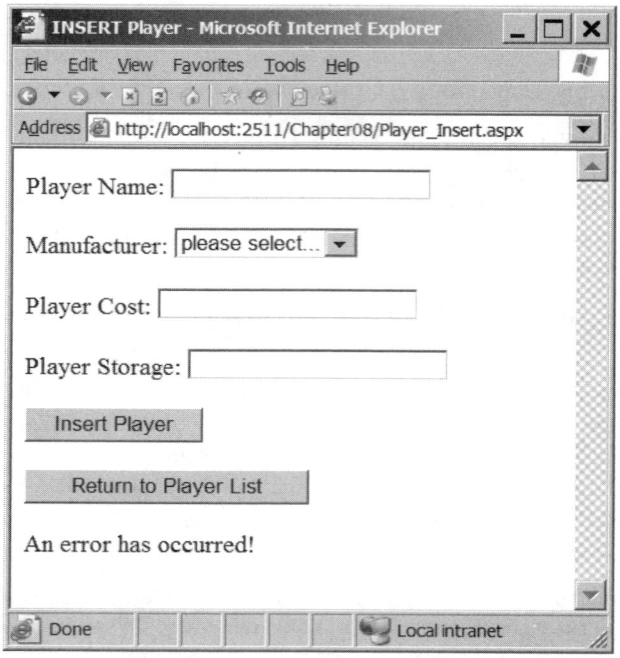

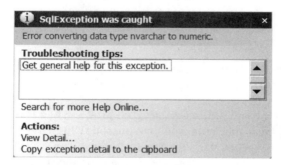

Figure 8-4. *Invalid data causes exceptions, which thankfully are trapped.*

SqlException was caught   ×

Error converting data type nvarchar to numeric.

Troubleshooting tips:

Get general help for this exception.

Search for more Help Online...

Actions:
View Detail...
Copy exception detail to the clipboard

Figure 8-5. *When debugging, you can see the details of the raised exception.*

Database Record Insertion

The part of the example of particular interest is the `SubmitButton_Click` event handler:

```
protected void SubmitButton_Click(object sender, EventArgs e)
{
  // save the player to the database
  int intPlayerID = SavePlayer();
```

```
// did an error occur?
if (intPlayerID == -1)
{
  QueryResult.Text = "An error has occurred!";
}
else
{
  // show the result
  QueryResult.Text = "Save of player '" + intPlayerID.ToString()
    + "' was successful";

  // disable the submit button
  SubmitButton.Enabled = false;
}
}
```

The SubmitButton_Click event handler calls the SavePlayer() method to save the Player to the database, and this method returns the PlayerID value for the new Player, or it returns -1 if an error has occurred. If you don't have a valid PlayerID, you know that something has gone wrong, and you display an error message to the user. If the returned PlayerID is valid (not equal to -1), you can assume that the Player has been added to the database, and you display a success message showing the PlayerID of the Player just added to the database. If the Player has been added successfully, you also disable the SubmitButton, so that you can't save the details for the same Player twice by accident. (Of course, there is nothing stopping the user from adding the exact same Player again and again!)

The SavePlayer() method is responsible for taking the details entered by the user and saving these details, using an INSERT query to the database:

```
INSERT Player (PlayerName, PlayerManufacturerID, PlayerCost, PlayerStorage)
VALUES (@Name, @ManufacturerID, @Cost, @Storage);
```

This should look familiar, as it was the example used in the earlier introduction to the INSERT query, but instead of having actual values in the *column value list*, you're using parameters that you add using the AddWithValue method:

```
// add the parameters
myCommand.Parameters.AddWithValue("@Name", PlayerName.Text);
myCommand.Parameters.AddWithValue("@ManufacturerID",
  ManufacturerList.SelectedValue);
myCommand.Parameters.AddWithValue("@Cost", PlayerCost.Text);
myCommand.Parameters.AddWithValue("@Storage", PlayerStorage.Text);
```

You're using a parameterized INSERT query in the interest of security. You could just build the query with string concatenation, but as you learned in Chapter 4, parameters prevent users from trying to harm your database by sending malevolent SQL instructions through the TextBox.

Once the Command object is created and the parameters added correctly, you execute the query against the database. But if you look at the code for the page, you'll see that the query that you're going to execute isn't quite what you just saw. In fact, the query that you send to the database is actually a *query batch* of two separate SQL queries: an INSERT and a SELECT query:

```
INSERT Player (PlayerName, PlayerManufacturerID, PlayerCost, PlayerStorage)
  VALUES (@Name, @ManufacturerID, @Cost, @Storage);
SELECT SCOPE_IDENTITY();
```

When sending a query to a SQL Server 2005 database, you can actually send multiple queries, separated by semicolons. You want to insert the Player into the database, but you also want to know the PlayerID of the Player that you've added. In this example, you display the PlayerID as a confirmation that the Player has been added to the database. In the next example, you'll use this PlayerID when adding the details of the Formats that the Player supports.

When using a column defined as an identity column, you can use the SCOPE_IDENTITY() function to retrieve the value of that column. In order to return the value from this function, you can use it as a column in a SELECT query.

■**Note** The system variable @@IDENTITY returns the value of the identity column last entered. In this instance, both the SCOPE_IDENTITY() function and the @@IDENTITY system variable would return the same value. However, in cases when you're using triggers, the @@IDENTITY system variable may return the wrong value; if the trigger also does an INSERT, it may return the identity value from a different table, whereas the SCOPE_IDENTITY() function returns the identity value from the original table. You should always use the SCOPE_IDENTITY() function to prevent any problems if triggers are added to your tables later.

Thus, when you execute this query, you do so by calling ExecuteScalar() rather than ExecuteNonQuery() so you can capture the new PlayerID. ExecuteScalar() returns a generic object, rather than a string or an integer, so you cast it to an integer to make it easier to handle:

```
// execute the query
intPlayerID = Convert.ToInt32(myCommand.ExecuteScalar());
```

If there was an error when inserting the Player, an exception is thrown. You catch this and set the PlayerID to -1 to indicate that the INSERT query failed:

```
catch
{
  // return -1 to indicate error
  intPlayerID = -1;
}
```

Although all you're doing here is setting a flag to indicate that there has been an error, you're free to perform any other actions you want. If you want to send an e-mail message to the Web site administrator informing her that a problem has occurred, you can do so. Just be careful that your error-handling code doesn't throw an exception, as that would cause a runtime error to be displayed to the user!

Once you've executed the query and returned the PlayerID, you exit from the SavePlayer() method and either display an error message or a confirmation to the user. At this point, the user can return to the list of Players to confirm that the new Player has been added and to add another Player if desired.

Queries in MySQL 5.0 and Microsoft Access

Before we move on to the next example and add the Format information, we'll quickly look at two areas where SQL Server 2005 differs from MySQL 5.0 and Microsoft Access:

- Only when using the SQL Server data provider to connect to SQL Server 2005 can you use named parameters. Neither the ODBC data provider when connecting to MySQL 5.0 nor the OLE DB data provider (which we use to connect to Microsoft Access) support named parameters. With those data providers, you need to add parameters in the order in which they appear in the query.

- Neither MySQL 5.0 nor Microsoft Access allows multiple queries to be executed as part of the same query batch, and neither supports the SCOPE_IDENTITY() function.

Parameters and Queries in MySQL 5.0 and Microsoft Access

As you've learned in earlier chapters, you can't use named parameters with MySQL 5.0 or Microsoft Access using the Odbc or OleDb data providers. You need to change the query that you want to execute and add the parameters to the parameters collection in the correct order.

For MySQL 5.0, replace the named parameters with the question mark character:

```
INSERT Player (PlayerName, PlayerManufacturerID, PlayerCost, PlayerStorage)
VALUES (?, ?, ?, ?)
```

The query required for Microsoft Access is similar, except you must also specify the INTO keyword:

```
INSERT INTO Player (PlayerName, PlayerManufacturerID, PlayerCost,
  PlayerStorage)
VALUES (?, ?, ?, ?)
```

Once the query is defined correctly, the parameters are added in the order in which they're required:

```
myCommand.Parameters.AddWithValue("?", PlayerName.Text);
myCommand.Parameters.AddWithValue("?", ManufacturerList.SelectedValue);
myCommand.Parameters.AddWithValue("?", PlayerCost.Text);
myCommand.Parameters.AddWithValue("?", PlayerStorage.Text);
```

Identity Values and MySQL 5.0 and Microsoft Access

Retrieving the identity value for a new row in a table requires two different queries to be executed. SQL Server 2005 allows you to execute these queries as part of the same query batch to the database by separating the queries with semicolons. However, neither MySQL 5.0 nor Microsoft Access supports this functionality. Therefore, you need to make two distinct queries to the database: the INSERT query to add the Player and a SELECT query to return the PlayerID.

For MySQL 5.0, this is relatively easy, as there is a corresponding function: LAST_INSERT_ID() returns the value you're after. So, you create two queries and execute these one after the other:

```
// create the INSERT query
string strQuery1 = "INSERT Player (PlayerName, PlayerManufacturerID, ➥
  PlayerCost, PlayerStorage) VALUES (?, ?, ?, ?);";
OdbcCommand myCommand1 = new OdbcCommand(strQuery1, myConnection);

// add the parameters
myCommand1.Parameters.AddWithValue("?", PlayerName.Text);
myCommand1.Parameters.AddWithValue("?", ManufacturerList.SelectedValue);
myCommand1.Parameters.AddWithValue("?", PlayerCost.Text);
myCommand1.Parameters.AddWithValue("?", PlayerStorage.Text);

// create the SELECT query
string strQuery2 = "SELECT LAST_INSERT_ID();";
OdbcCommand myCommand2 = new OdbcCommand(strQuery2, myConnection);

// open the connection
myConnection.Open();

// execute the queries we need to execute
myCommand1.ExecuteNonQuery();
intPlayerID = Convert.ToInt32(myCommand2.ExecuteScalar());

// close the connection
myConnection.Close();
```

You'll still wrap all of the above code in a try..catch..finally block, so that if there is a problem, you can set the PlayerID value to -1 to indicate that an error occurred.

To get the identity value in Microsoft Access, you can use the @@IDENTITY system variable. So, simply execute a different query to return the identity value:

```
// create the SELECT query
string strQuery2 = "SELECT @@IDENTITY;";
OleDbCommand myCommand2 = new OleDbCommand(strQuery2, myConnection);

// open the connection
myConnection.Open();

// execute the queries we need to execute
myCommand1.ExecuteNonQuery();
intPlayerID = Convert.ToInt32(myCommand2.ExecuteScalar());
```

You'll see these versions of getting the value of the PlayerID column in the code download for this book.

Try It Out: Setting the Player's Supported Formats

Now that we've looked at how to add the basic details for the Player, let's see how to add the Player's supported Formats.

1. Open `Players_Insert.aspx` and switch to the Design view.

2. Add a new `CheckBoxList` before the Insert Player button. Rename it `FormatList`, set its `RepeatColumns` property to 4 and its `RepeatDirection` to Horizontal. The layout should now be as shown in Figure 8-6.

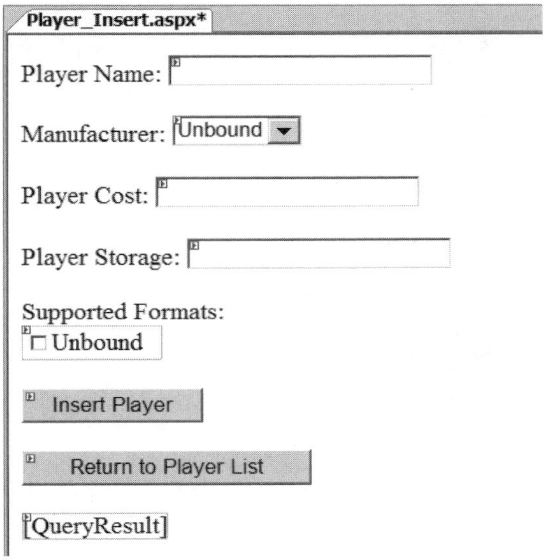

```
Player_Insert.aspx*

Player Name: [ ]

Manufacturer: [Unbound ▼]

Player Cost: [ ]

Player Storage: [ ]

Supported Formats:
  □ Unbound

  [ Insert Player ]

  [ Return to Player List ]

[QueryResult]
```

Figure 8-6. *The new layout showing the Supported Formats CheckBoxList*

3. Switch to the Source view and modify the `Page_Load` event as follows:

```
protected void Page_Load(object sender, EventArgs e)
{
  if (Page.IsPostBack == false)
  {
    // populate the list of manufacturers
    PopulateManufacturers();

    // populate the list of formats
    PopulateFormats();
  }
}
```

4. Add the new `PopulateFormats()` method:

```
private void PopulateFormats()
{
  // create the connection
  string strConnectionString = ConfigurationManager.
    ConnectionStrings["SqlConnectionString"].ConnectionString;
  SqlConnection myConnection = new SqlConnection(strConnectionString);
```

```
      try
      {
        // query to execute
        string strQuery = "SELECT FormatID, FormatName FROM Format ➥
          ORDER BY FormatName";

        // create the command
        SqlCommand myCommand = new SqlCommand(strQuery, myConnection);

        // open the database connection
        myConnection.Open();

        // run query
        SqlDataReader myReader = myCommand.ExecuteReader();

        // set the data source and bind
        FormatList.DataSource = myReader;
        FormatList.DataTextField = "FormatName";
        FormatList.DataValueField = "FormatID";
        FormatList.DataBind();

        // close the reader
        myReader.Close();
      }
      finally
      {
        // always close the database connection
        myConnection.Close();
      }
    }
```

5. Modify the SubmitButton_Click event handler as follows:

```
protected void SubmitButton_Click(object sender, EventArgs e)
{
  // save the player to the database
  int intPlayerID = SavePlayer();

  // did an error occur?
  if (intPlayerID == -1)
  {
    QueryResult.Text = "An error has occurred!";
  }
  else
  {
```

```
// save the formats for the player
bool blnError = SaveFormats(intPlayerID);

// did an error occur?
if (blnError == true)
{
  QueryResult.Text = "An error has occurred!";
}
else
{
  // show the result
  QueryResult.Text = "Save of player '" + intPlayerID.ToString()
    + "' was successful";

  // disable the submit button
  SubmitButton.Enabled = false;
}
    }
  }
}
```

6. Add the new SaveFormats() method as follows:

```
private bool SaveFormats(int intPlayerID)
{
  bool blnError = false;

  // create the connection
  string strConnectionString = ConfigurationManager.
    ConnectionStrings["SqlConnectionString"].ConnectionString;
  SqlConnection myConnection = new SqlConnection(strConnectionString);

  try
  {
    // query to execute
    string strQuery = "INSERT WhatPlaysWhatFormat(WPWFPlayerID, ➥
      WPWFFormatID) VALUES (@PlayerID, @FormatID)";

    // create the command
    SqlCommand myCommand = new SqlCommand(strQuery, myConnection);

    // add the two parameters
    myCommand.Parameters.AddWithValue("@@PlayerID", intPlayerID);
    myCommand.Parameters.Add("@FormatID", System.Data.SqlDbType.Int);

    // open the connection
    myConnection.Open();
```

```
      // loop through each of the formats
      foreach (ListItem objFormat in FormatList.Items)
      {
        // save if selected
        if (objFormat.Selected == true)
        {
          // set the parameter value
          myCommand.Parameters["@FormatID"].Value = objFormat.Value;

          // execute the query
          myCommand.ExecuteNonQuery();
        }
      }
    }
    catch
    {
      // indicate that we have an error
      blnError = true;
    }
    finally
    {
      // close the connection
      myConnection.Close();
    }

    // return the error flag
    return(blnError);
}
```

7. Save the page, and then open the Web site in your browser. In the list of Players, click the Add Player link, and you'll see that the list of Formats is populated. Enter the details for a new Player, and this time, specify the Formats that the Player supports.

8. Click the Insert Player button to save the Player to the database, along with the Formats it supports, as shown in Figure 8-7.

9. To see that the Format details have been saved to the database correctly, you can perform a SELECT query against the WhatPlaysWhatFormat table. The Player added has a PlayerID of 27, so look for this in the WPWFPlayerID column. As you can see in Figure 8-8, the two Formats have been added correctly.

Figure 8-7. *The supported Formats are also saved.*

19	4
20	4
20	2
20	6
27	3
27	2

Figure 8-8. *The supported Formats have been saved to the database.*

How It Works

With a bit more work, you've added the ability to save the supported Formats for a Player to the database. In order to do this, you need to perform two steps:

- Display the options on the page that may be selected in a suitable Web control.

- Save the selected options correctly to the database.

Because of the way that you structured the code for the first example, you can quite easily perform these two steps by adding two new functions: PopulateFormats() and SaveFormats().

The PopulateFormats() method displays the available Formats. You're showing a list of Formats, so you're going to be using one of the Web controls that support list binding, as described in Chapter 6. You need to allow the user to select multiple options, so you have only two choices: a CheckBoxList or a ListBox. You've used a CheckBoxList as it allows the selection of multiple entries with a single click, so the user doesn't need to use a combination of keyboard presses and mouse clicks to select multiple Formats.

The code within the PopulateFormats() method should be familiar to you by now. You return a list of FormatID and FormatName pairs using a simple query, and then set the DataTextField and DataValueField properties on the CheckBoxList.

It's within the SaveFormats() method that the real work occurs. The first part of the method should be familiar by now. You create a Connection object to connect to the database and a Command object populated with the correct INSERT query:

```
INSERT WhatPlaysWhatFormat(WPWFPlayerID, WPWFFormatID)
VALUES (@PlayerID, @FormatID)
```

Both parameters are then added to the Parameters collection:

```
// add the two parameters
myCommand.Parameters.AddWithValue("@PlayerID", intPlayerID);
myCommand.Parameters.Add("@FormatID", System.Data.SqlDbType.Int);
```

You already know the @PlayerID parameter value, as you retrieved it from the SavePlayer() method, and it is fixed for this Player, so you can use the AddWithValue() method to add it. But the @FormatID parameter is different. You're allowing the user to select multiple values, so you can't just add the parameter value and execute the query. You can add the parameter without a value using the Add() method, and then set its value later before you execute the query.

You check which Formats have been selected by using a foreach loop to work through all of the possible Formats (returned as ListItem objects from the Items collection of the CheckBoxList) and execute the INSERT query for each Format that is selected:

```
// loop through each of the formats
foreach (ListItem objFormat in FormatList.Items)
{
  // save if selected
  if (objFormat.Selected == true)
  {
    // set the parameter value
    myCommand.Parameters["@FormatID"].Value = objFormat.Value;

    // execute the query
    myCommand.ExecuteNonQuery();
  }
}
```

If the Format is selected, the Selected property will return true, and you can set the parameter value to be the Value of the ListItem. The ExecuteNonQuery() method is then used to execute the INSERT query against the database.

Note that you open the connection to the database only once, and you close the database connection only once. You're reusing the connection for each of the INSERT queries that you're executing. Now this goes a little against my "open late, close early" mantra, as you're keeping the connection open for longer than is necessary. However, in this case, the foreach loop is quick enough for the open connection to not be an issue.

Validating Data

The previous two examples have demonstrated how to add data to the database using INSERT queries. You also saw that it's quite easy to cause runtime errors by not entering valid data. Although you trapped these errors and handled them before the user saw the dreaded ASP.NET runtime error page, it would be much better to guard against these errors before they occur. You need to *validate* the data that the user enters before you attempt to insert the data into the database. The same is also true when you update data, as you'll see later in this chapter.

Whether you want to ensure that the user has entered a value of the required format (such as an e-mail address), entered a value within a range (such as a number between 1 and 10), or entered any value, ASP.NET provides Web controls to perform validation for you. The different validation Web controls are shown in Table 8-1. In addition to the Web controls for actually validating the user's input, another Web control displays the results of the validation: ValidationSummary.

Table 8-1. *The Validation Controls*

Name	Description
CompareValidator	The CompareValidator compares the value entered by the user with either a constant value or the value entered in another Web control.
RangeValidator	The RangeValidator checks that the value entered is between two specified values.
RegularExpressionValidator	The RegularExpressionValidator checks that the value entered matches the specified regular expression.
RequiredFieldValidator	The RequiredFieldValidator checks that a Web control contains a value.
CustomValidator	If none of the other four validators match your requirements, the CustomValidator allows you to define your own validation routines.

Each of the validation Web controls can be executed either at the client or at the server. If you choose to use client-side validation (the default), a postback will not occur, giving a richer user experience. However, in certain cases, a postback must occur before validation can continue. For example, if you're validating for a unique username when creating a user account, you must check against the database that the username hasn't already been used.

■**Caution** In the default state of the validation Web controls, the validation is performed at the client as well as at the server. However, it is quite possible for users to disable JavaScript in their browser and turn off the client-side validation, and post the page to the server with invalid data. The validation always runs at the server, even if you have client-side validation turned on. You should always check that any validation has been done before allowing changes to be made to the database.

The validation Web controls all expose a `ControlToValidate` property that specifies the ID of the Web control that is to be validated. The Web controls that can be validated automatically are shown in Table 8-2. For those Web controls that don't support automatic validation, you'll need to use a `CustomValidator` control for validation. For example, since there's no way to automatically validate that a user selected a value from a `CheckBoxList`, in our example, you'll have to write a `CustomValidator` to ensure that the user has selected at least one supported Format for the new Player.

Table 8-2. *Controls That Can Be Validated Automatically*

Control	Property Validated
DropDownList	SelectedItem
FileUpload	FileBytes
HtmlInputFile	Value
HtmlInputPassword	Value
HtmlInputText	Value
HtmlSelect	Value
HtmlTextArea	Value
ListBox	SelectedItem
RadioButtonList	SelectedItem
TextBox	Text

Table 8-2 also lists the property of the Web control that the validator accesses to perform the validation. At this point, warning signs should be flashing. How can you use the `SelectedItem` from a `ListBox` with a `RegularExpressionValidator`? The validation Web controls are a little more clever than you may initially think, and for the Web list controls, the validator will actually look at the `Value` property of the `SelectedItem`.

Now let's try using the various validation Web controls to improve the page for entering a new Player.

Try It Out: Validating Entered Data

In this example, you'll update the previous example to add validation Web controls to prevent the user from entering incorrect data into the database.

1. Open `Players_Insert.aspx` and switch to the Design view.

2. Add a `ValidationSummary` from the Validation tab of the Toolbox to the top of the page.

3. Add a `RequiredFieldValidator` to the start of the Player Name line. Set its `Display` property to `Dynamic`, `Text` property to `*`, and `ErrorMessage` property to **You must enter a name**. Finally set the `ControlToValidate` property to PlayerName. The page should look like the one shown in Figure 8-9.

Figure 8-9. *Adding the first validation Web controls*

4. Save the page, and then view it in your browser. Try saving a Player without a name. As soon as you click the Insert Player button, you'll receive an error, as shown in Figure 8-10, without a postback to the server being made.

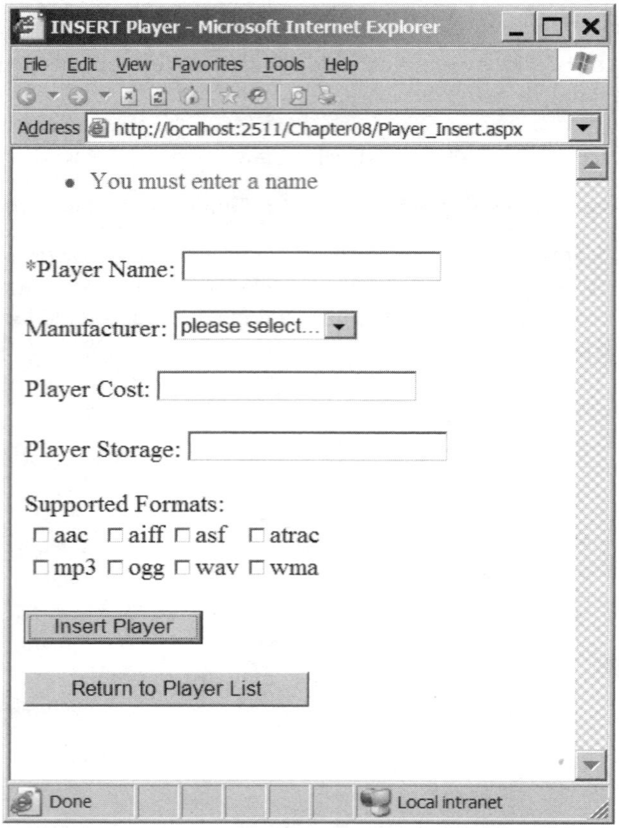

Figure 8-10. *The validation Web controls in action*

5. Add a CompareValidator to the start of the Manufacturer line. Set its properties as follows:

- Display: Dynamic

- Text: *

- ErrorMessage: You must select a manufacturer

- ControlToValidate: ManufacturerList

- Operator: NotEqual

- ValueToCompare: 0

6. Add a `RequiredFieldValidator` to the start of the Player Cost line. Set its properties as follows:

   - `Display`: Dynamic

   - `Text`: *

   - `ErrorMessage`: You must enter a cost

   - `ControlToValidate`: PlayerCost

7. Add a `RegularExpressionValidator` to the start of the Player Cost line. Set its properties as follows:

   - `Display`: Dynamic

   - `Text`: *

   - `ErrorMessage`: You must specify the cost as a decimal

   - `ControlToValidate`: PlayerCost

   - `ValidationExpression`: ^\d+(\.\d\d)

8. Add a `RequiredFieldValidator` to the start of the Player Storage line. Set its properties as follows:

   - `Display`: Dynamic

   - `Text`: *

   - `ErrorMessage`: You must enter a storage type

   - `ControlToValidate`: PlayerStorage

9. Add a `CustomValidator` to the start of the Supported Formats text. Set its properties as follows:

   - `Display`: Dynamic

   - `Text`: *

   - `ErrorMessage`: You must select at least one format

10. Double-click the `CustomValidator` to add the server-side validation event. Add the following code to the event handler:

```
protected void CustomValidator1_ServerValidate(object source,
  ServerValidateEventArgs args)
{
  if (FormatList.SelectedIndex == -1)
  {
    args.IsValid = false;
  }
}
```

11. Save the page, and then view it in your browser. Try testing the different combinations of validators. You'll see that they won't let you save the Player until all of the data entered is valid. But there's still a problem. Enter the data correctly, but don't select any Formats. As you can see in Figure 8-11, you'll get the correct validation error, but the Player will still been saved.

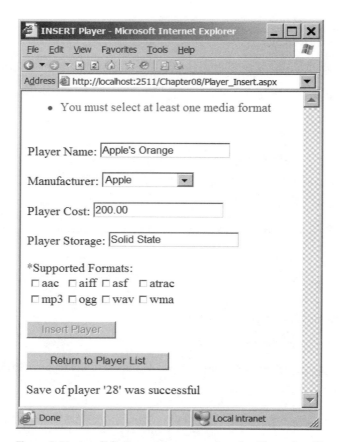

Figure 8-11. *A validation error occurs, but the Player is still saved.*

12. You want to save the page only if all of the validators on the page are valid. Modify the SubmitButton_Click event handler as follows:

```
protected void SubmitButton_Click(object sender, EventArgs e)
{
  // only save if valid
  if (Page.IsValid == true)
  {
    // save the player to the database
    int intPlayerID = SavePlayer();
```

```
      // did an error occur?
      if (intPlayerID == -1)
      {
        QueryResult.Text = "An error has occurred!";
      }
      else
      {
        // save the formats for the player
        bool blnError = SaveFormats(intPlayerID);

        // did an error occur?
        if (blnError == true)
        {
          QueryResult.Text = "An error has occurred!";
        }
        else
        {
          // show the result
          QueryResult.Text = "Save of player '" + intPlayerID.ToString()
            + "' was successful";

          // disable the submit button
          SubmitButton.Enabled = false;
        }
      }
    }
  }
}
```

13. Rerun the page, and now try to save the new Player without any Formats selected. This time, the Player won't be saved. Select at least one Format, and the page will now add the Player to the database.

How It Works

In this example, you used four out of the five available validators to prevent the user from saving a Player to the database with incorrect data, and you used both client and server-side validators.

Validator Properties

Although you used four different validator types on this page, three properties are common across all of the validators:

- Display: This determines how the validator is displayed on the page. The default value of Static always reserves space for the Web control on the page, even if it isn't being displayed. Setting this property to None will not show the Web control on the page (although the ErrorMessage will appear in a ValidationSummary). Setting it to Dynamic displays the Web control only if it's invalid.

- ErrorMessage: The ErrorMessage property sets the text that will be displayed in a ValidationSummary (if one exists on the page) if the validation for the Web control fails.

- Text: The Text property sets the text displayed as the validator when validation fails. When you're using a ValidationSummary, the Text property is usually used simply to highlight which validator has failed.

All of the validation Web controls, other than the CustomValidator, also set the ControlToValidate property. This specifies the ID of the Web control that is being validated. You can also set this property for a CustomValidator, but in the majority of cases, it won't be used. If you're using a CustomValidator because a normal validator won't work, you'll need to interrogate the Web control directly in code.

The ValidationSummary Web Control

The first Web control that you have on the page is the ValidationSummary. It is here that the different validation Web controls display their ErrorMessage if the validation fails. It isn't necessary to have this Web control on the page for validation to work, but it provides a handy location for all of the validation errors to be displayed.

The RequiredFieldValidator Web Control

The RequiredFieldValidator needs no configuration other than the Display, ErrorMessage, Text, and ControlToValidate properties that we've already discussed. As you saw in the example, if you don't specify a value for a Web control that has a RequiredFieldValidator attached to it, the validation will fail.

The CompareValidator Web Control

The CompareValidator allows you to compare the value of the attached Web control against either another Web control (using the ControlToCompare property) or against a specific value (using the ValueToCompare property). In this example, you need to ensure that a Manufacturer has been selected, and you can use a specific value comparison, since you know that the "please select..." entry has a value of 0 (zero). You can then set the ValueToCompare property to 0 and set the Operator property to NotEqual to ensure that the user has selected a value that isn't equal to 0.

As well as checking for NotEqual comparisons, the Operator also allows you to perform various other checks:

- Equal (default)

- GreaterThan

- GreaterThanEqual

- LessThan

- LessThanEqual

- NotEqual

The CompareValidator also allows you to perform a further validation check. By setting the Operator property to DataTypeCheck, you can check that the value of the ControlToValidate is of a specific type. If you choose this type of check, the ControlToCompare and ValueToCompare properties are ignored, and only a check for a value that is of the correct type is performed. You specify the type allowed using the Type property, which can be one of the following values:

- Currency

- Date

- Double

- Integer

- String (default)

■**Note** In this example, you could have used a CompareValidator to ensure that the cost of the Player was entered correctly. However, you used a RegularExpressionValidator rather than a CompareValidator, simply because it demonstrated another type of validator.

The RegularExpressionValidator Web Control

The RegularExpressionValidator allows you to check that the value entered matches a specific regular expression by setting the ValidationExpression property to the regular expression you want to use.

Any valid regular expression can be used, and Visual Web Developer provides you with several standard ones (an e-mail address and Web address, for instance). You're checking that the entered value is a decimal, so you need to define your own regular expression as follows:

```
^\d+(\.\d\d)
```

A decimal is any number of digits followed by a decimal point, then two decimal digits.

■**Tip** A good place to look for regular expressions that meet your requirements is http://www. regexlib.com. Also refer to *Regular Expression Recipes for Windows Developers: A Problem-Solution Approach* by Nathan A. Good (1-59059-497-5; Apress, 2005).

The CustomValidator Web Control

The CustomValidator allows you to perform any validation that you require. You can perform this validation on the client side if you write a function in JavaScript and then pass its name to the ClientValidationFunction property. However, in most cases, you'll run the validation on the server by providing an implementation for the ServerValidate event.

Within the ServerValidate event, if the validation fails, you indicate this by setting the IsValid property of the passed-in ServerValidateEventArgs parameter to false.

In this example, you determine if the user has selected a Format by checking the SelectedIndex property of the FormatList control. When validating, you're not actually concerned with what the user has selected, just that she has selected something. So the validation fails if the user hasn't selected anything—if the SelectedIndex is equal to -1:

```
if (FormatList.SelectedIndex == -1)
{
  args.IsValid = false;
}
```

Although the validation check that you're performing here is quite simple, there are no limits to the validation that you can perform in the ServerValidate event. As long as you set the IsValid property to false, you can make the validation as complex and complete as you require.

The Page IsValid Check

The final change to the code for the page is to change the SubmitButton_Click handler to save the page only if the page was valid:

```
// only save if valid
if (Page.IsValid == true)
{
  // save player
}
```

Without this check, as you saw, the data will be saved to the database, even if one of the validators—in this case, the CustomValidator—failed. When committing changes to the database, you need to make sure that the submitted page is valid before actually saving the changes.

Caution Always check that the page IsValid before inserting or updating data in the database. Never rely on the fact that the client-side validators will prevent incorrect data from being transmitted. All validators run the validation routines, even if the check is also made client side, and this extra check will make sure that malicious users don't deliberately send false data to your page.

Deleting Data from the Database

After completing the previous examples in this chapter, you have a number of extra Players in the database. So, you'll want to know how to delete data from tables in a database.

When you remove data, you still need to follow the rules laid out by the database, but this time, you must consider how a database deals with deleting data:

- Unlike Windows, databases don't have a Recycle Bin. Once a user says delete some data, it's gone; the only way to get it back is to reinsert it.

- The foreign key constraints you set on your tables may cause the database to delete additional data from related tables or prevent you from deleting data from a table.

Because of these considerations, users need to be absolutely sure that they want to delete information before they actually do, and you want to warn them if any other data will be removed. In fact, you could even take it out of their hands and not give them the opportunity to delete data in the first place.

Another possibility is that you won't actually want to delete the data, but instead *pretend* to delete the data. For example, you might decide to no longer display a Player to the users, but you need to keep the details for historical purposes. By adding an extra Boolean column to the Player table called Deleted, you can hide data from the user. If it's false, the row is available to the user. If it's true (the user has "deleted" the Player), the data is not available.

In the example here, you're going to really delete the data so that you can see the DELETE query in action, and also see some of the issues related to relationships that deleting data can cause. If you were following the "pretend delete" route, you wouldn't actually execute a DELETE query, but would instead execute an UPDATE query. We'll look at the UPDATE query in the "Updating Data in the Database" section later in this chapter.

The DELETE Query

Like any other database operation, data deletion is handled by sending a SQL query to a database—in this case, a DELETE query. The DELETE query is quite simple:

```
DELETE [FROM] <table name>
[ WHERE <constraints> ]
```

The DELETE query has four parts:

- The keyword DELETE denotes the action to the database.

- The optional keyword FROM makes the query more readable.

- The *table name* identifies the table from which the data will be deleted.

- An optional list of *constraints* as a WHERE clause constrains the rows to which the DELETE query applies.

Like the INSERT query, DELETE can work on only one table at a time, which is probably a good thing. A rogue query such as DELETE * could wipe out all the data at once, if it were a valid query, a bit like del *.* would do in a DOS prompt. Indeed, DELETE works with whole rows only. You never delete single columns from a row. If you needed to remove a column from a row, you would change the column to an empty value or null, if the database allowed it.

Sympathy for the User: GridView ButtonField Columns

In the INSERT example, you used a collection of individual Web controls to let the user specify the column values for a new Player, and then displayed the new Player in a GridView as confirmation. You could carry on using simple Web controls in this exercise—perhaps binding Player names to a DropDownList and deleting the one selected in the list when a button is clicked—but you can easily code a more elegant solution, which you'll look at here.

The GridView can display much more than just the results of a SELECT query. In fact, to make it more interactive, you can add columns of buttons and links to it, allowing you to work with a row of data in the grid, given the button that was clicked. In this special case, you'll use a button to indicate that a row should be deleted from the database. Depending on the purpose of your page, the button could signify that the row should be added to a shopping cart, copied to another location, or selected to have an e-mail message sent to it.

The object that enables you to do all this is the `<asp:ButtonField>` object, which you add to the GridView's Columns collection, like so:

```
<asp:GridView id="GridView1" runat="server">
  <Columns>
    <asp:ButtonField Text="Delete" ButtonType="Button"
     CommandName="DeletePlayer" />
  </Columns>
</asp:GridView>
```

When you DataBind() to the DataGrid, any auto-generated columns will appear as usual, but there will now also be a column of buttons to the left displaying the value of the ButtonField's Text property, as shown in Figure 8-12.

Figure 8-12. *The ButtonField as rendered in a GridView*

The `<asp:ButtonField>` object has two other key properties that should be given values: ButtonType and CommandName. ButtonType lets you specify whether the new column contains actual buttons or hyperlink-like buttons. CommandName identifies the action associated with the button and ties into the event handler called when the button is clicked.

By default, when a button in a ButtonField is clicked, the GridView raises an event called RowCommand. Within this event handler, you're free to implement whatever code you require.

Note There is one exception to the event mechanism when using a `ButtonField`. Setting the `CommandName` to `Cancel`, `Delete`, `Edit`, `Insert`, `New`, `Page`, `Select`, `Sort`, or `Update` has a slightly different effect than simply raising the `RowCommand` event. For instance, setting `CommandName` to `Delete` will actually raise the `RowDeleting` event and, after deleting the row, the `RowDeleted` event. However, in all cases, the `RowCommand` event also fires, so be aware if you're using multiple button columns that you need to check the `CommandName` to ensure that you're running the correct code. If you can avoid it, don't use a predefined `CommandName`.

Try It Out: Deleting Players with DELETE

Now that you know how to select a row for deletion in a `GridView`, let's build a page that demonstrates the technique. In this example, you'll add a `ButtonField` that sends the user to a new page that confirms that the Player is to be deleted.

1. Open `Players.aspx`. In the Design view, set the `DataKeyNames` property of the `GridView` to PlayerID.

2. Switch to the Source view and add a `BoundField` to the `Columns` collection of the `GridView`:

```
<Columns>
  <asp:BoundField DataField="PlayerID" HeaderText="PlayerID" />
  <asp:BoundField DataField="PlayerName" HeaderText="Name" />
  <asp:BoundField DataField="PlayerCost" DataFormatString="{0:n}"
    HeaderText="Cost" />
  <asp:ButtonField Text="Delete" ButtonType="Button"
    CommandName="DeletePlayer" />
</Columns>
```

3. Switch to the Design view and add a `RowCommand` event to the `GridView`. Add the following code to the event handler:

```
protected void Grid1View_RowCommand(object sender,
  GridViewCommandEventArgs e)
{
  // get the PlayerID
  int intIndex = Convert.ToInt32(e.CommandArgument);
  string strPlayerID = Convert.ToString(GridView1.DataKeys[intIndex].Value);

  // perform the correct action
  if (e.CommandName == "DeletePlayer")
  {
    Response.Redirect("./Player_Delete.aspx?PlayerID=" + strPlayerID);
  }
}
```

4. Add a new Web Form to the Web site called `Player_Delete.aspx` and change the page title to **DELETE Player**.

5. Add a confirmation question to the page and two buttons, called `SubmitButton` and `ReturnButton`. You'll also need a `Label`, called `QueryResult`, to show the results from the query that was actually executed. You can see how the Web controls are laid out in Figure 8-13.

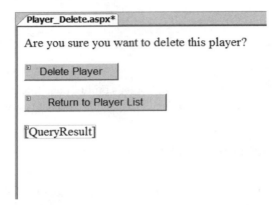

Figure 8-13. *You should always confirm deletions.*

6. Add a `Click` event for the `ReturnButton` control and add the following code to the event handler:

```
protected void ReturnButton_Click(object sender, EventArgs e)
{
  Response.Redirect("./Players.aspx");
}
```

7. Add the required namespace declaration to the top of the page:

```
<%@ Import Namespace="System.Data.SqlClient" %>
```

8. Add a `Click` event for the `SubmitButton` and add the following code to the event handler:

```
protected void SubmitButton_Click(object sender, EventArgs e)
{
  // create the connection
  string strConnectionString = ConfigurationManager.
    ConnectionStrings["SqlConnectionString"].ConnectionString;
  SqlConnection myConnection = new SqlConnection(strConnectionString);
```

```
try
{
  // query to execute
  string strQuery = "DELETE FROM WhatPlaysWhatFormat WHERE ➥
    WPWFPlayerID = @PlayerID; DELETE FROM Player ➥
    WHERE PlayerID = @PlayerID;";

  // create the command
  SqlCommand myCommand = new SqlCommand(strQuery, myConnection);

  // add the parameter
  myCommand.Parameters.AddWithValue("@PlayerID",
    Request.QueryString["PlayerID"]);

  // open the connection
  myConnection.Open();

  // execute the query
  myCommand.ExecuteNonQuery();

  // show the result
  QueryResult.Text = "Delete of player '" +
    Request.QueryString["PlayerID"] + "' was successful";

  // disable the submit button
  SubmitButton.Enabled = false;
}
catch (Exception ex)
{
  // show the error
  QueryResult.Text = "An error has occurred: " + ex.Message;
}
finally
{
  // close the connection
  myConnection.Close();
}
}
```

9. Save both pages, and then start the Web site. Click the Delete button for a Player, and you'll be presented with the confirmation page. Clicking the Delete Player button will call the event handler to delete the Player and return a confirmation, as shown in Figure 8-14.

10. If you now click the Return to Player List button, you'll be able to confirm that the Player has indeed been deleted.

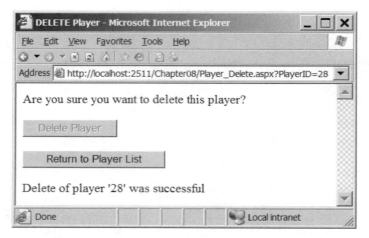

Figure 8-14. *Confirmation that the Player has been deleted*

How It Works

Adding button columns to a GridView isn't especially tricky. However, you should be aware of a couple of potential "gotchas" when you implement the event handler.

In this example, you're deleting only a row at a time, so the onus is on you to identify the row that has been selected for deletion using the primary key of the table and to relay that to the DELETE query. By using the primary key, you can ensure that only one row is deleted at a time. So, you discover the PlayerID for the row to be deleted and work with that. You append the PlayerID to the request for the Delete page as the PlayerID parameter:

```
Player_Delete.aspx?PlayerID=28
```

As you saw in Chapter 7, you can retrieve the ID of the row that you're dealing with from the DataKeys collection, as long as you've set the DataKeyNames property for the GridView. You can then extract the correct row from the collection:

```
int intIndex = Convert.ToInt32(e.CommandArgument);
string strPlayerID = Convert.ToString(GridView1.DataKeys[intIndex].Value);
```

Within Player_Delete.aspx, you first give the users the option of canceling the deletion by confirming that they wish to delete the Player. Remember that there is no Recycle Bin, so you should always confirm deletions before actually performing the DELETE. By clicking the Delete Player button, the SubmitButton_Click event handler is executed, and you can build the query to delete the Player from the database.

From the brief discussion of the DELETE query, you should be able to build a DELETE query to delete the Player relatively easily:

```
DELETE FROM Player WHERE PlayerID = @PlayerID
```

But if you look at the code, you'll see that this isn't the query that you execute. Now if you just ran this DELETE query by itself, you would get an error from the database saying that you can't delete the Player row because there are rows in the WhatPlaysWhatFormat table that depend on this one, and it violates the relationship you set between the two when you built the database. The key then is to delete these dependent rows from the WhatPlaysWhatFormat table *before* you delete the row from the Player table. Fortunately, all you need to do for this is use the PlayerID again as the WPWFPlayerID column, so you can create the DELETE FROM WhatPlaysWhatFormat query, and then tack on the DELETE FROM Player query at the end:

```
DELETE FROM WhatPlaysWhatFormat WHERE WPWFPlayerID = @PlayerID;
DELETE FROM Book WHERE BookID = @PlayerID
```

The actual code is straightforward. You create a Connection object and a Command object containing the DELETE query. After adding the @PlayerID parameter, you call ExecuteNonQuery() on the Command object to execute the query.

Here are a couple of things to consider about this example:

Concurrency problems: You're executing two DELETE queries as a query batch, and if the second query fails (for whatever reason), the first query will still succeed. This causes quite a large concurrency problem, as you've deleted the supported Formats for the Player but not the actual details of the Player itself. What you need to do is ensure that either both queries succeed or both queries fail. You do this by using a transaction, as discussed in Chapter 12.

Deletions even after changes: What happens if changes are made by another user to the Player while you're confirming that you want to delete it? The other user's changes are made to the Player, and then you delete it! This may be what you want to happen, but it also may be incorrect. You may want to not allow the deletion if the data has changed. By creating a slightly more complex DELETE query, you can prevent any deletions from occurring if the Player has changed. We'll look at concurrency issues such as this in Chapter 12.

Checks for the number of rows deleted: You don't actually check that you're deleting the correct number of rows from the table. From the Web site's design, you know that if you delete a Player, you should affect only one row in the Player table. You could also check that this is true by looking at the number of rows affected returned from ExecuteNonQuery(). However, when executing a query batch, as you do here, the rows affected are the sum of all of the queries that are executed, so you couldn't use this value at the moment. You could split the two DELETE queries into separate calls to the database and ensure that the DELETE query against the Player table deleted only one row. If it didn't, you would have an error (and if you were using a transaction, you could then abort the transaction and prevent the deletion from occurring).

Deleting data is a relatively simple thing to do, but it's also the most final. It's worth repeating that you need to be careful when implementing deletions.

■**Note** The code in the download for MySQL 5.0 and Microsoft Access both implement the DELETE functionality. However, as with the INSERT example, these databases can't handle multiple queries in the same query batch and don't support named parameters.

Updating Data in the Database

Suppose you want to allow users to edit data already in the database. You've designed the database to reduce the number of data-entry errors you may make, but that won't stop users from making mistakes, so you'll need to provide some way to correct them. Even if there aren't errors in your data, you still may need to update data. For example, an inventory system needs to keep updating the number of items in stock at any one time or the number of items sold; personalization systems need to update data when users update their preferences; and so on.

The process of editing data is much like adding it, except that you're starting the process with values that already exist. You still need to work with the rules of the database—the keys, the constraints, and so on. And you must try to use the best Web control for each column to allow users to edit the data. You may prefer to use a list Web control for foreign key values or a check box for Boolean values, rather than a text box.

The UPDATE Query

As usual, the whole operation of editing data comes down to generating and running a SQL query. In this case, it's an UPDATE query, which has the following syntax:

```
UPDATE < table name >
SET column1 name = expression1,
    column2 name = expression2,
        .
        .
        .
    columnM name = expressionM
[ WHERE <constraints> ]
```

The UPDATE query has the following five basic components:

- The keyword UPDATE denotes the action to the database.

- The *table name* determines the table from which the data will be updated.

- The keyword SET denotes the start of the updated information.

- A comma-separated list of assignments sets individual columns to given values.

- The WHERE clause constrains the number of rows that the UPDATE query affects.

UPDATE isn't limited to working with one table at a time, but it's probably easier to use it that way to start. Also, you may want to validate potential new values for the database before you update it, in the same fashion as when adding new rows.

Try It Out: Updating a Player with UPDATE

In this example, you'll add the final page to our solution so that Player details can be modified.

1. Open `Players.aspx` and add another `<asp:ButtonField>` to the `GridView`:

```
<asp:ButtonField Text="Edit" ButtonType="Button"
  CommandName="EditPlayer" />
```

2. Modify the `RowCommand` event of the `GridView` and add the following code:

```
protected void Grid1View_RowCommand(object sender,
  GridViewCommandEventArgs e)
{
  // get the PlayerID
  int intIndex = Convert.ToInt32(e.CommandArgument);
  string strPlayerID = Convert.ToString(
    GridView1.DataKeys[intIndex].Value);

  // perform the correct action
  if (e.CommandName == "DeletePlayer")
  {
    Response.Redirect("./Player_Delete.aspx?PlayerID=" + strPlayerID);
  }
  else if (e.CommandName == "EditPlayer")
  {
    Response.Redirect("./Player_Update.aspx?PlayerID=" + strPlayerID);
  }
}
```

3. In the Solution Explorer, copy `Player_Insert.aspx` and rename the copy `Player_Update.aspx`.

4. Change the page title to **UPDATE Player**, and change the `Text` property of the `SubmitButton` to **Update Player**.

5. Switch to the Source view and modify the `Page_Load` event as follows:

```
protected void Page_Load(object sender, EventArgs e)
{
  if (Page.IsPostBack == false)
  {
    // populate the list of manufacturers
    PopulateManufacturers();

    // populate the list of formats
    PopulateFormats();

    // retrieve existing player
    RetrieveExistingPlayer();
  }
}
```

6. Add the code for the RetrieveExistingPlayer()method:

```
private void RetrieveExistingPlayer()
{
  // create the connection
  string strConnectionString = ConfigurationManager.
    ConnectionStrings["SqlConnectionString"].ConnectionString;
  SqlConnection myConnection = new SqlConnection(strConnectionString);

  try
  {
    // create the first SELECT command
    string strQuery1 = "SELECT PlayerName, PlayerManufacturerID, ➥
      PlayerCost, PlayerStorage FROM Player WHERE PlayerID=@PlayerID;";
    SqlCommand myCommand1 = new SqlCommand(strQuery1, myConnection);
    myCommand1.Parameters.AddWithValue("@PlayerID",
      Request.QueryString["PlayerID"]);

    // create the first SELECT command
    string strQuery2 = "SELECT WPWFFormatID FROM WhatPlaysWhatFormat ➥
      WHERE WPWFPlayerID = @PlayerID;";
    SqlCommand myCommand2 = new SqlCommand(strQuery2, myConnection);
    myCommand2.Parameters.AddWithValue("@PlayerID",
      Request.QueryString["PlayerID"]);

    // open the connection
    myConnection.Open();

    // execute the first query
    SqlDataReader myReader1 = myCommand1.ExecuteReader();

    // if we have results, then we need to parse them
    if (myReader1.Read() == true)
    {
      PlayerName.Text = myReader1.GetString(
        myReader1.GetOrdinal("PlayerName"));
      ManufacturerList.SelectedValue = myReader1.GetInt32(
        myReader1.GetOrdinal("PlayerManufacturerID")).ToString();
      PlayerCost.Text = myReader1.GetDecimal(
        myReader1.GetOrdinal("PlayerCost")).ToString();
      PlayerStorage.Text = myReader1.GetString(
        myReader1.GetOrdinal("PlayerStorage"));
    }

    // close the first data reader
    myReader1.Close();
```

```
  // execute the second query
  SqlDataReader myReader2 = myCommand2.ExecuteReader();

  // if we have results, then we need to parse them
  while(myReader2.Read() == true)
  {
    foreach(ListItem objFormat in FormatList.Items)
    {
      if (objFormat.Value == myReader2.GetInt32(
        myReader2.GetOrdinal("WPWFFormatID")).ToString())
      {
        objFormat.Selected = true;
        break;
      }
    }
  }

  // close the second data reader
  myReader2.Close();
}
finally
{
  // close the connection
  myConnection.Close();
}
}
```

7. Change the code within the SubmitButton_Click event handler to the following:

```
protected void SubmitButton_Click(object sender, EventArgs e)
{
  // only save if valid
  if (Page.IsValid == true)
  {
    // save the player to the database
    bool blnPlayerError = SavePlayer();

    // did an error occur?
    if (blnPlayerError == true)
    {
      QueryResult.Text = "An error has occurred!";
    }
    else
    {
      // save the formats for the player
      bool blnFormatError = SaveFormats();
```

```
      // did an error occur?
      if (blnFormatError == true)
      {
        QueryResult.Text = "An error has occurred!";
      }
      else
      {
        // show the result
        QueryResult.Text = "Update of player '" +
          Request.QueryString["PlayerID"] + "' was successful";

        // disable the submit button
        SubmitButton.Enabled = false;
      }
    }
  }
}
```

8. Modify the SavePlayer() method as follows:

```
private bool SavePlayer()
{
  bool blnError = false;

  // create the connection
  string strConnectionString = ConfigurationManager.
    ConnectionStrings["SqlConnectionString"].ConnectionString;
  SqlConnection myConnection = new SqlConnection(strConnectionString);

  try
  {
    // query to execute
    string strQuery = "UPDATE Player SET PlayerName = @Name, ➥
      PlayerManufacturerID = @ManufacturerID, PlayerCost = @Cost, ➥
      PlayerStorage = @Storage WHERE PlayerID = @PlayerID;";

    // create the command
    SqlCommand myCommand = new SqlCommand(strQuery, myConnection);

    // add the parameters
    myCommand.Parameters.AddWithValue("@Name", PlayerName.Text);
    myCommand.Parameters.AddWithValue("@ManufacturerID",
      ManufacturerList.SelectedValue);
    myCommand.Parameters.AddWithValue("@Cost", PlayerCost.Text);
    myCommand.Parameters.AddWithValue("@Storage", PlayerStorage.Text);
    myCommand.Parameters.AddWithValue("@PlayerID",
      Request.QueryString["PlayerID"]);
```

```
        // open the connection
        myConnection.Open();

        // execute the query
        myCommand.ExecuteNonQuery();
    }
    catch
    {
        // indicate that we have an error
        blnError = true;
    }
    finally
    {
        // close the connection
        myConnection.Close();
    }

    // return the error flag
    return (blnError);
}
```

9. Modify the SaveFormats() method as follows:

```
private bool SaveFormats()
{
    bool blnError = false;

    // create the connection
    string strConnectionString = ConfigurationManager.
        ConnectionStrings["SqlConnectionString"].ConnectionString;
    SqlConnection myConnection = new SqlConnection(strConnectionString);

    try
    {
        // create the DELETE query
        string strQuery1 = "DELETE FROM WhatPlaysWhatFormat WHERE ➥
            WPWFPlayerID = @PlayerID;";
        SqlCommand myCommand1 = new SqlCommand(strQuery1, myConnection);
        myCommand1.Parameters.AddWithValue("@PlayerID",
            Request.QueryString["PlayerID"]);

        // create the INSERT query
        string strQuery2 = "INSERT WhatPlaysWhatFormat ➥
            (WPWFPlayerID, WPWFFormatID) VALUES (@PlayerID, @FormatID)";
        SqlCommand myCommand2 = new SqlCommand(strQuery2, myConnection);
        myCommand2.Parameters.AddWithValue("@PlayerID",
            Request.QueryString["PlayerID"]);
        myCommand2.Parameters.Add("@FormatID", System.Data.SqlDbType.Int);
```

```csharp
    // open the connection
    myConnection.Open();

    // execute the DELETE query
    myCommand1.ExecuteNonQuery();

    // loop through each of the formats
    foreach (ListItem objFormat in FormatList.Items)
    {
      // save if selected
      if (objFormat.Selected == true)
      {
        // set the parameter value
        myCommand2.Parameters["@FormatID"].Value = objFormat.Value;

        // execute the INSERT query
        myCommand2.ExecuteNonQuery();
      }
    }
  }
  catch
  {
    // indicate that we have an error
    blnError = true;
  }
  finally
  {
    // close the connection
    myConnection.Close();
  }

  // return the error flag
  return (blnError);
}
```

10. Save the two pages, and then start the Web site. If you edit a Player, you'll see that the modified details are saved to the database. Also notice that the validation routines prevent incorrect data from being entered.

How It Works

This example has more code than you've seen in the previous examples, but it just builds on those examples.

When editing data in the database, two tasks are paramount:

- Show the data that is already in the database so that the user can make the necessary changes.

- Save the data to the database, making sure that the modified data is saved and any old results are removed.

Due to the way that the Insert page is designed, you can add the ability to modify an existing Player by adding a new method, RetrieveExistingPlayer(), to populate the Web controls on the page with the existing details for the Player. Then you modify the SavePlayer() and SaveFormats() methods to handle updating the existing data, rather than adding new data.

We'll look at each of these methods in turn.

Note In most cases, you'll have only one page that is used for both adding and updating data. You'll see this when we look at the DataSet examples later in this chapter. However, you should be able to combine the Player_Insert.aspx, Player_Update.aspx, and Player_Delete.aspx pages together to have one page in the same way, as you will for the DataSet examples.

Retrieving the Existing Player

The RetrieveExistingPlayer()method is responsible for retrieving the existing details for the Player from the database and showing these details on the page. In order to retrieve the Player from the database, you need to execute two queries, because the required data is stored in two different tables. The first query returns all of the information from the Player table:

```
SELECT PlayerName, PlayerManufacturerID, PlayerCost, PlayerStorage
FROM Player
WHERE PlayerID = @PlayerID
```

The @PlayerID parameter is set to the value retrieved from the query string using the AddWithValue() method of the Parameters collection:

```
myCommand1.Parameters.AddWithValue("@PlayerID",
  Request.QueryString["PlayerID"]);
```

To populate the Web controls on the page, you return the results of the query as a DataReader and attempt to fill the Web controls only if you've returned results. You can check this by using the Read() method, which returns true if there is a row of data:

```
if (myReader1.Read() == true)
{
  PlayerName.Text = myReader1.GetString(
    myReader1.GetOrdinal("PlayerName"));
  ManufacturerList.SelectedValue = myReader1.GetInt32(
    myReader1.GetOrdinal("PlayerManufacturerID")).ToString();
  PlayerCost.Text = myReader1.GetDecimal(
    myReader1.GetOrdinal("PlayerCost")).ToString();
  PlayerStorage.Text = myReader1.GetString(
    myReader1.GetOrdinal("PlayerStorage"));
}
```

You use the GetXXX methods of the DataReader to return the required column in the correct format. For PlayerName, PlayerCost, and PlayerStorage, you use text boxes to enter the data, so you can set the Text property of the TextBox to the string version of the column.

The PlayerManufacturerID column is a little trickier. You're showing the list of Manufacturers in a `DropDownList`, so you need to set the `SelectedValue` property. The only caveat for setting this property is that you need to have populated the Web control before you can set the `SelectedValue` (you'll get a runtime error if you don't, as the value that you're trying to select won't be one of the values that the Web control is displaying). If you take a look at the `Page_Load` event handler, you'll see that `PopulateManufacturers()` is called before you retrieve the Player from the database.

The `Page_Load` event also calls `PopulateFormats()` to populate the `CheckBoxList` with all of the available Formats before you retrieve the Player. That should give you a big hint as to the second query that you need to execute.

The second query retrieves the supported Formats for the Player from the database. All you require is the list of FormatID values for the required Player:

```
SELECT WPWFFormatID
FROM WhatPlaysWhatFormat
WHERE WPWFPlayerID = @PlayerID
```

Again, the `@PlayerID` parameter is set directly from the query string value and you retrieve the results as a DataReader. However you're returning multiple results into a list Web control that supports the selection of multiple items, so you can't simply set the `SelectedValue` for the Web control as you did for the `ManufacturerList` control. You need to step through each of the returned values and set the individual items within the `CheckBoxList`. You step through all of the returned results in the DataReader using the `Read()` method in conjunction with a while loop:

```
while(myReader2.Read() == true)
{
```

Then you loop through all of the `ListItem` entries in the `CheckBoxList` and set the `Selected` property of the `ListItem` to true if the `Value` of the `ListItem` is the FormatID from the DataReader:

```
  foreach(ListItem objFormat in FormatList.Items)
  {
    if (objFormat.Value == myReader2.GetInt32(
      myReader2.GetOrdinal("WPWFFormatID")).ToString())
    {
      objFormat.Selected = true;
      break;
    }
  }
}
```

If you select the `ListItem`, you'll see that you use break to exit from the foreach loop immediately. You're looping through every entry in the `CheckBoxList` for each Format that you retrieve from the database, and using break allows you to stop executing when you're never going to select another `ListItem`.

This is quite a convoluted way of setting the entries in the `CheckBoxList`. Because you're allowing the reader to select multiple values from the list, you must manually select the individual items. You don't have the luxury of using the SelectedValue property, as you do for the ManufacturerList control.

Saving the Updated Player

In order to save the modified Player details to the database, you need to execute an UPDATE query to modify the existing Player in the database:

```
UPDATE Player
SET PlayerName = @Name, PlayerManufacturerID = @ManufacturerID,
  PlayerCost = @Cost, PlayerStorage = @Storage
WHERE PlayerID = @PlayerID
```

You're updating the Player table, and by adding the WHERE clause, you're constraining the UPDATE query to work only against the PlayerID that you require (which again takes its value from the query string).

The SET part of the query specifies the actual updating. You're updating the PlayerName, PlayerManufacturerID, PlayerCost, and PlayerStorage columns with the values from the @Name, @ManufacturerID, @Cost, and @Storage parameters.

You already know how to add parameters to the query, and you're simply specifying the reverse of the Web control population in the RetrieveExistingPlayer() method. You add the four parameters that take their values from the Web controls on the page:

```
myCommand.Parameters.AddWithValue("@Name", PlayerName.Text);
myCommand.Parameters.AddWithValue("@ManufacturerID",
  ManufacturerList.SelectedValue);
myCommand.Parameters.AddWithValue("@Cost", PlayerCost.Text);
myCommand.Parameters.AddWithValue("@Storage", PlayerStorage.Text);
```

And you also add the @PlayerID parameter from the query string value:

```
myCommand.Parameters.AddWithValue("@PlayerID",
  Request.QueryString["PlayerID"]);
```

Once you've added the five parameters to the query, you open the connection to the database and execute the query using the ExecuteNonQuery() method. If an error occurs, you trap it and set the error flag, causing any further processing of the update to be halted.

One thing you're not doing is checking that the UPDATE query has worked. You could use the return value from this method to determine the number of rows that were updated, and check that to determine if the update was a success—if you haven't updated a single row, then something has gone wrong. And if, in this instance, you've updated more than one row, then something has gone more wrong.

You're also not taking into account any changes that may be made by another user. What happens if changes are made by another user to the Player while you're making your changes? Whoever updates the Player first will lose those changes, and only the latest changes will be stored in the database. This may be what you want to happen, but it also may be incorrect. You may not want to allow the second update if the data has changed. By creating a slightly more complex UPDATE query, you can prevent any changes from occurring if the Player has changed. We'll look at this in Chapter 12.

Saving the Modified Formats

In order to save the supported Formats for the Player, you can't simply save the details of the selected Formats directly to the database. You need to insert multiple rows of information into the WhatPlaysWhatFormat table, and you can't do this using an UPDATE query. You saw how to add the Format details to the database using an INSERT query earlier, when you added a new Player. You use the same INSERT query to save the Formats to the database, but here, you can't simply add new information to the database; if you did, you might encounter the following problems:

- You add a Format that is already in the database, and you get a primary key error, as you're trying to add the same primary key (the combination of PlayerID and FormatID) into the WhatPlaysWhatFormat table.

- You manage to add the new information into the database (if you don't have a Format selected that was retrieved from the database initially), but now have incorrect data, as the Player will appear to support the original list of Formats as well as the new list of Formats that you saved.

To avoid these problems, you must remove the existing information from the database before you can add the new information. You execute a DELETE query to remove the existing Format details for the Player:

```
DELETE FROM WhatPlaysWhatFormat WHERE WPWFPlayerID = @PlayerID
```

Once the existing Format information has been saved to the database, you can then add the new information into the database. If you compare the SaveFormat() method in this page with the method you saw earlier in Player_Insert.aspx, you'll see that the method for adding the new information to the database is indeed the same.

Using a DataSet to Make the Changes

We've spent quite a considerable amount of time looking at how to insert, update, and delete data from the database by calling ExecuteNonQuery() and ExecuteScalar() on the Command object to propagate the changes to the database. Now we'll explore how to use a DataSet to make changes to the database. In the next chapter, you'll learn yet another way to edit data in a database: using the SqlDataSource with the GridView, DetailsView, and FormView.

As you learned in Chapter 5, the DataSet is disconnected from the database and allows you to make changes to the database and then propagate those changes back to the database in one go.

The key to making everything work is the DataAdapter (or to be provider-specific, the SqlDataAdapter, OdbcDataAdapter, and OleDbDataAdapter) being used in conjunction with INSERT, UPDATE, and DELETE queries. When using the DataAdapter to retrieve data, you set the SelectCommand to a Command object containing a SELECT query. You can do the same for INSERT, UPDATE, and DELETE queries by setting the InsertCommand, UpdateCommand, and DeleteCommand to the Command objects that you want to execute. You also have the option of letting a CommandBuilder (the SqlCommandBuilder, OdbcCommandBuilder, or OleDbCommandBuilder) automatically generate the INSERT, UPDATE, and DELETE queries based on the SELECT query that you use to populate the DataTable.

But how do you actually perform the changes? As you know, the DataAdapter has a `Fill()` method that populates a `DataTable` with the results of the `SelectCommand`. It also has a corresponding `Update()` method that propagates any changes made (either to the specified `DataTable` or to the `DataSet` as a whole) back to the database.

We'll start by looking at how the DataAdapter knows what changes need to be propagated to the database, and then see how the `DataRow` stores the changes that are made to its columns. Once we've finished this, admittedly brief, tour of the DataAdapter and `DataRow`, you'll build an example that allows you to insert, update, and delete Manufacturers.

■**Note** This section provides only an introduction to what is possible using a `DataSet` to modify the database. For more information, see *Professional ADO.NET 2.0* by Sahil Malik (1-59059-512-2; Apress, 2005).

The Role of the DataAdapter

To make changes to the database, the DataAdapter needs to know what has actually changed so that it knows which of the SQL queries it needs to execute. It does this by looking at the `RowState` for each `DataRow` in the `DataTable`.

The `RowState` is set to a value from the `System.Data.DataRowState` enumeration. Table 8-3 shows the possible values for the `DataRowState` enumeration, as well as the Command object that will be used during the call to `Update()`.

Table 8-3. *The DataRowState Enumeration Values*

Name	Description	Command
Added	The `DataRow` has been added to the `DataTable`.	InsertCommand
Deleted	The `DataRow` has been deleted by calling the `Delete()` method of the `DataRow`.	DeleteCommand
Detached	A `DataRow` is detached when it is first created and before it is added to a `DataTable` (at which point, its state changes to Added).	N/A
Modified	The `DataRow` has been modified.	UpdateCommand
Unchanged	The `DataRow` hasn't been modified.	None

On calling the `Update()` method, each `DataRow` is interrogated for its `RowState`, and the necessary Command object used to propagate the changes to the database. After the changes have been propagated to the database, the `RowState` is set to Unchanged for added and modified rows, and any deleted rows are actually removed from the `DataTable`.

■**Note** It is possible to turn off the modifications to the DataTable during an Update() by setting the AcceptChangesDuringUpdate property to false (it has a default of true). If you do this, the changes will have been made to the database, but the DataTable will still show that it has rows that have been changed. In order to accept the changes, you would need to call the AcceptChanges() method to complete the update of the DataTable. You can also call AcceptChanges() on an individual DataRow to commit any changes to that row, without affecting any other rows in the table.

The Role of the DataRow

As you've just learned, the DataRow knows that it has changed, and its RowState property tells you what change has been made. The DataRow also keeps a track of the value that it originally contained, as well as the value that it currently contains.

You can retrieve the value of a column from a DataRow by specifying either the column's index or its name. For example, to retrieve the ManufacturerName from a DataRow, you would use the following:

```
ManufacturerName.Text = drManufacturer["ManufacturerName"].ToString();
```

It is also possible to retrieve the value that the column originally contained:

```
ManufacturerName.Text =
  drManufacturer["ManufacturerName",DataRowVersion.Original].ToString();
```

Along with these two versions of the data, you can also retrieve two other versions. Table 8-4 shows the four versions you can retrieve.

Table 8-4. *The DataRowVersion Enumeration Values*

Name	Description
Current	The default, which returns the value that will be propagated to the database or returned when you don't specify a DataRowVersion. When the DataRow is created the Current and Original values are the same. When the column is modified the Current value will change.
Default	Returns either the Current version (if the RowState is Added, Modified, or Deleted) or the Proposed version (if the RowState is Detached).
Original	Returns the value that was retrieved from the database. You can use the Original version to check that the row you're updating or deleting hasn't changed before setting its value to the Current version (see Chapter 12).
Proposed	Returns the value that is proposed for the column.

Try It Out: Inserting Data Using a DataSet

In this example, you'll add a page that allows you to add Manufacturers in the database. You'll first create a page to view the Manufacturers that are in the database.

1. Add a new Web Form to the Web site called Manufacturers.aspx. Make sure that the Place Code in Separate File check box is unchecked.

2. In the Source view, find the <title> tag within the HTML at the bottom of the page and change the page title to **Manufacturers**.

3. Switch to the Design view and add a SqlDataSource to the page. Choose to configure the data source and use SqlConnectionString to connect to the database. Select the ManufacturerID, ManufacturerName, and ManufacturerCountry columns from the Manufacturer table to configure the SELECT query.

4. Switch back to the Source view and add the following markup after the declaration of the SqlDataSource:

```
<asp:HyperLink ID="HyperLink1" runat="server"
  NavigateUrl="./Manufacturer_Edit.aspx">Add manufacturer</asp:HyperLink>
<br /><br />
<asp:GridView ID="GridView1" runat="server" AutoGenerateColumns="False"
  DataSourceID="SqlDataSource1">
  <Columns>
    <asp:BoundField DataField="ManufacturerID"
      HeaderText="ManufacturerID" />
    <asp:BoundField DataField="ManufacturerName"
      HeaderText="ManufacturerName" />
    <asp:BoundField DataField="ManufacturerCountry"
      HeaderText="ManufacturerCountry" />
  </Columns>
</asp:GridView>
```

5. Add a new Web Form to the Web site called Manufacturer_Edit.aspx. Make sure that the Place Code in Separate File check box is unchecked.

6. In the Source view, find the <title> tag within the HTML at the bottom of the page and change the page title to **Edit Manufacturer**. Then add the required Import statements to the top of the page:

```
<%@ Page Language="C#" %>
<%@ Import Namespace="System.Data" %>
<%@ Import Namespace="System.Data.SqlClient" %>
```

7. Add the Web controls to allow the addition of a Manufacturer to the database. Add a Button to save the Manufacturer; a Button to return to the list of Manufacturers; and four TextBox controls for the user to add the Manufacturer's name, country, e-mail address, and Web site address. Name these SaveButton, ReturnButton, ManufacturerName, ManufacturerCountry, ManufacturerEmail, and ManufacturerWebsite, respectively. Also add a Label, called QueryResult, to show the results from the query that was executed. You can see how the Web controls are laid out in Figure 8-15.

```
Manufacturer_Edit.aspx*

Manufacturer Name: [    ]

Manufacturer Country: [    ]

Manufacturer Email: [    ]

Manufacturer Website: [    ]

[  Save Manufacturer    ]

[  Return to Manufacturer List  ]

[QueryResult]
```

Figure 8-15. *The Web control layout for Manufacturer_Edit.aspx*

8. Switch to the Source view and add the following variable declarations to the top of the `<script>` block:

```
SqlDataAdapter myAdapter;
DataSet myDataSet;
```

9. Add the private method to retrieve the Manufacturers from the database:

```
private void RetrieveManufacturers()
{
  // set the SQL query we need to get the manufacturers
  string strQuery = "SELECT ManufacturerID, ManufacturerName, ➥
    ManufacturerCountry, ManufacturerEmail, ManufacturerWebsite ➥
    FROM Manufacturer";

  // create the Connection to the database
  string ConnectionString = ConfigurationManager.
    ConnectionStrings["SqlConnectionString"].ConnectionString;
  SqlConnection myConnection = new SqlConnection(ConnectionString);
```

```
    // create the DataAdapter
    myAdapter = new SqlDataAdapter(strQuery, myConnection);

    // set up the INSERT/UPDATE/DELETE queries
    SqlCommandBuilder myCommandBuilder = new SqlCommandBuilder(myAdapter);

    // create a new DataSet
    myDataSet = new DataSet();

    // fill the DataSet
    myAdapter.Fill(myDataSet, "Manufacturer");

    // now add the primary key details
    DataColumn[] myPrimaryKey = {
      myDataSet.Tables["Manufacturer"].Columns["ManufacturerID"] };
    myDataSet.Tables["Manufacturer"].PrimaryKey = myPrimaryKey;
}
```

10. Switch to the Design view and double-click the Save Player button to add the Click
    event handler. Add the following code:

```
protected void SaveButton_Click(object sender, EventArgs e)
{
  // only save if valid
  if (Page.IsValid == true)
  {
    // get the Manufacturers
    RetrieveManufacturers();

    // create a new DataRow
    DataRow drManufacturer = myDataSet.Tables["Manufacturer"].NewRow();

    // now set the column values
    drManufacturer["ManufacturerName"] = ManufacturerName.Text;
    drManufacturer["ManufacturerCountry"] = ManufacturerCountry.Text;
    drManufacturer["ManufacturerEmail"] = ManufacturerEmail.Text;
    drManufacturer["ManufacturerWebsite"] = ManufacturerWebsite.Text;
```

```
      // add a temporary primary key value
      drManufacturer["ManufacturerID"] = "-1";

      // add the DataRow to the table
      myDataSet.Tables["Manufacturer"].Rows.Add(drManufacturer);

      try
      {
        // now update the database
        myAdapter.Update(myDataSet, "Manufacturer");

        // show the result
        QueryResult.Text = "Save of manufacturer was successful";

        // disable all the controls we don't want to allow changes to
        SaveButton.Enabled = false;
        ManufacturerName.Enabled = false;
        ManufacturerCountry.Enabled = false;
        ManufacturerEmail.Enabled = false;
        ManufacturerWebsite.Enabled = false;
      }
      catch (Exception ex)
      {
        // show the error
        QueryResult.Text = "An error has occurred: " + ex.Message;
      }
    }
  }
}
```

11. Switch back to the Design view and add the `Click` event handler for the Return to Manufacturer List button. Add the following code:

```
protected void ReturnButton_Click(object sender, EventArgs e)
{
  Response.Redirect("./Manufacturers.aspx");
}
```

12. Save both pages, and then open `Manufacturers.aspx` in your browser. Click the Add Manufacturer link, and then enter the details for a new Manufacturer on the `Manufacturer_Edit.aspx` page.

13. Click the Save Manufacturer button to the database, and you'll see that the Manufacturer has been saved, as shown in Figure 8-16.

Figure 8-16. *Adding a new Manufacturer to the database*

How It Works

As you can see, using a DataSet to add to the database requires substantially less code than the equivalent page for the earlier Player example.

The addition of a new Manufacturer to the database requires three basic steps:

- Retrieve the existing Manufacturers from the database into a DataTable within the DataSet.

- Add a new DataRow to the DataTable and populate it correctly with the information entered by the user.

- Save the changes made by to the DataTable to the database using the DataAdapter.

We'll look at each of these steps in turn.

Retrieving the Manufacturers

Before you can add a new Manufacturer to the DataTable, you need to know the structure of the DataTable. As you saw in Chapter 5, you can build the DataTable from scratch, populate it, and send the changes back to the database. However, you didn't do that here. Instead, you retrieve the existing Manufacturer table from the database to ensure that you have the correct format.

You retrieve the list of Manufacturers using the RetrieveManufacturers() method, which you call before you attempt to add a new row to the DataTable. It may seem a little strange that you're doing this in its own method and storing the DataSet and DataAdapter as global variables for the page. You use this approach because it allows you to use the same code to retrieve the list of Manufacturers for updating and deleting data as well.

The first thing that you do within the RetrieveManufacturers() method is to create the SQL for the SELECT query and create the Connection object.

```
// set the SQL query we need to get the manufacturers
string strQuery = "SELECT ManufacturerID, ManufacturerName, ➥
  ManufacturerCountry, ManufacturerEmail, ManufacturerWebsite ➥
  FROM Manufacturer";

// create the Connection to the database
string ConnectionString = ConfigurationManager.
  ConnectionStrings["SqlConnectionString"].ConnectionString;
myConnection = new SqlConnection(ConnectionString);
```

You then create the DataAdapter that you're going to use to propagate any changes back to the database, passing in the SELECT query and the Connection that you want to use:

```
// create the DataAdapter
myAdapter = new SqlDataAdapter(strQuery, myConnection);
```

Once you have a DataAdapter object, you can then use a CommandBuilder to automatically create the INSERT, UPDATE, and DELETE queries. All you need to do is create a new instance of the CommandBuilder, passing the DataAdapter to the constructor. You don't even need to keep a reference to the CommandBuilder after it has been created:

```
// set up the INSERT/UPDATE/DELETE queries
SqlCommandBuilder myCommandBuilder = new SqlCommandBuilder(myAdapter);
```

You then create a new DataSet and use the Fill() method of the DataAdapter to fill the correct table:

```
// create a new DataSet
myDataSet = new DataSet();

// fill the DataSet
myAdapter.Fill(myDataSet, "Manufacturer");
```

Next, you need to add the primary key details for the DataTable. You create a new array of DataColumn objects and add the required columns—in this case, ManufacturerID—to the array. You can then set the PrimaryKey property on the DataTable:

```
// now add the primary key details
DataColumn[] myPrimaryKey = {
  myDataSet.Tables["Manufacturer"].Columns["ManufacturerID"] };
myDataSet.Tables["Manufacturer"].PrimaryKey = myPrimaryKey;
```

You don't manually open or close the connection to the database within the RetrieveManufacturers() method. Instead, you let the DataAdapter open and close the connection as it requires. It will do this when it needs to Fill() or Update() the DataSet, and will open the connection only when it is required.

Adding a New Row to the Table

We've already looked at how to add a new row to a DataTable in Chapter 5. The code that you execute here is the same apart, from one little caveat.

You first call the NewRow() method on the Manufacturer DataTable to return a new DataRow object (which has its RowState set to Detached):

```
// create a new DataRow
DataRow drManufacturer = myDataSet.Tables["Manufacturer"].NewRow();
```

You can then set the values of the four columns directly from the TextBox controls from the page:

```
// now set the column values
drManufacturer["ManufacturerName"] = ManufacturerName.Text;
drManufacturer["ManufacturerCountry"] = ManufacturerCountry.Text;
drManufacturer["ManufacturerEmail"] = ManufacturerEmail.Text;
drManufacturer["ManufacturerWebsite"] = ManufacturerWebsite.Text;
```

Then you need to add a ManufacturerID to the DataRow, even though it's a primary key and an auto-generated column in the database. By setting the primary key on the DataTable, you're no longer allowed to have a null value for the ManufacturerID column, so you choose a value that cannot appear in the database:

```
// add a temporary primary key value
drManufacturer["ManufacturerID"] = "-1";
```

By using the value of -1, you don't risk picking a value that is (or could be) a ManufacturerID value in the database. This value is never sent to the database and is ignored, as the INSERT query that is generated doesn't pass it to the database.

You can then add the DataRow to the DataTable, changing its RowState to Added in the process:

```
// add the DataRow to the table
myDataSet.Tables["Manufacturer"].Rows.Add(drManufacturer);
```

Now that you've added the DataRow to the DataTable, you can propagate the changes to the database.

Saving the Changes to the Database

You propagate the changes to the database by calling the Update() method of the DataAdapter specifying the DataSet and the name of the DataTable you want to update. Then you inform the user that the save was successful:

```
// now update the database
myAdapter.Update(myDataSet, "Manufacturer");
```

```
// show the result
QueryResult.Text = "Save of manufacturer was successful";
```

Although the code looks simple, quite a lot of work is going on under the covers. The DataAdapter loops through all of the DataRows in the DataTable and checks the RowStatus. If the status is Added, Modified, or Deleted, the changes are propagated back to the database using the InsertCommand, UpdateCommand, or DeleteCommand, respectively.

As you've made only one change the DataTable, you have only one change to propagate to the database. As it's a DataRow addition, the InsertCommand will be used.

The CommandBuilder created the InsertCommand automatically, and as you saw in the example, it works. It's not all magic though, and it is possible to view the query that is being executed by tapping into the events that the DataAdapter raises.

As in common with most of the other data-access Web controls and classes in ASP.NET, the DataAdapter has before and after events concerned with updating the database:

- RowUpdating: This event occurs before the update takes place. The event arguments allow you to inspect the query that is being executed.

- RowUpdated: Once the update has taken place, the RowUpdated event allows you to see the query that has been executed, as well see the number of RecordsAffected by the update.

These two events are common to each type of update (INSERT, UPDATE, or DELETE).

If you wanted to, you could add the event handler. Visual Web Developer makes it very easy to do this, and it will auto-complete most of the code to add the event handler (and will even add the signature for the event handler itself if you press Tab when asked). You can add the following to add the event handler:

```
myAdapter.RowUpdating += new
  SqlRowUpdatingEventHandler(myAdapter_RowUpdating);
```

And then do whatever you want within the event handler itself.

If you look at the query that is executed (e.Command.CommandText), you'll see that it is a quite simple INSERT query:

```
INSERT INTO Manufacturer (ManufacturerName, ManufacturerCountry,
  ManufacturerEmail, ManufacturerWebsite)
VALUES (@p1, @p2, @p3, @p4)
```

The CommandBuilder has created an INSERT query simply from the definition of the SELECT query. The CommandBuilder has parameterized it as well, and if you look at the Parameters collection, you'll see that it picks up the values from the DataTable automatically using the SourceColumn and SourceVersion properties of the SqlParameter. You'll learn more about these properties a little later in this chapter, in the "Manually Creating the Commands" section.

Try It Out: Updating Data Using a DataSet

You'll now modify the example so that it also allows you to update an existing Manufacturer. In the earlier Player examples, a lot of the code was repeated in the INSERT and UPDATE examples. By combining the two pages, you can remove a lot of repeated code.

1. Open Manufacturers.aspx. In the Design view, set the DataKeyNames property of the GridView to ManufacturerID.

2. Switch to the Source view and add a ButtonField to the Columns collection of the GridView:

```
<Columns>
  <asp:BoundField DataField="ManufacturerID"
    HeaderText="ManufacturerID" />
  <asp:BoundField DataField="ManufacturerName"
    HeaderText="ManufacturerName" />
  <asp:BoundField DataField="ManufacturerCountry"
    HeaderText="ManufacturerCountry" />
  <asp:ButtonField Text="Edit" ButtonType="Button"
    CommandName="EditManufacturer" />
</Columns>
```

3. Add a `RowCommand` event to the `GridView`. Add the following code to the event handler:

```
protected void Grid1View_RowCommand(object sender,
  GridViewCommandEventArgs e)
{
  // get the ManufacturerID
  int intIndex = Convert.ToInt32(e.CommandArgument);
  string strManufacturerID = Convert.ToString(
    GridView1.DataKeys[intIndex].Value);

  // perform the correct action
  if (e.CommandName == "EditManufacturer")
  {
    Response.Redirect("./Manufacturer_Edit.aspx?ManufacturerID=" +
      strManufacturerID);
  }
}
```

4. Open `Manufacturers_Edit.aspx` and add a `Load` event to the page. Add the following code to the event handler:

```
protected void Page_Load(object sender, EventArgs e)
{
  if (Page.IsPostBack == false)
  {
    // only load if we have a manufacturer
    if (Request.QueryString["ManufacturerID"] != null)
    {
      // load all the manufacturers
      RetrieveManufacturers();

      // find the one we're after
      DataRow drManufacturer = myDataSet.Tables["Manufacturer"].
        Rows.Find(Request.QueryString["ManufacturerID"]);
```

```
            // set the four controls
            ManufacturerName.Text =
                drManufacturer["ManufacturerName"].ToString();
            ManufacturerCountry.Text =
                drManufacturer["ManufacturerCountry"].ToString();
            ManufacturerEmail.Text =
                drManufacturer["ManufacturerEmail"].ToString();
            ManufacturerWebsite.Text =
                drManufacturer["ManufacturerWebsite"].ToString();
        }
    }
}
```

5. Modify the SaveButton_Click event handler as follows:

```
protected void SaveButton_Click(object sender, EventArgs e)
{
  // only save if valid
  if (Page.IsValid == true)
  {
    // get the Manufacturers
    RetrieveManufacturers();

    // create new or use existing?
    DataRow drManufacturer = null;
    if (Request.QueryString["ManufacturerID"] == null)
    {
      // create a new DataRow
      drManufacturer = myDataSet.Tables["Manufacturer"].NewRow();
    }
    else
    {
      // find the one we're after
      drManufacturer = myDataSet.Tables["Manufacturer"].Rows.
        Find(Request.QueryString["ManufacturerID"]);
    }

    // now set the column values
    drManufacturer["ManufacturerName"] = ManufacturerName.Text;
    drManufacturer["ManufacturerCountry"] = ManufacturerCountry.Text;
    drManufacturer["ManufacturerEmail"] = ManufacturerEmail.Text;
    drManufacturer["ManufacturerWebsite"] = ManufacturerWebsite.Text;

    // if new, must add to table
    if (Request.QueryString["ManufacturerID"] == null)
    {
      // add a temporary primary key value
      drManufacturer["ManufacturerID"] = "-1";
```

```
    // add the DataRow to the table
    myDataSet.Tables["Manufacturer"].Rows.Add(drManufacturer);
}

try
{
    // now update the database
    myAdapter.Update(myDataSet, "Manufacturer");

    // show the result
    QueryResult.Text = "Save of manufacturer was successful";

    // disable all the controls we don't want to allow changes to
    SaveButton.Enabled = false;
    ManufacturerName.Enabled = false;
    ManufacturerCountry.Enabled = false;
    ManufacturerEmail.Enabled = false;
    ManufacturerWebsite.Enabled = false;
}
catch (Exception ex)
{
    // show the error
    QueryResult.Text = "An error has occurred: " + ex.Message;
}
}
}
```

6. Save both pages, and then open Manufacturer.aspx in your browser. Clicking any of the Edit buttons in the GridView will allow you to modify the selected Manufacturer. You can confirm the changes have been made by looking at the complete list of Manufacturers.

How It Works

You've added the ability to edit Manufacturers with only minimal changes to the page. We'll look at each of these changes in turn.

Populating the Controls on Load

Now that you're editing an existing Manufacturer, rather than adding a new Manufacturer, you must retrieve the list of Manufacturers and then select the correct Manufacturer. This is accomplished quite easily by using the Find() method of the Rows collection for the DataTable and specifying the primary key for the row that you want to retrieve:

```
// find the one we're after
DataRow drManufacturer = myDataSet.Tables["Manufacturer"].
  Rows.Find(Request.QueryString["ManufacturerID"]);
```

This returns a DataRow that you can interrogate to retrieve the column values that you're after and set the TextBox controls correctly.

Editing a Row in the Table

When editing a row, you no longer need to add a new DataRow to the DataTable; you can use the existing row. Therefore, you check whether you're performing an insert or an update by checking to see if there is a ManufacturerID in the query string. If there isn't, you want to create a new row, as before:

```
if (Request.QueryString["ManufacturerID"] == null)
{
  // create a new DataRow
  drManufacturer = myDataSet.Tables["Manufacturer"].NewRow();
}
```

If the query string does have a ManufacturerID, you retrieve the existing DataRow using the primary key to find the correct ManufacturerID:

```
else
{
  // find the one we're after
  drManufacturer = myDataSet.Tables["Manufacturer"].Rows.
    Find(Request.QueryString["ManufacturerID"]);
}
```

You then set the column values based on the TextBox controls in exactly the same way as before.

Next, you check to see if you're adding or editing a Manufacturer. If you're adding one, you set the temporary primary key value and add the new DataRow to the DataTable.

Saving the Changes to the Database

The code to save the changes to the database is exactly the same as before. The Update() method commits all changes to the database and chooses the UpdateCommand in this instance.

If you look at the query in the RowUpdating event handler, you'll see that the UPDATE query is a lot more complex than you might expect:

```
UPDATE Manufacturer SET ManufacturerName = @p1 WHERE
((ManufacturerID = @p2) AND (ManufacturerName = @p3)
AND ((@p4 = 1 AND ManufacturerCountry IS NULL) OR
(ManufacturerCountry = @p5)) AND ((@p6 = 1 AND
ManufacturerEmail IS NULL) OR (ManufacturerEmail = @p7)) AND
((@p8 = 1 AND ManufacturerWebsite IS NULL)
OR (ManufacturerWebsite = @p9)))
```

This is the query generated when you change only the ManufacturerName. If you changed all four values (name, country, e-mail address, and Web site address), the query becomes even more complex, with twelve parameters rather than the nine here. The UPDATE query is generated on the fly and updates only the columns that have been modified, but does it really need to be this complex?

Although this UPDATE query works, it isn't as efficient as it could be. You'll see shortly that you can add your own queries, rather than using the CommandBuilder auto-generated ones.

Try It Out: Deleting Data Using a DataSet

You'll now add the final part of the page to delete Manufacturers from the database.

1. Open `Manufacturers_Edit.aspx`. In the Design View, add a new `Button` called `DeleteManufacturer` to the page beside the Save Player button. You can see how the Web controls are laid out in Figure 8-17.

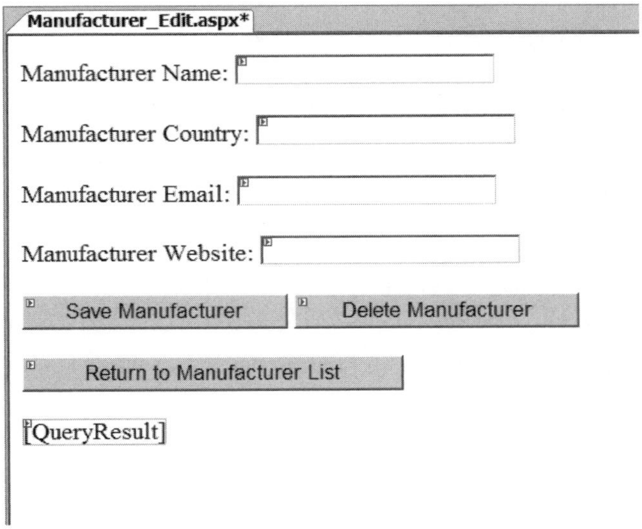

Figure 8-17. *The new Web control layout for Manufacturer_Edit.aspx*

2. Double-click the Delete Manufacturer button to add the `Click` event, and add the following code to the event handler:

```
protected void DeleteButton_Click(object sender, EventArgs e)
{
  // load all the manufacturers
  RetrieveManufacturers();

  // find the one we're after
  DataRow drManufacturer = myDataSet.Tables["Manufacturer"].Rows.
    Find(Request.QueryString["ManufacturerID"]);
```

```csharp
      // delete it
      drManufacturer.Delete();

      try
      {
        // now update the database
        myAdapter.Update(myDataSet, "Manufacturer");

        // show the result
        QueryResult.Text = "Delete of manufacturer was successful";

        // disable all the controls we don't want to allow changes to
        SaveButton.Enabled = false;
        DeleteButton.Enabled = false;
        ManufacturerName.Enabled = false;
        ManufacturerCountry.Enabled = false;
        ManufacturerEmail.Enabled = false;
        ManufacturerWebsite.Enabled = false;
      }
      catch (Exception ex)
      {
        // show the error
        QueryResult.Text = "An error has occurred: " + ex.Message;
      }
    }
```

3. Modify the Page_Load event handler to disable the Delete Manufacturer button if you're adding a new Manufacturer, as follows:

```csharp
protected void Page_Load(object sender, EventArgs e)
{
  if (Page.IsPostBack == false)
  {
    // only load if we have a manufacturer
    if (Request.QueryString["ManufacturerID"] != null)
    {
      // load all the manufacturers
      RetrieveManufacturers();

      // find the one we're after
      DataRow drManufacturer = myDataSet.Tables["Manufacturer"].
        Rows.Find(Request.QueryString["ManufacturerID"]);

      // set the four controls
      ManufacturerName.Text =
        drManufacturer["ManufacturerName"].ToString();
      ManufacturerCountry.Text =
        drManufacturer["ManufacturerCountry"].ToString();
```

```
        ManufacturerEmail.Text =
          drManufacturer["ManufacturerEmail"].ToString();
        ManufacturerWebsite.Text =
          drManufacturer["ManufacturerWebsite"].ToString();
      }
      else
      {
        // we want to disable the delete button
        DeleteButton.Enabled = false;
      }
    }
  }
}
```

4. Modify the end of the SaveButton_Click event handler and add the code to disable the Delete Manufacturer button:

```
// disable all the controls we don't want to allow changes to
SaveButton.Enabled = false;
DeleteButton.Enabled = false;
ManufacturerName.Enabled = false;
ManufacturerCountry.Enabled = false;
ManufacturerEmail.Enabled = false;
ManufacturerWebsite.Enabled = false;
```

5. Save the page, and then open Manufacturers.aspx in your browser. If you click the Edit button for a Manufacturer, you'll see that you can now delete the Manufacturer.

How It Works

Once again, you see that deleting is the easiest thing to do. First, you retrieve the DataRow that you're after:

```
// find the one we're after
DataRow drManufacturer = myDataSet.Tables["Manufacturer"].Rows.
  Find(Request.QueryString["ManufacturerID"]);
```

And then you delete it:

```
// delete it
drManufacturer.Delete();
```

This changes the RowState to Deleted. When the Update() method is called, the DeleteCommand is used, and the following auto-generated query is executed:

```
DELETE FROM Manufacturer WHERE ((ManufacturerID = @p1)
AND (ManufacturerName = @p2) AND ((@p3 = 1
AND ManufacturerCountry IS NULL) OR (ManufacturerCountry = @p4))
AND ((@p5 = 1 AND ManufacturerEmail IS NULL) OR
(ManufacturerEmail = @p6)) AND ((@p7 = 1 AND
ManufacturerWebsite IS NULL) OR (ManufacturerWebsite = @p8)))
```

As with the UPDATE query, the DELETE query works, but is perhaps overly complex. You should be able to delete a Manufacturer using one parameter (the ManufacturerID), but this DELETE query has nine parameters! It's definitely time to look at creating your own queries.

Manually Creating the Commands

You've seen in the previous three examples that you can use a CommandBuilder to automatically create the INSERT, UPDATE, and DELETE queries. Although the INSERT query was quite acceptable, the UPDATE and DELETE queries are a little complex (to say the least!).

It is easy to create your own INSERT, UPDATE, and DELETE queries, rather than letting a CommandBuilder do it for you. As an example, let's look at how to add an UPDATE query.

■**Caution** If you're not using a CommandBuilder and don't define a Command object for the operation that you're performing, you'll get an InvalidOperationException if you try to perform that operation.

You first need to define the Command object that you want to use (assuming that myConnection is already defined as a Connection object):

```
// query to execute
string strQuery = "UPDATE Manufacturer SET
  ManufacturerName = @ManufacturerName,
  ManufacturerCountry = @ManufacturerCountry,
  ManufacturerEmail = @ManufacturerEmail,
  ManufacturerWebsite = @ManufacturerWebsite,
  WHERE ManufacturerID = @ManufacturerID;";

// create the command
SqlCommand myCommand = new SqlCommand(strQuery, myConnection);
```

You then need to add all of the parameters to the Command object. But how do you know what the values are? How do you query the DataTable to get the correct parameters? You need to use the SourceColumn property to determine the specific column from the DataTable and the SourceVersion property to specify which version of the column (Current or Original) you're after. So, the ManufacturerName parameter is created as follows:

```
SqlParameter myNameParameter = new SqlParameter();
myNameParameter.ParameterName = "@ManufactuereID";
myNameParameter.SourceColumn = "ManufacturerID";
myNameParameter.SourceVersion = DataRowVersion.Current;
```

And then added to the Parameters collection as follows:

```
myCommand.Parameters.Add(myNameParameter);
```

The remaining four columns are created in the same way. You specify the SourceColumn as the name of the column and the SourceVersion to be the Current version.

Note When we look at concurrency in Chapter 12, you'll see that you sometimes use the Original version of a column to ensure that the data that you're changing hasn't changed between deciding to change the data and actually getting around to changing the data.

Creating your own INSERT and UPDATE queries follows the same pattern.

Summary

While a SQL query is at the center of every data operation—SELECT, INSERT, UPDATE, or DELETE— you have many ways to get that SQL query defined and executed, and its results examined. You can do almost anything you like as long as you form the SQL correctly and obey the rules of the database you've defined.

You shouldn't regard the examples in these chapters as the dogmatic way to do any one particular task. Their purpose is to present various techniques that you may or may not choose to use in your own pages. Whether you use any one block of code is up to you, but you do at least now know where some code works and where other code doesn't work.

In the next chapter, we'll move away from writing code to modify the database and see that the GridView (and its siblings the DetailsView and FormView) allows you to write pages that will automatically propagate the changes to the database, provided that you specify the correct INSERT, UDPATE, and DELETE queries.

CHAPTER 9

■ ■ ■

The GridView Family

In a superhero sort of way, the GridView has been hiding a second life from you. In the previous chapters, you've been using the GridView to simply display data, but it can do much more than that. In Chapter 7, you saw that with a minimum of work (translated as "very little code"), you can also sort and page the results. In this chapter, you'll see that, again with very little work, you can use the GridView to edit the data that it displays.

As you'll see as you work through this chapter, the GridView allows you to edit and delete data. However, it doesn't allow you to add new data. For that task, you'll need to use one of its siblings—the DetailsView or FormView. Both the DetailsView and FormView allow you to add new data, as well as edit and delete data.

Although the GridView, DetailsView, and FormView are what are displayed on the page, without a data source, they would be rather useless—no data means nothing to display. In the previous chapters, we've looked at using a SqlDataSource to provide the data to the GridView, and we've also looked at using code to handle the connection to the database. The SqlDataSource also has the ability to modify the contents of database. In the majority of cases when using the GridView, DetailsView, and FormView to modify the contents of the database, you'll use a SqlDataSource to do it. You could write all the necessary code to do so, but why reinvent the wheel?

This chapter covers the following topics:

- An introduction to the updatable features of the SqlDataSource

- An overview of the GridView and DetailsView and the Field Web controls that they support

- How to edit and delete existing data in a GridView

- How to use a DetailsView with a GridView, as well as use a DetailsView to edit, delete, and add data

- How to use a FormView, which is similar a DetailsView but allows more control over the way that the information is presented to the user

- How to add validation Web controls to prevent the user from entering incorrect data

The Updatable SqlDataSource

So far, when you've used a SqlDataSource, you've specified a SELECT query and, depending on what you were doing, a set of parameters for that query. For example, to return all the Players for a given Manufacturer, you would define the following SqlDataSource:

```
<asp:SqlDataSource ID="SqlDataSource1" runat="server"
  ConnectionString="<%$ ConnectionStrings:SqlConnectionString %>"
  SelectCommand="SELECT PlayerID, PlayerName FROM Player
    WHERE Player.PlayerManufacturerID = @ManufacturerID">
  <SelectParameters>
    <asp:ControlParameter ControlID="ManufacturerList"
      Name="ManufacturerID" PropertyName="SelectedValue" />
  </SelectParameters>
</asp:SqlDataSource>
```

The names that you use should give the game away a little. You have a SelectCommand property specifying the query that you want to execute, and a SelectParameters collection that contains the parameters, if any, for the query.

The SqlDataSource also supports INSERT, UPDATE, and DELETE queries. Not surprisingly, these have matching names to the SELECT query:

- The INSERT query is specified in the InsertCommand property, and its parameters are specified in the InsertParameters collection.

- The UPDATE query is specified in the UpdateCommand property, and its parameters are specified in the UpdateParameters collection.

- The DELETE query is specified in the DeleteCommand property, and its parameters are specified in the DeleteParameters collection.

By setting the necessary property and adding the parameters, you enable the SqlDataSource to perform the corresponding action. But that's not the end of the story. The SqlDataSource defines the queries but doesn't execute them. The Web control that's making use of the SqlDataSource actually executes the query.

The SqlDataSource exposes a method that allows the corresponding query to be executed. The SelectCommand is executed by calling the Select() method, the InsertCommand by calling the Insert() method, the UpdateCommand by calling the Update() method, and the DeleteCommand by calling the Delete() method. Before calling one of these methods, the GridView (or DetailsView or FormView) populates the necessary parameters for the query.

Each of the four queries also has two events that you can handle if necessary: a before action event and an after action event. For example, the Update() method first raises the Updating event, then executes the UPDATE query, before raising the Updated event. Similar events exist for the Select(), Insert(), and Delete() methods.

Within the before event (Selecting, Inserting, Updating, or Deleting), you can perform whatever processing is needed. Maybe you need to check the parameter values and block any incorrect actions. The after event (Selected, Inserted, Updated, or Deleted) allows you to check how many rows were affected by the query and inspect any exceptions that were raised by the query.

In the examples in this chapter, you won't use the `SqlDataSource` events, or even manually call the `SqlDataSource` to execute a query. The `GridView`, `DetailsView`, and `FormView` provide the required functionality for you.

We're going to spend the majority of this chapter looking at the `GridView` and `DetailsView`. We'll cover the `FormView` as well, but in less detail. Once you know how the `DetailsView` works, you'll be able to use a `FormView` without any problems.

The GridView and DetailsView

As you've already seen, the `GridView` is used to show a set of results in a table. In the table, one row of data is one row from the database. In contrast, the `DetailsView` is used to show a single row from the database in a table. One row in the table is, generally, one column from the selected row in the database.

The easiest way to think of these two Web controls is that they have a master-detail relationship. The `GridView` is used to show the list of results, and the `DetailsView` shows a single row from the results in more detail. That's not to say that you must use them in conjunction; each can be used separately.

The Field Controls

One of the things that the `GridView` and `DetailsView` have in common is that they both contain a collection of Field Web controls. The `GridView` has a `Columns` collection, and the `DetailsView` has a `Fields` collection. The Field Web controls were introduced in Chapter 7 (see Table 7-5). However, three of the Field Web controls are of special interest when editing or updating data: `BoundField`, `CheckBoxField`, and `TemplateField`.

The `BoundField` appears as a string of text when viewing data. When editing or updating data, it's displayed as a `TextBox`. The `CheckBoxField` is shown as a disabled `CheckBox` when viewing data, and is enabled when editing or inserting data.

As you learned in Chapter 7, the `TemplateField` is the most customizable of the Field Web controls. Within the `TemplateField`, you're free to define whatever look and feel you want for the different parts of the display and also what to display, depending on the mode of the `GridView` or `DetailsView`. The templates for the `GridView` that support displaying data were introduced in Chapter 7 (see Table 7-7). The following are the two additional templates for editing data:

- `EditItemTemplate`: Specifies the content to be displayed when the `GridView` or `DetailsView` is editing data. If not specified when editing data, the `ItemTemplate` (or `AlternatingItemTemplate`) will be used, effectively making the Field read-only.

- `InsertItemTemplate`: Specifies the content to be displayed when adding new data in a `DetailsView`. If not specified, the `EditItemTemplate` will be used when adding new data. If there is no `EditItemTemplate`, the `ItemTemplate` (or `AlternatingItemTemplate`) will be used instead, making the Field effectively read-only.

The EmptyDataTemplate

What if the `SELECT` query that is executed returns no results? The `GridView` and `DetailsView` won't have any data to display, so nothing will appear on the page. It's true that the `GridView` and DetailsView can't make things appear when there's no data, but that doesn't help the user. It would be better to show them some sort of message indicating that no results were returned.

In previous versions of ASP.NET, you were left with a "hack" of using a hidden Web control that you made visible manually if no results were present, to inform the user that there had been a problem. The GridView and DetailsView make this process a little easier by allowing you to add an EmptyItemTemplate, which is displayed whenever there is no data to display.

Here is a very simple declaration for an EmptyItemTemplate:

```
<asp:GridView ID="GridView1" runat="server" ...>
  <EmptyItemTemplate>
    <B>There are no manufacturers to display</B>
  </EmptyItemTemplate>
  <Columns>
    ...
  </Columns>
</asp:GridView>
```

As you'll see in the examples in this chapter, you can also make the EmptyItemTemplate quite functional, rather than just serving as a placeholder for messages.

The Eval() and Bind() Methods

In Chapter 7, when we looked at table binding, you saw that ASP.NET 2.0 added a shorthand method of binding data from the data source to the Web control. The Eval() method gives you easy access to the columns from the data source:

```
<%# Eval("[ManufacturerWebsite]") %>
```

And if you need to format the value from the column, you can add a format string to the Eval() method as well:

```
<%# Eval("[ManufacturerEmail]", "mailto:{0}") %>
```

The Eval() method is fine when all you want to do is show the column. But when you want to allow inline editing, the Eval() method doesn't work.

ASP.NET 2.0 introduces a new method, Bind(), that allows data to flow both ways: from the database to populate the Web control, and then back from the Web control when its value is required to send to the database. It has the same two overloads as the Eval() method. If you want to retrieve the column as it is, you specify the column name:

```
<%# Bind("[ManufacturerWebsite]") %>
```

And if you want to format the column, you specify a format string as well:

```
<%# Bind("[ManufacturerEmail]", "mailto:{0}") %>
```

You should use the method that is most appropriate. When the column is read-only, use the Eval() method. For example, in an ItemTemplate or AlternatingItemTemplate you should use Eval(), as the data will be read-only. If the column is read-write, use the Bind() method. For example, in an EditItemTemplate or an InsertItemTemplate for a column that is to be updated, use the Bind() method. If the column is not going to be updated, use the Eval() method.

As you learned in Chapter 7, all table-binding Web controls can use the `Eval()` method. However, a couple of restrictions apply to using the `Bind()` method:

- Only the `GridView`, `DetailsView`, and `FormView` support the `Bind()` method.

- You can use the `Bind()` method only if the data source is specified using the `DataSourceID` property; that is, if you're using a `SqlDataSource` to query the database.

The examples in this chapter follow both these rules, so you'll be able to use the `Bind()` method without any problems.

Editing Data in a GridView

The `GridView` doesn't support the addition of new data itself. It needs to be combined with the `DetailsView` or `FormView` to allow new data to be added. However, the `GridView` does allow you to update and delete existing data. We'll start out by creating a page for updating data.

Try It Out: Updating Data in a GridView

In this example, we'll use a `GridView` in a simple page that allows the basic details for a Player to be edited.

1. In Visual Web Developer, create a new Web site at `C:\BAND\Chapter09` and delete the auto-generated `Default.aspx` file.

2. Add a new `Web.config` file to the Web site and add a new setting to the `<connectionStrings />` element:

   ```
   <add name="SqlConnectionString"
       connectionString="Data Source=localhost\BAND;Initial Catalog=Players;
           Persist Security Info=True;User ID=band;Password=letmein"
       providerName="System.Data.SqlClient" />
   ```

3. Add a new Web Form to the Web site called `Players_Basic.aspx`. Make sure that the Place Code in Separate File check box is unchecked.

4. In the Source view, find the `<title>` tag and change the page title to **Players**.

5. Switch to the Design view and add a `SqlDataSource` to the page. From the Tasks menu, select Configure Data Source.

6. Select `SqlConnectionString` as the data connection, and then click the Next button.

7. Create a query that selects the PlayerID, PlayerName, PlayerManufacturerID, PlayerCost, and PlayerStorage columns from the Player table.

8. Click the Advanced button. In the Advanced SQL Generation Options dialog box, click the Generate INSERT, UPDATE, and DELETE statements check box, as shown in Figure 9-1.

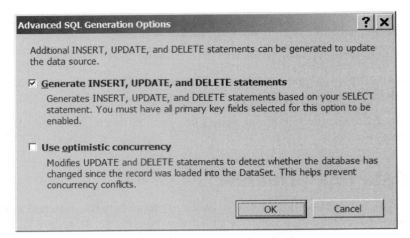

Figure 9-1. *Auto-generating INSERT, UPDATE, and DELETE queries*

9. Click the OK button to close the dialog box, and then click the Next button in the Configure Data Source dialog box. You can test the SELECT query if you wish on the next step. Click the Finish button to close the Configure Data Source wizard.

10. Add a GridView to the page and select SqlDataSource1 as the data source for the Web control. Select the Enable Editing and Enable Deleting options. This will configure the columns correctly for the GridView based on the SELECT query and also add Edit and Delete links to each row, as shown in Figure 9-2.

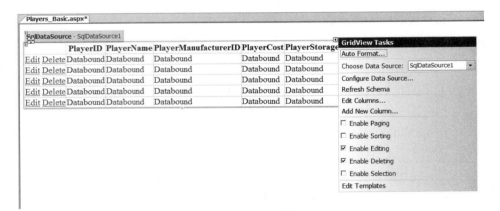

Figure 9-2. *Enabling editing and deleting for a GridView*

11. On the `GridView` Tasks menu, click the Edit Templates option. You'll now see that you can enter the details for the `EmptyDataTemplate`, as shown in Figure 9-3.

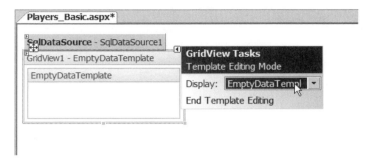

Figure 9-3. *Defining the EmptyDataTemplate*

12. Enter **There are no players to display** for the `EmptyDataTemplate`, and then click the End Template Editing option on the Tasks menu.

13. Save the page, and then open it in your browser. As shown in Figure 9-4, you'll see the list of all of the Players in the database, along with Edit and Delete links for each row.

	PlayerID	PlayerName	PlayerManufacturerID	PlayerCost	PlayerStorage
Edit Delete	1	iPod Shuffle	1	99.00	Solid State
Edit Delete	2	MuVo V200	2	96.00	Solid State
Edit Delete	3	iFP-700 Series	3	149.00	Solid State
Edit Delete	4	iFP-900 Series	3	149.00	Solid State
Edit Delete	5	MegaPlayer 521	4	199.00	Solid State
Edit Delete	6	Forge	5	93.00	Solid State
Edit Delete	7	Digital Audio Player	6	119.00	Solid State
Edit Delete	8	Network Walkman NW-E99	7	135.00	Solid State
Edit Delete	9	iPod	1	209.00	Hard Disk
Edit Delete	10	iPod Mini	1	169.00	Hard Disk

Figure 9-4. *Each row in the GridView has Edit and Delete links.*

14. Click the Edit link for the first row in the table. The page will be posted back to the server and the row placed into `Edit` mode, as shown in Figure 9-5.

15. Change the data and click the Update link. The page will refresh, and the `GridView` will be updated to reflect the changes.

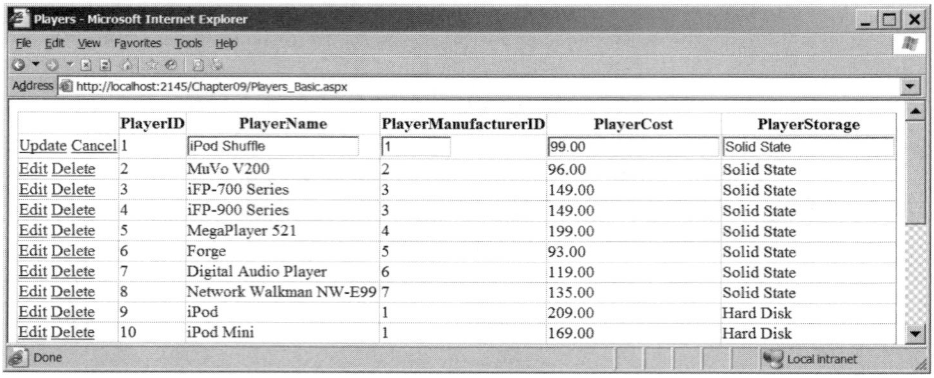

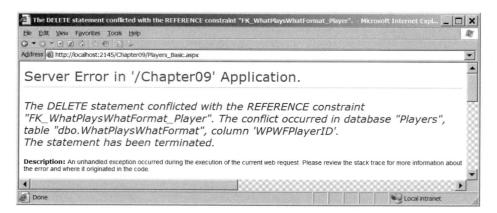

Figure 9-5. *Rows can be edited inline.*

16. Click the Delete link for the first row. Maybe you won't be surprised to see that you get a runtime error, as shown in Figure 9-6.

Figure 9-6. *We can't delete Players from the database.*

17. Switch back to the Design view in Visual Web Developer and add a Label between the SqlDataSource and GridView. Set its ID to lblError, Visible to False, ForeColor to Red, and remove the Text value.

18. Add a RowDeleted event to the GridView and add the following code to the event handler:

```
protected void GridView1_RowDeleted(object sender,
  GridViewDeletedEventArgs e)
{
  if (e.Exception != null)
  {
    lblError.Visible = true;
    lblError.Text = e.Exception.Message;
    e.ExceptionHandled = true;
  }
}
```

19. Also add a `Page_Load` event, and then add the following code to the event handler:

```
protected void Page_Load(object sender, EventArgs e)
{
  lblError.Visible = false;
}
```

20. Save the page. Now try to delete a Player. Instead of the ASP.NET error message, you'll receive a nicer warning, as shown in Figure 9-7.

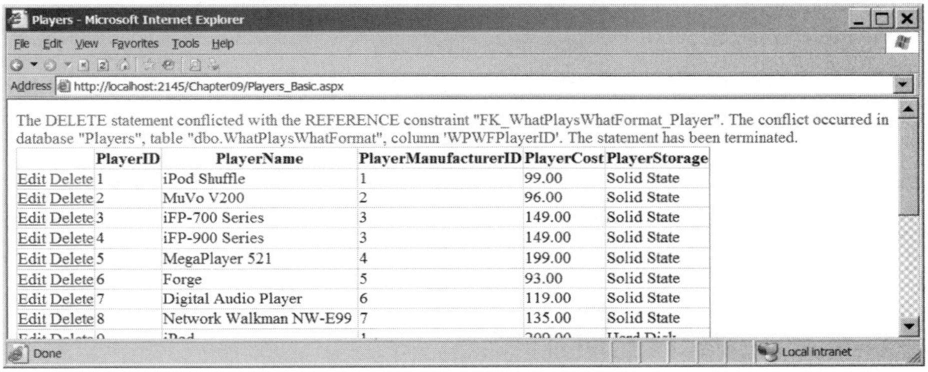

Figure 9-7. *Handling errors that occur during database operations*

How It Works

With only a few lines of code, you've built a page that allows you to edit information for the Players in the database. It's not perfect though, as the error you received when trying to delete a Player from the database shows.

Deleting Players from the database isn't the only problem, however. The page that you've built has at least four problems:

- **The page isn't very user-friendly**. Instead of showing the name of the Manufacturer, you're showing the PlayerManufacturerID. Now you may know that a value of 1 for PlayerManufacturerID corresponds to Apple, but what about the others?

- **You can't delete a Player from the database**. As you learned in Chapter 8, whenever you modify the database, you're bound by the database rules. In the sample database, Players are part of a relationship with the WhatPlaysWhatFormat table. As the error in Figure 9-6 shows, the Player is part of a relationship with the WhatPlaysWhatFormat table, and the constraints in the database prevent you from deleting a Player without deleting the referencing rows from the WhatPlaysWhatFormat table first.

- **You can't add a new Player to the database**. Although the GridView allows you to edit and delete data, it doesn't allow you to add new data.

- **You can't deal with the Player's supported Formats**. The GridView allows you to handle details from the Player table and, with a little more work, also the relationship to the Manufacturer of the Player, but it doesn't allow you to handle the many-to-many relationship with the Formats that the Player may support.

The first two problems can be resolved by making some modifications to the way that you use the GridView, as you'll see in the next two examples. In order to add a new Player to the database, you need to use one of the GridView's siblings: either a DetailsView or a FormView. We'll look at both of these Web controls later in the chapter and build a new example that allows you to add new Players to the database.

The supported Formats cause the most problems. How do you deal with the Formats that the Player supports? Recall that the Player and Format tables are involved in a many-to-many relationship. This is mapped to two one-to-many relationships via the WhatPlaysWhatFormat table, as shown in Figure 9-8.

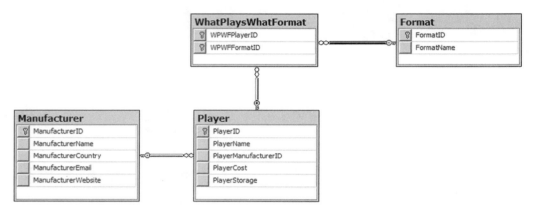

Figure 9-8. *The relationships in the database*

You can handle the Player-to-Manufacturer relationship by allowing the user to change the value of the PlayerManufacturerID value in the Player table. At the moment, the user must change the value manually, but in the next example, you'll see how to make the interface more user-friendly.

It's the Player-to-Format relationship that causes the problem. It's a many-to-many relationship, via the WhatPlaysWhatFormat intermediary table, and you can't model this automatically. You saw in Chapter 8 that you need to write some relatively complex code to model this relationship.

The GridView can't handle this relationship easily. When dealing with a complex database relationship such as this, you're better off using an alternative. Indeed, the examples that you saw in Chapter 8 are the best way to handle modifications to the Player table.

■**Note** In the code download for this chapter, you'll find two pages, Manufacturers_Details.aspx and Formats_Details.aspx, that allow you to manage the Manufacturer and Format tables. Here, you used the Player table, because that demonstrates more of the GridView's capabilities. The other tables contain only text.

Now that we've established that there are problems with the GridView and why it's not suitable in all cases, we'll look at what it actually does.

Auto-Generated SQL Queries

When adding a `SqlDataSource` that supports modifications to the database, you follow the normal process for adding the Web control. The Configure Data Source wizard allows you to define the `SELECT` query that you want to execute, and you can also test that this is returning the correct results by testing the query. However, you also need to define `INSERT`, `UPDATE`, and `DELETE` queries in order for the changes to be propagated back to the database.

You can define these queries manually, or you can ask the Configure Data Source wizard to generate these queries automatically by checking the Generate INSERT, UPDATE, and DELETE statements check box in the wizard, as shown earlier in Figure 9-1. If you select this option, you'll see that the wizard has not only added the `SelectCommand` property to the `SqlDataSource`, but also `InsertCommand`, `UpdateCommand`, and `DeleteCommand` properties as well:

```
<asp:SqlDataSource ID="SqlDataSource1" runat="server"
  ConnectionString="<%$ ConnectionStrings:SqlConnectionString %>"
  DeleteCommand="DELETE FROM Player WHERE PlayerID = @PlayerID"
  InsertCommand="INSERT INTO Player (PlayerName, PlayerManufacturerID,
    PlayerStorage, PlayerCost) VALUES (@PlayerName,
    @PlayerManufacturerID, @PlayerStorage, @PlayerCost)"
  SelectCommand="SELECT PlayerID, PlayerName, PlayerManufacturerID,
    PlayerStorage, PlayerCost FROM Player"
  UpdateCommand="UPDATE Player SET PlayerName = @PlayerName,
    PlayerManufacturerID = @PlayerManufacturerID, PlayerStorage =
    @PlayerStorage, PlayerCost = @PlayerCost WHERE PlayerID = @PlayerID">
```

The wizard has automatically determined what the different queries should be from the information that you've supplied for the `SELECT` query. It also had to query the structure of the table to work out the primary key. If you look at the `DeleteCommand` and `UpdateCommand` properties, you'll see that the queries are constrained by a `WHERE` clause for the PlayerID column.

You'll see that the three auto-generated queries are parameterized, and the wizard has also queried the database for the types of these parameters and added the parameters to the `SqlDataSource` definition:

```
<DeleteParameters>
  <asp:Parameter Name="PlayerID" Type="Int32" />
</DeleteParameters>
<UpdateParameters>
  <asp:Parameter Name="PlayerName" Type="String" />
  <asp:Parameter Name="PlayerManufacturerID" Type="Int32" />
  <asp:Parameter Name="PlayerStorage" Type="String" />
  <asp:Parameter Name="PlayerCost" Type="Decimal" />
  <asp:Parameter Name="PlayerID" Type="Int32" />
</UpdateParameters>
<InsertParameters>
  <asp:Parameter Name="PlayerName" Type="String" />
  <asp:Parameter Name="PlayerManufacturerID" Type="Int32" />
  <asp:Parameter Name="PlayerStorage" Type="String" />
  <asp:Parameter Name="PlayerCost" Type="Decimal" />
</InsertParameters>
```

The wizard has auto-generated the three required queries automatically and added the parameters to the SqlDataSource definition. But there may be instances where you want to define your own INSERT, UPDATE, and DELETE queries. You can do this manually by modifying the relevant Command property and adding the correct parameters for the query. If you use stored procedures (which we'll look at in Chapter 10), you'll usually need to create the queries for the SqlDataSource manually and specify the parameters to be passed to the query.

Another option when specifying the different queries for the SqlDataSource is to use the Command and Parameter Editor. You've already seen this in action for building SELECT queries, but it also handles INSERT, UPDATE, and DELETE queries.

If you look at the properties for the SqlDataSource, you'll see that, as well as the SelectQuery property, you also have DeleteQuery, InsertQuery, and UpdateQuery properties. Clicking the ellipsis for any of these properties launches the Command and Parameter Editor dialog box, as shown in Figure 9-9 for the UpdateQuery property.

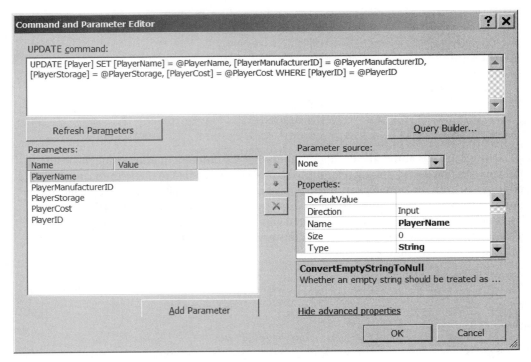

Figure 9-9. *Parameters can be defined using the Command and Parameter Editor dialog box.*

The Command and Parameter Editor dialog box allows you to define the query that you want to execute, and then define the parameters for it as well. A quick shortcut is to specify the query, and then click the Refresh Parameters button to automatically extract the parameters and populate the Parameters collection. By clicking the Show Advanced Properties link, you can also further modify the parameters. The wizard has defined the types for each of the parameters, as you can see in Figure 9-9.

You can also graphically design the query by clicking the Query Builder button. This will launch the Query Builder dialog box, as shown in Figure 9-10.

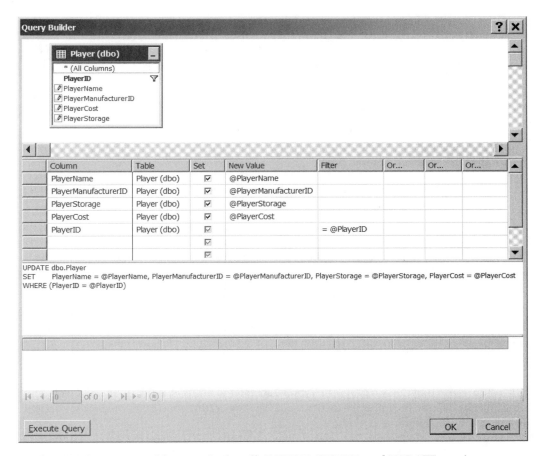

Figure 9-10. *The Query Builder can also handle DELETE, INSERT, and UPDATE queries.*

You can also test the query by clicking the Execute Query button. Be careful when testing INSERT, UPDATE, and DELETE queries, as you're going to be modifying the data in the database, and any changes you make are permanent.

Once you're happy with the query, you can close the Query Builder dialog box, and then use the Refresh Parameters button in the Command and Parameter Editor dialog box to build the correct Parameters collection.

The Editable GridView

Once the SqlDataSource has been configured correctly, you can use it as the data source for a GridView. The easiest way to do this is to select the data source from the Tasks menu for the GridView.

We've already looked at binding a SqlDataSource to a GridView. However, when you have an editable SqlDataSource, something else happens:

```
<asp:GridView ID="GridView1" runat="server" AutoGenerateColumns="False"
  DataKeyNames="PlayerID" DataSourceID="SqlDataSource1">
```

The DataKeyNames property has been added and set to the primary key, PlayerID, from the SELECT query that is being executed. This property is used by the GridView (and the DetailsView and FormView) to enable the INSERT, UPDATE, and DELETE queries to function. If you don't set this property correctly, the INSERT, UPDATE, and DELETE queries will not work.

A couple of properties are applied to the PlayerID BoundField as well:

```
<asp:BoundField DataField="PlayerID" HeaderText="PlayerID"
  InsertVisible="False" ReadOnly="True" SortExpression="PlayerID" />
```

The two highlighted properties are related to the fact that the PlayerID column is the primary key for the table that you're modifying:

- ReadOnly: You can't modify the primary key column for a row of data. Setting the ReadOnly property to True prevents the GridView from making this column editable.

- InsertVisible: When entering new data, you don't normally specify the primary key. By setting the InsertVisible property to False, you hide the column when you're adding new data to the database. With the GridView, this property doesn't affect anything, as you can't add new data using the GridView. However, when we look at using the DetailsView later in this chapter, you'll see this property in action.

Setting the GridView to allow editing and deleting has also added a new column, a CommandField, to the Columns collection. This column specifies which of the automatic actions you want the GridView to perform. In this case, you want Edit and Delete links:

```
<asp:CommandField ShowDeleteButton="True" ShowEditButton="True" />
```

You'll notice that the two properties you've set refer to buttons, rather than links. This isn't a mistake. By default, the GridView displays a LinkButton, rather than a Button. So, they appear as links on the pages you're building.

The CommandField column has several different properties that you can set. Not only can you add a couple other buttons, but you can also specify the text that the buttons show (the DeleteText and UpdateText properties) and change the type of button (using the ButtonType property). You'll see some of the other properties as we progress through this chapter.

■**Note** For a full discussion of the CommandField, refer to http://msdn.microsoft.com/en-us/library/system.web.ui.webcontrols.commandfield.aspx.

Editing a Row

Clicking the Edit link for a row of data posts the page back to the server and switches the GridView into Edit mode. Figure 9-11 shows the first row in Edit mode.

	PlayerID	PlayerName	PlayerManufacturerID	PlayerCost	PlayerStorage
Update Cancel	1	iPod Shuffle	1	99.00	Solid State

Figure 9-11. *A row in the GridView in Edit mode*

As you'll recall, the PlayerID column is specified as a ReadOnly column, so you can't modify this column. However, the remaining four columns have been turned into text boxes that can be modified.

A BoundField, when in Edit mode, is shown as a TextBox. There is no way to change this. If you need to use a different Web control, you'll need to change the column to a TemplateField and create the necessary templates. You'll do this in the next example.

The other change when in Edit mode is that the CommandField column has changed to show Update and Cancel links. If you decide you don't want to make any changes, click Cancel. If you're happy with the changes that you've made, click Update. Either way, the page is posted back to the server. If you clicked Update, the changes are made to the database, and the GridView is switched back into View mode. Any changes you've made will be visible immediately.

So how does the Update link work? The GridView populates the UpdateParameters collection in the bound SqlDataSource, and then calls the Update() method.

Handling Errors

As you saw, if you click the Delete link, an error is thrown by the database. Showing the ASP.NET error page to the user is not advisable and, if there is an error, you need to handle this gracefully and let the user know that an error has occurred without breaking the Web site.

The GridView (and the DetailsView and FormView) make this very simple. The after action events (Inserted, Updated, and Deleted) allow you to check to see if any errors have occurred and handle those errors. You can then tell the GridView that you've handled the error so that it isn't rethrown and the ASP.NET error page shown.

In this example, you just show the error message that is generated in a Label. In a real Web site, you may want to log the error to a file or by e-mail.

The error that you're dealing with arises when the DELETE query is called, so you need to add the Deleted event handler to the GridView (the same principal applies if you're executing an INSERT or UPDATE query and using the Inserted or Updated event handlers).

The argument to the Deleted event handler, a GridViewDeletedEventArgs object, has an Exception property that contains the exception that was raised, or null if no exception was raised. If the Exception property is not null, you know an error has occurred, and you can show this to the user:

```
if (e.Exception != null)
{
  lblError.Visible = true;
  lblError.Text = e.Exception.Message;
  e.ExceptionHandled = true;
}
```

You first make sure the Label is visible, and then show the exact Message to the user. You also set the ExceptionHandled property of the GridViewDeletedEventArgs object to true to indicate that you've handled the error.

By saying that you've handled the error, you're telling the GridView not to worry about it, and the users won't see the ASP.NET error page. Instead, they will see your nice, red error message.

■**Note** You'll notice that you haven't added error handling for the UPDATE query to this example. Nor do you add any new error handling to any of the examples from this point forward. The process for handling errors is the same for INSERT, UPDATE, and DELETE, so once you've seen it, adding it again (and again and again) to the examples will just make them longer for no added benefit.

Try It Out: Changing Controls Used for Editing

In this example, you'll expand on the previous example by changing the Web control that is used for setting the Manufacturer for a Player. Rather than using a TextBox, you'll populate a DropDownList with the list of Manufacturers and let the users select which Manufacturer they want.

1. Open Players_Basic.aspx from the previous example.

2. Add a second SqlDataSource to the page (this will be given an ID of SqlDataSource2). Use the SqlConnectionString to connect to the correct database, and set the SelectCommand to the following:

```
SELECT ManufacturerID, ManufacturerName
FROM Manufacturer
ORDER BY ManufacturerName
```

3. Switch to the Source view and change the SelectCommand for SqlDataSource1 to the following:

```
SELECT PlayerID, PlayerName, ManufacturerName,
  PlayerManufacturerID, PlayerStorage, PlayerCost
FROM Player INNER JOIN Manufacturer
  ON Player.PlayerManufacturerID = Manufacturer.ManufacturerID
```

4. Replace the PlayerManufacturerID BoundField with the following TemplateField:

```
<asp:TemplateField HeaderText="Manufacturer"
  SortExpression="ManufacturerName">
  <ItemTemplate>
    <asp:Literal ID="litManufacturer" runat="server"
      Text='<%# Eval("ManufacturerName") %>'>
    </asp:Literal>
  </ItemTemplate>
  <EditItemTemplate>
    <asp:DropDownList id="lstManufacturer" runat="server"
      DataSourceID="SqlDataSource2"
      DataTextField="ManufacturerName" DataValueField="ManufacturerID"
      SelectedValue='<%# Bind("PlayerManufacturerID") %>'>
    </asp:DropDownList>
  </EditItemTemplate>
</asp:TemplateField>
```

5. Save the page and view it in your browser. You'll see that the Manufacturer column now appears with the name of the Manufacturer, rather than the ID value, as shown in Figure 9-12.

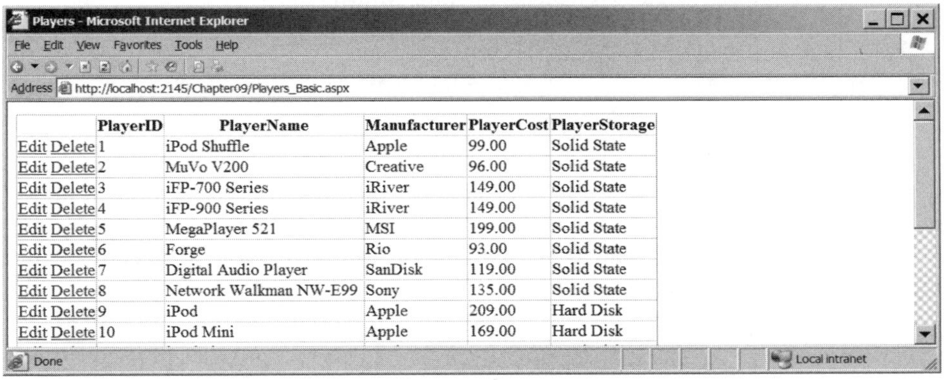

Figure 9-12. *The Manufacturer is now shown in a meaningful fashion.*

6. Click the Edit option. You'll see that the Manufacturer can now be selected from a DropDownList, as shown in Figure 9-13.

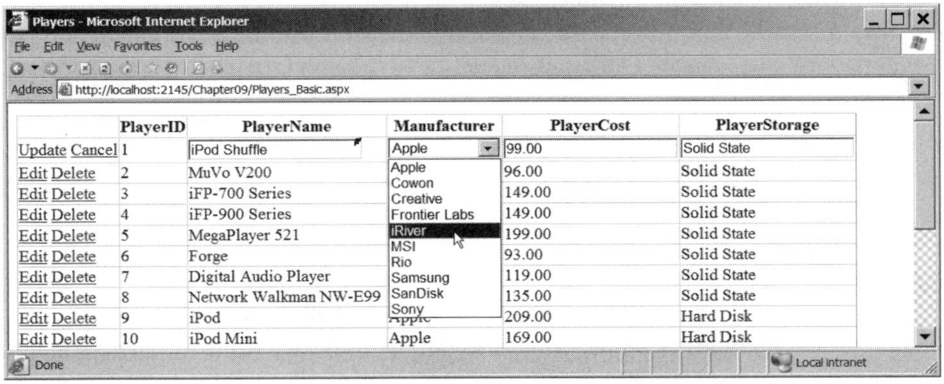

Figure 9-13. *You can now select the Manufacturer from a DropDownList.*

How It Works

Rather than forcing the user to remember all of the different values for the Manufacturers, you're allowing the user to select the Manufacturer from a DropDownList. You need to populate this DropDownList with a list of Manufacturers, so you use a second SqlDataSource to return the Manufacturers with a simple SELECT query:

```
SELECT ManufacturerID, ManufacturerName
FROM Manufacturer
ORDER BY ManufacturerName
```

You'll use this shortly to populate the DropDownList, but you also change the SelectCommand query to populate the GridView with all of the Players. Although you have the PlayerManufacturerID and can use this to set the DropDownList to the correct value, the value is not meaningful to the user. So, you modify the existing SELECT query to return the ManufacturerName, as well as the PlayerManufacturerID:

```
SELECT PlayerID, PlayerName, ManufacturerName,
  PlayerManufacturerID, PlayerStorage, PlayerCost
FROM Player INNER JOIN Manufacturer
  ON Player.PlayerManufacturerID = Manufacturer.ManufacturerID
```

You've changed only the SELECT query and not modified the INSERT, UPDATE, or DELETE queries. You're going to modify only the Player table, and the fact that you're returning the ManufacturerName is irrelevant as far as modifying the Player table is concerned. You return this only for display to the user.

In order to display a DropDownList, you need to replace the BoundField with a TemplateField:

```
<asp:TemplateField HeaderText="Manufacturer"
  SortExpression="ManufacturerName">
```

You set the HeaderText property to something meaningful and set the SortExpression to the values that you're going to show when the GridView is in View mode. Although you haven't enabled sorting or paging in this example, you'll notice that all of the BoundField columns have a SortExpression, and you add one here for completeness.

As you've seen in previous examples, within the TemplateField, you can define several different templates. The first one that you define here is the ItemTemplate displayed when the GridView is in View mode:

```
<ItemTemplate>
  <asp:Literal ID="litManufacturer" runat="server"
    Text='<%# Eval("ManufacturerName") %>'>
  </asp:Literal>
</ItemTemplate>
```

Within the ItemTemplate, you want to show the ManufacturerName, and you use a Literal to do this. You set the Text property to the ManufacturerName using the Eval() method. You don't need to edit the ManufacturerName, so you can use the Eval() method, as this allows one-way binding.

You also define an EditItemTemplate that will be displayed when the GridView is in Edit mode:

```
<EditItemTemplate>
  <asp:DropDownList id="lstManufacturer" runat="server"
    DataSourceID="SqlDataSource2"
    DataTextField="ManufacturerName" DataValueField="ManufacturerID"
    SelectedValue='<%# Bind("PlayerManufacturerID") %>'>
  </asp:DropDownList>
</EditItemTemplate>
```

We looked at data binding the DropDownList in some depth in Chapter 7. You're using SqlDataSource2 as the data source, and then specifying the DataTextField and the DataValueField correctly. The property that we're really interested in here is SelectedValue.

You're going to set the SelectedValue to the value returned as the PlayerManufacturerID. By using the Bind() method, you can perform two-way data binding. When an update occurs, the currently selected value in the DropDownList will be passed to the PlayerManufacturerID parameter.

Try It Out: Deleting Data in a GridView

As you saw earlier, the Player table is part of a relationship with the WhatPlaysWhatFormat table, and the constraints in the database prevent you from performing deletions from the Player without deleting the referencing rows from WhatPlaysWhatFormat table. Now you will update the earlier example to allow Players to be deleted from the database.

1. Open Players_Basic.aspx from the previous example.

2. Add the required Import statement to the top of the page:

```
<%@ Import Namespace="System.Data.SqlClient" %>
```

3. In the Design view, select the GridView. From the Properties window, add the RowDeleting event. Within the RowDeleting event handler, add the following code:

```
protected void GridView1_RowDeleting(object sender,
  GridViewDeleteEventArgs e)
{
  // create the connection
  string strConnectionString = ConfigurationManager.
    ConnectionStrings["SqlConnectionString"].ConnectionString;
  SqlConnection myConnection = new SqlConnection(strConnectionString);

  try
  {
    // query to execute
    string strQuery = "DELETE FROM WhatPlaysWhatFormat ➥
      WHERE WPWFPlayerID = @PlayerID;";

    // create the command
    SqlCommand myCommand = new SqlCommand(strQuery, myConnection);

    // add the parameter
    myCommand.Parameters.AddWithValue("@PlayerID", e.Keys["PlayerID"]);

    // open the connection
    myConnection.Open();
```

```
      // execute the command
      myCommand.ExecuteNonQuery();
    }
    catch (Exception ex)
    {
      lblError.Visible = true;
      lblError.Text = ex.Message;
      e.Cancel = true;
    }
    finally
    {
      // close the connection
      myConnection.Close();
    }
  }
```

4. Save the page, and then view it in your browser. If you now delete one of the Players, you'll see that the page no longer reports an error. The Player is deleted from the database.

How It Works

As you've learned, the main constraint when modifying the contents of the database is that you must work to the database rules. You can't delete from the Player table if there is related data in the WhatPlaysWhatFormat table. You must delete that data before you delete the Player itself.

When you click the Delete link, there is no more interaction from the user, and the GridView takes full control. It populates the DeleteParameters collection of the bound SqlDataSource, and then calls the Delete() method. A couple of events are raised, as well as the DELETE itself being performed:

- The RowDeleting event is raised.

- The DELETE query (via the SqlDataSource) is executed.

- The RowDeleted event is raised.

As you must make changes to the database before you allow the Player itself to be deleted, you need to use the RowDeleting event to delete the related information.

Within the RowDeleting event handler, you perform a simple DELETE from the WhatPlaysWhatFormat table:

```
DELETE FROM WhatPlaysWhatFormat
WHERE WPWFPlayerID = @PlayerID
```

You have a parameterized query that requires the PlayerID. You don't have direct access to this value, but you can retrieve it from the GridViewDeleteEventArgs parameter. The Keys collection contains all of the keys for the row in question, as specified by the DataKeyNames property of the GridView.

You can retrieve the current value for the specified key by indexing on the name of the column:

```
myCommand.Parameters.AddWithValue("@PlayerID", e.Keys["PlayerID"]);
```

You then use the `ExecuteNonQuery()` method to execute the `DELETE` query. This deletes the related data from the WhatPlaysWhatFormat table, and you can then let the `GridView` delete the data from the Player table.

■**Note** It's fine to simply delete the related data within the database when you delete a Player. The Formats that the Player supports are owned by the Player, so deleting the related data doesn't affect any data that it shouldn't. The same isn't true for the Manufacturer and Format tables: you can't delete a Manufacturer or a Format if they're in use. In the code download, you'll find that `Manufacturers_Details.aspx` and `Formats_Details.aspx` prevent any deletions from being made if the Manufacturer or Format is in use.

You'll notice that you're also catching any errors that may occur during the `DELETE` against the WhatPlaysWhatFormat table:

```
catch (Exception ex)
{
  lblError.Visible = true;
  lblError.Text = ex.Message;
  e.Cancel = true;
}
```

As with the earlier example, whenever there is an error, you display the error to the user using the `Label`. You're also setting the `Cancel` property of the `GridViewDeleteEventArgs` object to `true`. This tells the `GridView` that you don't want the `DELETE` operation to take place—as there has been an error, you don't want another error to potentially occur when you try to delete the data from the Player table.

■**Note** As I've already pointed out, we're not going to add error handling to all of the examples that you're going to build. The techniques for dealing with errors are exactly the same for the `GridView`, `DetailsView`, and `FormView`. You should be able to add error handling to the different Web controls easily, now that you know how it is accomplished.

Using the DetailsView

Although you now have an editable `GridView`, you don't have a way to add new Players to the database. You could build a new page to do this, as you saw in Chapter 8. Alternatively, you could use a `DetailsView` in conjunction with the `GridView` to allow new Players to be added. However, the `DetailsView` actually allows you to edit and delete data, as well as add it.

Try It Out: Showing Data in a DetailsView

In this first example, you'll build a new page that uses a GridView and a DetailsView to show the Players in the database. The following examples will build on this to allow the user to edit, delete, and add Players.

1. Add a new Web Form to the Web site called Players_Details.aspx. Make sure that the Place Code in Separate File check box is unchecked.

2. In the Source view, find the <title> tag within the HTML at the bottom of the page and change the page title to **Players**.

3. Switch to the Design view and add a SqlDataSource to the top of the page. Use the SqlConnectionString to connect to the database. On the Configure the Select Statement step, click the Specify a Custom SQL Statement or Stored Procedure option, and then click the Next button.

4. Enter the following SQL query:

```
SELECT PlayerID, PlayerName, ManufacturerName
FROM Player INNER JOIN Manufacturer
  ON Player.PlayerManufacturerID = Manufacturer.ManufacturerID
```

5. Click Next, and then click Finish to close the Configure Data Source wizard.

6. Switch to the Source view and add the following table definition to the page after the SqlDataSource markup:

```
<table>
  <tr>
    <td valign="top"></td>
    <td valign="top"></td>
  </tr>
</table>
```

7. Switch back to the Design view and add a GridView to the page in the first cell of the table. From the Tasks menu, set the data source to SqlDataSource1 and check the Enable Selection check box.

8. From the Tasks menu, select the Auto Format option and select a format, such as Colorful.

9. Switch to the Source view and add a DataKeyNames property to the GridView:

```
<asp:GridView ID="GridView1" runat="server" AutoGenerateColumns="False"
  DataSourceID="SqlDataSource1" DataKeyNames="PlayerID">
```

10. Add a second SqlDataSource to the page (which will be called SqlDataSource2 auto-matically). Again, use the SqlConnectionString to connect to the database. On the Configure the Select Statement step, click the Specify a Custom SQL Statement or Stored Procedure option, and then click the Next button.

Enter the following SQL query:

```
SELECT PlayerID, PlayerName, ManufacturerName, PlayerCost, PlayerStorage
FROM Player INNER JOIN Manufacturer
  ON Player.PlayerManufacturerID = Manufacturer.ManufacturerID
WHERE (PlayerID = @PlayerID)
```

11. Click Next. On the Define Parameters step, set the Parameter Source to Control and the ControlID to GridView1, as shown in Figure 9-14.

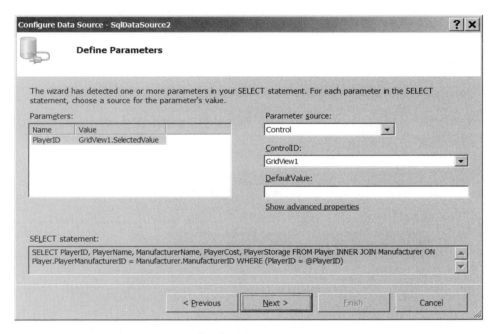

Figure 9-14. *Setting the parameters for the SELECT query*

12. Click Next, and then click Finish to close the Configure Data Source wizard.

13. Add a DetailsView to the page in the second cell of the table. Set its data source to SqlDataSource2.

14. Switch to the Source view and add an EmptyDataTemplate to the DetailsView:

```
<EmptyDataTemplate>
  Please select a player from the list
</EmptyDataTemplate>
```

15. Save the page, and then view it in your browser. Initially, no Player will be selected, so the DetailsView will show the EmptyDataTemplate, as shown in Figure 9-15.

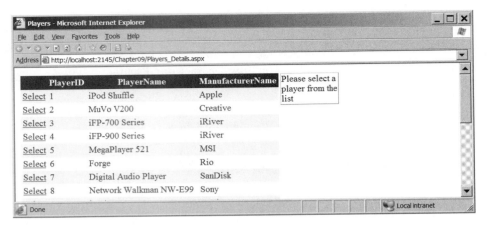

Figure 9-15. *If no Player is selected, the EmptyDataTemplate is displayed.*

16. Click the Select link for a row, and you will see the details for the Player in the DetailsView, as shown in Figure 9-16.

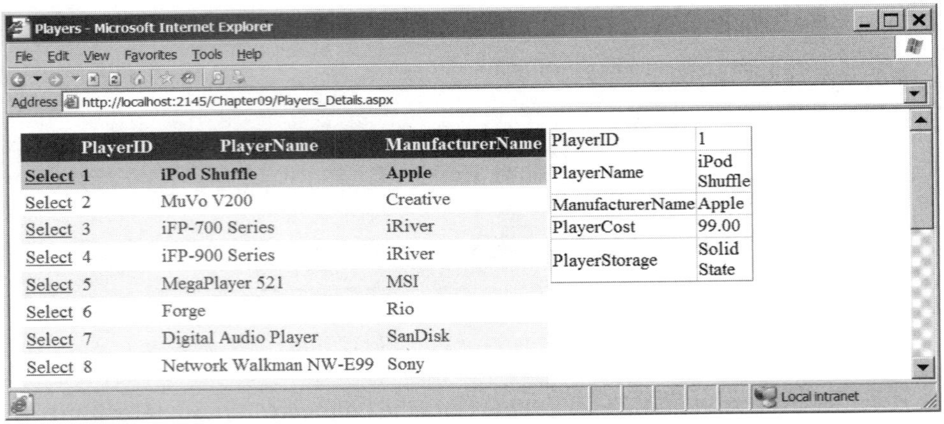

Figure 9-16. *Viewing the details for the Player*

How It Works

In this example, you use a GridView to show the list of Players and then a DetailsView to show the details for the Player. If you haven't selected a Player from the GridView, the DetailsView shows the EmptyDataTemplate. When you do select a Player, the DetailsView shows the details for that Player.

Rather than show all of the details for the Players in the GridView, you show only a subset, using the following SELECT query:

```
SELECT PlayerID, PlayerName, ManufacturerName
FROM Player INNER JOIN Manufacturer
  ON Player.PlayerManufacturerID = Manufacturer.ManufacturerID
```

This is a simple query, and you use this as the data source for the GridView. However, this time, you need to manually set the DataKeyNames property. Because it's not a query from a single table, the GridView is unable to work out what the primary key is for the query (is it the PlayerID from the Player table or the ManufacturerID from the Manufacturer table?), so you must manually specify that PlayerID is the primary key:

```
<asp:GridView ID="GridView1" runat="server" AutoGenerateColumns="False"
  DataSourceID="SqlDataSource1" DataKeyNames="PlayerID">
```

The DetailsView also uses a SqlDataSource as its data source. As you're selecting only a single Player from the table, you need to use a parameterized query:

```
SELECT PlayerID, PlayerName, ManufacturerName, PlayerCost, PlayerStorage
FROM Player INNER JOIN Manufacturer
  ON Player.PlayerManufacturerID = Manufacturer.ManufacturerID
WHERE (PlayerID = @PlayerID)
```

Using the Configure Data Source wizard, you also specified the details for the parameter, and this added a parameter to the SelectParameters collection:

```
<SelectParameters>
  <asp:ControlParameter Name="PlayerID" ControlID="GridView1"
    PropertyName="SelectedValue" />
</SelectParameters>
```

You're using the SelectedValue property of the GridView as the value of the parameter. And this is where the Select link in the GridView rows is used.

By clicking the Select link, you're causing a postback to occur, and the GridView to select the row. As you have a SelectedRowStyle defined (by virtue of selecting a format from the Auto Format dialog box), you can visually see that the row in the GridView has been selected.

Selecting a row in the GridView also sets the SelectedValue property. As the GridView has the PlayerID value set for the DataKeyNames property, the PlayerID for the selected row is returned as the SelectedValue, and this is used as the parameter to the filtered SqlDataSource.

■**Note** By default, the SelectedValue of a GridView is null, and when the page is first loaded, this value is passed to the filtered query when the DetailsView is data-bound. As none of the Players have a null value as a PlayerID, no data is returned, and the DetailsView displays the EmptyDataTemplate. However, the query to the database is still executed.

If you look at the `Fields` collection for the `DetailsView`, you'll see that it is remarkably similar to the `Columns` collection for the `GridView` in the previous example. As you've learned, the Fields are interchangeable between the two Web controls:

```
<Fields>
  <asp:BoundField DataField="PlayerID"
    HeaderText="PlayerID" SortExpression="PlayerID"
    InsertVisible="False" ReadOnly="True" />
  <asp:BoundField DataField="PlayerName"
    HeaderText="PlayerName" SortExpression="PlayerName" />
  <asp:BoundField DataField="ManufacturerName"
    HeaderText="ManufacturerName" SortExpression="ManufacturerName" />
  <asp:BoundField DataField="PlayerCost"
    HeaderText="PlayerCost" SortExpression="PlayerCost" />
  <asp:BoundField DataField="PlayerStorage"
    HeaderText="PlayerStorage" SortExpression="PlayerStorage" />
</Fields>
```

Now that you've seen how easy it is to view data in a `DetailsView`, let's turn our attention to editing the details. As you're using the same Web Field controls in both the `GridView` and `DetailsView`, you've probably guessed that editing in a `DetailsView` is very similar to editing in a `GridView`.

Try It Out: Editing Data in a DetailsView

You'll expand the previous example by adding the ability to edit the selected Player.

1. Open `Players_Details.aspx` from the previous example.

2. Switch to the Design view and select Configure Data Source from the Tasks menu for `SqlDataSource2`.

3. Click Next twice to skip to the Define Custom Statements or Stored Procedures step in the wizard.

4. Modify the `SELECT` query as follows:

   ```
   SELECT PlayerID, PlayerName, ManufacturerName, PlayerManufacturerID,
     PlayerCost, PlayerStorage
   FROM Player INNER JOIN Manufacturer
     ON Player.PlayerManufacturerID = Manufacturer.ManufacturerID
   WHERE (PlayerID = @PlayerID)
   ```

5. Click the UPDATE tab and enter the following query:

   ```
   UPDATE Player SET PlayerName = @PlayerName,
       PlayerManufacturerID = @PlayerManufacturerID,
       PlayerStorage = @PlayerStorage, PlayerCost = @PlayerCost
   WHERE PlayerID = @PlayerID
   ```

6. Click the Next button, and then click the Finish button to close the Configure Data Source wizard. Click No if prompted to Refresh Fields and Keys for DetailsView1.

7. From the Tasks menu for the DetailsView, select the Enable Editing option. You'll see that there is now an Edit link at the bottom of the DetailsView.

8. From the Properties window, add an event handler for the ItemUpdated event and add the following code to the event handler:

```
protected void DetailsView1_ItemUpdated(object sender,
  DetailsViewUpdatedEventArgs e)
{
  GridView1.DataBind();
}
```

9. Add a third SqlDataSource to the page (which will be called SqlDataSource3 automatically) and use SqlConnectionString to connect to the correct database. Use the following query to return the list of Manufacturers from the database:

```
SELECT ManufacturerID, ManufacturerName
FROM Manufacturer
ORDER BY ManufacturerName
```

10. Switch to the Source view and, in the DetailsView, replace the BoundField for the ManufacturerName with the following TemplateField:

```
<asp:TemplateField HeaderText="Manufacturer"
  SortExpression="ManufacturerName">
  <ItemTemplate>
    <asp:Literal ID="litManufacturer" runat="server"
      Text='<%# Eval("ManufacturerName") %>'>
    </asp:Literal>
  </ItemTemplate>
  <EditItemTemplate>
    <asp:DropDownList id="lstManufacturer" runat="server"
      DataSourceID="SqlDataSource3"
      DataTextField="ManufacturerName" DataValueField="ManufacturerID"
      SelectedValue='<%# Bind("PlayerManufacturerID") %>'>
    </asp:DropDownList>
  </EditItemTemplate>
</asp:TemplateField>
```

11. Save the page, and then view it in your browser. Clicking the Select link for a row will show the details for the Player in the DetailsView, as you saw in the previous example. Clicking the Edit link will allow you to edit the Player, as shown in Figure 9-17.

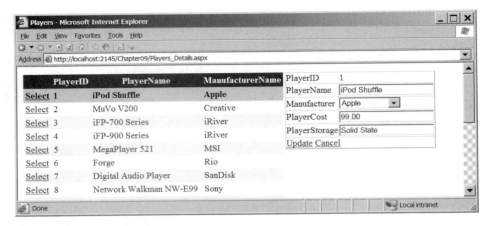

Figure 9-17. *Editing the details for the Player*

12. Change the details and click the Update link. You'll see that the changes are made to the database, and the GridView is updated to show the changes.

How It Works

All the changes you've made here should be familiar to you by now. The SELECT query that you're executing to populate the DetailsView is the same query that you used in the GridView example previously. Also, the UPDATE query is the same (and it probably won't come as a shock that the next example uses the same DELETE query).

The one thing that is slightly different is the UpdateParameters collection. Although the collection has been created with the correct parameters, none of them have a Type specified:

```
<UpdateParameters>
  <asp:Parameter Name="PlayerName" />
  <asp:Parameter Name="PlayerManufacturerID" />
  <asp:Parameter Name="PlayerStorage" />
  <asp:Parameter Name="PlayerCost" />
  <asp:Parameter Name="PlayerID" />
</UpdateParameters>
```

Because you've manually specified the UPDATE query that you want to execute, rather than letting the wizard auto-generate the query, the wizard has no idea of the types of the columns. It has parsed the query correctly and identified the parameter names, but not their types. Thankfully, you don't actually need the types, but if you want to add a Type property for each of the parameters, you can.

You'll also notice that the TemplateField definition is the same one that you used earlier to show the Manufacturer details in a more user-friendly manner. The SqlDataSource that the DropDownList binds to should also be very familiar, since it's the same query you used earlier to return a list of Manufacturers.

That's not to say that you've seen everything here before. There are a couple of new things to consider!

The first is the configuration of the DetailsView. Once you've added an UPDATE query to the SqlDataSource, the DetailsView acquires a new option on its Tasks menu: Enable Editing. Selecting this option adds a CommandField to the Fields collection:

```
<asp:CommandField ShowEditButton="True" />
```

Not surprisingly, this has the same effect in the DetailsView as it does in the GridView: it switches the DetailsView into Edit mode. You can then modify the data as you require and click either the Update or Cancel link to return to view mode, or as the DetailsView likes to think of it, ReadOnly mode.

Clicking the Update link saves the changes to the database, and you then need to ensure that the GridView is showing the updated data. In order to do this, you use the ItemUpdated event of the DetailsView:

```
protected void DetailsView1_ItemUpdated(object sender,
  DetailsViewUpdatedEventArgs e)
{
  GridView1.DataBind();
}
```

This will ensure that the GridView binds to the updated data in the database. If you don't call the DataBind() method, the GridView will still show the old data. The GridView will request data from the database only on the initial page load, and it will still show the old data unless you tell it that it needs to retrieve new data. Manually calling the DataBind() method forces the GridView to retrieve new data from the database.

Try It Out: Deleting Data in a DetailsView

Now that you know how to edit data, let's look at how to delete data.

1. Open Players_Details.aspx from the previous example.

2. Add the required Import statement to the top of the page:

   ```
   <%@ Import Namespace="System.Data.SqlClient" %>
   ```

3. Switch to the Design view and select Configure Data Source from the Tasks menu for SqlDataSource2.

4. Click Next twice to skip to the Define Custom Statements or Stored Procedures step in the wizard.

5. Select the DELETE tab and enter the following query:

   ```
   DELETE FROM Player
   WHERE PlayerID = @PlayerID
   ```

6. Click the Next button, and then click the Finish button to close the Configure Data Source wizard.

7. From the Tasks menu for the DetailsView, select the Enable Deleting option. You'll see that there is now a Delete link at the bottom of the DetailsView.

8. In the Properties window, add an ItemDeleting event for the DetailsView. Add the following code to the event handler:

```
protected void DetailsView1_ItemDeleting(object sender,
  DetailsViewDeleteEventArgs e)
{
  // create the connection
  string strConnectionString = ConfigurationManager.
    ConnectionStrings["SqlConnectionString"].ConnectionString;
  SqlConnection myConnection = new SqlConnection(strConnectionString);

  try
  {
    // query to execute
    string strQuery = "DELETE FROM WhatPlaysWhatFormat ➡
      WHERE WPWFPlayerID = @PlayerID;";

    // create the command
    SqlCommand myCommand = new SqlCommand(strQuery, myConnection);

    // add the parameter
    myCommand.Parameters.AddWithValue("@PlayerID", e.Keys["PlayerID"]);

    // open the connection
    myConnection.Open();

    // execute the command
    myCommand.ExecuteNonQuery();
  }
  finally
  {
    // close the connection
    myConnection.Close();
  }
}
```

9. Add an ItemDeleted event handler for the DetailsView and add the following code to the event handler:

```
protected void DetailsView1_ItemDeleted(object sender,
  DetailsViewDeletedEventArgs e)
{
  GridView1.SelectedIndex = -1;
  GridView1.DataBind();
}
```

10. Save the page, and then view it in your browser. Clicking the Select link for a row will show the details for the Player in the DetailsView, as you saw in the previous example. Clicking the Delete link will delete the Player from the database and update the list of Players displayed by the GridView.

How It Works

You've added a new button to the CommandField, and you're now displaying a Delete link as well as an Edit link:

```
<asp:CommandField ShowEditButton="True" ShowDeleteButton="True" />
```

As you're still working to the database rules, you need to make sure that you're deleting any data in the WhatPlaysWhatFormat table before you delete the data from the Player table. The GridView has a RowDeleting event, and the DetailsView has a corresponding ItemDeleting event. In this event, you use the same code as you saw in the RowDeleting event earlier to delete any related data that is in the WhatPlaysWhatFormat table.

When you click the Delete link and delete the data from the database, you also need to make sure that the GridView is binding to the latest version of the data in the database, and you use the ItemDeleted event of the DetailsView to call the DataBind() method of the GridView. You also set the SelectedIndex of the GridView to -1, so that your previous selection is removed. If it isn't, the "next" Player in the GridView will be selected, as it now has the row index of the deleted Player.

Try It Out: Adding Data in a DetailsView

Now that you can edit and delete data from the database, it's time to look at the final piece in the puzzle: adding a new Player to the database.

1. Open Players_Details.aspx from the previous example.

2. Switch to the Design view and select Configure Data Source from the Tasks menu for SqlDataSource2.

3. Click Next twice to skip to the Define Custom Statements or Stored Procedures step in the wizard.

4. Select the INSERT tab and enter the following query:

```
INSERT INTO Player
    (PlayerName, PlayerManufacturerID, PlayerCost, PlayerStorage)
VALUES (@PlayerName, @PlayerManufacturerID, @PlayerCost, @PlayerStorage)
```

5. Click the Next button, and then click the Finish button to close the Configure Data Source wizard. Click No if prompted to Refresh Fields and Keys for DetailsView1.

6. From the Tasks menu for the DetailsView, select the Enable Inserting option. You'll see that there is now a New link at the bottom of the DetailsView.

7. In the Properties window, add an `ItemInserted` event handler for the `DetailsView` and add the following code to the event handler:

```
protected void DetailsView1_ItemInserted(object sender,
  DetailsViewInsertedEventArgs e)
{
  GridView1.SelectedIndex = -1;
  GridView1.DataBind();
}
```

8. Save the page, and then view it in your browser. Clicking the Select link for a row will show the details for the Player in the `DetailsView` as you saw in the previous example. If you then click the New link, you'll be able to add a new Player to the database, as shown in Figure 9-18.

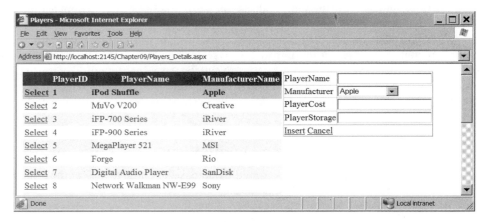

Figure 9-18. *Adding a new Player to the database*

9. Click Insert to add a new Player to the database and update the list of Players shown in the `GridView`.

How It Works

In this example, you've added the ability to add a new Player to the database with very little extra effort. You've added an `INSERT` query to the `SqlDataSource` and checked an extra option for the `DetailsView`, much as you did for the `UPDATE` and `DELETE` queries in the two previous examples.

When using a `BoundField` to interact with the database, the same Web control is used for the `SELECT`, `UPDATE`, and `INSERT` actions. For the `SELECT` query, you'll recall that a column is returned from the database that matches the `DataField` property of the `BoundField`. For the `UPDATE` and `INSERT` queries, the `UpdateParameters` and `InsertParameters` collections have a parameter that has the same name. You saw this earlier with the `UpdateParameters` collection, and here you have a similar `InsertParameters` collection:

```
<InsertParameters>
  <asp:Parameter Name="PlayerName" />
  <asp:Parameter Name="PlayerManufacturerID" />
  <asp:Parameter Name="PlayerCost" />
  <asp:Parameter Name="PlayerStorage" />
</InsertParameters>
```

You'll notice that the InsertParameters collection is missing the PlayerID parameter. This shouldn't come as a great surprise, as it's the auto-generated primary key and isn't present in the INSERT query that you're executing. When adding a new Player to the database, the PlayerID BoundField isn't shown because its InsertVisible property is set to False:

```
<asp:BoundField DataField="PlayerID" HeaderText="PlayerID"
  InsertVisible="False" ReadOnly="True" SortExpression="PlayerID" />
```

The other thing to notice is that you're not using the InsertItemTemplate within the TemplateField row. If you recall from the earlier discussion of templates for editing, the InsertItemTemplate is available when you're adding new data using a DetailsView. When an InsertItemTemplate isn't specified, the DetailsView will use the EditItemTemplate when adding new data.

All you're doing in the TemplateField is allowing the user to select the Manufacturer of the Player, and the process is the same for both editing and adding a Player. If you don't need to do anything different, then adding an InsertItemTemplate is just another place for errors to creep into your pages. Stick to the one template and use only an EditItemTemplate.

■**Note** Although the EditItemTemplate is used when inserting if an InsertItemTemplate hasn't been defined, the same isn't true if you have an InsertItemTemplate and no EditItemTemplate. If you don't specify an EditItemTemplate, when you switch the Web control into Edit mode, the TemplateField will still appear in ReadOnly mode. If no EditItemTemplate is defined, the ItemTemplate is used in its place.

The one thing that you can't do in this example is specify the Formats that the Player supports. In reality, adding a new Player to the database is a more complex task than shown here. You saw a much better way of handling the addition of Players in Chapter 8. Although the DetailsView allows you to build quite complex pages very simply, this is one example of its limitations.

Tidying Up the User Interface

If you've been working through the examples so far, you may have noticed a problem related to adding a new Player to the database. If you haven't spotted the problem, open Players_Details. aspx in your browser. The page you'll see is shown earlier in Figure 9-15.

Still can't see the problem? How exactly do you add a new Player to the database? There's no Add button anywhere. It's only when you actually view an existing Player that you're presented with the ability to add a new Player, as shown in Figure 9-19.

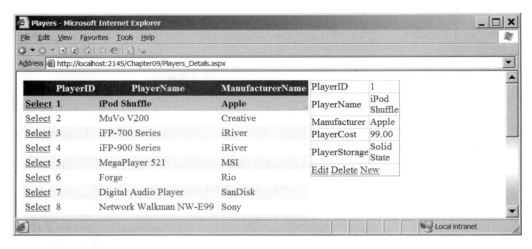

Figure 9-19. *Do you really want to have to view an existing Player to add a new one?*

Although the GridView and DetailsView interact, it's hardly an ideal setup. What you really want is an Add New Player link that allows you to add a new Player to the database. It's fine for the Edit and Delete links to be shown when you've selected a Player in the GridView, but you don't want the New link to appear.

You can accomplish this with a few little changes to the way that the Web controls interact.

Try It Out: Manually Adding an Add New Player Link

In this example, you'll modify the previous example to make it possible for the user to add a new Player to the database without having to select an existing Player first.

1. Open Players_Details.aspx from the previous example.

2. Select the DetailsView and from its Tasks menu, unselect the Enable Inserting option.

3. Add a new LinkButton (above the table containing the GridView and DetailsView) and change its Text property to **Add New Player**.

4. Double-click the LinkButton to add the Click event handler and add the following code:

```
protected void LinkButton1_Click(object sender, EventArgs e)
{
  DetailsView1.ChangeMode(DetailsViewMode.Insert);
}
```

5. Switch back to the Design view and add the SelectedIndexChanged event for the GridView. Add the following code to the event handler:

```
protected void GridView1_SelectedIndexChanged(object sender, EventArgs e)
{
  DetailsView1.ChangeMode(DetailsViewMode.ReadOnly);
}
```

6. Switch back to the Design view and add the PreRender event for the DetailsView. Add the following code to the event handler:

```
protected void DetailsView1_PreRender(object sender, EventArgs e)
{
  if (DetailsView1.CurrentMode == DetailsViewMode.Insert)
  {
    DetailsView1.AutoGenerateInsertButton = true;
  }
  else
  {
    DetailsView1.AutoGenerateInsertButton = false;
  }
}
```

7. Save the page, and then view it in the browser. You'll see that clicking the Add New Player link allows you to add a new Player to the database without viewing an existing Player first, as shown in Figure 9-20.

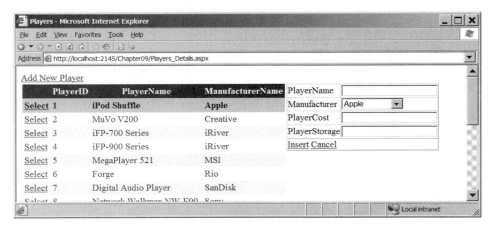

Figure 9-20. *Adding a new Player without viewing an existing Player*

8. Choose to view an existing Player. As shown in Figure 9-21, you'll see that when you do this, you no longer have the New link.

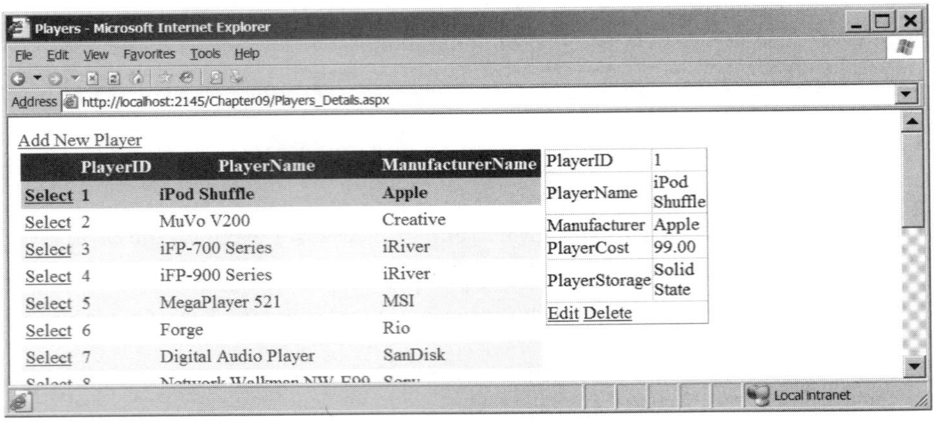

Figure 9-21. *Viewing an existing Player no longer shows the New link.*

How It Works

In order to tidy up the user interface when using the GridView and DetailsView, you've resorted to a little bit of trickery. You no longer let the DetailsView decide when to show a link to add a new Player. Instead, you add your own link.

In order to do this, you need to manually tell the DetailsView that it is inserting a new Player. In previous examples, the DetailsView switched itself into Insert mode when you clicked the New link. As you don't have this link here, you need to do this manually:

```
protected void LinkButton1_Click(object sender, EventArgs e)
{
  DetailsView1.ChangeMode(DetailsViewMode.Insert);
}
```

So when the user clicks the Add New Player link, the Click event handler is executed, and the ChangeMode method of the DetailsView is used to switch into Insert mode.

Once you switch into Insert mode, the DetailsView will remain in that mode until it's told to be in a different mode. If you clicked a Select link, the DetailsView would still be in Insert mode, not in ReadOnly mode, as you would expect. So, when a Select link is clicked, you need to switch the DetailsView back into ReadOnly mode.

When a row is selected in the GridView, not only does the SelectedValue property get set correctly, but also the SelectedIndexChanged event is fired. You can use this event handler to switch back to ReadOnly mode:

```
protected void GridView1_SelectedIndexChanged(object sender, EventArgs e)
{
  DetailsView1.ChangeMode(DetailsViewMode.ReadOnly);
}
```

You can change the mode of the Web control in the event handlers, as the GridView and DetailsView will be automatically data-bound after the OnPreRender event has fired. User-requested events are fired before you get to this stage, so you're free to change the status of the

DetailsView without creating an extra load on the database due to any data binding occurring before you change the mode.

All this talk of the page life cycle leads us nicely into the last change you made to the page. You actually added an event handler for the OnPreRender event to the DetailsView:

```
protected void DetailsView1_PreRender(object sender, EventArgs e)
{
  if (DetailsView1.CurrentMode == DetailsViewMode.Insert)
  {
    DetailsView1.AutoGenerateInsertButton = true;
  }
  else
  {
    DetailsView1.AutoGenerateInsertButton = false;
  }
}
```

The first change that you made to the DetailsView was to turn off the automatic creation of the New link. Indeed, if you look at the definition for the CommandField, you'll see that you no longer have a ShowInsertButton property. However, you still need to add the New link when you're in Insert mode. You do this as late as you can—immediately before the Web control is rendered—so that the mode has been set correctly by either of the event handlers.

The AutoGenerateInsertButton property, when set to true, automatically adds a CommandField with a New link to the DetailsView. If you're not in Insert mode (you're in Edit or ReadOnly mode), then you don't want to show the New link, so you set the AutoGenerateInsertButton to false. But you never see a New link—or do you?

In the previous examples, you've seen that the Edit link automatically turns into Update and Cancel links when the DetailsView is in Edit mode. The same is also true for the New link. It turns into Insert and Cancel links when the DetailsView is in Insert mode.

As you've switched the DetailsView into Insert mode and told it to show the New link, you get the Insert and Cancel links. Being in Insert mode also hides the Edit and Delete links, as they're only shown when the Web control is in Edit or ReadOnly mode.

Using the FormView

As you've just seen, the DetailsView is quite powerful and allows you to build a page that allows editing, deleting, and adding data quite easily with a minimal amount of code.

However, the DetailsView does have one major problem: it is tabular. You're limited to adding Field Web controls (BoundField, CommandField, and so on), and they appear as a table of data. Granted, you can use a TemplateField to achieve quite a lot of customization, but in some cases, you may not want to be restricted to a tabular layout. Enter the FormView.

The FormView, like the DetailsView, allows you to edit, delete, and add new data. Unlike the DetailsView, however, the FormView allows you complete control over its layout. This comes with a downside though, as you need to do a little more work when you're setting up the Web control. But after you've completed the setup, you'll see that the FormView is remarkably similar to the DetailsView in the way that it works. Indeed, the SqlDataSource that you use as the data source for the DetailsView can be used with the FormView with no changes whatsoever.

In the code download for this chapter, you'll find another page, Players_Form.aspx, that uses a FormView to perform the same functions as you saw in the DetailsView examples.

Using Templates with the FormView

The FormView is completely controlled by templates. Think of it as being similar to one big TemplateField. You define an ItemTemplate that you want to use when the Web control is in ReadOnly mode, an EditItemTemplate when in Edit mode, and an InsertItemTemplate when in Insert mode.

Within each of the templates, you must then define what you want to be displayed on the screen. If you look at Players_Form.aspx, you'll see that all three templates have been defined. For the ItemTemplate, I've chosen to use a table with a light blue background, which distinguishes it from the Player list, as shown in Figure 9-22.

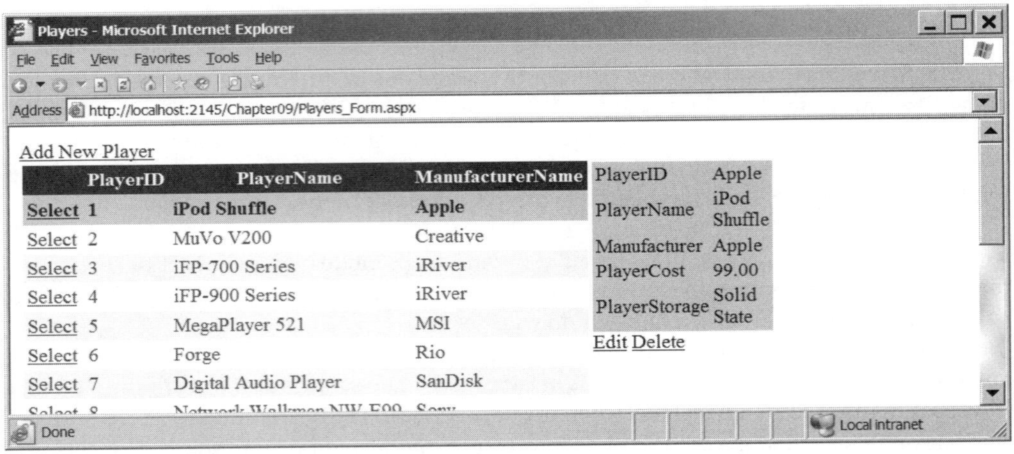

Figure 9-22. *Using a FormView to view an existing Player*

The ItemTemplate here is defined as follows:

```
<ItemTemplate>
  <table bgcolor="LightBlue">
    <tr>
      <td>PlayerID</td>
      <td><asp:Literal ID="litPlayerID" runat="server"
        Text='<%# Eval("ManufacturerName") %>'></asp:Literal></td>
    </tr>
    <tr>
      <td>PlayerName</td>
      <td><asp:Literal ID="litPlayerName" runat="server"
        Text='<%# Eval("PlayerName") %>'></asp:Literal></td>
    </tr>
```

```
    <tr>
      <td>Manufacturer</td>
      <td><asp:Literal ID="litManufacturer" runat="server"
        Text='<%# Eval("ManufacturerName") %>'></asp:Literal></td>
    </tr>
    <tr>
      <td>PlayerCost</td>
      <td><asp:Literal ID="litPlayerCost" runat="server"
        Text='<%# Eval("PlayerCost") %>'></asp:Literal></td>
    </tr>
    <tr>
      <td>PlayerStorage</td>
      <td><asp:Literal ID="litPlayerStorage" runat="server"
        Text='<%# Eval("PlayerStorage") %>'></asp:Literal></td>
    </tr>
  </table>
  <asp:LinkButton ID="btnEdit" runat="server"
    CommandName="Edit" Text="Edit" />
  <asp:LinkButton ID="btnDelete" runat="server"
    CommandName="Delete" Text="Delete" />
</ItemTemplate>
```

As you can see, you no longer have available the niceties of the BoundField to automatically show the data retrieved from the SqlDataSource. Instead, you need to manually output the columns you require. The ItemTemplate shows data only in ReadOnly mode, so you can use the Eval() method to do this.

The one thing to notice is that you also must manually add whatever buttons you need. The FormView is template-based and has no way to automatically generate the buttons to add the Edit and Delete links (nor any other links that are required). You therefore need to add a Button, in this case a LinkButton, which takes the CommandName of the action you require. The pertinent actions are shown in Table 9-1.

Table 9-1. *The FormView Command Buttons*

CommandName	Action
Cancel	Causes the Insert or Update operation to be canceled and returns the FormView to ReadOnly mode.
Delete	Causes the current item to be deleted from the underlying database. Raises the ItemDeleting and ItemDeleted events.
Edit	Switches the FormView into Edit mode, displaying the EditItemTemplate.
Insert	Causes the new item to be added from the underlying data source. Raises the ItemInserting and ItemInserted events.
New	Switches the FormView into Insert mode, displaying the InsertItemTemplate.
Update	Causes the current item to be updated in the underlying data source. Raises the ItemUpdating and ItemUpdated events.

As you can see from Table 9-1, it is possible to add buttons to perform whatever action you require. For the ItemTemplate, you want the user to be able to edit or delete the selected item, so you add buttons for those two actions.

You'll also see that this example follows the same pattern for the InsertItemTemplate and the EditItemTemplate. You must define the layout that you require for the template, and then provide the necessary buttons to enable the user to complete the action.

The InsertItemTemplate has Insert and Cancel buttons:

```
<asp:LinkButton ID="btnInsert" runat="server"
  CommandName="Insert" Text="Insert" />
<asp:LinkButton ID="btnCancel" runat="server"
  CommandName="Cancel" Text="Cancel" />
```

And the EditItemTemplate has Update and Cancel buttons:

```
<asp:LinkButton ID="btnUpdate" runat="server"
  CommandName="Update" Text="Update" />
<asp:LinkButton ID="btnCancel" runat="server"
  CommandName="Cancel" Text="Cancel" />
```

Switching Modes

You saw in the DetailsView example earlier that you can manually change the mode for the Web control by calling the ChangeMode() method. This also works for the FormView.

You have a LinkButton on the page that allows the user to add a new Player to the database. In its Click event handler, you change the mode to Insert:

```
protected void LinkButton1_Click(object sender, EventArgs e)
{
  FormView1.ChangeMode(FormViewMode.Insert);
}
```

And you switch the FormView back into ReadOnly mode if the user selects a different Player:

```
protected void GridView1_SelectedIndexChanged(object sender, EventArgs e)
{
  FormView1.ChangeMode(FormViewMode.ReadOnly);
}
```

This is exactly the same as you saw for the DetailsView. What you don't need to do when using the FormView is turn the New link on and off. Since you have no way of automatically adding buttons to a FormView, you explicitly specify the actions that you allow the user to take within the definition of the InsertItemTemplate and the EditItemTemplate.

Validating User Responses

The one thing missing from all of the examples that you've seen so far is validation. Nothing stops you, at the moment, from entering invalid data. You saw in Chapter 8 that you can use various validation Web controls to force the user to enter valid data before any changes to the database are attempted.

You can use the same validation Web controls when you're using a `FormView` without any work other than adding the Web controls to the page and configuring them. With the `GridView` and the `DetailsView`, however, things are a little more complex, because the validation Web controls won't work in conjunction with a `BoundField` or a `CheckBoxField`. The solution is to convert the `BoundField` or `CheckBoxField` into an equivalent `TemplateField`.

The `DetailsView` example includes several `BoundField` controls. One of these is used to display the PlayerName column:

```
<asp:BoundField DataField="PlayerName"
  HeaderText="PlayerName" SortExpression="PlayerName" />
```

Converting this to a `TemplateField` is very simple. You need to add an `ItemTemplate` that displays the PlayerName using a `Literal` and an `EditItemTemplate` that has a `TextBox` that allows the PlayerName to be edited:

```
<asp:TemplateField HeaderText="PlayerName"
  SortExpression="PlayerName">
  <ItemTemplate>
    <asp:Literal ID="litPlayerName" runat="server"
      Text='<%# Eval("PlayerName") %>'></asp:Literal>
  </ItemTemplate>
  <EditItemTemplate>
    <asp:TextBox id="txtPlayerName" runat="server"
      Text='<%# Bind("PlayerName") %>'></asp:TextBox>
  </EditItemTemplate>
</asp:TemplateField>
```

With a `DetailsView`, you could also add an `InsertItemTemplate` to use when inserting a new record. If you don't specify an `InsertItemTemplate`, the `EditItemTemplate` will be used when the `DetailsView` is in Insert mode. For that reason, you may still need to use the `InsertVisible` property on the `TemplateField` to indicate that the Field is not to be displayed when adding a new record.

The one `BoundField` property that isn't supported is `ReadOnly`. If you need to have a `ReadOnly` Field, then simply leave the `BoundField` as it is. It will always be displayed, and the user will never be able to modify it. You could also mimic its functionality by defining only an `ItemTemplate`. If the `DetailsView` or `GridView` is in Edit mode and no `EditItemTemplate` is defined, the `ItemTemplate` is used. If it's in Insert mode and no `InsertItemTemplate` or `EditItemTemplate` is defined, then the `ItemTemplate` is used.

Once you've converted all of your `BoundField` controls to `TemplateField` controls. you can then add the required validation to the page. When you try to edit or add data to the database, the validation will occur. If it fails, the action will be canceled and the validation results shown.

We'll now look at how you can change the `DetailsView` from earlier to add validation to the page.

■**Note** Adding validation Web controls to the `GridView` and `FormView` is similar to adding validation to the `DetailsView`. In the code download, you'll find two extra pages, named `Players_Basic_Validation.aspx` and `Players_Form_Validation.aspx`, which have validation added to them.

Try It Out: Adding Validation to the DetailsView

In this example, you'll modify the existing DetailsView example to add validation Web controls to the page. You'll also see that Visual Web Developer provides a handy means of editing templates through the graphical designer.

1. Copy Players_Details.aspx and rename the copy Players_Details_Validation.aspx.

2. In the Source view, find the HTML markup for the DetailsView and replace the PlayerName, PlayerCost, and PlayerStorage BoundField controls with TemplateField controls.

3. Replace the PlayerName BoundField with the following:

```
<asp:TemplateField HeaderText="PlayerName"
  SortExpression="PlayerName">
  <ItemTemplate>
    <asp:Literal ID="litPlayerName" runat="server"
      Text='<%# Eval("PlayerName") %>'></asp:Literal>
  </ItemTemplate>
  <EditItemTemplate>
    <asp:TextBox id="txtPlayerName" runat="server"
      Text='<%# Bind("PlayerName") %>'></asp:TextBox>
  </EditItemTemplate>
</asp:TemplateField>
```

4. Replace the PlayerCost BoundField with the following:

```
<asp:TemplateField HeaderText="PlayerCost"
  SortExpression="PlayerCost">
  <ItemTemplate>
    <asp:Literal ID="litPlayerCost" runat="server"
      Text='<%# Eval("PlayerCost") %>'></asp:Literal>
  </ItemTemplate>
  <EditItemTemplate>
    <asp:TextBox id="txtPlayerCost" runat="server"
      Text='<%# Bind("PlayerCost") %>'></asp:TextBox>
  </EditItemTemplate>
</asp:TemplateField>
```

5. Replace the PlayerStorage BoundField with the following:

```
<asp:TemplateField HeaderText="PlayerStorage"
  SortExpression="PlayerStorage">
  <ItemTemplate>
    <asp:Literal ID="litPlayerStorage" runat="server"
      Text='<%# Eval("PlayerStorage") %>'></asp:Literal>
  </ItemTemplate>
```

```
<EditItemTemplate>
  <asp:TextBox id="txtPlayerStorage" runat="server"
    Text='<%# Bind("PlayerStorage") %>'></asp:TextBox>
</EditItemTemplate>
</asp:TemplateField>
```

6. Switch to the Design view and add a ValidationSummary after the Add New Player link, as shown in Figure 9-23.

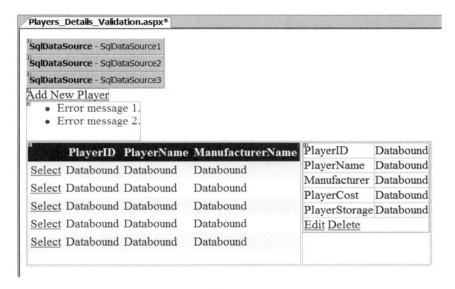

Figure 9-23. *Adding a ValidationSummary to the page*

7. Select the DetailsView and open its Tasks menu. Select the Edit Templates option. The DetailsView will change its appearance. If you expand the Display drop-down list in the Tasks menu, you'll see that you can switch to the different TemplateField controls and the different Web controls within each TemplateField, as shown in Figure 9-24.

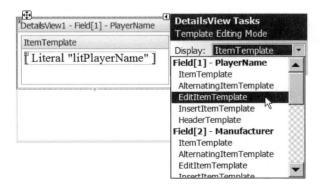

Figure 9-24. *Selecting the correct TemplateField and template to edit*

8. Select `EditItemTemplate` from beneath the PlayerName `TemplateField`, and you'll see the `EditItemTemplate` showing a `TextBox`.

9. Add a `RequiredFieldValidator` to the `EditItemTemplate`. Set its `Display` property to `Dynamic`, `Text` property to *****, and `ErrorMessage` to **You must enter a name**. Finally, set the `ControlToValidate` property to `txtPlayerName`. The `EditItemTemplate` should now look similar to Figure 9-25.

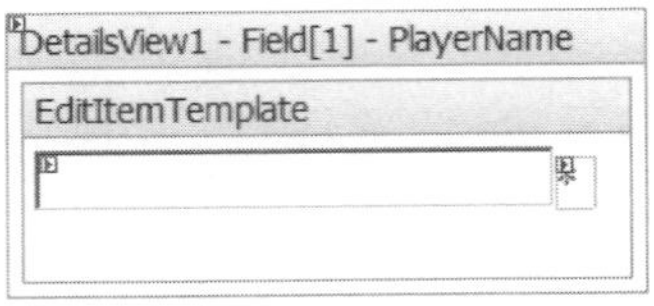

Figure 9-25. *Adding a RequiredFieldValidator to the EditItemTemplate*

10. Switch to the PlayerCost `EditItemTemplate` and add a `RequiredFieldValidator` to the template. Set its properties as follows:

- `Display:` Dynamic
- `Text:` *
- `ErrorMessage:` You must enter a cost
- `ControlToValidate:` txtPlayerCost

11. Add a `CompareValidator` to the template and set its properties as follows:

- `Display:` Dynamic
- `Text:` *
- `ErrorMessage:` You must specify the cost as a decimal
- `ControlToValidate:` txtPlayerCost
- `Operator:` DataTypeCheck
- `Type:` Currency

12. Switch to the PlayerStorage `EditItemTemplate` and add a `RequiredFieldValidator` to the template. Set its properties as follows:

- `Display:` Dynamic
- `Text:` *
- `ErrorMessage:` You must enter a storage type
- `ControlToValidate:` txtPlayerStorage

13. From the `DetailsView` Tasks menu, select the End Template Editing option to switch the `DetailsView` back to its normal view.

14. Set the `CausesValidation` property of the Add New Player `LinkButton` to `false`.

15. Save the page, and then view it in the browser. You'll find that it is now impossible to edit a Player or add a new Player if you haven't specified all of the required values. If you try to do this, you'll see that the validators report the errors, as shown in Figure 9-26.

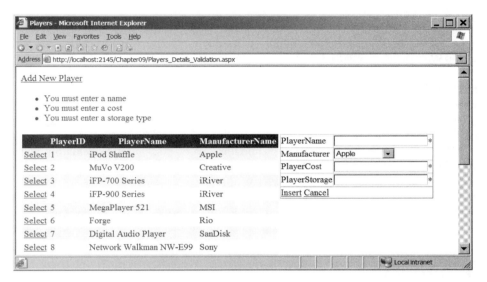

Figure 9-26. *The validators fire if the data is incorrect.*

How It Works

The validators you've added to the different templates are the same as the validators that you added to the examples in Chapter 8. You add three `RequiredFieldValidator` controls to make sure that the user enters all of the required data. You've used a `CompareValidator` to ensure the PlayerCost is entered as a valid currency.

As we've already discussed, you need to turn any `BoundField` controls that you want to validate into `TemplateField` controls with the correct templates defined. If you don't want to edit a `BoundField` or have no reason to validate the user's entry, then you can leave it as a `BoundField` (with the `ReadOnly` and `InsertVisible` properties set correctly).

In this example, you can leave the PlayerID `BoundField` as it is. It's already set as `ReadOnly`, so you can't edit it, and it's also set so that it doesn't appear when you're inserting a Player. The other three `BoundField` controls are converted to `TemplateField` controls quite easily (although it can quickly become quite tedious).

Once the required templates are added, you can use the design-time features of the `DetailsView` to configure the validators. By selecting the Edit Templates option, you can use the normal design-time tools to edit the individual templates within the Web control. (If you've ever had to deal with templates in earlier version of the development tools, you'll appreciate how much of an improvement this actually is.)

Note The GridView works exactly the same as the DetailsView when editing templates: you need to pick the Field you require, and then choose the template within that Field. The FormView is slightly different as it has no concept of Fields, so you can select only the template.

Selecting a template within a TemplateField turns that template into its own little design area, showing only that template and none of the others. You can use the normal tools available in Visual Web Developer within this template.

The important thing to remember is that when editing a template, any Web controls within the template can see only other Web controls within that template. If you look at any of the validation Web controls and expand the ControlToValidate drop-down list, you'll see that only the TextBox in the template is available. The TextBox controls defined in other templates aren't visible.

The validators run at both the client and the server. The client-side validators completely stop the page from being posted back to the server if it has any errors. If the client-side validators accept the page, it is posted back to the server, and the server-side validators are processed before any other events. If the server-side validation fails, the IsValid property of the Page is set to false. As the Page is now invalid, the insert or update action is canceled. The ItemInserting/ItemInserted or ItemUpdating/ItemUpdated events are no longer fired, and the INSERT or UPDATE isn't attempted.

Summary

In this chapter, we've looked at using the GridView, DetailsView, and FormView for modifying data in the database.

From working through the chapter, you may have the impression that the GridView, DetailsView, and FormView are the ideal answer when you need to interact with the database. However, you saw two examples of when this isn't the case. The design of our database includes a many-to-many relationship between the Player table and the Format table, and this causes problems.

When deleting a Player from the database, you had to add a second DELETE query to delete any related data in the WhatPlaysWhatFormat table. This can't be handled automatically by any of the Web controls that you've used. The SqlDataSource can handle only a single query in the DeleteStatement property.

The WhatPlaysWhatFormat table also causes problems when you want to add and edit data in the database. Because it's a many-to-many relationship, you must handle it slightly differently. As you saw in Chapter 8, you need to write extra code to retrieve the available Formats from the database and then determine which of those is supported by the Player. You then had to write extra code to massage the user's selection back into the database. The SqlDataSource just can't deal with this many-to-many relationship.

That's not to say that the Web controls we've looked at in this chapter aren't worthwhile. The Manufacturer and Format tables are ideal candidates for these Web controls, and the code download includes two pages, named Manufacturers_Details.aspx and Formats_Details.aspx, that show that the Web controls are suitable in some situations.

As with all design choices you make, you need to look carefully at what you're trying to accomplish and choose the right paradigm for the job at hand.

You're nearly ready to start building your own Web sites. At the moment, you can build your own pages that use various Web controls and data-binding techniques to display data to the user, as well as allow adding, editing, and deleting data in the database.

In the next chapter, I'll introduce you to stored procedures. Until now, you've always included the SQL query that you want to execute within the page. If another page wanted to execute the same query, you would need to repeat the SQL for the query on the other page as well. If a third page required the same query, you would have yet another copy of the same SQL query. What if you now discover that the query is actually incorrect? You would need to change it in all three places. Stored procedures solve this problem.

CHAPTER 10

■■■

Stored Procedures

All of the SQL queries you've executed against the database in previous chapters have been contained within the page where the execution will apply. Although you saw that this works effectively with simple SELECT, INSERT, UPDATE, and DELETE queries, formulating a query this way isn't always a suitable solution for more complex requirements.

Stored procedures provide another solution for executing queries against a database. Put simply, a stored procedure is a construct to store queries on the server, so the same query is available for any application that wants to use it.

SQL Server 2005 and MySQL 5.0 support stored procedures, and we'll look at both of them in this chapter. Microsoft Access has its own form of stored procedures, which are called, confusingly, *queries*. We won't look at Microsoft Access queries, because you need a copy of Microsoft Access to create them; however, if you do have a copy of Microsoft Access, you'll see that it does have quite a good query designer that bears a resemblance to the Visual Web Developer Query Builder.

This chapter covers the following topics:

- Advantages of using stored procedures

- How to create stored procedures and give users access to them

- How to execute stored procedures through a Command object

- How to alter and delete stored procedures you've already created

- How to make stored procedures more flexible using input parameters

- How to return information from stored procedures using output parameters

Why Should You Use Stored Procedures?

The queries you've looked at so far have always been single queries that performed only one action; for example, you've performed SELECT queries that return one set of results and INSERT queries that insert data into a single table. When you step into more complex data (and need more complex results), you'll find this way of working constrictive.

Stored procedures can contain just single SQL queries, and when they do so, they're naturally direct replacements for single queries. However, stored procedures are a powerful tool that can deliver much more than this. As you'll learn in this chapter, stored procedures can increase the performance of your queries and make maintaining Web sites a whole lot easier. They may contain multiple queries and exploit the power of SQL itself.

In a nutshell, using stored procedures gives you the following benefits:

Maintenance: Hard-coded queries on individual pages mean a string of SQL on each and every one of those pages. If you use the same query on several pages and need to change the query, you have to make the changes in every page. Stored procedures make maintaining the site easier by having only one copy of the query.

Security: Allowing direct access to the tables within the database to applications, as you've already seen in Chapter 2, forces you to grant "too much" access to the database. By using stored procedures, you allow the user access to the tables only through stored procedures, and you can apply suitable controls.

Speed: Depending on the database server that you're using, you may also gain a speed advantage from using stored procedures. If you're using MySQL 5.0 and pass a query to the server, the query must be parsed and an execution plan calculated for the query. If you pass the same query three times, MySQL 5.0 calculates the execution plan three times. MySQL 5.0 stored procedures are cached when they're created, and thereafter the precached versions are used. With SQL Server 2005, stored procedures do not process much more quickly than queries, because it also caches and reuses the execution plans of queries passed directly.

Reduced network traffic: Stored procedures allow you to process the results at the database and return only the required results to the page.

■**Note** This chapter won't present all the intricacies of SQL and all the different queries that are supported. You can find an introduction to SQL in Appendix B. It also will not cover the ability to write stored procedures in C# that was introduced with SQL Server 2005, as it's an extremely advanced topic. If you're interested, see *Pro SQL Server 2005 Assemblies* by Robin Dewson and Julian Skinner (1-59059-566-1; Apress, 2005).

Configuring MySQL 5.0 to Use Stored Procedures

When using SQL Server 2005 to connect to a database, it works "straight out of the box." By specifying the correct connection string, you can call stored procedures; no other configuration is required.

When using MySQL 5.0, things aren't as simple. The Odbc data provider that you've been using doesn't support the full range of features that are available in MySQL 5.0. In particular, the support for stored procedures isn't adequate and won't allow you to use stored procedures to their fullest extent.

To work around this limitation, you're not going to use the Odbc data provider for connecting to MySQL 5.0; instead, you're going to use the native provider for MySQL. The MySqlClient data provider, MySQL Connector/Net, handles stored procedures in the same way as the SQL Server 2005 data provider does.

■**Note** As I said earlier in this book, if there is a native data provider, you should always use that provider. We've been using the Odbc data provider to connect to MySQL 5.0 only to show all three of the supplied data providers in action.

Download Connector/Net from http://dev.mysql.com/downloads/connector/net/1.0.html. Once you've installed Connector/Net (by running the installer), configure it as follows:

- Give the account you're using permission to SELECT from a table in the mysql database. The mysql database is the *master* database that controls the operation of the database server, and you must give SELECT permission on the proc table. You can do this by executing the following query in MySQL Query Browser:

  GRANT SELECT ON mysql.proc TO band

- Add a reference to Connector/Net to your Web site by selecting Add Reference from the context menu for the Web site. Click the Browse tab and navigate to C:\Program Files\ MySQL\MySQL Connector Net 1.0.7\bin\.NET 2.0 (your directory will be different if you have a different version of Connector/Net installed). The DLL that you want to reference is MySql.Data.dll, as shown in Figure 10-1.

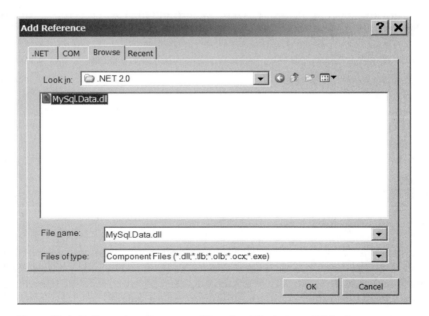

Figure 10-1. *Referencing Connector/Cased as Net in your Web site*

Once you've added the correct reference to your Web site, you can use Connector/Net in the same way as you would any other data provider.

As you've already seen, the different data providers all define their own objects, and Connector/Net is no different. All of the classes are contained in the MySql.Data.MySqlClient namespace and are prefixed with MySql. So you have MySqlConnection, MySqlCommand, and so on.

The one thing that the current version of Connector/Net doesn't handle is being used by the SqlDataSource. At the moment, you're limited to using Command or DataAdapter objects to access the database.

■**Note** Although this chapter includes the steps for creating stored procedures in MySQL Query Browser, we're not going to walk through code examples for using Connector/Net. As you've seen in previous chapters, the process for using all of the different data providers is the same. In the code download for the chapter, you'll find the three Command-based pages rewritten using Connector/Net in the mysql folder.

Creating Stored Procedures

To create a stored procedure, you must use a Data Definition Language (DDL) query. You'll look at DDL queries in more detail in Chapter 11, but for now, all you need to know is that DDL queries allow you to change the structure of the database.

The DDL query to create stored procedures is CREATE PROCEDURE. Both SQL Server 2005 and MySQL 5.0 use the same query to create a stored procedure, but their syntax is slightly different.

For SQL Server 2005, CREATE PROCEDURE in its simplest form is as follows:

```
CREATE PROCEDURE <name>
AS
<queries>
```

You give the stored procedure a name, and you can include whatever SQL queries you want after the AS statement. Any parameters that are required by the stored procedure are defined between the stored procedure's name and the AS statement.

For MySQL 5.0, the corresponding query to create a stored procedure is as follows:

```
CREATE PROCEDURE <name> ()
BEGIN
  <queries>
END;
```

The actual structure of the CREATE PROCEDURE query itself is quite similar to the SQL Server 2005 equivalent. You give the stored procedure a name, and you can include whatever SQL queries you want between the BEGIN and END statements. Any parameters to the stored procedure are defined within the brackets after the stored procedure's name.

We'll now look at creating a simple stored procedure in both SQL Server 2005 and MySQL 5.0.

Try It Out: Creating a Stored Procedure in SQL Server 2005

In this example, you'll use SQL Server Management Studio to create a stored procedure that returns all the Manufacturers from the database. You'll see that the tools you have at your disposal make it quite easy to create stored procedures.

1. Open SQL Server Management Studio and connect to the localhost\BAND database server using the sa account (the password is bandpass). In the Object Explorer, expand the Databases node, the Players database node, and then the Programmability node.

2. Right-click the Stored Procedures node and select New Stored Procedure from the context menu. This will load a template in the main design window, as shown in Figure 10-2.

```
localhost\BAND....- SQLQuery1.sql
-- ================================================
-- Template generated from Template Explorer using:
-- Create Procedure (New Menu).SQL
--
-- Use the Specify Values for Template Parameters
-- command (Ctrl-Shift-M) to fill in the parameter
-- values below.
--
-- This block of comments will not be included in
-- the definition of the procedure.
-- ================================================
SET ANSI_NULLS ON
GO
SET QUOTED_IDENTIFIER ON
GO
-- ================================================
-- Author:      <Author,,Name>
-- Create date: <Create Date,,>
-- Description: <Description,,>
-- ================================================
CREATE PROCEDURE <Procedure_Name, sysname, ProcedureName>
    -- Add the parameters for the stored procedure here
    <@Param1, sysname, @p1> <Datatype_For_Param1, , int> = <Default_Value_For_Param1, , 0>,
    <@Param2, sysname, @p2> <Datatype_For_Param2, , int> = <Default_Value_For_Param2, , 0>
AS
BEGIN
    -- SET NOCOUNT ON added to prevent extra result sets from
    -- interfering with SELECT statements.
    SET NOCOUNT ON;

    -- Insert statements for procedure here
    SELECT <@Param1, sysname, @p1>, <@Param2, sysname, @p2>
END
GO
```

Figure 10-2. *SQL Server Management Studio makes the creation of stored procedures a breeze.*

3. Replace the auto-generated template with the following stored procedure declaration:

```
CREATE PROCEDURE spGetManufacturers
AS

SELECT ManufacturerName
FROM Manufacturer
ORDER BY ManufacturerName
```

4. Click Execute on the toolbar to run the query and create the stored procedure.

5. Return to the Object Explorer and expand the Stored Procedures node. You'll see that the spGetManufacturers stored procedure has been added, as shown in Figure 10-3. (You may need to click Refresh on the Stored Procedures node to update the Object Explorer.)

Figure 10-3. *The new stored procedure has been saved to the SQL Server 2005 database.*

6. Right-click `spGetManufacturers` and select Execute from the context menu. This is a parameterless query, so in the Execute Procedure dialog box, click OK. You'll see the Output window with the results of executing the query, as shown in Figure 10-4.

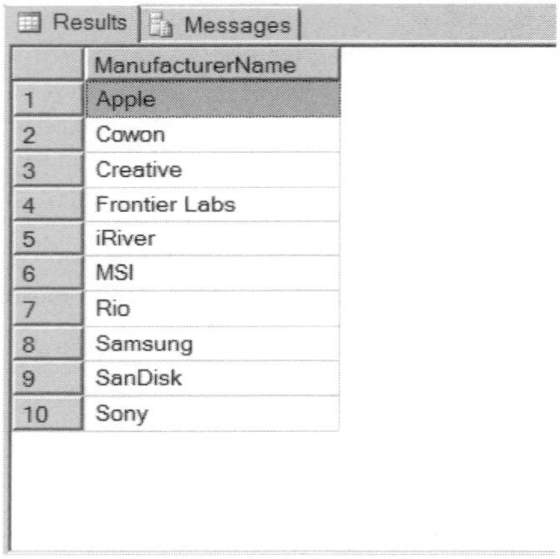

	ManufacturerName
1	Apple
2	Cowon
3	Creative
4	Frontier Labs
5	iRiver
6	MSI
7	Rio
8	Samsung
9	SanDisk
10	Sony

Figure 10-4. *SQL Server Management Studio can also execute stored procedures.*

7. In the Object Explorer, right-click the Players database node and select New Query from the context menu. Enter the following query:

```
GRANT EXEC ON spGetManufacturers TO band
```

8. Click Execute to execute the `GRANT` query against the database. If this query executes correctly, the Results pane will change to show a success message, as shown in Figure 10-5.

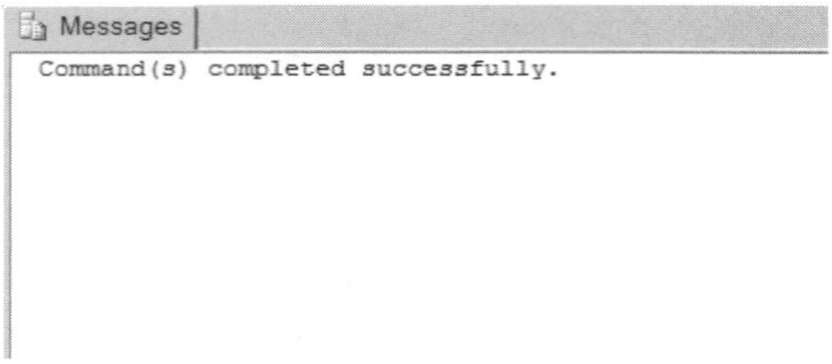

```
Command(s) completed successfully.
```

Figure 10-5. *Confirmation that the GRANT query has executed correctly*

How It Works

In this example, you've created your first stored procedure in SQL Server 2005. Granted, it's a simple stored procedure wrapping a query that you've already seen, but it does demonstrate the basic concept.

The first thing to look at is the account you use to connect to the database. To execute DDL queries, you must use an account with administrator privileges within the database. In this case, you're using the sa account, because the band account has permissions only on certain objects and doesn't have any administrator privileges.

As you saw in step 2, SQL Server 2005 automatically creates a stored procedure template for you. This template contains the basic definition of the stored procedure and hints at some of the possibilities, such as parameters, that we'll look at later in this chapter. However, it is quite a complex template, and there is a lot that you need to delete for most stored procedures. It's sometimes easier to simply discard the template and enter the stored procedure declaration from scratch, as you did in this example.

You created the following query in this example:

```
CREATE PROCEDURE spGetManufacturers
AS

SELECT ManufacturerName
FROM Manufacturer
ORDER BY ManufacturerName
```

This is a simple SELECT query that returns all of the Manufacturers in the database.

The one point to note is the name of the stored procedure. Although you created the stored procedure with the name spGetManufacturers, the name in Object Explorer is actually dbo.spGetManufacturers. All objects in the database need to be *owned*, and the name of the object is prefixed with the owner of the object. As you didn't specify the owner when creating the stored procedure, SQL Server Management Studio used the details of the currently logged-in user, sa, to determine the owner, dbo.

When specifying the owner of an object in SQL Server 2005, you don't actually specify a login as the owner of the object, but instead specify a schema. Schemas are quite an advanced topic but basically are a level of abstraction that SQL Server 2005 uses between logins and database objects. The sa login actually belongs to the dbo (database owner) schema, and that is why the spGetManufacturers stored procedure becomes dbo.spGetManufacturers.

Although the name of the stored procedure is prefixed with its owner, the name of the stored procedure is still spGetManufacturers, which is the name you use when you run the stored procedure.

After you click the Execute button, SQL Server Management Studio runs the query to create the stored procedure. If the query executes correctly, the stored procedure will be added to the database and be shown in the Object Explorer underneath the Stored Procedures entry. If, however, there's a problem with the query to create the stored procedure, an error message is returned, as shown in Figure 10-6.

Once any errors are corrected, the stored procedure will be created, and you can execute the stored procedure to check that it's working correctly. Once you're happy that the stored procedure performs as intended, you need to turn your attention to allowing users to access it.

```
Messages
Msg 102, Level 15, State 1, Procedure spGetManufacturers, Line 3
Incorrect syntax near 'SELECTS'.
```

Figure 10-6. *Errors are returned if you try to create an invalid stored procedure.*

By default, this stored procedure won't be available for use with any of the accounts in the database other than the stored procedure's owner—in this case, the sa account. As you've already seen, running applications using this account isn't recommended. You have a login called band that you're using to access the database from your Web pages. You can give an account permission to execute the stored procedure by granting it the EXEC permission using a GRANT similar to the ones you saw in Chapter 2, like so:

```
GRANT EXEC ON spGetManufacturers TO band
```

As the GRANT query doesn't return any results, the only indication that the stored procedure has executed correctly is the confirmation in the Results pane. All you really want to know is that the query has executed, so the confirmation is adequate.

Try It Out: Creating a Stored Procedure in MySQL 5.0

To demonstrate creating stored procedures in MySQL 5.0, you will use MySQL Query Browser to create a stored procedure that returns all the Manufacturers from the database.

1. Open MySQL Query Browser and connect to the localhost database server using the root account (the password is bandpass).

2. In the Schemata pane, right-click the Players database and select Create New Procedure / Function from the context menu. Enter a name of spGetManufacturers in the dialog box, as shown in Figure 10-7.

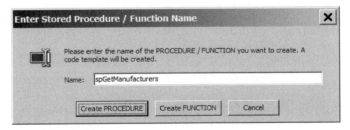

Figure 10-7. *MySQL requires the stored procedure name to be specified in advance.*

3. Replace the auto-generated template with the following stored procedure declaration:

```
DELIMITER $$

CREATE PROCEDURE spGetManufacturers ()
BEGIN
```

```
    SELECT ManufacturerName
    FROM Manufacturer
    ORDER BY ManufacturerName;
END $$

DELIMITER ;
```

4. Click Execute on the toolbar to run the query and create the stored procedure.

5. Return to the Schemata pane and expand the Players database. You'll see that the stored procedure has been added to the database, as shown in Figure 10-8.

Figure 10-8. *The stored procedure has been saved to the MySQL 5.0 database.*

6. Double-click the spGetManufacturers stored procedure. The query window at the top of the page will be populated with the correct SQL to execute the stored procedure, as shown in Figure 10-9.

Figure 10-9. *The SQL required to execute the stored procedure*

7. Click Execute to run the stored procedure. The results will be displayed, as shown in Figure 10-10.

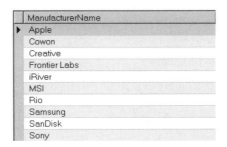

Figure 10-10. *MySQL Query Browser can also execute stored procedures.*

8. In the Schemata pane, right-click the Players database node and select New Query from the context menu. Enter the following query:

```
GRANT EXECUTE ON PROCEDURE spGetManufacturers TO band
```

9. Click Execute to execute the GRANT query against the database. The only sign that the query has executed correctly will be that you don't receive an error, and MySQL Query Browser indicates that the "Query returned no resultset."

How It Works

As you can see, creating your first stored procedure in MySQL 5.0 is no more difficult than creating the stored procedure in SQL Server 2005.

Again, MySQL Query Browser provides a template that you can use to create the stored procedure. It's slightly more complete, as you've already provided the name of the stored procedure. You could modify this to suit your purposes, but it is often easier to specify the query from scratch, as you've done here:

```
DELIMITER $$

CREATE PROCEDURE spGetManufacturers ()
BEGIN
  SELECT ManufacturerName
  FROM Manufacturer
  ORDER BY ManufacturerName;
END $$

DELIMITER ;
```

You're using the same SELECT query as the previous example, but this time you have to do a little more work to create the stored procedure.

Because MySQL 5.0 uses the semicolon to delimit the end of a query, you can't actually use it within the body of the CREATE PROCEDURE query. Each query within the stored procedure needs to be delimited correctly, and as soon as the semicolon is added, the CREATE PROCEDURE query is seen as complete—at the point of the semicolon, and not after the closing END where it should be. To solve this problem, you need to use the DELIMITER query to change the character that is being used (in this case, to $$) to allow the CREATE PROCEDURE query to contain semicolons. Once the CREATE PROCEDURE query is complete, the delimiter is then set back to the semicolon.

Once the stored procedure has been created, it is available only to the account that created it—in this case, the root account. You need to grant permission to execute the stored procedure by granting the EXECUTE permission:

```
GRANT EXECUTE ON PROCEDURE spGetManufacturers TO band
```

This has a slightly different syntax than the GRANT query in SQL Server 2005 does.

Granting Permissions for Stored Procedures

As you know, you must explicitly grant permissions for users to access the objects in the database. In Chapter 2, you saw that to enable a SELECT query to be executed against a table, you needed to give the user specific permissions to SELECT information from the table. So to give the band account SELECT permissions on the Manufacturer table, you would execute the following:

```
GRANT SELECT ON Manufacturer TO band
```

You would also need to give similar permission if you wanted to grant the band account INSERT, UPDATE, or DELETE permissions on the table.

Stored procedures also must have permissions applied in order for an account to be able to execute them. Stored procedures don't have SELECT, INSERT, UPDATE, or DELETE permissions, but instead have a single permission: EXEC in SQL Server 2005 and EXECUTE in MySQL 5.0. The syntax to grant this permission for a stored procedure is the same as granting any other permission. In SQL Server 2005, you grant the EXEC permission as follows:

```
GRANT EXEC ON spGetManufacturers TO band
```

And in MySQL 5.0, the syntax for granting the EXECUTE permission is as follows:

```
GRANT EXECUTE ON PROCEDURE spGetManufacturers TO band
```

Similarly, if you want to remove an existing permission, you can use the REVOKE query to remove the permission. For SQL Server 2005, the syntax for REVOKE is as follows:

```
REVOKE EXEC ON spGetManufacturers FROM band
```

For MySQL 5.0, use this syntax:

```
REVOKE EXECUTE ON PROCEDURE spGetManufacturers FROM band
```

SQL Server 2005 also allows you to explicitly deny the EXEC permission on a stored procedure with the following DENY query:

```
DENY EXEC ON spGetManufacturers TO band
```

■Note Once a user has been granted execute permissions on a stored procedure, no other permissions are required for that user to execute the stored procedure. The user executing the stored procedure doesn't need any permissions to access the tables used by the stored procedure. The database assumes that the stored procedure is correct and allows it access to all the tables within the database.

Calling Stored Procedures

You now have a stored procedure that will return all the Manufacturers in the database. Next, you need to look at how you call the stored procedure for execution instead of passing a query. Thankfully, calling a stored procedure is similar to passing a query.

When accessing the database in code in previous chapters, you've just passed the query into the Command object and used the correct execute method. For example, to return a DataReader containing the results of the query, you would use the following code:

```
string myCommandText = "SELECT ManufacturerID, ManufacturerName ➥
  FROM Manufacturer ORDER BY ManufacturerName";

SqlCommand myCommand = new SqlCommand();
myCommand.Connection = myConnection;
myCommand.CommandText = myCommandText;

SqlDataReader myReader = myCommand.ExecuteReader();
```

The same is true when using a DataAdapter. Instead of returning a DataReader from the Command object, you would create a new DataAdapter and use that to fill a DataSet:

```
SqlDataAdapter myAdapter = new SqlDataAdapter(myCommand);
DataSet myDataSet = new DataSet();
myAdapter.Fill(myDataSet, "Manufacturers");
```

Similarly, when using a SqlDataSource, you've set the Command property (SelectCommand, DeleteCommand, InsertCommand, or UpdateCommand) to the query to be executed:

```
<asp:SqlDataSource ID="SqlDataSource1" runat="server"
  ConnectionString="<%$ ConnectionStrings:SqlConnectionString %>"
  SelectCommand="SELECT ManufacturerID, ManufacturerName
    FROM Manufacturer ORDER BY ManufacturerName">
</asp:SqlDataSource>
```

To use a stored procedure in place of a query, you need to set the command type property. Both the Command object and the SqlDataSource object assume that the command passed is a query and use the default value of Text for the command type property. As this is the default, you don't need to set it, which is why you have not seen this property before.

To call a stored procedure, you simply pass the name of the procedure instead of a SQL query and specify the command type as StoredProcedure. When using a Command object, you pass the name of the stored procedure to the Command object and specify the correct CommandType:

```
string myCommandText = "spGetManufacturers";

SqlCommand myCommand = new SqlCommand();
myCommand.Connection = myConnection;
myCommand.CommandText = myCommandText;
myCommand.CommandType = CommandType.StoredProcedure;
```

For the SqlDataSource, you follow the same pattern and simply tell the Web control that you're passing the name of a stored procedure using the SelectCommandType, DeleteCommandType, InsertCommandType, or UpdateCommandType property:

```
<asp:SqlDataSource ID="SqlDataSource1" runat="server"
  ConnectionString="<%$ ConnectionStrings:SqlConnectionString %>"
  SelectCommand="spGetManufacturers"
  SelectCommandType="StoredProcedure">
</asp:SqlDataSource>
```

■Note Although I've intimated that the enumeration value that you're setting for the Command object and
`SqlDataSource` command type properties is the same, this is not the case. The Command object uses
values from the `System.Data.CommandType` enumeration, whereas the `SqlDataSource` object uses the
`System.Web.UI.WebControls.SqlDataSourceCommandType` enumeration. Both of these enumerations
contain `Text` and `StoredProcedure` values.

Try It Out: Using a Command Object to Call a Stored Procedure

Now that you have a stored procedure in the database and have set its permissions correctly, you
can use that stored procedure in place of a SQL query within a page. In this example, you'll use the
stored procedure with SQL Server 2005 to create a simple page that lists all of the Manufacturers in
the database.

1. Create a new Web site at `C:\BAND\Chapter10` and delete the auto-generated `Default.aspx`
   file.

2. Add a new `Web.config` file to the application and add a new setting to the
   `<connectionStrings>` element:

   ```
   <add name="SqlConnectionString"
     connectionString="Data Source=localhost\BAND;Initial Catalog=Players;
       Persist Security Info=True;User ID=band;Password=letmein"
     providerName="System.Data.SqlClient" />
   ```

3. Add a new Web Form to the application called `Calling_DataReader.aspx`. Set the
   `<title>` of the page to **Calling a Stored Procedure Using a DataReader**.

4. In the Design view, add a `GridView` to the page.

5. Switch to the Source view and make sure you've included the correct namespaces at the
   top of the page:

   ```
   <%@ Page Language="C#" %>
   <%@ Import Namespace="System.Data.SqlClient" %>
   ```

6. Add a `Page_Load` event to the page:

   ```
   protected void Page_Load(object sender, EventArgs e)
   {
     // create SqlConnection object
     string ConnectionString = ConfigurationManager.
       ConnectionStrings["SqlConnectionString"].ConnectionString;
     SqlConnection myConnection = new SqlConnection(ConnectionString);

     try
     {
       // create the command
       SqlCommand myCommand = new SqlCommand();
       myCommand.Connection = myConnection;
   ```

```
          // set up the command
          myCommand.CommandText = "spGetManufacturers";
          myCommand.CommandType = CommandType.StoredProcedure;

          // open the connection
          myConnection.Open();

          // run query
          SqlDataReader myReader = myCommand.ExecuteReader();

          // set up the grid
          GridView1.DataSource = myReader;
          GridView1.DataBind();

          // close the reader
          myReader.Close();
        }
        finally
        {
          // close the connection
          myConnection.Close();
        }
      }
```

7. Execute the page. You'll see that the stored procedure you've created is executed and that the results are returned as expected, as shown in Figure 10-11.

Figure 10-11. *Results from executing the spGetManufacturers stored procedure*

How It Works

The code for the Page_Load event is almost identical to the code that you've been using to access the database. The two lines of code that are of particular interest here are as follows:

```
myCommand.CommandText = "spGetManufacturers";
myCommand.CommandType = CommandType.StoredProcedure;
```

Instead of a SQL query, you give the name of the stored procedure as the CommandText of the Command object. You then tell the Command object that what you're passing in is the name of a stored procedure and not a SQL query by setting the CommandType property to CommandType.StoredProcedure.

▪Note If you don't set the CommandType correctly for the stored procedure, the stored procedure will still execute because the database makes an intelligent guess; figuring that an invalid query is probably a stored procedure name. However, if you explicitly instruct the database that you're passing in a stored procedure name, it makes your code not only more readable but also slightly quicker because you're removing the cost of forcing the database to choose a "best fit" from the instruction it receives. There is one caveat to this and that concerns the use of parameters. If you pass parameters to the stored procedure and forget to change the CommandType to CommandType.StoredProcedure, you'll get a runtime error.

Choosing an Execute Method

As you learned in the earlier chapters, you can use three execute methods to execute a query against the database. Which one you use depends on what the query that you're executing is doing. To recap, the three methods that you can use are as follows:

- ExecuteNonQuery(): Use this when the query doesn't return any results from the database. It is typically used when you're executing INSERT, UPDATE, or DELETE queries.

- ExecuteReader(): Use this when you want to return a result set from a SELECT query.

- ExecuteScalar(): Use this when you want to return only the first column from the first row of the returned result set. This is almost always used to return the results of a scalar query. You also have the same choice when you use stored procedures, and you should choose the method that matches what the stored procedure does.

▪Note You also have the option of using the Command object to create a new DataAdapter to populate a DataSet. As you've seen in earlier chapters, the code to use a DataAdapter and a DataSet is very similar to the code to use a DataReader, so it should be easy for you to use a stored procedure this way.

Try It Out: Calling a Stored Procedure in a SqlDataSource

In this example, you'll use a SqlDataSource to call your stored procedure.

1. Add a new Web Form to the application called Calling_DataSource.aspx. Set the <title> of the page to **Calling a Stored Procedure in a SqlDataSource**.

2. Switch to the Design view and add a SqlDataSource to the page. In the Properties window, set the ConnectionString to SqlConnectionString and set the SelectCommandType property to StoredProcedure.

3. Click the ellipsis for the SelectQuery property and enter spGetManufacturers as the SELECT command.

4. Add a GridView to the page and set SqlDataSource1 as its data source.

5. Execute the page. You'll see that the GridView shows the same list of Manufacturers as you saw in Figure 10-11.

How It Works

You can see how easy it is to use a stored procedure rather than a SQL query when using a SqlDataSource. If you look at the markup that is generated, you'll see that the SelectCommand has been changed to the name of the stored procedure and the SelectCommandType has changed to reflect the fact that you're executing a stored procedure:

```
<asp:SqlDataSource ID="SqlDataSource1" runat="server"
  ConnectionString="<%$ ConnectionStrings:SqlConnectionString %>"
  SelectCommand="spGetManufacturers"
  SelectCommandType="StoredProcedure">
</asp:SqlDataSource>
```

■**Note** As with the SqlCommand object, if you don't set SelectCommandType correctly for the stored procedure, the database will make an intelligent guess and check that what you're after is a stored procedure. If you're using parameters, you must set SelectCommandType to StoredProcedure.

Altering and Deleting Stored Procedures

Being able to add stored procedures to your database is all well and good, but you also need some way of modifying or deleting them. You can accomplish both of these tasks using two other DDL commands.

To modify a stored procedure, you use the ALTER PROCEDURE query, specifying the name of the stored procedure you want to modify as well as the complete new contents of the stored procedure, like so:

```
ALTER PROCEDURE <name>
AS
<new queries>
```

To delete a stored procedure from the database, you simply use the DROP PROCEDURE query, like so:

```
DROP PROCEDURE <name>
```

SQL Server Management Studio and MySQL Query Browser provide options to complete both of these tasks from the user interface. If you select a stored procedure and open the context menu, you'll see that there are options for editing and deleting stored procedures: the Modify and Delete options in SQL Server Management Studio, and the Edit Procedure and Drop Procedure options in MySQL Query Browser.

Deleting a stored procedure is straightforward. Simply right-click the procedure and select Delete or Drop Procedure from the context menu. You'll see a dialog box that asks you to confirm that you want to delete the stored procedure.

In the following examples, you'll see how to modify existing stored procedures.

Try It Out: Modifying a Stored Procedure in SQL Server 2005

In this example, you'll change the stored procedure you've already created using SQL Server Management Studio.

1. Open SQL Server Management Studio and connect to the localhost\BAND database server using the sa account.

2. Expand the Databases, Players, Programmability, then Stored Procedures node. Right-click the dbo.spGetManufacturers entry and select the Modify option to modify the spGetManufacturers stored procedure. Figure 10-12 shows the SQL that is generated to modify the current stored procedure.

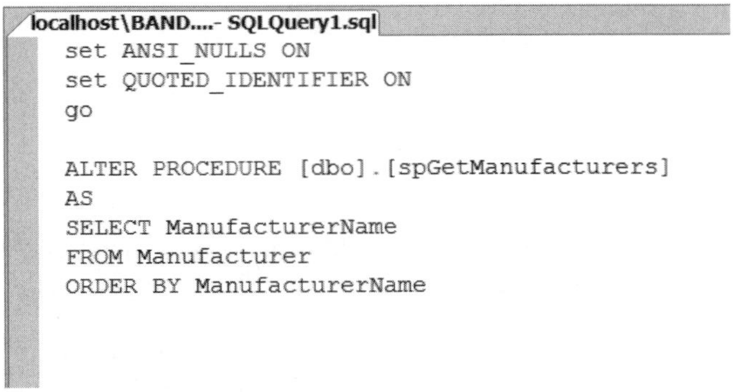

```
localhost\BAND....- SQLQuery1.sql
    set ANSI_NULLS ON
    set QUOTED_IDENTIFIER ON
    go

    ALTER PROCEDURE [dbo].[spGetManufacturers]
    AS
    SELECT ManufacturerName
    FROM Manufacturer
    ORDER BY ManufacturerName
```

Figure 10-12. *Modifying an existing stored procedure in SQL Server Management Studio*

3. Change the stored procedure to the following:

```
ALTER PROCEDURE dbo.spGetManufacturers
AS

SELECT ManufacturerID, ManufacturerName
FROM Manufacturer
ORDER BY ManufacturerName
```

4. Click the Execute button on the toolbar to run the query and modify the stored procedure.

5. Open either of the pages that you've created from the earlier examples. As shown in Figure 10-13, this will return the results from the stored procedure, with the addition of the ManufacturerID column.

Figure 10-13. *Results from executing the modified stored procedure*

How It Works

You've specified the new query for the stored procedure and saved it to the database. When you now execute the page and call the spGetManufacturers stored procedure, you get the results from the new query rather than the old one.

Editing a stored procedure in SQL Server Management Studio opens the stored procedure in the designer with the stored procedure ready to be modified as shown in Figure 10-12. It's then a simple task to modify the stored procedure.

Notice that you don't need to add any permissions for the stored procedure. As this is a modification of an existing stored procedure, any permissions that were applied to the original stored procedure will still be applied to the new stored procedure.

Try It Out: Modifying a Stored Procedure in MySQL 5.0

Modifying stored procedures in MySQL Query Browser is also quite simple. But, as you'll see, you don't use the ALTER PROCEDURE query.

1. Open MySQL Query Browser and connect to the localhost database server using the root account.

2. Expand the Players node in the Schemata pane. Right-click the spGetManufacturers entry and select the Edit Procedure option to modify the spGetManufacturers stored procedure. Figure 10-14 shows the SQL that is generated to modify the current stored procedure.

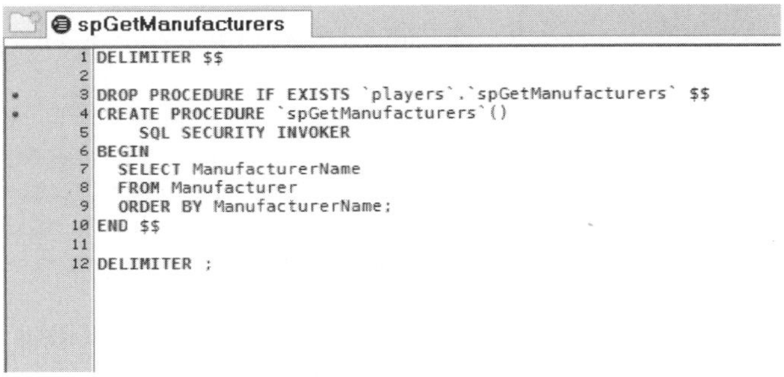

```
 1 DELIMITER $$
 2
 3 DROP PROCEDURE IF EXISTS `players`.`spGetManufacturers` $$
 4 CREATE PROCEDURE `spGetManufacturers`()
 5     SQL SECURITY INVOKER
 6 BEGIN
 7   SELECT ManufacturerName
 8   FROM Manufacturer
 9   ORDER BY ManufacturerName;
10 END $$
11
12 DELIMITER ;
```

Figure 10-14. *Modifying an existing stored procedure in MySQL Query Browser*

3. Change the query between the BEGIN and END statements to the following:

```
SELECT ManufacturerID, ManufacturerName
FROM Manufacturer
ORDER BY ManufacturerName;
```

4. Click the Execute button on the toolbar to run the query and modify the stored procedure. The only sign that the stored procedure has been modified is that you did not receive an error.

5. Execute the stored procedure in MySQL Query Browser. You'll see that it has been modified, as shown in Figure 10-15.

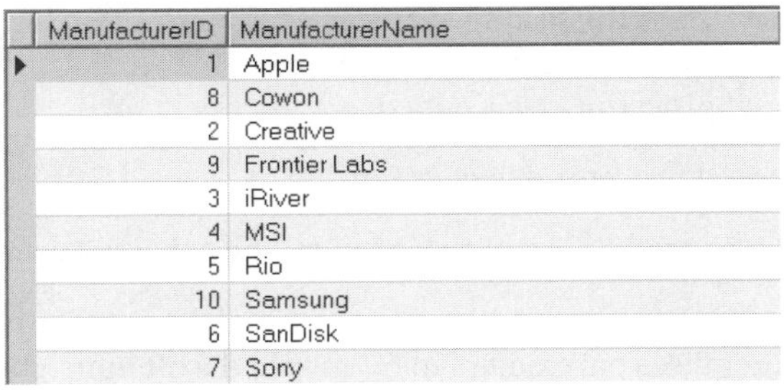

ManufacturerID	ManufacturerName
1	Apple
8	Cowon
2	Creative
9	Frontier Labs
3	iRiver
4	MSI
5	Rio
10	Samsung
6	SanDisk
7	Sony

Figure 10-15. *Results from executing the modified stored procedure in MySQL Query Browser*

6. You now need to add the permissions for the new stored procedure. In the Schemata pane, right-click the Players database node and select New Query from the context menu. Enter the following query:

```
GRANT EXECUTE ON PROCEDURE spGetManufacturers TO band
```

7. Click Execute to execute the GRANT query against the database.

How It Works

MySQL Query Browser isn't as user-friendly as SQL Server Management Studio, but it still gets the job done, just not in the same way. It doesn't modify the existing stored procedure; it deletes it and creates a new one!

The first line changes the delimiter, and then the stored procedure is dropped if it exists:

```
DROP PROCEDURE IF EXISTS 'players'.'spGetManufacturers'
```

The naming is slightly different here than SQL Server 2005. Instead of the owner, the name of the stored procedure is prefixed with the database that contains the stored procedure.

Once the existing stored procedure has been deleted, the stored procedure is re-created using a CREATE PROCEDURE query. After the new stored procedure has been created, you then need to add the permissions again.

This simple stored procedure returns all the Manufacturers in the database. This is just the beginning of the story. By responding dynamically to users and their interaction with your pages, you can impart real power to your applications. You can do this by using parameters with your stored procedures, as you'll learn in the remainder of this chapter.

Creating Stored Procedures with Input Parameters

In Chapter 4, you looked at two methods of modifying the queries when connecting to the database in code. You've also looked at using parameters when dealing with the SqlDataSource in Chapter 3 to pass values into the queries that were automatically executed. You pass parameters into stored procedures in the same way as you pass them to queries.

Whether using code or a SqlDataSource, you've been using *input parameters*—parameters that pass information to the query that being executed. SQL Server 2005 and MySQL 5.0 also define another type of parameter: an output parameter. Output parameters allow data to be returned from the stored procedure, as well as the results of any SELECT queries that have been executed. We'll look at using output parameters later in this chapter.

Using input parameters with stored procedures is a two-stage process:

- Define the parameters in the stored procedure declaration.

- Add the parameters to the SqlCommand or SqlDataSource before the call is made to execute the stored procedure.

Creating a stored procedure that requires parameters to be supplied isn't more complex than creating a stored procedure that doesn't accept parameters. You need to modify the stored procedure declaration slightly to list the parameters that are required.

For SQL Server 2005, you define the stored procedure as follows:

```
CREATE PROCEDURE <name>
<parameters>
AS
<queries>
```

For MySQL 5.0, you define the stored procedure like this:

```
CREATE PROCEDURE <name> (<parameters>)
BEGIN
  <queries>
END;
```

The parameters list is simply a list giving the name of the parameter and its type. If you have multiple parameters, separate them with commas.

SQL Server 2005 requires parameter names to be prefixed with the @ symbol. It's customary to put each parameter on its own line (it makes the stored procedure a lot more readable when editing), like so:

```
@name1 type,
@name2 type
```

MySQL 5.0 doesn't allow the @ prefix, so you use the name without the prefix:

```
name1 type, name2 type
```

All parameters that you include in the stored procedure declaration must be passed to the stored procedure by the calling application; if they aren't, an error is thrown.

SQL Server 2005 also allows you to override this default behavior. If you're sure you don't want to pass the parameter, you can override this behavior by giving the parameter a default value, as follows:

```
@name3 type = default
```

This will be used if the parameter isn't supplied a value by the calling application. If you always want a value to be passed to the stored procedure, then you don't specify a default value.

■Note Although you can use default values with stored procedures in SQL Server 2005, you're perhaps better off not doing so. Personally, I find that they're another place that an error can creep into a Web site. It's too easy to forget to pass the parameter, and this may cause the stored procedure to give incorrect results. When using the SqlDataSource, you can't use default values set within the stored procedures; the default values must be set on the parameters themselves within the page.

You'll now look at creating a stored procedure that accepts a parameter that modifies the results that are returned as part of the query. This stored procedure will also introduce you to the idea of flow control. You'll see how to use the IF statement to control what actions the stored procedure takes.

Try It Out: Creating a Stored Procedure with Input Parameters in SQL Server 2005

In this example, you'll create a new stored procedure that accepts a ManufacturerID and returns a list of Players or, if the ManufacturerID is passed as zero, returns all the Players in the database.

1. Open SQL Server Management Studio and connect to the `localhost\BAND` database server using the `sa` account.

2. Expand the Databases, then Players, then Programmability node. Select New Stored Procedure from the Stored Procedure node's context menu.

3. Give the stored procedure the following declaration:

```
CREATE PROCEDURE spGetPlayersByManufacturer
@manufacturer int
AS

IF (@manufacturer = 0) BEGIN
  SELECT Player.PlayerID, Player.PlayerName, Player.PlayerStorage,
    Player.PlayerCost, Manufacturer.ManufacturerName
  FROM Player INNER JOIN Manufacturer
    ON Player.PlayerManufacturerID = Manufacturer.ManufacturerID
  ORDER BY Player.PlayerName
END ELSE BEGIN
  SELECT PlayerID, PlayerName, PlayerStorage, PlayerCost
  FROM Player
  WHERE PlayerManufacturerID = @manufacturer
  ORDER BY Player.PlayerName
END
```

4. Click Execute to run the query and create the stored procedure.

5. In the Object Explorer, expand the Stored Procedures node and then expand the spGetPlayersByManufacturer stored procedure (you may need to refresh the Stored Procedures node to see the new stored procedure). Expand the Parameters node, and you'll be able to see the parameters for a stored procedure, without needing to open the stored procedure declaration, as shown in Figure 10-16.

6. Select the spGetPlayersByManufacturer stored procedure and select Execute Stored Procedure from the context menu. You'll be prompted to enter the values for the parameters, as shown in Figure 10-17.

7. Enter a value of 0 for the @manufacturer parameter and click OK. You'll see that all of the Players in the database are returned. Rerun the stored procedure and enter a value of 1 for the @manufacturer parameter, and you'll see that only the Players made by Apple are returned.

```
□ 🗀 Programmability
   □ 🗀 Stored Procedures
      ⊞ 🗀 System Stored Procedures
      ⊞ 🗐 dbo.spGetManufacturers
      □ 🗐 dbo.spGetPlayersByManufacturer
         □ 🗀 Parameters
               @ @manufacturer (int, Input, No default)
               🗊 Returns integer
   ⊞ 🗀 Functions
   ⊞ 🗀 Database Triggers
   ⊞ 🗀 Assemblies
   ⊞ 🗀 Types
   ⊞ 🗀 Rules
   ⊞ 🗀 Defaults
```

Figure 10-16. *You can easily view the parameters for a stored procedure in SQL Server Management Studio.*

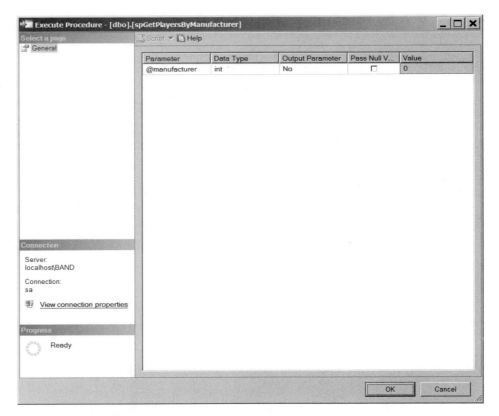

Figure 10-17. *SQL Server Management Studio allows you to test parameterized stored procedures.*

8. In the Object Explorer, right-click the Players database node and select New Query from the context menu. Execute the following query to set the permissions for the spGetPlayersByManufacturer stored procedure:

```
GRANT EXEC ON spGetPlayersByManufacturer TO band
```

How It Works

The way you've created this new stored procedure is the same way you created the spGetManufacturers stored procedure, and, unsurprisingly, you'll create every stored procedure this way. Here, you're interested in the structure of the stored procedure.

You add the parameters to the stored procedure definition between the stored procedure name and the AS statement, like so:

```
CREATE PROCEDURE dbo.spGetPlayersByManufacturer
@manufacturer int
AS
```

You have only one parameter in this particular query, and it's called @manufacturer. The name must be prefixed by the @ symbol to indicate that it's a user variable (as opposed to a system variable, which will have a prefix of @@). As you'll see when you call the stored procedure in the next example, this is the name you'll need to use when adding the parameter to the Command object and the SqlDataSource.

After the name of the parameter, you have the parameter's type. For types that require a size as well (such as the varchar type), you also need to include the size you're expecting.

Once you have declared the parameter, you can then use the parameter within the stored procedure. In this example, you use the parameter value to determine the results that are returned from the stored procedure.

If you don't want to filter the Players that are returned as part of the query, you can assume that a ManufacturerID of zero is passed to the stored procedure. You can use the ManufacturerID to determine the route through the stored procedure by using the IF statement:

```
IF (@manufacturer = 0) BEGIN
  <queries>
END ELSE BEGIN
  <queries>
END
```

As in C#, the IF statement lets you control what's executed within the stored procedure. As the condition of the IF statement, you can use any valid SQL that returns a Boolean value. You can do simple comparisons as you have here (all the usual operators are available), or you can use scalar functions (such as EXISTS) to control execution.

Depending on whether the condition evaluates to true or false, you take a different path. If it's true, you follow the path before the ELSE statement. If it's false, you follow the path after the ELSE statement.

■**Note** The BEGIN and END statements in SQL Server 2005 are equivalent to the opening and closing braces in C#. As with C#, you don't need them if you have only one query as part of the conditional path, but it makes the stored procedure a lot easier to read if they're present.

If you have a @manufacturer value of 0, you know that you don't want to filter the query, and you execute a SELECT query that returns the PlayerID, PlayerName, PlayerStorage, PlayerCost, and ManufacturerName for all the Players in the database.

```
SELECT Player.PlayerID, Player.PlayerName, Player.PlayerStorage,
  Player.PlayerCost, Manufacturer.ManufacturerName
FROM Player INNER JOIN Manufacturer
  ON Player.PlayerManufacturerID = Manufacturer.ManufacturerID
ORDER BY Player.PlayerName
```

If, however, you have a nonzero value for @manufacturer, indicating that a value has been passed into the stored procedure, you use this to constrain the SELECT query and return a slightly different list of columns, like so:

```
SELECT PlayerID, PlayerName, PlayerStorage, PlayerCost
FROM Player
WHERE PlayerManufacturerID = @manufacturer
ORDER BY Player.PlayerName
```

Try It Out: Creating a Stored Procedure with Input Parameters in MySQL 5.0

You'll now create the corresponding spGetPlayersByManufacturer stored procedure in MySQL 5.0.

1. Open MySQL Query Browser and connect to the localhost database server using the root account (the password is bandpass).

2. In the Schemata pane, right-click the Players database and select Create New Procedure / Function from the context menu. Enter a name of **spGetPlayersByManufacturer** and click the Create PROCEDURE button.

3. Enter the following stored procedure declaration:

```
DELIMITER $$

CREATE PROCEDURE spGetPlayersByManufacturer (manufacturer int)
BEGIN
  IF (manufacturer = 0) THEN
    SELECT Player.PlayerID, Player.PlayerName, Player.PlayerStorage,
      Player.PlayerCost, Manufacturer.ManufacturerName
```

```
       FROM Player INNER JOIN Manufacturer
         ON Player.PlayerManufacturerID = Manufacturer.ManufacturerID
       ORDER BY Player.PlayerName;
     ELSE
       SELECT PlayerID, PlayerName, PlayerStorage, PlayerCost
       FROM Player
       WHERE PlayerManufacturerID = manufacturer
       ORDER BY Player.PlayerName;
     END IF;
   END $$
   DELIMITER ;
```

4. Click Execute on the toolbar to run the query and create the stored procedure.

5. Expand the Players database in the Schemata pane. Expand the spGetPlayersByManufacturer stored procedure, and you'll see the parameters that the stored procedure requires, as shown in Figure 10-18.

Figure 10-18. *You can easily view the parameters for a stored procedure in MySQL Query Browser.*

6. Double-click the spGetPlayersByManufacturer stored procedure. The query window at the top of the page will be populated with a SQL query to execute the stored procedure.

7. Enter a value of **0** between the brackets and click Execute to run the stored procedure. A list of all of the Players in the database will be returned.

8. Change the query and enter a value of **1** between the brackets, and then click Execute to run the stored procedure. This time, the list of Players will be filtered for Apple.

9. In the Schemata pane, right-click the Players database node and select New Query from the context menu. Enter the following query:

```
GRANT EXECUTE ON PROCEDURE spGetPlayersByManufacturer TO band
```

10. Click Execute to execute the GRANT query against the database.

How It Works

When creating a parameterized stored procedure in MySQL 5.0, the parameters are specified between the brackets of the CREATE PROCEDURE query, as follows:

```
CREATE PROCEDURE spGetPlayersByManufacturer (manufacturer int)
```

Any value that is passed for the ManufacturerID will be available as the manufacturer variable (note the lack of the @ prefix), and you can then use this value to determine the SELECT query that is executed:

```
IF (manufacturer = 0) THEN
  <queries>
ELSE
  <queries>
END IF;
```

This is slightly different from the SQL Server 2005 IF construct, but it should be readily apparent what is happening.

Passing Parameters to Stored Procedures

You were introduced to passing parameters to a SqlDataSource in Chapter 3 and to Command objects in Chapter 4. You've also made extensive use of them in the intervening chapters to pass parameters into queries that you sent directly to the database. You use the same techniques to pass parameters to stored procedures.

When using the Command object, you need to create a Parameter object and set the name, type, and value before adding it to the Parameters collection. The SqlDataSource allows you to add parameters that can automatically bind to a variety of different values.

We'll look at both of these situations in turn to create pages that can accept a ManufacturerID as a query string parameter and modify the Players list that is displayed accordingly.

Try It Out: Using Input Parameters with a Command Object

You'll now build a slightly more complex example that displays the Players in the database and uses the spGetPlayersByManufacturer stored procedure to filter for which Manufacturer you're returning the Players.

1. Open Visual Web Developer. Open the Calling_DataReader.aspx page and save it as Input_DataReader.aspx.

2. Switch to the Source view and modify the code in the Page_Load event as follows:

```
// set up the command
myCommand.CommandText = "spGetPlayersByManufacturer";
myCommand.CommandType = CommandType.StoredProcedure;

// get the manufacturer value from the querystring
string strManufacturerID = Request.QueryString["manufacturerid"];

// determine the correct value as an integer
int intManufacturerID = 0;
if (strManufacturerID != null)
```

```
    {
      intManufacturerID = Convert.ToInt32(strManufacturerID);
    }

    // create the parameter
    SqlParameter myParameter1 = new SqlParameter();
    myParameter1.ParameterName = "@manufacturer";
    myParameter1.SqlDbType = SqlDbType.Int;
    myParameter1.Value = intManufacturerID;

    // add it to the command object
    myCommand.Parameters.Add(myParameter1);

    // open the database connection
    myConnection.Open();

    // run query
    SqlDataReader myReader = myCommand.ExecuteReader();
```

3. Execute the page. You'll see that the list of Players returned includes all of the Players in the database, as shown in Figure 10-19.

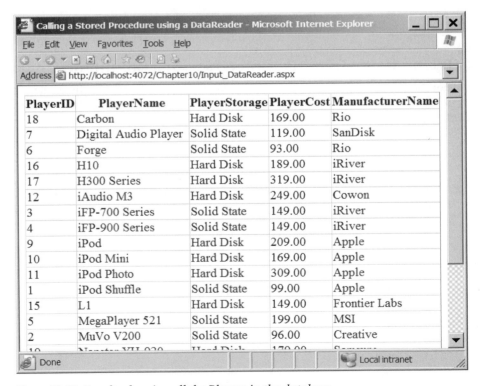

Figure 10-19. *Results showing all the Players in the database*

4. Modify the address that you're viewing and add ?manufacturerid=1 to the URL. Press Enter to load the page. You see all the Players manufactured by Apple, as shown in Figure 10-20.

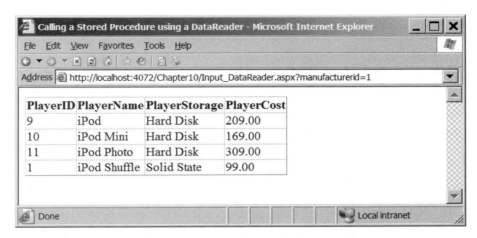

Figure 10-20. *Results showing the Players for a particular Manufacturer*

How It Works

This simple example demonstrates that passing parameters to stored procedures is the same as passing parameters to queries.

You call a stored procedure by creating a Command object. You set the CommandText to the name of the stored procedure, spGetPlayersByManufacturer, and the CommandType to CommandType. StoredProcedure. You then check to see whether a ManufacturerID has been added to the query string. As you know, Request.QueryString returns null if the requested value isn't present, and you use this fact to default to a ManufacturerID of 0 if the query string value isn't present:

```
// do we need to add the @manufacturer parameter
string strManufacturerID = Request.QueryString["manufacturerid"];

// determine the correct value as an integer
int intManufacturerID = 0;
if (strManufacturerID != null)
{
  intManufacturerID = Convert.ToInt32(strManufacturerID);
}
```

You then need to add the parameter to the Command object. You create a SqlParameter object and give it the correct name. Because you're using the SqlCommand object, you need to use the name that the stored procedure expects, so you use @manufacturer, like so:

```
// create the parameter
SqlParameter myParameter1 = new SqlParameter();
myParameter1.ParameterName = "@manufacturer";
```

You then specify the type of the parameter from the `SqlDbType` enumeration and set the value of the parameter to the value from the query string, like so:

```
myParameter1.SqlDbType = SqlDbType.Int;
myParameter1.Value = intManufacturerID;
```

Once the parameter has been created and correctly populated, you can add it to the `Parameters` collection of the `SqlCommand` object, like so:

```
// add it to the command object
myCommand.Parameters.Add (myParameter1);
```

You then use the `ExecuteReader()` method of the `SqlCommand` object to return a `SqlDataReader` object and bind this to the data grid.

When the stored procedure is executed, the route that's taken depends on the value passed as the parameter to the `SqlCommand` object, as discussed when you created the stored procedure in the previous example.

Try It Out: Using Input Parameters with a SqlDataSource

In this example, you'll build the same page as you saw in the previous example, but this time, you'll use a `SqlDataSource`.

1. Open Visual Web Developer. Open the `Calling_DataSource.aspx` page and save it as `Input_DataSource.aspx`.

2. Switch to the Design view and select the `SqlDataSource`. In the Properties window, click the ellipsis next to the `SelectQuery` property.

3. Change the `SELECT` query to `spGetPlayersByManufacturer`.

4. Click the Add Parameter button and change the name of the added parameter to `manufacturer`.

5. Change the `Parameter` source to `QueryString` and set the `QueryStringField` value as `manufacturerid`. Enter a default value of **0**.

6. Click OK to close the Command and Parameter Editor dialog box.

7. Execute the page. You'll see that the list of Players returned includes all of the Players in the database, as shown earlier in Figure 10-18.

8. Modify the address that you're viewing and add `?manufacturerid=1` to the URL. Press Enter to load the page. You'll see that it displays only Players manufactured by Apple, as shown earlier in Figure 10-19.

How It Works

In Chapter 3, you learned that you can automatically pass several different types of parameters to the various commands of the `SqlDataSource`. In this case, you're using the `manufacturerid` query string value:

```
<SelectParameters>
  <asp:QueryStringParameter DefaultValue="0" Name="manufacturer"
    QueryStringField="manufacturerid" Type="Int32" />
</SelectParameters>
```

The only new detail to the QueryStringParameter is the addition of the DefaultValue property. The DefaultValue allows you to specify the value that you want to pass into the stored procedure when, in this example, the query string value that you're after doesn't exist. For this stored procedure, you need to pass a value of 0 for the @manufacturer parameter when you don't have a manufacturerid value specified in the query string.

Using Parameters with MySQL 5.0

As you saw in earlier chapters, when using parameters in SQL Server 2005, you can add parameters to the SqlCommand object in whatever order you like, because the SqlCommand object supports named parameters. When connecting to MySQL 5.0 using the Odbc data provider, the parameters must be added in the correct order. Thankfully, using Connector/Net when connecting to MySQL 5.0 removes this limitation, as it does support named parameters.

You saw when creating the parameterized query in MySQL 5.0 that you specify parameters in brackets after the stored procedure name. In MySQL 5.0, local variables aren't prefixed with a @ as they are in SQL Server 2005, so the definition of spGetPlayersByManufacturer is as follows:

```
CREATE PROCEDURE spGetPlayersByManufacturer (manufacturer int)
```

To add the manufacturer parameter to the MySqlCommand object, you need to use the parameter name prefixed with ?, as follows:

```
MySqlParameter myParameter1 = new MySqlParameter();
myParameter1.ParameterName = "?manufacturer";
myParameter1.MySqlDbType = MySqlDbType.Int32;
myParameter1.Value = intManufacturerID;
myCommand.Parameters.Add(myParameter1);
```

Other than those few little changes, parameters—both input and output—work the same way in MySQL 5.0 as they do in SQL Server 2005.

Returning Data Using Output Parameters

Although you've now seen how you can pass parameters to a stored procedure, this isn't the end of what you can do with parameters. You can also use them to return values from a stored procedure.

You've already looked at two ways of returning data from the database: using the ExecuteReader() and ExecuteScalar() methods of the Command object, and by data binding when using a SqlDataSource.

Sometimes, however, you want to execute a query that doesn't return any results directly but returns information detailing what you've just done. If you're inserting information into the database, you may want to return a key for what you've just inserted. Or you may want to return more information than can be returned within the scope of the normal SELECT query. *Output parameters* are the key to this.

You can modify the values of user variables within stored procedures, and if they're parameters, the changed value may be returned to the calling application. If the parameter is an input parameter, the value isn't returned. When you use output parameters, the changed value is returned.

■Note The name *output parameter* is perhaps a bit misleading because an output parameter is more accurately an input/output parameter. You can pass a value into a stored procedure using an output parameter, and any changes to the parameter will be reflected in the parameter once control has returned from the stored procedure.

To use output parameters instead of input parameters, you don't need to do a lot of work. You can accomplish it in the following two stages:

- Tell the stored procedure that the parameter is an output parameter.

- Tell the Command object or SqlDataSource that the stored procedure is an output parameter, and then retrieve the changed value from the parameter after the stored procedure has executed.

To use output parameters within the stored procedure you need to mark the definition of the parameter as being an output parameter. For SQL Server 2005, you use the OUTPUT statement with the definition of the parameter, like so:

```
@name type = default OUTPUT
```

In MySQL 5.0, you need to prefix the parameter declaration with OUT, like so:

```
OUT name type
```

You're free to mix input and output stored procedures however you want in the stored procedure declaration.

As with input parameters, SQL Server 2005 also allows you to give output parameters default values that will be used if the parameter isn't passed to the stored procedure by the calling application.

Try It Out: Creating a Stored Procedure with Output Parameters in SQL Server 2005

You'll now build on the stored procedure in the previous example to include an output parameter that returns the number of Players for the selected Manufacturer.

1. Open SQL Server Management Studio and connect to the localhost\BAND database server using the sa account.

2. Expand the Databases, Players, then Programmability node and select New Stored Procedure from the Stored Procedure node's context menu.

3. Add the following stored procedure declaration:

```
CREATE PROCEDURE dbo.spGetPlayersWithCountByManufacturer
@manufacturer int,
@rowcount int OUTPUT
AS

IF (@manufacturer = 0) BEGIN
  SELECT Player.PlayerID, Player.PlayerName, Player.PlayerStorage,
    Player.PlayerCost, Manufacturer.ManufacturerName
  FROM Player
    INNER JOIN Manufacturer
    ON Player.PlayerManufacturerID = Manufacturer.ManufacturerID
  ORDER BY Player.PlayerName

  SET @rowcount = @@ROWCOUNT
END ELSE BEGIN
  SELECT PlayerID, PlayerName, PlayerStorage, PlayerCost
  FROM Player
  WHERE PlayerManufacturerID = @manufacturer
  ORDER BY Player.PlayerName

  SET @rowcount = @@ROWCOUNT
END
```

4. Click Execute to run the query and save the modified stored procedure to the database.

5. Expand the Parameters node underneath the spGetPlayersByManufacturer stored procedure. You'll see that output parameters are also shown, but with a different icon, indicating that they're output parameters, as shown in Figure 10-21.

Figure 10-21. *Output parameters are displayed with a different icon in SQL Server Management Studio.*

6. In the Object Explorer, right-click the Players database node and select New Query from the context menu. Execute the following query to set the permissions for the spGetPlayersByManufacturer stored procedure:

```
GRANT EXEC ON spGetPlayersWithCountByManufacturer TO band
```

How It Works

As you can see from the stored procedure declaration, you've added the following output parameter of type int called @rowcount:

```
@rowcount int OUTPUT
```

You'll use this to return the count of the number of rows that are returned for the Manufacturer you've selected. You use the SET statement to assign values to variables, and you can set @rowcount to the number of rows returned using the @@ROWCOUNT system variable, like so:

```
SET @rowcount = @@ROWCOUNT
```

@@ROWCOUNT returns the number of rows that the previous SQL query returned or affected and is valid not only for SELECT, but also for DELETE, INSERT, and UPDATE.

Try It Out: Creating a Stored Procedure with Input Parameters in MySQL 5.0

You'll now create the corresponding spGetPlayersWithCountByManufacturer stored procedure in MySQL 5.0.

1. Open MySQL Query Browser and connect to the localhost database server using the root account (the password is bandpass).

2. In the Schemata pane, right-click the Players database and select Create New Procedure / Function from the context menu. Enter a name of spGetPlayersWithCountByManufacturer and click the Create PROCEDURE button.

3. Enter the following stored procedure declaration:

```
DELIMITER $$

CREATE PROCEDURE spGetPlayersByManufacturer (manufacturer int,
  OUT rowcount int)
BEGIN
  IF (manufacturer = 0) THEN
    SELECT Player.PlayerID, Player.PlayerName, Player.PlayerStorage,
      Player.PlayerCost, Manufacturer.ManufacturerName
    FROM Player INNER JOIN Manufacturer
      ON Player.PlayerManufacturerID = Manufacturer.ManufacturerID
    ORDER BY Player.PlayerName;
```

```
      SET rowcount = (SELECT COUNT(*) FROM Player);
    ELSE
      SELECT PlayerID, PlayerName, PlayerStorage, PlayerCost
      FROM Player
      WHERE PlayerManufacturerID = manufacturer
      ORDER BY Player.PlayerName;

      SET rowcount = (SELECT COUNT(*) FROM Player
       WHERE PlayerManufacturerID = manufacturer);
    END IF;
END $$
DELIMITER ;
```

4. Click Execute on the toolbar to run the query and create the stored procedure.

5. Expand the Players database in the Schemata pane, and then expand the spGetPlayersWithCountByManufacturer stored procedure. You can see the parameters that the stored procedure requires, as shown in Figure 10-22.

Figure 10-22. *Output parameters aren't shown differently in MySQL Query Browser.*

6. In the Schemata pane, right-click the Players database node and select New Query from the context menu. Enter the following query:

```
GRANT EXECUTE ON PROCEDURE spGetPlayersWithCountByManufacturer TO band
```

7. Click Execute to execute the GRANT query against the database.

How It Works

Adding an output parameter to a stored procedure in MySQL 5.0 is as simple as prefixing the parameter declaration with OUT:

```
OUT rowcount int
```

You'll use this to return the count of the number of rows that are returned for the Manufacturer you've selected. Unfortunately, the ROW_COUNT() function in MySQL doesn't work in stored procedures, so you need to use the COUNT scalar function to return the number of rows selected. For the unfiltered list, this is as follows:

```
SET rowcount = (SELECT COUNT(*) FROM Player);
```

The filtered list is returned the same way:

```
SET rowcount = (SELECT COUNT(*) FROM Player
  WHERE PlayerManufacturerID = manufacturer);
```

Returning Parameters from Stored Procedures

You've already seen how you add input parameters to the SqlCommand object and SqlDataSource. Adding output parameters is similar, except that you need to change the direction of the parameter. This is because parameters are defined as input parameters by default.

When using the SqlCommand object and the SqlDataSource, you specify the direction for a parameter using the Direction property and setting it to one of the values in the System.Data.ParameterDirection enumeration. The default value for the Direction property is Input. To specify it for an input parameter to the SqlCommand object, use this form:

```
myParameter.Direction = ParameterDirection.Input
```

Similarly, for an input parameter to a SqlDataSource, you would set the property as follows:

```
Direction="Input"
```

For output parameters, you can use either of the following for the Direction property:

- Output: Returns the value from the stored procedure, but any value you attempt to send to the stored procedure is ignored.

- InputOutput: Allows values to be passed into the stored procedure by the parameter and will return the parameter value from the stored procedure.

Although SQL Server and MySQL allow all OUTPUT parameters to accept an input value, ADO.NET makes a distinction between these two options.

If you declare a parameter as solely an Output parameter, then even if you give it a value before calling the stored procedure, the value will not be passed to the stored procedure. The output value will be set correctly, but any input value is completely ignored.

On the other hand, if you define the parameter as an InputOutput parameter, then any value you give it will also be passed to the stored procedure.

Note This is one of the few instances where passing parameters to SQL Server 2005 and MySQL 5.0 is different. If you're using a parameter direction of Output or InputOutput with MySQL 5.0, you don't need to provide a value for the parameter. However, if you're using SQL Server 2005, you must provide a value if the parameter is an InputOutput parameter. If you don't, an error will occur when you try to execute the stored procedure.

Try It Out: Using Output Parameters with a SqlCommand Object

In this example, you'll build on the previous example and return the number of rows from the spGetPlayersWithCountByManufacturer stored procedure using an output parameter.

1. Open Visual Web Developer. Open the Input_DataReader.aspx page and save it as Output_DataReader.aspx.

2. Add the following HTML immediately before the GridView:

```
<p>
Returned <asp:Label id="Label1" runat="server">0</asp:Label> players.
</p>
```

3. Modify the code in the Page_Load event to add the second parameter and retrieve the output parameter after the stored procedure. Add the following code after the declaration of the @manufacturer parameter:

```
// add the @rowcount parameter
SqlParameter myParameter2 = new SqlParameter();
myParameter2.ParameterName = "@rowcount";
myParameter2.SqlDbType = SqlDbType.Int;
myParameter2.Direction = ParameterDirection.Output;
myCommand.Parameters.Add (myParameter2);
```

4. Add the following to retrieve the output parameter after the line to close the DataReader:

```
// now get the output parameter
Label1.Text = Convert.ToString(myCommand.Parameters["@rowcount"].Value);
```

5. Execute the page. This will execute the stored procedure, return all the Players in the database, and update the count of the number of Players returned, as shown in Figure 10-23.

6. Modify the address that you're viewing and add ?manufacturerid=1 to the URL. Press Enter to load the page, displaying the Players manufactured by Apple as well as the count, as shown in Figure 10-24.

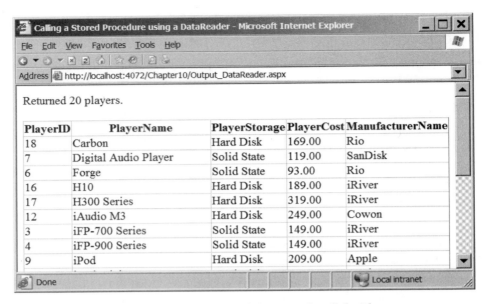

Figure 10-23. *Results showing the Players and the count for all the Players*

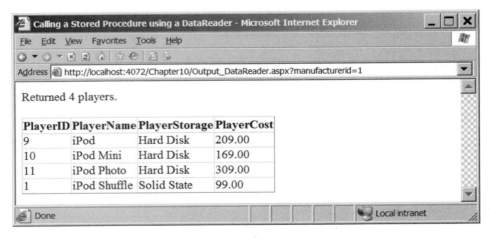

Figure 10-24. *Players and their count for a particular Manufacturer*

How It Works

The first change you make is to add the output parameter. You declare the parameter as you have all the other parameters you've used, but this time, you specify the direction of the parameter, like so:

```
// add the @rowcount parameter
SqlParameter myParameter2 = new SqlParameter();
myParameter2.ParameterName = "@rowcount";
myParameter2.SqlDbType = SqlDbType.Int;
myParameter2.Direction = ParameterDirection.Output;
myCommand.Parameters.Add (myParameter2);
```

You then execute the stored procedure as you normally would, bind the reader to the GridView, and then close the DataReader. Once the DataReader has been closed, you can retrieve the values of the output parameters simply by using the name of the parameter as the index to the Parameters collection of the Command object, like so:

```
// now get the output parameter
Label1.Text = Convert.ToString(myCommand.Parameters["@rowcount"].Value);
```

You're after the value of the parameter, so you use the Value property. This property returns an Object that you can then cast to whatever type you want. In this case, you want to set the Text property of a Label, so you convert the value to a string.

When using the Command object and output parameters, it's important to remember that you must close the DataReader object you're using before you can access the output parameters. If it isn't closed, the output parameters will not be populated with the results you expect.

■Note If you were using ExecuteScalar() or ExecuteNonQuery() to execute a stored procedure that has output parameters, you wouldn't have any problems and wouldn't need to worry about closing things before you could access the output parameters. This isn't strictly a "problem" with the implementation of the ExecuteReader() method, but it's a big enough issue to warrant its own Microsoft Knowledge Base article (http://support.microsoft.com/default.aspx?scid=kb;en-us;Q308621). Although the article is about ADO.NET 1.0, the problem still occurs in ADO.NET 2.0. The same problem also affects Connector/Net. So, you should always close the DataReader before you try to use any of the output parameters.

Try It Out: Using Output Parameters with a SqlDataSource

Now you'll build on a previous example to demonstrate using output parameters with a SqlDataSource.

1. Open Visual Web Developer. Open the Input_DataSource.aspx page and save it as Output_DataSource.aspx.

2. Add the following HTML immediately before the GridView:

```
<p>
Returned <asp:Label id="Label1" runat="server">0</asp:Label> players.
</p>
```

3. Switch to the Design view and select the SqlDataSource. In the Properties window, click the ellipsis for the SelectQuery property.

4. Click the Add Parameter to add a new parameter. Name the parameter rowcount.

5. Click the Show Advanced Properties link and set Direction to Output and Type to Int32.

6. Click OK to close the Command and Parameter Editor dialog box.

7. Switch to the Events view for the SqlDataSource and add a Selected event. Change the code within the event handler as follows:

    ```
    protected void SqlDataSource1_Selected(object sender,
      SqlDataSourceStatusEventArgs e)
    {
      Label1.Text = Convert.ToString(e.Command.Parameters["@rowcount"].Value);
    }
    ```

8. Execute the page. This will execute the stored procedure, return all the Players in the database, and update the count of the number of Players returned, as shown earlier in Figure 10-23.

9. Modify the address that you're viewing and add ?manufacturerid=1 to the URL, and then press Enter to load the page. You'll see the Players manufactured by Apple, as well as the count, as shown earlier in Figure 10-24.

How It Works

To return the value as the output parameter, you've created a new parameter without a parameter source and set its Direction to Output and its Type to Int32. You can see this more clearly if you look at the markup that is generated:

```
<SelectParameters>
  <asp:QueryStringParameter DefaultValue="0" Name="manufacturer"
    QueryStringField="manufacturerid" />
  <asp:Parameter Direction="Output" Name="rowcount" Type="Int32" />
</SelectParameters>
```

To access the output parameter, you need to catch the Selected event from the SqlDataSource. Each of the four operations that you can perform has a before and after event (such as Selecting and Selected), and you need to catch the after event, as you can look at the output parameter value only after the stored procedure has been executed.

Within the event, you access the parameters in much the same way as you do when manually accessing the Command object in code, except this time, you use the Command property of the event argument:

```
Label1.Text = Convert.ToString(e.Command.Parameters["@rowcount"].Value);
```

You need to get the Value property of the parameter. Because it's returned as an Object, you cast this to a string before setting the Text property for the label to display the count of the number of rows returned.

■Note You may be thinking that the syntax for accessing the parameters for the Command object and SqlDataSource are quite similar. In fact, they're identical. The Command property within any of the eight before and after events for the SqlDataSource actually returns the Command object that is being used internally to execute the stored procedure. Once you have the Command object, you're free to interrogate it as you would a Command object that you created yourself.

Using Stored Procedures with Other Queries

In this chapter, we've looked at stored procedures that return results; that is, those that contain SELECT queries. Stored procedures aren't limited to just SELECT queries, though. INSERT, UPDATE, and DELETE queries, which were introduced in Chapter 8, also are perfectly valid queries to use in stored procedures.

We're not going to walk through any step-by-step examples of using these other queries, as the procedure for creating the stored procedure is the same. Instead, we'll look at stored procedure replacements for some of the queries and query batches that we looked at in Chapter 8.

For instance, consider the UPDATE query that you used in Player_Update.aspx in Chapter 8. You would create the stored procedure using the following query:

```
CREATE PROCEDURE spPlayerUpdate
  @PlayerID int,
  @Name varchar(50),
  @ManufacturerID int,
  @Cost decimal(10,2),
  @Storage varchar(50)
AS

UPDATE Player SET PlayerName = @Name, PlayerManufacturerID = @ManufacturerID,
  PlayerCost = @Cost, PlayerStorage = @Storage
WHERE PlayerID = @PlayerID
```

If you look back to Chapter 8, you'll see that the UPDATE query itself is the same query as you passed to the database. Instead of passing the UPDATE query to the database, you would pass the name of the stored procedure and call ExecuteNonQuery() to execute the stored procedure.

You can call the stored procedure in the same way as the SQL query and also define the parameters in the same way:

```
myCommand.Parameters.AddWithValue("@PlayerID",
  Request.QueryString["PlayerID"]);
myCommand.Parameters.AddWithValue("@Name", PlayerName.Text);
myCommand.Parameters.AddWithValue("@ManufacturerID",
  ManufacturerList.SelectedValue);
myCommand.Parameters.AddWithValue("@Cost", PlayerCost.Text);
myCommand.Parameters.AddWithValue("@Storage", PlayerStorage.Text);
```

The spPlayerUpdate stored procedure, in this case, is a direct replacement for a single query that you passed to the database. You have five parameters to the SQL query, and you have the same five parameters to the stored procedure. As you're using named parameters, the order that you add the parameters doesn't matter, but it is good practice to keep the ordering consistent in the stored procedure and code. If nothing else, it makes it easier to see whether any of the parameters have been missed.

As you saw with the output parameters example, a stored procedure can do more than execute one query. You can use this to your advantage to simplify the Player_Insert.aspx page. When adding a new Player to the database, you need to return the PlayerID of the newly created Player. This requires two queries that you executed as a query batch in Chapter 8. But with a stored procedure, you can execute both of the queries in the same stored procedure:

```
CREATE PROCEDURE spPlayerInsert
  @Name varchar(50),
  @ManufacturerID int,
  @Cost decimal(10,2),
  @Storage varchar(50)
AS

INSERT Player (PlayerName, PlayerManufacturerID, PlayerCost, PlayerStorage)
VALUES (@Name, @ManufacturerID, @Cost, @Storage);

SELECT SCOPE_IDENTITY();
```

You first insert the Player into the database and then return the SCOPE_IDENTITY() value. This returns the PlayerID from the stored procedure, and you can access this using the ExecuteScalar() method. This is the same technique as you saw for retrieving the PlayerID from the query batch in Chapter 8:

```
intPlayerID = Convert.ToInt32(myCommand.ExecuteScalar());
```

The DELETE query from Player_Delete.aspx can also be used in a stored procedure very easily. In this stored procedure, you're again executing two queries that you previously ran as a query batch:

```
CREATE PROCEDURE spPlayerDelete
  @PlayerID int
AS

DELETE FROM WhatPlaysWhatFormat WHERE WPWFPlayerID = @PlayerID;
DELETE FROM Player WHERE PlayerID = @PlayerID;
```

Nothing to it! Following the procedures you learned in the various examples in this chapter, you'll be able to modify the pages that you created in Chapter 8 to use stored procedures.

Summary

This chapter started by looking at the advantages of using stored procedures. Depending on the database server that you're using, there are several reasons for using stored procedures:

- Simplified maintenance

- Increased security

- Increased performance

- Reduced network traffic

After looking at why you might use stored procedures over direct SQL queries, you then took a step back from the relative complexities of the previous chapters. You created several stored procedures that used the following options you have for passing and returning data to and from stored procedures:

- Returning data using a SELECT query

- Passing parameters using input parameters

- Returning data using output parameters

You also saw that there's very little difference between calling a stored procedure and executing a SQL query. You pass the stored procedure name as the query to execute and tell the Command object or SqlDataSource that you're executing a stored procedure by specifying StoredProcedure.

We then looked briefly at how to use stored procedures for executing INSERT, UPDATE, and DELETE queries. You saw the definitions of three stored procedures that are replacements for the SQL queries that were introduced in Chapter 8.

In the next chapter, we'll look at the DDL subset of SQL and see what it can do. As you'll see in the next chapter, you can use SQL to create the entire database, without ever going near a graphical tool.

CHAPTER 11

Modifying the Database Structure

In Chapter 2, you saw that you can execute three types of SQL queries. One type is Data Manipulation Language (DML) for querying data. These are the SELECT, INSERT, UPDATE, and DELETE queries you've worked with in the previous chapters. Another type is Data Control Language (DCL) queries for controlling access to the database, and you've used the GRANT query in the previous chapters to allow the band account to access tables and stored procedures in the database. The third type is Data Definition Language (DDL), which allows you to modify the structure of the database.

In Chapter 2, you looked at using SQL Server Management Studio to create the SQL Server database and MySQL Query Browser to create the MySQL database. Both of these graphical clients allow you to manipulate databases, shielding you from the majority of DDL queries. Under the covers, however, DDL queries are used to accomplish the task you specified in the graphical client.

In the intervening chapters, you concentrated on DML queries and built several examples that interacted with the database. In Chapter 10, you looked at a few DDL queries for creating stored procedures: CREATE PROCEDURE, ALTER PROCEDURE, and DROP PROCEDURE.

In this chapter, you'll turn your attention to DDL queries and learn what you can do with them. To work with DDL queries, you need to use a tool that allows you to enter queries and execute them directly against the database. As you've already seen, both SQL Management Studio and MySQL Query Browser allow you to do this. For most of the examples in this chapter, you'll use the graphical clients.

Sometimes, however, you can't use a graphical tool to query the database; in these cases, you need to dive into the murky world of command-line tools. Both SQL Server and MySQL have command-line clients that are installed by default. You'll briefly look at these before you begin examining the various DDL queries.

This chapter is intended as a brief introduction to DDL, not a complete reference work. Entire books have been written about the subject. For examples of more complex DDL, see the scripts provided in this book's code download. You'll see that this chapter doesn't cover a lot of advanced topics (and you'll probably agree that you don't want that much detail at this stage).

This chapter covers the following topics:

- The command-line tools

- DDL for creating databases

- DDL for creating tables

- DDL for adding, modifying, and removing table columns

- DDL for creating and deleting indexes

- DDL for creating and deleting table relationships

- DDL for deleting tables

- DDL for deleting databases

Using Command-Line Tools

Both SQL Server and MySQL install a command-line tool that can connect to both local and remote databases and allow SQL queries to be executed against the database. Although the tools are similar, they have differences. The following sections show each of these in turn.

■**Note** You have a lot more options for both SQLCMD and mysql.exe than what you'll see here. You can find more details about SQLCMD at http://msdn.microsoft.com/en-us/library/ms162773.aspx. For mysql.exe, refer to http://dev.mysql.com/doc/refman/5.0/en/mysql.html.

Using SQLCMD

SQLCMD is installed as part of the SQL Server installation, and if the default installation folder has been accepted, it will be in the C:\Program Files\Microsoft SQL Server\90\Tools\binn folder.

To use SQLCMD, you must specify the server to connect to and the security credentials you want to use for the connection.

To specify the server, use the -S parameter, followed by the server to which you want to connect. If you don't specify a server, SQLCMD will assume you want to connect to the default instance of SQL Server on the local machine.

The security credentials you specify depend on whether you're using Windows authentication or SQL authentication. If you want to use Windows authentication, you specify this with the -E parameter. If you want to use SQL authentication, you must specify the username and password by using the -U and -P parameters, respectively. So, to connect to the (local)\BAND server using Windows authentication, use the following command line:

```
SQLCMD -E -S (local)\BAND
```

To connect to the same server using SQL authentication and the band account, you need to specify the username and password you want to use, as follows:

```
SQLCMD -U band -P letmein -S (local)\BAND
```

If you're being security conscious, then typing a password in plain text is a big problem. You can force SQLCMD to ask you for the password rather than specifying it on the command line by simply omitting the -P parameter. Then you'll be prompted for the password before the connection is made.

```
SQLCMD -U band -S (local)\BAND
```

Although you can now connect to the server using the correct credentials, you still may not be connected to the correct database. If you don't specify a database, you'll connect to the default database for the user (in most cases, this will be the master database). You can specify the database to use once a connection has been made using the USE SQL query, but it's equally valid to specify this on the command line using the -d parameter followed by the database name. So, to connect to the Players database on the (local)\BAND server using the band account, use the following command:

```
SQLCMD -U band -S (local)\BAND -d Players
```

If the connection to the database is refused, the error message that's returned by SQLCMD is quite helpful. If you specified incorrect login details, you will get a "Login failed for user" message. If you specified an invalid database, you will get a "Cannot open database requested in login" message. You can fix the error noted in the message and then try to connect to the database again.

Try It Out: Querying a SQL Server Database via the Command Line

You'll begin your introduction to DDL using the SQLCMD command-line tool. You'll use this to execute a simple query against the Players database.

1. Open a command prompt, enter the following command, and then press Enter:

   ```
   SQLCMD -U band -S (local)\BAND -d Players
   ```

2. At the prompt, enter letmein as the password (your entry won't be echoed to the screen). This will open the SQLCMD command-line tool, as shown in Figure 11-1.

3. Enter the following at the 1> prompt, and then press Enter:

   ```
   SELECT * FROM Manufacturer ORDER BY ManufacturerName
   ```

4. At the 2> prompt, enter GO and press Enter. This will execute the command and return the results, as shown in Figure 11-2.

5. Close SQLCMD by entering EXIT or QUIT and pressing Enter.

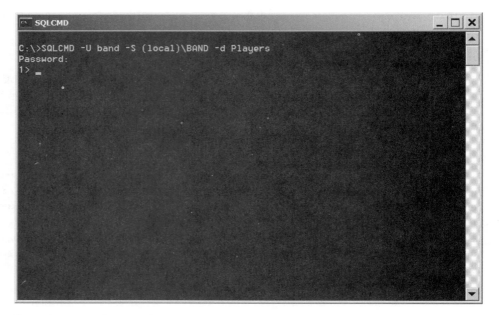

Figure 11-1. *SQLCMD ready to accept commands*

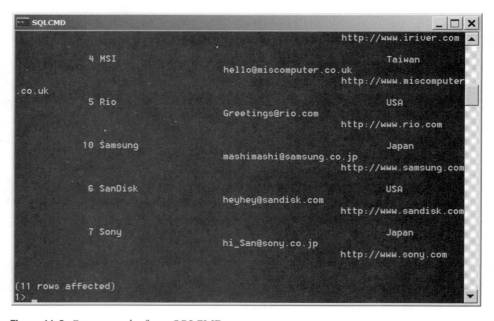

Figure 11-2. *Query results from SQLCMD*

How It Works

Even though SQLCMD is in a rather obscure folder, you can normally launch it from anywhere, because that folder has been added to the command-line execution path.

■**Note** The command-line execution path in Windows allows command-line tools to be executed regardless of the directory that contains the executable and the current directory. The SQL Server installer adds the correct path for SQLCMD to the end of the path variable, so you don't normally need to worry about its location.

On the command line, you specify the server, database, and user account you want to use and force SQLCMD to ask you for the password you want to use. This prevents anyone from looking over your shoulder and seeing the passwords you're using. This isn't a massive security risk, but you should be doing all you can to ensure that your database password remains secret.

Once you've connected to the database, you execute a simple SELECT query against the Manufacturer table and return all the entries in the table, as shown previously in Figure 11-2.

Using SQLCMD, you can enter several queries separated by semicolons, or you can spread one query across several different lines (which is quite valuable if you have complex queries). Only when SQLCMD sees a GO command does it execute the query or queries you've entered.

You close the connection to the database and SQLCMD by using either the QUIT or EXIT command. You can use these commands interchangeably.

Using mysql.exe

The MySQL 5.0 command-line tool is installed in the bin folder of the MySQL 5.0 installation. If the defaults have been accepted, it will be in the C:\Program Files\MySQL\MySQL Server 5.0\bin folder.

Specifying the server, database, and security credentials for mysql.exe is similar to SQLCMD.

To specify the server you want to connect to, you use the -h parameter, followed by the name of the server. If the server isn't specified, an attempt will be made to connect to MySQL on the local machine.

You specify the security credentials you want to use with the -u and -p parameters, as with SQLCMD, except that with mysql.exe, the switches themselves must be lowercase. If you want mysql.exe to prompt for the password, specify the -p parameter without a value.

You can specify the database you want to connect to by using the -D parameter or by simply adding the database name as the last thing on the command line. If you don't specify a database, you'll connect to the server but won't connect to a database; therefore, you must change to the database you want to access with the USE query.

So, to connect to the Players database on the local machine using the band account, use the following command line:

```
mysql -u band -p Players
```

Try It Out: Querying a MySQL Database via the Command Line

In this example, you'll use mysql.exe to connect to the Players database and execute a simple query to return all the Manufacturers in the database.

1. Open a command prompt and navigate to the C:\Program Files\MySQL\ MySQL Server 5.0\bin folder.

2. Enter the following command, and then press Enter:

   ```
   mysql -u band -p Players
   ```

3. At the prompt, enter letmein as the password. This will open the mysql.exe command-line tool, as shown in Figure 11-3.

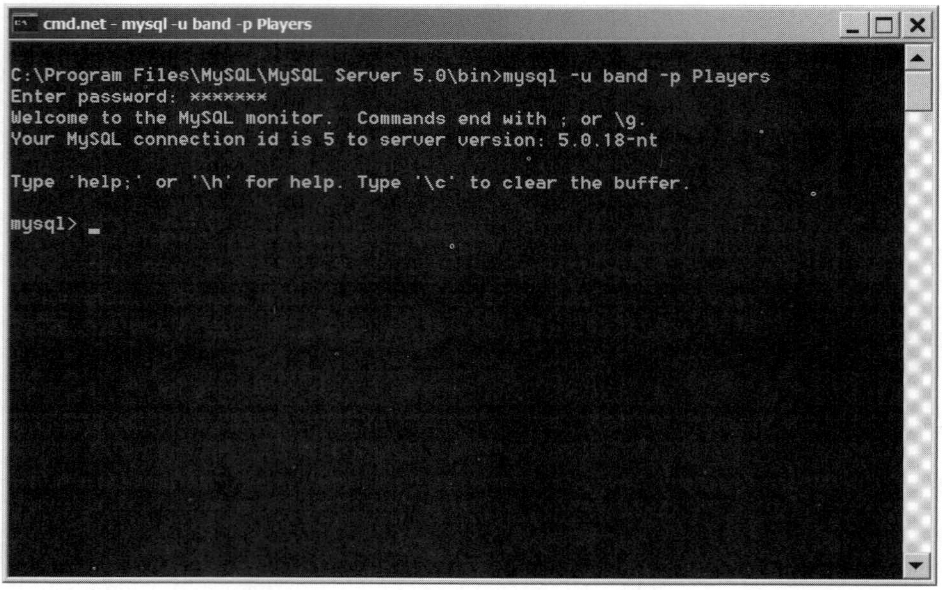

Figure 11-3. *mysql.exe ready to accept commands*

4. Enter the following query, and then press Enter:

   ```
   SELECT * FROM Manufacturer ORDER BY ManufacturerName;
   ```

5. This will execute the query and return the results, as shown in Figure 11-4.

6. Close mysql.exe by entering EXIT or QUIT and then pressing Enter.

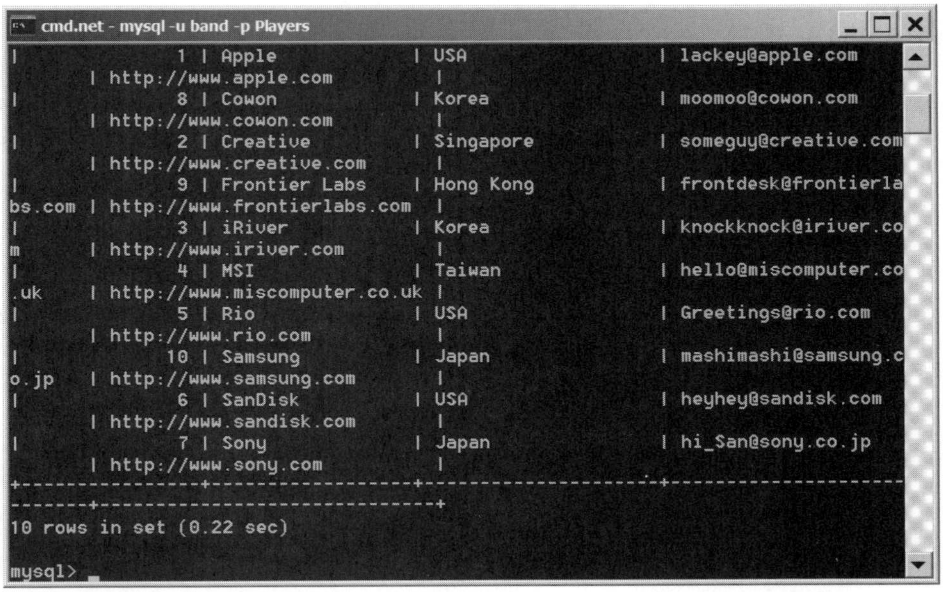

Figure 11-4. *Query results from mysql.exe*

How It Works

Unlike SQLCMD, the path to the mysql.exe executable isn't added to the path for you, so you must navigate to the correct folder before you can execute it. You could, of course, use the full path for the executable if you require.

■Note If you're going to use mysql.exe often, it's a lot easier to add the path to the executable in the Windows path. You can do this by adding C:\Program Files\MySQL\MySQL Server 5.0\bin to the end of the path in Windows in the autoexec.bat file or, in Windows 2000 onward, by modifying the PATH environment variable.

Once you've entered the password and connected to the database, you enter the queries you want to execute. After they're executed, the results are returned in a tabular format.

Unlike SQLCMD, you can enter only one query at a time, but it can again be across multiple lines. Instead of the GO command that SQLCMD uses, mysql.exe uses the semicolon to specify that a query is complete and should be executed.

As with SQLCMD, you can also use QUIT or EXIT to close the connection to the database and exit mysql.exe.

Creating Databases

The first DDL query you need to look at is the query to create a database. In Chapter 2, you briefly learned about CREATE TABLE. In Chapter 10, you looked at CREATE PROCEDURE. It should come as no surprise that there's a corresponding CREATE query for creating databases: CREATE DATABASE.

Try It Out: Creating a Database with CREATE DATABASE

The first DDL query you'll look at is CREATE DATABASE. You'll use this to build a database that you'll query in later examples without destroying the database you've been using in the previous chapters. As you've seen, when you use a command-line client, you enter a command and then press Enter to execute it. From now on, the instructions for entering commands won't repeat the "press Enter" part.

1. Open the command-line client for the database you want to use.

   - To connect to SQL Server, open a command prompt and execute the following:

     ```
     SQLCMD -U sa -S (local)\BAND
     ```

   - To connect to MySQL, open a command prompt, navigate to the C:\Program Files\MySQL\MySQL Server 5.0\bin folder, and then execute the following command:

     ```
     mysql -u root -p
     ```

2. At the password prompt, enter the correct password, which is bandpass for both SQL Server and MySQL.

3. At the command prompt, enter the query to create the database.

   - For SQL Server, enter the following on two separate lines:

     ```
     CREATE DATABASE PlayersTemp
     GO
     ```

   - For MySQL, enter the following command:

     ```
     CREATE DATABASE PlayersTemp;
     ```

4. The database will be created, and a confirmation message may be returned, depending on whether you're using SQL Server or MySQL.

   - For SQL Server, the database will be created, and no confirmation other than the lack of an error message is given, as shown in Figure 11-5.

   - For MySQL, you get a message saying that the query you've executed is correct, as shown in Figure 11-6.

5. Exit the command-line tool by entering either EXIT or QUIT.

Figure 11-5. *Database created successfully using SQLCMD*

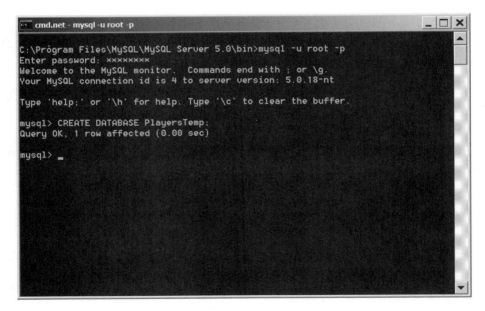

Figure 11-6. *Database created successfully using mysql.exe*

6. To verify that the databases have been created correctly, fire up the graphical tool you've been using. You'll see the database has been created.

- Open SQL Server Management Studio, and you'll immediately see the PlayersTemp database, along with the Players database you've been using, as shown in Figure 11-7.

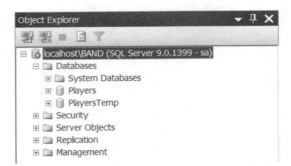

Figure 11-7. *SQL Server Management Studio showing that the database has been created*

- Open MySQL Query Browser, and you'll immediately see the PlayersTemp database, along with the Players database you've been using, as shown in Figure 11-8.

Figure 11-8. *MySQL Query Browser showing that the database has been created*

7. Close both graphical clients.

How It Works

The syntax for the query to create a database is the same whether you're using SQL Server or MySQL. As you'll see shortly, this is one of the few instances where you can use the same query with both SQL Server and MySQL.

Notice that before you execute the query, you're logged in to the server as the administrator account (the sa account for SQL Server and the root account for MySQL), rather than the band account you've been using to execute DML queries. As you saw in Chapter 2, you should always use an account that has only the privileges you need, and the ability to execute DDL queries should be one of the most jealously guarded privileges. You use the administrator account because this is the only account in the system that has permission to execute the DDL queries you need.

To create a database, you use the CREATE query, specifying that you want to create a database, and then follow this with the name of the database you want to create, as follows:

```
CREATE DATABASE PlayersTemp
```

So, with this one line of SQL, you're constructing a PlayersTemp database. When you execute this query, the database structure is created before control is returned to the client.

■**Note**   Although this version of CREATE DATABASE is the simplest you can get, you can apply a plethora of options to the query to modify how the database is constructed, and these options are different for SQL Server and MySQL. If you're interested, you can find further details for SQL Server at http://msdn. microsoft.com/en-us/library/ms176061.aspx and for MySQL at http://dev.mysql.com/doc/ refman/5.0/en/create-database.html.

Now that you've created the database, you can create the tables that make up the database.

Creating Tables

You briefly saw in Chapter 2 that CREATE TABLE is the DDL query for creating tables. For those of you who've been waiting for a fuller discussion, your prayers will now be answered!

The basic structure of the CREATE TABLE command is as follows:

```
CREATE TABLE <table-name>
(
  <column1-name column1-type column1-options>,
  <column2-name column2-type column2-options>,
  ...
  <columnN-name columnN-type columnN-options>,
  <table-options>
)
```

You specify the name of the table and then specify each of the columns that make up the table by giving the name of the column, the type of the column, and any other options you need for the column.

In the following examples, you'll create the four tables of the Players database in both SQL Server and MySQL using the graphical client you have available. As you'll see, the queries to create the tables are similar for the two databases, but they're different enough to warrant their own examples.

Try It Out: Creating Tables in SQL Server with CREATE TABLE

In this example, you'll switch from using the command-line to using SQL Server Management Studio. You'll use this graphical client to execute four CREATE TABLE queries to create the four tables that make up the PlayersTemp database.

1. Open SQL Server Management Studio and connect to the (local)\BAND database using the sa account.

2. Expand the Databases node in the Object Explorer and select New Query from the context menu for the PlayersTemp database.

3. In the query text area, enter the following:

```
CREATE TABLE Manufacturer (
  ManufacturerID int IDENTITY NOT NULL PRIMARY KEY,
  ManufacturerName varchar(50) NOT NULL,
  ManufacturerEmail varchar(50)
)
```

4. Click the Execute button. This will execute the query, and if all goes well, you'll receive a "Command(s) completed successfully" confirmation at the bottom of the Query Editor dialog box.

5. To verify that the Manufacturer table has been created, expand the PlayersTemp database in the Object Explorer, and then expand the Tables node. You'll see that the table has indeed been created. Expand the dbo.Manufacturer and Columns nodes, and you'll see that the columns have been created correctly. If the table isn't immediately present, select Refresh from the context menu for the Tables node, and it should appear, as shown in Figure 11-9.

6. Create the Player table by executing the following query:

```
CREATE TABLE Player (
  PlayerID int IDENTITY NOT NULL PRIMARY KEY,
  PlayerName varchar(50) NOT NULL,
  PlayerManufacturerID int NOT NULL
    CONSTRAINT FK_Player_Manufacturer
    REFERENCES Manufacturer(ManufacturerID),
  PlayerStorePrice decimal(10,2) NOT NULL,
  PlayerStorage varchar(50) NOT NULL
)
```

7. Create the Format table by executing the following query:

```
CREATE TABLE Format (
  FormatID int IDENTITY NOT NULL,
  FormatName varchar(50) NOT NULL,
  PRIMARY KEY (FormatID)
)
```

Figure 11-9. *After creating a table using SQL Server Management Studio, you can verify that it has been created correctly.*

8. Create the WhatPlaysWhatFormat table by executing the following query:

```
CREATE TABLE WhatPlaysWhatFormat (
  WPWFPlayerID int NOT NULL,
  WPWFFormatID int NOT NULL,
  PRIMARY KEY (WPWFFormatID, WPWFPlayerID)
)
```

9. You can verify that all four tables have been created correctly by refreshing the Tables node in the tree on the left side of the window.

How It Works

The queries you've just used have created all the tables you need.

After naming the table, you define the columns. A column definition contains the name of the column, its data type, and any options you want to apply to that column.

For example, for the Manufacturer table, you're creating the following three columns:

```
ManufacturerID int IDENTITY NOT NULL PRIMARY KEY,
ManufacturerName varchar(50) NOT NULL,
ManufacturerEmail varchar(50)
```

The column name and data type are fairly self-explanatory, but the column options need some explanation.

The IDENTITY option specifies that the column contains an identity value (in other words, one that automatically updates when you insert an entry into the table).

The NOT NULL option specifies that the column doesn't allow null values. By default, a column will accept null values. So, if you want to allow null values, you don't need to specify this option. You can see this if you look at the ManufacturerEmail column:

```
ManufacturerEmail varchar(50)
```

But if you want to be explicit in your definition of whether a column will accept null values, you can also specify this using the NULL option. The following line is functionally equivalent to the previous version:

```
ManufacturerEmail varchar(50) NULL
```

Another column option is PRIMARY KEY, which allows you to specify that the column in question is, not surprisingly, the primary key for the table. If you have a single column making up the primary key, you can specify PRIMARY KEY as a column option, as you do for the Manufacturer table:

```
ManufacturerID int NOT NULL IDENTITY PRIMARY KEY
```

The Player table also uses this method of specifying the primary key. However, you can also specify the primary key as a table option, as you do for the Format table:

```
PRIMARY KEY (FormatID)
```

You can use whichever method of specifying the primary key that you want. However, if the primary key is a composite key and contains more than one column, you must use the alternative syntax, as you do for the WhatPlaysWhatFormat table:

```
PRIMARY KEY (WPWFFormatID, WPWFPlayerID)
```

When specifying the columns for a composite key, you put the column names in a comma-separated list within the brackets of the PRIMARY KEY table option.

The Player table also uses the REFERENCES column option. This allows you to define foreign key constraints at the same time as the table declaration. In this case, you create a relationship called FK_Player_Manufacturer between the PlayerManufacturerID in the Player table and the ManufacturerID in the Manufacturer table:

```
PlayerManufacturerID int NOT NULL
  CONSTRAINT FK_Player_Manufacturer
  REFERENCES Manufacturer(ManufacturerID)
```

You can also add foreign key constraints by specifying a table option, as follows:

```
CONSTRAINT FK_Player_Manufacturer
  FOREIGN KEY (PlayerManufacturerID)
  REFERENCES Manufacturer(ManufacturerID)
```

You can specify both primary and foreign keys on an individual column or as a table option. You're free to choose either option. Personally, I prefer the table option version, as it keeps the keys separate and makes them a little easier to see. So, I would create the Player table as follows:

```
CREATE TABLE Player (
  PlayerID int IDENTITY NOT NULL,
  PlayerName varchar(50) NOT NULL,
  PlayerManufacturerID int NOT NULL,
  PlayerStorePrice decimal(10,0) NOT NULL,
  PlayerStorage varchar(50) NOT NULL,
  PRIMARY KEY (PlayerID),
  CONSTRAINT FK_Player_Manufacturer
    FOREIGN KEY (PlayerManufacturerID)
    REFERENCES Manufacturer(ManufacturerID)
)
```

This version has a few more lines of SQL, but the keys are a lot easier to spot and aren't hidden away among the column definitions.

Although SQL Server gives you the option when defining foreign keys, you'll soon see that MySQL isn't as flexible.

■**Note** For more information about the options you can supply for columns when using SQL Server, see http://msdn.microsoft.com/en-us/library/ms174979.aspx.

Try It Out: Creating Tables in MySQL with CREATE TABLE

In this example, you'll see that the SQL queries to create tables in MySQL are similar to those that you use when creating the tables in SQL Server, but there are differences.

1. Open MySQL Query Browser and connect to the local database using the root account.

2. Switch to the PlayersTemp database by double-clicking it in the Schemata pane.

3. Enter the following in the query area:

   ```
   CREATE TABLE Manufacturer (
     ManufacturerID int AUTO_INCREMENT NOT NULL PRIMARY KEY,
     ManufacturerName varchar(50) NOT NULL,
     ManufacturerEmail varchar(50)
   )
   ```

4. Click the Execute icon on the toolbar to execute the query. You'll see a success message, as shown in Figure 11-10.

Figure 11-10. *MySQL Query Browser provides a little more feedback.*

5. Expand the PlayersTemp database in the Schemata pane. You'll see that the table has been added, as shown in Figure 11-11. If the new table isn't immediately available, refresh the display by selecting Refresh from the PlayersTemp context menu.

Figure 11-11. *In MySQL Query Browser, you can verify that a table has been created correctly.*

6. Create the Player table by executing the following query:

```
CREATE TABLE Player (
  PlayerID int AUTO_INCREMENT NOT NULL PRIMARY KEY,
  PlayerName varchar(50) NOT NULL,
  PlayerManufacturerID int NOT NULL,
  PlayerStorePrice decimal(10,2) NOT NULL,
  PlayerStorage varchar(50) NOT NULL,
  CONSTRAINT FK_Player_Manufacturer
    FOREIGN KEY (PlayerManufacturerID)
    REFERENCES Manufacturer(ManufacturerID)
)
```

7. Create the Format table by executing the following query:

```
CREATE TABLE Format (
  FormatID int AUTO_INCREMENT NOT NULL,
  FormatName varchar(50) NOT NULL,
  PRIMARY KEY (FormatID)
)
```

8. Create the WhatPlaysWhatFormat table by executing the following query:

```
CREATE TABLE WhatPlaysWhatFormat (
  WPWFPlayerID int NOT NULL,
  WPWFFormatID int NOT NULL,
  PRIMARY KEY (WPWFFormatID, WPWFPlayerID)
)
```

9. You can verify that all four tables have been created correctly by refreshing the Schemata display.

How It Works

As you can see, the queries that you use to create the tables within the database are quite similar to the corresponding queries in SQL Server.

One of the things you need to watch out for is the different names that the different databases use for their data types. While most of the data types will be the same, sometimes the data types have different names or need to be specified slightly differently. See Appendix B for a comparison of the SQL Server and MySQL data types.

The options you can specify in MySQL and SQL Server are similar. The NOT NULL, NULL, and PRIMARY KEY notation for columns operate in the same way for MySQL as they do for SQL Server, and you can also specify primary keys and composite keys using the same terminology. The one column option that's different between SQL Server and MySQL is the IDENTITY option in SQL Server. In MySQL, you must specify this type of column using the AUTO_INCREMENT option.

The one major difference is the way that foreign keys are defined. Whereas SQL Server allows you to define the foreign key on the column, with MySQL you must specify the foreign keys as a table option. However, the syntax is the same, as in this example:

```
CONSTRAINT FK_Player_Manufacturer
   FOREIGN KEY (PlayerManufacturerID)
   REFERENCES Manufacturer(ManufacturerID)
```

This plays nicely into my preference for creating both primary and foreign keys as table options, rather than intermingled with the column definition:

```
CREATE TABLE Player (
  PlayerID int AUTO_INCREMENT NOT NULL,
  PlayerName varchar(50) NOT NULL,
  PlayerManufacturerID int NOT NULL,
  PlayerStorePrice decimal(10,0) NOT NULL,
  PlayerStorage varchar(50) NOT NULL,
  PRIMARY KEY (PlayerID),
  CONSTRAINT FK_Player_Manufacturer
    FOREIGN KEY (PlayerManufacturerID)
    REFERENCES Manufacturer(ManufacturerID)
)
```

■**Note** For more information about the options you can supply for columns when you're using MySQL, see http://dev.mysql.com/doc/refman/5.0/en/create-table.html.

Adding, Modifying, and Removing Columns

You've now seen how to create tables in both SQL Server and MySQL. This is fine as long as you've created the table correctly in the first place and as long as the requirements for the data that the table will hold don't actually change. If they do change, then you'll need some method of modifying the table.

The basic query to modify a table in the database is ALTER TABLE. Depending on what you actually want to do, the other details you must supply will change.

If you want to add a column to a table, you must use the ADD syntax of the query, specifying the new column you want to add, like so:

```
ALTER TABLE <table-name> ADD <column-name column-type column-options>
```

You specify the new column in the same way as you do when creating the table. All the options you have available when creating the table are also available here.

To delete a column, you use the DROP COLUMN syntax and specify the column you want to delete, like so:

```
ALTER TABLE <table-name> DROP COLUMN <column-name>
```

Sometimes, you'll also need to change the definition of a column. You accomplish this slightly differently in SQL Server and MySQL.

For SQL Server, you use the ALTER COLUMN syntax and specify the old column name and the new definition for the column, like so:

```
ALTER TABLE <table-name> ALTER COLUMN <column-name> <column-type column-options>
```

MySQL uses the CHANGE COLUMN syntax for this. You must specify the old name of the column, as well as the complete definition, including the column name, for the modified column, like so:

```
ALTER TABLE <table-name> CHANGE COLUMN <column-name>
  <column-name column-type column-options>
```

Be careful when modifying columns, because it's easy to lose data if you don't think things through fully—whether this is from a data-type conversion that was unintended or because a column's length has been reduced. Neither SQL Server nor MySQL will warn that this is about to occur; both will just assume you know what you're doing.

■**Note** The differences between the SQL Server and MySQL syntax for modifying columns is because this functionality isn't defined in the SQL specification. Most databases allow this functionality, but their implementations are all slightly different.

Try It Out: Changing a Table Definition with ALTER TABLE

In this example, you'll modify the Manufacturer table by adding two columns. You'll then modify one of the columns to increase the amount of information that can be stored within the column.

1. Open either SQL Server Management Studio or MySQL Query Browser and connect to the correct database.

   - For SQL Server Management Studio, connect to the (local)\BAND database using the sa account.

   - For MySQL Query Browser, connect to the localhost database using the root account.

2. Make sure you're working in the PlayersTemp database.

   - Expand the Databases node in the Object Explorer and select New Query from the context menu for the PlayersTemp database.

   - For MySQL Query Browser, select the PlayersTemp database by double-clicking its name in the Schemata pane.

3. Create two new columns on the Manufacturer table by executing three queries. The queries used by both SQL Server and MySQL are the same in this case, and they should be executed one at a time:

```
ALTER TABLE Manufacturer ADD ManufacturerCountry varchar(50)
ALTER TABLE Manufacturer ADD ManufacturerWebsite varchar(100)
ALTER TABLE Manufacturer ADD ManufacturerTelephone varchar(11)
```

4. Verify that the new columns have been added to the table.

   - For SQL Server Management Studio, expand the PlayersTemp node. Then expand the Tables node and select the Manufacturer table. Expand the Columns node, and you'll see that the new columns have been added and the details match those that you've given, as shown in Figure 11-12.

   - For MySQL Query Browser, expand the PlayersTemp database, and then expand the Manufacturer table. You'll see the columns for the table, including the new ones you've added, as shown in Figure 11-13.

Figure 11-12. *Verifying that the new columns have been added to the table in SQL Server Management Studio*

Figure 11-13. *Verifying that the new columns have been added to the table in MySQL Query Browser*

5. Modify the ManufacturerEmail column on the Manufacturer table by executing the appropriate query.

    •   For SQL Server Management Studio, execute the following query:

    ```
    ALTER TABLE Manufacturer ALTER COLUMN ManufacturerEmail varchar(100)
    ```

    •   For MySQL Query Browser, execute the following:

    ```
    ALTER TABLE Manufacturer CHANGE COLUMN ManufacturerEmail
        ManufacturerEmail varchar(100);
    ```

6. Verify that the length of the ManufacturerEmail column has indeed changed from 50 characters to 100 characters.

    •   For SQL Server Management Studio, you can see the new column width directly in the tree view.

    •   For SQL Query Browser, you'll need to look at the table definition. You can see this by selecting Edit Table from the context menu for the Manufacturer table.

7. Execute the command to delete the ManufacturerTelephone column you've just added. The command is the same for both SQL Server and MySQL.

    ```
    ALTER TABLE Manufacturer DROP COLUMN ManufacturerTelephone
    ```

8. Verify that the column has been deleted and that you now have only two new columns in the Manufacturer table: ManufacturerCountry and ManufacturerWebsite.

How It Works

In the example, you first added three columns to the database using the same queries for both SQL Server and MySQL:

```
ALTER TABLE Manufacturer ADD ManufacturerCountry varchar(50)
ALTER TABLE Manufacturer ADD ManufacturerWebsite varchar(100)
ALTER TABLE Manufacturer ADD ManufacturerTelephone varchar(11)
```

Two of these are the ManufacturerCountry and ManufacturerWebsite columns that are in the original database that you didn't include in the CREATE TABLE definition for the Manufacturer table in the previous example. The database wouldn't be the same if you didn't have them, so you've added them in this example. You also added a ManufacturerTelephone column that contains a string of up to 11 characters.

You then altered the ManufacturerEmail column for both databases. Fifty characters may not be enough to hold an e-mail address, so you double the size. Unlike adding columns, the two databases have slightly different query forms for this, but they both accomplish the same thing.

For SQL Server, you use the following ALTER COLUMN syntax:

```
ALTER TABLE Manufacturer ALTER COLUMN ManufacturerEmail varchar(100)
```

For MySQL, you use the following CHANGE COLUMN syntax:

```
ALTER TABLE Manufacturer CHANGE COLUMN ManufacturerEmail
  ManufacturerEmail varchar(100);
```

Because you're increasing the size of the column, you don't run the risk of losing any data. If you had reduced the size of the column from 100 characters to 50 characters, anything that was contained in the final 50 characters would be permanently lost, so be careful when changing column sizes. Once you've lost the information, you have no way to get it back.

As you probably suspected, you added that column that isn't in the Players database, ManufacturerTelephone, just so you could see how to delete it from the table. You do that with the following query:

```
ALTER TABLE Manufacturer DROP COLUMN ManufacturerTelephone
```

You simply specify the column you want to delete and execute the query. You don't get a confirmation, so make sure you're deleting the correct column before executing the query!

Note Although you've seen perhaps the three most important uses of the ALTER TABLE query, you can do a lot more using ALTER TABLE. If you want more information, refer to the documentation for SQL Server at http://msdn.microsoft.com/en-us/library/ms190273.aspx or for MySQL at http://dev.mysql.com/doc/refman/5.0/en/alter-table.html.

Creating and Deleting Indexes

Once you've created the necessary tables in the database, it's possible to create indexes on the tables. You've looked at how to create indexes for both SQL Server and MySQL using graphical tools in Chapter 2 (and learned about the index options in that chapter as well). You saw that the process was quite different for the different tools. However, even though the graphical tools are completely different, both SQL Server and MySQL support the same syntax for creating and deleting indexes.

Creating Indexes

You add indexes to the database using the following CREATE INDEX query:

```
CREATE INDEX <index-name> ON <table-name> ( <column-name> )
```

When creating an index, the first thing you need to specify is a name for the index. SQL Server defaults to using a name of the form IX_*column*, where *column* is the column that's being indexed. It's best to stick to a consistent naming scheme that is easy to understand if you need to return to the database in the future. The SQL Server naming scheme is as good as any.

You then specify the table you're adding the index to and the column you want to index.

■**Note** Both SQL Server and MySQL automatically add an index to a table when you define a primary key (either as a single column or a composite key) for the table. SQL Server calls this index PK__tablename, and MySQL calls it PRIMARY. Deleting this index will remove the primary key information from the table, so you probably don't want to delete it.

Try It Out: Creating Indexes with CREATE INDEX

You'll now add indexes to the four tables you created in the previous example. You'll add indexes for three different columns. You'll reuse two of these when we look at relationships shortly. You'll delete the third index in the next example.

1. Open either SQL Server Management Studio or MySQL Query Browser and connect to the correct database.

   • For SQL Server Management Studio, connect to the (local)\BAND database using the sa account.

   • For MySQL Query Browser, connect to the localhost database using the root account.

2. Make sure you're working in the PlayersTemp database.

   • Expand the Databases node in the Object Explorer and select New Query from the context menu for the PlayersTemp database.

   • For MySQL Query Browser, select the PlayersTemp database by double-clicking its name in the Schemata pane.

3. Execute the queries to create the indexes.

   • For SQL Server, you need to execute the following three queries. You'll receive a "Command(s) completed successfully" message for each:

```
CREATE INDEX IX_WPWFPlayerID ON WhatPlaysWhatFormat (WPWFPlayerID)
CREATE INDEX IX_WPWFFormatID ON WhatPlaysWhatFormat (WPWFFormatID)
CREATE INDEX IX_PlayerManufacturerID ON Player (PlayerManufacturerID)
```

   • For MySQL, you need to execute only the first two queries. You'll receive a "Query returned no resultset" message for each query:

```
CREATE INDEX IX_WPWFPlayerID ON WhatPlaysWhatFormat (WPWFPlayerID)
CREATE INDEX IX_WPWFFormatID ON WhatPlaysWhatFormat (WPWFFormatID)
```

4. You can use the graphical tools to check that the indexes have been created.

   • SQL Server Management Studio has an Indexes node for each table, which shows all the indexes for the table. Figure 11-14 shows the indexes for the Player table.

Figure 11-14. *Indexes are shown in the tree for SQL Server Management Studio.*

- MySQL Query Browser allows you to see the indexes that have been created by viewing the table definition, as shown in Figure 11-15.

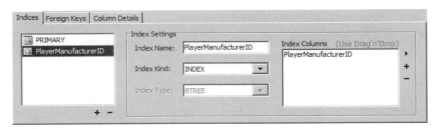

Figure 11-15. *MySQL Query Browser shows the indexes in the Table Editor.*

How It Works

As you can see, the CREATE INDEX queries are the same for both SQL Server and MySQL. You simply specify the name of the index, on what table you want the index created, and the columns in the index:

```
CREATE INDEX IX_WPWFPlayerID ON WhatPlaysWhatFormat (WPWFPlayerID)
```

You created three indexes in SQL Server and two indexes in MySQL. Yet MySQL actually has the index that you didn't create already defined, as you can see in Figure 11-15.

If you recall from Chapter 2, MySQL requires an index for any column that is a foreign key, and the column must be the first column in the index. When you added the foreign key in the `CREATE TABLE` query for the Player table, the index for the PlayerManufacturerID column was added automatically.

The other indexes that you added to the WhatPlaysWhatFormat table are required for adding relationships, as you'll do after the discussion of indexes. By creating them now, you've saved the work of having to create them later. However, you need to see how to delete indexes, so one of them has to go.

■**Note** You can find more information about the `CREATE INDEX` command for SQL Server at `http://msdn.microsoft.com/en-us/library/ms188783.aspx` and for MySQL, at `http://dev.mysql.com/doc/refman/5.0/en/create-index.html`.

Deleting Indexes

To delete an index, you use the `DROP INDEX` query. For SQL Server, the syntax is as follows:

```
DROP INDEX <table-name>.<index-name>
```

For MySQL, the syntax is slightly different:

```
DROP INDEX <index-name> ON <table-name>
```

In both versions, you must specify the name of the index and the table for the index. This will drop the index from the specified table without any warning, and you can't recover an index that has been deleted.

Try It Out: Deleting an Index with DROP INDEX

In this example, you'll delete one of the indexes you created in the previous example.

1. Open either SQL Server Management Studio or MySQL Query Browser and connect to the correct database.

   - For SQL Server Management Studio, connect to the `(local)\BAND` database using the `sa` account.

   - For MySQL Query Browser, connect to the `localhost` database using the `root` account.

2. Make sure you're working in the PlayersTemp database.

   - Expand the Databases node in the Object Explorer and select New Query from the context menu for the PlayersTemp database.

   - For MySQL Query Browser, select the PlayersTemp database by double-clicking its name in the Schemata pane.

3. Execute the query to drop the index.

- For SQL Server, execute this:

  ```
  DROP INDEX WhatPlaysWhatFormat.IX_WPWFFormatID
  ```

- For MySQL, execute this:

  ```
  DROP INDEX IX_WPWFFormatID ON WhatPlaysWhatFormat
  ```

4. You can verify that the index has been deleted by looking at the indexes for the table, as you did in the previous example. As an alternative, you can also execute the DROP INDEX query again. For SQL Server, you'll receive an error message explaining that the index doesn't exist, as shown in Figure 11-16. Figure 11-17 shows the error message for MySQL.

```
Messages
Msg 3701, Level 11, State 7, Line 1
Cannot drop the index 'WhatPlaysWhatFormat.IX_WPWFFormatID', because it does not exist or you do not have permission.
```

Figure 11-16. *Unknown index error message in SQL Server*

```
The query could not be executed.                                          Ed
! Description
!  Can't DROP 'IX_WPWFFormatID'; check that column/key exists
   1: 50
```

Figure 11-17. *Unknown index error message in MySQL*

How It Works

As you can see, deleting indexes is easy. Notice that you don't get any warning that you're about to delete an index. However, in this case, the lack of warning isn't really a problem, because you can simply re-create the index without any loss of data. When you look at deleting tables and databases later in this chapter, you'll see that the lack of warning can be a problem, though.

You may have noticed that you've deleted an index that I said was necessary, in MySQL, for the relationships that you are going to add. The key is the fact that the foreign key must be the first column in an index. If you look at Figure 11-18, you'll see that the WPWFFormatID column was already the first key in the PRIMARY index.

Figure 11-18. *The WPWFFormatID column was already in a suitable index.*

Recall that you created the WhatPlaysWhatFormat table with the following primary key definition:

```
PRIMARY KEY (WPWFFormatID, WPWFPlayerID)
```

A primary key always has an index created for it, and as you've specified the WPWFFormatID column first in the primary key, it becomes the first column in the index. Therefore, you don't need a separate index for it, so it's okay to delete the unnecessary index.

■**Note** You can find more information about the DROP INDEX command for SQL Server at http:// msdn.microsoft.com/en-us/library/ms176118.aspx and for MySQL at http://dev.mysql.com/ doc/refman/5.0/en/drop-index.html.

Creating and Deleting Relationships

In Chapter 2, you looked at the relationships between tables and saw how these relationships give databases their real power. After all, they wouldn't be called relational databases unless there was a relation in there somewhere.

Relationships aren't the be-all and end-all of databases, however. You can run a perfectly acceptable database solution without implementing any relationships in the database, and instead relying on the SQL queries you write. While this is perfectly acceptable and a lot of databases have no relationships explicitly defined, you should always use relationships if the database you're using implements them.

Creating Relationships

As you saw in Chapter 2, a relationship will exist between two columns. For the Player database, for example, you have a relationship between a Player and a Manufacturer—the PlayerManufacturer column in the Player table and the ManufacturerID column in the Manufacturer table. You added this relationship when you created the Player table by adding a FOREIGN KEY table option to the CREATE TABLE query.

It is also possible to add relationships to existing tables. To do this, you need a SQL query that can model this relationship. In this case, you can use the ADD CONSTRAINT syntax of the ALTER TABLE query.

■**Note** The ADD CONSTRAINT version of the ALTER TABLE query allows you to do more than simply add relationships to the table. You can add primary keys to tables using this method, and you can also specify indexes and keys that contain multiple columns using this command. For more information, refer to the ALTER TABLE syntax at http://msdn.microsoft.com/en-us/library/ms190273.aspx for SQL Server and at http://dev.mysql.com/doc/refman/5.0/en/alter-table.html for MySQL.

The syntax of the ADD CONSTRAINT version of the ALTER TABLE query is as follows:

```
ALTER TABLE <table-name>
  ADD CONSTRAINT <relationship-name>
  FOREIGN KEY ( <column-name> )
  REFERENCES <table-name> ( <column-name> )
```

This is a little more involved than the other DDL queries you've seen so far in this chapter, but it isn't that complex. If you refer to the CREATE TABLE queries earlier in this chapter, you'll see that it's very similar to the way that you added relationships when creating the table. Let's look at the query line by line.

First, you need to specify the table to which the relationship is being applied. You always apply a constraint to the foreign key side of the relationship, so for the Player to Manufacturer relationship, you add the constraint to the Player table, because you have multiple Players for only one Manufacturer.

You must then specify a name for the relationship. If you don't have a name, you can't ever refer to it, and in the database everything must have a name. SQL Server defaults to using a name of the form FK_table1_table2, where table1 is the table containing the foreign key and table2 is the table containing the primary key, but you're free to use whatever name you want (limited by the SQL naming conventions, of course). Again, for maintenance reasons, you should stick to a consistent naming scheme, and the SQL Server naming scheme is acceptable.

You then tell the database that you're creating a foreign key (using the fairly obvious FOREIGN KEY syntax) and specify, in brackets, which column you want as the foreign key.

Finally, you must let the database know with which table and column you're creating the relationship. You do this after the REFERENCES clause, and you specify the table name followed by the column name in brackets.

That's it. You now know how to add a relationship between two tables. Theory is one thing, but now you'll actually do it.

Try It Out: Creating Relationships with ALTER TABLE

In this example, you'll add the relationships that exist in the database using the ADD CONSTRAINT version of the ALTER TABLE query.

1. Open either SQL Server Management Studio or MySQL Query Browser and connect to the correct database.

   - For SQL Server Management Studio, connect to the (local)\BAND database using the sa account.

   - For MySQL Query Browser, connect to the localhost database using the root account.

2. Make sure you're working in the PlayersTemp database.

   - Expand the Databases node in the Object Explorer and select New Query from the context menu for the PlayersTemp database.

   - For MySQL Query Browser, select the PlayersTemp database by double-clicking its name in the Schemata pane.

3. Add the relationship between the WhatPlaysWhatFormat and Player tables by executing the following query:

```
ALTER TABLE WhatPlaysWhatFormat
ADD CONSTRAINT FK_WhatPlaysWhatFormat_Player
FOREIGN KEY (WPWFPlayerID)
REFERENCES Player (PlayerID)
```

4. Add the final relationship, between the WhatPlaysWhatFormat and Format tables, by executing the following query:

```
ALTER TABLE WhatPlaysWhatFormat
ADD CONSTRAINT FK_WhatPlaysWhatFormat_Format
FOREIGN KEY (WPWFFormatID)
REFERENCES Format (FormatID)
```

5. You can verify that the relationships have been created correctly by using the graphical tools.

- To view the relationships for SQL Server, you can either create a diagram containing the related tables (as you learned in Chapter 2) or use SQL Server Management Studio to view the relationships. If you view the table definition, you can select Relationships from the context menu to view the relationships for the table, as shown in Figure 11-19.

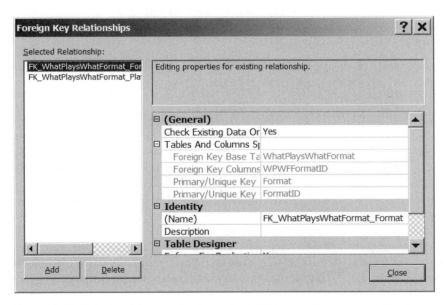

Figure 11-19. *Relationships can be viewed in SQL Server Management Studio.*

- You can view the relationships for MySQL using MySQL Query Browser. As shown in Figure 11-20, the Foreign Keys tab of the Edit Table dialog box shows all of the relationships where the table is the foreign key of the relationship.

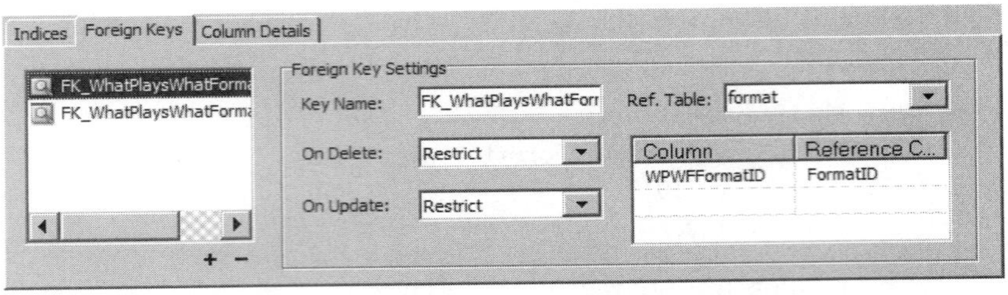

Figure 11-20. *MySQL Query Browser shows only foreign key relationships.*

How It Works

In this example, you've added the two relationships you require to the database using two separate ALTER TABLE queries.

The first query adds the relationship between Players and WhatPlaysWhatFormat:

```
ALTER TABLE WhatPlaysWhatFormat
ADD CONSTRAINT FK_WhatPlaysWhatFormat_Player
FOREIGN KEY (WPWFPlayerID)
REFERENCES Player (PlayerID)
```

You're creating a relationship between the WPWFPlayerID column in the WhatPlaysWhatFormat table and the PlayerID column in the Player table.

The second query follows a similar pattern. You're creating the relationship between the WPWFFormatID column in the WhatPlaysWhatFormat table and the FormatID column in the Format table:

```
ALTER TABLE WhatPlaysWhatFormat
ADD CONSTRAINT FK_WhatPlaysWhatFormat_Format
FOREIGN KEY (WPWFFormatID)
REFERENCES Format (FormatID)
```

These two relationships that the WhatPlaysWhatFormat table has with the Player and Format tables define the many-to-many relationship between the Player and Format tables. The relationships are both created on the WhatPlaysWhatFormat table because a Player can support several Formats and a Format will be supported by several different Players.

Finally, you viewed the relationships defined on the tables. SQL Server Management Studio allows you to view relationships in two ways. When you learned about database diagrams in Chapter 2, you saw that when a diagram contains two tables that are related, the relationship is shown. The relationships are also visible in the Relationships dialog box, as in Figure 11-19. You can also see that a column is a foreign key by looking at the columns in the Object Explorer. As shown in Figure 11-21, columns that are foreign keys are shown with a gray key icon.

Figure 11-21. *SQL Server Management Studio shows foreign keys in Object Explorer.*

MySQL Query Browser provides fewer tools for viewing the relationships than SQL Server Management Studio offers. Although you can't view the relationships where the table contains the primary key, you can view relationships for a table if the table contains the foreign key column.

Deleting Relationships

Once you've created relationships in the database, you may need to modify those relationships at some point in the future. Unlike with table columns, there's no concept of modifying a relationship in the database. If you need to change a relationship, you must delete the old one and then create the new one.

Deleting a relationship is slightly different depending on whether you're using SQL Server or MySQL, because they refer to relationships as different things and use different queries to delete relationships.

In SQL Server, a relationship is called a *constraint*, and you use the DROP CONSTRAINT version of the ALTER TABLE query, like so:

```
ALTER TABLE <table-name> DROP CONSTRAINT <relationship-name>
```

MySQL calls a relationship a foreign key and uses the DROP FOREIGN KEY version of ALTER TABLE, like so:

```
ALTER TABLE <table-name> DROP FOREIGN KEY <relationship-name>
```

You can simply drop a relationship by specifying the table that the relationship was created on and specifying the name of the relationship you want to delete.

■**Note** If you try to delete a relationship from the wrong table—in other words, from the primary key side of the relationship—an error will be thrown, as the relationship isn't defined on that table. But if you've followed my advice and used a consistent naming scheme that is easy to decipher, you can avoid a lot of these errors.

Try It Out: Deleting Relationships with ALTER TABLE

In this example, you'll start the process of dismantling the database you've built through the previous examples. You'll first delete the relationships in the database.

1. Open either SQL Server Management Studio or MySQL Query Browser and connect to the correct database.

   - For SQL Server Management Studio, connect to the (local)\BAND database using the sa account.

   - For MySQL Query Browser, connect to the localhost database using the root account.

2. Make sure you're working in the PlayersTemp database.

   - Expand the Databases node in the Object Explorer and select New Query from the context menu for the PlayersTemp database.

   - For MySQL Query Browser, select the PlayersTemp database by double-clicking its name in the Schemata pane.

3. Drop the relationship between the Player and Manufacturer tables.

   - For SQL Server, execute the following query. If the relationship is deleted correctly you'll receive a "Command(s) completed successfully" message.

     ```
     ALTER TABLE Player DROP CONSTRAINT FK_Player_Manufacturer
     ```

   - For MySQL, execute the following query. You'll receive a "Query returned no resultset" message if the relationship is deleted correctly.

     ```
     ALTER TABLE Player DROP FOREIGN KEY FK_Player_Manufacturer
     ```

How It Works

As in most cases, destroying something is much easier than creating it. To delete relationships, you simply specify the name of the relationship you want to delete and the table to which the relationship belongs. The only wrinkle is that you need to specify the relationship as a CONSTRAINT in SQL Server and a FOREIGN KEY in MySQL.

Deleting Tables

As with deleting relationships, deleting tables (and, as you'll see shortly, deleting databases) is a lot easier than creating them.

To delete a table from the database, use the DROP TABLE query, like so:

```
DROP TABLE <table-name>
```

Executing this query will delete the table without any warning, so be extremely careful that you're deleting the correct table and that deleting the table is indeed what you want to do.

Try It Out: Deleting Database Tables with DROP TABLE

In this example, you'll delete entire tables from the database. You'll delete only three of the four tables that are in the database, as you'll need at least one table for the next example.

1. Open either SQL Server Management Studio or MySQL Query Browser and connect to the correct database.

   - For SQL Server Management Studio, connect to the (local)\BAND database using the sa account.

   - For MySQL Query Browser, connect to the localhost database using the root account.

2. Make sure you're working in the PlayersTemp database.

   - Expand the Databases node in the Object Explorer and select New Query from the context menu for the PlayersTemp database.

   - For MySQL Query Browser, select the PlayersTemp database by double-clicking its name in the Schemata pane.

3. Execute the following query to drop the Manufacturer table. You'll get the success message that you've seen in the earlier examples.

   ```
   DROP TABLE Manufacturer
   ```

4. Enter the following query to drop the Player table:

   ```
   DROP TABLE Player
   ```

5. Executing this query will result in an error being thrown.

   - For SQL Server, the error is a FOREIGN KEY constraint error, as shown in Figure 11-22.

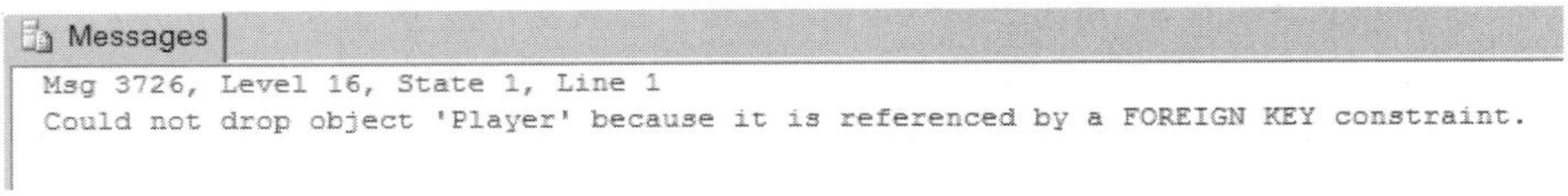

Figure 11-22. *SQL Server error if attempting to delete a table in a relationship*

   - For MySQL, the error is a foreign key constraint fails error, as shown in Figure 11-23.

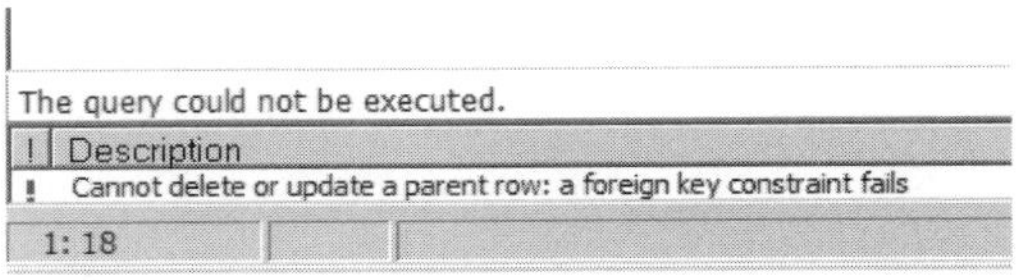

Figure 11-23. *MySQL error if attempting to delete a table in a relationship*

6. You can't delete the Player table because it has a relationship with the WhatPlaysWhatFormat table. The WhatPlaysWhatFormat table is the owner of the relationship, so you must delete that table first:

```
DROP TABLE WhatPlaysWhatFormat
```

7. This will delete the relationships owned by the WhatPlaysWhatFormat table, so you can now delete the Player table by executing the same query as you did in step 4:

```
DROP TABLE Player
```

8. To verify that the three tables have been deleted, use the graphical tool to see what tables are left in the database. You should have only one table left.

   - For SQL Server, expand the Object Explorer until you have expanded the Tables node for the PlayersTemp database. You'll see that you still have one table left, Format, as shown in Figure 11-24.

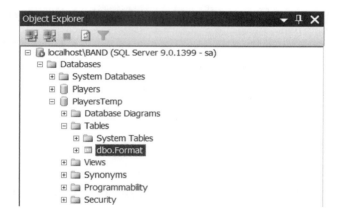

Figure 11-24. *Verifying that the tables have been deleted from the database in SQL Server*

   - For MySQL, refresh the PlayersTemp node in the Schemata pane. You'll see that you have only the Format table remaining, as shown in Figure 11-25.

Figure 11-25. *Verifying that the tables have been deleted from the database in MySQL*

How It Works

As you can see, deleting tables is simple and therefore dangerous! Be sure you're deleting the correct table!

The first table you've deleted from the database is the Manufacturer table:

```
DROP TABLE Manufacturer
```

Executing the query successfully deletes the table from the database. When you try to delete the Player table, however, you run into problems.

The Player table provides a primary key for a relationship within the database, so it can't simply be deleted. As you'll recall, you created a relationship between the WhatPlaysWhatFormat and Player table, like so:

```
ALTER TABLE WhatPlaysWhatFormat
ADD CONSTRAINT FK_WhatPlaysWhatFormat_Player
FOREIGN KEY (WPWFPlayerID)
REFERENCES Player (PlayerID)
```

Because the Player table provides the primary key in a relationship defined for the WhatPlaysWhatFormat table, you can't delete the Player table without first deleting the relationship. You could do this using a `DROP CONSTRAINT` or `DROP FOREIGN KEY` command, similar to those you've already looked at, but you use a different solution here.

You can't delete a table if it's providing the primary key in the relationship, but you can delete a table if it's the foreign key in the relationship, and doing so will delete all the foreign key relationships for the table. So, in deleting the WhatPlaysWhatFormat table, you deleted the `FK_WhatPlaysWhatFormat_Player` and `FK_WhatPlaysWhatFormat_Format` relationships. Once these relationships are deleted, you can delete the Player table.

You'll notice that you haven't had any problems deleting tables that have indexes on them. As you'll recall, you specified indexes on the WhatPlaysWhatFormat table, yet the table was deleted without any problems. Unlike relationships, an index deals with only one table, and deleting the table automatically deletes any indexes for the table.

■**Note** You can find more information about the `DROP TABLE` command for SQL Server at `http://msdn.microsoft.com/en-us/library/ms173790.aspx` and for MySQL at `http://dev.mysql.com/doc/refman/5.0/en/drop-table.html`.

Deleting Databases

If you thought deleting a table was easy and a good way to lose data, then deleting a database is just as easy—and with a lot more scope to delete a lot of data you didn't want deleted. So, you need to be especially careful when you decide to delete a database.

The query to drop a database is as follows:

```
DROP DATABASE <name>
```

This will delete the entire database along with any tables, relationships, and data that still exist in the database. SQL provides no safeguards against deleting entire databases, and this emphasizes why you need to restrict access to the database and, in particular, any administration privileges. If someone has the password for the administrator account, she can delete everything on the server easily. Keep your administrator password secure, and don't give any other account any administrator privileges.

Try It Out: Deleting a Database

To delete the database, you'll now switch back to using the command-line tools to execute a DROP DATABASE query. Follow these steps:

1. Open the command-line client for the database you want to use.

   - To connect to SQL Server, open a command prompt and enter the following:

   ```
   SQLCMD -U sa -S (local)\BAND
   ```

   - To connect to MySQL, open a command prompt, navigate to the C:\Program Files\MySQL\MySQL Server 5.0\bin folder and execute the following command:

   ```
   mysql -u root -p
   ```

2. At the password prompt, enter the correct password, which is bandpass for both SQL Server and MySQL.

3. At the command prompt, enter the query to delete the database.

   - For SQL Server, enter the following on two separate lines:

   ```
   DROP DATABASE PlayersTemp
   GO
   ```

   - For MySQL, enter the following command:

   ```
   DROP DATABASE PlayersTemp;
   ```

4. The database will be deleted. For SQL Server, no confirmation message is given, as shown in Figure 11-26. For MySQL, a brief message is returned, as shown in Figure 11-27.

SQLCMD
C:\>SQLCMD -U sa -S (local)\BAND
Password:
1> DROP DATABASE PlayersTemp
2> GO
1>

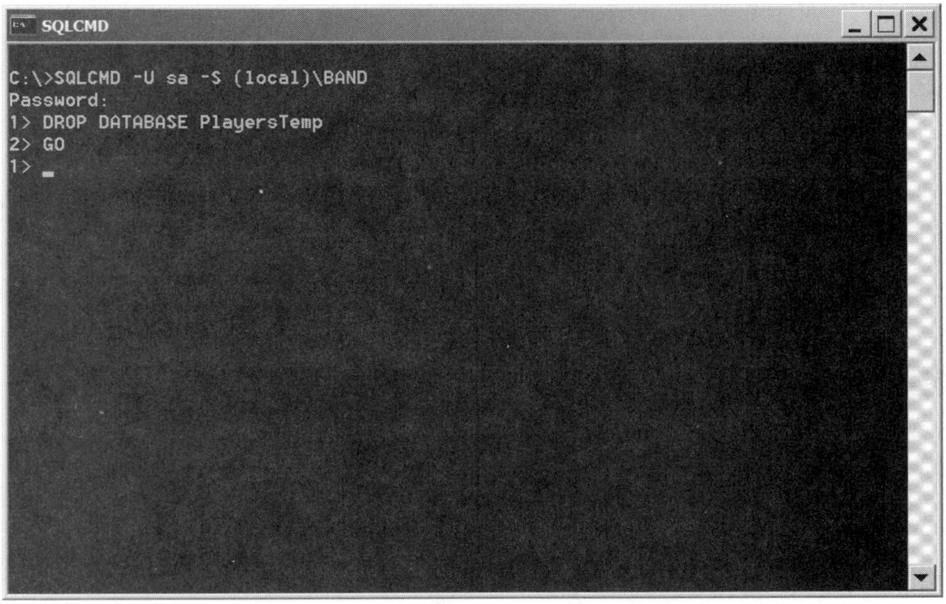

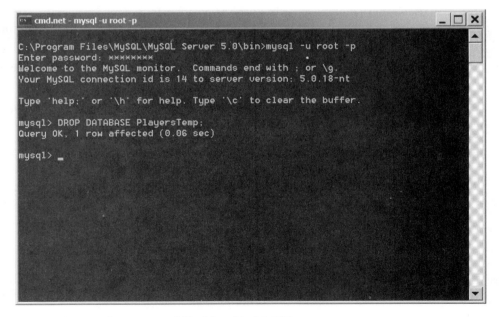

Figure 11-26. *Database successfully deleted in SQL Server*

cmd.net - mysql -u root -p
C:\Program Files\MySQL\MySQL Server 5.0\bin>mysql -u root -p
Enter password: ********
Welcome to the MySQL monitor. Commands end with ; or \g.
Your MySQL connection id is 14 to server version: 5.0.18-nt
Type 'help;' or '\h' for help. Type '\c' to clear the buffer.
mysql> DROP DATABASE PlayersTemp;
Query OK, 1 row affected (0.06 sec)
mysql>

Figure 11-27. *Database successfully deleted in MySQL*

How It Works

There isn't an awful lot to say—except be careful! The DROP DATABASE query deletes databases with no warning.

Note You can find more information about the DROP DATABASE command for SQL Server at http://msdn.microsoft.com/en-us/library/ms178613.aspx and for MySQL at http://dev.mysql.com/doc/refman/5.0/en/drop-database.html.

Summary

In this chapter, you've taken a whirlwind tour through the DDL "subset" of SQL, yet you've hardly scratched the surface. As I noted at the beginning of the chapter, if you look at the scripts provided in the code download, you'll see that even for this small database, the scripts are complex—certainly more complex than you've seen here.

You've looked at the basics of DDL, and you've seen how to create, modify, and delete databases and tables in both SQL Server and MySQL. You've also seen how you can create indexes on tables and relationships between the different tables in the database.

Remember the following points when using DDL:

- You usually have multiple ways to do the same thing; for example, you looked at two ways to create primary keys on tables. None of the ways to do something is more correct than the others, so choose the one you're comfortable using.

- Be extremely careful when deleting things from the database. It's easy to destroy a table or a database using just a single line of SQL.

You've just about finished with your look at databases, and in the next chapter you'll learn about several topics that will improve how you handle databases. You'll look at concurrency, caching, transactions, and multiple result sets and see that these more advanced topics can improve the Web sites that you're building quite dramatically.

CHAPTER 12

■■■

Useful Techniques

The past eleven chapters have covered quite a lot of ground and provided a good foundation in creating data-driven Web sites. This chapter covers several useful techniques to improve your Web site's use of databases.

When updating or deleting from the database, there is always the possibility that another user has managed to change the data in the database before you've had the chance to make your own changes. This potentially leaves the database in a bit of a mess, as the first set of changes will be lost and overwritten with the second set of changes, resulting in a data *concurrency* problem. We'll look at one solution to this problem, which prevents changes being made to the database if changes to the same data have already been made.

Next, we'll explore caching. In previous examples, you've always needed to make a round trip to the database to retrieve query results from the database. For frequently changing data, this is the only way that you can show up-to-date data. But for data that doesn't change that often, you can use the caching functionality of ASP.NET to store that data on the Web server and remove the relatively expensive trips to the database.

Our next topic is transactions. When you need to execute multiple related queries against the database (such as inserting, updating, or deleting a Player), you want all of the queries to succeed or you want all of the queries to fail. By default, each query you execute exists in its own little world, and as soon as it's executed, the database is updated with the changes. If a related query fails, then the database is left in an inconsistent state—is the data correct or is it incorrect? Transactions allow you to combine queries together so that they either all succeed or all fail.

Finally, we'll look at using multiple result sets. In previous chapters, you've looked at query batches, but they have either not returned any results or returned only one set of results. ASP.NET allows you to combine multiple SELECT queries into one query batch and deal with the results through a single DataReader.

This chapter covers the following topics:

- How to ensure data concurrency

- How to cache data on the Web server to avoid round trips to the database

- How to work with transactions to ensure that a set of queries either completely succeeds or completely fails

- How to combine multiple SELECT queries in a query batch

Concurrency

When we looked at modifying the database in Chapters 8 and 9, you saw that you can encounter problems in data concurrency when the data you are modifying has already been modified by someone else. Suppose both Alice and Bob are updating the same Manufacturer, say Apple, at the same time to change the e-mail address. At the start of the update, both Alice and Bob see the same e-mail address of lackey@apple.com. If Alice changes the Manufacturer e-mail address to someguy@apple.com and Bob changes the Manufacturer e-mail address to hello@apple.com, what value does the database show? It all depends on who saved the changes last. If Alice updated the e-mail address before Bob did, then Bob's changes would be in the database and any changes made by Alice would be lost.

In cases where only one person manages the content of the database, this may be the correct behavior. But what happens if you have several people who manage the content of the database? Do you want to take the "last-in" approach and overwrite any changes that are made? Or do you want to prevent the second change from taking effect—a sort of "first-in" approach?

As you've seen, by using the primary key value of the table that you're updating, the details in the table will always be updated (the last-in approach), as the only part of the WHERE clause matching the row to be updated is the primary key.

Consider the UPDATE query that we've looked at for Manufacturers:

```
UPDATE Manufacturer SET
  ManufacturerName = @ManufacturerName,
  ManufacturerCounty = @ManufacturerCountry,
  ManufacturerEmail = @ManufacturerEmail,
  ManufacturerWebsite = @ManufacturerWebsite
WHERE ManufacturerID = @ManufacturerID
```

Every time you run this query, the Manufacturer details will be updated. To ensure that the query succeeds only whenever none of the details for the Manufacturer have changed during the course of the query, you need to modify the WHERE clause to perform the update only if all the details match what you think they should be, based on your knowledge before you ran the query:

```
UPDATE Manufacturer SET
  ManufacturerName = @ManufacturerName,
  ManufacturerCountry = @ManufacturerCountry,
  ManufacturerEmail = @ManufacturerEmail,
  ManufacturerWebsite = @ManufacturerWebsite
WHERE ManufacturerID = @ManufacturerID
  AND ManufacturerName = @originalManufacturerName
  AND ManufacturerCountry = @originalManufacturerCountry
  AND ManufacturerEmail = @originalManufacturerEmail
  AND ManufacturerWebsite = @originalManufacturerWebsite
```

With the modified query, the Manufacturer will be updated only if all of the details for the Manufacturer match what they were before you started updating. So, in the Alice and Bob example, the second update, made by Bob, won't be applied, as the ManufacturerEmail column will be someguy@apple.com, not the original lackey@apple.com.

So, the update won't be applied, and you need to inform the user that the update hasn't been made. If you're using a Command object to make the update, you can check the return from the ExecuteNonQuery() method. If it returns zero, there have been no updates to the database, and you can assume that the details have already been changed. If you're making the update in a GridView, you can check the AffectedRows property of the GridViewUpdatedEventArgs in the RowUpdated event (the same is also true for the DetailsView and FormView, except that the event is ItemUpdated).

We'll look at handling concurrency errors using a Command object to make the update, and then you'll see that you can also handle concurrency errors when using a SqlDataSource to populate a DetailsView.

■**Note** Before you can follow the examples in this chapter, you need to download the code for this chapter from the Apress Web site (http://www.apress.com). In the code download, you'll find a folder called original, which contains several pages that you'll use as you work through the chapter. These are pages that we've already looked at in earlier chapters. Here, you'll add the functionality discussed in this chapter. You could rebuild these pages from scratch in this chapter, but I'm sure that you would rather concentrate on the new information, without needing to rebuild the same pages over and over again.

Try It Out: Handling Concurrency Using Command Objects

We'll first look at handling concurrency issues when using a Command object to connect to the database.

1. In Visual Web Developer, create a new Web site at C:\BAND\Chapter12 and delete the auto-generated Default.aspx file.

2. Add a new Web.config file to the Web site and add a new setting to the <connectionStrings /> element:

```
<add name="SqlConnectionString"
  connectionString="Data Source=localhost\BAND;Initial Catalog=Players;
    Persist Security Info=True;User ID=band;Password=letmein"
  providerName="System.Data.SqlClient" />
```

3. Copy Manufacturers_DataSource.aspx from the original folder in the code download to the root of the Chapter12 Web site.

4. Add a new Web Form to the Web site called Manufacturers_Edit_Command.aspx. Make sure that the Place Code in Separate File check box is unchecked.

5. In the Source view, find the <title> tag and change the page title to **Edit Manufacturer Using Command**.

6. Add the correct Import statement to the top of the page:

```
<%@ Import Namespace="System.Data.SqlClient" %>
```

7. Switch to the Design view and add a Label to the page. Set its ID to lblError, ForeColor to Red, and Visible to false. Remove the value from the Text property.

8. Switch to the Source view and add the following markup after the Label:

```
<table>
  <tr>
    <td>Name:</td>
    <td><asp:TextBox ID="txtName" runat="server"></asp:TextBox></td>
  </tr>
  <tr>
    <td>Country:</td>
    <td><asp:TextBox ID="txtCountry" runat="server"></asp:TextBox></td>
  </tr>
  <tr>
    <td>Email:</td>
    <td><asp:TextBox ID="txtEmail" runat="server"></asp:TextBox></td>
  </tr>
  <tr>
    <td>Website:</td>
    <td><asp:TextBox ID="txtWebsite" runat="server"></asp:TextBox></td>
  </tr>
</table>
```

9. Switch back to the Design view and add two Button controls after the table. The first Button should have its ID set to btnUpdate and it Text property set to Update. The second should have its ID set to btnCancel and its Text property set to Cancel. Your page should look similar to Figure 12-1.

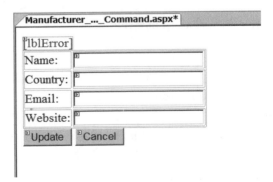

Figure 12-1. *Page design to add a new Manufacturer*

10. Add a Load event to the page and add the following code to the Page_Load event handler:

```
protected void Page_Load(object sender, EventArgs e)
{
  lblError.Visible = false;
```

```
    if (Page.IsPostBack == false)
    {
      LoadManufacturer();
    }
  }
```

11. Add the LoadManufacturer() method:

```
private void LoadManufacturer()
{
  // create the connection
  string strConnectionString = ConfigurationManager.
    ConnectionStrings["SqlConnectionString"].ConnectionString;
  SqlConnection myConnection = new SqlConnection(strConnectionString);

  try
  {
    // create the SELECT command
    string strQuery = "SELECT ManufacturerName, ManufacturerCountry, ➥
      ManufacturerEmail, ManufacturerWebsite ➥
      FROM Manufacturer WHERE ManufacturerID = @ManufacturerID";
    SqlCommand myCommand = new SqlCommand(strQuery, myConnection);
    myCommand.Parameters.AddWithValue("@ManufacturerID",
      Request.QueryString["ManufacturerID"]);

    // open the connection
    myConnection.Open();

    // execute the query
    SqlDataReader myReader = myCommand.ExecuteReader();

    // if we have results then we need to parse them
    if (myReader.Read() == true)
    {
      txtName.Text = myReader.GetString(
        myReader.GetOrdinal("ManufacturerName"));
      txtCountry.Text = myReader.GetString(
        myReader.GetOrdinal("ManufacturerCountry"));
      txtEmail.Text = myReader.GetString(
        myReader.GetOrdinal("ManufacturerEmail"));
      txtWebsite.Text = myReader.GetString(
        myReader.GetOrdinal("ManufacturerWebsite"));

      // save values into viewstate
      ViewState["ManufacturerName"] = txtName.Text;
      ViewState["ManufacturerCountry"] = txtCountry.Text;
      ViewState["ManufacturerEmail"] = txtEmail.Text;
      ViewState["ManufacturerWebsite"] = txtWebsite.Text;
    }
```

```
      // close the reader
      myReader.Close();
    }
    catch (Exception ex)
    {
      lblError.Text = ex.Message;
      lblError.Visible = true;
    }
    finally
    {
      // always close the connection
      myConnection.Close();
    }
  }
```

12. Add a Click event to the Update button and add the following code to the btnUpdate_Click event handler:

```
protected void btnUpdate_Click(object sender, EventArgs e)
{
  if (Page.IsValid == true)
  {
    SaveManufacturer();
  }
}
```

13. Add the SaveManufacturer() method:

```
private void SaveManufacturer()
{
  // create the connection
  string strConnectionString = ConfigurationManager.
    ConnectionStrings["SqlConnectionString"].ConnectionString;
  SqlConnection myConnection = new SqlConnection(strConnectionString);

  try
  {
    // create the UPDATE command
    string strQuery = "UPDATE Manufacturer SET ➥
      ManufacturerName = @ManufacturerName, ➥
      ManufacturerCountry = @ManufacturerCountry, ➥
      ManufacturerEmail = @ManufacturerEmail, ➥
      ManufacturerWebsite = @ManufacturerWebsite ➥
      WHERE ManufacturerID = @ManufacturerID ➥
      AND ManufacturerName = @originalManufacturerName ➥
      AND ManufacturerCountry = @originalManufacturerCountry ➥
      AND ManufacturerEmail = @originalManufacturerEmail ➥
      AND ManufacturerWebsite = @originalManufacturerWebsite";
    SqlCommand myCommand = new SqlCommand(strQuery, myConnection);
```

```
// add the parameters
myCommand.Parameters.AddWithValue("@ManufacturerID",
  Request.QueryString["ManufacturerID"]);
myCommand.Parameters.AddWithValue("@ManufacturerName",
  txtName.Text);
myCommand.Parameters.AddWithValue("@ManufacturerCountry",
  txtCountry.Text);
myCommand.Parameters.AddWithValue("@ManufacturerEmail",
  txtEmail.Text);
myCommand.Parameters.AddWithValue("@ManufacturerWebsite",
  txtWebsite.Text);
myCommand.Parameters.AddWithValue("@originalManufacturerName",
  ViewState["ManufacturerName"]);
myCommand.Parameters.AddWithValue("@originalManufacturerCountry",
  ViewState["ManufacturerCountry"]);
myCommand.Parameters.AddWithValue("@originalManufacturerEmail",
  ViewState["ManufacturerEmail"]);
myCommand.Parameters.AddWithValue("@originalManufacturerWebsite",
  ViewState["ManufacturerWebsite"]);

// open the connection
myConnection.Open();

// execute the query
int intCount = myCommand.ExecuteNonQuery();

// no records affected is error
if (intCount == 0)
{
  lblError.Text = "No update was made.  Concurrency problem.";
  lblError.Visible = true;
}
else
{
  // disable controls
  txtName.Enabled = false;
  txtCountry.Enabled = false;
  txtEmail.Enabled = false;
  txtWebsite.Enabled = false;
  btnUpdate.Enabled = false;
```

```
        // change the cancel to continue
        btnCancel.Text = "Continue";
      }
    }
    catch (Exception ex)
    {
      lblError.Text = ex.Message;
      lblError.Visible = true;
    }
    finally
    {
      // always close the connection
      myConnection.Close();
    }
  }
```

14. Add a Click event to the Cancel button and add the following code to the btnCancel_Click event handler:

```
protected void btnCancel_Click(object sender, EventArgs e)
{
  if (Request.QueryString["Type"] == "DS")
  {
    Response.Redirect("./Manufacturers_DataSource.aspx");
  }
  else if (Request.QueryString["Type"] == "DR")
  {
    Response.Redirect("./Manufacturers_DataReader.aspx");
  }
}
```

15. Save the page, and then open Manufacturers.aspx in your browser. Click the Edit Command button for a Manufacturer and make some changes to the Manufacturer. You'll see that the update works as you would expect.

16. Open another instance of Internet Explorer by selecting File ➤ New ➤ Window from the Internet Explorer menu. You'll now have two instances of Internet Explorer viewing the list of Manufacturers.

17. Click to edit the same Manufacturer in both instances of Internet Explorer. In one of the instances, you'll be able to make changes, and these will be saved, as shown in Figure 12-2.

18. Try to modify the Manufacturer in the other instance of Internet Explorer. This time, the change will be rejected and a warning will be shown, as you can see in Figure 12-3.

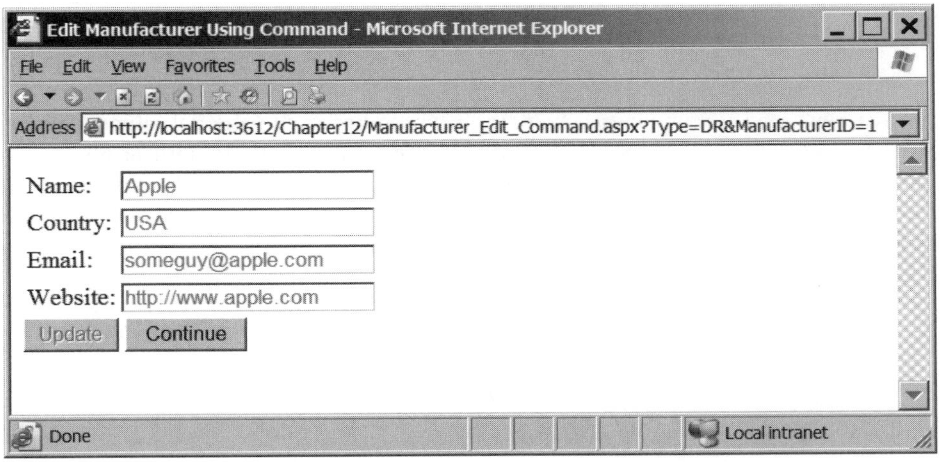

Figure 12-2. *You can make changes in one instance of Internet Explorer.*

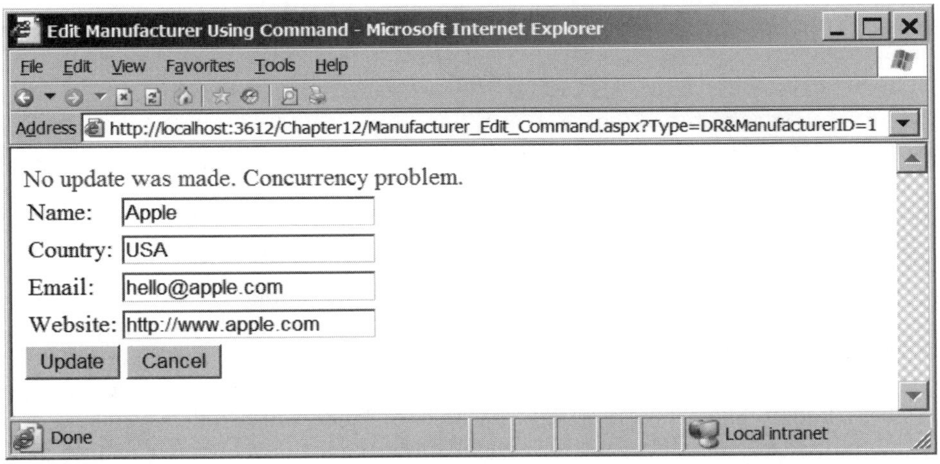

Figure 12-3. *You cannot make changes if they cause a data concurrency problem.*

How It Works

In Chapter 8, you saw how to send an UPDATE query to the database, and that's effectively all you're doing here. Granted, it's a more complex UPDATE query, but it's still just an UPDATE query:

```
UPDATE Manufacturer SET
  ManufacturerName = @ManufacturerName,
  ManufacturerCountry = @ManufacturerCountry,
  ManufacturerEmail = @ManufacturerEmail,
  ManufacturerWebsite = @ManufacturerWebsite
WHERE ManufacturerID = @ManufacturerID
  AND ManufacturerName = @originalManufacturerName
```

```
AND ManufacturerCountry = @originalManufacturerCountry
AND ManufacturerEmail = @originalManufacturerEmail
AND ManufacturerWebsite = @originalManufacturerWebsite
```

The key to the handling of concurrency is remembering the original values so that you can use them to populate the WHERE clause correctly. You can store them quite easily in ViewState, and they'll always be available to the page. So, in the LoadManufacturer() method, you retrieve the values that you need from the database and set the four TextBox controls' Text properties. Rather than accessing the DataReader twice, you then use the TextBox control Text properties to save the correct values into ViewState:

```
// save values into viewstate
ViewState["ManufacturerName"] = txtName.Text;
ViewState["ManufacturerCountry"] = txtCountry.Text;
ViewState["ManufacturerEmail"] = txtEmail.Text;
ViewState["ManufacturerWebsite"] = txtWebsite.Text;
```

You can then use the values stored in ViewState when you add the parameters to the Command object:

```
myCommand.Parameters.AddWithValue("@originalManufacturerName",
  ViewState["ManufacturerName"]);
myCommand.Parameters.AddWithValue("@originalManufacturerCountry",
  ViewState["ManufacturerCountry"]);
myCommand.Parameters.AddWithValue("@originalManufacturerEmail",
  ViewState["ManufacturerEmail"]);
myCommand.Parameters.AddWithValue("@originalManufacturerWebsite",
  ViewState["ManufacturerWebsite"]);
```

Once you've added all the parameters correctly, you can then execute the UPDATE query. If the query fails, the ExecuteNonQuery() method will return zero, indicating that no rows were affected by the UPDATE. You tell the user about the problem, as shown in Figure 12-3.

The Cancel button has its text changed so you can use it for both the cancel and continue purposes. Rather than having two buttons with two Click event handlers, you have only one.

Within the event handler, you have slightly more code than you might expect:

```
if (Request.QueryString["Type"] == "DS")
{
  Response.Redirect("./Manufacturers_DataSource.aspx");
}
else if (Request.QueryString["Type"] == "DR")
{
  Response.Redirect("./Manufacturers_DataReader.aspx");
}
```

Don't worry about it! If you look at the URL for the page, you'll see that it has a type as part of the query string. You're actually going to use these edit pages a little later, and you need the Cancel/Continue button to be able to return to the correct page. You've added the Type parameter so that you can control which of the Manufacturers pages you're returned to.

■**Note** In the examples here, you'll work with only the UPDATE query, and not the DELETE query. The process for handling concurrency problems with the DELETE query is the same as with the UPDATE query.

Try It Out: Handling Concurrency Using the SqlDataSource

The SqlDataSource also handles data concurrency and will generate the correct UPDATE query to force concurrency.

1. Add a new Web Form to the Web site called Manufacturer_Edit_DataSource.aspx. Make sure that the Place Code in Separate File check box is unchecked.

2. In the Source view, find the <title> tag and change the page title to **Edit Manufacturer Using DataSource**.

3. Switch to the Design view and add a SqlDataSource to the page (which will be called SqlDataSource1). From the Tasks menu, select Configure Data Source.

4. Select SqlConnectionString as the data connection to use and click the Next button.

5. Create a query that selects the ManufacturerID, ManufacturerName, ManufacturerCountry, ManufacturerEmail, and ManufacturerWebsite columns from the Manufacturer table.

6. Click the WHERE button and add a WHERE clause for ManufacturerID that uses the ManufacturerID QueryString value, as shown in Figure 12-4. Click OK to close the Add WHERE Clause dialog box.

7. Click the Advanced button. In the Advanced SQL Generation Options dialog box, click both the Generate INSERT, UPDATE, and DELETE Statements check box and the Use Optimistic Concurrency check box, as shown in Figure 12-5. Click OK to close the Advanced SQL Generation Options dialog box.

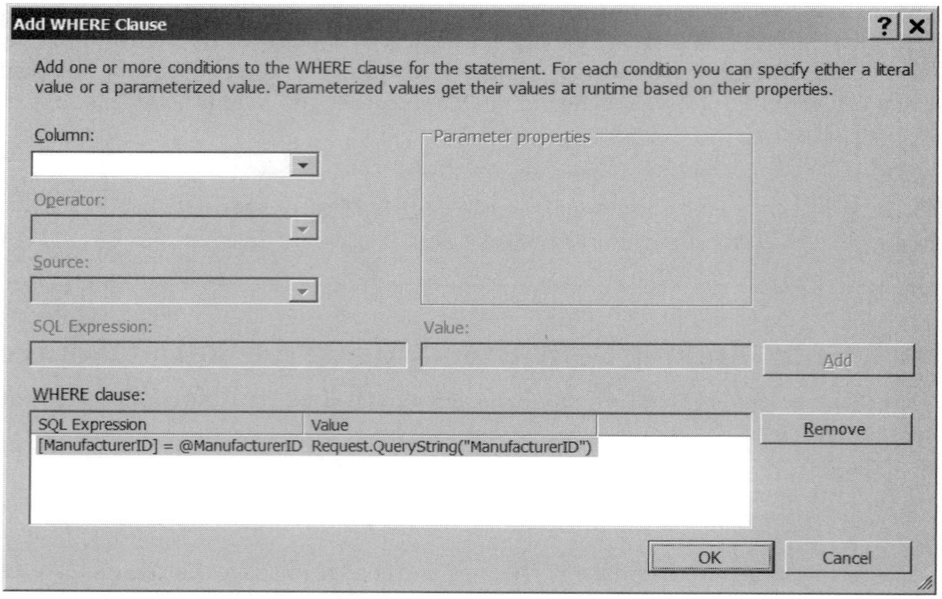

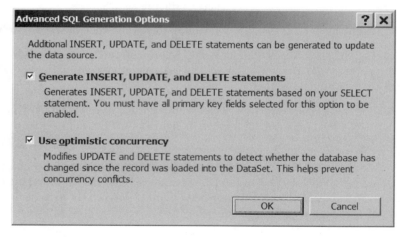

Figure 12-4. *Using the QueryString value to constrain the SqlDataSource*

Figure 12-5. *Auto-generating concurrency-proof UPDATE and DELETE queries*

8. Click Next, and then click Finish to close the Configure Data Source wizard.

9. Add a Label to the page. Set its ID to lblError, ForeColor to Red, and Visible to false. Remove the value from the Text property.

10. Add a DetailsView to the page and use SqlDataSource1 as the DataSource from the Tasks menu.

11. Switch to the Source view and remove the first BoundField from the Fields collection of the DetailsView.

12. Add the following FooterTemplate to the DetailsView:

```
<FooterTemplate>
  <asp:Button ID="btnUpdate" CommandName="Update"
    runat="server" Text="Update" />
  <asp:Button ID="btnCancel" CommandName="Cancel"
    runat="server" Text="Cancel" />
</FooterTemplate>
```

13. Add a Load event to the page and add the following code to the Page_Load event handler:

```
protected void Page_Load(object sender, EventArgs e)
{
  lblError.Visible = false;

  if (Page.IsPostBack == false)
  {
    DetailsView1.ChangeMode(DetailsViewMode.Edit);
  }
}
```

14. Add the ItemUpdated event to the DetailsView and add the following code to the DetailsView1_ItemUpdated event handler:

```
protected void DetailsView1_ItemUpdated(object sender,
  DetailsViewUpdatedEventArgs e)
{
  if (e.Exception != null)
  {
    lblError.Text = e.Exception.Message;
    lblError.Visible = true;
    e.ExceptionHandled = true;
    e.KeepInEditMode = true;
  }
  else if (e.AffectedRows == 0)
  {
    lblError.Text = "No update was made.  Concurrency problem.";
    lblError.Visible = true;
    e.KeepInEditMode = true;
  }
}
```

15. Add the ItemCommand event to the DetailsView and add the following code to the
    DetailsView1_ItemCommand event handler:

```
protected void DetailsView1_ItemCommand(object sender,
  DetailsViewCommandEventArgs e)
{
  if (e.CommandName == "Cancel")
  {
    if (Request.QueryString["Type"] == "DS")
    {
      Response.Redirect("./Manufacturers_DataSource.aspx");
    }
    else if (Request.QueryString["Type"] == "DR")
    {
      Response.Redirect("./Manufacturers_DataReader.aspx");
    }
  }
}
```

16. Add the DataBound event to the DetailsView and add the following code to the
    DetailsView_DataBound event handler:

```
protected void DetailsView1_DataBound(object sender, EventArgs e)
{
  // set the buttons correctly
  if (DetailsView1.CurrentMode == DetailsViewMode.ReadOnly)
  {
    ((Button)DetailsView1.FooterRow.FindControl("btnUpdate")).
      Enabled = false;
    ((Button)DetailsView1.FindControl("btnCancel")).Text = "Continue";
  }
}
```

17. Save the page, and then open Manufacturers_DataSource.aspx in your browser. Click
    the Edit DataSource button for a Manufacturer and make some changes to the Manu-
    facturer. You'll see that the update works as you would expect.

18. Open another instance of Internet Explorer by selecting File ➤ New ➤ Window from the
    Internet Explorer menu. You'll now have two instances of Internet Explorer viewing the
    list of Manufacturers.

19. Click to edit the same Manufacturer in both instances of Internet Explorer. In one of the
    instances, you'll be able to make changes, and these will be saved, as shown in Figure 12-6.

20. Try to modify the Manufacturer in the other instance of Internet Explorer. This time, the
    change will be rejected and a warning will be displayed, as shown in Figure 12-7.

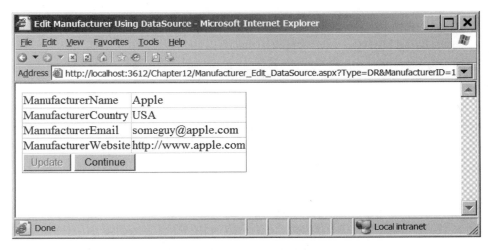

Figure 12-6. *Using a DataSource, changes can be made as you would expect.*

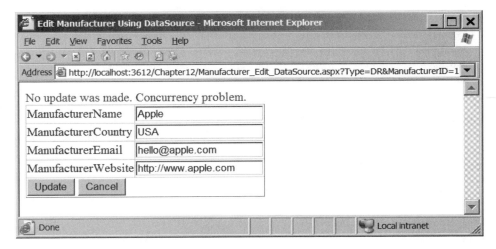

Figure 12-7. *You cannot make changes if they cause a data concurrency problem.*

How It Works

As you've just seen, enabling concurrency protection for the SqlDataSource is as simple as checking a box in the Configure Data Source wizard. It may have looked as though there was more than that, but a lot of the code that you added was to control the DetailsView and make it work in a "solo" way when it's not being used in a master-detail situation with a GridView.

When configuring the SqlDataSource, you have the option of enabling the control for concurrency. You've already seen how the SqlDataSource will generate INSERT, UPDATE, and DELETE queries if you tell it to do so. By checking the Use Optimistic Concurrency check box in the Advanced SQL Generation Options dialog box, you've also told the SqlDataSource that you want to use concurrency. You'll see that the UpdateCommand for the SqlDataSource is no longer a simple UPDATE query, but is now the query to support concurrency that you've already seen:

```
UPDATE Manufacturer SET
  ManufacturerName = @ManufacturerName,
  ManufacturerCountry = @ManufacturerCountry,
  ManufacturerEmail = @ManufacturerEmail,
  ManufacturerWebsite = @ManufacturerWebsite
WHERE ManufacturerID = @original_ManufacturerID
  AND ManufacturerName = @original_ManufacturerName
  AND ManufacturerCountry = @original_ManufacturerCountry
  AND ManufacturerEmail = @original_ManufacturerEmail
  AND ManufacturerWebsite = @original_ManufacturerWebsite
```

And the `UpdateParameters` collection also has the extra parameters specified:

```
<UpdateParameters>
  <asp:Parameter Name="ManufacturerName" Type="String" />
  <asp:Parameter Name="ManufacturerCountry" Type="String" />
  <asp:Parameter Name="ManufacturerEmail" Type="String" />
  <asp:Parameter Name="ManufacturerWebsite" Type="String" />
  <asp:Parameter Name="original_ManufacturerID" Type="Int32" />
  <asp:Parameter Name="original_ManufacturerName" Type="String" />
  <asp:Parameter Name="original_ManufacturerCountry" Type="String" />
  <asp:Parameter Name="original_ManufacturerEmail" Type="String" />
  <asp:Parameter Name="original_ManufacturerWebsite" Type="String" />
</UpdateParameters>
```

The `SqlDataSource` and `DetailsView` manage the concurrency checks and the necessary parameter values automatically. All that you need to deal with is the control of the user interface.

Because you're using the `DetailsView` on its own page, you want it only in `Edit` mode. You've chosen to edit the Manufacturer on the previous page so, in `Page_Load`, you always switch the `DetailsView` into `Edit` mode:

```
if (Page.IsPostBack == false)
{
  DetailsView1.ChangeMode(DetailsViewMode.Edit);
}
```

You're also don't want to rely on the automatic buttons that the `DetailsView` offers. These don't quite fit the purposes here, so you add your own buttons into the `FooterTemplate`:

```
<FooterTemplate>
  <asp:Button ID="btnUpdate" CommandName="Update"
    runat="server" Text="Update" />
  <asp:Button ID="btnCancel" CommandName="Cancel"
    runat="server" Text="Cancel" />
</FooterTemplate>
```

As you'll recall from Chapter 7, by using a `CommandName` of `Update`, you can force the `DetailsView` to perform an update. By using `Cancel`, you can force the `DetailsView` to cancel the current operation.

When canceling, you want to return to the list of Manufacturers, so in the `ItemCommand` event handler, you check that it was the Cancel button that was clicked. If it was, you return to the correct list of Manufacturers:

```
if (e.CommandName == "Cancel")
{
  if (Request.QueryString["Type"] == "DS")
  {
    Response.Redirect("./Manufacturers_DataSource.aspx");
  }
  else if (Request.QueryString["Type"] == "DR")
  {
    Response.Redirect("./Manufacturers_DataReader.aspx");
  }
}
```

If the user clicks the Update button, the `DetailsView` will perform the update and then raise the `ItemUpdated` event. As you'll recall from Chapter 9, this event allows you to check if there were any exceptions raised during the update and to also check how many rows were updated by the query. You need to handle both of these conditions and gracefully let the user know what is happening.

If you have an exception during the update, the `Exception` property of the `DetailsViewUpdatedEventArgs` will be set to the exception that was raised. You'll show the details of the problem to the user and let the `DetailsView` know that you've handled the exception. You're also setting the `KeepInEditMode` property to `true`, since the update hasn't been made and you don't want to leave `Edit` mode:

```
if (e.Exception != null)
{
  lblError.Text = e.Exception.Message;
  lblError.Visible = true;
  e.ExceptionHandled = true;
  e.KeepInEditMode = true;
}
```

If no exception was raised, there may be concurrency issues to handle. The `AffectedRows` property will return zero if no rows were updated. If this happens, you let the user know that a concurrency problem has occurred:

```
else if (e.AffectedRows == 0)
{
  lblError.Text = "No update was made.  Concurrency problem.";
  lblError.Visible = true;
  e.KeepInEditMode = true;
}
```

The final piece of code is again concerned solely with the user interface and how you use a `DetailsView` on its own. If the `DetailsView` is in `ReadOnly` mode, it means that the update has been successful. You don't want to allow the user to click the Update button again, so you disable it. The user can no longer cancel the update, so you change the text of the Cancel button to Continue. Both of these occur in the DataBound event:

```
protected void DetailsView1_DataBound(object sender, EventArgs e)
{
  // set the buttons correctly
  if (DetailsView1.CurrentMode == DetailsViewMode.ReadOnly)
  {
    ((Button)DetailsView1.FooterRow.FindControl("btnUpdate")).
      Enabled = false;
    ((Button)DetailsView1.FindControl("btnCancel")).Text = "Continue";
  }
}
```

As you can see, the SqlDataSource handles all of the logic for concurrency issues automatically. All you have to do to enable concurrency protection is check the appropriate check box in the wizard. You had to add a little code within the ItemUpdated event handler to deal with any exceptions or concurrency problems that arose, but the tasks of generating the UPDATE query, handling the original values, and passing these values to the query are handled automatically.

Caching

As you know by now, actually accessing the database is an expensive operation. Making the connection and then executing a query takes time. If there are instances where you don't need to query the database, consider caching results on the Web server so you can avoid that round trip to the database.

As you're aware, ASP.NET provides a cache for you to store information that will be used several times. The ideal types of objects to store on the cache are those that take a long time to create, so you don't need to re-create them.

So what results should be stored in the cache? Although you can cache anything that you want, storing regularly changing data there is a little pointless, since it will soon be invalidated. Data that changes infrequently is suitable for caching. In the sample database, new Manufacturers won't be added that often, so the list of Manufacturers is an ideal candidate for caching. However, you need to ensure that the data that is cached doesn't become invalid. If a new Manufacturer is added to the database, then the cached version of the list of Manufacturers will be incorrect.

Adding objects to the cache is very simple. The Page object provides direct access to the cache using the Cache property. You can add data to the cache using either the Add() or Insert() method. For the Insert() method, as a minimum, you need to specify a key for the object and the object itself:

```
dsManufacturers.RemotingFormat = SerializationFormat.Binary;
Cache.Insert("Manufacturers", dsManufacturers);
```

This adds a DataSet, dsManufacturers, to the cache indexed on the Manufacturers key. It sets the RemotingFormat of the DataSet to Binary, as this is the most efficient format in which you can store the DataSet. (You're storing this in the memory of the Web server, so you need to use as little space as possible.) It uses the Insert() method, which will automatically overwrite an existing item with the same key; the Add() method would throw an error.

You can access objects in the cache by using the key as the index to the Cache object itself. The cached object is returned as an Object, so it will need to be cast to the correct type:

```
DataSet dsManufacturers = (DataSet)Cache["Manufacturers"];
```

But that's not the end of the story. After you've added things to the cache, do they stay there forever? Certainly not! There are several instances where a cached object may be removed, including the following:

- ASP.NET removes the object automatically because there are resourcing issues with the Web site. As the memory of the Web server is used, ASP.NET will remove objects from the cache as required to ensure that the Web server operates correctly.

- You can specify that the objects can be cached for a fixed period of time or that the object is removed if it isn't used for a specified period of time.

- You can manually remove objects from the cache using the Remove() method.

So, if the item isn't in the cache, how do you detect that it isn't there? You can't perform a check on the cache directly to see if the object is there (it has no Contains() method as you would expect from a collection). Instead, you need to check that you actually have an object returned. For example, to test if the list of Manufacturers is in the cache, perform the following check:

```
DataSet dsManufacturers = (DataSet)Cache["Manufacturers"];
if (dsManufacturers == null)
{
  // rebuild DataSet
  // add DataSet to cache
}
```

If the DataSet isn't in the cache, the object returned will be equal to null. In that case, you would need to rebuild the DataSet and then make sure that it's added to the cache to be reused next time.

We'll now look at the two options for specifying the period of time that an object will remain cached. Then you'll work through an example where you cache the results from a DataReader and see that the queries to the database are reduced. Caching a DataSet is broadly similar, so we'll just look at the differences. Finally, you'll see how to use the Remove() method to ensure that when the database is modified, there are no cached objects that are invalid.

■**Note** Caching is a massive topic. MSDN provides information and examples covering all the different types of caching at http://msdn.microsoft.com/en-us/library/726btaeh.aspx. ASP.NET provides a series of Quickstart tutorials at http://www.asp.net/QuickStart/aspnet/doc/caching/default.aspx.

Specifying the Life Span of a Cached Object

When caching objects, you can allow the object to exist on the server until ASP.NET decides that it needs to be removed, but this isn't ideal. Although you're caching only data that changes infrequently, there aren't any guarantees that the cached data will be reused, and storing it in memory on the Web server when it isn't used isn't necessary.

You therefore need some way of specifying that the object that you're caching is valid for only a specified period of time. ASP.NET supports two types of time-based expiration:

- With *absolute expiration*, you specify a specific date and time that the data in the cache will become invalid.

- *Sliding expiration* allows you to specify a period of time that the object will remain in the cache since it was last accessed.

For example, to add a list of Manufacturers, stored in a `colManufacturers` object, to the cache, use the following:

```
Cache.Insert("Manufacturers", colManufacturers, null,
  DateTime.Now.AddMinutes(5), Cache.NoSlidingExpiration);
```

The fourth parameter to this overload of the `Insert()` method allows you to specify the absolute time that the cached object expires. This example takes the current time and adds 5 minutes to it. Once those 5 minutes are up (from the moment you called the `Insert()` method), the object is removed from the cache. Because you're using absolute expiration, you set the final parameter to `Cache.NoSlidingExpiration`.

To use sliding expiration, you use a similar call to the `Insert()` method:

```
Cache.Insert("Manufacturers", colManufacturers, null,
  Cache.NoAbsoluteExpiration, TimeSpan.FromMinutes(5));
```

This version sets the absolute expiration to `Cache.NoAbsoluteExpiration` and specifies a sliding expiration. In this case, `TimeSpan` is set as 5 minutes in the future. The list of Manufacturers will be cached for 5 minutes after it was last used and then discarded. If the list was accessed before it was invalidated, even if that access takes place after 4 minutes and 59 seconds, the object would remain in the cache for a further 5 minutes. And if it was accessed again? It has another 5 minutes before it is invalidated. The expiration slides!

■**Note** The third parameter to the `Insert()` method (passed as `null` in the examples here) allows you to add cache dependencies to the added object, so that it can be invalidated automatically if the dependent object is invalidated as well. For some good examples of cache dependencies, see the MSDN documentation referenced earlier, at `http://msdn.microsoft.com/en-us/library/726btaeh.aspx`.

Try It Out: Caching the Manufacturers

In this first example of caching, you'll build a new page that retrieves the list of Manufacturers using a DataReader and show the results in a GridView. You'll start with a basic page from the code download and modify this to add caching to reduce the number of queries made against the database.

1. Copy Manufacturers_DataReader.aspx from the original folder in the code download to the root of the Chapter12 Web site.

2. Open Manufacturers_DataReader.aspx and modify the Page_Load event as follows:

```csharp
protected void Page_Load(object sender, EventArgs e)
{
  if (Page.IsPostBack == false)
  {
    // retrieve the Manufacturers from cache
    ArrayList colManufacturers = (ArayList)Cache["Manufacturers"];

    // only load if not cached
    if (colManufacturers == null)
    {
      // create the connection
      string strConnectionString = ConfigurationManager.
        ConnectionStrings["SqlConnectionString"].ConnectionString;
      SqlConnection myConnection = new SqlConnection(strConnectionString);

      try
      {
        // query to execute
        string strQuery = "SELECT ManufacturerID, ManufacturerName, ➥
          ManufacturerCountry, ManufacturerEmail, ManufacturerWebsite ➥
          FROM Manufacturer ORDER BY ManufacturerName";

        // create the command
        SqlCommand myCommand = new SqlCommand(strQuery, myConnection);

        // open the database connection
        myConnection.Open();

        // run query
        SqlDataReader myReader = myCommand.ExecuteReader();
```

```
            // create a new collection
            colManufacturers = new ArrayList();
            foreach (System.Data.Common.DbDataRecord objRecord in myReader)
            {
              colManufacturers.Add(objRecord);
            }

            // close the reader
            myReader.Close();

            // cache the collection
            Cache.Insert("Manufacturers", colManufacturers, null,
              Cache.NoAbsoluteExpiration, TimeSpan.FromMinutes(5));
          }
          finally
          {
            // always close the database connection
            myConnection.Close();
          }
        }

      // set the data source and bind
      GridView1.DataSource = colManufacturers;
      GridView1.DataBind();
    }
}
```

3. Save the page and set Manufacturers_DataReader.aspx as the start page for the Web site.

4. Add a breakpoint to the first line of the Page_Load event handler and start debugging the application. When the page first loads, the collection of Manufacturers will not be present in the cache, as shown in Figure 12-8, so the database will be queried. If you continue to step through the code by pressing F10, you'll see this happening.

```
if (Page.IsPostBack == false)
{
    // retrieve the Manufacturers from cache
    ArrayList colManufacturers = (ArrayList)Cache["Manufacturers"];

    // only load if not cached
    if (colManufacturers == null)
    {                      ⊞  ◆ colManufacturers  null
        // create the connection
```

Figure 12-8. *On first load, the list of Manufacturers is not in the cache.*

5. Once the page has loaded and the list of Manufacturers is displayed in the GridView, press F5 to reload the page.

6. This time, when the breakpoint is hit, step through the code. You'll see that the list of Manufacturers has been retrieved from the cache, as shown in Figure 12-9. If you continue to step through the code, the database will not be queried.

```
if (Page.IsPostBack == false)
{
    // retrieve the Manufacturers from cache
    ArrayList colManufacturers = (ArrayList)Cache["Manufacturers"];

    // only load if not cached
    if (colManufacturers == null)
    {                    ⊞ ♦ colManufacturers  Count = 10
        // create the connection
```

Figure 12-9. *Subsequent loads retrieve the list of Manufacturers from the cache.*

7. Wait 5 minutes (go and make a cup of tea!), and then refresh the page. Step through the code, and you'll see that the list of Manufacturers has been removed from the cache and the database will be requeried.

How It Works

This example demonstrated that caching data is quite simple, as is dealing with the cache, as you'll see shortly. First, though, let's look at what you're actually storing on the cache.

As you know, the DataReader object is connected to the database while it is being used, and it provides forward-only, read-only access to the data. Because it is connected at all times, there is no way you can cache it without massaging it beforehand. You can't directly cache the DataReader; instead, you cache the results that it has returned.

The DataReader object returns the results from the query as a series of DbDataRecord objects. A DbDataRecord, once created by the DataReader, is not connected to the database and you can store it in the cache and reuse it as required.

As you're going to use the collection for data binding to the GridView, you use an ArrayList. The ArrayList supports the ICollection interface, so you can directly use it for data binding:

```
GridView1.DataSource = colManufacturers;
GridView1.DataBind();
```

To populate the ArrayList, you can iterate through the DataReader and simply add each DbDataRecord to the collection:

```
colManufacturers = new ArrayList();
foreach (System.Data.Common.DbDataRecord objRecord in myReader)
{
  colManufacturers.Add(objRecord);
}
```

After you've constructed the ArrayList that contains your massaged results, you can cache it and reuse it whenever you need it.

Adding the ArrayList to the Cache is accomplished in one line of code:

```
Cache.Insert("Manufacturers", colManufacturers, null,
  Cache.NoAbsoluteExpiration, TimeSpan.FromMinutes(5));
```

As you've already seen, you can cache data until a certain date and time using absolute expiration, or you can use sliding expiration to cache the data for a set period of time. In this case, you cache the list of Manufacturers for 5 minutes since it was last used.

You can check if the list of Manufacturers is present in the cache by using the key for the object you're retrieving, and cast the object to the correct type:

```
ArrayList colManufacturers = (ArrayList)Cache["Manufacturers"];
```

If there is a matching object in the cache, it will be returned and cast to the correct type. If there is no matching object—either because this is the first load of the page and you've never cached the ArrayList or it has been removed (for whatever reason)—the Cache object will return null. If you don't have a cached ArrayList, you query the database and construct the collection and cache, so that it's available in the future.

Caching a DataSet

Caching a DataSet is even easier than caching a DataReader. Because the DataSet is disconnected from the database, you can add it directly to the cache without any of the extra coding that was required to massage the DataReader into a cacheable collection.

So, in the previous example, the code to retrieve the list of Manufacturers would now look like this:

```
// retrieve the Manufacturers from cache
DataSet dsManufacturers = (DataSet)Cache["Manufacturers"];

// only load if not cached
if (dsManufacturers == null)
{
  // fill the DataSet as you'd normally do

  // set to Binary serialization
  dsManufacturers.RemotingFormat = SerializationFormat.Binary;

  // cache the DataSet
  Cache.Insert("Manufacturers", dsManufacturers, null,
    Cache.NoAbsoluteExpiration, TimeSpan.FromMinutes(5));
}

// now populate the GridView
GridView1.DataSource = dsManufacturers;
GridView1.DataBind();
```

As you can see, the code is very similar to the code that you used for the DataReader earlier. You construct the object to cache, in this case a DataSet, and then add it to the cache.

The actual cache statement again specifies a 5-minute sliding expiration, so it will be removed from the cache 5 minutes after the last access (or earlier if ASP.NET decides it needs to be removed or you remove it manually).

When caching a DataSet, you need to use the most efficient method of storing it. By default, the DataSet is serialized as XML, and this isn't very efficient. By setting the RemotingFormat to SerializationFormat.Binary, you use the most efficient serialization method available.

Removing Objects from the Cache

When using time-based cache expiry, there is always the chance that the data that you've cached isn't the same as the data in the database. If you've cached a list of Manufacturers and another user has added a new Manufacturer, then the database and the cache no longer contain the same list of Manufacturers. In these cases, you need to remove the cached object so that the results are requeried from the database.

Removing an item from the cache manually is simplicity itself. As you know the key of the object that you want to remove, you simply call the Remove() method:

```
Cache.Remove("Manufacturers");
```

This will remove the specified object from the cache. An attempt to remove an object that isn't in the cache won't cause any problems; it will just be ignored. ASP.NET may remove cached objects automatically, so the object may have been removed without your knowledge.

Try It Out: Removing Cached Objects Manually

In this example, you'll add code to the pages for editing a Manufacturer to remove the list of Manufacturers if you modify a Manufacturer. The process for removing an object from the cache is the same whether you're using a Command object or a SqlDataSource. The only difference is when you call the Remove() method.

1. Open Manufacturers_Edit_Command.aspx and switch to the Source view.

2. Modify the SaveManufacturers() method as follows:

```
        // change the cancel to continue
        btnCancel.Text = "Continue";

        // remove from the Cache
        Cache.Remove("Manufacturers");
    }
}
catch (Exception ex)
{
    lblError.Text = ex.Message;
    lblError.Visible = true;
}
```

3. Open Manufacturers_Edit_DataSource.aspx and switch to the Source view.

4. Modify the `ItemUpdate` event for the `DetailsView` as follows:

```
else if (e.AffectedRows == 0)
{
  lblError.Text = "No update was made.  Concurrency problem.";
  lblError.Visible = true;
  e.KeepInEditMode = true;
}
else
{
  // remove from the Cache
  Cache.Remove("Manufacturers");
}
```

5. Open `Manufacturers_DataReader.aspx` and, if you don't already have one, add a break-point to the first line of code in the `Page_Load` event handler.

6. Save all three pages and set `Manufacturers_DataReader.aspx` as the start page for the Web site.

7. Press F5 to start debugging. When the code hits the breakpoint for the first time, step through the code, and you'll see that the database is queried for the list of Manufacturers.

8. Let the page finish loading and press F5 to refresh it. Step through the code, and you'll see that the cached version of the results is used.

9. Click the Edit Command button for one of the Manufacturers. On the next page, click Update to make a change (even though nothing has actually changed) to the database. Click the Continue button to return to the list of Manufacturers. The breakpoint will be hit again. This time, the cache won't contain the list of Manufacturers, because the list was removed when you updated the Manufacturer on the previous page.

10. Let the page finish loading, and then press F5 to refresh it and confirm that the list of Manufacturers has again been cached.

11. Click the Edit DataSource button for a Manufacturer. On the next page, click Update to force a database update. Click the Continue button to return to the list of Manufacturers.

12. Step through the code again. You'll see that the list of Manufacturers has again been removed from the cache.

How It Works

Although there were quite a few steps to the example, you've made only two code changes (well, actually the same change in two different places). The majority of the example was proving that the list of Manufacturers had indeed been removed from the cache.

Of interest is this line of code:

```
// remove from the Cache
Cache.Remove("Manufacturers");
```

You're removing the object with the key of `Manufacturers` from the cache. In this case, that's the list of Manufacturers.

For the Command object version of the edit page, you remove the object from the cache if you've updated the database. In this example, you're checking for any concurrency errors when updating, so you remove the list from the cache only when you've modified a row in the database:

```
// no records affected is error
if (intCount == 0)
{
  // ...
}
else
{
  // ...

  // remove from the Cache
  Cache.Remove("Manufacturers");
}
```

The `SqlDataSource` version of the page is similar in that you remove the list from the cache only if the update has been successful. In this case, you need to check if you don't have an exception raised and you've modified a row in the `ItemUpdated` event handler:

```
if (e.Exception != null)
{
  // ...
}
else if (e.AffectedRows == 0)
{
  // ...
}
else
{
  // remove from the Cache
  Cache.Remove("Manufacturers");
}
```

Once you've removed the object from the cache, the list of Manufacturers is repopulated when the `GridView` is displayed.

If you actually wait long enough (5 minutes), the list of Manufacturers will already have been removed from the cache before you call the `Remove()` method. This won't cause a problem. As stated earlier, if the object that you're trying to remove from the cache doesn't exist, `Remove()` is simply ignored.

Transactions

When you looked at inserting, updating, and deleting Players in Chapter 8, you saw that these tasks require two queries: one to handle the Player table and another to handle the

WhatPlaysWhatFormat table. In fact, you saw that updating an existing Player actually requires three queries to be executed.

When inserting or updating, you trap any errors that occur and continue the save only if the previous query executed correctly. Consider the Click event handler for the Save button:

```
// only save if valid
if (Page.IsValid == true)
{
  // save the player to the database
  bool blnPlayerError = SavePlayer();

  // did an error occur?
  if (blnPlayerError == true)
  {
    QueryResult.Text = "An error has occurred!";
  }
  else
  {
    // save the formats for the player
    bool blnFormatError = SaveFormats();

    // did an error occur?
    if (blnFormatError == true)
    {
      QueryResult.Text = "An error has occurred!";
    }
    else
    {
      // show the result
      QueryResult.Text = "Save of player '" +
        Request.QueryString["PlayerID"].ToString() +
        "' was successful";

      // disable the submit button
      SubmitButton.Enabled = false;
    }
  }
}
```

If the SavePlayer() method fails, you'll tell the user that there is an error and not attempt to execute the SaveFormats() method. If the SavePlayer() method succeeds, then the SaveFormats() method is called.

But what if the SaveFormats() method fails? The SavePlayer() method has already made its changes to the database, and only the second set of changes fail. The result is that the Player stored in the database is now incorrect.

What you need to happen is for all queries to the database to succeed. If any of the queries that are being executed fail, then they must all fail. What you need is a transaction.

Transactions are a way to group different queries so that they all complete or they all fail—it's all or nothing.

To use the correct terminology, you *begin*, or *start*, a transaction, and then perform whatever steps you need to take as part of the transaction. If everything went as you wanted it to, you then *commit* the transaction, and all modifications are saved to the database. If something has gone wrong, a *rollback* of the transaction takes place, and the database isn't modified—it will appear as though the SQL queries you executed never took place.

Transactions, as with most things in the computing world, have their own acronym: ACID. It's not some throwback to the 1960s, but the first letters of the four properties that all transactions must exhibit:

Atomic: All queries within the transaction should succeed or fail. The archetypal example that's always used is a bank transfer scenario. If money is being transferred between two bank accounts, the tasks of taking the money from the source account and putting the money in the destination account both must succeed or both must fail. You can't have money removed from the source account but not added to the destination account, and you can't have money appearing in the destination account without the money being removed from the source account.

Consistent: A transaction transforms the database from one consistent state to another consistent state.

Isolated: A transaction that's currently executing will not see the results of any other transaction until the other transaction has completed.

Durable: A committed transaction should remain committed in the database, even if a failure occurs after the transaction has been committed.

Transactions can be handled in the following three places:

- You can handle transactions in the database. With SQL Server 2005 and MySQL 5.0, it is possible to implement transactions within stored procedures and ensure that all the queries that are to be executed are indeed executed.

- You can handle transactions in your code. Using ADO.NET, you can enlist different Command objects using the same connection to be part of a transaction using a Transaction object (SqlTransaction, OdbcTransaction, or OleDbTransaction). This allows you to execute several different queries or stored procedures and commit the results to the database only if they all execute correctly.

- You can use an External Transaction Manager. .NET makes it possible to run transactions across several different database connections (which may be on one machine or across several machines) and to also include nondatabase resources. In previous versions of .NET, you could perform transactions using COM+ using the System.EnterpriseServices namespace, but this is quite complex. .NET 2.0 introduces the System.Transactions namespace, which makes implementing distributed transactions a lot easier.

One thing to bear in mind when using transactions is that they impart a performance penalty on execution. During the lifetime of the transaction, any resources that are used are locked until the transaction is completed or rolled back. Any other queries trying to access those resources will be blocked and will have to wait until the transaction is over before the resource can be used.

Think carefully about whether to use transactions. Obviously, sometimes you must use transactions to ensure that the data is correct and can't be left in a state that you don't want it in. Don't, however, assume that every SQL query you're executing must be explicitly defined within a transaction. Transactions reduce the performance of the database, so if you don't need a transaction, don't use one.

Defining Database Transactions

Every query that you execute in the database will have an implicit transaction associated with it. As it's only a single query, you're never aware that it is running as a transaction, and you can, effectively, forget the fact that it is a transaction.

The simplest transaction that you will define is one that is "complete" within one stored procedure—either everything you're trying to do is committed to the database or it's all rolled back.

Consider the example of deleting a Player from the database. You need to make sure that the data is deleted from both the Player and WhatPlaysWhatFormat tables or from neither of them.

In SQL Server 2005, transactions are controlled using the BEGIN TRANSACTION, COMMIT TRANSACTION, and ROLLBACK TRANSACTION queries. In MySQL 5.0, you use the corresponding START TRANSACTION, COMMIT, and ROLLBACK queries.

Deleting a Player in SQL Server 2005 is as simple as executing the following queries:

```
-- start the transaction
BEGIN TRANSACTION

-- first delete
DELETE FROM WhatPlaysWhatFormat WHERE WPWFPlayerID = @PlayerID

-- second delete
DELETE FROM Player WHERE PlayerID = @PlayerID

-- commit the transaction
COMMIT TRANSACTION
```

First, you use the BEGIN TRANSACTION query to instruct the database that you want to start a transaction. After you execute the two DELETE queries, you then call COMMIT TRANSACTION to commit the changes to the database. It's only at this point that the data is actually deleted from the database.

You'll notice that you don't have a ROLLBACK TRANSACTION in the stored procedure. If a transaction is started and an error is raised, the ROLLBACK TRANSACTION is executed automatically by the database, which causes any changes to be rolled back. In this case, you wouldn't have an element that was partially deleted.

Although you don't need a ROLLBACK TRANSACTION if you have an error, you do need the COMMIT TRANSACTION at the end of the stored procedure. If the stored procedure reaches the COMMIT TRANSACTION, everything has gone correctly and you can commit the transaction. Although the transaction is rolled back automatically if an error has occurred, it won't be committed automatically; you must call COMMIT TRANSACTION. Failure to commit or roll back a transaction that has been started will result in an error being raised and the transaction rolled back, which will not be what you wanted if you forgot to call COMMIT TRANSACTION.

■**Note** The rollback of the transaction will not always be done by the database and may sometimes be handled by your code or ADO.NET. One example is adding a null value into a NOT NULL column in SQL Server 2005. This is not a fatal error as far as SQL Server is concerned and the rollback will be performed by ADO.NET.

Using a Transaction Object

Database transactions are handled in code using a Transaction object (either a SqlTransaction, an OdbcTransaction, or an OleDbTransaction). To use a Transaction object, you just need to tell the Command object that it's part of the transaction. As explained in Chapter 4, one of the Command object constructors takes a Transaction object as a parameter. For example, you can create a SqlCommand object as follows:

SqlCommand(string, SqlConnection, SqlTransaction)

Once you have a Transaction object, it's simple to enlist a Command object in the transaction by passing the object to the Command object constructor, or you can set the Transaction property after you've created the Command object. However, starting the transaction is not as simple as creating a new Transaction object.

You cannot create a Transaction object directly; you must use the BeginTransaction() method of the Connection object. Calling this method creates the necessary Transaction object and tells the Connection object that it needs to be transactional.

You can then use the created Transaction object with all the Command objects that you want to include in the transaction. Every Command object that uses the Connection object must also use the same Transaction object—once a Connection object is transactional, every related Command object must also be transactional. If they're not, an error will be raised when you try to execute a query on the nontransactional Command object.

When the transaction is complete, you call Commit() on the Transaction object to commit the transaction to the database or call Rollback() to abort the transaction.

The process for using transactions in code is simple and can be broken down into the following six steps:

1. Open the connection to the database.

2. Call the BeginTransaction() method on the Connection object to start the transaction and store the Transaction object for later use.

3. Create a Command object, and then specify the Transaction object that you want to use.

4. Use the Command object as you normally would.

5. Loop steps 3 and 4 as often as required.

6. Either commit or roll back the transaction by calling the Commit() or Rollback() method on the Transaction object.

You may have noticed the limitation with using the Transaction object: it works only across a single connection, and you cannot use a Transaction object with a Command object that uses a different connection. If you attempt to use the same Transaction object across different connections, you'll receive an error. If you want to run a transaction across different connections, you need to use the System.Transactions method of handling distributed transactions, as described in the "Implementing Distributed Transactions" section later in this chapter.

Try It Out: Using a Transaction Object

In this example, you'll modify the INSERT Player page from Chapter 8 to support transactions. You'll first modify one of the queries to force an error so that you can see the problems that occur when you don't have having transactions. By modifying the pages to use transactions, you'll show that the changes are rolled back when the error occurs.

1. Open Visual Web Developer and copy Players.aspx and Players_Insert.aspx from the original folder in the code download to the root of the Chapter12 Web site.

2. From the Solution Explorer, set Players.aspx as the start page for the Web site.

3. Open Players_Insert.aspx and modify the INSERT query in the SaveFormats() method as follows:

```
// query to execute
string strQuery = "INSERT WhatPlaysWhatFormats ➡
  (WPWFPlayerID, WPWFFormatID) VALUES (@PlayerID, @FormatID)";
```

4. Save the page, and then start debugging for the Web site.

5. Click the Add Player link and fill in the details for a new Player. Select some Formats, and then click the Insert Player button. You know that there's going to be an error (as you've forced an incorrect INSERT query in the SaveFormats() method), and the error is handled, as shown in Figure 12-10.

6. Open SQL Server Management Studio and connect to the localhost\BAND database server. Navigate to the Tables node from the Players database.

7. Open the Players table. You'll see that the new Player has been added, as shown in Figure 12-11 (Pear, in this example).

8. Open the WhatPlaysWhatFormat table. You will not see the Formats that you selected. The error has prevented the Formats from being added, but the Player has still been added. You need a transaction to avoid the problem.

9. Close Internet Explorer and switch back to Visual Web Developer. Open Players_Insert.aspx.

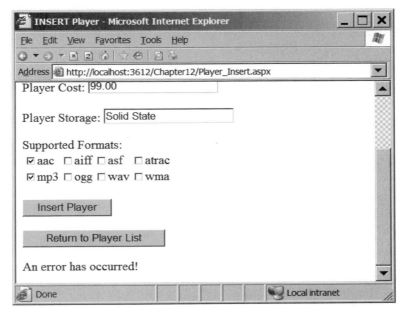

Figure 12-10. *The error is trapped but it isn't accurate.*

16	H10	3	189.00	Hard Disk
17	H300 Series	3	319.00	Hard Disk
18	Carbon	5	169.00	Hard Disk
19	Napster YH-920	10	179.00	Hard Disk
20	Network Walkman NW-HD3	7	215.00	Hard Disk
21	Pear	1	99.00	Solid State

Figure 12-11. *The Player has been added.*

10. Replace the Click event handler for the SubmitButton with the following:

```
protected void SubmitButton_Click(object sender, EventArgs e)
{
  // only save if valid
  if (Page.IsValid == true)
  {
    // create the connection
    string strConnectionString = ConfigurationManager.
      ConnectionStrings["SqlConnectionString"].ConnectionString;
    SqlConnection myConnection = new SqlConnection(strConnectionString);

    try
    {
      // open the connection
      myConnection.Open();
```

```
            // begin the transaction
            SqlTransaction myTransaction = myConnection.BeginTransaction();

            // save the player
            int intPlayerID = SavePlayer(myConnection, myTransaction);

            // save the formats
            SaveFormats(intPlayerID, myConnection, myTransaction);

            // commit the transaction
            myTransaction.Commit();

            // show the result
            QueryResult.Text = "Save of player '" +
              intPlayerID.ToString() + "' was successful";

            // disable the submit button
            SubmitButton.Enabled = false;
          }
          catch
          {
            // show the error
            QueryResult.Text = "An error has occurred!";
          }
          finally
          {
            // always close the connection
            myConnection.Close();
          }
        }
      }
```

11. Replace the SavePlayer() method with the following:

```
private int SavePlayer(SqlConnection myConnection,
  SqlTransaction myTransaction)
{
  // query to execute
  string strQuery = "INSERT Player (PlayerName, PlayerManufacturerID, ➥
    PlayerCost, PlayerStorage) VALUES (@Name, @ManufacturerID, @Cost, ➥
    @Storage); SELECT SCOPE_IDENTITY();";

  // create the command
  SqlCommand myCommand = new SqlCommand(strQuery, myConnection,
    myTransaction);
```

```
    // add the four parameters
    myCommand.Parameters.AddWithValue("@Name", PlayerName.Text);
    myCommand.Parameters.AddWithValue("@ManufacturerID",
      ManufacturerList.SelectedValue);
    myCommand.Parameters.AddWithValue("@Cost", PlayerCost.Text);
    myCommand.Parameters.AddWithValue("@Storage", PlayerStorage.Text);

    // execute the query
    int intPlayerID = Convert.ToInt32(myCommand.ExecuteScalar());

    // return the ID
    return (intPlayerID);
}
```

12. Replace the SaveFormats() method with the following (notice that it still has the error in the INSERT query):

```
private void SaveFormats(int intPlayerID, SqlConnection myConnection,
  SqlTransaction myTransaction)
{
  // query to execute
  string strQuery = "INSERT WhatPlaysWhatFormats ➥
    (WPWFPlayerID, WPWFFormatID) VALUES (@PlayerID, @FormatID)";

  // create the command object
  SqlCommand myCommand = new SqlCommand(strQuery, myConnection,
    myTransaction);

  // add the two parameters
  myCommand.Parameters.AddWithValue("@PlayerID", intPlayerID);
  myCommand.Parameters.Add("@FormatID", System.Data.SqlDbType.Int);

  // loop through each of the formats
  foreach (ListItem objFormat in FormatList.Items)
  {
    // save if selected
    if (objFormat.Selected == true)
    {
      // set the parameter value
      myCommand.Parameters["@FormatID"].Value = objFormat.Value;

      // execute the query
      myCommand.ExecuteNonQuery();
    }
  }
}
```

13. Save the page and open Players.aspx. Again choose to add a new Player to the database.

14. Enter the details for a new Player and click the Insert Player button. Again, the error will be trapped (Figure 12-10). However, if you query the database, you'll see that neither the Player or WhatPlaysWhatFormat table shows any details for the failed insertion.

15. Go back to Visual Web Developer and fix the broken INSERT query in SaveFormats() as follows:

```
// query to execute
string strQuery = "INSERT WhatPlaysWhatFormat ➥
  (WPWFPlayerID, WPWFFormatID) VALUES (@PlayerID, @FormatID)";
```

How It Works

Although it looked like you modified quite a lot of code in this example, that really wasn't the case! Most of the changes in the SavePlayer() and SaveFormats() methods were to remove code, and we'll look at these shortly. The really interesting code, at least from a transactional point of view, is in the SubmitButton_Click event handler.

Handling the Transaction

When using a Transaction object, all of the queries need to operate over the same connection. But before you create that connection, you check that the page is valid (that is, all the validators that you may have added have passed):

```
// only save if valid
if (Page.IsValid == true)
{
  // create the connection
  string strConnectionString = ConfigurationManager.
    ConnectionStrings["SqlConnectionString"].ConnectionString;
  SqlConnection myConnection = new SqlConnection(strConnectionString);

  try
  {
    // ...
  }
  catch
  {
    // show the error
    QueryResult.Text = "An error has occurred!";
  }
  finally
  {
    // always close the connection
    myConnection.Close();
  }
}
```

You've also added the error-handling code that you've come to expect. If you have an error anywhere while using the Connection object, you display an error message to the user (in the catch block) before always closing the connection (in the `finally` block).

A transaction can only be created on an open connection, so the first thing you need to do is open the connection:

```
// open the connection
myConnection.Open();
```

Once you have an open connection, you can create a transaction by calling the `BeginTransaction()` method of the Connection object:

```
// begin the transaction
SqlTransaction myTransaction = myConnection.BeginTransaction();
```

The `BeginTransaction()` method returns a Transaction object that you can use to enlist Command objects into the transaction, as you'll see when we look at the `SavePlayer()` and `SaveFormats()` methods shortly.

The next two lines are the calls to the two methods to save the Player to the database. In both cases, you need to pass the Connection and Transaction objects to the methods:

```
// save the player
int intPlayerID = SavePlayer(myConnection, myTransaction);

// save the formats
SaveFormats(intPlayerID, myConnection, myTransaction);
```

As all the queries need to use the same connection and same transaction, you need the two methods to be able to see the Connection and Transaction objects in order to use them. You could have made them available as global variables to the page, but they should be available only where they're needed, so you pass them to the two methods.

If both methods execute correctly, then you want to commit the transaction by calling the `Commit()` method of the Transaction object:

```
// commit the transaction
myTransaction.Commit();
```

This will make the changes to the database. Then you proceed to close the connection in the `finally` block.

But, where's the call to the `Rollback()` method if there's an error? There isn't one! If an error occurs anywhere within the `try` block, execution jumps to the `catch` block, and the `Commit()` method is never called. The Transaction object is pessimistic. If it isn't committed, then when it is disposed of (as it will be when it goes out of scope with the jump to the `catch` block), the `Rollback()` method is automatically called.

So, if there's an error, the changes are rolled back automatically. This is exactly what you saw happen in the example.

Saving the Player and the Formats

You've removed all error handling from the `SavePlayer()` method. You've moved all of the necessary error handling to the `SubmitButton_Click` event handler, so that you can handle the commit and rollback of the transaction from a central location.

Apart from the lack of error handling, you've made only two changes to the method. You've removed the creation of a connection to the database (as you're now passed the Connection object to use), and you've changed the way that the Command object is constructed:

```
// create the command
SqlCommand myCommand = new SqlCommand(strQuery, myConnection,
  myTransaction);
```

As well as specifying the query to execute and the existing Connection object, you're also passing in the Transaction object that you want to use. Any queries executed by this Command object will now be enlisted in the transaction and will be committed or rolled back with all the other queries enlisted in the transaction.

The changes to the `SaveFormats()` method follow the same pattern as the `SavePlayer()` method. You've removed all the error handling, you no longer create the connection to the database, and when creating the Command object, you enlist it in the provided transaction:

```
// create the command object
SqlCommand myCommand = new SqlCommand(strQuery, myConnection,
    myTransaction);
```

Whenever the query is executed (which it will be once for each Format that the Player supports), it will be enlisted in the transaction and committed only if all of the other queries execute successfully.

Implementing Distributed Transactions

As you've just seen, using a Transaction object to control transactions is ideal and will allow you to perform multiple queries across the same connection. However, not all transactions occur to the same database or across the same connection. Indeed, the `Players_Insert.aspx` page originally used two different connections to the same database. You modified the page to use the same connection so that you could use a Transaction object.

However, you may not always be able to modify the code to allow the use of the Transaction object. In this case, you need to enable a distributed transaction.

Put simply, a *distributed transaction* is a transaction that needs to run across more than one database connection. The different connections may be to the same database, they may be to different databases on the same server, or they may be connections to different database servers altogether. The key is that as soon as you use a different Connection object, the transaction becomes distributed.

In ASP.NET 1.1, you would need to write code to deal with the `System.EnterpriseServices` namespace in order to implement a distributed transaction. In ASP.NET 2.0, you can now use the `System.Transactions` namespace, which provides various objects to make distributed transactions quite simple. In order to use a distributed transaction, all you need to do is create a `TransactionScope` object:

```
using (TransactionScope objTransScope = new TransactionScope())
{
  // any database interaction here is transactional

  // must commit the transaction
  objTransScope.Complete();
}
```

Any code that executes against a database connection within the using statement is automatically enlisted in the transaction. If an error occurs and the Complete() method isn't called, the transaction will be rolled back automatically.

You don't always need to use the using statement to control what is enlisted in the transaction. You can also use a normal try..catch..finally statement to handle the transaction:

```
TransactionScope objTransScope = new TransactionScope()

try
{
  // any database interaction here is transactional

  // must commit the transaction
  objTransScope.Complete();
}
finally
{
  objTransScope.Dispose();
}
```

This is equivalent to the preceding code. Any errors in the try block will cause the Complete() method to be skipped and the transaction to be rolled back when the Dispose() method is called.

■**Note** Currently, only SQL Server 2005 is designed to be used with the System.Transactions namespace. Neither Microsoft Access nor MySQL 5.0, at the time of printing, can be used in conjunction with the System.Transactions namespace. Microsoft Access will throw an error if you try it, and MySQL 5.0 will simply ignore the transaction scope and execute each query individually. With these databases, you're stuck with using the OleDbTransaction and OdbcTransaction objects to enforce transactions across the same Connection object. But in the future, you can expect the namespace to be used in a lot more cases. For more details about using System.Transactions, see http://msdn.microsoft.com/en-us/library/0abf6ykb.aspx.

Although the System.Transactions namespace is designed to support distributed transactions, not every transaction that it handles is distributed. A transaction under System.Transactions starts its life under the Lightweight Transaction Manager (LTM) and, if the transaction is not distributed, will remain under the control of the LTM. If the transaction needs to be distributed, it must be under the control of the Distributed Transaction Coordinator (DTC), and using this adds an overhead to the transaction.

Thankfully, .NET 2.0 manages the transaction for you. It decides when a transaction needs to be under the control of the DTC and promotes the transaction from being a local transaction to a full-blown distributed transaction.

So when does a transaction require the DTC to control it? For our purposes, this occurs whenever you use a second Connection object. When a connection is first used within the TransactionScope, it is initially under the control of the LTM. Since it's using only one connection, there is no need to add the overhead of making the transaction distributed. If no other connections are used, then all the queries will be executed under the control of the LTM; the DTC is never used.

As soon as a different Connection object tries to enlist in the transaction, it is promoted to being a distributed transaction under the control of the DTC. However this requires that you have the Distributed Transaction Coordinator service running; otherwise, the transaction cannot be promoted and an error will be generated.

We'll now look at both of these scenarios: local and distributed transactions.

Try It Out: Using a Local Transaction

In order for a transaction to be under the control of the LTM, you need to use the same connection for all queries within the transaction. In this example, you'll modify the DELETE Player page from Chapter 8 to use the System.Transactions namespace and implement a local transaction.

1. Open the Administrative Tools folder of Control Panel and open the Services application. Find the Distributed Transaction Coordinator in the list of services. If it is running, stop it (either from the context menu or from the toolbar).

2. Open the Chapter12 Web site in Visual Web Developer and a reference to System.Transactions to the Web site.

3. Copy Players_Delete.aspx from the original folder in the code download to the root of the Web site.

4. Open Players_Delete.aspx in the root of the Web site and add the correct Import statement to the top of the page:

```
<%@ Import Namespace="System.Transactions" %>
```

5. Replace the SubmitButton_Click event handler with the following (there is an intentional error in the second DELETE query):

```
protected void SubmitButton_Click(object sender, EventArgs e)
{
  // create the connection
  string strConnectionString = ConfigurationManager.
    ConnectionStrings["SqlConnectionString"].ConnectionString;
  SqlConnection myConnection = new SqlConnection(strConnectionString);
```

```
try
{
  using (TransactionScope objTransScope = new TransactionScope())
  {
    // create the first query
    string strQuery1 = "DELETE FROM WhatPlaysWhatFormat ➡
      WHERE WPWFPlayerID = @PlayerID;";
    SqlCommand myCommand1 = new SqlCommand(strQuery1, myConnection);
    myCommand1.Parameters.AddWithValue("@PlayerID",
      Request.QueryString["PlayerID"]);

    // create the second query
    string strQuery2 = "DELETE FROM Players WHERE PlayerID = @PlayerID;";
    SqlCommand myCommand2 = new SqlCommand(strQuery2, myConnection);
    myCommand2.Parameters.AddWithValue("@PlayerID",
      Request.QueryString["PlayerID"]);

    // open the connection
    myConnection.Open();

    // execute the queries
    myCommand1.ExecuteNonQuery();
    myCommand2.ExecuteNonQuery();

    // show the result
    QueryResult.Text = "Delete of player '" +
      Request.QueryString["PlayerID"] + "' was successful";

    // disable the submit button
    SubmitButton.Enabled = false;

    // must commit the transaction
    objTransScope.Complete();
  }
}
catch (Exception ex)
{
  // show the error
  QueryResult.Text = "An error has occurred: " + ex.Message;
}
finally
{
  // close the connection
  myConnection.Close();
}
}
```

6. Save the page, and then start debugging to load Players.aspx.

7. Click the Add Player link. Add a new Player to the database, and then click Continue to return to the list of Players.

8. Find the Player that you've just added and click the Delete button. When Players_Delete.aspx is loaded, click the Delete Player button to confirm the deletion. As shown in Figure 12-12, an error has occurred.

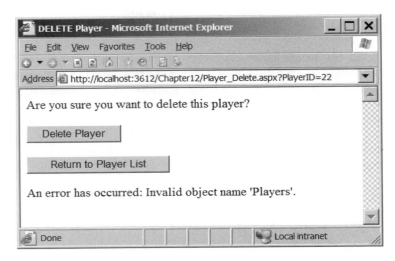

Figure 12-12. *The Player cannot be deleted.*

9. Open SQL Server Management Studio. You'll see that the Player is still present in the Players table and also in the WhatPlaysWhatFormat table, as shown in Figure 12-13.

	22	3
	22	4
	22	5
	22	6

Figure 12-13. *The Player is still in the database.*

10. Stop debugging. Modify the second query in the SubmitButton_Click event handler so that it is now correct:

```
// create the second query
string strQuery2 = "DELETE FROM Player WHERE PlayerID = @PlayerID;";
```

11. Load the Web site again. You'll be able to delete the Player, and the transaction will commit to the database. If you check the Player and WhatPlaysWhatFormat tables, you'll see that the Player has indeed been deleted.

How It Works

Once again, you've used an existing page to reduce the work that you need to do in order to see the desired results.

Within the SubmitButton_Click event handler, you're executing two DELETE queries against the database. The first thing you need is a connection to the database, so you create a Connection object, myConnection, as you've done in previous examples. You then wrap the remainder of the database access code in a try..catch..finally block so that you can handle any errors that occur.

To make all the queries executed against the database transactional, you wrap all of the database interactions within a using statement (only the pertinent parts of the code are shown here):

```
using (TransactionScope objTransScope = new TransactionScope())
{
  // create the first query
  SqlCommand myCommand1 = new SqlCommand(strQuery1, myConnection);

  // create the second query
  SqlCommand myCommand2 = new SqlCommand(strQuery2, myConnection);

  // open the connection
  myConnection.Open();

  // execute the queries
  myCommand1.ExecuteNonQuery();
  myCommand2.ExecuteNonQuery();

  // must commit the transaction
  objTransScope.Complete();
}
```

Once you have a TransactionScope object, you can create the two Command objects that you want to execute. Notice that they're both using the same Connection object, myConnection, so this transaction will remain under the control of the LTM, rather than being promoted to a distributed transaction under the control of the DTC.

After you've created the two Command objects, you open the connection to the database, execute the queries, and then Complete() the transaction.

If all goes well, the changes to the database will be made when you call Complete(). However, if there's an error, as in this case, the call to the Complete() method will be skipped, and the transaction will be rolled back automatically.

Let's backtrack to the very beginning of this example. The first thing that you did was turn off the Distributed Transaction Coordinator service, which effectively turns off distributed transactions. This proves that the transaction that you created remained a local transaction under the control of the LTM. If the transaction had needed to be promoted to a distributed transaction, an error would have been thrown. You'll see this in the next example.

Try It Out: Using a Distributed Transaction

You're now going to build an example that requires a distributed transaction. You'll see how the transaction is promoted to distributed only when a second Connection object is used.

1. Open Visual Web Developer and copy `Players_Update.aspx` from the `original` folder in the code download to the root of the `Chapter12` Web site.

2. Open `Players_Update.aspx` in the root of the Web site and add the correct `Import` statement to the top of the page:

```
<%@ Import Namespace="System.Transactions" %>
```

3. Modify the `SubmitButton_Click` event handler as follows (the changed code is in bold):

```
protected void SubmitButton_Click(object sender, EventArgs e)
{
  // only save if valid
  if (Page.IsValid == true)
  {
    using (TransactionScope objTransScope = new TransactionScope())
    {
      // save the player to the database
      bool blnPlayerError = SavePlayer();

      // did an error occur?
      if (blnPlayerError == true)
      {
        QueryResult.Text = "An error has occurred!";
      }
      else
      {
        // save the formats for the player
        bool blnFormatError = SaveFormats();

        // did an error occur?
        if (blnFormatError == true)
        {
          QueryResult.Text = "An error has occurred!";
        }
        else
        {
          // show the result
          QueryResult.Text = "Save of player '" +
            Request.QueryString["PlayerID"].ToString() + "' was successful";

          // disable the submit button
          SubmitButton.Enabled = false;
```

```
                    // must commit the transaction
                    objTransScope.Complete();
                }
            }
        }
    }
}
```

4. Add a breakpoint to the using statement that you've added to SubmitButton_Click.

5. Save the page, and then start debugging to load Players.aspx.

6. Click the Edit button for one of the Players in the list. Click the Update Player button to start the update process and hit the breakpoint you've added.

7. Step through the code and step into the SavePlayer() and SaveFormats() methods. You'll be able to step through SavePlayer() without any problems, and the UPDATE query in that method will execute without any problems. However the SaveFormats() method isn't as cooperative. As soon as you try to open the new SqlConnection object, an error is thrown, as shown in Figure 12-14.

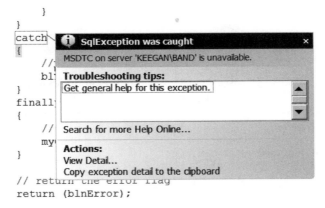

Figure 12-14. *The transaction can't be promoted to a distributed transaction.*

8. Press F5 to continue execution, and Players_Update.aspx will show an error. If you use SQL Server Management Studio, none of the changes that you've made will have been committed to the database.

9. Open the Services application from the Administrative Tools folder of the Control Panel and start the Distributed Transaction Coordinator service.

10. Save the changes to the Player. You'll be able to step through the code without any problems, and the transaction will be committed to the database.

How It Works

As explained earlier, a transaction is promoted to being distributed whenever it uses more than one database connection, and a distributed transaction is controlled by the DTC. This example has shown both of these features.

In the previous example, you stopped the Distributed Transaction Coordinator service to demonstrate that if you use the same connection to the database, you don't create a distributed transaction; it remains a local transaction. By starting this example with the service still stopped, you've seen that the transaction that you're executing does indeed need to be promoted.

You've wrapped all of the code to access the database inside a using statement, and any queries that you execute will be automatically enlisted within the TransactionScope you specified. This is true for code that runs directly within the using statement (as you saw in the previous example) or any code that runs in methods that are called from within the using statement.

Both SavePlayer() and SaveFormats() create their own Connection object and, even though these are to the same database, because you have more than one Connection object, it will automatically become a distributed transaction. The interesting thing to notice is that it doesn't become a distributed transaction until the second Connection object is required. The SavePlayer() method actually runs as a local transaction. It isn't until the SaveFormats() method tries to use its own Connection object that the transaction needs to be distributed. At that point, the transaction is automatically promoted from a local transaction to a distributed transaction and, as the Distributed Transaction Coordinator service isn't running, an error is thrown.

Multiple Result Sets

As you've learned in previous chapters you can execute several different queries as part of the same query batch to the database. For example, when you add a new Player to the database, you're executing an INSERT query to add to the Player table and then a SELECT query to return the PlayerID of the newly added Player:

```
INSERT Player (PlayerName, PlayerManufacturerID,
  PlayerCost, PlayerStorage)
VALUES (@Name, @ManufacturerID, @Cost, @Storage);
SELECT SCOPE_IDENTITY();
```

One thing that all of the examples that we've looked at so far have in common is that they contain only one SELECT query. When you've needed to execute two SELECT queries, you've executed these using two different SqlCommand objects. However, as noted in Chapter 8, you can actually execute multiple SELECT queries as part of the same query batch. For example, to retrieve all of the details for a Player at the same time, you could execute the following query batch:

```
SELECT PlayerName, PlayerManufacturerID, PlayerCost, PlayerStorage
  FROM Player WHERE PlayerID=@PlayerID;
SELECT WPWFFormatID FROM WhatPlaysWhatFormat
  WHERE WPWFPlayerID = @PlayerID;
```

If you executed this query batch through the ExecuteReader() method, the results of both queries would be returned within the same DataReader. You would need to use the NextResult() method to access the results of the second query.

■Note Only SQL Server 2005 allows you to use a query batch to execute multiple SELECT queries. Neither Microsoft Access nor MySQL 5.0 supports query batches. With those databases, you need to use separate SELECT queries.

Try It Out: Executing Two SELECT Queries in a Query Batch

In this example, you'll update the Players_Update.aspx page to query the database only once when retrieving an existing player. You will use a query batch to execute the two SELECT queries, and then use the NextResult() method to access the results of the second query.

1. Open Visual Web Developer and open Players_Update.aspx in the root of the Web site.

2. Replace the RetrieveExistingPlayer() method with the following:

```
private void RetrieveExistingPlayer()
{
  // create the connection
  string strConnectionString = ConfigurationManager.
    ConnectionStrings["SqlConnectionString"].ConnectionString;
  SqlConnection myConnection = new SqlConnection(strConnectionString);

  try
  {
    // create the query batch
    string strQuery = "SELECT PlayerName, PlayerManufacturerID, ➥
      PlayerCost, PlayerStorage FROM Player WHERE PlayerID = ➥
      @PlayerID; SELECT WPWFFormatID FROM WhatPlaysWhatFormat ➥
      WHERE WPWFPlayerID = @PlayerID;";
    SqlCommand myCommand = new SqlCommand(strQuery, myConnection);
    myCommand.Parameters.AddWithValue("@PlayerID",
      Request.QueryString["PlayerID"]);

    // open the connection
    myConnection.Open();

    // execute the query batch
    SqlDataReader myReader = myCommand.ExecuteReader();

    // if we have results then we need to parse them
    if (myReader.Read() == true)
    {
      PlayerName.Text = myReader.GetString(
        myReader.GetOrdinal("PlayerName"));
      ManufacturerList.SelectedValue = myReader.GetInt32(
        myReader.GetOrdinal("PlayerManufacturerID")).ToString();
```

```
          PlayerCost.Text = myReader.GetDecimal(
            myReader.GetOrdinal("PlayerCost")).ToString();
          PlayerStorage.Text = myReader.GetString(
            myReader.GetOrdinal("PlayerStorage"));
        }

        // get the next results
        myReader.NextResult();

        // if we have results then we need to parse them
        while (myReader.Read() == true)
        {
          foreach (ListItem objFormat in FormatList.Items)
          {
            if (objFormat.Value == myReader.GetInt32(
              myReader.GetOrdinal("WPWFFormatID")).ToString())
            {
              objFormat.Selected = true;
              break;
            }
          }
        }

        // close the reader
        myReader.Close();
      }
      finally
      {
        // close the connection
        myConnection.Close();
      }
    }
```

3. Save the page, and then start debugging the Web site. Click to edit one of the Players, and you'll see that the details of the existing Player are returned as expected.

How It Works

In this example, you've modified the RetrieveManufacturer() method to execute a query batch containing two SELECT queries:

```
SELECT PlayerName, PlayerManufacturerID, PlayerCost,
  PlayerStorage FROM Player WHERE PlayerID = @PlayerID;
SELECT WPWFFormatID FROM WhatPlaysWhatFormat
  WHERE WPWFPlayerID = @PlayerID;";
```

When executing a query batch containing several SELECT queries, the DataReader is initially connected to the results of the first SELECT query.

So, initially, you have access to the details for the individual Player. You need to first check that you have results for this query using the Read() method (the HasRows property would work equally as well) before you parse the results and set the controls on the page:

```
// if we have results then we need to parse them
if (myReader.Read() == true)
{
  // ...
}
```

Once you're finished with the first set of results, you can move on to the results for the second SELECT query by calling the NextResult() method:

```
// get the next results
myReader.NextResult();
```

The NextResult() method advances to the next set of results in the DataReader. In this case, you're returning the media Formats that the Player supports, and you can parse through the rows returned:

```
// if we have results then we need to parse them
while (myReader.Read() == true)
{
  // ...
}
```

That's all there is to it. For every SELECT query, there is a result set in the DataReader that you can access. Even if the SELECT query doesn't return any results, it will still have a result set that has the HasRows property set to false.

Summary

In this chapter, we've looked at a few topics that will broaden your knowledge and help you build better Web sites. Here, you learned the following:

- With a few changes to the UPDATE query, you can prevent changes from being made to the database if the data in the database is different from what you were expecting.

- By caching data that changes infrequently, you can improve performance by reducing the number of queries made against the database.

- By placing several queries in the same transaction, you can commit or roll back the changes as a whole to ensure that the database isn't left in an inconsistent state.

- By placing several SELECT queries in the same query batch, you can return several sets of results using the same DataReader.

This chapter completes this book's coverage of specific techniques for building data-driven Web sites. The next and final chapter provides some guidance on how to put it all together into a well-designed and well-implemented application.

CHAPTER 13

■■■

Application Design and Implementation

The contents of the book thus far have taught you the individual techniques of database access. This chapter aims to help put all you've learned into a more real-world context. You may now know how the different objects in a data provider work together and are put to use, and you may have learned how to produce a page that will do the tasks you want it to perform, but taking that next step forward and putting together a whole data-driven Web site requires an extra set of skills.

Let's start with what you do know and then think bigger. As you develop more complex data-driven pages, you start to section database functionality into functions, so that they can be called time and time again, rather than written out in full. This is good programming practice that saves you time and space, even on a single page. If you take the time to design your Web site well, you can make such common functions available to every page rather than just individual ones—more time, space, and resources saved. In fact, the benefits are exponential. Indeed, a well-designed and well-implemented application is easier to maintain, test, debug, and extend than one grown a page at a time.

In this chapter, you'll look at some of the concepts in the *development life cycle* of a data-driven Web site. The point here is to give you an idea of the issues to be aware of and the questions to ask yourself as you build your Web site, rather than tell you exactly what to do and when.

This chapter covers the following topics:

- An overview of the Web site development life cycle

- Client requirements and Web site development tools

- Database and application design

- Best practices for implementing code

- Unit testing and performance measurements

- Common Web site maintenance tasks

This chapter is intended as a pause for thought before you begin building your own Web sites; it contains no actual code or examples. Instead, it introduces many concepts and refers you to books and Web sites where you can find more details and examples. Think of this not as the *Encyclopaedia Galactica* on the subject but, rather, as the *Hitchhiker's Guide*—useful, common information only. So, with the mandatory warning—don't panic!—let's begin.

The Software Life Cycle

From initial ideas to postrelease, the main stages of software development are as follows:

Requirements gathering and analysis: This stage involves defining what functionality a Web site will have, and how people and machines will interact with the Web site. You also need to develop the tests, or metrics, for measuring the performance of your Web site.

Design: This is when you design a namespace and class structure for the Web site that's clean, flexible, and easily extendable. You'll also design an equally efficient and extendable database structure (building on the techniques you learned in Chapter 2).

Implementation: This stage involves writing code over the class structure, taking into account the good practices you've learned thus far in the book.

Testing and debugging: You'll need to test each module to see whether it passes the benchmarks you laid out for it in the analysis phase, and then track down those annoying bugs.

Maintenance: Once the Web site has gone live, that isn't the end of the story. All Web sites need to be maintained. Bugs may need to be fixed, and there will always be areas where things aren't quite right. Additionally, unless you're extremely lucky, clients will request new features after the Web site is live.

Several different life cycle methodologies are available, and there isn't any "right" way to do things. Every project has its own unique qualities.

Analysis

It would be unwise to jump straight into coding a Web site without taking some time first to consider what the Web site needs to do. If a Web site doesn't perform to a client's standards, others may think again about contracting you to build something for them, and you certainly won't get any further business from the original client either. Even if you're working on something for yourself—a portfolio piece, if you will—you want to code it well if it will be on display for others to see; this is doubly so if it's an open source project where the standard of your coding will be judged.

Client Requirements

Your first job will be to work on a list of requirements for the Web site. If this is a contracted job, you need to sit down with your clients to draft this. But what kind of requirements are you after? Well, you can broadly categorize them as described in the following sections.

Contents and Functionality

The Web site contents and functionality requirements are concerned with the main aims for the Web site, the intended users, and the tasks it should be performing. Specifically, you should consider the following questions:

- What kind of Web site is it? Is it a personal site for a friend, a reference site for a business, an e-commerce site for a retail company, or a showy site for a rock band?

- Is the Web site envisaged as an intranet site, an extranet site, or a public Web site on the Internet?

- How many pages will the Web site include? What will they do? What information is being provided in these pages to the users? Once you understand the pages that are required, you should be able to draw a site map that shows how all of the pages fit together.

- What information is being provided to the Web site's owners about the users? Will the user habits and logins need to be tracked?

While the clients are trying to describe how they would like the Web site to run, your goals are to try to identify the items and events that could be modeled in a database and to pin the clients down on the distinct functionality of the Web site that you can translate into a class structure. Now, this latter point won't actually happen because, unless the Web site is remarkably trivial, clients will continue to change their minds, adding and removing features as you try to make progress. However, the core functionality of the Web site should be possible to pin down, and you should be able to produce a site map showing how the different pages of the site fit together.

User Roles and Access

User roles and access requirements involve getting to know more about who will use the Web site and how they will use it. Specifically, you should consider the following questions:

- Will the Web site interface with any other application? How will this interaction be achieved, and to what other applications will it be available?

- Who is going to be using the Web site? Will the user base be confined to a single company if it's an intranet site or a known set of users (if it's an extranet), or can anyone access it (if it's on the Internet)?

- Of those users, can you distinguish the roles they may have? For example, in a forum Web site, guests may only read posts, members may write posts, and moderators may approve and reject posts.

- What are the use cases? Can you determine how people in various roles will try to perform a task and how the Web site will behave in response? For example, in a forum Web site, how will a member look for a post on a topic and reply to it? What happens if a guest tries the same thing?

Use cases can be tricky to write, but they become invaluable when it comes to coding pages that are applicable to them. You need to worry as much about what the page does as how to implement it. Use cases also provide a useful mechanism for double-checking against the site map and the Web site's contents list that the client provides. Can the pages the clients want to see actually perform the tasks the use cases have demarcated?

■**Note** Use cases are typically written in English and then more formally in a graphical notation known as Unified Modeling Language (UML). Read more about UML in *Fast Track UML 2.0* by Kendall Scott (1-59059-320-0; Apress, 2004).

Security issues also need to be considered here. Use cases should include when users without sufficient permissions for a task are denied access by the Web site. You also want to establish how the different roles for a Web site map onto its different users and the type of user authentication strategy you may use. If you're working on an intranet site, Windows authentication may be fine. If you're working on an Internet site, Forms-based authentication or even Microsoft Passport-based authentication may be more appropriate.

Available Resources and Performance Targets

You need to ascertain what resources the Web site will have available to it and whether those resources will be able to perform as the clients would have them do. Specifically, you need to consider the following:

- Who will be hosting the Web site and where? Will the developers get physical access to the servers (hopefully not, as developers normally can't stop fiddling)? What specification are they using? Which database is running? What is the connection speed?

- What's in the budget for the day-to-day running of the Web site?

- Will this Web site use proprietary or open source software (besides ASP.NET)?

- Roughly how many users are expected to use the Web site at any one time? How quickly does the client expect the number of users to rise, and how fast does the client think the amount of data to be stored and retrieved in the database will increase?

The majority of clients will already have a hosting solution in place and presumably ASP.NET, too.

■**Note** If your clients are already using Java or PHP, now may be a good time to go and get another book, say on Java database programming, and put this one down. Either that, or start extolling the virtues of ASP.NET.

The key in this part of the requirements analysis is to establish the kind of performance and scalability targets your clients want to achieve and whether their hosting solution will accommodate that. In concert with this, you also need to devise the tests, or metrics, that will allow you to measure whether your code has attained those standards. For example, if you're working on a project with a SQL Server database containing 200,000 records that will need to be referenced and may be updated every day between 10 p.m. and 6 a.m, an obvious benchmark is the speed with which this database scan can be done.

If your clients are relying on you to provide a hosting solution as well as the Web site itself, the onus is on you to work with their budget and their performance targets to find the solution that best suits them. Typically, you need to establish a compromise between the price you pay for a database, the size of the connection you can use, the level of support provided for the servers if they're located off site, and so on. (You'll find a quick guide to choosing a database in the "The Right Data Source" section, coming up shortly.) If the client's budget stretches to it, you could investigate using and extending a commercially available piece of software as the backbone of the Web site.

Future Needs

Understanding how the client may want to extend the Web site in the future will have an influence on how you design the Web site, and you need to answer questions regarding how new content and functionality are to be added, as well as how maintenance is to be performed after the initial delivery. Specifically, you should consider the following questions:

- Is the Web site a one-off, or will it be refactored as a different Web site with the same purpose but different content, as is the case with http://www.dotnetjunkies.com and http://www.sqljunkies.com?

- How will the Web site continue to grow? Will it be a case of existing functionality being refined, or will completely new aspects of the Web site be added?

- How will content and data be added to the Web site and maintained? Will a user add it through a Web page or with a Windows application? Will data be updated automatically from system to system (for example, as one application pulls current stock prices from Wall Street)?

- How will Web site upgrades be applied? Will they be applied from a CD directly on the server? Or will upgrades be done online—perhaps via FTP, via some source versioning control system, or even via a set of Web services?

You should have resolved all the bugs you can find in the Web site before you release it to the client, but that won't mean there won't be more. Consider the case of Microsoft Windows. That's been in continuous development for more than ten years, and you can still find bugs all over the place. Maintainability isn't just about considering how the client will keep the Web site and the data it consumes current. It's also about how you can make bug fixes and small alterations to the Web site with the least interference to its uptime.

Maintainability is also about leaving yourself with the path of least resistance when it comes to upgrading a Web site with new features or reapplying the site design to some new purpose. The key is to design an open class structure so that new functionality can be "plugged into" the Web site without disrupting anything else. It's also vital to make sure the code is well documented and commented so that other developers who may work on the site later can see how it works and write their upgrades in a way to blend with your code. You may also be able to reuse code you've already written for other projects or use code online.

Last, but not least, it may not be a bad idea here to profile the clients yourself and see if there's anything they've missed or may want to add to the Web site in the second version. Forewarned is forearmed, as they say. And don't be afraid to ask clients for clarifications to their requirements list, especially when they revise them in the middle of the whole process. If they can bother you, you can bother them—especially if it means you go one way or another with the Web site's design.

We'll take a closer look at some maintenance issues in the "Maintenance" section later in this chapter.

The Right Tools

With a set of requirements from a client, you can start deciding on the basic building blocks for the Web site. You've already decided on ASP.NET as the framework of choice and effectively standardized on Internet Information Services (IIS), but what about the database containing the Web site's data, and even the tools you'll use to create the Web site? If the client has predetermined the database, that's fine; it leaves you with just your development tools to pick.

The Right Data Source

Although it may sound strange to ask, but does the Web site actually need to use a relational database as its data source? Would it suffice to use an alternative data source such as a set of XML files, Excel spreadsheets, .csv files, or perhaps an alternative type of database, XML-based or object-oriented?

Looking on such open source Web sites as SourceForge (http://www.sourceforge.net) or even GotDotNet workspaces (http://workspaces.gotdotnet.com), it's not too difficult to find applications with the same goal but different approaches to data storage. Take the example of two blogging engines, dasBlog and .Text. Both are designed to make blogging easy for users, but dasBlog uses XML files to store recent entries, and .Text uses SQL Server. dasBlog is more portable and easier to host. .Text can provide blogging for many users once the blog is set up. dasBlog works for one user per installation.

As this example implies, all the decisions you make are trade-offs—one requirement against another. You're inevitably forced to make financial decisions based on your time and the client's budget, and to balance the issues of performance, scalability, maintainability, and availability based on the requirements and the tools you're using. Your choice of database, if you have one, reflects that balance. The following are some of the factors that may influence your decision:

Price: SQL Server 2005 Express Edition is free to download, Access is part of Microsoft Office, and SQL Server 2005 varies in price from expensive to very expensive depending on which version you want to use. MySQL 5.0 is free to download, but you'll need to pay for phone support, if you need it.

Performance: Access (*.mdb) files are easy to create and use but are slow compared to actual database servers such as SQL Server 2005 and MySQL 5.0. MySQL's emphasis is on fast data retrieval, but SQL Server beats it for performance at enterprise levels.

Maintenance: Can the database server be backed up easily? Does it support automatic failover to a different database server if the main database server fails? A server failure can happen any time, and you need to be prepared for the worst-case scenario.

Data provider: Where possible, use a database with its own data provider rather than using the generic OleDb or Odbc data providers supplied by Microsoft. For example, although we've used the Odbc data provider to connect to MySQL 5.0 in the majority of the examples in this book, that was only for demonstration purposes. If you're working with MySQL 5.0, you should use its native data provider, Connector/NET, which you can download from http://dev.mysql.com/downloads/connector/net/1.0.html.

Ease of use: All databases work fine with ASP.NET, but some are easier to administer than others. For example, you've used both SQL Server Management Studio and MySQL Query Browser in this book. While these tools are certainly an improvement over the previously available tools, they still have their limits. Similarly, how easy is it to migrate a database across to a new installation or even a new version of the database?

Functionality: Relational databases all have the same core functionality because they're all built according to the 12 rules of relational database design originated back in the early 1970s. What you need to look for are the extensions to the core that the database vendor has decided to add that may help you in building your Web site. Does it handle XML, transactions, and stored procedures? What extensions to the SQL standard does it support? How does its error handling work? What about user roles, security, and backup tools? Establish what functionality you need from the database and shop around for the one that does the best job providing it.

Support: Last, but not least, how well is this database supported by the vendor if something goes wrong and you have no choice but to ask for help? Newsgroups and FAQs can be helpful, but phoning technical support is sometimes the only solution.

The Right Development Tools

You've used the free (for the time being) Visual Web Developer 2005 Express Edition for the ASP.NET development work in this book. It's a perfectly acceptable tool, works particularly well with C# and VB .NET, and is a subset of the functionality afforded by Visual Studio 2005.

If you're new to programming and aren't used to any development tool yet, stick with Visual Web Developer for the time being and download evaluation copies of a few others. Although Visual Studio 2005 has by far the best support for .NET development of all these tools—with features such as the class browser, integrated data explorer, and IntelliSense—it's still a very expensive piece of software.

Design

As Web developers, you may tend to regard Web sites as groups of pages. However, it's far wiser to approach them as traditional applications. Bearing this in mind, it's safe to say that Web sites are subject to the following usual tenets of software engineering:

- A software application—whether it's Web-based, desktop-based, or even designed for a mobile platform—is implemented by dividing the tasks it must perform into smaller and smaller tasks until they can't be reduced any further. These atomic tasks are represented as a line of code in the application, and where atomic tasks are often called in the same sequence, they're grouped into methods.

- A software application of any size is subject to bugs and the client's desire to upgrade it. Dividing the functionality of an application into classes and namespaces that can be debugged and upgraded individually lessens the downtime for the application as a whole. It also has the added bonus that, because several people can work on individual classes and namespaces simultaneously as long as the public application programming interfaces (APIs) are as agreed, development time will be quicker.

The purpose of analyzing the requirements for an application is to identify the common tasks it will execute, how well they should execute, and the various ways in which you can segregate its functionality into manageable chunks—what you'll implement as namespaces and classes. In the design phase, your goal is to translate those requirements into a class and namespace structure and a supporting database design that will make your Web site work efficiently and be easy to maintain. You can then use the metrics you created for the Web site to check that the various chunks of the Web site work as well as required.

You should split this phase of development into two parts: designing the table structure for the database that underlies the Web site, and then designing its namespace and class structure.

Database Design

As with every other subject in this chapter, whole books have been written about database design. Many people make a very good living from just designing and administering databases. Here, I'll touch on the salient points.

Database design in general is all about efficiency. If you can correctly identify and model the various objects and events the Web site needs to keep details on, the Web site will have the following benefits:

- It will be easier to write.

- It will run faster because fewer queries need to be made to the database.

- It will be easier to maintain and upgrade because the SQL will be easier to work with.

- It will be easier to add new tables into the database if you need to do so.

The database design should be completed before any work starts on building the pages of the Web site. Discovering that the database hasn't been completed or is incorrect can cause problems if you've already started coding the Web site. It may even require you to throw away the pages that you've already written because they don't work with the changed database.

At this basic level, you're most concerned with modeling the Web site's data correctly. As you learned in Chapter 2, a lot of good database design is simply a result of paying attention to the details. However, it all bears repeating here.

Your core job at this stage is to correctly identify the individual types of objects and events you'll model in the database underlying your Web site. For example, in a blogging Web site, you need to model messages, users, and comments. Don't forget the following simple tips toward this end:

- Each table in the database should contain details about one object or event. Don't try to match up two objects that are roughly the same—for example, buildings and companies. The ploy may work at first, but it would require you to split them later when the Web site is up and running, which would mean you would need to take the Web site offline while this was being done.

- Pay attention to the names of the tables and columns as they're conceived. Using plurals and words such as *or* and *and* could indicate that a column needs to be split into its own table that has a one-to-many or many-to-many relationship with the original. Try to make every column and table name unique.

Of course, you have a more formal way to achieve a streamlined database design, called *normalization*.

Normalization

The basic rules of normalization have been around since 1972. They've been tweaked and added to since then, but the same goal remains: to improve the performance of a database by eliminating duplicate data and therefore the chance of any errors occurring when information is added, updated, or deleted. A normalized database will also make searching easier because it won't have to deal with redundant copies of data.

Consider the sample database we've used in this book. We chose to include the storage format for each Player as text inside each row in the Players database, but as you saw in Chapters 8 and 9, this made some aspects of working with this particular column quite troublesome. It's also a waste of time and a source of potential errors to enter the storage format by hand for each Player. Why not just enter the storage formats once, and then refer to which one of them the Player uses? This would also remove the possibility of a user misspelling a storage format—mistakes that make accurate searches trickier. By using normalization, you identify duplicate data that could be stored in separate tables.

Using normalization to improve the design of a database is a three-step process. The result of each step is known as a *normal form*. (There are extra steps beyond the first three, but those are rarely used in the real world.)

First Normal Form

The goal of the first normal form (1NF) is to eliminate repeating groups of data in a table. You create a separate table for each related set of data and identify each table with a primary key.

> *A relation is in 1NF if and only if all underlying simple domains contain only atomic values.*

In more practical terms, a database table is in 1NF only if all values in all columns can't be split any further into separate columns—in other words, they're *atomic*. Furthermore, atomic values shouldn't be repeated over various columns.

For example, Figure 13-1 shows the Player table as it was originally. The original Player table isn't in 1NF for a number of reasons, but the most obvious reason is that the PlayerManufacturer column contains two pieces of information that should be split into two separate columns: the name of the Player and its Manufacturer. The PlayerFormats column also contains more than one piece of information depending on how many Formats the Player supports.

Table Name: Player

PlayerID	PlayerManufacturer	PlayerCost	PlayerStorage	PlayerFormats
1	iPod Shuffle (Apple)	99.00	Solid State	wav, mp3, aac
more rows...				

Figure 13-1. *The Player table not in 1NF*

To obey the first half of the 1NF rule, the Player table should look like Figure 13-2.

Table Name: Player

PlayerID	PlayerName	ManufacturerName	PlayerCost	PlayerStorage	Format1	Format2	Format3
1	iPod Shuffle	Apple	99.00	Solid State	wav	mp3	aac
more rows...							

Figure 13-2. *Splitting atomic values*

The only problem is that this table still isn't in 1NF. The second half of the rule states that atomic values shouldn't be repeated over more than one column in the same table. The three columns Format1, Format2, and Format3 violate this rule. Figure 13-3 shows how to achieve 1NF by splitting this information into two tables.

Table Name: Player

PlayerID	PlayerName	ManufacturerName	PlayerCost	PlayerStorage
1	iPod Shuffle	Apple	99.00	Solid State
more rows...				

Table Name: Format

FormatID	PlayerID	PlayerName	FormatName
1	1	iPod Shuffle	wav
2	1	iPod Shuffle	mp3
3	1	iPod Shuffle	aac
more rows...			

Figure 13-3. *1NF achieved*

By creating the Format table, you now have a FormatName column containing individual Format names. Both tables are in 1NF.

Note how the tip for accurately naming columns can help in identifying whether a table is in 1NF. A pluralized name indicates that perhaps the column should be separated from the table. Any sign of an *or* or an *and* would indicate that a column may be better as two or more columns.

Second Normal Form

The second step in the normalization process, second normal form (2NF), seeks to identify relationships between entities in a database and to model them correctly.

A relation is in 2NF if and only if it's in 1NF and every nonkey attribute is fully dependent on the primary key.

The first part of this definition is a given. You shouldn't be moving onto 2NF if you haven't made your database design 1NF already. The second part of the definition warrants attention, however. In plainer English, if a column isn't uniquely related to the primary key in a table, it should be elsewhere.

Let's take a look at the Player and Format tables, which are both in 1NF. The primary key for the Player table is the PlayerID, so you need to establish which of the values for the four other columns are linked directly to the PlayerID. The answer is that only the PlayerName and PlayerCost column are; both ManufacturerName and PlayerStorage aren't dependent on the Player having a certain PlayerID. As you've seen, many Players may have the same Manufacturer or Storage, so to satisfy 2NF, you'll have to split them into a different table. Neither column relies on the other either, so you'll need to create one table each for them, as shown in Figure 13-4.

Table Name: Player

PlayerID	PlayerName	ManufacturerID	PlayerCost	StorageID
1	iPod Shuffle	1	99.00	1
more rows...				

Table Name: Manufacturer

ManufacturerID	ManufacturerName
1	Apple
more rows...	

Table Name: Storage

StorageID	StorageName
1	Solid State
more rows...	

Figure 13-4. *Putting the Player table in 2NF*

■**Note** The Player table that we've been using is not fully in 2NF. The PlayerStorage column was deliberately left incorrect to highlight the problems that you will have if the database is not correctly designed.

Like the Player table, the Format table isn't in 2NF. The FormatName column is fully dependent on the FormatID column, which is the primary key, but the PlayerID and PlayerName columns aren't; the wav Format will probably be supported by more than just the iPod Shuffle, for example. You need to introduce a third table to express the many-to-many relationship between Formats and Players, and thus satisfy 2NF, as shown in Figure 13-5.

Table Name: Format

FormatID	FormatName
1	wav
2	mp3
3	aac
more rows...	

Table Name: WhatPlaysWhatFormat

WPWFPlayerID	WPWFFormatID
1	1
1	2
1	3
more rows...	

Figure 13-5. *Putting the Format table in 2NF*

The Format table is now in 2NF because the FormatName is dependent on the FormatID column, and the WhatPlaysWhatFormat table is in 2NF because it has a compound key comprising both columns.

Third Normal Form

The third and final step, third normal form (3NF), looks specifically at tables with compound primary keys.

A relation is in 3NF if and only if it's in 2NF and every nonkey attribute is nontransitively dependent on the primary key.

In plain English, this rule basically says that a column in a table must depend on all the elements in a primary key. So if a table has a simple primary key (that is, the primary key is only one column) and is in 2NF, it's also in 3NF. If a table has a compound primary key, however, you'll need to take a closer look.

For example, what if the WhatPlaysWhatFormat table had two more columns, as in the slightly contrived Figure 13-6?

Table Name: WhatPlaysWhatFormat

WPWFPlayerID	WPWFFormatID	ImplementationUrl	PlayerUrl
1	1	http://www.apple.com/ipod/wav	http://www.apple.com/ipod
1	2	http://www.apple.com/ipod/mp3	http://www.apple.com/ipod
1	3	http://www.apple.com/ipod/aac	http://www.apple.com/ipod
more rows...			

Figure 13-6. *Removing the PlayerUrl column will leave this table in 3NF.*

Both the ImplementationUrl and the PlayerUrl columns are dependent on the primary key in this table, so it's still in 2NF. But whereas the ImplementationUrl column depends on both WPWFPlayerID and WPWFFormatID columns for context, the PlayerUrl column relies only on the WPWFPlayerID column. This partial dependence is also referred to as *transitive dependence*, which means the table isn't in 3NF. The PlayerUrl column should be moved to the Player table for the whole database to be in 3NF.

Normalizing a database will make it faster to sort and search through by reducing the chance of redundant data in the database. In particular, the database will need fewer indexes, which will improve the performance of INSERT, UPDATE, and DELETE queries.

However, normalization can increase the complexity of joins required to retrieve the data. This, in some cases, may hinder performance. Sometimes, databases are denormalized to reduce the complexity of joins and to get quicker query response times (one of the reasons why fourth and fifth normal forms aren't often used). As always, you need to strike a balance between flexibility and speed. This is just another juggling act you'll encounter as you implement the Web site.

Other Modeling Considerations

Normalization is a great tool for laying the groundwork in your database design, but just because your tables are all in 3NF doesn't mean you've modeled the data the best you can for the Web site. The following are a few more database design considerations.

Naming: The database server doesn't care how tables and columns are named as long as they're identified unambiguously in SQL queries. However, for your own benefit, you should try to name them all sensibly and uniquely, as you did in the sample database. You only have to look at the number of columns that could be called ID in the sample database to see that it's always a good idea to give them all unique names so you don't get confused as you write your code. Here, you used the simple method of prefixing the name column with the name of the table: PlayerID, ManufacturerID, and FormatID.

Foreign keys: You've identified the various tables in the database and the relationships they have between each other, but when you're setting up the foreign key constraints, you need to consider how a child table should be affected when a row in the parent table is updated or deleted. Are the database's defaults fine, or should the implications cascade down into the child table?

Data types: You've identified the various columns in each table of the database, but what type should they be and what length? Should ID columns be automatically generated integers or globally unique identifiers (GUIDs)? How long should each string be? Should the database store the image or just the image's file name?

Views: Will it be of any benefit to you to create distinct views over the database for querying? It does mean that you can keep your SQL queries simple, but at what cost? Each time a view is queried, the query to create that view must first be executed, so there are actually two queries being used here for the sake of one.

When you've considered these issues, you can start to determine how to speed up database access and secure the database against both the malevolent and the stupid.

Application Design

While design of any kind is somewhat in the eye of the beholder and subject to a person's own preference for doing things a certain way, it's good to know that database designs won't vary that much among architects given the same list of requirements. The design of an application's class structure, on the other hand, can be much more divergent.

Not only must you marry functionality to pages, you must also see that the classes you design reflect the database design you've just achieved and obey the second software tenet. For those of you who missed it earlier, this means that to make the Web site as quick to implement, easy to debug and maintain, and straightforward to upgrade as possible, you need to divide the tasks of the Web site into clearly defined sections that you can then map to namespaces and classes. So, for example, you can split such easy-to-define sections of a Web site as forums, polls, shopping carts, product browsing, and so on. However, it isn't so obvious how to split potential namespaces into individual classes.

Fortunately, a great deal of practice and trial and error by a great many people have shown that you can think of a Web site (and indeed most applications) as split across several tiers.

Tier Definition

Splitting the functionality of the Web site into separate modules—polls, forums, carts, newsletters, and so on—means that you can add new modules to the Web site at any time and that individual modules can be shut down for maintenance without affecting the rest of the Web site. To make things easier, you can split the tasks each module performs into the following three tiers:

Data access tier: Code in the data access tier deals solely with sending commands to and retrieving data from the database, checking that the current user has permissions, and handling any database-related errors. If code in either of the two other tiers needs to interact with the database, it must do so through the data access tier.

Business rules tier: The business rules tier is where the majority of the work happens. Here, the Web site will determine how to react to a user's request, log the request for future reference, start the process of creating a new page by requesting information from the data access tier, and then interpret that new data into something a user will be able to understand. For example, when a user requests the home page of a Web site, the business rules tier may take care of such tasks as retrieving user preferences, determining what's new on the Web site since the user last visited, and telling the presentation tier (described next) how to react accordingly.

Presentation tier: Code in the presentation tier deals exclusively with the Web site's user experience and the generation of pages when requested. It will use the business rules and data access tiers to retrieve the content for a page, and then use its own code to assemble it on the page. No code from the business rules tier or data access tier should directly alter the user interface of the Web site.

Splitting a code module into tiers and then into classes within those tiers gives you great flexibility. Suppose you were writing an e-commerce cart module and were told to provide front ends for both Web and mobile users. You could write separate classes for the module's presentation tier: one for browsers and one for mobile devices. They would both interface with the business rules tier in the same way, but each would optimize the presentation of content for their respective device.

In the same way, you could write individual modules for the different ways to pay for the items in the shopping cart. To the users, this would be invisible, but to the owners of the e-commerce store, this would be invaluable. Should they choose to barter Visa transactions with a different merchant bank, for example, you could take down and revise just the Visa class in the e-commerce module, leaving the cash, Mastercard, and other modules up and running. Compare this to a situation where all transactions are run through a single class or as a single monolithic piece of code. To update the Visa functions, you would need to take down the whole shopping cart.

Similarly, you could write new classes for working against a new database rather than rewriting the old ones.

As long as the public interface to each class remains the same (it may expand to include new public calls, too), so you don't have to worry about other classes calling functions that no longer exist, you could work with as many different databases, credit cards, banks, and interfaces as you like. Good application design gives you this kind of flexibility, and separating an application into these three tiers is the first step to achieving it.

Note Depending on how complex your Web site or a module for your Web site is, its code may split logically into only one or two tiers. Don't worry about this and go searching for the third tier. Three is just the standard number; there are always exceptions to the rule.

Structure Definition

Now that you understand how a Web site may be split into data, business rules, and presentation tiers, a question arises. Say you're building a community Web site and, from the site map, have identified a number of modules you'll eventually want to add to it, as shown in Figure 13-7. What translates into a namespace and the classes inside it?

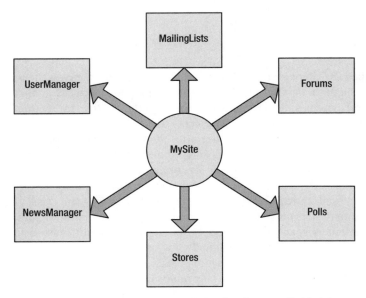

Figure 13-7. *A Web site and its modules, but how to divide it?*

Do you have three namespaces for each tier of the Web site and a class for each relevant section of forums, polls, and so on inside those namespaces? Or are the individual modules modeled better as namespaces with the tiers split inside them into classes? The latter is the best route. Taking the long view, if you design a uniform class structure and API for working with the core of the Web site for each, you get a nice plug-in API from which it's easy to add or remove functionality. If you keep the core of the Web site separate, you can come up with a namespace structure looking something like Figure 13-8.

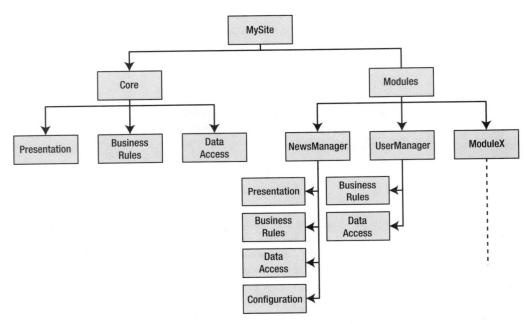

Figure 13-8. *A clean namespace structure for MySite*

Depending on how detailed the client requirements are and how complex the Web site is, you may want to encapsulate the three tiers within classes rather than namespaces. Note that you'll need to tailor the creation of namespaces to the functionality of the module, rather than arbitrarily creating presentation, business rules, and data access namespaces and attempting to wedge all functionality into those. In Figure 13-8, for example, the UserManager module won't return any on-screen information per se, so it won't need a presentation tier. Meanwhile, the NewsManager module acquires an additional namespace for configuration to keep track of news feeds being used. In the same way, a shopping cart may have a separate namespace for negotiating sales with merchant banks, with each bank being dealt with in a separate class.

With any luck, the requirements list you've already procured will give you plenty of clues as to what the classes within each namespace will encompass. If not, take the opportunity to go back to the client and ask for more details on any functionality that isn't clear.

Remember that some classes will reflect the objects and events you're modeling in the database, and some will simply be utility classes, which may not be immediately foreseeable. Work through the use cases for each module in turn. Understand which pieces of data they will require and the way in which the sequence of events within them will flow.

It would be nice to say that every enumeration and class will come forth in a Zen-like way from the pattern of the Web site, but they won't initially. Just don't get frustrated when this happens. You can't identify every single facet of the design until you've implemented and looked at it again in hindsight. That's why you prototype and postmortem your projects.

■**Note** Like every subject in this chapter, good class design is a topic that warrants its own book. Good ones in this case are siblings: the *C# Class Design Handbook* by Richard Conway (1-59059-257-3; Apress, 2003) and the *Visual Basic .NET Class Design Handbook* by Damon Allison, Andy Olsen, and James Speer (1-59059-275-1; Apress, 2003).

Techniques such as using design patterns to drill down into individual classes also apply at this stage. However, even though these techniques are handy, a lot of this step comes down to your own experience and what you can learn from the experiences of other developers. Remember that however you choose to design (and implement) your Web site, the whole point of breaking it up into components is to give it a flexible, efficient structure that's easy to program and extend.

Implementation

Lest we forget that this book is aimed squarely at introducing you to developing pages using a database to supply the content, the following sections on implementing your design focus on the basic issues of writing code for working with the database, or issues related to the data tier. How you choose to present information on a page isn't the issue here, and neither are any business rules you may be adding.

Prototypes

It's a good idea to prototype a Web site to prove and refine an initial design. Although it won't help you identify and deal with every issue concerning elements that seemed reasonable on paper but don't translate across into code, it will catch many problems. It also has the added advantage of giving you something to show your clients and get their feedback on, which can't be a bad thing. Inevitably, on seeing even the first iteration of their commission, customers often have opinions and questions that may affect the final product, so it's worth building a prototype at least once to validate your design and pacify clients, if nothing else.

Exactly how much detail you include in a prototype is up to you, but from a data access point of view, you definitely want to validate the following pieces of the design:

- The Web site core

- The database design

- The various SQL queries to the database that are most likely to be made and the classes you'll create to wrap these queries

Security always seems to get put aside in favor of the noticeable functionality of the Web site, but try to prototype the user registration and login to make sure that each user role has the correct set of permissions for access to the database. You could even use the metrics you've designed previously to test the prototype and see how far away you are from your performance goals.

Stored Procedures

When you send a SQL query to a database, the database checks that its syntax is correct, making sure that the tables, columns, constraints, and so on that it references actually exist. Finally, it figures out how best to execute the query, and then does it. Depending on the database server, this whole process is repeated for each new query (SQL Server 2005 actually caches the execution plan for the SQL query to speed things, whereas MySQL 5.0 performs the same steps every time). Even with a small number of concurrent users, those three steps can quickly mount up and burden the database. Fortunately, there's a solution.

Most relational database management systems now offer the ability to create and save stored procedures. As you learned in Chapter 10, a stored procedure is a SQL query saved in the database server, so that rather than the database working through three steps, the stored procedure requires only one step (the execution of the stored procedure). It's not hard to see that using stored procedures can offer the promise of a significant performance increase. However, not everything works better as a stored procedure. There's a small overhead associated with actually retrieving and then executing the stored procedure. In some cases, simple SQL queries (for example, selecting data from a single table) may actually perform better when they come from the code directly. In general, though, stored procedures are a good thing to use if the database server supports them.

Stored procedures also give you an extra level of flexibility when it comes to retrieving data. When you get to the inevitable decision of whether to use a DataSet or DataReader to build your pages, you can also consider using a stored procedure's output parameters to retrieve single values straight into a variable, without the need for either a DataSet or DataReader.

Stored procedures also give you a more structured way to introduce error handling and transactions into a SQL query. By using SQL aggregate functions, you can use stored procedures to perform quite a few calculations that you may have thought only ASP.NET could do for you.

Code Issues

Designing a Web site well will help a project along, but it's making informed implementation decisions on the spot based on the design and your experience that really counts. The following are some of the most common data-related issues that will crop up:

DataReader vs. DataSet: By now, you know the advantages and disadvantages of both approaches. Browse to http://msdn.microsoft.com/library/en-us/vbcon/html/ vbconDecidingOnDataAccessStrategy.asp for details on some additional issues; refer to Chapters 5, 6, 7, and 8 of this book; and make the choice.

SqlDataSource: As you saw in Chapter 9, you can accomplish quite complex editing using a SqlDataSource. However, the SqlDataSource doesn't fit into the tiered application model described earlier in this chapter. It connects to the database directly from the presentation tier, skipping the data access and business rules tiers completely. That doesn't mean you shouldn't use it, but you should consider its limitations before you do.

Data provider: It sounds obvious, but you need to consider the actual data provider you use in your code. For example, MySQL has a solid, stable ODBC driver, and you can take advantage of that using the `Odbc` data provider, which is also stable. However, is this the best solution? As noted earlier, MySQL has a native data provider that is a better choice.

Data modeling: If speed is of the essence, then the amount of data retrieved from a database is surely one of the key factors in keeping the speed up, so finding ways of packing information into smaller pieces is always handy. Reducing the maximum length of a column is always a risk, but take the case of an ISBN for a published book. This is a ten-digit string consisting of nine integers and a tenth-check digit that's either another integer or an X. The check digit is always calculated in the same way, so do you store the ISBN as a ten-character string that's held by 10×8 bits = 80 bits, or as a nine-digit integer that can be held comfortably in 32 bits, and create the check digit programmatically when required?

Security: It's easier to write code that does the job required and then add security measures after the fact, but coding securely is an art in itself; in fact, it's something you should always try to do. You've already seen some good practices in earlier chapters. Hide your database connection strings in `Web.config` to keep them from prying eyes. Try not to use the query string for values being sent to and from the database. Work with multiple database servers rather than just one. If you're using a DataReader, close it with `Close()` as quickly as possible.

Of course, you'll have to make many more trade-offs and decisions as you implement your design. But rather than tread in places that have been well covered by books devoted to the topic, let's move on to the next phase of the software life cycle: testing and debugging your Web site.

Testing and Debugging

Nothing is more annoying than installing a new application, starting to work in it, and seeing a dialog box pop up to inform you that an error has occurred and the application will now shut down. You've now lost all the work you were doing and have given yourself a nasty injury after kicking the desk in frustration. If the application had been debugged more thoroughly, that may not have happened.

This phase of the software life cycle is certainly as crucial as the others, yet it's usually written about less because it's almost impossible to describe how to debug specific errors; further, writing for the generic case isn't very helpful. However, without going into the debugging process itself, you can try to factor a handful of useful techniques into your development process.

■**Note** For a complete guide to .NET debugging strategies, see *Debugging Strategies for .NET Developers* by Darin Dillon (1-59059-059-7; Apress, 2003) or (if you can find it) *Visual Basic .NET Debugging Handbook* by Jan Narkiewicz and Thiru Thangarathinam (1-86100-729-9; Wrox Press, 2002). The latter is out of print but packed with gems of information.

Unit Testing

As mentioned earlier, one of the benefits of writing code as individual modules is that you can write them in parallel. But it goes further than that. You can debug and test them individually as well.

Back in the analysis phase of the software life cycle, you devised a set of benchmarks and use cases that could measure the performance of your Web site as it was built. By isolating the relevant user scenarios and benchmarks, and writing some code (a *test harness*) that reflects the metrics you designed to test the Web site against those benchmarks, you can prove the utility of this module before you move on to the next. This process is known as *unit testing*.

One of the more frustrating aspects of this process is that as requirements change and targets are realigned, modules that you've already written and tested will need to be altered and retested. Indeed, this cycle of rebuilding and retesting is quite short, so a few utilities now allow you to automate the unit testing process. The best of these is NUnit (`http://www.nunit.org`).

NUnit is the standard unit testing framework for .NET applications and was itself written in C#. By itself, NUnit comes with a choice of a rudimentary command-line interface or a rudimentary graphical interface, which both do the job, albeit not in a particularly attractive way. NUnit on its own is great for testing business rules and data access code, but it needs help to test Web pages because they can't be "run" inside the NUnit framework. In this case, you need to use NUnitASP (`http://nunitasp.sourceforge.net/download.html`), which essentially hooks into ASP.NET and gives NUnit a view of the intrinsic objects (Context, Response, Request, and so on) to use. You can find a great introduction to using NUnitASP at `http://www.theserverside.net/articles/showarticle.tss?id=TestingASP`.

■**Note** NUnit is a free, stand-alone application that's great if you continue to use Visual Web Developer. If you use Visual Studio 2005, however, you'll be pleased to know that you can run NUnit as an add-in, using TestRunner for Visual Studio .NET (`http://www.mailframe.net/Products/TestRunner`). Visual Studio 2005 also has its own testing environment (and a whole lot more) called Visual Studio Team System. Team System is currently in the final stages of its beta process and should be available soon. For more details about Team System, see `http://msdn.microsoft.com/vstudio/teamsystem/default.aspx`.

Unit testing applies to only single modules, but you need to account for the way modules interact with each other, as well. Do they successfully share session and user information, for instance? If one module makes a call to another, is that call being made for the purpose the method was originally intended, or is it being forced into the engine of another car? If the latter is the case, you may want to investigate why this is being done and how better to achieve the desired results before continuing.

Measuring Performance

As is the case with most development, the strategies you use to measure the performance of your Web site are formed by the experience you've had using different techniques in previous projects and whether they have worked for you. You can then define the target metrics for a Web site and the tests you know will be able to prove that those benchmarks have been achieved.

But where do you begin? What methods can you use to stress test your Web site and retrieve results? Can you continue to work on your Web site without buying an IDE? Of course you can. Microsoft even tells you how. Refer to the ASP.NET performance page at `http://msdn.microsoft.com/asp.net/using/understanding/perf/default.aspx`. This page links to many articles, each covering a different aspect of performance you may not have considered and the various ways to measure and improve it. In particular, look first at the articles entitled "ASP.NET Performance Monitoring, and When to Alert Administrators," "MyTracer Monitors and Traces ASP.NET Apps," and "Real-World Load Testing Tips to Avoid Bottlenecks When Your Web App Goes Live." For a great resource on testing and improving the performance of a database, look no further than `http://www.sql-server-performance.com`. It focuses specifically on SQL Server, but a lot of the information applies to other databases as well.

■**Note** You can also find several good books that cover performance issues and testing. See *Performance Tuning and Optimizing ASP.NET Applications* by Jeffrey Hasan and Kenneth Tu (1-59059-072-4; Apress, 2003) and *Test-Driven Development in Microsoft .NET* by James W. Newkirk and Alexei A. Vorontsov (0-73561-948-4; Microsoft Press, 2004).

Maintenance

Once your site has been implemented, tested, and deployed, that isn't the end of the story. There will always be some element of maintenance to your Web site. Unlike the other steps in the life cycle, the maintenance step will go on forever (well, until the Web site is switched off).

The main part of maintenance will be fixing any bugs that occur in the operation of the site. Most bugs affect the end user's experience of using the site and will, normally, need to be addressed as soon as possible.

However, that won't be the only part of the maintenance task. Your client will request changes to existing functionality and even the addition of new functionality. You'll need to handle and manage these feature requests.

Bug Fixes

All software, once completed, will have some bugs in it. No matter how thoroughly you test the Web site before it goes live, there will be problems. Like death and taxes, it's one of the few things in life that can be guaranteed.

When a bug is discovered, you need some way of being informed of the issue. In most cases, this will be an e-mail message informing you that an end user has experienced a problem. Or maybe you're using the `Error` event of the `Application` in `Global.asax` to automatically log the error (into a log file, by e-mail, or even directly into the database). However you're notified of the error, you need to deal with it.

The first step in bug fixing is to reproduce the error. Once you can do that, you can then investigate how to fix the problem. If you can't reproduce the error, then you'll need to communicate with the user who raised the error (if there was one) to get more details.

Fixing the problem may require changes to the database, as well as changes to the pages of the Web site. As noted earlier, any changes to the database structure have the potential to cause havoc in the Web site. A code change in a page will normally affect only that page, but if you're making changes to the database, you need to make sure that the database change hasn't affected anything else.

The key part of bug fixing is testing. All changes to fix bugs in the Web site must be tested as rigorously as the Web site was tested before it went live. It is very easy for a simple change to impact parts of the Web site that you didn't think would be affected.

Feature Requests

When you released the Web site, you met all of the client's requirements. However, at some point, clients will find something that doesn't work quite as they wanted and request that you change the functionality. You'll also get requests for new features that weren't part of the original requirements (and you should be able to charge the client for this new work).

Whether the change is a small or a large change to the Web site, just as with bug fixes, you must consider the impact on the rest of the Web site. Some changes will be quite minor, requiring very little work in the analysis, design, and implementation stages. Others may be quite fundamental and require large changes to the Web site that can take a considerable amount of time to implement.

As with bug fixing, you should always fully test your changes to the Web site. Even a relatively minor change can impact parts of the Web site that you wouldn't expect and cause problems.

Issue Tracking

When maintaining a Web site, you can stick to the e-mail and post-it note solution, but that can very quickly degenerate into chaos. You need a better way to track issues.

Microsoft is planning to release an application that supports issue tracking, Team Foundation Server, as an add-on for Visual Studio. It integrates directly into the Visual Studio IDE, and as well as issue tracking, it also provides a complete source control system and allows the end-to-end tracking of issues (from the issue being raised to the individual code changes to fix the issues). For more information, see http://msdn.microsoft.com/vstudio/teamsystem/team/default.aspx.

Another option for issue tracking is FogBugz, available from http://www.fogbugz.com. Although it doesn't integrate into the Visual Studio IDE, it is a perfectly capable issue-tracking system.

Summary

In this chapter, you looked at some of the issues you'll face each time you start a new project. Working with a client on the specifications can be fruitless if you don't have a specific agenda. The more information you have, the more responsive your design can be to the resources you have available and the tasks you're trying to achieve. You can use the three-tier design to make your Web site more flexible and easier to develop. You can iron out more wrinkles in both design and specifications by building prototypes to prove the concept and showing those to the client.

When it comes to implementing the design, you need to keep in mind the good practices you've learned in this book and apply them evenly to improve security and performance.

But this is just the beginning. As you become more experienced, you'll quickly start to build an appreciation of what does and doesn't work. Web site development is a continually evolving skill. There will always be that "new way" of doing something that is slightly better than the way you done something in the past. Learn from your mistakes and don't repeat them!

■ ■ ■

Installation Instructions

In this appendix, you'll find instructions for installing the following applications:

- .NET Framework 2.0

- Microsoft Jet Engine

- Visual Web Developer 2005 Express Edition

- SQL Server 2005 Express Edition

- SQL Server 2005 Management Studio Express

- MySQL 5.0

- MySQL Query Browser 1.1

- MySQL Connector/ODBC 3.51

- MySQL Connector/NET 1.0

.NET Framework 2.0 Installation

Before you can install any of the other applications, you'll need to install .NET Framework 2.0. Follow these steps:

1. Download the .NET 2.0 Redistributable Package installer from the Microsoft site at `http://msdn.microsoft.com/netframework/downloads/updates/default.aspx`. Follow the quick link for .NET Framework 2.0 and download the correct version of the redistributable package. (`dotnetfx.exe` is 22.4MB.)

2. After the package has downloaded, double-click it and let the installer run.

Microsoft Jet Engine Installation

Since the release of Microsoft Data Access Components (MDAC) 2.6, the Jet engine isn't installed by default. Therefore, if you don't have Microsoft Access installed, you may not have the Jet engine. To install the latest version, follow these instructions:

1. Download the latest version of the Jet engine from the Microsoft Jet Security Bulletin MS04-014 page of Microsoft TechNet, `http://www.microsoft.com/technet/security/bulletin/ms04-014.mspx`.

2. After the package has downloaded, double-click the installer and let it run.

Visual Web Developer 2005 Express Edition Installation

All of the examples in the book are built using Visual Web Developer 2005 Express Edition. At the time of writing, you can download it for free.

■**Note** Visual Web Developer Express Edition is available free for only a *limited period*, which as yet doesn't have a specified end date. Microsoft has been saying "for the next year," so you should be able to get the free version until at least the end of December 2006.

Follow these instructions to download and install Visual Web Developer Express Edition.

1. Download the latest version of Visual Web Developer from `http://msdn.microsoft.com/vstudio/express/vwd`. (`vwdsetup.exe` is a little under 3MB.)

2. After the package has downloaded, double-click the installer to run it.

3. The first step of the wizard offers the Help Improve Setup option. This doesn't affect the installation process at all. You can check what information is sent to Microsoft by visiting `http://msdn.microsoft.com/vstudio/products/privacy`. Once you've made your choice, click the Next button.

4. Accept the terms of the license agreement and click the Next button.

5. You don't need to install any of the extra packages, but you can choose to if you want them. The documentation may come in quite handy, but it is a hefty download at 248MB. Do not install SQL Server 2005 Express Edition, as some of the options that you'll need to set are not available if you install via this route. Click the Next button.

6. Click the Install button to start the installation. The installer will connect to the Internet to download the necessary components (40MB for Visual Web Developer on its own). If you want to get a cup of coffee, now is your chance.

7. Once setup is complete, you can choose to register your copy of Visual Web Developer for a few extras. To decide if you want to register, see `http://msdn.microsoft.com/vstudio/express/register/default.aspx`.

SQL Server 2005 Express Edition Installation

To run the SQL Server 2005 versions of the examples in the book, you'll need to install SQL Server 2005 Express Edition and SQL Server 2005 Management Studio Express.

SQL Server 2005 Express Edition is a freely available, cut-down version of Microsoft's SQL Server 2005 Enterprise Database Server. To install it, follow these steps:

1. Download SQL Server 2005 Express Edition from `http://msdn.microsoft.com/vstudio/express/sql/default.aspx`. (`SQLEXPR.EXE` is 53.5MB, so make sure there is enough space on your hard drive, and have another cup of coffee handy.)

2. After the package has downloaded, double-click it. The necessary files will be extracted, and the installer will be run automatically.

3. Accept the terms of the license agreement and click the Next button.

4. The SQL Server 2005 Express Edition prerequisites will now be installed. This will take a couple of minutes. Once the prerequisites have been installed, click the Next button.

5. The installer will scan your computer's configuration and then run the "real" installer. Click the Next button to proceed with the installation.

6. The installer will now perform a system configuration check to ensure that the minimum installation requirements are met. Click the Next button to continue with the installation. It is quite common at this point to have a Pending Reboot Requirement specified, halting the installation. In this case, reboot your computer and run the installer again.

7. On the next step, enter your registration information and uncheck the Hide Advanced Configuration Options check box. Click the Next button.

8. Accept the selected features by clicking the Next button.

9. You're going to install SQL Server 2005 Express as a named instance, so select the Named Instance option and enter BAND, as shown in Figure A-1. (You can have multiple instances of SQL Server 2005 running on the same machine, and you've used an instance named BAND to keep the databases for this book separated from others.) Click the Next button.

10. On the Service Account step, select the default option of using the Network Service account by clicking the Next button.

11. On the Authentication Mode step, switch the authentication mode of the database to Mixed Mode by clicking the correct radio button and entering the password that you want for the sa account. For the purposes of this book, enter **bandpass** as both the password and its confirmation, as shown in Figure A-2. (You can use a different password if you prefer, but then you must make sure that you use the password you have chosen instead of the one in the instructions throughout the examples in this book.) Click the Next button.

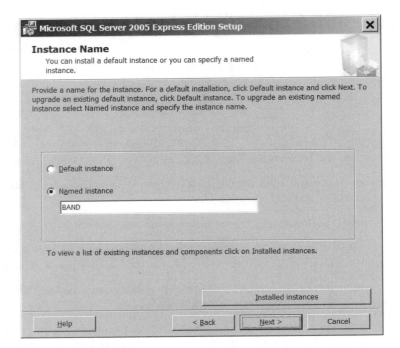

Figure A-1. *Specifing the name of the SQL Server instance to create*

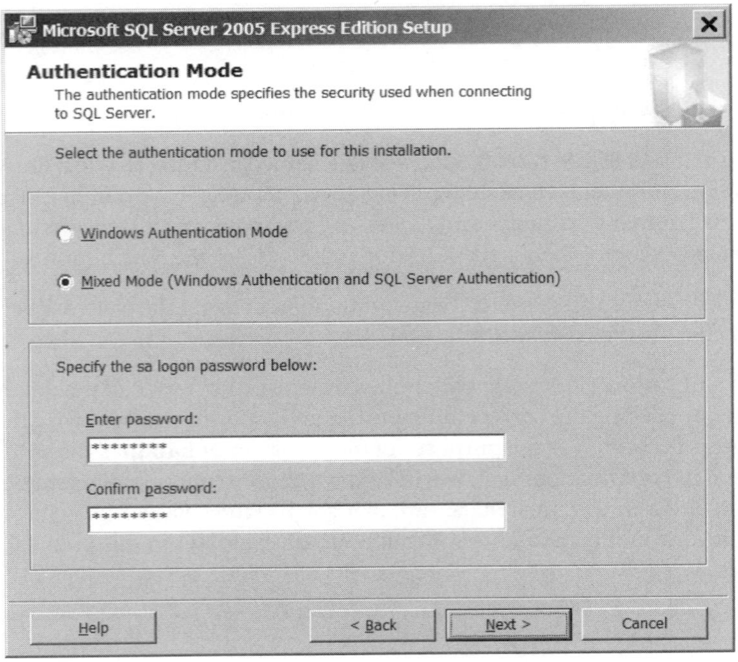

Figure A-2. *Entering the login details for the sa account*

12. On the Collation Settings step, select the default options by clicking the Next button.

13. Click Next to allow user instances of SQL Server.

14. On the Error and Usage Reporting Settings step, you can choose to turn on reporting if you wish. Once you've made your choice, click the Next button.

15. Click the Install button to begin installation of SQL Server 2005 Express Edition.

16. The installation may take a little time. Once it is finished, click the Next button to continue to the Summary step. Click Finish to close the installer.

17. You may need to restart your machine once the installer has finished.

You now need to check that SQL Server 2005 Express Edition has installed correctly. The way to do this differs across platforms, but for Windows XP, you can find it by selecting Start Menu ➤ Settings ➤ Control Panel ➤ Administrative Tools ➤ Services. This launches the Services tool, as shown in Figure A-3.

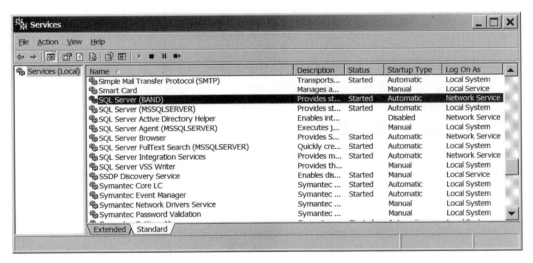

Figure A-3. *The Services tool shows the new instance of SQL Server 2005 Express Edition.*

Look for a service called SQL Server (BAND) in the list. This is your installation of SQL Server 2005 Express Edition. As you can see in Figure A-3, there are two instances of SQL Server 2005 installed on the machine: the instance that you've just installed (BAND) and the default instance on this machine (MSSQLSERVER). Make sure the Status and Startup Type options are set to Started and Automatic, respectively. The Startup Type setting will ensure that SQL Server 2005 Express Edition starts automatically whenever your computer is rebooted.

■**Note** You can install several instances of SQL Server 2005 side by side on one machine. In fact, you can even install different versions of SQL Server on the same machine. The one for this book is named BAND (for Beginning ASP.NET Databases), and as it's a SQL Server 2005 database, it's called SQL Server (BAND).

SQL Server 2005 Management Studio Express Installation

SQL Server 2005 Management Studio Express is a graphical front-end tool for administering SQL Server 2005. Although the current free version is a Community Technical Preview, it is very stable. It's a cut-down version of the tool that is provided with the full version of SQL Server 2005. To install it, follow these steps:

1. Go to `http://msdn.microsoft.com/vstudio/express/sql/default.aspx` and click the Download SQL Server Management Studio Express link. Then download the correct installer. (`SQLServer2005_SSMSEE.msi` is slightly under 30MB, so you'll need your third cup of coffee here.)

2. After the package has downloaded, open the installer by double-clicking it.

3. Skip past the Welcome step by clicking the Next button, accept the terms and conditions on the next step, and click the Next button again.

4. Enter your registration details and click the Next button.

5. Click the Next button to accept the selected features, and then click the Install button to begin the installation.

6. Once the installation has completed, click the Finish button to close the installer.

MySQL 5.0 Installation

To build and run the MySQL 5.0 examples, you'll need to install MySQL 5.0, as well as MySQL Query Browser and MySQL Connector/ODBC. To follow the stored procedure examples in Chapter 10, you'll need to install MySQL Connector/NET.

To install the database server, follow these steps:

1. Download the Community Edition - Windows Essentials installer from `http://dev.mysql.com/downloads/mysql/5.0.html`. (`mysql-essential-5.0.18-win32.msi` is 16.8MB.)

2. After the package is downloaded, double-click it. The files needed will be extracted, and the installer will run automatically.

3. Click the Next button on the Welcome step and accept the Typical installation options by clicking the Next button on the following step. Click the Install button to start the actual installation.

4. On the Sign Up step, you can choose to log in or create an account to MySQL.com. Alternatively, you can click the Skip Sign-Up option. Once you've made your selection, click the Next button.

5. Click the Finish button to configure the newly installed database server.

6. Click the Next button on the first step of the Configuration wizard and choose the Standard Configuration on the following step. Click the Next button.

7. Make sure that both the Install As Windows Service and Include Bin Directory in Windows PATH options are checked, and then click the Next button.

8. Enter a **bandpass** as both the password and its confirmation. Then click the Next button.

9. Click the Execute button to perform the configuration.

10. Once the configuration is completed, click the Finish button to close the Configuration wizard.

To check that MySQL 5.0 has installed correctly, you need to verify that the service is installed and is running. Open the Services tool by selecting Start Menu ➤ Settings ➤ Control Panel ➤ Administrative Tools ➤ Services. In the list of services, look for the MySQL service, as shown in Figure A-4. Make sure the Status and Startup Type options are set to Started and Automatic, respectively. The Startup Type setting will ensure that MySQL 5.0 is started automatically whenever your computer is rebooted.

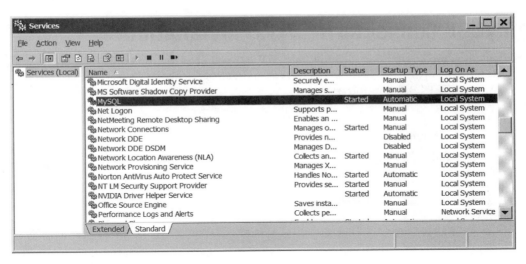

Figure A-4. *The Services tool shows the MySQL service.*

MySQL Query Browser 1.1 Installation

MySQL Query Browser 1.1 is a graphical front-end tool for administering MySQL 5.0. To install it, follow these instructions:

1. Download the Windows installer from `http://dev.mysql.com/downloads/query-browser/1.1.html`. (`mysql-query-browser-1.1.19-win.msi` is 5.1MB.)

2. After the package has downloaded, double-click it. The necessary files will be extracted, and the installer will run automatically.

   3. Accept the terms of the license agreement.

   4. On the Setup Type step of the installation wizard, choose to perform a Complete installation.

MySQL Connector/ODBC 3.51 Installation

In order to use MySQL 5.0 with the Odbc data provider, you need to install the MySQL ODBC driver. To install Connector/ODBC 3.51, follow these steps:

   1. Download the Windows MSI package from http://dev.mysql.com/downloads/ connector/odbc/3.51.html. (mysql-connector-odbc-3.51.12-win32.msi is 2.3MB.)

   2. After the package has downloaded, double-click it. The necessary files will be extracted, and the installer will run automatically.

   3. Accept the terms of the license agreement.

   4. On the Setup Type step of the installation wizard, choose to perform a Typical install.

MySQL Connector/NET 1.0 Installation

In order to execute stored procedures in MySQL 5.0, you need to install the MySqlClient data provider. (The MySQL ODBC driver doesn't support all of the necessary features.) To install Connector/NET 1.0, follow these steps:

   1. Download the Source and Binaries ZIP file from http://dev.mysql.com/downloads/ connector/net/1.0.html. (mysql-connector-net-1.0.7.zip is 545KB.)

   2. Open the downloaded ZIP file, and then double-click the MySql.Data.msi installer to run the installer.

   3. On the Setup Type step of the installation wizard, choose to perform a Typical installation.

SQL Data Types

Databases support the same core set of data types as defined in the SQL standard, but annoyingly, they call these data type different things. This appendix provides an easy reference to the data types defined in SQL Server 2005, MySQL 5.0, and Microsoft Access. In this appendix, the data types are grouped as follows:

- Text types

- Numeric types

- Date and time types

- Binary types

- Miscellaneous types

Text Types

Several text-based types are defined in SQL and are distinguished by the following two main characteristics:

- Does it support Unicode?

- Does it have a fixed length or a variable length?

If you choose a fixed-length type for a field, and the string it contains is smaller than that length, the string is padded with spaces to make it the correct length. This padding won't occur if you use a variable-length data type, but you must specify a maximum length for the string using the Length/Size property for the field.

char

The char type maps to a string (System.String) in C# and is defined as follows:

- In SQL Server, char represents a fixed-length string of up to 8,000 non-Unicode characters. You should use the SqlDbType.Char type identifier for parameters of this type.

- In MySQL, char represents a fixed-length string of up to 255 non-Unicode characters. Depending on the data provider, you should use the OdbcType.Char or MySqlClient.String type identifiers for parameters of this type.

- In Microsoft Access, the char type is called Text and represents a variable-length string of up to 255 Unicode characters. You should use the OleDbType.Char type identifier for parameters of this type.

longtext

The longtext type maps to a string (System.String) in C# and is defined as follows:

- In MySQL, longtext represents a variable-length string of up to 2^{32}-1 (4,294,967,295) non-Unicode characters. Depending on the data provider, you should use the OdbcType.Text or MySqlClient.String type identifiers for parameters of this type.

- There is no equivalent in SQL Server or Microsoft Access.

mediumtext

The mediumtext type maps to a string (System.String) in C# and is defined as follows:

- In MySQL, mediumtext represents a variable-length string of up to 2^{24}-1 (16,777,215) non-Unicode characters. Depending on the data provider, you should use the OdbcType.Text or MySqlClient.String type identifiers for parameters of this type.

- There is no equivalent in SQL Server or Microsoft Access.

nchar/national char

The nchar/national char type maps to a string (System.String) in C# and is defined as follows:

- In SQL Server, nchar represents a fixed-length string of up to 4,000 Unicode characters. You should use the SqlDbType.NChar type identifier for parameters of this type.

- In MySQL, national char represents a fixed-length string of up to 255 Unicode characters. Depending on the data provider, you should use the OdbcType.NChar or MySqlClient.String type identifiers for parameters of this type.

- There is no equivalent in Microsoft Access.

nvarchar/national varchar

The nvarchar/national varchar type maps to a string (System.String) in C# and is defined as follows:

- In SQL Server, nvarchar represents a variable-length string of up to 4,000 Unicode characters. You should use the SqlDbType.NVarChar type identifier for parameters of this type.

- In MySQL, national varchar represents a variable-length string of up to 65,535 Unicode characters. Depending on the data provider, you should use the OdbcType.NVarChar or MySqlClient.String type identifiers for parameters of this type.

- There is no equivalent in Microsoft Access.

SQL Server 2005 defines a new type nvarchar(max) that allows 2^{30}-1 (1,073,741,823) Unicode characters to be stored. This is still a string in C#, but you should use the SqlDbType.NText type identifier for parameters of this type.

ntext

The ntext type maps to a string (System.String) in C# and is defined as follows:

- In SQL Server, ntext represents a variable-length string of up to 2^{30}-1 (1,073,741,823) Unicode characters. You should use the SqlDbType.NText type identifier for parameters of this type.

- There is no equivalent in MySQL or Microsoft Access.

text

The text type maps to a string (System.String) in C# and is defined as follows:

- In SQL Server, text represents a variable-length string of up to 2^{31}-1 (2,147,483,647) non-Unicode characters. You should use the SqlDbType.Text type identifier for parameters of this type.

- In MySQL, text represents a variable-length string of up to 65,535 non-Unicode characters. Depending on the data provider, you should use the OdbcType.Text or MySqlClient.String type identifiers for parameters of this type.

- In Microsoft Access, the text type is called Memo and represents a variable-length string of up to 2^{31}-1 (2,147,483,647) Unicode characters. You should use the OleDbType.Char type identifier for parameters of this type.

tinytext

The tinytext type maps to a string (System.String) in C# and is defined as follows:

- In MySQL, tinytext represents a variable-length string of up to 255 non-Unicode characters. Depending on the data provider, you should use the OdbcType.Text or MySqlClient.String type identifiers for parameters of this type.

- There is no equivalent in SQL Server or Microsoft Access.

varchar

The varchar type maps to a string (System.String) in C# and is defined as follows:

- In SQL Server, varchar represents a variable-length string of up to 8,000 non-Unicode characters. You should use the SqlDbType.VarChar type identifier for parameters of this type.

- In MySQL, varchar represents a variable-length string of up to 65,535 non-Unicode characters. Depending on the data provider, you should use the OdbcType.VarChar or MySqlClient.String type identifiers for parameters of this type.

- There is no equivalent in Microsoft Access.

SQL Server 2005 defines a new type varchar(max) that allows 2^{31}-1 (2,147,483,647) non-Unicode characters to be stored. This is still a string in C#, but you should use the SqlDbType.Text type identifier for parameters of this type.

Numeric Types

Like .NET types, data types are available in SQL Server and MySQL for both integer and floating-point values. However, there's a difference in implementation. Both databases assume by default that these types are signed—that is, they have negative values—but only MySQL gives you the option to make a type unsigned (by clicking the UNSIGNED check box in MySQL Query Browser).

In addition, all numeric types are fixed-length data types. If a field contains a value that doesn't use all of its allocated value, it's padded with spaces. In MySQL Query Browser, if you click the ZEROFILL check box, numeric values are padded with zeros instead of spaces.

Autonumbers

Supporting the notion that primary key fields must contain unique values, all three database types can auto-generate unique integer values for ID (primary key) fields. They can also generate globally unique ID fields (GUIDs)—128-bit hexadecimal numbers that are both random and unique. The following are the various ways to do this:

- To auto-generate integers in SQL Server, set the field's data type to one of the integer values and set IsIdentity to true. The properties IdentitySeed and IdentityIncrement let you set the first value to be generated for the field and the difference between each subsequent value, respectively.

- To auto-generate GUIDs in SQL Server, set the field's data type to `uniqueidentifier` and its default value to `newid()`.

- To auto-generate integers in the Jet engine, set the field's data type to `AutoNumber`.

- To auto-generate GUIDs in the Jet engine, set the field's data type to `ReplicationID` and then set `Autogenerate` to `true`.

- MySQL supports only auto-generated integers. Set the field's data type to one of the integer data types and set `AUTO_INCREMENT` to `true`.

Integer Types

Integer types are those types that can hold only nondecimal numbers.

bigint

You should use `bigint` only if you're absolutely sure that the integers you need to store cannot fit in an `int` data field. The `bigint` type represents an 8-byte integer and maps to a `long` (`System.Int64`) in C#. It is defined as follows:

- In SQL Server, `bigint` can take values between -2^{63} (-9,223,372,036,854,775,808) and 2^{63}-1 (9,223,372,036,854,775,807). You should use the `SqlDbType.BigInt` type identifier for parameters of this type.

- For a signed `bigint`, MySQL allows the same range of values as SQL Server. An unsigned `bigint` can represent a range of integers between 0 and 2^{64} (18,446,744,073,709,551,616). Depending on the data provider, you should use the `OdbcType.BigInt` or `MySqlClient.Int64` type identifiers for parameters of this type.

- There is no equivalent in Microsoft Access.

bit

The `bit` type is typically used as the data type to store Boolean values. Columns of type `bit` can't have indexes on them. The `bit` type maps to a `bool` (`System.Boolean`) in C# and is defined as follows:

- In SQL Server, `bit` is an integer type that can take two values: 0 or 1. You should use the `SqlDbType.Bit` type identifier for parameters of this type.

- In MySQL, `bit` is an integer type that can take two values: 0 or 1. It's also known as `bool` or `boolean`. Depending on the data provider, you should use the `OdbcType.Bit` or `MySqlClient.Bit` type identifiers for parameters of this type.

- In Microsoft Access, `bit` is called `Yes/No` and can take the values of Yes (1) or No (0). You should use the `OleDbType.Boolean` type identifier for parameters of this type.

int

The int type represents a 4-byte integer and maps to an int (System.Int32) in C#. It is defined as follows:

- In SQL Server, an int represents a range of integers between -2^{31} (-2,147,483,648) and 2^{31}-1 (2,147,483,647). You should use the SqlDbType.Int type identifier for parameters of this type.

- For a signed int, MySQL uses the same definition as SQL Server. An unsigned int can represent a range of integers between 0 and 2^{32} (4,294,967,296). Depending on the data provider, you should use the OdbcType.Int or MySqlClient.Int32 type identifiers for parameters of this type.

- In Microsoft Access, an int type is represented as a Number data type and a Long Integer field size. It supports the same range of values as SQL Server, and you should use the OleDbType.Integer type identifier for parameters of this type.

mediumint

The mediumint type represents a 3-byte integer and has no direct mapping in .NET. The closest is an int in C#. It is defined as follows:

- A signed mediumint in MySQL represents a range of integers between -2^{23} (-8,388,608) and 2^{23}-1 (8,388,607). An unsigned mediumint can represent a range of integers between 0 and 2^{24} (16,777,216). Depending on the data provider, you should use the OdbcType.Int or MySqlClient.Int24 type identifiers for parameters of this type.

- There is no equivalent in SQL Server or Microsoft Access.

smallint

The smallint type represents a 2-byte integer and maps to a short (System.Int16) in C#. It is defined as follows:

- In SQL Server, a smallint represents a range of integers between -2^{15} (-32,768) and 2^{15}-1 (32,767). You should use the SqlDbType.SmallInt type identifier for parameters of this type.

- For a signed smallint, MySQL uses the same definition as SQL Server. An unsigned smallint can represent a range of integers between 0 and 2^{16} (65,536). Depending on the data provider, you should use the OdbcType.SmallInt or MySqlClient.Int16 type identifiers for parameters of this type.

- In Microsoft Access, a smallint type is represented as a Number data type and an Integer field size. It supports the same range of values as SQL Server, and you should use the OleDbType.SmallInt type identifier for parameters of this type.

tinyint

The `tinyint` type represents a 1-byte integer and maps to a `sbyte` (`System.SByte`) in C#. It is defined as follows:

- In SQL Server, a `tinyint` represents a range of integers between 0 and 255. You should use the `SqlDbType.TinyInt` type identifier for parameters of this type.

- For an unsigned `tinyint`, MySQL uses the same definition as SQL Server. A signed `tinyint` can represent a range of integers between -128 and 127. Depending on the data provider, you should use the `OdbcType.TinyInt` or `MySqlClient.Byte` type identifier for parameters of this type.

- In Microsoft Access, a `tinyint` type is represented as a `Number` data type and a `Byte` field size. It supports the same range of values as SQL Server, and you should use the `OleDbType.TinyInt` type identifier for parameters of this type.

decimal

The `decimal` type represents a number range defined by a maximum number of digits (its *precision*) and the maximum number of digits that can be used to the right of the decimal point (its *scale*). It maps to a `decimal` (`System.Decimal`) in C# and is defined as follows:

- In SQL Server, the `decimal` type can have a maximum precision of 38. The default precision is 18, and the default scale is 0. You should use the `SqlDbType.Decimal` type identifier for parameters of this type.

- In MySQL, the `decimal` type can have a maximum precision of 65 and a maximum scale of 30. The default precision is 10, and the default scale is 0. Depending on the data provider, you should use the `OdbcType.Decimal` or `MySqlClient.Decimal` type identifier for parameters of this type.

- In Microsoft Access, the `decimal` type is represented as a `Number` data type and a `Decimal` field size. The default precision is 18, and the default scale is 0. You should use the `OleDbType.Number` type identifier for parameters of this type.

Variable-Size Floating-Point Numbers

The `decimal` type specifies a fixed number of digits both before and after the decimal point, and will always store the number you want exactly as you enter it. With variable-size floating-point numbers, the value that is stored may be imprecise. The more bytes that are used to store the number, the more precise it will be.

4-Byte Floating-Point Numbers

A 4-byte (32-bit) floating-point number represents a fixed range of values between $3.40E^{38}$ to $-1.18E^{-38}$ for negative values, zero, and $1.18E^{-38}$ to $3.40E^{38}$ for positive values. It maps to a float (System.Single) in C# and is defined as follows:

- In SQL Server, a 4-byte floating-point number is a real. You should use the SqlDbType.Real type identifier for parameters of this type.

- In MySQL, a 4-byte floating-point number is a float. Depending on the data provider, you should use the OdbcType.Real or MySqlClient.Float type identifier for parameters of this type.

- In Microsoft Access, a 4-byte floating-point number is represented as a Number data type and a Single field size. You should use the OleDbType.Single type identifier for parameters of this type.

8-Byte Floating-Point Numbers

An 8-byte (64-bit) floating-point number represents a fixed range of values between $1.79E^{308}$ to $-2.23E^{-308}$ for negative values, zero, and $2.23E^{-308}$ to $1.79E^{308}$ for positive values. It maps to a double (System.Double) in C# and is defined as follows:

- In SQL Server, an 8-byte floating-point number is a float. You should use the SqlDbType.Float type identifier for parameters of this type.

- In MySQL, an 8-byte floating-point number is a double. Depending on the data provider, you should use the OdbcType.Double or MySqlClient.Double type identifier for parameters of this type.

- In Microsoft Access, an 8-byte floating-point number is represented as a Number data type and a Double field size. You should use the OleDbType.Double type identifier for parameters of this type.

Date and Time Types

All three databases support "instance-in-time" fields, but only MySQL supports time unit types.

date

The date type maps to a System.DateTime in C# without a time specified (00:00:00). It is defined as follows:

- In MySQL, a date represents a date between 1000-01-01 and 9999-12-31. Depending on the data provider, you should use the OdbcType.Date or MySqlClient.Date type identifiers for parameters of this type.

- There is no equivalent in SQL Server or Microsoft Access.

datetime

The datetime type maps to a System.DateTime in C# and is defined as follows:

- In SQL Server, datetime represents a date and time combination between 00:00:00 on Jan. 1, 1753, through to 23:59:59 on Dec. 31, 9999. You should use the SqlDbType.DateTime type identifier for parameters of this type.

- In MySQL, datetime represents a date and time combination between 00:00:00 on Jan. 1, 1000, through to 23:59:59 on Dec. 31, 9999. Depending on the data provider, you should use the OdbcType.DateTime or MySqlClient.Datetime type identifier for parameters of this type.

- In Microsoft Access, a datetime is represented as a Date/Time data type and represents a date and time combination between 00:00:00 on Jan. 1, 1000, through to 23:59:59 on Dec. 31, 9999. You should use the OleDbType.DBDate type identifier for parameters of this type.

smalldatetime

The smalldatetime type maps to a System.DateTime in C# and is defined as follows:

- In SQL Server, smalldatetime represents a date and time combination between 00:00:00 on Jan. 1, 1900, through to 23:59:59 on June 6, 2079. You should use the SqlDbType.SmallDateTime type identifier for parameters of this type.

- There is no equivalent in MySQL or Microsoft Access.

time

The time type maps to a System.TimeSpan in C# and is defined as follows:

- In MySQL, time represents a period of time in the format *HH:MM:SS* between -838:59:59 and 838:59:59. Depending on the data provider, you should use the OdbcType.Time or MySqlClient.Time type identifier for parameters of this type.

- There is no equivalent in SQL Server or Microsoft Access.

timestamp

The timestamp type maps to a byte array in C# and is defined as follows:

- In SQL Server, a timestamp represents an automatically generated 8-byte binary number (which is guaranteed to be unique within a database) given to the field when its row is added to the table or modified. More information can be found at http://msdn.microsoft.com/en-us/library/ms182776.aspx. You should use the SqlDbType.Timestamp type identifier for parameters of this type.

- In MySQL, a `timestamp` is a date and time value automatically generated and given to the field when its row is added to the table or modified. More information can be found at `http://dev.mysql.com/doc/refman/5.0/en/timestamp-4-1.html`. Depending on the data provider, you should use the `OdbcType.Timestamp` or `MySqlClient.Timestamp` type identifier for parameters of this type.

- There is no equivalent in Microsoft Access.

year

The year type maps to an `int` (`System.Int32`) in C# without a day, month, or time specified. It is defined as follows:

- In MySQL, a year represents a range of years from 1901 to 2155 if you're using four digits and 1970 to 2066 if you're using two digits. Depending on the data provider, you should use the `OdbcType.Int` or `MySqlClient.Year` type identifier for parameters of this type.

- There is no equivalent in SQL Server or Microsoft Access.

Binary Types

All databases define a few data types for binary data for storing items such as compiled programs, images, and audio. You'll see the rather unflattering acronym for binary data in general—BLOBs, for Binary Large OBjects.

SQL Server Binary Types

SQL Server has three binary types: `binary`, `image`, and `varbinary`.

binary

The `binary` type maps to a `byte` array in C# and represents a fixed-length binary sequence of up to 8,000 bytes. You should use the `SqlDbType.Binary` type identifier for parameters of this type.

image

The `image` type maps to a `byte` array in C# and represents a variable-length binary sequence of up to 2^{31}-1 (2,147,483,647) bytes. You should use the `SqlDbType.Image` type identifier for parameters of this type.

varbinary

The `varbinary` type maps to a `byte` array in C# and represents a variable-length binary sequence of up to 8,000 bytes. You should use the `SqlDbType.VarBinary` type identifier for parameters of this type.

MySQL Binary Types

MySQL has four binary types: `blob`, `longblob`, `mediumblob`, and `tinyblob`.

blob

The `blob` type maps to a `byte` array in C# and represents a variable-length binary sequence of up to 65,535 bytes. Depending on the data provider, you should use the `OdbcType.VarBinary` or `MySqlClient.Blob` type identifier for parameters of this type.

longblob

The `longblob` type maps to a `byte` array in C# and represents a variable-length binary sequence of up to 2^{32}-1 (4,294,967,295) bytes. Depending on the data provider, you should use the `OdbcType.VarBinary` or `MySqlClient.LongBlob` type identifier for parameters of this type.

mediumblob

The `mediumblob` type maps to a `byte` array in C# and represents a variable-length binary sequence of up to 2^{24}-1 (16,777,215) bytes. Depending on the data provider, you should use the `OdbcType.VarBinary` or `MySqlClient.MediumBlob` type identifier for parameters of this type.

tinyblob

The `tinyblob` type maps to a `byte` array in C# and represents a variable-length binary sequence of up to 255 bytes. Depending on the data provider, you should use the `OdbcType.VarBinary` or `MySqlClient.TinyBlob` type identifier for parameters of this type.

Microsoft Access Binary Data

Microsoft Access handles binary data through a single type, `OLE Object`, which allows you to store as much binary data as there is space on disk. You should use the `OleDbType.VarBinary` type identifier for parameters of this type.

Miscellaneous Types

Several types aren't easily classifiable into the previous categories. These include `enum('value1','value2',...)`, `money`, `set('value1','value2',...)`, `smallmoney`, and `uniqueidentifier`.

enum('value1','value2',...)

The `enum('value1','value2',...)` type, defined only in MySQL, allows you to define a column that contains one of the values defined for the `enum`. For more information, see `http://dev.mysql.com/doc/refman/5.0/en/enum.html`.

money

The money type maps to a decimal (System.Decimal) in C# and is defined as follows:

- In SQL Server, money represents a range of monetary values from -922,337,203,685,477.5808 to 922,337,203,685,477.5807 with an accuracy of four decimal places. You should use the SqlDbType.Money type identifier for parameters of this type.

- In Microsoft Access, the money type is specified as a Currency data type and supports the same range of values as SQL Server. You should use the OleDbType.Currency type identifier for parameters of this type.

- There is no equivalent in MySQL.

set('value1','value2',...)

The set('value1','value2',...) type, defined only in MySQL, allows you to define a column that contains up to 64 of the values defined for the set. For more information, see http://dev. mysql.com/doc/refman/5.0/en/set.html.

smallmoney

The smallmoney type, defined only in SQL Server, maps to a decimal (System.Decimal) in C# and allows you to hold a monetary value from -214,748.3648 to 214,748.3647 with an accuracy of four decimal places. You should use the SqlDbType.SmallMoney type identifier for parameters of this type.

uniqueidentifier

The uniqueidentifier type maps to a System.Guid in C# and is defined as follows:

- In SQL Server, uniqueidentifier denotes that the field will hold a GUID. You should use the SqlDbType.Uniqueidentifier type identifier for parameters of this type.

- In Microsoft Access, a uniqueidentifier is represented as a Number data type and a Replication ID field size. You should use the OleDbType.Guid type identifier for parameters of this type.

- There is no equivalent in MySQL.

■ ■ ■

SQL Primer

This appendix summarizes the basic syntax for SELECT, INSERT, UPDATE, and DELETE queries. This isn't intended as a full reference, but as a recap of how to use the queries in ASP.NET, as demonstrated in the examples in this book.

In this appendix, the SQL keywords are shown in all uppercase letters. Optional elements of a query are surrounded by brackets. User-defined elements of a query are in *italics*.

Note that SQL keywords don't need to be in uppercase, and the queries don't need to be separated over many lines, as they are shown in this appendix. These conventions just make it easier to read and understand them. SQL is case-insensitive, except for cases where the database server insists that table and column names *are* case-sensitive, which depends on how your database server is configured. If you've followed the installation instructions in Appendix A, then both SQL Server 2005 and MySQL 5.0 are case-insensitive. However, you should endeavor to be consistent in your letter casing, because it will reduce the chances of problems cropping up later.

You can find Microsoft's Transact-SQL reference online at http://msdn.microsoft.com/en-us/library/ms189826.aspx. You can find MySQL's SQL reference online at http://dev.mysql.com/doc/refman/5.0/en/sql-syntax.html. Each section in this appendix includes links relevant to the specific query from these references.

■Tip Two good books on SQL in general are *The Programmer's Guide to SQL* by Cristian Darie and Karlie Watson (1-59059-218-2; Apress, 2003) and *Teach Yourself SQL in 10 Minutes* by Ben Forta (0-67232-567-5; Sams, 2004). Both are good introductory guides to the subtleties of SQL not covered here.

SELECT

The purpose of a SELECT query is to return some information from the database. This information may be any of the following:

- A single scalar value returned as an object by a call to ExecuteScalar()

- A table of values returned as a single result inside a DataReader object by a call to ExecuteReader()

- A set of tables of values returned as multiple results inside a DataReader object

- A table returned into a DataSet via a DataAdapter's Fill() method

- A set of results returned from a SqlDataSource

The syntax of the SELECT query looks like this:

```
SELECT <select column list>
FROM <table>
  [ <join expression> ]
[ WHERE <constraints> ]
[ ORDER BY <order column list> ]
```

This query has the following five pieces:

- A *select column list* to be retrieved from the database. Generally, this is a comma-separated list of column names from the database, the * wildcard (meaning every column in the given table should be returned), or an aggregate function on a set of columns such as COUNT() or TOP().

- The name of the *table* from which the selection should originate.

- An optional *join expression* determining how other tables should be linked to the information in the *table*. There can be as many *join expression* statements as needed to retrieve the required data from other tables in the database.

- An optional *constraints* prefixed by the WHERE clause that allow you to filter the data to be returned. The *constraints* isn't a comma-separated list. Each condition is joined by one of the three Boolean conditions OR, AND, or NOT and is a comparison of a column to either a literal value or another column.

- An optional comma-separated *order column list* indicating which columns the results of the SELECT query should be ordered by. By default, they're organized into ascending order. Adding the keyword DESC to a column in the ORDER BY clause will sort that column in descending order.

For example, to retrieve the names of all the family members in a genealogy database, use the following query:

```
SELECT MemberName FROM familymember
```

If you want to retrieve all the details about the dogs in the family, use the following query:

```
SELECT * FROM familymember
WHERE MemberSpecies = 'dog'
```

To retrieve the Social Security number for every member of the family born before 1987, use the following query:

```
SELECT familymember.MemberName, financialdetail.SSN
FROM familymember
  INNER JOIN financialdetail
  ON financialdetail.MemberID = familymember.MemberID
WHERE MemberBirthdate < '01/01/1987'
```

Note that some of the elements of SELECT have been left out for simplicity's sake and because they aren't covered in the book. For a complete look at SELECT, check out the following links:

- SQL Server: `http://msdn.microsoft.com/en-us/library/ms189499.aspx`

- MySQL: `http://dev.mysql.com/doc/refman/5.0/en/select.html`

INSERT

The purpose of an INSERT query is to add some new information to a table in a database. This new data must conform to the rules and constraints already laid out on the table, or an error will be returned. INSERT queries are called through a DataAdapter's Update() method, executed by calling ExecuteNonQuery() on a Command object (which returns the number of rows in the table the query has added), or called through a SqlDataSource.

The syntax of the INSERT query looks like this:

```
INSERT [INTO] <table name> [ ( <column list> ) ]
VALUES ( <column value list> )
```

This query has the following five pieces:

- The optional keyword INTO to make the query more readable.

- The *table name* that determines the table to which the information will be added.

- The optional (comma-separated) *column list* that names the columns in the new row to which you're giving values. This list must be surrounded by parentheses.

- The keyword VALUES that separates the *column list* from the *column value list*.

- The (comma-separated) *column value list* that contains a value for each of the columns in the *column list* for the new row. Each value can be a literal, an expression saying how a value is to be determined from the values of other columns (firstname + ' ' + surname, for example), the keyword DEFAULT indicating that the column should take its default value as defined in the database, or NULL. This list must be surrounded by parentheses.

The number of the items in the *column list* should equal the number of items in the *column value list* and be ordered in the same way. Thus, the first column named in the *column list* will be filled with the first value in the *column value list*, the second with the second, and so on. If a *column list* isn't supplied, the *column value list* must supply a new value for every column in the table.

For example, to add a newcomer to a family database, use the following query:

```
INSERT INTO familymember
   (MemberID, MemberName, MemberBirthdate, MemberSpecies)
VALUES (25, 'Spot', '14/04/04', 'Cat')
```

For more information about the INSERT query, try these links:

- SQL Server: `http://msdn.microsoft.com/en-us/library/ms174335.aspx`

- MySQL: `http://dev.mysql.com/doc/refman/5.0/en/insert.html`

UPDATE

The purpose of an UPDATE query is to modify some already existing information in a table in the database. UPDATE queries are called through a DataAdapter's Update() method, executed by calling ExecuteNonQuery() on a Command object (which returns the number of rows in the table the query has modified), or called through a SqlDataSource.

The syntax of the UPDATE query looks like this:

```
UPDATE <table name>
SET column1 name = expression1,
    column2 name = expression2,
        .
        .
        .
    columnM name = expressionM
[ WHERE <constraints> ]
```

This query has the following four pieces:

- The *table name* that identifies the table in which data will be updated.

- The keyword SET to denote the start of the updated information.

- A comma-separated list of assignments where individual columns are set to given values.

- An optional *constraints* prefixed by the WHERE clause that allows you to filter the data to be updated.

For example, to change a female family member's name in the family database, use the following query:

```
UPDATE familymember
SET MemberName = 'Jane Maharry'
WHERE MemberName='Jane Randall'
```

For more information about the UPDATE query, try these links:

- SQL Server: http://msdn.microsoft.com/en-us/library/ms177523.aspx

- MySQL: http://dev.mysql.com/doc/refman/5.0/en/update.html

DELETE

The purpose of a DELETE query is to remove one or more rows of information from a table in a database. DELETE queries are called through a DataAdapter's Update() method, executed by calling ExecuteNonQuery() on a Command object (which returns the number of rows in the table the query has deleted), or called through a SqlDataSource.

The syntax of the DELETE query looks like this:

```
DELETE [FROM] <table name>
[ WHERE <constraints> ]
```

This query has the following three pieces:

- The optional keyword FROM to make the query more readable.

- The *table name* that determines the table from which data will be deleted.

- An optional *constraints* prefixed by the WHERE clause that allows you to filter the data to be deleted.

For example, to remove all cats from the family database, use the following query:

```
DELETE FROM familymember
WHERE MemberSpecies = 'Cat'
```

Note that calling DELETE without a WHERE clause removes all the rows from a table but does not remove the table itself. Also, you should check whether your databases will DELETE data regardless of whether the DELETE query breaks referential integrity constraints. Some do; some don't.

For more information about the DELETE query, try these links:

- SQL Server: http://msdn.microsoft.com/en-us/library/ms189835.aspx

- MySQL: http://dev.mysql.com/doc/refman/5.0/en/delete.html

■ ■ ■

Sample Database Tables

This appendix contains the complete structure of and data for the four tables in the sample database used in the examples in this book. Use it in conjunction with the instructions given in Chapter 2 to build the sample database. Alternatively, use the instructions at the end of this appendix for generating the databases automatically.

Note that if you're creating a MySQL database, all tables must be InnoDB-type tables.

In SQL Server 2005 and MySQL 5.0, the sample database has a user account called BAND attached to it. Refer to Chapter 2 to see how to add this user account to the database.

The Manufacturer Table

The Manufacturer table contains the columns listed in Table D-1 and the data listed in Table D-2. Table D-1 also lists the properties of each column that you should set (or ensure that they're set as specified).

Table D-1. *Columns in the Manufacturer Table*

Column Name	Microsoft Access	SQL Server 2005	MySQL 5.0
ManufacturerID	DataType: Autonumber PrimaryKey: true	DataType: int PrimaryKey: true Is Identity: true Allow Nulls: false	DataType: integer PrimaryKey: true AUTO_INCREMENT: true Not Null: true
ManufacturerName	DataType: Text Size: 50 Required: Yes	DataType: varchar Length: 50 Allow Nulls: false	DataType: varchar Length: 50 Not Null: true
ManufacturerCountry	DataType: Text Size: 50 Required: No	DataType: varchar Length: 50 Allow Null: true	DataType: varchar Length: 50 Not Null: false
ManufacturerEmail	DataType: Text Size: 100 Required: No	DataType: varchar Length: 100 Allow Null: true	DataType: varchar Length: 100 Not Null: false
ManufacturerWebsite	DataType: Text Size: 100 Required: No	DataType: varchar Length: 100 Allow Null: true	DataType: varchar Length: 100 Not Null: false

Table D-2. *Data in the Manufacturer Table*

ManufacturerID	ManufacturerName	ManufacturerCountry	ManufacturerEmail	ManufacturerWebsite
1	Apple	USA	lackey@apple.com	http://www.apple.com
2	Creative	Singapore	someguy@creative.com	http://www.creative.com
3	iRiver	Korea	knockknock@iriver.com	http://www.iriver.com
4	MSI	Taiwan	hello@msicomputer.co.uk	http://www.msicomputer.co.uk
5	Rio	USA	greetings@rio.com	http://www.rio.com
6	SanDisk	USA	heyhey@sandisk.com	http://www.sandisk.com
7	Sony	Japan	hi_san@sony.co.jp	http://www.sony.com
8	Cowon	Korea	moomoo@cowon.com	http://www.cowon.com
9	Frontier Labs	Hong Kong	frontdesk@frontierlabs.com	http://www.frontierlabs.com
10	Samsung	Japan	mashimashi@samsung.co.jp	http://www.samsung.com

The Player Table

The Player table contains the columns listed in Table D-3 and the data listed in Table D-4. Table D-3 also lists the properties of each column that you should set (or ensure that they're set as specified).

Table D-3. *Columns in the Player Table*

Column Name	Microsoft Access	SQL Server 2005	MySQL 5.0
PlayerID	DataType: Autonumber PrimaryKey: true	DataType: int PrimaryKey: true Is Identity: true Allow Nulls: false	DataType: integer PrimaryKey: true AUTO_INCREMENT: true Not Null: true
PlayerName	DataType: Text Size: 50 Required: Yes	DataType: varchar Length: 50 Allow Nulls: false	DataType: varchar Length: 50 Not Null: true
PlayerManufacturerID	DataType: Number Field Size: Long Integer Required: Yes	DataType: int Allow Null: false	DataType: integer Not Null: true
PlayerCost	DataType: Number Field Size: Decimal Required: Yes	DataType: decimal Size: 10, 2 Allow Null: false	DataType: decimal Size: 10, 2 Not Null: true
PlayerStorage	DataType: Text Size: 50 Required: Yes	DataType: varchar Length: 50 Allow Null: false	DataType: varchar Length: 50 Not Null: true

Table D-4. *Data in the Player Table*

PlayerID	PlayerName	PlayerManufacturerID	PlayerCost	PlayerStorage
1	iPod Shuffle	1	99.00	Solid State
2	MuVo V200	2	96.00	Solid State
3	iFP-700 Series	3	149.00	Solid State
4	iFP-900 Series	3	199.00	Solid State
5	MegaPlayer 521	4	93.00	Solid State
6	Forge	5	119.00	Solid State
7	Digital Audio Player	6	135.00	Solid State
8	Network Walkman NW-E99	7	138.00	Solid State
9	iPod	1	209.00	Hard Disk
10	iPod Mini	1	169.00	Hard Disk
11	iPod Photo	1	309.00	Hard Disk
12	iAudio M3	8	249.00	Hard Disk
13	Zen Micro	2	138.00	Hard Disk
14	Zen Touch	2	169.00	Hard Disk
15	L1	9	149.00	Hard Disk
16	H10	3	189.00	Hard Disk
17	H300 Series	3	319.00	Hard Disk
18	Carbon	5	169.00	Hard Disk
19	Napster YH-920	10	179.00	Hard Disk
20	Network Walkman NW-HD3	7	215.00	Hard Disk

The Format Table

The Format table contains the columns listed in Table D-5 and the data listed in Table D-6. Table D-5 also lists the properties of each column that you should set (or ensure that they're set as specified).

Table D-5. *Columns in the Format Table*

Column Name	Microsoft Access	SQL Server 2005	MySQL 5.0
FormatID	DataType: Autonumber PrimaryKey: true	DataType: int PrimaryKey: true Is Identity: true Allow Nulls: false	DataType: integer PrimaryKey: true AUTO_INCREMENT: true Not Null: true
FormatName	DataType: Text Size: 10 Required: Yes	DataType: varchar Length: 10 Allow Nulls: false	DataType: varchar Length: 10 Not Null: true

Table D-6. *Data in the Format Table*

FormatID	FormatName
1	wav
2	mp3
3	aac
4	wma
5	asf
6	ogg
7	atrac
8	aiff

The WhatPlaysWhatFormat Table

The WhatPlaysWhatFormat table contains the columns listed in Table D-7 and the data listed in Table D-8. Table D-7 also lists the properties of each column that you should set (or ensure that they're set as specified).

Table D-7. *Columns in the WhatPlaysWhatFormat Table*

Column Name	Microsoft Access	SQL Server 2005	MySQL 5.0
WPWFPlayerID	DataType: Number Field Size: Long Integer PrimaryKey: true Required: Yes	DataType: int PrimaryKey: true Allow Nulls: false	DataType: integer PrimaryKey: true Not Null: true
WPWFFormatID	DataType: Number Field Size: Long Integer PrimaryKey: true Required: Yes	DataType: int PrimaryKey: true Allow Nulls: false	DataType: integer PrimaryKey: true Not Null: true

Table D-8. *Data in the WhatPlaysWhatFormat Table*

WPWFPlayerID	WPWFFormatID	WPWFPlayerID	WPWFFormatID
1	1	11	1
1	2	11	2
1	3	11	8
2	2	12	1
2	4	12	2
3	2	12	4
3	4	12	5
3	5	12	6
3	6	13	2
4	2	13	4
4	4	14	1
4	5	14	2
4	6	14	4
5	1	15	1
5	2	15	2
5	4	15	4
6	2	16	2
6	4	16	4
7	2	17	1
7	4	17	2
8	2	17	4
8	7	17	5
9	1	17	6
9	2	18	2
9	3	18	4
9	8	19	2
10	1	19	4
10	2	20	2
10	3	20	4
10	8	20	6

Using the Database Scripts

In the code download for this book (available from the Apress Web site, http://www.apress.com), you'll find a scripts folder, which contains two script files: sqlserver.sql and mysql.sql. You can use these to automatically build the databases in SQL Server 2005 and MySQL 5.0, as described in the following sections.

The code download also includes a Microsoft Access database, players.mdb, in the root of the download. You can use this immediately as the data source for your pages.

■**Caution** By running these scripts, you erase any changes made to the contents of the database since its creation. Therefore, save any changes you may want to keep before running these scripts.

Using a Script to Build the SQL Server 2005 Database

To refresh the SQL Server 2005 database, follow these steps:

1. Open SQL Server Management Studio and cancel any attempt to connect to an existing database.

2. Select File ➤ Open ➤ File and select the sqlserver.sql file from the scripts folder download (from wherever you've saved the files onto your machine).

3. When the Connect dialog box appears, connect to the localhost\BAND database server using the sa account (which, if you've followed the setup instructions in Appendix A, will have a password of bandpass).

4. Click the Execute button on the toolbar to run the script and refresh the database.

5. If this is a database refresh, you may receive the error shown in Figure D-1, but don't worry about it. The script is designed to build the database completely, and as you already have the user account created (either manually or from the script previously), you can't create it again.

```
Messages

(1 row(s) affected)

(1 row(s) affected)

(1 row(s) affected)

(1 row(s) affected)

(1 row(s) affected)
Msg 15025, Level 16, State 1, Line 1
The server principal 'band' already exists.
Msg 15023, Level 16, State 1, Line 1
User, group, or role 'band' already exists in the current database.
```

Figure D-1. *You can't re-create the user login if it already exists.*

Using a Script to Build the MySQL 5.0 Database

To refresh the MySQL 5.0 database follow these steps:

1. Open MySQL Query Browser and connect to the localhost database server using the root account (which, if you've followed the setup instructions in Appendix A, will have a password of bandpass).

2. Select File ➤ Open Script and select the mysql.sql file from the scripts folder download (from wherever you've saved the files onto your machine).

3. Click the Execute button on the toolbar to run the script and refresh the database.

Index